CITIZEN AND SELF IN ANCIENT GREECE

This study examines how the ancient Greeks decided questions of justice as a key to understanding the intersection of our moral and political lives. Combining contemporary political philosophy with historical, literary, and philosophical texts, it examines a series of remarkable individuals who performed "scripts" of justice in Early Iron Age, Archaic, and Classical Greece. From the earlier periods, these include Homer's Achilles and Odysseus as heroic individuals who are also prototypical citizens, and Solon the lawgiver, writing the scripts of statute law and the jury trial. In democratic Athens, the focus turns to dialogues between a citizen's moral autonomy and political obligation in Aeschylean tragedy, Pericles' citizenship paradigm, Antiphon's sophistic thought and forensic oratory, the political leadership of Alcibiades, and Socrates' moral individualism.

Vincent Farenga has taught Classics and Comparative Literature at the University of Southern California since 1973. He served as head of the Comparative Literature Department from 1985 to 1991.

CITIZEN AND SELF IN ANCIENT GREECE

INDIVIDUALS PERFORMING JUSTICE AND THE LAW

VINCENT FARENGA

University of Southern California

CAMBRIDGE UNIVERSITY PRESS
Cambridge, New York, Melbourne, Madrid, Cape Town, Singapore, São Paulo

Cambridge University Press
40 West 20th Street, New York, NY 10011-4211, USA

www.cambridge.org
Information on this title: www.cambridge.org/9780521845595

First published 2006

Printed in the United States of America

A catalog record for this publication is available from the British Library.

Library of Congress Cataloging in Publication Data
Farenga, Vincent, 1947–
Citizen and self in ancient Greece : individuals performing justice and the law / Vincent Farenga.
p.   cm.
Includes bibliographical references and index.
ISBN-10: 0-521-84559-9 (hardcover)
ISBN-13: 978-0-521-84559-5 (hardcover)
1. Justice – Greece – Athens – History – To 1500.   2. Democracy – Greece – Athens –
History – To 1500.   3. Citizenship – Greece – Athens – History – To 1500.
4. Justice, Administration of (Greek law).   5. Greek literature – History and criticism.
6. Law and literature.   7. Justice in literature.   I. Title.
JC75.J8F37   2006
320.938′5′011–dc22   2005002862

ISBN-13   978-0-521-84559-5 hardback
ISBN-10   0-521-84559-9 hardback

À Nicole, qui m'a conduit à la victoire,
et à Stéphane, qui l'a couronnée

CONTENTS

ACKNOWLEDGMENTS

I HAVE BEEN TEACHING CLASSICS AND COMPARATIVE LITERATURE at the University of Southern California since 1973. Over the years I have benefited from the inspiration and support of many colleagues and students, some of whom I've come to hold in particular esteem and affection. Among former Classics colleagues from a deepening past, I wish to acknowledge Jane Cody, the late David S. Wiesen, Richard Caldwell, Carolyn Dewald, Jeffrey Henderson, the late George Pilitsis, William Levitan, Martha Malamud, and Donald T. McGuire, and, from a shallower past, Phiroze Vasunia and Catherine Gilhuly. Among present colleagues, I continue to draw on the insights, energies, and encouragements of W. G. Thalmann, Thomas Habinek, A. J. Boyle, Bryan Burns, and Claudia Moatti.

Among colleagues outside USC, I received support and encouragement at an early stage of my career from John Peradotto, Pietro Pucci, and the late Charles Segal. An NEH Fellowship for College Teachers in 1984–85 provided an opportunity for research on Archaic Greek culture, some of which has contributed (in a revised context) to arguments in Chapter 4. More recently, I owe much to the anonymous readers of Cambridge University Press, whose comments and criticisms have had a major impact on the final version of this project.

Friendships old and new have continued to provide resources vital to completing this work. Among old friends I thank Glenn Embrey, John House, and David Eidenberg; among newer friends, Ron Scheer. I owe my greatest debt to family members whose love and support seem boundless: my sisters Marie Danziger and Catherine Behrens, my son Stéphane, but beyond all others my wife Nicole Dufresne.

INTRODUCTION

◎▣◎

PERFORMING CITIZENSHIP AND ITS SCRIPTS IN DEMOCRATIC ATHENS

A new field has emerged over the past fifteen years out of the perennial interest ancient historians and classicists have shown in the Athenian democracy of 508–322 BC; we might call it "Athenian democracy studies."[1] Reasons for its popularity are not hard to identify in an era devoted to the ideal of interdisciplinary research, but its developing contours already demonstrate how complex a topic democratic society can be, especially if we inquire into ways human subjects experience it through democratic citizenship. And so not surprisingly Athenian democracy studies are expanding rapidly right now, propelled by variety in evidence and eclecticism in methodology as scholars seek out Athenian cultural practices and beliefs peculiar to the democracy – and devise new ways to scrutinize them. For one manifestation of this variety and eclecticism we need only look to the "smorgasbord" essay collections by multiple authors that proliferate in so many fields today: major collections on Athenian democracy keep multiplying, at least in English.[2] One effect of these collections is to suggest that scholars find it difficult to forge a single, interdisciplinary approach to the Athenian democracy. They may also encourage readers to believe – mistakenly, I

---

[1] All dates in this study referring to developments in Greek history are BC. All translations from languages ancient and modern are mine unless otherwise noted.

[2] See Rhodes 2004, Goldhill and Osborne 1999, Cartledge, Millett, and von Reden 1998, Morris and Raaflaub 1998, Boedeker and Raaflaub 1998, Ober and Hedrick 1996, Euben, Wallach, and Ober 1994, Boegehold and Scafuro 1994, and Osborne and Goldhill 1994. For multilingual essay collections see David Cohen 2002, Kinzl and Raaflaub 1995, and Eder 1994.

1

think – that democratic community and citizenship are too multiform and confusing to accommodate a single line of inquiry.

About a decade ago a neat bifurcation distinguished old and new paradigms for studying Athenian democracy and citizenship. Older studies were grounded in a constitutional sense of legal status and participation in political institutions, while more recent studies emphasized ideological questions of social behavior, values, and attitudes affecting citizens and noncitizens alike.[3] Today, however, the dynamism of Athenian democracy studies has caused that bifurcation to ramify into an array of options. One is methodological, a version of the "theory question" many classical scholars and ancient historians face these days: "Should my approach be cross-fertilized by contemporary political, social, and cultural theory, or should it remain 'empirically' based in traditional senses of 'what life was like in democratic Athens'?"[4]

Scholars who choose a theoretically informed approach also face the Pandora's box of eclecticism: "Should I draw on a mix of thinkers and theories or stay grounded in one primary approach?"[5] The choice of

---

[3] Scafuro discusses this bifurcation (1994: 2–8); Manville proclaims the "new paradigm" (1994 and 1990); Ober's work is most representative of the focus on ideology (1998, 1996, 1994 and 1989).

[4] Studies using cross-fertilization include Ober 1998, 1996 and 1989, Hunter 1994 and Euben 1990. Equally valuable empirically based contributions include Hansen 1987 and 1991, Stockton 1990, Sinclair 1988, and Ostwald 1986. M. I. Finley practically created the field of contemporary Athenian democracy studies, serving as both an inspiration and bridge for scholars of both approaches (e.g., 1983, 1985a, and 1985b). Rhodes divides the methodological possibilities of this field into eight neat categories (2003a: 70–71).

[5] Typical ingredients for the theory mix include Foucault, Bourdieu, and Searle. Sagan (1991) examines Athenian democracy and paranoia through a classically psychoanalytic lens; Saxonhouse (1992) uses gender theory to assess the democracy; McClure (1999) and Lape (2004) do also for Athenian democracy and drama, with Lape combining ideologies of gender and race (2003). Loraux's work eclectically draws on multiple models (Foucault, structuralism, poststructuralism, feminism, psychoanalysis, etc.) (e.g., 2002a, 2002b, 1998).

how widely to gather evidence also presents an option: "If my study is empirically grounded, do I draw on a wealth of evidence for democratic life in Athenian politics, law, religion, warfare, economy, gender relations, philosophy, and so on, or do I limit myself to a single cultural practice?"[6] More materially based research might focus solely on artistic or archaeological evidence for democratic practices or on interpretive models grounded in archaeology and visual theories.[7] Yet another option, pursued only sporadically, combines the questions of methodology and evidence, asking, "Should I set Athenian democracy and citizenship into dialogue with contemporary studies of democratic theory and practice in fields such as political science, sociology, policy and planning, and law?" To put it more bluntly, "Can the realities and theories of ancient, modern, and postmodern democracies inform one another?"[8] This last project might prompt some scholars self-consciously to wonder to what degree their own nationalist traditions influence the ways they approach and evaluate ancient democracy.[9]

[6] The approaches featured in the 1996 Ober and Hedrick anthology draw on a wide spectrum of evidence; one popular choice for a single cultural practice has been litigation in Athens' democratic courts, as in studies by Allen 2000, Johnstone 1999, Christ 1998, and the essays in Hunter and Edmonson 2000, and Cartledge, Millett, and Todd (1990).

[7] Studies in art history and Athenian democracy include Neer 2002, Hurwit 1999, and Castriota 1992; see also the majority of essays in Boedeker and Raaflaub 1998. See the archaeological evidence covered in the essays edited by Coulson (1994), where Brenne's study of *ostraka* is a good example. For interpretive models see the discussion by Small and Morris in the Morris and Raaflaub collection (1998: 217–46).

[8] Rhodes tackles this broad methodological question, providing partial answers (2003a). Recent studies include Colaico 2002, Wallach 2001, Villa 2001, and Mara 1997 on Socrates and/or Plato; for more limited attempts see contributions in Ober and Hedrick 1996, Ober 1996: 161–87, Wolin 1994, and passages in McAfee 2000 (1–18), and Farrar 1988 (e.g., 3–14 and 273–78). But see now Samons 2004 and Ober 2005.

[9] Rhodes misleads us when he characterizes all modern scholars as epigones locked into their respective national democratic traditions (2003a: 34–53). This pigeonholing ignores individuals whose personal and educational histories are multinational and

These options within Athenian democracy studies create the false impression that ancient democracy and its citizenship are not amenable to a unified set of questions, definitions, or concepts. The polyphony of issues concerning methodology and evidence might even discourage us from asking what democratic citizenship (ancient, modern, and postmodern) is, and encourage us to conclude that there couldn't be a fundamental nature behind the heterogeneous ways subjects experienced it in antiquity and after. However, one recent development in Athenian democracy studies has taken a step toward a more conceptually unified approach, one employing a mix of theories to study an array of cultural practices in Athens. Its key innovative strategy links democratic citizenship in Athens to what we call today "performance studies." In a helpful introduction to the essay collection *Performance Culture and Athenian Democracy* (Goldhill and Osborne 1999), Simon Goldhill offers a detailed explanation for this link. A quick look at his enthusiastic "Programme Notes" (1999) provides an Ariadne's thread to lead us past the variety, eclecticism, and apparent confusion surrounding ancient democratic citizenship.

According to Goldhill, performance theory, springing about thirty years ago from such fields as ethnography and theater studies, then migrating to gender studies, and finally infiltrating classics, constitutes a sort of royal road to understanding democratic citizenship in Athens.[10] He "maps" the "intellectual space" of performance as a "heuristic category" to connect such varia of Athenian life as theatrical spectacle, law court debate, deliberation in the citizen assembly, civic religious festival, gatherings at symposia and gymnasia, social rituals

---

multicultural; it also flirts with a subjective indulgence in national stereotypes (54–69). On Athenian democracy and modern nationalism and nation building, see Anderson 2003.

[10] See Goldhill's survey of theoretical approaches in performance studies, with bibliogaphy (1999: 10–20); for performance and Greek culture, see Mackie 2004, Faulkner, Felson, and Konstan 1999, Bassi 1998, Edmunds and Wallace 1997, and Martin 1994.

like homoerotic courtship, and the use of inscriptions both public and private. From the unifying perspective of performance, then, Goldhill implies that these multiple practices derive their coherence from some sort of key social action at the core of citizenship. While he never says so, we're invited to envision citizenship as a kind of performance *tout court*. He grounds Athens' performance culture in a single social scenario of actions by individuals who make competitive displays of self-presentation so that their social standing (*timê*) can then be collectively evaluated (4, 5) and judged (5, 6, 8) by others. This "dynamic of self-presentation" or "self-promotion" occurs in four master citizen actions of Greek social life: *agôn* or competition; *epideixis* or display; *schêma* or appearance (also "posture," "pose") and *theôria* or "spectating" (2–8).

This abstract, synthetic description of four citizen actions implies that Athenians sustained their democratic citizenship performatively – and it further suggests that, to understand the nature of that citizenship, we need a unified theory of citizen action. But this action, though unified, could not be a simple one because its multiple practices contribute to the "construction" of "the public discourse of democracy. . . ." (8). In other words this action must be composite and at least in part linguistic (I prefer to call it "communicative"). In it Goldhill sees another dimension too, offering nothing less than the key to Athenian subjectivity itself, or "the construction of the [democratic] self" and "self-consciousness" (1–10). For it is through the four master citizen actions that the "self" or "political subject of democracy" is somehow "constructed" (9) or "negotiated" (4). So, in addition to action and language, citizenship somehow contributes to forming individual subjects, and this justifies an impressive scope of theoretical resources on which performance studies can draw.[11] "Performance" thus seems poised to

---

[11] Among others, Goldhill suggests Bakhtin, Victor Turner, Erving Goffman, Austin and Searle, Freudian-Lacanian "gaze theory," Foucault, new historicism, and Clifford's poststructural anthropology. On performance and gender see Butler 1990.

display for classicists the aura of those overarching, master concepts in contemporary cultural theory, such as "violence" in the seventies, "power" in the eighties, and "the body" in the nineties.

But like these blockbuster concepts, performance seems to me fuzzy and a little crude as a theoretical passe-partout. Goldhill acknowledges that it owes some of its allure to a heavily composite nature: as he puts it, "Indeed, for all the claims of 'performance studies' to be a discipline, it remains a bricolage" (15). As an amalgamated methodology, performance studies and its object, the amalgamated activity of citizenship, are therefore congruent; and this goes a long way toward answering the question of whether Athenian democracy studies should be eclectic in both evidence and methodology with an emphatic "Yes, they must!" But how should we refine the concept of performance so that classicists and ancient historians, when using performance studies to illuminate Athens' "performance culture" (8, 10), might understand more clearly the relation between citizenship and performance? Goldhill for the most part sees performance as an instrument or vehicle for enacting citizenship, or as one element in a mix that constitutes citizenship: it's "part of the exercise of citizenship" (1); through it the "public discourse" of Athenian democracy is in part "constructed, articulated and reflected on" (8); and the democracy's development has had at least one "focus" in "performative elements" (10).

But we can relate performance to citizenship in a more fundamental way – a way that will also enable us to benefit from a wide spectrum of contemporary theoretical work on citizenship and democratic community. I propose going farther than Goldhill, for whom the Athenian democracy "might *depend* on performance in specific and special ways" (1; my emphasis). I'd like to entertain the more radical possibility that performance and democratic citizenship are one, that citizenship actually *is* performance.

What might this mean? Performance studies employ the term "performance" in a wide range of culturally defined contexts embracing, for example, ethnographic observations of rituals and genealogical recitations, theatrical presentations in Western or non-Western societies, and the sociology of encounters (e.g., through role-playing) in everyday modern life. What's essential is that someone enact some sort of "script," within a specific framework of time, space and agency, which guides speaker and listeners to interpret a shared sense of its possible meanings.[12] Applied to Athens, this should prompt us to think of democratic citizenship as the know-how to perform a repertoire of significant actions before others who possess similar knowledge, or as a shared understanding between people about how to behave, communicate, and respond to one another at various times and places in the public and private spheres. It shouldn't matter whether the script in question is played out formally in a courtroom, in the citizen assembly, while participating in a religious procession, or more informally while at the theater, performing a ritual at one's family hearth, or conversing at a symposium with fellow members of one's phratry (a local political, social and religious organization of citizens).[13]

The ability to perform citizen scripts as "rules of engagement," I maintain, was not invented wholesale in the early years of the democracy; instead Athenians developed these scripts piecemeal from a cultural storehouse of prescribed behavior inherited from earlier stages

---

[12] For a folklorist and anthropological notion of "script," see Bauman 1977: 9.

[13] On the various citizen organizations in the democracy, see Jones 1999. How distinctive were citizen scripts compared to scripts played out by noncitizens? E. Cohen challenges long-standing assumptions that: (1) Athenian citizens saw themselves as markedly different from noncitizen metics (resident aliens) and slaves; (2) inhabitants of Attica (the territory of Athens) regularly distinguished citizens from noncitizens in daily encounters; (3) citizens' relations to others were fundamentally power relationships; (4) citizens and noncitizens in daily life pursued significantly different goals (2000). Despite Cohen's at times persuasive arguments, Athenians did distinguish citizens from noncitizens in scripts played out in the political and cultural spheres, especially when deliberating and deciding questions of justice and public policy, verifying membership in the citizen body, and practicing certain cults and civic performances.

of political life. In recent years a few classicists have begun connecting research in cognitive psychology and discourse analysis to early Greek poetry with the goal of understanding how the early Greeks stored cultural knowledge in narrative "scripts" that enabled them to retrieve and express that knowledge in stereotypical bits and chunks.[14] The terminology these scholars use can at times be confusing, for they speak of "frames," "scripts," "scenarios," "schemas," "plans," etc., to describe the "shared seeing" of a world between performer and audience. I'll adopt their use of "script" to designate a fixed, stereotypical representation of knowledge incorporating a sequence of actions, speech acts and situations. For example, today a static stereotype such as the "automobile" can be scripted various ways into "at the auto show," "at the carwash," "buying a new car," "buying a second-hand car," or "fatal automobile accident." Or, in Homer, scripts take the form of narrative themes that transform a stereotype such as "weapon" into "a hero arms for battle," or "meal" into "a meal of hospitality shared by host and guest.[15] From these scholars' perspective, we might then want to know, for example, whether Goldhill's four master citizen actions constitute "citizen scripts" of this sort.[16]

PERFORMING SELFHOOD

The notion of citizenship as the ability or privilege to perform certain roles in citizen scripts accounts well for the collective identity citizens share. But if we recall Goldhill's suggestion that performing citizenship led Athenians to a "construction of the self" as "the

---

[14] I have in mind Minchin 2001 and 1992, Russo 1999, Bakker 1997a, 1997b, 1993, and Rubin 1995.

[15] See Minchin 1992: 233–35, esp. 235, n. 29, adapting the term from Schank and Abelson 1977. See also Brown and Yule 1983: 241–43.

[16] I use "script" to include the more complex organization of what some discourse analysts and classicists call a "schema" (Russo 1999; Brown and Yule 1983) or a "scenario" (Sanford and Garrod 1981).

political subject of democracy" (9), we'll want to know whether performance can also serve as a royal road to understanding how Athenians experienced their individuality. And by this I mean not just bringing an idiosyncratic style to playing a certain role but enacting a selfhood distinct from others who might share that same role.[17] To achieve this, performance needs to account for the similarities and differences between ancient and modern conceptions of selfhood. This gap, Goldhill realizes, has become problematic today because we are increasingly sensitive to ways in which classicists of previous generations anachronistically evaluated the Greek self through Cartesian and Kantian models of subjectivity, but the remedy he proposes sidesteps the most important issues.[18] Because of work bridging classics and moral philosophy by scholars such as Nussbaum (1986), B. Williams (1993), Gill (1996), and others, it's become clear that contemporary theories of the self influence our capacity to appreciate whether or not the Greeks, from Homer to the Classical period, could achieve selfhood in the modern sense, or genuinely deliberate and exercise a will, or possess any degree of individual moral autonomy, or, to our mind, be held morally responsible for their actions. These scholars show us, in other words, the need to theorize about the self comparatively if we wish to determine how close or distant Greek selves are from our

[17] On the various meanings of our modern notion of the self, see Gill 1996: 1, with his discussion of the methodological problems we face when we apply these meanings to the Greeks (2ff.). See also the typology of modern individuals and its application to the Greek city-state in Gribble 1999: 7–23, and the essays in Pelling 1990.

[18] Goldhill thinks we can avoid projecting modern notions of "inwardness, privacy and individual personality" onto Athenians if we provide a "historically specific and nuanced account of the constitution of the citizen as a political subject across and through a range of particular social practices and discourses" (1999: 9–10); cf. Rhodes' warnings on scholarly "subjectivity" (2003a: 9–17). For discussion of increased scholarly sensitivity to confusing ancient and modern notions of self, Goldhill cites Pelling 1990 and Gill 1996.

own – and somehow performance would have to accommodate this theorizing.[19]

We've seen, for example, effective criticisms of Snell's contentions that Homeric individuals lack a true self in the sense of a self-conscious agent possessing psychic unity and a true will, and that they are therefore "deficient" in moral autonomy.[20] It's also harder now to uphold M. I. Finley's contention that nowhere in Homer do we find "rational discussion" and deliberation in the form of "a sustained, disciplined consideration of circumstances and their implications" (1979 [1954]), whether by individuals or groups.[21] We've learned as well to recognize in the practical conflicts faced by tragic characters, such as Aeschylus' Agamemnon, moral dilemmas consistent with a modern understanding of this term, and appreciate how individual characters, such as Homer's Penelope and the female protagonists of Athenian tragedy, function as moral agents in senses both ancient and modern.[22] And Gill has recently facilitated this effort to shuttle between ancient and modern selves by devising a classificatory scheme to distinguish Cartesian- and Kantian-inspired types of self, which he calls "subjective-individualist" because they are centered around the "I" as the subject of

[19] Alford's *The Self in Social Theory* (1991) offers a comparative, psychoanalytic approach to theorizing about the self from Homer and Plato to Hobbes, Locke, Rousseau, and John Rawls. Villa (2001) reconstructs Socrates' notion of the citizen as an individual center of moral and intellectual agency and then relates this ideal to modern notions of citizenship in J. S. Mill, Nietzsche, Weber, Arendt, and L. Strauss.

[20] See, e.g., Sharples 1983, Gaskin 1990, B. Williams 1993: 21–49, Gill 1996: 29–41, and Hammer 1998. Vernant's has been the most influential recent argument for the Greeks' lack of a true will and moral decision-making in the modern sense (1988).

[21] On rational deliberation and decision making in Homer, see in particular Schofield 1986, in addition to Sharples 1983, Gaskins 1990, B. Williams 1993: 35–36, Teffeteller 2003, and Barnouw 2004; 7–120.

[22] On conflicts like Agamemnon's, see Nussbaum 1986: 25–50; for Penelope and female tragic protagonists, see Foley 1995 and 2001: 107ff.

self-consciousness, from other approaches to the self, which he calls "objective-participant" because they are grounded in a more objectively based understanding of individuals as psychological entities that participate in interpersonal, collective relationships (1996: 1–13, esp. 11–12).

So my retooling of performance, if it is to account for degrees of identity that are both shared with others and distinct from them, must embrace ancient and modern understandings of self. It also needs to enrich the notion of a script from discourse analysis in order to accommodate ancient and modern theories of citizenship.[23] Interestingly, most of the scholars who are adept at theorizing the Greek and modern selves have little to say about citizenship in connection to selfhood, whether in ancient Greece or the modern world. And since, as we've seen, most scholars of citizenship in Athenian democracy studies don't engage much in dialogue with contemporary theories of citizenship, they likewise don't incorporate theories of self into their work. I propose, however, to relate the Greeks' experience of how citizenship and selfhood overlap to attempts in contemporary political theory to understand their interconnection, for this field explores ways we might pursue our individuality today and still retain or renew our capacity for citizenship.[24] Simultaneously maintaining both ancient and modern perspectives on citizenship and selfhood is essential, I believe, because we find already embedded in every theory or model of citizenship a

---

[23] I generally agree with Rhodes' dictum that contemporary approaches to ancient history need to "do justice" to the past by avoiding a simple projection of our concepts and needs (our "subjectivity") onto the ancients (2003a: 17). But his criteria for regulating the scope of our interpretations oversimplifies the variety of meanings an action, text, or object may have in its original context and when seen in other contexts (9–17).

[24] See Kymlicka 2002: 284ff. for a survey of major trends in contemporary citizenship theory.

particular concept of self. And this self relies on performing a finite number of scripts to enact its relation, whatever that might be, to a community of speakers.

SELF AND COMMUNITY: THREE CONTEMPORARY VISIONS AND THEIR SCRIPTS

Three particularly coherent visions of how self and community should be interconnected have emerged in contemporary political theory since the early 1970s: revised liberal models of society and the individual; the communitarian critique of these models; and most recently the alternative vision of deliberative democracy. Liberal thinkers have long tended to conceive of individuals as closed, "atomist" or "unencumbered" beings constituted prior to interaction with others by their individual preferences and willful choice of self-interest. In the liberal vision communal ties to one another result from contractual agreements secured by inalienable rights designed to protect individual freedoms and by a "thin," minimal consensus about collective needs.[25] Beginning in the 1980s, communitarian thinkers began questioning the coherence of this vision of individuals and their communities, arguing for the notion of a more interpersonal self whose nature was constituted by moral choices conditioned by ties to others and by historically defined traditions, and calling for revival of a "thick" sense of collective identity not unlike classical forms of republicanism.[26] By the 1990s an alternative to the communitarian critique of liberalism

---

[25] I'm referring to the liberalism of Rawls 1971 and 1993, and to neo-republican versions of liberalism like Dagger 1997. For an overview of Rawlsian liberalism in the context of contemporary political philosophy, see Kymlicka 2002: 53–101, with bibliography.

[26] See Sandel 1998 and 1984, Taylor 1995, 1994, 1989, 1985a, and 1985b, and Walzer 1990. For an overview of communitarianism in its contemporary context, see Kymlicka 2002:

became apparent through a "deliberative turn" in democratic theory, which identified democratic legitimacy with the ability of individuals and groups to participate in decisions about public values and policies through a discourse free from coercion, manipulation, or deception.[27] At the heart of this ability lies the process by which diverse individuals and groups reach agreement or consensus, and here some proponents of deliberative democracy characterize the self as not merely interpersonal but "intersubjective."[28] Some deliberative democrats also maintain that universal participation in forming consensus even has the potential to transform a self whose decision making was previously impaired.[29]

Each of these contemporary visions depends for its vigor on different theories of the self and community; and each contributes to debate today in democratic theory centering around features of selfhood and

208–83, with bibliography. From a liberal perspective, Phillips uses four criteria of community in thinkers like MacIntyre (1984), Sandel, Taylor, and Walzer to evaluate democratic Athens – and finds the totality of Athenian society falling far short of that ideal (which he considers a historical illusion) (1993: 122–48 and 10–21).

[27] See, e.g., Warren 2001 and 1995, Dryzek 2000, Elster 1998, Bohman and Rehg 1997, Bohman 1996. I also include Habermas' major contribution to deliberative democracy (1996a, 1996b, 1992, 1990, 1987, and 1984).

[28] I use this term in connection with the need of one self and another to cooperate if they are to produce meaningful utterances, especially according to G. H. Mead's (1934) theory. For Mead, communication occurs only when a speaker chooses an utterance because of the meaning he or she believes it will have for an addressee: meaning thus emerges not from the privileged position of a self (or subject) but only when self and other meet to share positions mutually; cf. Bakhtin's "communicative function" of language (1986: 67–68). For thinkers like Habermas intersubjectivity accurately reflects the process of individuation that produces the self, and it also describes the necessary communicative dynamics behind the rational exchange of ideas that produces understanding. See, e.g., Habermas 1987: 10–11 and 58–60; 1992: 149–204. For the term's pervasive importance to Habermas' work, see Rehg 1994, and for its Habermasian use in contemporary citizenship theory, see McAfee 2000: 23–55.

[29] Warren 1995: 184–88.

community that sometimes compete and sometimes overlap. The tendency of the liberal, communitarian, and deliberative democrat visions to contradict as well as converge with one another strikes me as particularly fruitful, especially where we can recognize similar patterns of contradiction and convergence in the Greeks' experiences as citizens and selves. In this study I identify these patterns in a finite number of citizen scripts that were practiced at particular historical moments in the development of Greek polity. These range from very early scripts, which predate citizenship itself in the state's Formative period (the Middle to Late Geometric periods, ninth to eighth centuries); they include scripts from oligarchic city-states in the Archaic period (seventh to late sixth centuries); and they conclude with scripts from the Athenian democracy of the fifth and fourth centuries. And so, just as modern theories of the self can clarify our perceptions of Greek selfhood, I believe that arguments among liberal, communitarian, and deliberative democrat understandings of self and community can inform our understanding of how the Greeks experienced these two dimensions of identity.

The Liberal Script: The Citizen as Self

If there is a particular notion of self embedded in every theory or model of citizenship, and if the self enacts its relation to a community in performing a script, then each script asks the following question: How autonomous is the self? It's important to note at the outset that autonomy, in the basic senses of self-legislation and self-determination, has acquired a plurality of meanings that sometimes mix political, social and moral dimensions, and that this was true for its ancient[30] as well as

---

[30] We'll see in Chapter 5 that Athenians didn't begin using the word *autonomia* until the 460s or 450s, and then in a restricted sense to designate one city-state's freedom from a more powerful ally's interference in its domestic politics (Ostwald 1982: 1–46; cf. the critique in Farrar 1988: 30, n. 54, and 103–6). But soon enough the term could

modern and contemporary uses.[31] So performing a citizen script invokes a cluster of ancient and modern concerns about the self's autonomy – and ways to qualify it when the self enacts its tie to community. For an example we can see how the history of these concerns links ancient and modern thinkers if we compare the moral autonomy Socrates defends in the *Apology* to the modern liberal tradition's understanding

refer to the social and political freedoms (*eleutheria, isêgoria, parrhêsia*) democratic Athenians enjoyed in their public and personal lives – positive freedoms of speech, conduct, and thought, and negative freedoms from political control and social censure. These senses are distinct from the moral autonomy that enabled them collectively to determine the values and "goods" characteristic of their community and individually to decide how to pursue a life dedicated to self-determined values and "goods." On the *eleutheria* enjoyed by Athenians both collectively and individually, see Wallace 1996 and 1994, Hansen 1996 (esp. 94), and Raaflaub 1983. For the Athenians' practice of individual autonomy in the moral sense, in addition to Farrar 1988 see Nussbaum 1986 (as "self-sufficiency"), and B. Williams 1993: 75–102.

[31] On the role of autonomy in the history of modern moral philosophy up to and including Kant, see, for example, Schneewind 1998. Contemporary discussions of post-Kantian autonomy as individual self-determination tend to intertwine social, political, and moral visions. The concept remains the "true core … the inner citadel" of liberalism upon which its notion of moral responsibility depends (Kekes 1997: 15 and 1–22); see Norton 1991: 8 and 44ff., for a liberal version of autonomy influenced by communitarian critique. Individual and collective autonomy provide the battleground for the communitarian critique of liberalism, inspiring some liberal and neo-republican thinkers to conceptualize a hybrid "liberal republicanism" whose individual autonomy rests on "interdependence" with others, not independence from them. See Macedo's notion of an autonomous individual whose public and private virtues are "interdependent" (1990: 265); Norton's definition of interdependence as "determining for oneself what one's contributions to others will be, and determining for oneself which values from the self-actualizing lives of others to utilize, and how" (1991: 113); and Dagger, for whom "autonomy entails *inter*dependence," transforming the liberal autonomous person from a "lone rights-bearer" into "someone who depends upon others" for substantial independence (1997: 39). For deliberative democracy both senses of autonomy constitute democracy's "fundamental norm" or "good"; see Warren, who argues for autonomy as a *political* good while trying to suppress its moral dimensions (2001: 62 and 236, n. 2 [with references]). Others stress that citizens in a democracy must recognize one another as "equal moral persons" (J. Cohen 1998: 18).

of individual autonomy. The latter is envisioned as a script enacted by an agent resembling Kant's transcendental subject, with free access to an autonomous will when deciding questions of justice on the basis of universal categories of duty or prohibition. And for Kant these categories, above all, cannot be defined by practical circumstances or fixed notions of the good (1788).

Contemporary liberal thinkers have adapted this Kantian subject in various ways, most notably in Rawls' formulation of the "unencumbered self" who is free from the accidents of birth and circumstance (familial, ethnic or racial, religious, etc.) and so may enact the "original position" when deciding questions of distributive justice (1971). As a script the original position establishes for Rawls a context of time, space, and agency that preserves the self's autonomous will by positing real, and not transcendental, beings who exercise the right to decide about justice behind a "veil of ignorance" concerning their own or anyone else's place in society, assets, abilities, or specific purposes, ends, and conceptions of the good (Rawls 1971: 12). In this way each agent of justice is free to choose principles that are not informed or constrained by knowledge that might foster privilege or prejudice. Rawls' is a script, then, where the "right" of a radically autonomous self to choose is, above all, prior to any "good" it or others might choose; and it justifies the pursuit of a diversity of goods.

As a citizen script the original position and its unencumbered self are designed to ensure a particularly liberal vision of distributive justice in our contemporary, multicultural societies.[32] But the script has antecedents, not only in the modern liberal tradition of social contract theory, but in democratic Athens, where Socrates enacted a dissident form of citizenship whose goals were to avoid two moral faults: com-

---

[32] See Kymlicka's lucid description and defense of Rawls' original position (2002: 60–70).

mitting injustice, and contradicting one's own moral commitments. In Chapter 7 I will discuss attempts by today's ancient historians, philosophers and political theorists to justify the democratic citizenship Socrates enacts in such texts as the *Apology*, *Crito*, and *Gorgias*. They readily acknowledge its foundation in a new theory of the self's relation to community – in "an individual's private decision to behave ethically" (Ober 1998: 181), or in the "moral individualism" Socrates invented (Villa 2001: 1).[33] To achieve "genuine autonomy" for a human being (Farrar 1988: 1988), or "the thinking individual's relative moral independence" (Villa 2001: 41), Socrates had to preach a "partial estrangement" (14) of the self from the collective, shared norms of democratic citizenship outlined by Pericles in his Funeral Oration and experienced by Athenians through the citizen scripts they played out in the Assembly, law courts, and so forth (5–12). And the sort of knowledge this required, again according to Villa, was nonexpert and not dependent on the transcendental truths and realities later endorsed by Plato (28–29). We therefore could make a case for Socrates (at least in the *Apology* and *Gorgias*) as a fair Athenian equivalent to Rawls' unencumbered self in the original position. But how can we evaluate Socrates' aberrant achievement as a citizen and self if we don't locate it within a dialogue between ancients and moderns that embraces both moral theory about the self and political theory about citizenship?[34]

[33] See Ober on Socrates the citizen within the context of Athenian politics of the late fifth and fourth centuries BC (1998: 166–213); cf. Colaico 2002. See Wallach on the historical Socrates' influence on the Platonic art of politics (2001: 92–119), esp. his summary (116–18, nn. 193 and 194) of scholarly opinion on Socrates' relation to democracy (e.g., Wood and Wood 1978, Euben 1990, Vlastos 1991 and 1994, Kraut 1984, and Irwin 1977 and 1995). Villa discusses Socrates' dissident citizenship in light of its influence on later political thinkers (2001: 1–58).

[34] Villa acknowledges Socrates' founding role in liberal thinking (e.g., 2001: 306), and casually refers to him as hostile to the contemporary notion of an "encumbered" self (23), but his discussion avoids detailed engagement with contemporary ideologies

The Communitarian Script: The Self as Citizen

By the 1980s Rawls' original position, with its "priority of the right over the good," had come under attack by communitarian thinkers such as Michael Sandel, who pinpoints contradictions in the key actions that constituted the self and its relations to others.[35] In particular Sandel finds illusory the claim that the unencumbered self posseses a radical autonomy "individuated in advance" of contact with others and with "bounds [that] . . . are fixed in advance," arguing instead that the self must be both "intersubjective" (constituted by ties to others in various senses of community) and "intrasubjective" (constituted by competing, multiple identities within a single person) (1998: 62–63). Most importantly, Sandel challenges Rawls' notion of the self as an exclusively "voluntarist" agent. By this he means that, if we understand human agency as "the faculty whereby the self comes by its ends" (58), then for Rawls the self in the original position exists prior to its ends – and yet it defines itself by the willful act of choosing its ends. We can, Sandel suggests, alternatively conceive of the self as an agent whose ends are given in advance – by the norms and traditions of its community, for example – and in this case self-definition is achieved through reflection and introspection about which ends one might "own up to," as I prefer to phrase it. Such a self-constitution Sandel calls "cognitive," in

like liberalism and communitarianism. Santas explores Platonic and Aristotelian conceptions of the ultimate good in light of Rawls' diversity of goods, especially in relation to theories of justice (2001). Wallach places Platonic political theory within an ancient–modern context (2001: 396–401), suggesting that we look to a "rehistoricized" Plato as a superior theorist of deliberative democracy compared to contemporaries like Rawls and Habermas (400–10). Mara tries to cast Plato's Socrates as the Athenian equivalent of a contemporary deliberative democrat who is also a "liberal ironist" (1997, esp. 251–59).

[35] See Sandel 1998. Sandel 1984 provides a brief introduction to his critique of Rawls' original position.

this special sense, and its script focuses on the act of discovering within oneself senses of the good (58ff.).[36]

This communitarian critique of liberalism's script in the 1980s and 1990s clearly draws on models of the self anchored in the ideology of classical civic republican communities like Athens and Rome (often described as "Aristotelian republicanism").[37] And Sandel's "voluntarist" and "cognitive" types of the self in relation to its ends (and in relation to community) clearly resonate with a history of the self, from Homer onward, which moral philosophers and classicists can trace. If we take these voluntarist and cognitive types of self as different dimensions of, or elements within, the self, we can find the tension between them in two heroic prototypes for the Greek citizen, Homer's Achilles and Odysseus. Chapters 1 and 3 of my study demonstrate the first stage in such a history of citizenship and selfhood, when each hero experiences a version of the unencumbered self in a moment of moral duress. Each needs to decide a question of justice concerning his own *timê*, the relative rank or reward he deserves from authoritative others in his society. Both Achilles in his tent at Troy and Odysseus on Calypso's isle use voluntarist elements of self to define themselves through ends they might obtain from others, but each in different ways briefly hypothesizes about the kind of self he might *wish* to be. The self each chooses to become, however, is not entirely self-fashioned by voluntarist elements – as a liberal self would be – but one they own up

---

[36] Rawls defends the "original position" in *Political Liberalism* (1993), jettisoning a Kantian conception of the self in favor of a self split into two discontinuous roles: a private individual free to pursue whatever moral ends it might choose, and a political, public identity as a citizen deliberating autonomously about justice in a public arena free from anyone's personal conceptions of the good. Sandel challenges this script centered on a self bifurcated into private and political roles (1998: 184–218)

[37] See Kymlicka's discussion of the civic republican strand in contemporary citizenship theory (2002: 294–99; cf. Kymlicka and Norman 1995: 293–94).

to when, responding to cognitive elements, their will accepts ends and attachments provided by others.

Later chapters (6 and 7) extend this history to democratic Athens, where we'll see Socrates and his contemporaries play out similar inner conflicts between voluntarist and cognitive elements of the self. The divide between today's liberals and communitarians serves as a helpful lens to examine the ideal of democratic citizenship engineered from about 450 to the 420s by the sophist Protagoras and statesman Pericles – and also to understand how alternatives to their paradigm of citzen and self could be performed by Athenians as diverse as the sophist and speechwriter Antiphon (ca. 480–411), and the statesman, general and bon vivant Alcibiades (ca. 450–407), in addition to Socrates (ca. 469–399). As alternative paradigms, all three of these emerged in the shadow of the citizenship and selfhood endorsed by Protagoras and Pericles, and I'll relate these shadow citizens and selves to the possibilities for moral autonomy opened up by the *nomos/physis* controversy and by different styles of a democratically narcissistic personality.

But in the 1980s and 1990s other voices besides Sandel's have been contributing to the communitarian critique of liberal scripts of selfhood and citizenship. Some of these foreground more fundamentally linguistic or communicative questions about the self's constitution and ties to others, and these voices will enable us to: return closer to performance as a royal road to understanding ancient and modern citizen scripts; and find a few paths of convergence linking the liberal, communitarian and deliberative democrat visions. Charles Taylor, in a range of essays, has challenged liberalism's radically autonomous self by insisting on the self's anchorage in a linguistic tie to others, so that "one cannot be a self on one's own. I am a self only in relation to certain interlocutors . . . . only within . . . 'webs of interlocution'" (1989: 36). For Taylor this crucible of language determines the very nature of human agency, or what it means to be a "person," because it enables

us to interpret our lives and make the choices we use to define ourselves (1985a). (It's in these choices enacting personhood and autonomy that we'll find possible convergences between Rawlsian liberalism
and the communitarianism of Taylor and Sandel.[38]) For Taylor language also provides the sole medium we have to achieve "recognition"
of our unique identity from "significant others" (here Taylor adapts
G. H. Mead's term "generalized other") with whom we struggle in dialogical relationships.[39]

Using Taylor's concept of the person, I derive two fundamental, programmatic questions about Greek individuality from the moral dilemmas about justice confronted by Achilles, Odysseus, the democratically ideal citizen of Protagoras-Pericles, his "shadows" in Antiphon,
Alcibiades, and Socrates, and others. These questions are: "If I am to
decide this question of justice, what kind of person must I become?"
And: "If I am to decide this question of justice, what kind of person do
I wish to become?" The negotiation between this imperative and this

---

[38] In this act of choice that defines us as a person, we find a potential overlap between
the Rawlsian self and the self of communitarians like Taylor and Sandel. Kymlicka
points out that the distinction in these three thinkers' concept of the self boils down
to "where, within the person, to draw the boundaries of the self" (2002: 227), and
how to understand the conditions under which we exercise autonomy (245–46).
It would not be inaccurate to describe the self of Taylor and Sandel as a hybrid
liberal–communitarian self alternately dominated by its voluntarist and cognitive
dimensions.

[39] Taylor 1994: 32–33. Mead's "generalized other" is the organization of all the attitudes
which members of a community or social group may legitimately adopt toward
one another and the group as a whole. Each fully developed self must learn to
internalize the attitudes not only of particular others he or she encounters but
of the group as a whole (1934: 152–64). Mead uses an analogy from game-playing:
before each move, the individual chess player must keep in mind not only his or her
opponent's possible moves but those moves that all competent chess players might
legitimately make at that moment. In this study I use "dominant social other" as a
synonym for Mead's "generalized other." Cf. Joas on game-playing and the "role,"
self, and generalized other in Mead (1985: 118–20).

imaginative hypothesis, and the self-transformation each implies, is a major focus of the study.

Taylor helps us move away from a preoccupation with individuality and toward community because his communitarian script insists that the interpersonal linguistic link between speaker and listener has the capacity to create public space: "But the crucial and highly obtrusive fact about language, and human symbolic communication in general, is that it serves to found public space, that is, to place certain matters before *us*" (1985a: 259, emphasis in the original). He describes this achievement as a "move" into the "for-us," and he regards this "move into public space" as "one of the most important things we bring about in language . . ." and as "essential" to the "sense of a shared immediate common good" characteristic of republics ancient and modern (1995: 190–91). To exemplify how language forges a shared, "for-us" reality, he in fact points to democratic Athens, suggesting that visiting Persians would have been befuddled by the political sense Athenians created for such ordinary words as "equal" and "like" (*isos, homoios*). While not unfamiliar with the simple concepts of equality or likeness as an attribute of many things, the Persians' "horizon of values" would not have enabled them to articulate the Athenian idiom in a linguistic currency that had meaning for the Persian political experience (1985a: 275–77).

A key critical voice that points to both contradictions and convergences within liberal and communitarian thinking, offering a bridge between these visions and deliberative democracy, belongs to Jürgen Habermas. From as far back as the 1970s he too has located the self's origins and its tie to the dominant social other (i.e., Mead's "generalized other") in language – and here we return to performance and my promise to retool it. As Goldhill implied when he identified four master-actions of Athenian citizenship, the performance linking citizen and self to others enacts a fundamentally linguistic relation. But Habermas makes this more explicit by borrowing the term "performative" from

Austin's speech act theory to designate a dimension within an utterance that enacts rather than proposes a certain state of affairs – as expressed, for example, by stating, "I hereby declare the games of this Thirtieth Olympiad open." The performative thrust of an utterance helps transform its "propositional" dimension, which states something to be the case from a third-person, objective perspective, into an "illocutionary" dimension enabling a first-person speaker to communicate how he/she intends a second-person listener to interpret it – in this case, by "declaring" the games open rather than merely stating that they're open or "denying," "forbidding," or "lamenting" their opening.[40] So in the performative utterance a first-person speaker affirms to a second-person listener that a certain state of affairs is "hereby" the case – and in the process establishes an intersubjective relation between them to serve as a basis for reaching understanding.[41]

To see how the performative quality of an utterance works hand-in-glove with its illocutionary force, recall how at *Iliad* 9.132–33 Homer dramatically transforms the proposition "Agamemnon never climbed into bed and made love to Briseis" (Achilles' prize captive) into the old warlord's performative declaration of a *promise* to *swear an oath* to Nestor and the other chiefs: "*And I will swear a mighty oath* that I *never* climbed into bed and made love to her"). By promising "hereby" to swear that

[40] See, e.g., Habermas 1979: 43ff., where he distinguishes between these two dimensions of a speech act in this way: illocutionary meaning emerges when we intersubjectively share an interpersonal relation with a first-person speaker. We tend to grasp a speech act's propositional content through the objective, third-person attitude of an observer (48). See also Habermas 1984: 111. Petrey provides useful definitions and descriptions of performative utterances (1990: 4–21), and he indicates how Austin's notion of an utterance's "illocutionary force" and meaning conform to social conventions that are in effect for a particular social group at a particular historical moment (12–15).

[41] For Habermas the illocutionary component of a speech act relies on a performative sentence to carry it out, usually in a present indicative affirmation to a second person, and accompanied explicitly or implicitly by an expression meaning "hereby" (1979: 36).

"hereby" he has never, Agamemnon, with a first performative utterance, a promise ("I will swear"), endows with certainty a state of affairs, namely, that a second performative utterance will occur ("a mighty oath "). And this second performative utterance endows with certainty the proposition that he never slept with Briseis. All three utterances are bound with an illocutionary force made doubly explicit through the promise and the oath. In this way he assumes a "performative attitude" toward his community, one anchoring his interlocutors and himself in the shared set of norms they rely on to reach mutual understandings.

In effect, Habermas isolates the performative attitude accompanying the illocutionary dimension of speech acts to see it as the key element in a script conferring (or confirming) both individuality and one's social relation to others. And while he explicitly sees it at work in the "illocutionary mode" of modern genres such as the confession, diary, and autobiography, its communicative dynamics match well enough the competitive displays of self-presentation in the four master citizen actions of competition, display, appearance and spectating that, according to Goldhill, enabled Athenian citizens to have their social standing (*timê*) collectively evaluated and judged by others (1999: 4–6, 8). Habermas describes this performative attitude in terms consistent with Taylor's understanding of what constitutes a "person" and the person's need for recognition from a "significant other" (what I call the "dominant social other"): "it is not a matter of *reports* and descriptions from the perspective of an observer, not even of *self-observations*; rather, it is a matter of interested *presentations of self*, with which a complex claim presented to second persons is justified – a claim to recognition of the irreplaceable identity of an ego manifesting itself in a conscious way of life" (1992: 167; emphasis in the original).[42]

---

[42] There's a congruence here with the script Taylor outlines for modern identity in his essay on the "politics of recognition" (1994), especially concerning the self's

This notion of a performative attitude, when it accompanies illocutionary statements in an act of self-presentation, holds the key to understanding how performing certain cultural scripts enables individuals to negotiate with others recognition of both citizenship and selfhood. By identifying and describing how it operates within a given script, we should be able to see how this use of language opens up a public, "for-us" space that is intersubjectively shared by interlocutors, and that may well exclude others – Persians visiting Periclean Athens, for example – who cannot participate in the performative attitude struck by Athenian speakers of equality. (In fact the Persians' perplexity when Athenians use words for equality describes the corresponding performative attitude of the Asiatic foreigner.) Also, if we wish to determine degrees of the self's autonomy vis-à-vis others and their community traditions, this performative attitude should serve as an index: at one extreme the self may be entirely constituted by the discourse of others and of traditions; at another it may establish itself as an outsider, essentially distinct from their discourse and traditions; or it may discover intermediate positions between these poles.[43]

To appreciate the importance of performative attitudes embedded in the illocutionary force of what citizens say, let's look at the act that inaugurated Athenian citizenship. This act required an individual to cross over an illocutionary threshold by performing a speech genre: swearing

---

dependence on others for its identity. For Habermas the ego itself "retains an intersubjective core because the process of individuation from which it emerges runs through the network of linguistically mediated interactions" (1992: 170). For Taylor "my discovering my own identity doesn't mean that I work it out in isolation, but that I negotiate it through dialogue, partly overt, partly internal, with others" (1994: 34).

[43] My use of "performative attitude" lends more flexibility to the positions individuals may take vis-à-vis the dominant social other. Compare, e.g., Gill's rigid distinctions between "subjective-individualist" and "objective-participant" selves (1996: 11–12 and *passim*).

an oath.[44] When young men between the ages of eighteen and twenty served as apprentice citizens (ephebes), they received military training, religious instruction, and moral guidance from elders.[45] After passing scrutiny at a formal ceremony called a *dokimasia* on both the local and state levels – we'll discuss this script at greater length in Chapters 5 and 7 – they took an oath at the sanctuary of the god Aglaurus.[46] Note in the following epigraphic version of the oath how each ephebe presents himself to the dominant social other by using the promissory part of the oath to represent persons and objects listening to him as the citizen body he will soon join; they occupy the subject position of third-person observers (future comrades in the hoplite phalanx, state officials, weapons, and state institutions). Also note how he then uses the oath's invocation to establish an I–you relationship with ancient divinities and the land itself (its boundaries marked by fields of key agricultural products); these he configures as second-person interlocutors called to witness the promise. As a composite speech genre, the oath combines the promise and invocation into one illocutionary component and into a performative attitude that constructs two spatiotemporal frames, one

[44] Bakhtin defines a speech genre as a stable type of utterance with a characteristic use of thematic content, style, and structure (1986: 60). See Hirzel's basic study of the oath in Greek literature and society (1966). See the more recent Sealey 1994: 95–100 (primarily on Homeric oaths), Loraux 2002a (oaths and civic strife from Hesiod to democratic Athens), and Cole 1996 (oaths used to define and enact citizenship in Athenian democracy). In Sealey's simplified scheme, a typical Greek oath consists of: invocation (to a deity), content (a promise or statement of fact), and imprecation (a curse the speaker calls down on himself if he fails his promise or lies in stating facts) (1994: 96).

[45] Pseudo-Aristotle's *Constitution of the Athenians* provides the most detailed description of the ephebate as it existed in the fourth century (*Ath.Pol.*42). On the traditional nature of the ephebate and its probable establishment early in the democracy, see Pélékides 1962, esp. 78, and my discussion (with additional references) in Chapter 5.

[46] For the time of the oath's administration, see Pélékides 1962: 111 and Rhodes 1981: 506.

nested inside the other: the larger frame of Athens' community memory over which divine agents and the land preside, and the smaller frame of each ephebe's own life as a citizen.

To echo Taylor, the oath creates in just a few words a "web of interlocution," a "for-us" reality; to echo Habermas, the oath uses all three subject positions (first, second and third persons) to transform the ephebe from an outsider into a privileged member of the community. In my sense of citizenship as performance, it splices the "performative" of speech act theory into the performance of a social script by aligning individuals, groups, and temporal-social spaces into performative attitudes and subject positions. The end result has the speaking self and the dominant social other he invokes reciprocally recognize one another. The inscription reads:

> *This is the ancestral oath the ephebes must swear:*
> *"I will not disgrace these sacred weapons, nor will I abandon the man*
> *at my side wherever [in the line] I may be stationed. I will protect our*
> *sacred and public institutions, and I will not pass on my fatherland in*
> *worse condition but greater and better, by myself or with everyone's help.*
> *And I will obey those who for now hold authority reasonably, and the*
> *established laws, and those they will establish reasonably in the future.*
> *If anyone should try to do away with them, I will not let them, either by*
> *myself or with everyone's help. And I will respect our ancestral sacred*
> *institutions. As witnesses I name the gods Aglaurus, Hestia, Enyo,*
> *Enyalius, Ares and Athena Areia, Zeus, Thallo, Auxo, Hegemone,*
> *Heracles, and the boundaries of the fatherland: wheat, barley, vines,*
> *olive trees, fig trees."*[47]

---

[47] This version of the oath was inscribed in the deme of Acharnae in the fourth century; I've modified Siewert's translation (1977: 103).

But the performative attitude within an illocutionary statement can generate other, more innovative or flexible types of individual identity and community membership. Let's return to Taylor's example of Persian visitors in Athens. Does their perplexity inevitably exclude them from ever participating in the sense of community Athenian citizens share? Ideally, according to Habermas, these Athenian speakers and their Persian listeners *could* align their performative attitudes to reach mutual understanding through a type of reasoning he calls "communicative." In this case they would overcome their cultural and linguistic divide by, first, understanding one another's utterances about equality as interpretations of their respective worlds, and, second, "negotiat[ing] common definitions of the situation" as a basis for generating a "communicative action" they might jointly carry out concerning a mutually acceptable notion of equality – perhaps in the diplomatic form of a peace treaty, or an agreement to form common cause against a third party (Habermas 1984: 95). Under these circumstances, their realignment of performative attitudes would have resulted in the creation of a new, if perhaps fragile, form of community, through a script we might call "forming an alliance" (*summakhia*).

Taylor helps us develop this example further by pointing to another term in the classical Athenian vocabulary with which visiting Persians would have struggled: "freedom" (*eleutheria*). For a person from a despotic culture, Taylor explains, "This notion of freedom, as a status within a certain kind of practice of self-rule, seems utterly devoid of sense. . . . What our Persian observer [can] not see . . . is the way in which 'equal,' 'like,' 'free,' and such terms as 'citizen,' help define a horizon of value. . . . They articulate the citizen's sensitivity to the standards intrinsic to this ideal and this way of life" (1985a: 276). In other words such propositions as "The freedom of Athenians makes them superior to other peoples," or "Athenians are fortunate to possess their kind of freedom," or "Freedom to an Athenian is worth more than any other possession," while perfectly comprehensible to the speaker and listeners of Pericles' Funeral Oration in 430, might provoke only a shake of the head from a Persian interlocutor – unless of course one could imagine a bilingual, bicultural Persian capable of exercising communicative reason and sharing common cause with Athenians and other Greeks who prized this freedom. The Athenian historian Xenophon tell us that this is more or less what the Persian prince Cyrus the Younger displayed in 401, when, in a doomed attempt to wrest the throne from his half-brother Artaxerxes, he exhorted his ten thousand Greek mercenaries before the battle of Cunaxa near Babylon. Note how he transforms versions of the three propositions about freedom into the illocutionary statements I italicize. In this way Cyrus uses self-presentation to enact a performative attitude which, at least momentarily, places him within a new, if fragile, community that is both Persian and Greek as he leads freedom-loving Greeks into this battle – now a genuinely Greco-Persian communicative action:

> *Men of Greece, I'm not leading you as my allies* [summakhous] *because I lack non-Greek men; rather, I've taken you with me because* I acknowledge [nomizôn] you to be braver and stronger than non-Greeks. *And so be worthy of the freedom you've come to possess and* for which I consider you to be fortunate [eudaimonizô]. *Know well that* I would prefer [heloimên an] to have that freedom *in exchange for many times more than all my other possessions. (Anabasis 1.7.3–4)*[48]

The Script of Deliberative Democracy: Citizen, Self, and Discourse

Through speeches like this we see how language uses such resources as illocutionary force and performative attitudes to transform the identity of both individuals and communities: Cyrus and his Greek mercenaries briefly metamorphose into Greco-Persians, hybrid versions of

---

[48] See Dillery's discussion of this passage in the context of panhellenic community, and others like it by fifth- and fourth-century Greek writers (1995: 60–61).

one another. This self-transformative potential in discourse leads us finally to a third contemporary voice in democratic theory, deliberative democracy. Habermas has been the most influential contributor to the strand of deliberative democracy nourished by the tradition of critical theory, usually called "discourse theory."[49] He contends that the liberal model of democracy, compared to the discourse theory model, defines the citizen's autonomy as too narrowly constricted by a series of negative rights to secure freedom from compulsion. The citizen's autonomy in communitarian models, he claims, may guarantee positive freedoms to participate in public deliberations, but such deliberations are "ethically constricted" because individuals ideally can discover who they are (or wish to be) only by drawing on fixed cultural or national traditions that converge toward common senses of the good (1996a: 23–25). Discourse theory better suits the diversity of today's democracies; rather than aim toward self-discovery, individual or collective, it forms public opinion by seeking out procedures of argument and reasoning that include the deliberative techniques of every political, ethnic, or moral tradition represented by those who will be affected by the outcome. And its ultimate goal should be, not a moral-political consensus, but a legal consensus on questions of justice in the form of law (25–30).

Discourse theory's self-transformative nature also offers the advantage of a field where political theory and psychology overlap, for it asks what impact participation in democratic discourse might have on "self-realization," or individuation, and on developing a more autonomous citizenry as well as self.[50] Warren has recently tried to explain democracy in terms of "democratic self-rule" or autonomy, which for him

[49] See Dryzek's account of the various "strands" in deliberative democracy (2000: 1–30).
[50] I have in mind studies like Warren 2000, 1995, and 1992, McAfee 2000, Seligman 1997, J. Cohen and Arato 1992, and Alford 1991.

includes ideals of equal access to the "power to make collective decisions" and to participate in "collective judgment." Within the latter,
he suggests, we find individual and collective identity interrelated:

> *First, democracy implies processes of communication through which
> individuals come to know* as individuals *what they want or think is
> right. Individuals should be the owners of their beliefs and preferences,
> meaning that beliefs and preferences should not be the result of
> manipulation or received opinion but rather the result of considered
> adherence. Second, democracy implies processes of communication
> through which a collectivity comes to know what it wants or thinks is
> right* as a collectivity. Collective *judgment indicates that individuals
> have given due consideration to what each wants* as a member of the
> collectivity, *enabling the collective to form a will or "public opinion."*
> (2001: 60; emphasis in the original)

In other words both senses of collective judgment depend on the exercise of autonomy at the individual and political levels. For individuals
today this might include the sense of a unique life history, the ability to
project goals from the past and present into the future while retaining
a reflexive core of self-identity, the ability to create projects and ideas,
and a capacity to separate oneself from circumstances like traditions
or institutions, perhaps by exercising self-reflexive evaluation of one's
own inner thoughts and emotions (Warren 2001: 63–65; cf. 1995: 172–75).
For communities, political autonomy implies a corresponding ability
to create a public will through processes of reasoning and justification
that incorporate individual judgments into consensual criteria for the
validity of opinions and reasons (Warren 2001: 65–67).

Deliberative democracy therefore contains its own conception of
a self whose participation in communicative interactions with others
promises degrees of change and even transformation. Some of these
changes may realize the personal, "voluntarist" ideal of liberalism, to

define oneself by the ends one chooses, but other changes will more closely correspond to the communitarian's ideal of a "cognitive" self reaching self-understanding through the traditions and norms of established communities – and owning up to them. Still other changes will result from the more innovative outcomes of communicative actions formed in debate and discussion with groups and individuals "foreign" to one's own experience. It is the interaction of all three of these dimensions of self – voluntarist, cognitive, and deliberative – that completes the notion of performance I see as the key to citizenship and selfhood.

How Greek Citizens and Selves Use Deliberation to Perform Justice and the Law

But did the Greeks engage in genuine deliberation by our contemporary standards? Some of today's deliberative democrats, such as Jon Elster, claim that the Athenians merely "mimicked" genuine deliberation (1998:1–2). And some historians, such as M. I. Finley, claim that nowhere in Homer do the Greeks deliberate in the modern sense of a sustained, rational discussion of competing courses of action, with clear consideration of their advantages and disadvantages (1979: 114–15). In this study I maintain that, starting with Homeric epic, the Greeks certainly deliberated in our sense of the term, and that they used deliberation to negotiate their identities as citizens and selves with varying degrees of individual freedom and political autonomy. The gallery of remarkable individuals already mentioned (Homer's Achilles and Odysseus; the Athenian democrats Protagoras, Pericles, Antiphon, Alcibiades, and Socrates) each performed selfhood and citizenship as a kind of deliberation. I also suggested that an important part of that deliberation tries to determine self-worth by taking the hypothetical form of such questions as "What sort of person must I become?" and "... do I wish to become?" But that deliberation is not just – or even primarily – about self-evaluation. More often, deciding a question of justice demands that an individual or group decide about the relative *timê* of others.

As a result this study tells the history of how the Greeks deliberated not just as individuals concerned with self-worth but as individuals and groups concerned with evaluating the worth of others in their community – both what sort of rank others should have and what sort of person others should be. In some form or other the citizen scripts "how citizens deliberate" and "rendering a judgment" therefore provide a thread I follow in each chapter – a blueprint congruent with Aristotle's in-a-nutshell definition of citizenship as "nothing else but participating in judgment and in exercising state authority" (*metekhein kriseôs kai arkhês, Pol.*3.1.4), which he further boils down to serving as a juror (*dikastês*) and member of a citizen assembly (*ekklêsiastês*, 3.1.8). In this study we'll see how the history I describe intertwines citizenship and individual autonomy in Greek states[51] in ways demonstrating that we cannot regard Aristotle's definition of citizenship as an attribute subordinate to selfhood or vice-versa: the two interconnect like the surfaces on a Moebius strip. We'll see that to be a Greek citizen one must enjoy the following privileges: a measure of individual *timê* deserving sufficient recognition from others to maintain a positive public image; a qualified personal autonomy permitting exercise of the will in individual and family self-interest so long as community welfare isn't damaged; and a set of deliberative freedoms including participation with peers in freedoms of speech, assembly, and an exchange of reason giving.

---

[51] By "Greek state" I mean both the city-state (the *polis*, pl. *poleis*) and the regionally defined state (the *ethnos*, pl. *ethnê*). For the distinction between them in the Archaic period (ca. 800–500), see Snodgrass 1980: 28–31 and 42–47; more generally, see Fouchard 2003: 9–70. Recent scholarship disputes this neat distinction, preferring to see these types as "tiers of identity" a community could adopt for various reasons at various times (see C. Morgan 2003: 1–16, and Hansen 1998).

In contrast to Achilles' discovery of a new kind of self in Chapter 1, Chapter 2 examines ways of performing justice in the prestate and early state periods (ninth to seventh centuries), when judicial chiefs (*basileis*) orchestrate deliberation in dispute settlement. Here the chief tries to lead disputants and their supporters to an agreement (a "straight" *dikê*) incorporating the interests of each side and in accord with tradition. We'll see, though, that the judicial chief achieves this sort of consensus through a cognitive virtuosity linking his performance to that of epic bards and compromising the autonomy of the dispute's participants.

In Chapter 3 I argue that Odysseus' self-transformation enables him, in comparison with the judicial chief, to play a very different agent of justice when he takes revenge on Penelope's suitors. He models for Homer's audiences around 700 one of the primary roles individual citizens will play when soon after 650 they begin administrating state justice as magistrates and jurors in a law court. It's the development of written, statute law, however, that permits a new citizen script, the jury trial, to emerge with its particular form of deliberation. Chapter 4 ties statute law to another sort of remarkable individual: the lawgiver. None of these legendary figures is more remarkable (or unique) than Solon of Athens (ca. 590), and this chapter explores how he combines role-playing as a lawgiver, politician, and poet in order to demonstrate to citizens the deliberative and cognitive arts they need in order to "perform the law" as magistrates and jurors. Because Solon's figure looms large over Athens' legal and political history, I extend Chapter 4's scope to the fifth and fourth centuries, where we can appreciate changes in the law as a performance tradition. We'll see that forensic oratory (Antiphon, Demosthenes, and Aeschines) prompts jurors to practice types of mimesis that carry on Solon's lawgiving in ways that respond differently to the democracy's changing political ideologies.

What are the risks to individuals, to the collective citizen body, and to the community's well-being when citizens deliberate about justice and the worth (*timê*) of others? Chapter 5 claims that Aeschylus dramatizes these questions on the tragic stage of democratic Athens in his play *Suppliants* (ca. 463–61). I argue that the key dilemma of the play (and the trilogy it belongs to) is alliance formation, by which I mean a decision about whether to recognize that one's own well-being coincides with another's. Aeschylus stages the need to make this judgment as a test his spectators face in evaluating others who are noncitizens (specifically, foreigners and females) – and they do this in the double register of a heroic legend's fictional world and Athens' contemporary world of democratic imperialism. He forces his spectators to deliberate over justice as both individuals and citizens, divided on one hand by private emotions such as compassion and fear, and on the other hand by collective reason-giving under the guidance of elite leaders. The first kind of justice prompts them as individual human beings to identify with others in a nonpolitical sense of community; the second kind demands they use strategic reasoning to further their community's interest over that of their rivals and preserve its autonomy.

The subsequent history of Athenian democracy from around 450 onward continued developing ways for citizens to define themselves and their interests individually and collectively. I've already alluded to changing paradigms of citizenship and selfhood under the Periclean regime (from the 450s to the early 420s) and in the remaining years of the fifth century. I explore alternatives to the Periclean paradigm – its "shadows," I call them – in Chapters 6 and 7 through deliberations that are increasingly interior to the individual and based on self-interest or criteria such as Socrates' commitment to "self-regarding" rather than "other-regarding" virtues (Irwin 1977: 255). I use the sophistic opposition between *nomos* (law, social custom) and *physis* (nature, human nature, individual personality) to set for us the terms of a conflict between "communitarian" values based on owning up to the ends others provide us and more "liberal" values that seek a moral shelter conducive to self-fashioning. But since Antiphon, Alcibiades, and the historical Socrates enact forms of moral autonomy that are radical and elite, their social negotiability is questionable. And so both chapters explore strategies each of these remarkable individuals uses to play the game of citizenship; we'll also consider ways ordinary Athenians try to make sense of such hyperintelligent scripts based on inner deliberation.

The Conclusion considers whether we can see in the history we've traced a convergence between the paths of performing justice as a self-evaluation and as an evaluation of others. We return briefly to fourth-century oratory, to an unusual speech (Demosthenes 25, written in 338–24) that struggles to harness competing legal and political ideologies in persuading jurors how to perform the law and evaluate the defendant correctly. This struggle recalls our competing contemporary scripts of liberalism, communitarianism and deliberative democracy; it also indicates how in performing justice the Greeks and ourselves enact the interdependence of citizenship and selfhood.

1 JUSTICE TO THE DEAD: PROTOTYPES OF THE CITIZEN AND SELF IN EARLY GREECE

⊙▣⊙

BEFORE THE FORMATION OF THE CITY-STATE AND ETHNOS-STATE, what kinds of script and what kinds of self enabled Greek communities to perform justice? Did these scripts and selves undergo changes when the state and its citizens emerged in the early eighth century? My goals in this chapter are to recover a likely version of the earliest pre-citizen script, including its cognitive dimensions (especially the sort of reasoning) and its communicative dimensions (especially key speech acts, speech genres, and performative attitudes), and to identify a kind of performer we can consider a prototype for the earliest citizens, including his or her degrees of social and moral autonomy. Given the nature of the evidence at our disposal, my argument must remain hypothetical. I claim that, first, Early Iron Age communities created a heroic self when they used funerary ritual, especially lamentation, to render justice to deceased warrior chiefs (*basileis*); and, second, that around the time of state formation this heroic self achieves a degree of autonomy when performances of the *Iliad* enable Homer's Achilles to manipulate scripts of lament and deliberation, effecting a self-transformation into a prototype for the citizen.

I divide my inquiry into three unequal parts. The first, "Doing Justice to the Dead in Early Iron Age Communities," outlines key social features of typical communities in Early Iron Age Greece (ca. 1100–700), particularly in the state's "Formative Era," the Early to Middle Geometric periods (ca. 900–760).[1] Here I argue that the worldview of

---

[1] For this "Formative Era" see Donlan and Thomas 1993: 5. My use of the term Early Iron Age refers to the period ca. 1100–700, although most classicists and historians

these prestate communities probably depended on narratives about ancestors, and I identify a "script" (as defined in the Introduction) that establishes justice in funerary ritual for warrior chiefs – in particular lament. The second part, "Performing Justice in Homeric Lament," uses the *Iliad* to identify an additional script that communities in the Formative period used to establish justice: I call it "how leaders deliberate" and contrast its cognitive and communicative dimensions with those of lament. The third and longest part, "Achilles' Self-transformation," focuses on this Iliadic performer at three moments in the poem where he tries to transform "how leaders deliberate" into a deliberative script that can accommodate a new, more autonomous self, which I identify with the prototypical citizen. The key to Achilles' effort is his self-transformation through the adaptation of traditional lament: in Books 1, 9, and 24, he progressively splices lament for a fallen leader and the deliberation of leaders into a unique, hybrid discourse, a "self-lament." Through it he determines his own *timê* autonomously, publicly proclaims it as consistent with a just fate, and demands its recognition by peers. He is thus the first in this study's gallery of remarkable individuals to frame the programmatic questions, "What sort of person must I become if I am to decide this question of justice? And what sort of person do I wish to become?"

I   DOING JUSTICE TO THE DEAD IN EARLY IRON AGE COMMUNITIES
A Profile of Early Iron Age Communities
To identify scripts and performers for establishing justice in Greece's prestate communities, we need to outline key features of their worldview(s). Material evidence, crosscultural ethnographic models, and Homeric epic enable us to approximate the categories of time, space,

still prefer "Dark Age" when referring to roughly the same period (ca. 1100–ca. 800); on the different terms, cf. Antonaccio 1995a: 2, n. 4. (My profile of Early Iron Age communities revises arguments and updates data in Farenga 1998.)

and human agency behind their understanding of the world. We can also, with some accuracy, identify typical settlement patterns, population levels, modes of production, degrees of social stratification, and forms of authority. This composite evidence highlights specific dilemmas in material and social life and in ideology, all of which made a coherent worldview problematic: dilemmas of settlement instability and survival, a potential crisis over the death of a community leader, and contradictions in the hybrid form of his big-man and chieftain authority. In particular this dilemma of leadership challenged communities to construct a stable and coherent social persona for the *basileus*, one to which an individual's achievement could justly be assimilated upon his death. But these communities possessed symbolic resources to meet these problems, among them an understanding of time and space grounded in stories about ancestors and funerary ritual for individuals of high status. These resources transformed the Early Iron Age warrior chief from an "indebtor" into an "indebted" self. I use these terms to describe a leader who in life actively sustains his social persona through exchange relations that bind followers in obligation to him, but who in death passively owes his social identity in community memory to their obligation to repay him.

Greece's Early Iron Age settlements were for the most part villages conforming to the dominant settlement pattern throughout the Bronze Age, in which an extended family's household (*oikos*) joined with several others to form a "nucleated" hamlet or village cluster; and these villages remained independent, much as they had been in the Bronze Age, except for the relatively brief period of palace-state formation in the Late Bronze Age.[2] Generally speaking, these autonomous villages

[2] Donlan and Thomas 1993: 61–2; for Crete see Haggis 1993 and Cavanaugh et al. 1998. For Greece as a whole see recent archaeological surveys by Whitley (2001: 80–101) and Morris (2000: 201ff.; 1998a); cf. Thomas and Conant's profile of six Dark Age sites (1999). See Thalmann's portrait of Dark Age social life in relation to Homeric

(re)appeared within a generation or two of the Mycenaean collapse, around the start of the Protogeometric period (ca. 1050), flourished around 900, and lasted until the state emerged between 800 and 750. They can be characterized by peaceful prosperity, by a considerable level of economic activity, and in some locations by contacts with the Near East. Instability characterized most individual settlements, which were inhabited for anywhere from fifty to three hundred years, although a few (Athens, Knossos, and Argos) were stable, and inhabited continuously from the Bronze Age to the Archaic period.[3] Population density tended to be low, with most people living in hamlet groups of thirty to fifty individuals, although villages whose population numbered in the hundreds were not unusual, and a few communities (again, Athens, Knossos, and Argos) probably numbered in the low thousands.[4] The "domestic mode of production" prevailed everywhere, driving a subsistence economy mixing pastoralism with agriculture;[5] and its ideal of the self-sufficient *oikos* applied to the "autarkic and autonomous" village as well.[6]

The typical Early Iron Age community prior to 800 was therefore an isolated village of thirty-five to one hundred and fifty inhabitants occupying its site for about one hundred and fifty years.[7] Despite a

society (1998: 249–55) and Hammer's overview of evidence for Dark Age political community, with profiles of three sites (2002: 29–43).

[3] Whitley 1991a: 346–47, 1991b: 184, and 2001: 88–89. See Haggis 1993 on stability in East Crete's small village clusters.

[4] Garnsey and Morris 1989: 99; Morris 1991: 33; Donlan 1994: 34. On modeling demographic expansion from the tenth century onward, see Scheidel 2003.

[5] See Johnson and Earle's adaptation of Sahlins' "domestic mode of production" (2000: 23–24); Donlan 1989: 7–12 on the Dark Age *oikos*; Snodgrass 1987: 193–209 on pastoralism; Morris 1987: 23 and Garnsey and Morris 1989: 99 on pastoralism and agriculture.

[6] Donlan and Thomas 1993: 64.

[7] See Snodgrass 1987: 190–92 on the average life-span. Donlan and Thomas see hamlets and villages as the "normal community for most inhabitants" of Dark Age Greece

diversity of settlements, one general conclusion may be drawn: the fundamental problem for the typical community was long-term survival, especially at the lower end of so-called "local groups," as well as for other settlements on the spectrum where households and the community strove for economic autonomy.[8] For the continuously inhabited "big three," perhaps for settlements like Lefkandi, which survived from the Bronze Age to perhaps 700,[9] and for isolated village clusters like those in East Crete, stability rather than survival was the challenge. For despite prosperity and economic development, the long-term material resources of even the larger settlements varied due to climate and the intermittent contacts of exchange, long-distance trade, warfare, and migration.[10]

These problems of survival and stability were compounded for all settlements by two additional features: degrees of social stratification and forms of authority. Both resist precise understanding – especially forms of authority – because material evidence presents an incomplete

---

(1993: 63). Whitley concludes, "it would not be unreasonable to say that, in general, Dark Age settlements were small . . . scattered across the landscape; and that the population was, compared to later periods, low" (2001: 89). Nevertheless, the broader perspective of political anthropology indicates that the Early Iron Age knew a variety of prestate polities on an ever-shifting spectrum of evolution and devolution. Cf. Ferguson on the Dark Age's "hybrid polities" (1991: 170–71); Farenga 1998: 181, and Thalmann 1998: 249, on evolution and devolution; and Whitley 2001: 90 on diverse settlement patterns. Edwards makes a similar point to characterize Hesiod's Ascra around 700 as a sparsely populated, autonomous village typical of Dark Age settlements (2004: 6, 33, 37).

[8] "Local groups," consist of multiple families in village or regional settlements five to ten times the size of the "family-level groups," which ranged from 5–8 persons to 25–35 (Johnson and Earle 2000: 33–34 and 123–40).

[9] For the end of settlement at Lefkandi, see Thomas and Conant 1999: 88 and 102; settlement was perhaps briefly interrupted from ca. 1100 to 1050 (92–93; 103).

[10] Whitley's division into "stable" and "unstable" seems too rigid, especially the claim that each type experienced "quite different" social formations (1991b: 184); Thomas and Conant also reject this rigid distinction (1999: 102).

picture of class differences and leadership. Also, crosscultural, ethno-graphic models of authority and leadership don't correspond with great precision to Aegean communities. We can say that social stratification in the smaller and more unstable communities (between the "family-level" and "local" groups of Johnson and Earle 2000) must have been minimal; in these "homogeneous" hamlets, ranking appeared only in the form of the village headman, who may have been called a *basileus*.[11] But in larger settlements, or as smaller settlements grew, local village groups of 100 to 300 would have experienced increased segmentation and ranking; and when local village groups of 300 to 500 appeared, more common by the Middle Geometric period (850–760), they demon-strate incipient stratification.[12] (The largest communities, Athens and Knossos, likely preserved their Late Bronze Age social hierarchy.[13]) So it's reasonable to conclude with Thalmann that "Hierarchy – at least in the simple form of a line between elite and commoners – evidently per-sisted" from the Bronze Age (1998: 250); but we should allow for varying degrees of stratification in relation to population, so that "hierarchies shifted constantly" (Whitley 2001: 90) and were not "elaborate, rigid hierarchies" (97).[14]

---

[11] See Donlan and Thomas 1993: 63–5, and Donlan 1994: 35. A good example of such a settlement is Nichoria, with a population of about 60 (13–14 families) in its first Early Iron Age phase (ca. 1075–975) (Thomas and Conant 1999: 36–37, drawing on MacDonald, Coulson, and Rosser 1983: 322–25; see also Donlan and Thomas 1993: 64).

[12] Donlan and Thomas 1993: 65; cf. Morris 1991: 43 on "complex, stratified society" at Lefkandi and Naxos. Tandy in a general sense recognizes stratification in Iron Age communities, but he points mainly to the eighth century (1997: 93).

[13] Morris 1991: 27–40, 42. He sees Iron Age societies as stratified between an elite (one-quarter to one-third of the population) and serf-like peasants (1987: 173–83; 1989b: 506).

[14] E.g., Nichoria's population of about 60 in its first Early Iron Age phase (1075–975) shows no material evidence of stratification and looks like a largely acephalous "local group" without perceptible degrees of status distinction and leadership until

This varying degree of social stratification vexes the question of how to categorize the typical leaders of these changing communities. As with settlement types and diversity, we are probably better off conceiving of Early Iron Age leadership along a developmental spectrum from village headman to big man to chieftain, with many leaders combining features of any two of these ethnographic types.[15] We might imagine any profile we draw of Early Iron Age leadership to possess the fluid proportions of one of those computer-generated, composite photographs that one moment seems to represent a recognizably real individual and the next moment doesn't. This is particularly so when we try to use models to distinguish the functions of a big man from a chieftain,[16] or when we

its second phase, when its population of about 200 sees the construction of the "chieftain's house." Nevertheless, despite this building's conspicuous dimensions and functions, "minimal distinctions separated the families" (Thomas and Conant 1999: 57).

[15] In a typical Iron Age village of 35–150 people, a headman may or may not have organized the village's households for productive and ritual activity. But as some village groups increased in population toward 300, headmen would have functioned as incipient big men through more intergroup, regional efforts at clan-like organization for the purposes of reducing production risks, focusing ceremonial activity, defending territory, and initiating personal networks of exchange (Johnson and Earle 2000: 33–34 and 126; cf. 203ff. for profiles of three typical big-man systems). See Edwards' argument for lack of a local leader in Hesiod's Ascra (2004: 118–23). Contra Thomas and Conant, I don't believe Nichoria's "chieftain's house" signals the transition from big-man to chieftain leadership since a village of about 200 persons is not large enough for a transition from personally constructed to institutionally based leadership (1999: 56–57). Even at the height of its growth (ca. 900 BC), Nichoria's leader was still a would-be big man. When village groups of 500 became more common in the Middle Geometric, their big men would have operated on a wider regional scale as well and projected the function of the chieftain, whose authority compromises the autonomy of individual communities in a region and relies on a more institutionally secured than personally maintained basis.

[16] See Johnson and Earle 2000: 265–67 on simple chiefdoms and 276–77 on intermediate forms combining big-man/chieftain systems. Earle defines the chiefdom as "a regional polity with institutional governance and some social stratification organizing a population of a few thousand to tens of thousands of people. . . . Chiefdoms are

expect Greek leadership in this Formative period to conform neatly to ethnographic models. (For example, these communities' would-be and bona fide chieftains did not provide regional centers for storage and redistribution, suggesting that the Aegean leadership departed in fundamental ways from a key feature in classic ethnographic models.[17]) Because these communities grew, and sometimes shrank again, and had varying degrees of social stratification, they likely generated a hybrid leadership whose social persona combined features of headman, big-man and chieftain authority.[18]

Not surprisingly, some of the earliest scholars to apply ethnographic models to Iron Age and Homeric *basileis* soon enough recognized the instability of settlements and leaders as a principal characteristic: Donlan and Qviller in the early 1980s attributed it to the predominance

---

intermediate-level polities, bridging the evolutionary gap between small, village-based polities and large, bureaucratic states." (1997: 14). In contrast to the classic chiefdoms of Polynesia, Whitley thinks we can "exclude the possibility that many communities in Early Iron Age Greece were 'chiefdoms' . . ." (2001: 97) but after 900 Athens, Knossos, and Argos look to me like "immature chiefdoms" in Donlan's (1982a, 1982b) and Qviller's (1981) sense. Earle's profile of chiefdoms in the Thy region of Late Neolithic and Bronze Age Denmark (ca. 2300–1300) may offer parallels to Early Iron Age Greece (1997: 18–33, and *passim*).

[17] Donlan and Thomas 1993: 66. Garnsey and Morris note in passing that early Greek states show no evidence of "large concentrations of storage facilities" for the presumed surplus production of elites (1989: 100). Thalmann points out how difficult it is to see the Homeric *basileus* as a redistributor along the lines of the big-man and chieftain models (1998: 262–62). Tandy assumes that redistribution increased in Greece after around 850 (1997: 111), but he offers no material evidence and adduces Homeric examples whose scope and applicability to existing social realities are unclear (cf. Schaps 1998).

[18] Thalmann addresses this hybridism in assessing Homeric leadership, asking, "Is status achieved (as with big-men) or ascribed (as in chiefdoms)?" (1998: 268). He concludes that the epics' elite ideology makes this simple opposition undecidable and that perhaps both types of authority coexisted (269–71). Whitley sees Early Iron Age communities as "rank" rather than "stratified" and status as achieved, not ascribed (2001: 90).

of "immature chiefdoms" in Dark Age and Homeric societies.[19] Donlan subsequently began to emphasize how "notoriously unstable" these polities were; not only could their populations shift allegiances from one local big man's kin- or clanlike "pyramid" of authority to another's, but local big men could in turn shift allegiance toward or away from a regional pyramid "constructed" by a paramount chief or his rivals.[20] More recently he has characterized what was a "fatal defect" of these chiefdoms (1989: 25) in stronger terms as an "underlying contradiction" based on the "conflicting claims of egalitarianism and authoritarianism which are inherent in chiefdoms" (1994: 45). In other words, as general system problems, the survival and instability of settlements both small and large appear tied to the figure of the *basileus*, whose authority raised ideological questions about the legitimacy of power while it simultaneously attempted to manage the economic flux of uncertain resources, such as exchange, trade, and climate.

As a focus for both economic stress and ideological contradiction, the Iron Age *basileus* must have, I think, provoked his followers to find cognitive resources to resolve material dilemmas linked to instability so that they might render his social persona and their world ideologically more coherent. Until recently not much attention has been paid to the type of thinking, reasoning, and argumentation that impelled inhabitants of prestate communities to establish or abandon

---

[19] Donlan 1982a: 172, 173 and 1982b: 3–7; Qviller 1981: 120. Cf. Ferguson on "overlapping, layered and linked authority patterns" before and after statehood (1991: 171), and Earle 1987: 282 and Johnson and Earle 2000: 268 on continuity between non-Greek big-man systems and chiefdoms. Whitley rigidly assigns big men to unstable and chiefs to stable communities (1991a: 352 and 1991b: 192).

[20] Donlan 1985a: 304–5 and 1989: 22; cf. Donlan and Thomas 1993: 65–69. For Thalmann, power in Homeric society rests on a "more secure basis" than Donlan's assessment of unstable leadership suggests (1998: 266). But I doubt that the "stable social organization" he sees in the poems existed in most communities prior to the eighth century.

settlements, to legitimate or chafe against degrees of social stratification, or to explain the flux of material and symbolic resources. Political anthropology has begun to explore the function of cognition, ideology and symbolic thinking in chiefdoms, and Earle in particular has examined the ways that chiefdoms manipulate the economic, military, and ideological sources of power to legitimize their regional political control. He assigns a primary role to the process he calls "materialization," which is "the transformation of ideas, values, stories, myths and the like into a physical reality that can take the form of ceremonial events, symbolic objects, monuments, and writing" (1997: 151). Through these forms of materialization, chieftains manipulate ideology to give concrete form to a worldview, to its principles of moral and religious order, and to its understandings of what is just (144).

Earle specifically recognizes materialization at work in the elite use of symbolic objects and monuments to establish narrative senses of time and place (155ff.). This links his work to the efforts of classical archaeologists who explore the ways Early Iron Age communities manipulated time and space as a cognitive resource to sustain their worldviews. Studies by Morris (1987, 1989a, 1989b, 1998a, 2000), Whitley (1991a, 2001), Antonaccio (1993, 1994, 1995a and 1995b), and Sourvinou-Inwood (1981, 1983, 1995), to name a few, have called attention to the funerary sphere as the principal symbolic resource of Early Iron Age communities of around 1100–800. Their work has illuminated the considerable amounts of labor and wealth these communities invested in the privileges of formal burial, in the manufacture, disposition and decoration of grave goods, in the periodic practice of tomb cult, and in the use or disposal of iron. But I believe these communities utilized a more fundamental symbolic resource without whose categories of time, space, and agency these other activities would have been inconceivable and incomprehensible: storytelling, or the formulation and reformulation of oral narratives about *basileis* both living and deceased.

Funerary Ritual and Its Scripts

A link between storytelling and burials – especially those that appear "heroic" – helps explain how Early Iron Age communities before 800 could establish continuity between the present, the past, and the near future, where discontinuity in fact had been (and likely would continue to be) more common. As the evidence of tomb cult suggests, some communities needed to reinvent over and again, in the face of present difficulties and an uncertain future, a "shallow" past emerging from stories of ancestors and events spanning no more than two or three generations.[21] Such stories could also use ancestors to invent ties to other communities within or outside a given region as patterns of trade, warfare and migration changed, making more coherent the tension between purely local interaction and its sometime expansion to regional and interregional levels. Stories about *basileis* and ancestors could also evaluate a recently deceased leader's achievement in light of the social persona of an ancestral *basileus*: Was the man an ethical success or failure? Has his community thrived or failed? Does he merit praise or blame for its fate? These sorts of stories would have operated ideologically within a wider and more abstract sphere, that of the cosmic framework of justice. So if "instability" or "variability" in social life typified these communities, what more valuable resource for rendering justice could they possess than storytelling's ability to fashion a coherent worldview as they grappled with survival, instability, war, and an ideologically flawed leadership?

Recent reinterpretations of physical evidence for Early Iron Age burials do suggest that the funerary sphere used elite burials to anchor narratively based worldviews.[22] In communities with a shallow

---

[21] "Tomb cult" refers to occasional (or even unique) visits and offerings at grave sites; see Antonaccio 1995a: 6 and 264ff., 1994: 401–2, and 1993: 63.

[22] Morris' survey of post-Mycenaean burial practices infers a use of oral traditions about ancestors (2000: 201ff. and 225). After 1050 communities may have restricted archaeologically recoverable burials to adults of rank, with cemeteries organized

genealogical memory of about three generations, funerary ritual and/or tomb cult seem intent on merging in the nonspecific category of "ancestors" the recent dead with the unknown dead who inhabited the location in a distant past.[23] These symbolic resources were thus marshaled to configure a time, space and agency projected backward to forge a vital if uncertain continuity between past and present, perhaps to legitimate a kinlike group that, not lacking rivals, faced a far from certain future.[24] Some historians and classical archaeologists have begun to probe the possibility that narratives about ancestors and use of funerary ritual provided cognitive resources for Early Iron Age social problems. Sourvinou-Inwood surmised that the death of even one adult member constituted an unwelcome event for which funerary ritual provided a cognitive tool for restoring continuity and order:

> *In the small Dark Age villages, community life was* de facto *disrupted*
> *by each death, and each dead person had inevitably had social*
> *relationships with all the rest of the community which needed severing*
> *and consequent adjustment, so the whole community was* de facto

along kinship lines (1987 and 1989a; cf. Humphreys' critique [1990], and Morris' reply [1998b: 27–29]). At about this time communities either prepared new tombs for elites, with evidence of tomb cult, reused Mycenaean (or earlier) tombs for burial and tomb cult of their own dead, or made offerings to unknown occupants of earlier graves (Antonaccio 1993: 46–70 and 1995a: 6–7). After 925 more wealth, new decorative styles (Geometric) and disposal techniques suggest increased competition among elites (Morris 1987: 42 and 181–82; Whitley 1991b: 136–37; Antonaccio 1995a: 257ff.). Tomb cult, often of short duration, may reflect these changes and pressures (Antonaccio 1993: 48–56, 1994: 401–2, and 1995a: 245–46).

[23] See Antonaccio 1993: 63–64, 1995a: 252–53 and 264–65; cf. Lambrinoudakis 1988: 245.

[24] Antonaccio 1993: 64; cf. 1994: 410 (though burials and tomb cult may not always have been restricted to elites; 403.) On tomb cult as competition for the past both locally and panhellenically, see Antonaccio 1994: 408; cf. Whitley 1995: 49–50 on the Dark Age use of the past to legitimate the present. Morris sees eighth-century tomb and hero cult as "ambiguous, meaning different things to different people" (1988: 758).

> *involved in each death-ritual. Moreover, in those years, the survival of*
> *the (vulnerable and depopulated) community was the top priority. (1981:*
> *29; cf. 1983: 42)*

More threatening for communities large or small, with a hybrid headman/big-man/chieftain authority, was the leader's death.[25] Because of mixed degrees of achieved and ascribed authority, these communities lacked institutional procedures for an orderly succession of power, and so the leader's demise would have thrown the community's stability, or even its future, into doubt. Calligas (1988) suggested that communities of the "Lefkandi Period" (ca. 1050–830) originated the heroic narrative tradition we associate with Greek epic; and he linked storytelling to the funerary sphere by arguing that narratives extended "heroic" burials for leaders and prolonged their legitimacy into the future. More recently, Morris has suggested that the great warrior burial at Lefkandi (ca. 950) actually initiated the Greeks' belief in the gap separating themselves as an impoverished Iron Age race from their heroic ancestors (2000: 228–37).

Thomas and Conant have in a broader sense stressed the role that oral memory and narration probably played in "honoring the deeds of local ancestors" in Nichoria, and in "mold[ing] fundamental conceptions of the world and the role of humans in it," including "maintaining proper order" and the "communal business of justice" (1999: 49, 50). They've also pointed to the heroic burials at Lefkandi from 950 to 825 as expressions of materialization in Earle's sense because the burials testify to a "heroic" worldview centered around warfare, adventure, and "an obsession with honor and prestige (*timê*)" (108–9). This obsession with *timê*, they suggest, also depends on an oral, "remembered tradition"

---

[25] See Sourvino-Inwood 1981; 30, n. 53, for the greater impact of a leader's death and a difference in the scale of symbolic expression for his funerary ritual.

about *basileis* at Lefkandi that will enable its inhabitants "to deal with the present" (109).[26]

All these possibilities become more concrete if we ask what sort of scripts Early Iron Age communities might have developed in funerary ritual to cast the deceased *basileus* as a heroic self. These scripts would have relied on narratives to generate *timê* for a recently deceased leader by linking him to ancestors, and cognitively they would have enacted a collective, rationalizing effort we might call "stocktaking." Its function would have been to restore coherence when experiences such as a leader's death disrupted community life or its preestablished patterns of understanding. In particular, by reaching back to the experiences of previous generations, individuals and communities would have used the interplay of these narratives to understand how the deceased helps link them and their predecessors intersubjectively through a sort of "cognitive relay,"[27] especially when recent events threatened faith in the self-evident effectiveness or appropriateness of, for example, social hierarchy or forms of authority.[28]

But what kinds of narratives would scripts of stocktaking have utilized within the funerary sphere? And what kind of communicative interaction would these scripts and narratives establish between those who framed a particular tale for a leader's funerary ritual and/or tomb

---

[26] Antonaccio also connects the later heroic burials in the Toumba cemetery at Lefkandi with efforts to establish the rank of a deceased warrior in relation to the powerful *basileus* buried in the "funerary feasting hall" (1995b: 18–19).

[27] For these terms and cognitive framework see Carr 1986: 86–94 and 113.

[28] Horton's notions of "traditionalist knowledge" and "consensual elaboration of theory" suggest that oral, premodern or non-Western societies resist the disruptive effect of novel experiences and ideas by judging them inconsistent with ancestral beliefs and values (1993: 329–30; 338–40). Or, if established beliefs must conform to new realities, storytelling can defuse innovation by removing the novel idea from active reflection and projecting it backwards after several generations to the time of ancestors.

cult – that is, the "speakers" of a particular burying group – and those for whom the tale was meant – the "listeners" inhabiting the local village or region? As one archaeologist puts it, "Obviously, archaeology cannot recover oral . . . accounts of kinship or genealogy, nor such practices as prayer." (Antonaccio 1994: 401). Nevertheless, Bakhtin's theory of speech genres and his "communicative function of language" help us hypothesize that: each type of narrative about ancestors and *basileis* constituted a speech genre, a stable form of utterance absorbing simpler kinds of direct utterances from daily life into conventions of theme, composition and style (1986: 60–65); each speech genre in the funerary sphere took account of listeners' anticipated responses in producing its meanings; and so the social relation between the speakers' intentions and the listeners' responses, and the worldviews of each group, played a role in the formation of funerary ritual's speech genres (77, 90). Depending on how compatible or dissonant these worldviews might be, funerary speech genres would display varying degrees of dialogism: in some cases speakers and listeners might be almost identical groups sharing a worldview, in others the listeners may have been hostile, foreign, or subordinate to speakers (95). Degrees of social or ethnic otherness would therefore have been crucial, deserving particular attention as Early Iron Age communities expand or contract in population, acquire or lose access to vital resources and external trade, intensify or lessen warfare, and so on.

In kin-based societies scripts and narratives that determine a leader's *timê* would normally draw upon that vast storehouse of unquestioned, unproblematic beliefs Habermas and others call a "lifeworld" (*Lebenswelt*). This provides traditional societies with a "horizon of understanding" for reaching consensus when problematic situations arise, and it functions as a "conservative counterweight" to disagreements and anomalous or dissonant events (Habermas 1984: 70). But there is some likelihood that Early Iron Age communities, faced with instability, survival, and ideologically problematic leadership, would find their ancestral lifeworld challenged or "decentered" by the world-view of a competing or contentious group. In such cases the script of stocktaking loses its safe mooring in the lifeworld of ancestors, and deliberation becomes an option. By "deliberation" I mean a kind of dialogic interaction where participants try to resolve disagreement or contradiction by making more explicit their reasons for or against competing views, perhaps by interpreting a problematic situation in ways that require spontaneously *shared* criteria for rationality instead of criteria the lifeworld has set in advance (70–71). In other words, a script of stocktaking that admits deliberation into its narratives may articulate novel forms of reasoning and criteria for rationality.

As we've seen, Calligas (1988) and Thomas and Conant (1999) infer that burying groups in communities like Lefkandi and Nichoria used epic or proto-epic narratives to evaluate the *timê* of a deceased *basileus* in relation to ancestors. This is surely a likely conjecture. Tandy goes farther in proposing a sweeping, antagonistic scenario in which eighth century elites used heroic burials (among other strategies): to separate themselves from commoners and traditional sources of wealth; and to disguise this breach between the present and the heroic past by claiming descent from traditional epic figures (1997: 149–65).

But these same groups throughout the Early Iron Age must also have enacted scripts of stocktaking that included a potent resource that is likewise archaeologically difficult to document: the emotional, musical, and verbal performance we call lamentation. We nevertheless do have iconographic evidence of a "striking indication of continuity" in the attitude, gestures, and ritual centrality of lamentation from the Mycenaean period to the Middle to Late Geometric (760–690).[29] As

---

[29] Cavanaugh and Mee (1995: 58) confirm the "unbroken continuity of funerary imagery and behavior" that Vermeule saw from the Bronze Age to the classical period (1979: 63).

a ritualized form of mourning, lament would have restored to Early Iron Age burying groups a psycho-physiological sense of order through the passive, collective experience of suffering. It would have served the bereaved as a kind of therapy for their grief, enabling them both to share in and then separate themselves from the experience of death.[30] And so through lament the group would have enacted a stocktaking with three goals: to restore coherence when a leader's death disrupts a village's everyday experience of human relationships (its "social organization"); to reinforce its ideal conception of how individuals and groups should interconnect (its "social structure") – in other words, to provide reasons for that death as just or unjust within a cosmic framework consistent with the lifeworld; and to evaluate the deceased so that his social persona might pass from the fluctuating identity typical of a living individual to the fixed identity assigned the dead. All three goals program the notion of "doing justice" to a great man's death.[31]

But if lament included a script of stocktaking to evaluate leaders, it also included storytelling to the same purpose. How in this regard did lament differ from epic tales? And if we look for degrees of deliberation, do we find significant differences in the reason-giving, rationality criteria, and performative attitudes in each speech genre's attempt to do justice to a leader by evaluating his *timê?*

II Performing Justice in Homeric Lament
The Communicative Dynamics of Lament
We can answer these questions by turning to our one surviving indication of how Early Iron Age performers evaluated leaders, both dead

---

[30] See Sourvinou-Inwood 1981: 26–28 and 1983: 41–42. For the distinction between grief and mourning, see Derderian 2001: 4–5, with references.

[31] On the disruption of social organization and reinforcement of social structure, see Morris 1987: 39; on the transformation of the deceased's social persona in the Early Iron Age, see Sourvinou-Inwood 1995: 115; on the transition from fluctuating to stable identity, see Derderian 2001: 4, with references.

and alive, in narrative form: Homeric representations of lament for *basileis* and of deliberations about their relative rank. Derderian's recent study (2001) gives us a clearer, more systematic understanding of the various speech acts (verbal and nonverbal) and gestures comprising the composite speech genre of Homeric lament, and of the types of individuals and groups who customarily performed and listened to them. These speech acts included *akhnusthai*, which most often describes one elite male grieving for a fallen leader, companion or kin, usually as a representative of the deceased's social group, and grieving in a way that links the need to grieve to a competing need to take action on the group's behalf (e.g., revenge) (Derderian 2001: 17–22, with textual references). *Oduresthai* describes another speech act within lament, one expressing a more individualistic or "subjective" grief in isolation from one's group, a grief accompanied by a passive withdrawal from others (22–24, with references). I suggest that these two ways of articulating grief to others, labelled respectively by Derderian "collective-active" and "individual-passive" (24), each enacts different performative attitudes defining an individual's relation to others: with *akhnusthai*, the griever recovers a sense of self (and a degree of individual autonomy) in time to "answer to" or model a socially constructive group value; with *oduresthai*, the griever no longer maintains an autonomous sense of self that can answer to the demands of ordinary daily life.

Lament's narrative components occur in two other expressions of grief, both of which can themselves be called speech genres by Bakhtin's definition: *klaiein* (or the noun *klauthmos*) and *goan* (noun *goos*) (Derderian 2001: 24ff.). Men and women may use these to express grief spontaneously and informally, but women can also formally perform a ritual *goos*, and Homer cites such a performance seven times in the *Iliad* and once in the *Odyssey*.[32] More so than *akhnusthai* and *oduresthai*,

---

[32] See Derderian 2001: 33–34. The formally performed *gooi* occur at: *Il.*18.51ff.; 22.430–36; 22.477ff.; 23.19–23; 24.723–45; 24.748–59; 24.762–75; and *Od.*4.721–41. Achilles is the sole male to perform a formal *goos* (at *Il.*23.19–23).

klaiein and *goan* provide the basis for a script of stocktaking because both construct a narrative about the deceased *basileus* that employs the antithetical structure commonly found in elements of Greek funerary ritual, and this includes a communicative interaction between the kin-based mourning group and a wider audience of non-kin.[33] Both *klaiein* and *goan* therefore provide the burying group an occasion to conduct a narrative evaluation of its deceased leader's *timê* before the community. While *klaiein* tends to occur in more informal, domestic contexts and before smaller groups, and *goan* often has a more public setting, both are nevertheless private genres compared to the *thrênos*, whose performers were probably professionals in a more public setting, because they originate within the burying group's household (Derderian 2001: 31). With *klaiein* the performative attitude of an authority figure orchestrates the lamentation by regulating its beginning and end (27), while one of the deceased's female kin begins the formal *goan* in a "domestic or public setting" (33).

We can therefore think of the narrative component within *klaien* and *goan* as a carefully controlled dialogue between Early Iron Age family members and non-kin, one of whose goals is to merge these separate groups under the authority of the burying group's worldview. In local village groups and small chiefdoms, the non-kin audience would have been allies in the form of collateral kin, members of the community's lesser households who were economically tied to the dominant *oikos*

---

[33] On antithesis and a "balance of opposites" in lament, see Alexiou 1974: 165–84; cf. Sourvinou-Inwood 1981. The iconography of death ritual (Late Bronze Age to Geometric) indicates that female mourners predominate, with an antithetical arrangement of mourning family members, non-kin, their costume, gestures, and other forms of expression (Cavanaugh and Mee 1995). Of *klaiein* and *goan*, Derderian observes, "Both genres involve the creation of a narrative about the dead that mediates between his past life and present death within a group context. . . ." (2001: 25); *klaiein* is often more informally set than *goan*, but their "narrative content" is similar (30). For visual evidence from Archaic and Classical Athenian vase painting of female vs. male mourning behavior, and the possible influence of female lament on a burying group's family history and legal claims, see Stears 1998.

through exchange networks and so obliged to support it, or representatives of exploited, serflike groups compelled to contribute to their masters' status displays.[34] The kin-group members who performed *klaiein* and *goan* were attempting, I suggest, not just to evaluate the *timê* of their dead kinsman but to recruit non-kin to join them in this evaluation – and to join in ways that limited or suppressed the potential for a dialogic clash of opposing worldviews. The participation of non-kin recruits, in other words, would likely have precluded the expression of a reality at odds with the dominant *oikos*; and, though representing the community at large, they would not have been able to isolate in this script of stocktaking a paradox or contradiction to challenge the cognitive adequacy of the burying group's worldview. Both cognitively and socially the role of non-kin would have been assent and submission.[35]

This sort of controlled dialogue within the funerary sphere is consistent with Whitley's suggestion that the symbolic thrust behind Early Iron Age funerary ritual testifies to competitive stress among elites. It's clear in Homer that lament in the form of *klaiein* and/or *goan* constitutes part of the special symbolic reward due the elite dead, the *geras thanontôn*, along with rich grave goods, sacrifices, funerary meals, chariot processions, the burial mound, and stele, and so on.[36] And so, as

---

[34] Among the funerary offerings for Patroclus, Achilles promises the lamentation of the Trojan women he and Patroclus captured (*Il*.18.339–42). See Seaford 1994: 116, and Sourvinou-Inwood 1983: 43 on forced participation of non-kin in elite funerals in the Archaic period.

[35] *Mythos* is an "authoritative speech act" seeking a listener's submission, indignation, or fear (Martin 1989: 22); Hecuba's and Helen's laments are *mythoi* (*Il*.24.746–776).

[36] The *geras thanontôn* comprises, at *Il*.23.9, a chariot procession, funerary meal and *goan*; at *Od*.4.197 a performance of *klaiein*; and at *Od*.24.188–90 the preparation of the body for burial and performance of *goan*. Elsewhere it's mound and stele (*Il*.16.675). Cf. Derderian 2001: 34: "Each ritual lament [*goos*] is viewed as part of the *geras thanontôn* and often immediately precedes the ritual processing of the body, which includes the burning of the pyre, the funeral feast, and the erection of the burial mound."

scripts of stocktaking, laments linking the deceased to ancestors helped complete the relationship of general reciprocity tying chieftains to their followers, who in funerary ritual feel compelled to do justice to their leader by recognizing his *timê* in return for the protection and wealth he generated for them when he was alive.[37] In a radical sense the chieftain owes to his followers the self they create for him when they assimilate him to ancestors as part of the *geras thanontôn*: the final social persona he will enjoy in community memory is therefore largely a reflex of obligation. While alive he indebted them to him through exchange networks; after death, they repay him one last time – but now his self is indebted to their determination of its lasting identity. And this "indebted self" would not have emerged as a funerary offering to a leader in isolation from similar offerings by rival groups to their *basileis*. In the effort to recruit non-kin to participate in their elaboration of *klaiein* and *goan*, burying groups were in effect soliciting a community-wide performance devoted to constructing a heroic, indebted self patterned after a set of local rivals.[38]

But as scripts, where do these two genres derive the communal authority their speakers assume, whether male or female? Ideologically, what legitimates the lamenter's attempt to determine the fallen leader's *timê*? Speakers of *klaiein* and *goan* turn to narrative in order to recontextualize the meaning of a life that has just ended – a life now in transition between the flux of experience and the stability of

---

[37] See van Wees 1998: 42–44 on ways big men and chiefs use reciprocity to attract and sustain followers; Donlan 1998 and Postlethwaite 1998 for reciprocity in relations between Homeric leaders and followers, as well as competition between leaders, and Donlan's earlier, fundamental study of reciprocities in Homer (1982b).

[38] For a parallel see Whitley's description of the development of Geometric style in Attica during the ninth century, where funerary ritual served as an "arena of emulation and display" through a "common repertoire" of vase shapes and decorative motifs, whose "syntax" and "schemata" determined their combination (1991b: 118, 134).

the deceased's reputation (*kleos*) in community memory. Most often this reconfiguration occurs in the form of a dialogue between the first-person speaker and the deceased, who is imagined as somehow still present, not quite out of sound or sight of the speaker and audience.[39] But the conversation between speaker and fallen leader is, of course, anything but a private one: the speaker in effect publicly declares her or his recontextualization of the dead man's life and does so by super-imposing on the setting and activity surrounding the corpse a series of alternative "chronotopes," in Bakhtin's sense.

Chronotopes are the dominant representations of time, space and agency in verbal or visual artifacts; they define the parameters of physical and metaphysical reality as well as the logic enabling characters to interact with their environment and one another (Bakhtin 1981: 84–85). Typical chronotopes in heroic narratives, for example, are the battlefield, the war council, the sea journey, the hunt, the funeral, the chieftain's hall. While these heroic chronotopes are not absent from a genre like the formal *goos*, they are subordinated to chronotopes typical of female narratives, centered on birth, child-rearing, marriage, and female domestic space and activities (for example, weaving).[40] In effect these female speakers revise the meaning of the dead leader's life by switching the dominant chronotopes of his life from the masculine, heroic contexts of epic narrative to the contexts of the *oikos* where female authority presides. While scholars of Homeric lament have noted this

---

[39] Of the eight formal *gooi* in Homer, all but two utilize the dialogue format, referring in the third person to leaders who are still living: Thetis' for Achilles (*Il.*18.52–64) and Penelope's for Odysseus and Telemachus (*Od.*4.721–41).

[40] See, e.g., *Il.*22.510–14, where Andromache concludes her *goos* for Hector with reference to the many lavish robes she wove for him; she imagines they will never clothe him now but will serve as a funerary offering to symbolize his *kleos* among the Trojans. On this passage's connection between female weaving and male *kleos*, see Easterling 1991.

"overwriting" of masculine chronotopes by feminine, there is more in these two types of discourse about the hero than tension between gender roles and emotional states (Monsacré 1984) and more than a female "social commentary" or alternative form of commemoration of heroic values (Derderian 2001: 41, 51).

As part of a script of stocktaking that does justice through the *geras thanontôn*, a lament's chronotopal switching in *klaiein* and *goan* permits speakers to claim for themselves and the burying group's *oikos* the universal moral authority of one participating in the cosmic redistribution of fate: it permits them to establish divine justice performatively. A speaker here assumes the performative attitude of one who declares in the here and now (*nun*) the degrees of honor the community should attribute to the fallen leader, and likewise pronounces the miserable or fortunate nature of the fate (*moira*) or destiny (*aisa*, portion) awarded him, his family members and his enemies. After she witnesses Hector's death, for example, Hecabe describes in her formal *goos* the dimensions of the *kudos* her son has garnered among the Trojans (22.432–35), and then announces, "And now (*nun*) in effect his death and fate (*moira*) have arrived" (436). A few moments later Andromache, in her *goos*, pronounces her husband and herself to have been "born to the same destiny" (*aisêi*, 22.477), and she designates this three times as a "wretched" or "harsh" fate (*dusmoros*, 481; *ainomoron*, 481; *dusammoroi*, 485). And she extends her moral knowledge from the present and past to the future in predicting the misery awaiting their son (490–506). Later, in the three formal *gooi* performed at Hector's funeral, his female kin again publicly pronounce cosmic judgments: Hecabe declares Hector beloved by the gods "even in the portion of death [they provided you]" (*kai en thanatoio per aisêi*, 24.750) and on the spot heroizes him as one slain in battle by Apollo (758–59). Helen too, as Andromache had before, equates herself with Hector in sharing a wretched fate (*ammoron*, 24.773). Finally, in the *goos* Penelope performs for the absent Odysseus, she demarcates the dimensions of the *kleos* he has won "throughout wide Hellas and deep into Argos" (*Od*.4.726).

Clearly, as communicative actions these *gooi* derive their authority by invoking such forces and figures from the lifeworld as fate and the gods – after all, their female speakers claim a knowledge usually reserved for Zeus, who "knows well all things, the fortunate and wretched fates (*moiran t'ammoriên*) of men who are subject to death" (*Od*.20.75–76). In this respect female lament speakers assume the performative attitude of one authorized to mark the limits of a life in multiple senses. We've just seen them pronounce the moment of death as a limit to the warrior's life – and they mark that limit not so much temporally as socially. They also render an ethical judgment on that life as fortunate and successful or wretched and disastrous; and they immediately presume to know the extent of fame the warrior will enjoy in community memory. In all these senses these women claim to be no less agents and performers of *dikê* than Zeus himself, for this word's fundamental meaning is probably "to point out" or "mark" (*deiknunai*) a boundary or portion (*moira, aisa*) appropriate to a category of human or divine beings.[41] Note, however, that each female performance declaring a hero's fate (with its link to *dikê*) embeds these lifeworld forces within an essentially domestic dialogue between mother and son, wife and husband, sister- and brother-in-law, and so on. Through a feminized authoritative speech the burying group thus precludes the presentation of reasons for and against the rank (*timê*) and fame (*kleos*) proclaimed for its fallen loved one; their female representatives seek nothing like a consensus between speakers and listeners negotiated through mutual agreement on rationality criteria.[42]

---

[41] For the word's etymology, see Palmer 1950: 160–63; on its occurrences and contextual meanings in Homer, see Yamagata's comprehensive discussion (1994: 61–72 and 78–79). On Zeus as its primary agent in the *Iliad*, see Lloyd-Jones 1971: 1–27.

[42] Lifeworld concepts like fate keep oppositional or innovative thinking at bay, much as taboo operates by discouraging listeners from imputing to the fallen leader actions

What is more, the *goos'* dialogue format between the speaker and the deceased has serious consequences for the nature of the various selves engaged in its communicative network: the authoritative, collective self of the burying group, the individual, heroic self who is mourned and celebrated, and the self of the listener whose response the lament anticipates. The dialogue format confers on the kinswoman the performative attitude of an authoritative speaker who interacts with a silent interlocutor no longer capable of actively presenting himself to others: in effect the female performer exploits the liminality of the death ritual to transform the fallen leader from a once vigorous participant in deliberation and decisive action into a passive, third-person referent. She readily takes his place as a self-presenter inviting the listeners into a mother's or wife's subjective, inner world; but behind its verbal exchange between "I" and "you" this action camouflages a "we" (the burying group) who determine for others the appropriate *geras* for a "him" (the fallen *basileus*). The basic illocutionary statement accompanying the lament speaker's performative attitude therefore constitutes a kind of double-speak: "I – but also we, the burying group – now publicly declare you – but also him, this fallen leader – to be the recipient of such *timê*. And I – but also we, the burying group – declare that your – *but also his, this fallen leader's* – fate has determined your – but also his – *kleos* to be such in community memory."

Transforming Scripts: Lament into Deliberation

Performatively speaking, the heroic self who is lamented in Homer therefore seems to share with his Early Iron Age predecessors a reliance on others for evaluation of his *timê*: as an indebted self, he possesses in death no moral autonomy and no linguistic capacity for

that question the truth of the rank his kinswoman claims for him or that indicate deviation from ancestral norms; see Horton 1993: 245–46.

self-determination. As a script of stocktaking and doing justice, lament therefore looks like the polar opposite of deliberation, and death transforms the *basileus*, despite his role as a paramount when alive, into his burying group's passive instrument. Whereas in life he manipulated reciprocal exchange to control others, in death his former generosity is repaid with an absorption into the narrative world of ancestors and rivals that confers a *timê* and *kleos* beyond his control. Is there no way for such an Early Iron Age leader to enjoy greater autonomy in determining his own *timê* and *kleos* within the bounds of what is *dikê*? Consider this fantastic revision of the lament's script as a linguistic blueprint for the fallen leader to achieve the autonomy that his society and burying group deny him: What if the deceased *basileus* could rise up from his funerary bier to transform the lament's sham dialogue into an active dialogue between himself and his lamenters over the nature of his *timê*? Better yet, what if he could appropriate from his burying group and its female mouthpieces the lament's moral and ethical capacity to confer value – and then conduct a lament *for himself* to determine his *own* degree of *timê* and *kleos*? In a word can we imagine an individual hijacking the lament as a vehicle for deliberating with others about his own worth? Such a fantasy performance provides a key to understanding the self-transformation of Achilles in the *Iliad*. It will also bring us face to face with the autonomy generated by a new type of individual emerging from Achilles' self-transformation.

As Early Iron Age communities changed, there are signs that listeners could respond to the lament with something other than mere assent, acknowledgment and submission – in particular there's evidence they could exercise a more autonomous sense of self in their response. Here Homeric lament again proves indispensable, for we can discern within it two distinct psycho-physiological dynamics behind the burying group's effort to recruit fellow mourners. Each pivots around the question: What motivates non-kin who observe grieving to respond

with similar mourning behavior? And each demarcates a different relation between the kin who lament and the non-kin who are recruited to
join them. The first dynamic links a socially superior group to inferiors
and relies on what I'll call mimetic grief: this conforms to what we've
been describing as the burying group's desire to control the participation of non-kin in mourning. The second dynamic operates between
those who are in some important sense equals – that is, non-kin who
are nevertheless like kin or potential kin – and I'll characterize its
motivation as grieving out of compassion.[43]

As Derderian observes, *klaiein* in Homer is not in fact a discrete
mourning action but part of a communicative link intended to elicit a
response from observers in the form of a groaning or moaning sound
designated by *stenakhesthai* and *stenein*, or by a less particular mourning
behavior, *muresthai* (2001: 26–30) – and, we should add, this is true of
goan as well. We can see how this psycho-physiological response operates mimetically between kin and non-kin in ways consistent with
assent and submission when Achilles learns of Patroclus' death and prepares to lament for him (*Il*.18.22ff.). As soon as he begins to exhibit the
effects of grief (*akhos*, 22) through gestures of mourning, we hear the cries
of non-kin who are female subordinates, the *dmôiai* he and Patroclus
captured (28–31); they immediately assume his *akhos* (*akêkhemenai*, 29),
as though by contagion. Achilles' ally Antilochus, a non-kin who is
standing by his side, likewise responds, presumably because of intimate ties of *philotês* (32–33): he "grieved pouring forth tears" (*odureto
dakrua leibôn*, 32), takes Achilles' hands, "groaned out his mighty heart"

---

[43] These two dynamics within lament may reflect an eighth-century transition
between two types of political space, one grounded in the *basileus'* privileges, the
other in a more "collegial" space where followers need to recognize the justness
of the chief's authority (Hammer 2002: 121–29). Tandy's hypothesis suggests that
elites anticipate one dynamic with fellow elites, the other with more "peripheral"
groups they seek to exclude (1997).

(*estene kudalimon kêr*, 33), and shouts (*ôimôksen*, 35) for fear that Achilles, in his uncontrolled grief, might slit his own throat. True kin, Achilles' mother Thetis and her Nereid companions (35ff.), then model the family members' expression of grief, absorbing the mimetic participation of non-kin in their climactic performance, which includes shrieks (*kôkusen*, 37) and breast-beating and culminates in Thetis' intonation of the first formal *goos* (51ff.). In Book 23, non-kin react similarly when Achilles recounts his dream about Patroclus' ghost to the Greek army, and they all yield to the desire for lamentation (*goos*) (23.108 and 153).

In none of these cases do the mourners who are Patroclus' non-kin appear to participate with a genuine self-expression of sorrow over his death. As Sourvinou-Inwood emphasizes, lamentation is not spontaneous emotion but "repeated, prescribed behaviour" constituting a "socially meaningful act" (1983: 38 and 33–34). Here that meaning seems to emerge from their involuntary and mimetic response to the grief expressed by Achilles' physical proximity and powerful rendering of *akhos*. In acquiescing to it, these non-kin exhibit a performative attitude that makes the leader's grief their own. The illocutionary thrust of their response seems to say, "I accept your grief as my grief," and they submerge their own will in recognition, assent and submission to his authority. In terms of contemporary political philosophy, mimetic grief compels laments' listeners to surrender the voluntarist elements of self to others. It also deflects them from the cognitive task of deciding or owning up to who they are as persons – that is, of acknowledging their own goals and values – since they assume the burying group's criteria for personhood as represented by the fallen leader and his mourners. Needless to say, these listeners suppress any deliberative elements within the self that might challenge those criteria.

Yet the *Iliad* also dramatizes an alternative response on the part of non-kin to a kin's lamentation. In Book 19 the same captive *dmôiai* whose mourning in Book 18 expressed submission to Achilles' and Patroclus' authority react to the lament for Patroclus by Briseis, who functions both as Patroclus' "kin" and as their social equal, by "groaning over their very own [*sphôn d'autôn*] sorrows in reply" (*epi de stenakhonto*, 301–2). Just after this, as Achilles obstinately refuses to eat and continues to lament Patroclus, the elite of the Greek command – who, as *gerontes* (338), must be regarded as Achilles' social equals – likewise respond to his cries by "groaning in reply as each remembered those he had left behind in his halls" (*epi de stenakhonto*, 338–39). Here non-kin listen to and participate in a kin's lament in a communicative interaction essentially different from mimetic grief's "assent and submission."

I characterize this as compassion because the non-kin listeners see themselves in some way as the kin's equals and are moved to lament not by mimicking the kin's grief but by taking it as a simulacrum for their own sorrow. In so doing they maintain a degree of autonomy for a self who in effect declares, "I see in your grief a prompt to remind me of my own need to grieve."[44] In the third part of this chapter we'll see how compassion, when understood as an emotional and linguistic response, provides the climactic resolution to the problem of Achilles' personality and to the question of how much autonomy an individual leader should enjoy. Our attention will focus in particular on the moment in *Iliad* 24 when old King Priam dramatically supplicates Achilles in order to

---

[44] Non-kin who see themselves as in some way equal to kin therefore experience compassion as an *alternative form of grieving*. This needs emphasizing in light of Konstan's contention, following Aristotle (*Rhet*.2.8.2ff.) and contra Crotty (1994: 46), that close family members (*philoi*) can feel only grief for each other's misfortune and not compassion (pity) (2001: 61–63). Aristotle clarifies that those with family members are more liable to "consider" (*oiesthai*, 2.8.2) and "believe" (*nomizein*, 2.8.4) that they can feel compassion for others because their connection to loved ones leaves them vulnerable to the thought that another's misfortune might strike them or one of "their own" (2.8.2 and 2.8.5). This experiencing of another's grief or misfortune *as if it were* one's own or an intimate's constitutes the compassion we witness at *Il*.18.301–302 and 338–39 as a simulacrum of grief. Even by his rigid Aristotelian standards, Konstan is thus inaccurate to claim that compassion (pity) cannot be "reduc[ed] to a mere simulacrum of what another person feels" (2001: 73).

ransom Hector's body, and the two are seized with a "desire for *goos*" as each "remembers" his own loved ones who deserve grief (24.507, 509).

When we outlined the degrees of social stratification and authority in Early Iron Age communities and considered the material evidence of chieftain's houses or feasting halls at Nichoria and Lefkandi, we found evidence suggesting not only competition over rank and a concern for narrative ties to ancestors but also the role "discourse" played in these communities to "mold . . . conceptions of the world and the role of humans in it," and this included the establishment of "proper order" through "justice" (Thomas and Conant 1999: 50). So as a resource discourse enabled leaders to make of "verbal eloquence" a "mark of higher status" (50) – and just as the resources of funerary ritual (lament, rich grave goods, etc.) helped provide the appropriate *geras* for a fallen leader, skill at deliberation could accomplish the same for a leader while still alive.

Once again Homeric evidence proves indispensable because, in addition to dramatizing a pre-citizen script of stocktaking in the form of lament, it dramatizes a pre-citizen script we might call "how leaders deliberate." Now M. I. Finley, for one, claimed that nowhere in Homer do we find the modern equivalent of deliberation: a sustained, rational discussion of competing courses of action, with clear consideration of their advantages and disadvantages (1979: 114–15). But Schofield shows that rational discussion does indeed emerge as a "heroic ideal" in the *Iliad*'s councils, at times with "sustained and single-minded concentration on the rational solution of a problem" (1986: 24). He cogently argues that *euboulia* ("good judgment," "excellent counsel") emerges in the *Iliad*'s six important Achaean councils or assemblies as a "preeminent virtue of the Homeric chieftain" that may garner for him almost as much *timê* as prowess in battle.[45] Each council provides

---

[45] Schofield 1986: 9 and 13–16. Cf. Tandy on the Homeric *boulê* as "a regular forum, a place where one could exhibit nonmilitary *aretê* (excellence) and acquire *timê*"

an occasion where disputing individuals compete before their peers for a redistribution of *timê* that is subject to the sanction of a dominant *basileus* whose display of *euboulia* forges consensus. In addition Schofield attributes another quality to *euboulia*: the ability to understand a present situation in terms of both the past and the future, to introduce to deliberation a "point of view *external*" to the heroic code's insistence on *aretê* and *timê* (16, emphasis in the original).

And here we find a point of comparison for lament's script of stocktaking and the script of deliberation. A good counselor, Schofield says, must be able to manipulate both reason and the emotions to be persuasive: he may appeal to passions and desires but primarily as "considerations – that is, reasons – of one sort or another to the audience."[46] His ability to understand a present situation in terms of both the past and future in effect places the here-and-now cognitively in different frames that may take the form of prudence, compassion, or a sense of justice or propriety that has been overlooked by other deliberators (16). Sometimes, Schofield points out, a Homeric display of *euboulia* even invites a disputant to examine the conflict from his adversary's position – most notably in *Iliad* 1, when Nestor attempts to reconcile Agamemnon and Achilles in the argument over their respective *timai*: "Achilles and Agamemnon are invited to think not just of themselves and their own honour (*timê*), but of the other man's point of view, and what *his* position or situation entitles *him* to expect."[47] The script "how leaders deliberate," I suggest, therefore has the potential to compete with

---

(1997: 143). Gill argues that "deliberative" monologues by Iliadic heroes display patterns of reasoning consistent with those we find in the poem's deliberative councils (1996: 46ff.).

[46] 1986: 16. Schofield's best example is Polydamas, a foil for Hector's ill-advised decisions; his wise counsel succeeds because "he alone sees before and after" (*Il*.18.250).

[47] 1986: 28, emphasis in the original; Schofield points to Odysseus' similar reasoning when attempting to reconcile Agamemnon and Achilles at 19.181–83.

lament's script of stocktaking as a way to evaluate the heroic self by determining the extent of his *timê*.

III   ACHILLES' SELF-TRANSFORMATION

More importantly, as competing scripts, deliberation and lament can alter the way we understand the tension between lament as a female-dominated discourse and the male-dominated discourse of epic. The *Iliad*'s Achilles stands at the nexus of this tension since his exorbitant mourning for Patroclus – including his idiosyncratic performance of a formal *goos* for his fallen companion – seems to split his heroic persona into both a feminine lamenter and a masculine warrior. As Derderian puts it, "Achilles' violent transformation of lament and his fusion of lament and death ritual with his own heroic activity is central to his position as the epic protagonist" (2001: 57). This claim, as far as it goes, is accurate, but it overlooks Achilles' most important achievement when he *combines* the roles of warrior and lamenter in a unique performance in the poem of a self-definition in relation to others. We can trace the development of this performance at three moments when Achilles tries to situate himself in relation to others through a hybrid discourse merging elements of lament with the deliberation of leaders: in Book 1, when he turns from defeat in his quarrel with Agamemnon to seek his mother Thetis' help (348–427); in Book 9, in his great speech rejecting Agamemnon's offer of reconciliation (308–426); and in Book 24, when Priam succeeds in supplicating Achilles for the ransom of Hector's corpse (485–551). With increasing success in each scene Achilles uses lament's typical diction, performative attitude and illocutionary statements *to recode* versions of the script "how leaders deliberate" so that he might reverse the judgment at the poem's outset when he failed to obtain the *timê* he believed he justly deserved.

The uniqueness of Achilles – including his uniqueness as a performer – has certainly preoccupied Homeric scholars in recent years. In part my goal is to deepen our understanding of broad claims like those of Slatkin, who believes that, as Achilles confronts his own mortality, "the definition of the self comes urgently into question," specifically through "Achilles' discovery of his own identity – of values, of morality" (1991: 40, 39). Zanker too claims that during the *Iliad* Achilles undergoes "massive changes from his former self" and in particular a "radical change" in Book 24 (1994: 75, 121). Martin's demonstration of the ways Achilles fashions a uniquely "self-reflexive rhetoric" (1989:192) in his great speech of Book 9 (308–426) can be linked to Achilles' identity crisis and self-transformation: if this rhetoric really does amount to "creat[ing] the illusion of an interiorized, Achillean language" with an "explicitly new ethical bent" (Martin 1989: 196, 183), then it accompanies Achilles' achievement of a similarly innovative deliberative and moral autonomy.

Ultimately Achilles' self-transformation, "character development" (Macleod 1982: 23) or "ethical achievement" (Taplin 1992: 274) primarily concerns the nature of the autonomy he passionately pursues after his disgraceful defeat in deliberation with Agamemnon. In this regard my understanding of Achilles' autonomy concurs with Hammer's recent discussion of the hero's "self-sufficiency" as constitutive of a new political ethic (2002: 93–113), and it recognizes, with Zanker, Kim (2000) and Hammer, how emotional ties like compassion and friendship contribute to this political ethic. But my goal is to understand the moral dimensions of this individual autonomy in terms of citizenship's political and communicative (linguistic) components. So with help from G. H. Mead (1934, 1964) and Habermas (1979, 1984, 1987, 1990, 1992) I see Achilles replacing a leader's reciprocal relation to followers with a reciprocal exchange of self-representations rather than gifts or favors. And it is this that guarantees the autonomous participation of both self and other in a prototype of citizen interaction. I add one final perspective on Achilles' autonomy:

contemporary debates in political philosophy over individuality and citizenship.

Iliad 1

In the *Iliad*'s first enactment of the script "how leaders deliberate," Achilles fails during his quarrel with Agamemnon to impose his claim to a rightful *geras*. We might say he fails because, goaded by the voluntarist dimension within the self, he attempts to assert his will against a rival; and this attempt cannot prevail over Homeric society's conventional procedures governing a paramount leader's distribution of plunder among elite warriors. But Achilles himself says he is victimized by an act of hybris on Agamemnon's part (1.203) – a claim Athena endorses a few moments later when she speaks to him (214). In his 1917 thesis Louis Gernet (2001) identifies hybris as the archetypal Greek crime, the key to Greek moral and juridical thought; just as importantly for our purposes, he demonstrates how the concept, when grasped in its full semantic use, identifies an individual's relationship to social order and justice from Homer to the fourth-century Athenian law courts.[48] We can understand at least two important reasons why hybris has such signifying potency if we build on the basic sense Gernet finds in the term: "outrage or flagrant insult; excess or going beyond" (*outrage/outrance*) (4, 14). First hybris aligns two individuals or groups, its perpetrator(s) and its victim(s), in relation to the values of a dominant social group – a group, following Mead, I call the dominant social other; second, and more importantly, it encourages those who speak of hybris to scrutinize individuality in various ways in different eras because it isolates the

---

[48] On hybris as a key to Gernet's understanding of how the Greeks saw the individual and the moral autonomy of the person, see Cantarella 2001: ix–xiv. See Humphreys on the 1917 thesis in relation to the rest of Gernet's work and the intellectual milieu of Durkheim, Mauss, and others (Humphreys 1978: 76–106).

individual in two senses: the "subject" (the perpetrator) of hybris and its "object" (the victim) (Gernet 2001: 4).[49]

We do need, however, to draw on subsequent studies, such as those by Fisher (1992), Cairns (1996), Cantarella (2003) and MacDowell (1976), to reach a more accurate definition of the term. Fisher understands the core meaning of hybris from Homer to fourth-century Athens as a deliberate, frequently violent assault by one individual or group upon another, causing dishonor or shame, provoking anger and a need for revenge, and arising from the perpetrator's willful, often pleasurable, exercise of superiority over the victim. It also characterizes behavior associated with the young, the rich, and the socially powerful (1992: 1ff. and *passim*). MacDowell's earlier, less encyclopedic study encourages us to recognize in acts of hybris voluntary forms of indulgent, exuberant self-expression that threaten to damage social relations in society at large. These acts spring from an unregulated excess of life-energy, usually in the form of appetites for drink, food, and sex (1976: 21ff.). Cairns understands hybris not as a willful intent to commit such acts but as an individual's long-standing disposition to overvalue oneself without concern for others – an ingrained tendency to permit one's own *timê* to encroach an another's (1996: 8, 10, 17, 32). Cantarella underscores the tight link between hybris and *timê*: hybris in fact never lacks a victim (object), for it inevitably leads one elite individual's pursuit of *timê* to compromise someone else's ability to uphold a positive public self-image (2003: 110–20, esp. 119).

---

[49] Gernet sees the victim of hybris defining the social boundaries of a kin group or state because he or she arouses sympathy and provokes awareness of an individual's right to respect from others (*timê*). The perpetrator of hybris rouses a collective force of incrimination that draws social boundaries to exclude the criminal outsider and at the same time stimulates interest in the nature of the perpetrator's will (2001: 433–36; cf. 182–85).

Hybris in Homer describes acts which are not strictly speaking illegal but which offend the spiritual or moral values of a kin group's social
order (Gernet identifies this with *themis*) or of a wider social order shared
among kin groups (Gernet identifies this with *dikê*). And the victims
of Homeric hybris are usually individuals who qualify as *basileis*, leaders whose vulnerability to outrage suggests a weakened control over
local, kin-based social order (*themis*) (2001: 19–25; cf. 159). Now as soon
as Achilles declares himself an object (victim) of hybris, he attracts
collective interest in the nature of his individuality: Gernet describes
this as a combination of sympathy for an injured party's plight and a
more generalized concern over proper redistribution of social resources
(*eunomiê*) (2001: 21–22). We've already mentioned in passing how this
leads to Nestor's failed attempt at dispute settlement (1.247–84), where
the old man plays the role of an adjudicating *basileus* who tries to lead
the two "litigating" *basileis* to a resolution (a *dikê*). As we saw, Nestor
based this resolution on his own ability to assume each man's subject
position along with the objective, third-person perspective of community interest; he then tried to persuade each litigant to share the other's
position as well as the community's.

Because this attempt fails, Achilles must surrender his prize (*geras*),
the captive Briseis, to his rival. He then initiates an alternative attempt
to establish the "true" nature of his *timê*, an attempt I characterize
as an effort to establish publicly the validity of a self-evaluation. He
calls upon his mother Thetis (1.348ff.), and here Homer's description of
Achilles' appeal and Thetis' response is remarkable for the way it splices
an obvious concern with *timê* into the language and gestures of lament.
It also enables Achilles to evoke typically feminine chronotopes of
childbirth and to assume the typically feminine performative attitude
in lament, which, as we described it earlier, announces the leader's death
within a scheme of cosmic justice or apportionment. Once he isolates
himself from his comrades, Achilles begins to weep (*dakrusas*, 349) and

calls out in prayer to his mother as "you who bore me, even though it was to a short life" (352).[50] But he immediately links this typically feminine chronotope of childbirth to the question of the *timê* (353) he should therefore receive from Zeus, who now provides him with none (*nun d'oude me tutthon eteisen*, 354). To explain this, he then switches chronotopes to the masculine scene of the quarrel's deliberation, where Agamemnon "dishonored" (*etimêsen*) him and seized his *geras* (356). The speech ends with another description of Achilles' tears (357).

These lines programmatically introduce a hybrid discourse whose characteristics oscillate between lament and chieftain deliberation, and the remainder of the exchange between Achilles and Thetis maintains this oscillation. Thetis responds to her son's tearful prayer by taking his hand, not unlike a lamenting woman who makes physical contact with the fallen leader's corpse (cf. Derderian 2001: 28–29, 53). She identifies her son's behavior as *klaiein* (*ti klaieis*) and a display of sorrow (*penthos*, 362), and proposes that the two of them reach a common understanding of it (363). Achilles complies with a narrative (365–92) that has puzzled scholars both ancient and modern, for it seems too long and detailed in summarizing the genesis, dynamics and outcome of the quarrel with Agamemnon that Homer has just narrated (cf. Kirk 1985: 88–93). What commentators fail to notice, however, is that Achilles embeds this account of the deliberation within the speech genre of lament, specifically within the speech acts of *klaiein*, noted by Thetis, and *stenakhein*, noted by Homer, who describes Achilles' reply to his mother's question "Why are you grieving?" (*ti klaieis*, 362) with the formulaic "groaning deeply, he replied . . ." (*baru stenakhôn*, 364). The deliberation now conforms to the format within lament of a dialogue between a mother

---

[50] Achilles initially uses the speech genre of prayer to summon Thetis (*êrêsato*, with hands extended out over the sea, 351), but it turns out to be more a "complaint" (Kirk 1985: 89). I would describe it as a hybrid "prayer/lament."

and her deceased child, or between a wife and her deceased husband, though here the child is still alive and *it is he who inaugurates and leads the dialogue*. The two of them therefore open the possibility of meeting the improbable or fantastic revision of lament I suggested earlier, where a deceased *basileus* might rise up from his funerary bier to transform the lament's sham dialogue into an active dialogue between himself and his lamenter over the nature of his *timê*.

In his summary account of the deliberation (365–92), Achilles' narrative is at first rich in typical heroic actions like the sacking of Thebe's citadel and division of its plunder – actions the Homeric narrator curiously omits from his original account of the quarrel (cf. Kirk 1985: 91) – but then Achilles concentrates on the dynamics of the key speech acts by each participant in a chain of deliberative events leading up to and including the quarrel: the priest Chryses' supplication (374) and the Achaean assembly's consent to accept the ransom (376–77); Agamemnon's refusal in an abusively powerful speech (379); Chryses' plea for Apollo's aid and the god's answer to his prayer (380–81); the seer Calchas' public pronouncement about the meaning of the god-sent plague (385); Achilles' attempt to assume direction of the Achaean assembly (386); and finally Agamemnon's threat to take away Achilles' prisoner, Briseis (387–88).

But (at 393), after highlighting these deliberative exchanges among warriors, Achilles abruptly swerves back to his initial language of prayer/lament centered on dialogue between mother and child, with its chronotope of child-rearing: "But you – that is, if you are able – engulf your fine son in protection" (*alla su, ei dynasai ge, periskheo paidos heêos*). Thetis plays her part in the antiphonal structure of *stenakhein* by responding first with tears (413) and then plunging fully into lament's female performative attitude as we've described it: in effect she picks up Achilles' cue (at 352) about his short life and launches into a classic illocutionary statement – phrased in the form of a question – of the fallen leader's fate: "O my child, why did I raise you when all I gave birth to were terrible experiences?" (414).[51] She pronounces his portion or destiny (*aisa*) as lasting "just a little while, not at all long" (416), doomed to a swift death (*ôkumoros*) and wretched beyond anyone else's (417). "Why then did I bear you to such an evil destiny (*kakêi aisêi*)?" she concludes. And yet, despite what appears to be pure lament, Thetis turns back to deliberation with her promise to "persuade" (*peisesthai*) Zeus through supplication as soon as he returns home to Olympus (427).

In this long exchange mother and son indeed come to a mutual understanding: they conspire to find an alternative path circumventing the conventional outcome of the script "how leaders deliberate," which normally determines each leader's *timê* when plunder is divided. By recoding the judgment reached in the Achaean assembly within the language of lament – the only occasion and discourse where women may speak authoritatively about the *timê* of men – they try to replace the male exercise of *euboulia*, which often understands a present situation in terms of both the past and future, with the female mourner's prescient knowledge about the deceased's *timê* in the past, present and future, including its place within community memory (*kleos*) and within a cosmically just scheme of apportionment. Socially and historically speaking, the conspiracy of Achilles and Thetis opens the door to an even more momentous transformation: they reject the paramount *basileus* (Agamemnon) as the arbiter of *timê* among his comrades (*philoi*) and replace him with a mother-son duo comprising a novel, composite male-female lament speaker.

---

[51] Kirk connects Thetis' question and her statements that follow to the language of Homeric lament; he also helps us see the illocutionary dimension of her question as something like: "I cannot understand why I bore and raised such an unfortunate son!" (1985: 96).

(One of them, Thetis, is a powerful agent of cosmic justice in her own right.[52])

To use Mead's terminology, Achilles and Thetis supplant Agamemnon as the representative of the dominant social other whose authority determines the worth of all other social roles – the "me" roles all individuals must own up to as the indicator of their social identity. And even though Achilles' self is in a pretty abject state, having just been bested in the quarrel with Agamemnon, he and his mother take the first step in a process of individuation that promises him a self-transformation and autonomy unparalleled in Early Iron Age society. The key to its success lies in this innovative, hybrid discourse about himself that Achilles has just learned, a discourse that rewrites the script "how leaders deliberate" and whose temporal and cognitive frames and rationality criteria just might trump those of typical male deliberation.

Iliad 9

The quarrel between Agamemnon and Achilles lies dormant until Book 9, when the older chief reignites it by sending an embassy of Achaean chiefs to enumerate an extravagant offer of gifts designed to placate Achilles' anger and induce his reentry into battle. Clearly Thetis' supplication of Zeus has successfully turned the war against the Achaeans, rendering more credible Achilles' original arguments about the proper measure of his *timê*. The embassy scene offers a version of the script "how leaders deliberate" in which Achilles can now articulate alternative reasons for his earlier arguments by applying the lesson in hybrid discourse he learned from Thetis in Book 1. The embassy also attempts to settle the dispute by having authoritative figures like Odysseus and Phoenix play the role of an adjudicating *basileus*. Achilles

---

[52] See Slatkin 1991: 69–72. It's important to note that the *Iliad* only alludes to Thetis' powerful agency in order to foreground her role as a lament speaker (83–84).

once again adopts the performative attitude and temporal-cognitive frames typical of lament in an attempt to recode both the original deliberation with Agamemnon and the paramount chief's extravagant new offer – only now in a more subtle performance that posits for Homer's audience a hypothetical autonomy characteristic of membership in a new sort of community. Understanding the hypothetical nature of this autonomy will help clarify the perennial debate among scholars about the individualism of Achilles – whether his stance in the great speech (9.308–429) challenges the coherence of his heroic society's moral and social codes, and so situates him beyond them in a semblance of modern selfhood, or whether his stance, despite severely criticizing those codes, remains consistent with them.[53] (In Gill's terms, does Achilles articulate a Cartesian-Kantian "subjective–individualist" type of selfhood or an "objective–participant" one? [1996: 11–12]).

In this speech Achilles projects an autonomy that doesn't fit neatly into Gill's conceptual duality because it displays elements of selfhood found in both modern and premodern societies – and ultimately it will be judged an autonomy too radically individual for membership in any actual community. His great speech enacts the sort of self-presentation that redefines the self in a new attempt at individuation. This occurs in two stages, the first echoing the female lamenter's performative attitude and voice, and the second the novel performative attitude and voice of the dead leader himself. As we hypothesized earlier, it's as though he were to rise up from his bier to determine his own degree of *timê* before the mourners, as though he were to ask, "What sort of person must I become in order to decide the justice of my own *timê*?" In this first stage Achilles the self-lamenter understands his own identity as the identity he has for others in a social order – to Mead he sees himself in terms

---

[53] See, among others: Parry 1956, Whitman 1958, Claus 1975, Friedrich and Redfield 1978, Nimis 1986, Martin 1989, Rose 1992, Gill 1996, Hammer 2002, and Wilson 2002.

of a "me" role sanctioned by the dominant social other. In the second stage he willfully chooses to own up to this identity in a self-conscious claim to a personal life history.[54] But at the same time this willful choice briefly reveals a sense of the self's agency that usually remains concealed: what Mead calls the "I," the self as a speaking subject, an individual organism that is extra-social because, while it can reflect upon itself, it doesn't yet recognize itself in the ways others react and speak to it.[55] With the voice of the "I" Achilles will ask, "What sort of person do I wish to become in order to decide the justice of my own *timê*?"

This distinction between a socially mediated, self-conscious sense of self (the "me") and a self-reflexive but extra-social self (the "I") helps to explain why Achilles doesn't opt for a radical individuality outside any adherence to social codes and values, even when he steps outside the I-you reciprocal exchange relationship between elite warriors and the paramount chief. It also helps to explain how he can present himself to others as an "irreplaceable and distinctive person" (Habermas 1992: 168) – and insist that they recognize this socially unmediated identity. In discussing the speech I want to clarify the need for this seeming paradox within individuation, and to focus on one key to the success of his fantastic performance as a self-lamenter: his exploitation of the female lamenter's value-conferring voice, which enables him to replace the "devalued" sense he has as a warrior under Agamemnon with the demand that others recognize the value he confers on himself for the life he chooses to lead.

---

[54] See Habermas 1992: 152–53, where he describes this process: "The identity of social-ized individuals forms itself simultaneously in the medium of coming to an under-standing with others in language and in the medium of coming to a life-historical and intrasubjective understanding with oneself."

[55] For the distinction between the "me" and the "I," see Mead 1934: 173–86 and 1964: 138–41 and 142–45; see also Habermas 1992: 171–77.

Like Achilles' exchange with Thetis at *Il*.1.348–427, the great speech oscillates between versions of the scripts "how leaders deliberate" and lament. In its first ten lines (9.308–317) Achilles defines a deliberative strategy of his own in contrast to all the other warriors (and especially Agamemnon), one that places him outside any possibility of persuasion: he alone expresses straightforwardly what he thinks is best; anyone who conceals his true thoughts while saying something else is hostile to his ethical principles (*ekhthros*).[56] But the reason Achilles offers for this stance on deliberation derives not from typical scenes of deliberation but from a lamenter's cognitive perspective when she or he judges the fallen warrior's lot: "The portion [*moira*] is equal for he who lays low and for he who advances straight into battle; both the coward and the braveheart have equal *timê*; the do-nothing dies just the same as the achiever" (318–20).[57] Achilles then for the first time turns the language of lament toward himself when he judges, "Nothing extra is left for me, even though I've suffered pains in my heart, always risking my own life's breath (*emên psykhên*) to advance into battle" (321–22).

Martin identifies Achilles' reference here to his own *psykhê* as an instance of his "self-reflexive rhetoric" and a "shift toward an interior language," suggesting that Achilles adapts here the language of another speech genre, the boast, when a warrior claims he will transform the *psykhê* a dying enemy yields to him into a sign of his own superior

---

[56] For Martin, persuasion is the "leading theme" of Achilles' reply to the embassy (1989: 198ff.); for Gill it's a key to that reply's intelligibility (1996: 136ff.). For Wilson, Achilles' goal in the speech is to best Agamemnon in a rhetorical contest of definitions (2002: 10), a "tournament of definitions" (135) over which of two distinct types of exchange (and degrees of relative *timê*) will determine the relation between them. (The older chief offers his enticing gifts as "unlimited *apoina*" (compensation), but Achilles will try to recode this offer as *poinê*, retribution for the loss of *timê* Agamemnon has inflicted on him [2002: 75ff.]).

[57] As Griffin suggests, there's a double meaning to Achilles' use of *moira* here: not only a "share" of plunder from battle but the human "lot" of death (1995: 112).

status (1989: 192–93). But I believe Achilles' reference to his own *psykhê* adapts a particularly self-reflexive version of different speech genre, lament: this is the *psykhê*'s ability after death to lament itself and its own fate, to perform its own *goos*. At 16.856–7 we see Patroclus' *psykhê* leave his body on its way to Hades, "performing a *goos* over its own fate [*hon potmon gooôsa*] for it has left behind manhood and youth." Hector's *psykhê* does likewise (at 22.362–3). And (at 23.106) Patroclus' *psykhê* hovers all night over Achilles, "performing a *goos* and lamenting" (*gooôsa te muromenê te*).[58]

In keeping with lament's chronotopes of childbirth and child-rearing, Achilles then compares himself to a mother bird who self-lessly sacrifices her own needs to feed her brood (323–24) – a simile of animal affection for offspring that will reappear overtly as lament when Achilles leads the Achaeans in a *goos* for Patroclus, "groaning (*stenakhôn*) like a bearded lion whose cubs a deer hunter has snatched away" (18.318–22).[59] Achilles' self-representation as the mother bird not only evokes an image characteristic of a lament speaker, it also forms a bridge to a narrative description of his own heroic achievements (325–37) – and this enables him to take the posture of one performing his own *goos while still alive*. He thus utters these feats of conquest and plunder in an ambiguous rhetorical register: they resemble the account of the fallen warrior's life a female lamenter might provide in the nar-rative portion of a *goos* (cf. Hecabe on Hector, 22.432–35; Andromache

---

[58] The lamenter in a formal *goos* might also see the fallen warrior's *psykhê* as a precious possession his enemy steals from him, as Hecuba says of Hector (24.754).

[59] On these and other animal similes in the poem as indices of Achilles' peculiar set of heroic characteristics, see Zanker 1994: 15–16, with n. 33. Martin sees Achilles' self-comparison to the mother bird as a pathetic image from the discourse of augury, where at *Il*.2.311–315 a mother bird watches a snake devour her chicks (1989: 204–205). But this mother bird clearly laments (*oduromenê*, 315) her chicks as they are being devoured.

on Hector, 24.729–30), but they also match the account a warrior might provide of his own achievements when leaders deliberate over *timê* and *geras*. So in effect, as he did (at 1.365ff.) in his conversation with Thetis, Achilles succeeds in recoding the account of his heroism that failed to best Agamemnon in their quarrel. Now, however, he has more clearly evoked the performative attitude of the lamenter whose authoritative voice publicly proclaims a warrior's fate and ultimate portion.

If at this point in his speech Achilles engages in what Gill (adapting the term from Taylor and Frankfurt) calls "second-order" reasoning – a rational assessment of one's own reasons – it is because he has superimposed the cognitive frame of lament on the script "how leaders deliberate" (1996: 133). Unlike other heroes who engage in second-order reasoning – Gill compares Sarpedon's speech to Glaucus at 12.310–28 – Achilles the self-lamenter already stands beyond the limit of his life, and from this privileged point he can perform a self-evaluation that returns us to the paradox noted above: while clearly unique, it appears consistent with shared, communal norms for heroic conduct. How can this be? Specifically, it appears to echo the feminine voice of lament which Early Iron Age burying groups used to ventriloquize their values and prestige and to inspire in listeners assent and submission. So, as Gill insists, Achilles does not in this speech seem to take a true "outsider's" position rejecting the rational basis for participating in the generalized reciprocal exchange linking all the elite warriors. Nevertheless, he will provide reasons, especially at 337–43, for rejecting Agamemnon's version of an exchange network, reasons challenging such a network's typical heroic behavior, values and logic.

The key to understanding the paradox is to ask: "Which aspect of the self is capable of refusing the 'me' roles society enjoins us to play, including their underlying logic?" Mead identifies this dimension of the self's agency as the "I." Today we might call it a voluntarist impulse within the self that emerges spontaneously in naked support of our self-interest as an individual organism. But the "I" also identifies for Mead (and Habermas) the agent who performs the vocal gestures to which others respond as they communicate to the self the nature of its "me" roles (cf. Habermas 1992: 171–72). It unconsciously articulates presocial, instinctual drives which the self's "me" roles will soon have to control, but it also serves, in Habermas' words, as the "impulse of creative fantasy – or as the impetus for the innovative transformation of a way of seeing" (1992: 180). The "I" within the self is thus a fleeting apparition destined to be domesticated by the "me," but it provides a sort of safety valve for the "me" when the pressures of social differentiation or conflicting social roles motivate the self to resist rigid conventions. At this point the "I" spontaneously and impulsively envisions an alternative, "larger society" receptive to its needs, perhaps one that only posterity will realize. Or this society might be accessible only to those who share a counterfactual, universal discourse of reason, a way of thinking and speaking that can recognize the self's uniqueness before reabsorbing it into a now-expanded or redefined "me" role accommodating an individual's moral autonomy (183–86).

Achilles gives voice to this "I" within the self when his linguistic innovations begin to express, in Martin's phrase, an "explicitly new ethical bent" (1989: 183). Interestingly, he doesn't envision this new self (at 337ff.) as an absolutely autonomous individual – that would be a pure expression of the "I" – but as a new *type* of man defining a new "me" role. In view of his partiality for the female lament speaker, Achilles categorizes this type of man in terms of the value a woman has for him:

> *Why must Argives go to war with Trojans? Why did the son of Atreus gather an army and lead us here? Wasn't it because of Helen with her beautiful hair? Do the sons of Atreus alone among mortal men cherish their wives? Any man who is good and sensible cherishes his wife, just*

as I cherished my woman from my heart, even if I did win her with my
spear.

(9.337–43)

These lines certainly testify to the importance in Achilles' moral stance of emotional ties, such as affection (Zanker 1994: 89), and Martin's lexical evidence helps us see how Achilles' "obsession" with certain novel phrases is linked to the "theme of women" (1989: 184). But is this consistent, as Gill would have it, with any "objective-participant" social role we can identify in Early Iron Age society? Or does Achilles' use of the feminine voice of lament and his identification here with women in their roles as wives and mothers announce a break with early Iron Age social roles for men?

Achilles' rhetorical relation to women helps us to understand in what sense he's striving for moral autonomy.[60] Just as Early Iron Age burying groups used their female members as ideological spokespersons to persuade lament's listeners of a fallen leader's *timê*, so in these lines Achilles appropriates a female performative attitude in lament and, in the same breath, expresses it as a certain type of man's strong "personal" (in our modern sense) attachment to women. But what is it in the female lamenter's performative attitude that appears useful to male-dominated burying groups in the Early Iron Age and to Achilles in this speech? It's her ability to articulate publicly a moral agency rooted in what *she claims to be* her "subjective" experience of powerful emotion. To borrow a term from Habermas, in lament women supposedly display their grief publicly in actions that are "dramaturgical," that is, actions

---

[60] Loraux notes the self-centeredness of female lament in tragedy, claiming that Cassandra, Antigone, Helen, and Iphigenia use "lamentation for their own purposes and on own behalf" (2002b: 58–59). She links the wrath of Homer's Achilles to the wrath of tragedy's mourning mothers, seeing him as the sole male participant in an otherwise "female figure of memory" (2002a: 160).

whose rationality is not primarily based on teleological criteria like success or failure, or normative criteria like adherence to or deviance from norms, but on criteria of sincerity or deceptiveness (1984: 90–94).[61] The key questions the speech genre of lament addresses to its audience are, thus: "Do this lamenting woman's cries and statements strike us as authentic revelations of an inner world to which she has privileged access?" "Will her expression of grief invite us to share her highly subjective perception of the world and recognize it as in some way similar to our own?"[62]

By performing laments, women in Early Iron Age, Homeric and later state societies won recognition from the dominant social other as a true moral agent.[63] And by adopting their performative attitude, Achilles

---

[61] Mourning behavior of course has teleological and normative dimensions – i.e., it aims to accomplish ends and should follow prescribed rules. But as a performance it must at least lay claim to expressing inner emotion. While expressions of grief may be intended to deceive, feigned grief loses its primarily dramaturgical nature and should be judged teleologically or normatively. Stears considers the sincerity of female grief in lamentation in Archaic and Classical Athens, its "correct" display, and its use as a "social strategy" (1998: 122–26).

[62] A listener's ability to recognize when an individual displays privileged access to his or her inner world takes different forms in different societies. For Taylor this is essential to a modern sense of individual identity, especially that part of our self-understanding we call our "authenticity" as unique human beings (1994: 28). We engage others in recognizing our identity and authenticity when we reveal ourself most accurately as a "subject of significance": this is a special kind of agent who draws on emotions like shame, fear, or love to communicate a unique experience of subjectivity better than any other set of criteria, especially those based on teleological reason (1985a: 94–114). While we cannot simply identify Achilles with a version of modern selfhood, we should not allow his rhetorical performance in this speech to eclipse ethical dimensions of the self that emerge here. Wilson's emphasis on Achilles as a rhetorical subject denies any sincerity to his expression of affection for Briseis because mention of her "suits his rhetorical purpose" (2002: 88).

[63] On women as moral agents in the Greek tradition, see Foley 2001: 112ff., where tragic lamentation is the most conspicuous vehicle for women's recognition as moral agents.

induces his listeners to evaluate his recoded narrative of heroic exploits according to rationality criteria typical of such an agent, criteria that are no longer primarily teleological or normative but dramaturgical. His claims (in lines 341–43, "Any man who is good and sensible cherishes his wife, just as I cherished my woman from my heart, even if I did win her with my spear") cannot be judged right or wrong except as a sincere expression originating in a new type of person, a different sort of man, one who not only gives priority to "subjective" preferences originating in his inner world but expects others – including the dominant social other – to recognize the legitimacy of his preferences and to recognize in his expression of these preferences a simulacrum of their own.

With these words Achilles begins to clear a moral space for the moral and political autonomy of the Greek citizen in city-states and ethnos-states, a space that begins to insist on the three basic criteria for citizenship and selfhood outlined in my Introduction: an individual *timê* deserving recognition from others sufficient to maintain a positive public image; a qualified personal autonomy permitting one to exercise his will in individual and family interest without endangering community welfare; and deliberative freedoms that include participation with peers in assembling, speaking, and in the exchange of reason giving. Achilles' new man sees this as a space where an individual can establish the legitimacy of what is his own, where individual choice founds a partnership of male and female that stands apart from the generalized reciprocal exchange linking warriors to chieftains. Mead might say that Achilles' new man accommodates the impulsive or creative drives of the "I" within his "me" roles; Habermas might say that Achilles grounds this new man's identity in an "ethical self-understanding" that takes the form of a consciously chosen life history (1992: 168).

For today's political philosopher Achilles gives considerable freeplay to the self's voluntarist dimension – he highlights after all the act of choosing and cherishing a sexual partner regardless of what others may think – and he isolates the act of choice as characteristic of a certain type of man who does not depend on the dominant social other in the form of a *basileus*' who dictates the type of exchange network that determines his *timê*. This new man locates his worth, not in the authoritative reasons another might give when assessing his property or achievements in relation to a rival's, but in another's ability to recognize the validity of his choice based on criteria deriving from that choice itself, criteria that are intrinsic to it. Entry into this new class of men thus depends on one's ability to understand Achilles' claims as reasonable by the criteria of dramaturgical action.

Does Achilles Become an "Unencumbered Self"?

It is not, I believe, unreasonable to claim that Achilles' efforts to individuate a new type of self amount to an early Greek attempt to theorize about the self. And his "moves," rhetorical, logical, and ethical, are not dissimilar from attempts in contemporary political philosophy to individuate a self capable of enacting justice. I'm thinking of Rawls' desire to conceive of justice with a "theoretical basis" that is "individualistic," that is, enacted by distinct persons rather than a faceless collectivity (1971: 264; cf. Sandel 1998: 53). The self Rawls posits as the agent of justice is one that is "prior to the ends which are affirmed by it" (1971: 560): this is a self that can distance itself from its interests without detaching itself completely from them because its identity is secured independently of the choices that connect it to others. Sandel calls this a "subject of possession" that, while relating itself to something or someone through choice, at the same time marks a distance between itself and the object of that choice (1998: 54). Achilles too now thinks of himself that way, for he is staking his new self on his emotional attachment to Briseis, but he will shortly have little problem distancing himself from that choice to imagine an alternative mate (9.394). He therefore isolates the self as an "I" in its dramaturgical actions, in its will to choose its ends and interests, rather than in the ends themselves. Through privileged access to his inner life, he remains prior to his ends rather than constituted by them – and his self seems to have fixed boundaries defined by his "right" to choose his own conception of the good and his demand that others recognize its legitimacy (cf. Sandel 1998: 175).

Achilles appeals here to rational criteria he believes both cognitively and deliberatively superior to the criteria used in the traditional script "how leaders deliberate," and this precludes reaching agreement with anyone (including Agamemnon) still attached to the old criteria (344). Now he can characterize as patently inferior the tactics the chiefs have been using in their deliberations without him (346–55), and he repeats with renewed force the threats he uttered in Book 1 to leave Troy (356–63). He can also more confidently bestow *timê* on himself in a brief catalogue of the wealth he has stockpiled at home in Phthia as well as acquired at Troy, again as though he were performing a *goos* over himself and had no need of a social other to calculate this for him (363–66). His autonomy (performative, moral, and cognitive) inspires him to repeat from Book 1 his invective against Agamemnon, renewing his claim to be the object (victim) of hybris (368), only now these threats are recoded in his new language (367–77). And when he echoes back to the embassy the catalogue of Agamemnon's gifts, his novel expressions and furious rhetoric mockingly recode these items as devalued in light of his newly established rationality criteria (378–92): the gifts are morally repugnant (*ekhthra*) and, in a parody of lament speaking, they are worth "the portion of a scrap" (*en karos aisêi*, 378).

The great speech reaches its climax (starting at 386–87), when Achilles for the third time rejects the possibility that Agamemnon might persuade him. The theme of persuasion, as Martin, Gill, Wilson, and others claim, does seem to dominate the speech, but this is because for Achilles persuasion defines a moral and deliberative community of like-minded speakers and listeners. After declaring "not even then would Agamemnon yet persuade me" (386), he returns to the founding act of his new man, the pivotal choosing of a wife. Agamemnon had offered him one of his daughters in marriage, with a fabulous dowry, as a climactic inducement to return (9.142–56; 283–98): this offer Achilles now recodes as: "I will not marry a daughter of Agamemnon son of Atreus – not even if she rivaled Aphrodite in beauty or could compete in handiwork with gray-eyed Athena! Not even then would I marry her. Let some other Achaean take her, someone more suitable to him and more of a *basileus*" (388–92). Once again it is imperative that Achilles remain outside the exchange network engineered by this paramount *basileus*, whose rank constitutes the gold standard by which warriors under him share in degrees of chieftainship. Should he ever return home, he imagines a scenario for choosing a wife free from Agamemnon's interference. It also provides an alternative to his choice of Briseis at Troy, where he knows death may come at any time, but it retains at its core the pivotal act of personally choosing the kind of life one wishes to lead. Achilles imagines he will respect the priorities and protocol of his own family and permit his father Peleus to "seek out" by himself – that is, without Agamemnon's advice – a wife from among many candidates in Hellas (Thessaly) and Phthia. Nevertheless, Peleus' choice will become Achilles' own because "whichever one of these women [pre-selected by Peleus] I prefer, I will make my cherished wife" (397). And he emphasizes how, prior to arriving at Troy, he had at home repeatedly sought to find just the right sort of woman for proper marriage: "Back there [*entha*] my wild heart time and again urged me to marry a properly courted wife, a mate suitable to me, so that I might enjoy the possessions Peleus stored up for me" (398–400).[64]

---

[64] Griffin clarifies how the terms Achilles uses here, while originally referring to a sexual partner (*alokhos, akoitês*), mean in this context a "wedded wife" (1995: 123).

So in defining himself a "subject of possession" Achilles shows that the core of this new self can be detached from its particular choices so long as others recognize the legitimacy of its "right" to choose. Increasingly his stance, centered in Mead's "I," resembles a version of Rawls' unencumbered self defined prior to its ends. To emphasize his equation of self with the act of choosing, Achilles expands upon his earlier use of an "interior language" where "he speaks of the 'soul' and of his 'self' in the same breath" (Martin 1989: 192): "To me there is nothing equivalent in value to my soul [*psykhê*], not all they say was stored up in Ilium's well-built citadel before the Achaeans came, nor all the stone threshold of the archer Phoebus Apollo encloses at rocky Pytho" (401–5). He soon explains why: because the *psykhê* of any man, being immaterial, is "possessed" in life in a sense quite different from material possession ("A man's *psykhê* cannot come back again like something plundered or seized once it passes the barrier of his teeth," 408–9). Here the *psykhê* names a faculty for possessing that we must distinguish from the nature of particular possessions – one even implying a capacity for *disinterest* in the particular choices it or others make – and that renews itself so long as we are competent to make choices. This resembles the "deontological self" in Rawls' notion of the person: a "subject whose identity is given independently of the things I have, independently, that is, of my interests and ends and my relations with others" (Sandel 1998: 55).[65]

This ability to separate the act of choosing from a particular object of choice does not, I believe, impugn the sincerity of Achilles' present attachment to Briseis.

[65] For Hammer, Achilles' autonomy in book 9 "defines his own happiness apart from the mediating structures of warrior society" and implies that "social prescriptions and proscriptions do not meaningfully bind us to others" (2002: 96). But I disagree when he then separates "Achilles' unwillingness to bind himself to others" from "a new notion of the will that is internal" (103). Sandel's "self of possession" (1998: 54–59) shows how closely intertwined are the self's internal will and its ability to express disinterest in its ends.

These words mark Achilles' most pronounced declaration of personal autonomy, his most theoretical statement about the nature of individuation. Yet he insists that they describe a *type* of man with a life history situated in both time and space during the age of state formation. He insists that this "I" can be embodied in a more permanent, socially viable role as a "me" others will recognize. He places this man with some precision in an Aegean world whose exchange circuits rule out not only Agamemnon's current network at Troy but also circuits extending backward into the heroic past of Troy's legendary wealth and forward to Delphi's eighth-century prominence as an Aegean center for the deposit and display of treasure.[66] Achilles defines a self that will not suffer evaluation in terms either of the heroic past or the present's interregional competition among elites for panhellenic prestige. He will not invest himself in the accumulation and display of treasure-items (*keimêlia*) that in the Early Iron Age marked the wealth of *basileis* while they lived and that constituted their *geras thanontôn* upon death (cattle, sheep, tripods, horses [406–7]). Nor will he seek outside his own land and father's beneficence anything more than a wife and house peculiar to his own nature and needs.

Morally Achilles portrays this new man as an agent of volition, one who owes his identity to a self-willed act of creation. If we compare this new man to the indebted heroic self who was fashioned through his followers' lament as part of the *geras thanontôn*, we are looking at two creatures who are morally speaking almost opposites: the new man is neither an indebtor of others nor is he indebted to others for self-definition. Socially, we've just seen, there's no question that Achilles' act of self-creation locates this new type of man outside both the growing

---

[66] Griffin (1995: 123–24) adduces Burkert (1985: 49), Morgan (1990: 10), and Taplin (1992: 33–34) to date Delphi's panhellenic prominence to the latter half of the eighth century.

panhellenic circuits of elite exchange in the eighth century and the legendary past. Of what sort of historical world might a man with such a moral profile be typical? We can say this much: the great speech distances this type of man from the ideals and values of its "internal audience" of embassy chiefs (Odysseus, Ajax, and Phoenix). If the broader "implied audience" of Homer's eighth-century *Iliad* in any way differs from the internal audience of chiefs, then this new man may suit a society this broader audience recognizes, perhaps a society that has not yet fully emerged.[67] Despite a contemporaneity with ourselves, this new man is sociologically and politically at home as a citizen in the earliest oligarchic states, whether city-states or ethnos-states. In fact he and his new society meet the criteria Morris (1996), using Dahl's principles (1989), outlines for the "middling" ideology from which the Greek state emerged – and without predicting, causing or inhibiting developments like democracy three hundred years hence.

What is more, this self, defined by its own volition, clearly points to the future rather than the past; and, despite Achilles' aristocratic lineage, it points away from elite exchange circuits centered on Delphi. Now it's true that Achilles does not necessarily reject "the ethics of cooperative relationships between chieftains" (Gill 1996: 147), for he leaves open the possibility (at 387) that Agamemnon might repay him in some fashion for the painful insult he's inflicted, and he does not respond to the embassy chiefs as though they and he could never again inhabit the same ethical community (Gill 1996: 142–48). (And obviously he does return to this community and even reconcile with Agamemnon.) So in this sense Achilles does not define himself, as scholars such as Parry and Whitman had characterized him, as a social "outsider" (see

---

[67] In Chapter 3 we'll discuss further the difference between audiences that are "internal" to the narrative of Homeric epic and audiences we may posit as external to the narrative and so "implied" by it. For the distinction, see L. Dougherty 1995: 19.

Gill 1996: 124ff.). But Gill misses the significance of Achilles' second-order reasoning when the hero evaluates the self, his own person, in a unique manner that can have no exact equivalent in terms of what others value since it depends wholly on acts of personal preference and choice.[68] This does indeed opt out of any socially endorsed value system before or contemporary with the world of heroes represented in the poem.

The only world in which Achilles' words might ring true exists in the minds and hearts of individuals *outside* the poem's narrative – those for whom Homer fashions Achilles' speech. This world was undoubtedly coming to terms with state formation and citizenship, whether of city-states or ethnos-states. We'll see in Chapter 3 how well Achilles' stated preferences in Book 9 match ways the Odysseus of the *Odyssey* comes to value his wife, household, territory and aged father. But in these lines from *Iliad* 9 (and at 9.408–9) Achilles' sentiments also do not fall very far from those Archilochus was said to put into the mouth of Charon, a simple carpenter who endorsed the "middling values" of the city-state citizen when he evoked the seventh-century Aegean context of Delphic competition for wealth and prestige in order to declare: "Of no concern to me is the wealth of Gyges rich in gold. I feel no urge to compete [with him], nor am I jealous of his godlike achievements – and I do not desire supreme command over others [that is, tyranny]. These things are far from my eyes" (fr. 22; cf. Arist. *Rhet.*1418b.28).[69] At the same

---

[68] In his lengthy discussion of the great speech, Gill makes only passing reference to Achilles' valorization of his *psykhê*, and without mentioning the word (1996: 149; cf. 311, n. 276). Wilson argues that Achilles doesn't "discountenance" materially based *timê* in principle, or claim his honor is "incommensurable"; he claims only that his life (*psykhê*) can't be computed in material terms of *apoina* (the type of compensation Agamemnon offers) (2002: 92–94).

[69] Gyges of Lydia (687–62) was remembered as one of the first individuals to dedicate rich offerings at Delphi (Her.1.14).

time Achilles' use of this second-order reasoning anticipates another dissonant seventh-century voice: Sappho's famous declaration in poem 16 of personal preference and choice as the arbiter of value. There she uses the rhetorical device of the "priamel": "Some say the most beautiful thing is . . . others say . . ." (16.1–3 and 19–20), to evoke typically heroic, Aegean choices dictated by collective preferences. Like Achilles, things valued by such a dominant social other pale by comparison to her own choice: "But I say it is whatever one loves" (16.3–4).

Achilles prepares to conclude his speech by returning openly to the cognitive perspective from which its reasoning sprang: the female lament speaker's, and specifically his mother's. He explains how he owes his capacity to assign preeminent value to the act of choosing on one's own behalf to Thetis' transcendent moral position, where he first had recourse in Book 1 and which we can now say that, as a self-lamenter, he has thoroughly internalized. Through indirect statement, Achilles paraphrases or ventriloquizes for the embassy Thetis' words, whose diction anticipates the formal *gooi* that she, Hecuba, Andromache, and Helen (and Penelope in the *Odyssey*) will utter over their fallen men.[70] So here in the most literal sense he performs his own lament in the form of a *goos* announcing each of his two deaths, his two fates, and the two degrees of *kleos* others will attribute to them:

> My mother, silver-footed goddess Thetis, tells me that two fatal
> moments [kêras] carry me toward death's end: if I stay right here and
> wage war [amphimakhômai] around the Trojans' citadel, my
> homecoming [nostos] is lost to me, but I will have imperishable fame
> [kleos aphthiton]. If I should go homeward [oikad'] to my cherished
> fatherland, my noble fame is lost to me, but my life will last a long time,

---

[70] Martin claims that at 9.413 Achilles "is actually quoting Thetis," and he attributes the phrase *kleos aphthiton* to her authoritative, divine diction (1989: 183, n. 63).

and death's end [telos thanatoio] *will not come* [kikheiê] *to me*
quickly. (*410–16*)

Achilles anticipates in these lines Thetis' lament for him in Book 18,
when she hears his mighty groan for Patroclus and regrets "sending
him off to wage war [*makhêsomenon*] on Trojans, but now I will never
again welcome him at his homecoming [*nostêsanta*] when he returns
homeward [*oikade*] within Peleus' house" (18.59–60). And because of the
choice Thetis provides him, he can play here for himself the role Hecuba
will play shortly for her son Hector when she intones (at 22.436), "Now
in effect your death and fate [*thanatos kai moira*] have arrived [*kikhanei*]."

Once Achilles finishes speaking, his listeners remind us that they
have understood all he said within the frame of the script "how leaders deliberate." Their amazement at his forceful delivery (*krateros*, 431)
responds not only to the passion behind his words but to their content:
his vision of the self as a radically autonomous "I" which sees itself
as a "subject of possession," and his implication that such a self could
populate an entire community in the form of a "me" role. Not surprisingly, the embassy's *basileis* are hardly prepared to welcome this
new theoretical attempt to define individuation because it devalues the
rationality criteria of generalized reciprocity within the chieftain system and appeals to novel criteria based on dramaturgical action.[71] The
counter-arguments and counter-appeals voiced in advance of the great
speech by Odysseus (225–306), and after by Phoenix and Ajax (434–605;

---

[71] How closely does Achilles' dissonant voice approximate the "moral individualism"
Socrates displayed to his fellow Athenians? We'll see in Chapter 7 that in the *Apology*
he stakes his "new, individualist form of citizenship" (Villa 2001: 14) on a set of
rationality criteria peculiar to a person's inner life (*psykhê*); and as a "subject of
possession" like Achilles, he is willing to abandon previously chosen ends and
interests should they fail to meet the demands of those criteria (23, citing *Gorgias*
457d–458b, and characterizing this new, "dissident" citizen self as "unencumbered"
in Sandel's sense).

624–42), take aim directly at what they perceive to be the fatal flaw in Achillean individuation: it describes a self that cannot be a viable member of any community they know, either a *basileus*' individual household or a warrior-band united around its chief.

Iliad 24

Their appeals reintroduce the theme of compassion (pity), whose recurrence as a dominant motif in the poem Kim (2000) has recently demonstrated.[72] But Kim's thin definition of compassion inhibits an understanding of how this emotion opens a window into the constitution of the self.[73] When Phoenix reminds Achilles of the intense knot of emotions binding the two of them (and Peleus) in *philotês*, he dramatically juxtaposes a very different notion of selfhood to Achillean individuation. This is a self morally obliged to own up to those relationships that have constituted it, without which it would unravel, and which it "possesses" in a sense quite different from the way the self of possession chooses ends and interests from which it may some day detach itself. Thanks to the complex knot of chieftain generosity and obligation that have woven their lives together (438ff.), Phoenix blatantly asserts, "In this way I suffered so much and worked so hard for you, all the while worrying the gods would produce no offspring out of me. But I made you my son, godlike Achilles, so that you might someday protect me from disaster" (493–95). This is an Achilles so constituted by and indebted to others, who so belongs to them and they to him, that

---

[72] Kim sees compassion (pity) as the poem's central theme, dividing it into three parts: Achilles' argument with Agamemnon robs him of compassion for the Greeks in Books 1–8; he finally yields to pleas for compassion from his comrades in Books 9–16; and in Books 17–24 he ultimately reverses his lack of compassion for Trojans (2000: 69–71).

[73] Kim understands *oiktirein, eleein, eleairein, kêdesthai* and related words like *nêleês*, ("pitiless") in the *Iliad* to mean "to spare a life," "not to kill someone," and as terms necessarily relating a more powerful to a less powerful individual (2000: 39ff.).

he should not be able to say where the limits of his own self end and theirs begin. Sandel describes this as an alternative dynamics of possession, typical of a self "embedded" in ends, relations and circumstances that possess it more than it possesses them. This is a self whose ends are prior to it and whose limits therefore remain open or fluid. Its challenge is to "come by" these ends less by choice than by discovery (1998: 56–58) – by owning up to them, as I prefer to describe it. And Phoenix, along with Odysseus (at 302) and Ajax (at 632), designates compassion as the emotion whose cognitive thrust acknowledges an essential merging of one self's limits with the limits of others.

In Book 24 the old Trojan King Priam unexpectedly arrives at Achilles' tent as a suppliant seeking to ransom back his son Hector's body (468–676). Not only does the old king succeed in persuading Achilles to make this exchange, but he induces Achilles to treat him – a mortal enemy – as a guest-friend. Together the young hero and the old king then initiate Hector's death ritual and engage in joint lamentation – Priam for Hector and Achilles for Patroclus and his own father, Peleus. Their encounter has long been recognized as the poem's dramatic climax, but recent scholarship doesn't agree on any other particular context to explain the significance of what transpires between them. Some, for example, Crotty (1994), Griffin (1995), and Kim (2000), isolate the scene's dominant emotions of grief and compassion into aesthetic discussions of character and theme; they see no historical dimension related to nascent forms of citizenship.[74] Others, such as Seaford (1994) and Zanker (1994), find these emotions politically significant but offer no theoretical blueprint to account for the internal constitution

[74] Like Nussbaum I prefer "compassion" to "pity" because "pity" today connotes a condescension toward and superiority over the sufferer, which we don't find in *eleos*, *oiktos*, and their compounds (2001: 301–2). Konstan disagrees, assigning "compassion" to strong feelings we have for intimates (2001: 59) and "pity" (*eleos*, *oiktos*) to those with whom we maintain some distance and superiority (49ff.).

of the citizen self or for communicative interaction between citizen selves.[75] Only Hammer's recent discussion (2002: 170ff.) recognizes the expression of compassion as fundamental to the dynamics of the city-state as a "political field," and his reading is sensitive as well to some of the cognitive changes Achilles needs to undergo as a model for citizen behavior.

Nevertheless, our understanding of Achilles' ability to grieve with and feel compassion for Priam remains incomplete if we don't compare it to the moral autonomy he proclaimed in Book 9 and the new society he envisioned of like-minded selves grounded in an individual's choice of whatever (or whomever) he values. We attributed that expression of autonomy to ways the self-lamenter's "I" impulsively revealed his inner world through a dramaturgical action that calculated his own self-worth and solicited others to recognize the *timê* he knew he deserved. But we questioned whether this self could remain locked within the spontaneity of the "I" and still function as a social being. The embassy leaders clearly rejected that possibility in labeling Achilles a man incapable of compassion. To populate a society, this radically autonomous "I" needs to constitute a "me" role other individuals can assume as well; it needs to convey a performative attitude whose

---

[75] For Seaford, Priam and Achilles establish a reciprocity that generates "solidarity between potential enemies" and shows how "even hostile aliens are reconciled to each other by the integrative power of lamentation and death ritual" (1994: 176). While this "death ritual" (106–43) is an emotional and cognitive vehicle for promoting "models of action and feeling for the age of the polis" (177), it remains a composite rather than historically grounded behavior combining funerary practices in various eras for elites, citizens, and mythic figures. Nowhere does Seaford link its communicative dynamics with citizenship. For Zanker, Achilles' radical personality change culminates in a "pity" for Priam, expressing a unique "magnanimity" or altruism (1994: 122–30; 1998) going "beyond reciprocity" (1998: 81). He briefly links it to the needs of a suddenly "socially diverse" eighth-century society whose elites might find Homer's "unified code" of ethics and social institutions helpful in "crossing 'tribal' boundaries" (1994: 136).

meaning is acknowledged by both the self *and* someone else representing the dominant social other. For only when the self learns to take the
attitudes of those with whom it interacts can it escape its subjectivity
and become conscious of itself as a social object (Mead 1964: 283–84); only
then can both self and other live in a community of similar individuals
where each assumes the perspective of the other and expects "reciprocal
recognition" (Habermas 1992: 186). In Mead's succinct formulation, "We
must be others if we are to be ourselves" (1964: 292).

Mead's and Habermas' notions of individuation suggest that, when
the self takes a socially meaningful performative attitude, it needs to
loosen any strict limits it may have chosen for itself. It needs to
acknowledge that it is to some degree possessed by ties that preclude
self-fashioning because they enable others to fashion it, as childless
Phoenix made Achilles into his son. So I suggest that the reciprocity
Achilles and Priam enact is not primarily sociological or anthropological but cognitive and linguistic: it completes the exchange of the
performative attitude Achilles' "I" offered the Greek embassy when
he presented himself as a self-lamenter. His resulting moral isolation
from them will continue until he encounters in someone else a more
socially acceptable version of himself, of his own dramaturgical presentation to others as a self-lamenter, a self-evaluator, and a proclaimer
of his own destiny. Is it possible for him to recognize in Priam's performance of the scripts of supplication and ransoming a simulacrum of
his own selfhood? Can Priam succeed where Achilles' Greek comrades
failed?

From the moment in Book 22 when he witnessed Achilles slay his
son, the old king's grief dictated to him (at 22.416–28) the supplication
and ransoming he would perform at 24.469ff. Priam indicates clearly (at
22.417–22) the strategic importance of a self-presentation engineered to
elicit two emotions from Achilles: he begs his people to let him go to the
Achaean camp "so I might supplicate [*lissômai*] that deranged man who

does dark deeds, to see if he might somehow show respect for [*aidessetai*] my years and have compassion [*eleêsêi*] on my old age" (22.418–19). The first of these emotions, *aidôs*, recalls an individual to his or her social senses. Its two basic meanings of "to feel shame before" and "to have respect for" remind Homer's Greeks of the "internalized other" within themselves whose authoritative dictates they should heed.[76] Here in particular it summons Achilles' self to abandon the impulsive agency of the "I" and recognize that it must assume one or another of the "me" roles sanctioned by the dominant social other. *Aidôs* thus shatters the illusion that the self can remain isolated within the private, inner world expressed to others in a dramaturgical action, for it insists that such experiences can only be meaningful when others share them as versions of their own.

Priam will couple his insistence that Achilles heed the call of *aidôs* with a call for compassion. *Aidôs* is, properly speaking, a programmatic emotion: it alerts us to the dictates of the other within us and the possibilities of shared meaning, but it accomplishes nothing. Compassion complements *aidôs* because in a particularly dramatic way it invites the self to own up to the possible "me" roles open to it. In the suffering of another it holds up to the self a would-be sign or image meant to function as a potential mirror for the self; and it challenges the self to perform the cognitive actions – I'm thinking in particular of judgments – that are basic to achieving a consensus between self and

[76] For its meanings, see Cairns 1993: 1–47; for its meanings in Homeric society, see Cairns 1993: 48–146 and Yamagata 1994: 156–76. For Cairns, *aidôs* as shame requires an "other [who] may be wholly internalised, such that one can be an observer to himself" (1993: 18; also 144). B. Williams describes this as a real presence within the self of someone who is "indeed abstracted and generalised and idealised, but . . . potentially somebody rather than nobody, and somebody other than me" (1993: 84). For Redfield *aidôs* is "a vulnerability to the expressed ideal norm of the society . . . directly experienced within the self, as a man internalizes the anticipated judgments of others on himself" (1975: 116).

other.[77] This consensus holds that despite apparent differences (of rank, situation, gender, ethnicity, etc.), the self finds in the dramaturgical actions of a suffering other an equivalent to dramaturgical actions of its own.

The prospect of Achilles seeing in old Priam a figure equivalent to himself has not attracted much attention, probably because Priam's strategy to elicit compassion from the younger man takes a more circuitous, and dramatically more compelling, route. In the course of his opening appeal to Achilles he will encourage the younger man to recognize parts of himself in no less than three different individuals: Hector, Achilles' aging father Peleus, and himself. He draws our attention away from any direct equivalence between himself and Achilles when he initiates the verbal portion of his supplication with an overt comparison betweeen himself and Peleus. He had contemplated this in Book 22 when first conceiving the idea of pleading with Achilles, but now that the moment has arrived, he begs, "Remember your father, godlike Achilles, to whom I'm similar in years, on the grim threshold of old age" (24.486). This image of the two aged fathers, and the corresponding equivalence of Achilles and Hector as their sons, blinds us to a subtler connection between the older and younger man.

It's been pointed out that both Priam and Achilles at this moment suffer from an exile's isolation (Seaford 1994: 70) and that both had earlier expressed a willingness to die upon learning that the person dearest to them (Patroclus, Hector) had been killed (Zanker 1994: 121–22, n. 16). But the equivalence Priam invites Achilles to recognize between them

---

[77] Cairns notes how Homer often links *aidôs* and compassion (*eleos*) in pleas from a less fortunate individual to a more fortunate, as Priam shows at 24.503 (1993: 49, with n. 10). In addition see *Il.*21.74, 22.123–24 and 419, 24.44 and 207–8; and *Od.*14.388–89, 19.253–54, 22.312, and 344. On compassion and cognition, see Nussbaum 2001: 304–27 and Konstan 2001: 8–18; on memory, cognition, and supplication, see Crotty 1994: 77ff.

is primarily performative, for it links Achilles in his great speech of Book 9 to Priam in his present act of supplication: both present themselves to others as self-lamenters and self-evaluators who announce the uniqueness of their fate, both own up to this fate as their life history, and both seek confirmation from others that such a life may not be dissimilar from their own. Priam actually sketches out the sad fate of Peleus as a counterpoint to his own, contrasting Peleus' individual destiny with those of anonymous others, "somebodies" or "nobodies"; and he will do likewise in evoking Hector's and his own fate. Of Peleus he says, "No doubt those who live around him harass him, with no one to keep disaster and ruin at bay" (488–89). But Priam believes Peleus at least can hope to see his son return one day, which permits him to launch the first salvo of his self-lament: "But I have an all-wretched fate [*panapotmos*] since I bred outstanding sons throughout broad Troy and now I declare not one [*ou tina*] of them is left" (493–94).

This self-proclaimed isolation from others, locked into a destiny unique among mortals, recalls Achilles' similar self-portrait and self-proclamation in the great speech as an individual with an unprecedented moral profile (in his case, the need to choose one of two cosmic apportionments and degrees of *kleos*). At this point, however, Priam deflects attention from himself to remind Achilles of his fifty sons, most killed in battle, and in particular of the "one alone left to me to protect his city and his people, whom you killed as he defended his fatherland, Hector" (499–501). Priam represents Hector's fate too as unique: to be the last of his sons to fall to Achilles and the Greeks, and the only one whose corpse he will try to ransom back (501–2).[78] Priam's

---

[78] Macleod points out that Homeric warriors were normally ransomed while alive, not as corpses (1982: 20). When at 22.256–59 and 338–43 Hector tries to negotiate a pact with Achilles for each to permit the other's kin to ransom back his corpse, he thus creates an important component of his unique fate.

strategy thus isolates three individuals, Peleus, himself and Hector, for Achilles to ponder; and with all three in mind he now exhorts the hero, "Respect [aideio] the gods, Achilles, and have compassion [eleêson] for me as you remember your own father!" (503–4). Why, we might ask, does he first evoke three individuals and their different fates but then only seek compassion for one, himself? We'll see that Priam's grief does indeed induce him to believe he suffers an irreducibly different fate from the others. But despite this conviction his speech invites Achilles to look upon all three individuals as versions of himself.[79]

The call to practice aidôs, as we observed earlier, is programmatic: by itself it accomplishes nothing. It does however ask its recipient to shift his or her cognitive perspective or "frame" (in Goffman's sense – Goffman: 1974) to interpret the present circumstance. In this case Priam reminds Achilles of the divine protection the gods grant suppliants (Cairns 1993: 118), and this cognitive shifting of frames from the here-and-now to the transcendent narrative frame of Greek divinities, myths, and community memories always engineers the collective social control of individuals' behavior, as will be discussed further in subsequent chapters. But Priam intends his plea for compassion to trigger an emotional response that will complete a reciprocal *linguistic* exchange of one self, with its life history and destiny, for another that is ostensibly different. That is, it's intended to induce Achilles to judge Priam to be a version of that self he impulsively presented to the Greek embassy in Book 9 but to which those heroes refused "recognition" in Taylor's sense.

As Nussbaum describes it, compassion in the Greek and western traditions asks the self to perform three cognitive acts in response to another's misfortune: to judge that misfortune serious; to judge that

---

[79] In Chapter 3 Kohut's (1977, 1985) concept of the "selfobject" provides a psycho-analytic model for an individual's perception of him/herself in others.

misfortune undeserved; and, in the Aristotelian tradition, to judge the self as potentially liable to similar misfortune, or in Nussbaum's revision, to judge the self's well-being as vulnerable to the other's misfortune (2001: 304–21). Her eudaimonistic version of this final judgment captures particularly well compassion's attempt to secure a linguistic exchange in which one self does more than accept another's fate and life history as a version of a common "me" role shared by both. It underscores how the other's fate and life history are necessarily implicated in one's own, how they are necessary to complete one's own sense of a life worth living. In Sandel's terms compassion "proves" to the self that it can become so possessed by others that its own limits turn fluid and uncertain; and this helps explain, returning to Mead, why "We must be others if we are to be ourselves."[80]

Priam certainly expects Achilles to judge the fates and life histories of at least two of the three individuals because he immediately compares his own case to that of Peleus as "even more deserving of compassion" (*eleeinoteros per*, 504). But he insists too, as Achilles had in his great speech, on his uniqueness as a human, since "I have endured what no other mortal ever has: I drew to my mouth the hand of a man who killed my son" (505–6). This last remark insists that Achilles reflect on the gesture of supplication Priam has just performed silently, when he slipped unnoticed into Achilles' tent (477–79). In describing this moment, the Homeric narrator compares the old king in his isolation to a murderer who flees his own country to seek help elsewhere as

---

[80] Mead 1964: 292, Hammer makes a similar point when he distinguishes between Achilles' ability earlier in the poem to experience "suffering-from" another, when Agamemnon's dishonored him, and "suffering-with" another, when he learns of Patroclus' death and sees that "his own pain is connected to the suffering of another" (2002: 175–76; 180). Konstan insists that the subject of *eleos* and *oiktos* does not "merge" or "identify with" the object but always maintains an emotional distance (2001: 60, 65, 71–72).

a suppliant to a powerful man (480–82). And we should recall that Achilles evoked a similar life history, still in the grip of anger in Book 9, to characterize the shame he felt when Agamemnon treated him "like some refugee who has no *timê*" (9.648).

In our discussion of Book 9 this image of an outsider or outlaw lacking any social standing aptly expressed the radical autonomy and asociability of the "I": here it suits Priam's distraught, grief-induced conviction that his fate has projected him beyond all human community. Like Achilles in Book 9, he remains locked within his subjective experience of an inner world, and his words transform the ritual action of suppliance into a dramaturgical action whose "I" performatively calls out to others, as Achilles had, to recognize that radical autonomy. Because Achilles will respond (at 24.515) to Priam with compassion, he will provide the old man with what Phoenix, Ajax, and Odysseus denied him. For when he looks at Priam, Achilles stands face to face with an abject self who mirrors himself at the end of Book 1, weeping to his mother Thetis: dishonored, deprived of the person he says he most cherished, and completely dependent on a powerful someone else for assistance. In Priam's delusion of radical autonomy and self-proclaimed unique fate, Achilles recognizes a self that is interchangeable with his own. And unlike Priam he recognizes that Peleus, Hector, and Patroclus, despite different life histories, share that fate not as radically but as *relatively* autonomous individuals who have owned up to a "me" role thrust upon them by a script of cosmic apportionment beyond their control.[81]

---

[81] Hammer locates Achilles' ability to feel compassion for Priam in the internal dynamics of Achilles' self – again, in his loss of self-esteem when he experiences "suffering-with" upon Patroclus' death and then when he feels responsible for abandoning Peleus (2002: 185–86). Because he focuses on the internal calculation of self-worth, Hammer describes Achilles' compassion as his "ability to *imagine* himself in the position of another" (185; my emphasis). Because I emphasize the communicative and cognitive dynamics between Achilles and Priam – where lament

Achilles' act of compassion actually occurs in two phases. Before he displays any outward sign of compassion toward Priam, he first experiences in his own inner world an emotional response to Priam's grief. In fact, as Macleod suggests, Achilles at first seems to reject Priam's supplication (at 508) by pushing the old man away (1982: 130). But he is at this moment engrossed in taking Priam's grief over Hector as a cue for his own need to grieve for Peleus, who is still alive, and then for Patroclus. Priam's words trigger in Achilles an immediate desire (*himeron*) to perform a *goos* for Peleus (507), and so both men are seized by memories of their absent loved ones and spontaneously perform a lament, a *klauthmos:* "They both remembered, and one lamented [*klai'*] deeply for man-slaying Hector as he crouched before Achilles' feet, while Achilles lamented [*klaiein*] now for his own father, now for Patroclus. And their groaning [*stonakhê*] spread through the dwelling" (509–12).

Only when Achilles has quenched this need for what appears to be pure feeling beyond (or beneath) any need for words (513–14) does he enter the second phase of his compassion. Here the Homeric narrator describes the gestures that signify Achilles' acceptance of Priam as a suppliant: "He then rose from his chair and stood the old man up by his hand, for he felt compassion [*oiktirôn*] for both his gray head and gray chin" (515–16). What Achilles then puts into words outlines a moral and theological vision of justice that describes a human community whose paramount values seriously depart from the new social order he sketched out in his great speech of Book 9. There the individual appeared supreme in his or her ability to determine value based on what he or she most cherished – and seemed sovereign as well in

plays a dominant role – I describe Achilles' compassion as his *discovery* that internal calculations of self-worth have no meaning unless validated by those whose ends and purposes are constitutive of the self.

demanding that others recognize such a radical autonomy rooted in personal difference. Here Achilles abandons a cognitive frame founded on the privileged access of the "I" to its inner world for a frame whose Olympian perspective dwarfs the life of any one individual. Nevertheless, it provides a reasoned explanation for each person's fate, including Peleus' and Priam's. At the heart of this vision sits a cosmic, despotic agent of justice, Zeus, who allots from two jars portions of good and evil to each human life. Some humans lead lives of mixed blessings, like a Peleus or a Priam; others of pure misery, like the outsiders and outlaws who receive *timê* from neither mortals nor immortals; only the gods are entirely happy (525–51).[82]

This grim glimpse of cosmic justice recasts the shrilly egotistical and utopian order Achilles envisioned in his great speech in several ways, but most dramatically by pulverizing the individual's insistence that his or her identity rests on differences forged in the inner world of personal preference. Achilles' new vision reduces individual human fates to a few simple categories that render individual needs and desires irrelevant. But in its annihilation of difference it is no less utopian than the vision that exalted difference, for it renders reasonable the belief that each person's life history is more or less symbolically interchangeable with another's. The utopianism of this linguistic reciprocity has of course important social implications. Within the *Iliad*'s dramatic world the interchangeability of life histories certainly takes the form of a cosmopolitanism erasing the ethnic differences between Greeks and Trojans and a social revisionism erasing differences between rich and poor and between a territory's "insiders" and outsiders. Historically, in the social world of Homeric audiences straddling the prestate and early

---

[82] Teffeteller 2003 reinforces B. Williams 1993 in arguing that Homeric individuals display a reason-based, responsible, coherent concept of self when they attribute extraordinary conduct and outcomes (good or bad) to the gods.

state periods, nascent cosmopolitanism and social revisionism offer a rationale for questioning a social structure sustained by a warrior chief's acts of balanced or generalized reciprocity. The ends imputed to the moral life of such a *basileus*, as we've seen in the first and second parts of this chapter, were best expressed in the fate and degree of *kleos* his lamenters publicly proclaimed for him. Achilles' act of compassion for Priam is the fulcrum that implements this historically meaningful utopian order because it devalues the rationality of that claim: it renders more reasonable the prospect of sharing in a common or citizen life, where the fates of all we're likely to encounter in friendship or enmity are interchangeable.

How does compassion challenge the logic of relations governed by a chieftain's reciprocal exchange? Zanker has argued that Achilles' act of compassion and the hospitality it leads him to extend Priam are altruistic because they surpass the rewards he might expect from completing the reciprocal exchanges of supplication and ransom (1998: 73–85). Achilles also rejects, Zanker claims, any *timê* based on human evaluations and exchanges; his motives are rather more "personal" (87) because they originate in compassion for the suffering of a fellow human and result in a "magnanimity" we equate with altruism (90). We can again look to Mead if we wish to understand how a magnanimity "beyond reciprocity" might open a new cognitive perspective and type of communication worthy of the term "utopian." In his essay "Philanthropy from the Point of View of Ethics" (1964 [1930]), Mead recognizes in charitable giving both an "impulse" and a sense of "obligation" (393–95). The latter, he believes, places us within a social order where we "sympathize" or put "ourselves in the other's place" and also make a negative judgment about the social order that causes the other such distress (397–98). Our acts of sympathy and generosity imply or endorse a different social order, an ideal or universal one, that would result if only we could develop the "intelligence" latent in the present order – if only we could become "the sort of selves which society implies though it does not make them possible" (403). The generous donor therefore responds to the call of a "hypothetically different order" that functions as a "universe of discourse which transcends the specific order" because it places donor and recipient "outside of the community as it exists" and enables them to "agree upon changed habits of action and a restatement of values" (404).

Achilles and Priam dramatize the possibility of such a discursive universe for Homer's audiences, and their climactic interaction foregrounds the kind of reasoning that grants one access to it. This universe is indeed a social order, Mead insists, "for its function is a common action on the basis of commonly recognized conditions of conduct and common ends. Its claims are the claims of reason. It is a social order that includes any rational being who is or may be in any way implicated in the situation with which thought deals" (404). The key to gaining admission to the "commonwealth of rational beings" projected by Achilles and Priam lies simply in the ability to see in another's dramaturgical expression of his or her inner world and life history a simulacrum of one's own. More historically it means abandoning notions of indebted self-worth derived from Early Iron Age exchange with a chieftain in favor of a linguistic reciprocity in which relatively autonomous citizens choose "unique" life histories that are interchangeable with those of their peers. If this sounds paradoxical, Habermas helps clarify:

> The idealizing supposition of a universalistic form of life, in which everyone can take up the perspective of everyone else and can count on reciprocal recognition by everybody, makes it possible for individuated beings to exist within a community – individualism as the flip side of universalism. (1992: 186)

2 PERFORMING JUSTICE IN EARLY GREECE: DISPUTE SETTLEMENT IN THE *ILIAD*

◎⬛◎

AS PERFORMANCES OF JUSTICE, THE *ILIAD*'S SCRIPTS OF FUNERARY ritual (especially lamentation) and chieftain deliberation (especially when redistributing plunder) provide prototypes for the nascent state and its citizen because they succeed in exposing the *basileus* of the Formative period (ca. 900–760) as a problematic person. We've seen that an Agamemnon or an Achilles becomes controversial by exercising greater moral autonomy than others, especially within scripts designed to redistribute *timê* competitively. If their problematic decision making reflects with any accuracy the realities of this period, then by the eighth century a chieftain's attempt to evaluate his own worth in relation to social rivals often provoked criticism of his validity claims. But we must remember that the *basileus* enjoyed moral privileges not only in the *Iliad*'s wartime scripts but in peacetime too. As we saw in Chapter 1 the role of *basileus* is enacted as a center in exchange relationships of reciprocity and redistribution in village and regional polities, combining elements of the authority identified with a headman, big man, or chief. In this chapter we'll examine a script whose successful outcome was vital to the Formative period's fragile, village-based societies, which from time to time witnessed among their households and descent groups intractable disputes that threatened community stability. This is the earliest judicial script we can reconstruct; we might call it "rendering a *dikê*" or "rendering the 'straightest' *dikê*," which is the nonviolent solution most acceptable to all parties and most in conformity with tradition.

When such disputes arose, the *basileus* reassumed his role as a center for exchange relations, for here the path to maintaining stability lay in redistributing the *timê* or social standing of individuals and their groups. "Rendering a *dikê*" demanded from the *basileus* a virtuoso performance not unlike Nestor's brief, unsuccessful attempt to reconcile Agamemnon and Achilles (at *Il*.1.247–84), a performance capable of orchestrating the communicative roles (speech genres and acts, performative attitudes and subject positions) and cognitive actions of the disputants and their supporters, all of whom he hoped to induce to evaluate, recognize and negotiate competing claims to *timê*. As the judicial chief at the center of this script, he was therefore responsible for generating among the divided participants a unified moral consciousness from which consensus would emerge. Not surprisingly, as the center he also enjoyed privileges that endowed his speech with an illocutionary force unavailable to other participants – that is, unless or until he induced them to assume it. In examining the evidence for dispute settlement, I want to explore the dynamics behind the judicial *basileus*' relative performative autonomy and its capacity for consensus formation. In particular I am interested in understanding how his performance was ideologically contrived to suit consensus formation in big-man or chieftain societies as opposed to the type of proto-citizen agreement we saw forged in the compassionate exchange between Achilles and Priam in *Il*. 24.

This question assumes a pivotal importance because, as will be demonstrated in Chapters 3 and 4, at some point in the late seventh century the state transformed the script "rendering a *dikê*" into such scripts as civic arbitration by a judicial magistrate and, more importantly for our interests, into the jury trial by citizens. When this occurs, the script of the jury trial has to accommodate the script "how citizens deliberate" so that all participants in a dispute might achieve an intersubjective understanding by aligning themselves for and against positions that included objective facts, social norms, and the subjective experiences of the litigants in an alleged injustice. But before arriving there, it is necessary to understand how a consensus induced by the communicative and cognitive virtuosity of a *basileus*, and his privileged performative freedom, operated differently from the state's statute law and citizen autonomy – and paradoxically how this individual's talents forestalled their development and yet prepared their way. In a nutshell, my goal in this chapter is to understand how and why the judicial *basileus* was transformed from the early dispute settlement's arch-performer into a citizen and juror or judge.

JUDICIAL DIVERSIONS: THE *BASILEUS* AS PERFORMER OF JUSTICE

Intractable disputes over *timê* in the Formative period likely provided occasions for what Habermas calls a "decentered understanding of the world," that is, a collective experience in which once reliable, traditional truths and validity claims become detached from the certainties of a chiefdom's worldview that are implicit, unquestioned, and grounded in ancestors and their descent groups. Habermas describes this "decentration of worldviews" as follows:

> *The lifeworld ... stores the interpretive work of preceding generations. It is the conservative counterweight to the risk of disagreement that arises with every actual process of reaching understanding; for communicative actors can achieve an understanding only by taking yes/no positions on criticizable validity claims.* The relation between these weights changes with the decentration of worldviews. *The more the worldview that furnishes the cultural stock of knowledge is decentered, the less the need for understanding is covered in advance by an interpreted lifeworld immune from critique, and the more this need has to be met by the interpretive accomplishments of the participants themselves, that is, by way of risky (because rationally motivated) agreement, the more frequently we can expect rational action orientations. (1984: 70, emphasis in the original; cf. 1990: 138)*

Could this sort of decentered deliberation have occurred in eighth-century dispute settlement? I have already alluded to M. I. Finley's claim that nowhere in Homer do we find the modern equivalent of deliberation: a sustained, rational discussion of competing courses of action, with clear consideration of their advantages and disadvantages (1979: 114–15). But Schofield demonstrates that rational discussion does indeed emerge as a "heroic ideal" in the *Iliad*'s councils, at times with "sustained and single-minded concentration on the rational solution of a problem."[1] According to Schofield another quality of *euboulia* ("good judgment," "excellent counsel") as a heroic ideal is the ability to understand a present situation in terms of both the past and future – in effect, to place the here-and-now in different temporal frames that may take the form of prudence, pity, or a sense of justice or propriety that inject into deliberation a "point of view *external*" to the heroic code's insistence on *aretê* and *timê* (1986: 16; emphasis in the original).

If Schofield is right, then deliberation in Homeric society included a cognitive talent devoted to placing an event in different temporal frames. We can expand on this talent to propose that it helped resolve the problem of what I'll call the "ontological inadequacy" of an intractable dispute. By this I mean one where an impasse results because the everyday reality in which the offensive or criminal acts occurred, and in which the dispute itself unfolds, cannot provide sufficient truth value (e.g., key facts can't be ascertained) or decidability (two conflicting principles can't be reconciled) to produce a resolution. One way to bridge such an impasse is to draw upon an indispensable component of the lifeworld: the ability to frame

---

[1] 1986: 24. Compare Schofield's six particularly important assemblies and councils in the *Iliad* (1986: 8) to Hammer's sixteen scenes of shared decision making (2002: 230, n. 63).

both the disputed facts or principles and the dispute itself in terms of a reality that "trumps" the everyday experience of time, space, and agency. In the Early Iron Age a community's narrative world of myths about ancestors and gods provided such a reality, and in the eighth century elites expected the panhellenic heroic age to do the same.[2] Rendering a straight *dikê* may thus have turned on who could control the dispute's cognitive flow through privileged access to trumping realities and to the speech genres linking them to everyday life.

This question returns us to Tandy's revisionist focus on the relationship between the *basileus* and the *aoidos* (epic bard). Both these figures, he hypothesizes, colluded in the eighth century to legitimate the authority of a new kind of *basileus*, one who recently acquired impressive wealth through maritime trade outside his community. The key to this legitimation was to tie the new *basileus* to the men and exploits of the heroic past (1997: 166–89). We can sharpen that focus, however, to ask how on one hand these two figures may have colluded prior to the eighth century to produce (in Habermas' terms) an "understanding" that was "covered in advance by an interpreted lifeworld immune from critique," and how on the other hand, by 700, "this need [had] to be met by the interpretive accomplishments of the participants themselves." Gagarin took a step in this direction in his 1992 discussion of a familiar passage in Hesiod's *Theogony* juxtaposing the similar verbal talents of the *basileus* and the *aoidos* (*Th.* 79–104). Hesiod launches into this comparison after listing the nine Muses; Calliope ("Lovely Voice")

---

[2] In the *Iliad*'s opening dispute Nestor tries to render a *dikê* by switching ontological frames when he advises Achilles against quarreling with a *basileus* like Agamemnon, "to whom Zeus has given honor" (1.279), and when he adduces Achilles' divine genealogy (1.280). As Hammer puts it, Nestor realizes that "the criterion for effective leadership is the ability actively to engage different, even opposing, views" (2002: 92).

is last and most important (*propherestatê*, 79) because she "accompanies" (*opêdei*, 80) both *basileis* and bards. Then the poet elaborates how she does this for *basileis*:

> *Whenever great Zeus' daughters will honor and look upon a man as someone born of* basileis *raised by gods, they pour sweet dew on his tongue, and honey flows from his mouth. All the folk gaze on him when he makes decisions with straight settlements* (dikai) *while performing* themistes. *He addresses them without stumbling and quickly ends even an intractable* (mega) *dispute by using his intellect* (epistamenôs). *Because of this,* basileis *have keen understanding* (ekhephrones) *and easily make it come to pass in the agora that crimes against folk who are wronged will win them compensation because these* basileis *soothe with gentle words. When he reaches the assembly place, they treat him like a god with respect that flows like honey, and he stands out among the crowd. This is the sort of sacred gift the Muses bestow on humankind.*
> (Th. *81–93*)

Mention of this gift prompts Hesiod to think of *aoidoi* and lyre players, who like *basileis* enjoy divine favor since they too have voices sweetly flowing from their mouths and can put an end to human sorrows, not with judicial decisions but with stories of heroes and gods that induce listeners to forget their cares (*Th.* 94–104). Gagarin's discussion steers our understanding of the verbal gifts Hesiod attributes to these figures toward the communicative and cognitive abilities enacted by their rhetorical skills. Where he characterizes a *basileus'* expression of a *dikê* as "a speech act" (*logos*) (1992: 61), I suggest we think of "rendering a *dikê*" as a performance orchestrating a suite of speech genres to articulate the shifting cognitive and ontological perspectives necessary to produce a nonviolent solution acceptable to all. But Gagarin is on the mark in noting how the verbal talent of both *basileus* and *aoidos* is equated with sure knowledge: the *basileus* speaks in public "without stumbling" (or "in sure tones," *asphaleôs*, Th. 86), ends even an intract-able dispute (*mega neikos, Th.* 87) "by using his intellect" (*epistamenôs, Th.* 87), and "possesses understanding" (*ekhephrones, Th.* 88) when he easily turns a crime around into an act of restitution (*metatropa erga, Th.* 89) for the injured parties (*Th.* 88–89).[3]

Gagarin's most important point, however, concerns the words Hesiod uses, *paraiphamenoi* (*Th.* 90) and *paretrape* (*Th.* 103), to describe the effect of the *basileus'* and bard's words on his listeners: he "diverts" them or "leads them aside" from their current thoughts, or even "deceives" them. Gagarin explains the possibility of deceit as the use of "a certain degree of tactful diversion of the mind of each litigant away from issues that are most divisive and towards those on which the judge wishes to base an acceptable settlement" (1992: 66); but these two words resonate more richly if we see them describing a competi-tive tactic to control the cognitive flow of the ontological inadequacy of an intractable dispute. As Tandy suggested, if the bards "derive their legitimacy from access to special information" in the form of "special, divine knowledge," that knowledge must somehow be linked to the "special interests" of *basileis* (1997: 170, 175).

Hesiod's idealized description of the dovetailing talents of judicial chiefs and poets suggests that in the Early Iron Age lifeworld it is rea-sonable for a *basileus* to perform a *dikê* by translating, for litigants and bystanders, the difficult details of the dispute at hand into chrono-topes concerning ancestors and gods – chronotopes preserved in each community's memory of past feuds, and not unrelated to chronotopes found in local genealogical and epic tales. Just as oral poetics helps us to understand how bards traditionally represent the interests of elite

---

[3] Gagarin claims that, in Homer, speaking with skill and speaking the truth are equivalent (1992: 64–65), but the judicial *basileus'* communicative and cognitive skills are not concerned with perceiving the truth in our modern sense.

leaders by knowing how to "read" their audience's mood or needs, and then translate those interests into chronotopes chosen from appropriate "paths of song," the judicial *basileus* transfers an apparently insoluble dispute into "paths of adjudication" whose chronotopes divert the litigants' fixation on matters of the here-and-now toward an other-worldly, transcendent perspective.[4]

I believe we can reconstruct the communicative and cognitive details of this "diverting" (if not deceptive) performance. One key to its success at each stage will be the degrees of autonomy performers enjoy as they assume performative attitudes toward one another, and as speech genres foreclose or open to them the possibility of taking (to echo Habermas) "yes/no positions on criticizable validity claims" contributing to consensus. It will be necessary to reexamine a number of familiar terms in early Greek legal procedure to see how they are linked in a relay: at one end we'll find the unquestionable expressions of authority and privileged cognitive virtuosity typical of a mythologically based worldview, and at the other increasingly decentered speech genres and openly deliberative cognitive actions. These terms are: *themis*, the voice of cultural authority in the form of an illocutionary statement and normative action that curtails individual autonomy; *themistes*, the *basileus'* performance of rendering a *dikê* that "diverts" the minds of listeners by switching ontological frames; *thesmion* or its plural, *thesmia*, stories of paradigmatic crimes and their resolutions that constituted a community's legal memory bank; oath challenges, which served *basileis*

---

[4] On Homeric "paths of song," see Ford 1992: 40–42, esp. 42, n. 78. See Stoddard on the talent of the poet and judicial *basileus* here as a kind of *enargeia* ("poetic reenactment"): "The Muses grant poets the ability to make events seem to happen again before the eyes of the audience, hence these events are 'persuasive,' i.e., they appear real and make the listener forget about everything else.... Similarly ... [the *basileus*] ... employs *enargeia*: he makes the path of justice 'appear' ... before the eyes of his listeners by persuading the aggrieved party to accept a settlement" (2003: 12). See also Cantarella's discussion of the Homeric *basileus* as an agent of justice (2003: 279–88); cf. 1979: 251.

as a royal road linking disputes to trumping realities because they performatively situated litigants in a cultic sense of community that inhibited individual autonomy; *thesmos*, a norm or law rooted in a community's memory of canonical performances of *themistes* by a *basileus* (this was the term for the state's first true law, whether unwritten or written; it preserves a memory of *dikê* as an oral performance by a historical or legendary individual who serves as a "model of mimesis" for future citizen jurors); and finally *nomos*, the self-conscious framing of a law in about 500, now detachable from an individual's canonical performance and recognized solely as what results when citizens exercise collective autonomy through communicative action. Chapter 3 will examine *thesmia* more thoroughly, Chapter 4 *thesmos*, and Chapters 5 through 7, *nomos*.

The Dispute on Achilles' Shield

It has long been recognized that our most valuable pieces of written evidence for early procedures of dispute settlement in the period before and during state formation are: the dispute depicted on Achilles' shield over the payment of the penalty after a homicide (*Il*.18.497–508): the quarrel between Menelaus and Antilochus over second prize in a chariot race (*Il*.23.566–95); and Hesiod's dispute with his brother over their inheritance (*WD* 27–41).[5]

Before discussing our key pieces of evidence, however, we should acknowledge an observation by Eric Havelock in *The Greek Concept of Justice* (1978). Sociologically speaking, both of our surviving early Greek epics use a similar narrative frame to inaugurate their major conflicts: a public assembly (*agora*) at which two litigants seek a peaceful settlement

---

[5] How historically accurate are these scenes' representations of early Greek adjudication? See Gagarin 1986: 20, 42–43, Westbrook 1992, Todd 1993: 33–35, Thür 1996, and Carawan 1998: 51ff. We'll consider Hesiod's quarrel with his brother in Chapter 4.

(*dikê*) from community leaders over disputed possession of a woman. In each poem the woman symbolizes the litigant's *timê*, and in each conflict it is hoped that a settlement can be reached by inviting the gods to participate through the use of oaths (1978: 123–49). While it's easy to see within this frame Agamemnon and Achilles squaring off (in *Il.* 1) over Briseis, Havelock reminds us that (in *Od.* 2) Telemachus convenes an assembly to demand that the suitors cease pursuing Penelope and consuming his father's wealth. He also points out that (at *WD* 213–85) Hesiod uses a similar but more abstract scenario to describe the panhellenic pursuit of justice (1978: 194ff.).

Havelock's insight suggests that the Greek cultural memory associated dispute settlement among elites with a fundamental script capable of many narrative transformations. Not surprisingly, this script bears strong similarities to Goldhill's four "master actions" of democratic Athenian citizenship and scripts of "rendering a judgment" and "how citizens deliberate" (which was discussed in the Introduction). In Homer and Hesiod, this script requires an individual wishing to define himself as an elite to: enter a public arena and present himself in verbal conflict with a rival over possession of a symbolic object representing his status, in hope of a settlement (*dikê*) through the judgment of a *basileus* or *basileis*. Each narrative version of the script presumes that its audience will recognize this way of configuring a confrontation, or *agôn*.

In the dispute scene on Achilles' shield, the script "seeking/rendering a *dikê*" appears in the form of an *ekphrasis*, a verbal description of what has been portrayed visually.[6]

> *The people gathered as a crowd in the agora. There a quarrel had*
> *erupted, with two men quarreling over the payment of restitution for a*

---

[6] Homer contrasts this script to another on the shield, a joyful wedding, suggesting that the two scripts must be related in the minds of his audience – perhaps as "ceremonies of social solidarity and social conflict" in village life (Redfield 1975: 187).

murdered man. Now the one man publicly proclaimed he had paid
everything, the other refused to accept anything. Both pressed for an
adjudicator to determine the boundary line. The people encouraged both
men, supported both. And heralds held back the mass of people. Elders
sat on polished stone benches in the sacred circle, and they were holding
in their hands the loud-voiced heralds' staff. They each jumped to their
feet and in turn were rendering a dikê. *In their midst lay two talants of*
gold to be given to the one among them who could speak the straightest
dikê. *(Il.18.497–508).*

This dramatized dispute settlement permits us to reconstruct some universal details of the script in the minds of Homer's audience before and during the age of state formation: it was the prerogative of *basileis,* whom I equate with village elders (*gerontes*)[7]; their goal was to render publicly a "straight" decision (*dikê*) acceptable to the litigants, their families and supporters, and consistent with tradition; the acts of adjudication were orally delivered, ad hoc in nature, and were at times formulated in competition with other *basileis.*[8] From the perspective of the performance unfolding in the dispute on the shield, we may distinguish three general roles: the litigants, the crowd (probably their families and supporters), and the adjudicators.

WHAT IS *THEMIS*?

This outline of steps in a sequence of actions and the limited set of roles suggest that these disputes were not essentially different from other

[7] See Cantarella's argument and evidence from Homer for equating *gerontes* (elders) with *basileis* (chiefs), irregardless of chronological age (2003: 136–37).
[8] See Gagarin on a "well established procedure" for late Dark Age dispute settlement (1986: 20–45, esp. 42–43). Carawan suggests that Homer's brevity prompts the audience "to recognize the scene and visualize the figures in their proper roles" (1998: 53).

occasions for controlled competition (*agôn*) in Greek social life. From this perspective knowledge about controlled competition exerted a cultural authority the Greeks referred to by the term *themis*. Havelock, for instance, calls *themis* the "oral law" that permitted the murderer (or his kin) depicted on Achilles' shield to offer the victim's family reparation for the crime – and also the oral law forbidding Achilles to murder Agamemnon in *Il.* 1 (1978: 135). As a concept, its meaning is difficult to pin down because of its omnipresence as the very "oxygen" sustaining a preliterate culture's lifeworld. Jane Harrison thought of it in a Durkheimian manner as the Greeks' collective consciousness itself, their "herd instinct" providing both "social sanction and social imperative" (1912: 485). By contrast it's relatively rare in early Greek storytelling to evoke it by name since it designates what is usually never questioned in social life. But when personified as a goddess, Themis designates the desire in chieftain society for an assembly, whether restricted to a *boulê* of chiefs or open to a wider community (*agora*), or for a feast (*dais*); as Tandy observes, both occasions were used to form policy and distribute honors (*timai*) (1997: 142–44).[9] How then might the term incorporate both a religious and a political force vital to a prestate community's ability to enact decision making through some form of deliberation?

To answer this question, we need to consider wider meanings of *themis*, for when we examine its use as a common noun it serves as a portal to the unquestioned principles governing the lifeworld of chiefdoms, where its political usefulness is not yet differentiated from its religious force. In Homer and Hesiod, the formula *themis esti* (or its equivalent) ("it is according to *themis* that...") frequently refers to clearly prescribed, ritual actions: swearing an oath (either what one swears to be or not

---

[9] Tandy 1997: 142–44. See, e.g., *Il.*15.87, 16.387, 20.4; *Od.*2.68 and Hesiod *Th.* 901. See Vos on the goddess Themis in Homer, Homeric Hymns, and Hesiod (1979: 42ff.).

to be the case, or how one should swear)[10]; how to treat strangers in relations of *xenia*[11]; a decision not to wash while in mourning (*Il*.23.44); pouring a libation to a god (*Od*.3.45); or not sacrificing to the gods as mortals should (Hes.*WD* 137). But the formula can also confirm the correct performance of more informal, customary human behavior within the sphere of kinship and family, such as the inclination of men and women to sleep together (*Il*.9.134, 9.276, 19.177), of fathers to kiss their sons (*Od*.11.451), and of widows to weep for husbands who perish abroad (14.130). Occasionally the use of *themis* implies that an action risks violating the boundary between the divine and human spheres: mortal warriors shouldn't strike at the sight of Poseidon's sword in battle (*Il*.14.386); when Patroclus dies, godlike Achilles' helmet shouldn't fall bloodied into the dust (*Il*.16.796–99); and Aeolus shouldn't assist a man hated by the gods (*Od*.10.73).[12]

[10] At *Il*.9.134, 9.276, and 19.177, the formula characterizes the natural proclivity of men and women to sleep together, but it's embedded in Agamemnon's promise to swear an oath that, contrary to natural custom, he did not sleep with Achilles' captive Briseis. At 23.44 the formula refers to Achilles' oath that he will not wash with water until Patroclus is cremated. At 23.581 it sanctions the gestures Antilochus should use to touch the objects on which to swear that he did not willfully interfere with Menelaus' chariot during their race (on swearing oaths upon objects, see Sealey 1994: 97–98).

[11] At *Il*.1.779 the formula refers to Peleus' proper hospitality in providing copious food and drink for his guests; at *Od*.9.268 to the guest-gifts Odysseus expects from the Cyclops; at 14.56 to the *timê* Eumaeus should show his guest; and at 24.286 to the guest-gifts Laertes says Odysseus would provide anyone with whom he had ties of *xenia*.

[12] At the Hesiodic *Shield of Heracles* 22, the formula refers to the obligation a mortal has to fulfill an agreement witnessed by the gods; and at 244 Athena uses it to warn Ares he is not permitted to kill Heracles and strip his armor. Vos categorizes the use of *hê themis esti* in Homer and Hesiod (1979: 1–35) in ways largely consistent with mine. Of its positive uses he claims, "*Themis* is the norm regulating the way humans live together and in particular makes this possible; its character is absolute and universal" (13). The negative formula *ou themis* refers to "actions . . . that are not open to debate and that are for every human being completely impossible

In all cases the formula always expresses an *ought* or *should* and seems to derive its ethical force from this illocutionary element.[13] Also, it's usually intended by a speaker as an authoritative speech act to persuade others: it designates or implies that an action or state of affairs conforms to or deviates from a widespread cultural norm. But, as suggested above, Homer and Hesiod also use *themis esti* to legitimate a more properly political meaning when it refers to the authoritative conduct of *basileis*, differentiating their status from others. It justifies such prerogatives as speaking up at a council or assembly (*Il*.2.73, 9.33, 11.807) and helping plan policy (24.652).[14] It also sanctions communication between *basileis* or between a *basileus* and an inferior: this makes it right for Nestor to share with Telemachus information about *nostoi* (the fates of Achaean warriors after leaving Troy) (*Od*.3.187), and for Odysseus-the-old-beggar to express personal dismay to the young *basileus* Telemachus over the political misfortune of his household (16.91). Most notably, at Hesiod *Th*.389ff., it confirms a key tactic by which Zeus consolidated his power when he led the revolt against the Titans:

> For immortal Styx born of Ocean planned it like this on that day when
> the Olympian god of lightning summoned all the immortals to mighty
> Olympus and said that whoever among them fought with him against
> the Titans would not be deprived of a geras but would keep the timê
> he or she had enjoyed among the immortal gods up till then. And he
> said that whoever went without timê or geras under the rule of

---

[*unmöglich*] and inadmissable" [*unzulässig*] (13–14). Cantarella (1979: 246–47) and van Effenterre (1985: 156) note the appearance of both formulas in Linear B.

[13] Vos implicitly endorses *themis'* illocutionary force when he claims that the positive use of *themis esti* "always supports the reason why someone does something or allows it to be done" (1979: 7). The negative formula he terms "a universally valid, absolute prohibition" (15).

[14] Cf. Vos on *themis* as a personal privilege of Homeric "kings" and "princes" (1979: 1–6).

Cronus would be promoted to these – and that this was themis.
$(389–96)$[15]

Here it is impossible to separate the social force of *themis* from a fundamental source of chiefly power in the Dark Age world: this was his role
in redistributive exchange relations as the center who recruits followers and confers rewards on those who recognize his authority.[16] Once
again, the formula *themis esti* expresses the illocutionary force of an
ought or *should* rhetorically harnessed in speech acts which intend to
persuade.

   This last set of political examples returns us to the dispute settlement
on the shield: how might the elders competing to render a *dikê* use judicial authority to reinforce the ideology of an Early Iron Age chiefdom?
How might they be poised to exercise communicative and cognitive
privileges that will confirm their status as centers of a redistributive
network? To answer these questions, *themis* must mean more than "oral
law," and more too than a people's "collective consciousness" arising
from "social sanction and social imperative." Even Chantraine's translations of *themis esti* as "that which is the order established by the gods"
and "a practice or custom solidly implanted in reality" occlude its tie to
chiefly redistribution.[17] More helpful is Gernet's understanding of
themis as not only the sense of cosmic order peculiar to a descent group

---

[15] Interestingly, Hesiod includes this anecdote to explain why the river Styx, personified as a goddess, was the first divinity to decide (*ebouleuse, Th.*289) to ally herself
and her brood of children (Rivalry, Victory, Power, and Force) with Zeus in his
hall on Olympus. To reward (*timêse*, 399) her, Zeus made her the favorite object by
which the Olympians would swear oaths (399–403).

[16] Cf. Tandy 1997: 101ff., and Donlan 1994.

[17] See Chantraine 1953, where the formula is translated as "*quelque chose comme 'ce qui
est l'ordre établi par les dieux'*" (75) and the idea "*d'un usage ou d'une coutume solidement
implantée dans la réalité*" (76). Vos defines *themis* as "an archaic conceptualization that
basically means a world order [*die Ordnung in einer Welt*] that doesn't distinguish

(*genos*) but also as implemented by the group's leader – as "intrafamilial justice," in effect (2001 [1917]: 22–24; 159). More inclusive of its religious, political and (if Tandy is correct) economic persuasiveness is Corsaro's definition of the term as the traditional, orally maintained system of rules and norms guaranteeing a fair redistribution of lots and status (*moirai* and *timai*) so that no party feels damaged by what has been assigned to it.[18] Clearly, as a basis for social order, this definition opens up *themis* as a dynamic effort to share resources, one whose formulation each generation is compelled to repeat through reinterpretation and renegotiation.[19]

As a type of knowledge capable of achieving this, *themis* included all one ought to know how to do and say in order to uphold and reenact a "cosmically correct" balance of powers. And Corsaro at least implies that the term is always intended to arouse an assent among all present through which a universal moral community will be confirmed. This need not mean, however, that all participants at a dispute or assembly had access to this information. To the contrary, in Early Iron Age societies knowledge of what is *themis* did not enhance the individual autonomy of participants but rather inhibited it: its uses were meant

---

among the natural order, correct ways of behaving [*dem wesensrichtingen Benehmen*], the legal system [*der Rechtsordnung*] and the social and moral order" (1979: 29).

[18] For Corsaro *themis* is "the personification of a traditional system of rules and norms whose observance guarantees and maintains an order reflecting the equitable division [*equa ripartizione*] of portions [*moirai*], so that no one is disadvantaged by what's assigned to him. The idea of equitable division is fundamental to the notion of *themis*. The social order is based on the just redistribution [*distribuzione*] of *timai*; *eunomia* [beneficial rule of law] exists when the laws guarantee equitable division" (1988: 57–58).

[19] Hammer suggests we not understand *themis* primarily in connection with the privileges of *basileis* since it is rather what makes political relationships within public space possible: it is "constitutive of public space" and states a "claim to public reciprocity" (2002: 121, 116). He acknowledges it as the "performative dimension" political actors use for "the framing of rights" that need to be "negotiated" through "enactment of formally defined rituals and laws . . ." (126).

to emerge from the mouths of authoritative speakers whose autonomy vis-à-vis others was privileged or exaggerated.[20] The meaning of what one should know how to do or say on any given occasion was hardly transparent or comprehensive, for the petty details of present circumstances often blinded actors to how the ontologically diverse realities of the here-and-now and cosmic order might converge.

For this reason *themis* sometimes signified an oracular knowledge – a wishful projection into the future of the ability to understand *now* what will *later* turn out to be in accord with social benefit and cosmic harmony. We can more accurately characterize *themis* as by nature epistemologically split into two knowledge states: one that in the present may or may not be self-evident, but which at a future moment will in retrospect be clear to every sensible person. When uttered in the present its illocutionary force therefore rested on reasons that were not open to discussion – let's say, concerning facts that might be merely circumstantial, norms with contradictory imperatives, or incompatible versions of individual experiences. Its reasons lie outside such doubts, always contained in advance in its authoritative speaker's moral vision.[21]

Dispute Settlement as a "Joint Action"

And so in the scene on Achilles' shield the unfolding dispute may contain, despite its status as a script, uncertainties for the participants as

---

[20] Cf. *Od.*14.56, where the slave Eumaeus' use of the phrase underscores his moral excellence in welcoming the less fortunate, disguised beggar Odysseus; and 16.91, where the disguised Odysseus uses it apologetically to address his social superior, Telemachus. Vos describes *themis* at *Il.*2.73 and *themistas* at 1.198 as personal privileges of the *basileus* in order "to protect in the interest of all"; these included ". . . the right to come up with advice and to make decisions for others" (1979: 3). Gernet points to the precariousness of *themis* when a leader isn't strong enough to protect the interests of his household or *genos* against outsiders (2001: 25).

[21] My discussion of *themistes* differs from a traditional understanding (e.g., Vos 1979: 17–22) by identifying it as a type of oracular knowledge.

well as for us. What speech genres would participants in each of the three roles make use of, what cognitive actions would their performance provoke, and exactly how would this enable the litigants to represent themselves in a manner acceptable to all? Exactly how would one individual's authority achieve this? Given Homer's elliptical presentation of the dispute, it's significant that he foregrounds the adjudicators' role rather than the dispute's genesis, any earlier attempts to resolve it, the litigants' precise motives for seeking a settlement, and the exact nature of their opposing arguments. These lacunae are not accidental; and so inference must be our guide when we translate the event into the types of knowledge we moderns think essential to resolving legal quarrels. We can begin to understand the knowledge states in the minds of the figures on the shield by assuming that, according to *themis*, early Greek disputes commonly were a stage in a self-help action by the aggrieved party (the "plaintiff"), and not the result of an obligatory or voluntary recourse by the plaintiff and defendant to community arbitration.[22]

Self-help also clarifies which speech genre(s) the plaintiffs used to perform their actions. We may assume that each litigant performs an act of self-presentation before an audience that includes his own household, his supporters, and a wider public. In addition we can infer that this self-presentation must rely partly on a narrative and partly on genres of status assertion whose rationality is grounded in that narrative. Each performance of self-presentation must also relate dialogically (in a contradictory or conflictual way) to a corresponding self-presentation by the adversary. We can therefore identify on the

---

[22] On self-help, see Sealey 1994: 107–11 and Thür 1996: 58–62, partially reinforcing Wolff 1946 and contra Gagarin 1986. Here Carawan's reconstruction of early Greek dispute settlement concurs with Thür while contesting Wolff (1998: 49–68). (Self-help strikes me as consistent with the *basileus*' privileges and responsibility for maintaining and protecting his own *timê*, as Adkins described it, and characterizes as well his need to muster material and human resources to do so [1972: 15–16]).

shield the roles Habermas finds necessary for communicative action: speaker, addressee, and bystander (1990: 135). In addition, for us the shield includes all three of the senses of a "world" that come into play during a communicative action: an objective world of everyday reality to which the adjudicator's, litigants', and bystanders' speech acts refer; a social world created and sustained by interpersonal relations whose interactions are recognized as legitimate; and a subjective world to which each speaker claims privileged access through self-presentation (1990: 136; 1984: 70).

The first speaker (the "defendant") performs two speech acts to assert that he paid the entire blood-price for a homicide: he "solemnly avows" or "asserts" (*eukhomai*) it, using a heightened form of statement akin to prayer, and then "declares" it, demonstrates it or "makes it evident" (*piphauskô*) to the community.[23] Both acts form a narrative of self-presentation calculated to portray the speaker as someone who, though implicated in the killing, tries to conform to established custom in compensating for the loss of *timê* suffered by the murdered man and his family: the reparation (*poinê*) he claims to have a right to pay (or to have paid) in full symbolizes a restoration of lost *timê*. The plaintiff's speech act straightforwardly "denies" (*anainomai*) that he has taken any payment, or (more likely) he "refuses" to take it, in what has to be a narrative of self-presentation designed to contradict or otherwise conflict with the first narrative.[24] No information on the murder is given, the

---

[23] For *eukhomai* here, see Muellner 1976: 104, Westbrook 1992: 73, and Carawan, who translates, "he claimed *the right* to make full payment," arguing with Westbrook (1992: 74) that the procedure calls for the murderer's kin to make payment if they wish to (1998: 55, with n. 44).

[24] A long-standing tradition in Near Eastern dispute settlement permitted the victim's kin to choose ransom or revenge (death) as compensation unless the murder occurred under mitigating circumstances. Since custom permitted a fixed ransom in such a case, Westbrook believes the murderer (or his kin) on the shield are claiming this. The victim's kin must therefore be refusing the ransom, he argues, because they

guilt of the murderer is not in question, nor is there any indication about how justified the act was. No statements of status assertion are reported. By eliding these factual details, Homer's description foregrounds the plaintiff's intransigence, the impending act of judgment itself, and its agents, the elders. But the nature of their cognitive acts and how these acts unfold are still not apparent.[25]

Why does Homer leave suspended what interests us most: the conflict's origins in factual details, each litigant's expression of "validity claims" reflecting a partisan understanding of facts, norms and personal experiences, and some indication about the conflict's resolution? Perhaps the disputants could not: distinguish the "facts" of the case as an objective reality whose truth they could establish; isolate a principle intersubjectively shared by all members of the community about who is clearly in the "right" here; or believe that different individuals could have legitimately different, subjective "takes" on what happened or what must now be done. In other words, the lifeworld within which these participants move influences them to leave unexamined those independent senses of objective, social, and subjective worlds. And so they can have little interest in eliciting conflicting validity claims representing different world concepts that could only make sense to them through interpretations evaluating the quality of reasons for and against.[26] As a result, to us *themis* almost seems to blind them to issues we feel are "natural," pointing them toward a path darkened by what cannot be known when seeking a *dikê*.

consider the murder an "aggravated assault" and so insist on the choice of revenge or ransom (1992). See Wilson's elucidation of ransom (*apoina*) and revenge (*poinê*) as distinct "themes" within the "poetics of compensation" in the *Iliad* (2002: 14–17).

[25] Cf. the different speculations about the exact nature of the quarrel and what each litigant, the elders, and the supporters may have had "in mind": Carawan 1998: 55–56; Thür 1996: 66–69; Sealey 1994: 103–105; Gagarin 1986: 26–33; Nagy 1979: 109, with a key reference to Muellner 1976: 105–6.

[26] Cf. Habermas 1984: 51.

This inability or disinterest in distinguishing between independently objective, social, and subjective worlds helps bolster the recent scholarly contention that the goal of early Greek legal procedure was not to establish objectively guilt or innocence, or the "truth" of what happened, but to achieve through a *dikê* a "mode of proof" acceptable to all parties and capable of ending the dispute peacefully.[27] It may well be then that disputes were only brought before elders when a solution acceptable to all parties did not hinge on a fact that was easy to establish, and so a defendant had no recourse if he wished to interrupt the plaintiff's pursuit of self-help except an appeal to a local chief or chiefs. For this dispute Thür suggests that it isn't likely that the elders would be competing for the straightest *dikê* if the matter could have been decided by a simple factual alternative (e.g., the compensation was paid or not; it conformed to custom or not).[28]

So while it may disappoint us that disputes like the one on the shield did not immerse Dark Age village communities in a collective "whodunit," it should encourage us to appreciate how much more "creative," "poetic," and "prophetic" they could be than our jury trials and detective stories, for they were occasions for the performance not only of competing claims by litigants but also of competing paths of judicial discovery that pursued an elusive, unknown "proof" ultimately resulting in a reconfiguration of *timê* in the community.[29] And here the "proof" performed by the successful *basileus* had in some way to trump the performative skills of the litigants, their supporters, and his

---

[27] "Mode of proof" is Sealey's translation for *dikê* (1994: 101–4). In Gernet's words, "Negatively, what defines prelaw in particular is that there is no possibility of an objective truth that would support a verdict" (1981: 189).

[28] See Gagarin 1986: 32–33 and Thür 1996: 67 for opposing views on the problem with the payment.

[29] Carawan, too, comments on the relative lack of interest in "who-done-it" in Homeric and other legendary disputes (1998: 27).

rival *basileis*. Hesiod's analogy of *basileus* and bard (*aoidos*) at *Th.* 79–104 does, however, shed some light on the nature of the darkened path disputants had to take in search of a "proof," for, as performers, both bard and *basileus* competed against rivals to create a cognitive "diversion," a transport, away from present distress and toward a wishful, imagined achievement of transcendent order.

The nature of a *dikê* as a "mode of proof" and the epistemologically split nature of *themis* also tell us why Homer suspends the conflict's resolution: despite the existence of familiar scripts like "seeking" and "rendering a *dikê*," and despite the ritual certainty attending some uses of *themis*, the outcome of disputes unfolding in this period could never be known in advance. This unpredictability characterizes not only the litigants' and/or the crowd's choice of the elder who will produce the straightest *dikê* but also the terms of the settlement and the final social standing of each disputant. Who, in fact, will be judged responsible for preventing a "correct" payment of restitution for the homicide, the murderer (or his kinsman) or the victim's kinsman? Who then will be found culpable of encroaching on the *timê* of the other and of prolonging a destabilized social order?[30] These occasions were inherently dramatic because, in spite of their rule-governed nature, outcomes depended on an unforeseeable (and thus to a degree uncontrollable) sequence of provocations and responses by the three performance roles of the disputants, the divided public, and the elders. In our modern terms, rendering a *dikê* as a "mode of proof" was very much a question of negotiation.

To appreciate the impending settlement's open-endedness, we can compare it to a modern type of event John Shotter calls a "joint

---

[30] See Gernet's extended discussion of *timê* (2001: 281–302), Yamagata 1994: 121ff., and Sealey's succinct definition of Homeric *timê* as a person's "portion," "right" or "privilege" demanding community recognition (1994: 142–44).

action." These are interactions between persons which by nature can't be controlled by one participant or the other, and whose outcome can't be dictated or predetermined by preestablished rules and roles. In our culture this includes such encounters as informal conversations and discussions, labor negotiations, tutorials, insults, sporting events, and consultations (1980: 53). It's because we can distinguish objective, social, and subjective senses of reality that we frequently find ourselves in situations where we must interpret each other's words and acts, in effect reconstructing each other's social and personal worlds in dialogic fashion, to achieve a "consensual understanding" through "negotiation" of the other's account of his or her reasons for behaving this way rather than that.[31] These are, in other words, communicative actions in a minor key, in contexts both public and private, with consequences both significant and banal.

At first glance the early Greek lifeworld seems to hold no place for joint actions like this. As we've seen, at one extreme *themis* can indicate highly prescribed actions and interactions in the form of rituals, whose unfolding in rigid certainty was a matter of grave concern.[32] But *themis*

---

[31] Shotter 1980: 32–56, esp. 53; 1993: 3–4 and 108–11. Westbrook's (1992) cogent interpretation of the dispute on the shield unfortunately ignores the different degrees of centralized legal authority and control between early states (palace- or city-states) and prestate communities in Early Iron Age Greece.

[32] See, e.g., Burkert's definition of ritual as "a programme of demonstrative acts to be performed in set sequence and often at a set place and time – sacred insofar as every omission or deviation arouses deep anxiety and calls forth sanctions. As communication and social imprinting, ritual establishes and secures the solidarity of the closed group; in this function it has doubtless accompanied the forms of human community since the earliest of times" (1985: 8). In premodern societies, Shotter contrasts joint action with ritual loosely defined: "It is only in highly ritualistic, pre-established forms of social interaction that the direction and content of conduct can be explained by rule/role models; usually the direction and content of the exchange is fashioned out of what people in interaction have to deal with" (1980: 34).

couldn't have imparted this sort of certainty to dispute settlement if its outcome depended on a "diversion" that negotiated, in a manner consistent with a mythological worldview, between the interests of both parties and the community. From a broader perspective, in fact, some of the most dramatic scenes in early Greek literature develop this potential for a stereotypical script like "calling an assembly" to backfire on the instigator when it hemorrhages into an ancient sort of joint action.[33] In a fundamental way, therefore, the potential for an event's transformation into a joint action – an event free of strict, ritual protocol – challenges the stereotypical nature of scripts as structures of knowledge with a preestablished sequence of actions. A joint action short-circuits the automatic cognitive response a script is designed to elicit because it accommodates degrees of autonomy by participants, whether as individuals or collectively. And so every early Greek dispute settlement, even though its script is "fixed" in advance as a piece of cultural knowledge, has the potential to develop into a joint action so long as it guarantees its arch-performer considerable autonomy in responding cognitively to what the other performers think and say. In other words, once activated in performance, the scripts "seeking" and "rendering a *dikê*" contain within themselves at least the possibility of passing from cultural knowledge of how to restore social stability into a catalyst for further destabilization.

Now we can better appreciate why Homer foregrounds the adjudicator's role in the settlement process. For it is the interpretive skill of the elder who most accurately grasps the movement of this

---

[33] E.g., the assembly Achilles calls in *Il.* 1 to challenge Agamemnon's decision to refuse the ransom of Chryseis; Agamemnon's assembly in *Il.* 2 to test the loyalty of the troops; the assembly Telemachus calls in *Od.* 2 to seek the community's help.

give-and-take process between adversaries that will result (to use Shotter's terms) in a "consensual understanding" or "joint" way all parties can agree for "going on" with a settlement (1980: 50). In essence this elder will have recognized the dispute process as an attempt to "negotiate" in our modern sense rather than simply to "find" or "know" objectively the meaningful resolution, and he will understand that the individual social identity of each litigant (along with his family's) likewise must result from negotiation. He, and not the litigants or spectators, would assume the autonomous acts which citizens of a modern nation state might perform for themselves in the joint actions characteristic of our civil society, whose "zones of uncertainty" invite us to negotiate with one another by assuming responsibility for understanding how our differences and similarities (of gender, race, class, ethnicity), and our uniqueness as individuals, condition our experience of our social and individual reality.[34]

THE OATH AS A MODE OF PROOF

The elder on the shield must therefore in some way enjoy the privilege (and take on the burden) of assuming the litigants' individual autonomy and the community's collective autonomy. But how? The simplest answer is that each elder proposes a settlement (*dikazein*) concerning the point at issue, whether the victim's family should accept or refuse the reparation from the murderer or his kin, and the litigants

[34] Through joint action Shotter imagines citizenship and community as engaging in "'joint (formative) activities' producing over time imaginary objects 'subsisting' in the 'negotiations' between people, ephemeral objects serving the purpose merely of coordinating debate about what in the situation to do next" (1993: 134). This enables us "to adopt a critical, reflexive self-awareness, an awareness of what we are 'doing' in talking as we do, and a preparedness to recognize that all our cultural statements are constructed in this contradictory, ambivalent, and indeterminate time-space of negotiation" (134–35).

together with the crowd will determine which elder's solution is most acceptable.[35] But if we agree that a *dikê* constituted a mode of proof, then each elder must propose a settlement in the form of something one or both litigants perform before the crowd. That performance, according to Thür, Sealey and now Carawan, was most likely the improvisational composition of an oath for one or both litigants to swear. Each scholar speculates helpfully on the possible complexities of composing the best oath for the case, which certainly would have required a display by the winning elder of cognitive virtuosity or, as Sealey used the word, "ingenuity" (1994: 104).[36] Carawan suggests that each elder "will challenge the rival claimants to make formal proof of their claims by oath or testimony of witnesses or conceivably by some other test." This sort of judgment, he continues, "will defer to the claims of the litigants but challenge their good faith." Thus the *litigants themselves*, by their willing agreement or implicit consent, will determine the author of the "straightest justice."[37]

If Carawan is right, doesn't a solution based on a "willing agreement or implicit consent" honor each litigant's autonomy vis-à-vis the other and the community, especially if the settlement unfolds within the context of a self-help action? Aren't the litigants free to express elements of a voluntarist self that chooses its own ends? And doesn't this make the winning elder look anything but autonomous – more like a mere facilitator for a "consensual principle" that respects the autonomy of both

---

[35] See Gagarin 1986: 27–31.

[36] See Carawan 1998: 52, 57, 59–67, and 81 (without reference to Sealey 1994 or Thür 1996). On the use of oaths, cf. Gagarin's interpretation of this dispute as evidence that oath-swearing was not an "automatic" mode of proof in Homer and Hesiod but more a "rhetorical strategy" to outmaneuver one's opponent (1992: 76); see also Gagarin 2005b: 86–90. For an overview of oaths in arbitration and trials in fifth- and fourth-century Athens, see Allen 2000: 320–22.

[37] 1998: 57; my italics. This concurs with Thür (1996) and Sealey (1994: 104–5).

individuals and community? Homer's designation of this individual as an *istôr* seems to reinforce this, particularly if we take it to mean a "witness" to an oath or other mode of proof and not a "knowledge-expert."[38] And Carawan does argue that this performative solution is consistent with the earliest written law code at Gortyn on Crete, which may preserve the legal realities of the seventh century. This code consistently calls for judges to propose oaths or other proofs so that the disputants themselves may reach an agreement. As a result Carawan concludes that at Gortyn, "The outcome is not a verdict imposed by sovereign command upon one party or the other. Its social function is rather to reconcile the hostile parties: each is to recognize the claims of the other, thus disavowing the cycle of vendetta that would inevitably arise if one side were faced with an unacceptable outcome" (1998: 61).

To me this apparent respect for a "consensual principle" is nevertheless illusory. While it's not incompatible with state society in the sixth century and later, we cannot square it with a prestate community under the leadership of a *basileus*, especially if we accept Tandy's thesis of a legitimation crisis for the eighth century's new *basileis*. I believe the performance of oaths witnessed by a *basileus* very much constituted a "verdict imposed by sovereign command upon one party or the other," that it was designed to inhibit the litigants' individual autonomy as well as that of the community at large, and that, as an enactment of *themis*, it was consistent with the redistributive authority of the *basileus* as a center. Carawan inadvertently leads us in this direction when he aligns an important issue in this dispute with Draco's homicide legislation in Athens of around 620. That issue is whether the plaintiff on

---

[38] See Carawan 1998: 61–63. Sealey takes *istôr* to mean a "wise man," but his observation elsewhere that Greeks frequently swore oaths by calling upon a god "so that he/she might know" (*istô*) reinforces this interpretation of *istôr* as a witness to an oath or other proof (Sealey 1994: 103, with Homeric examples). See also Cantarella 2003: 284–86.

the shield is refusing to accept the reparation despite his family's prior agreement to accept it or a customary mandate that it be accepted – that is, whether this dispute was triggered by one man's recalcitrance.[39]

If so, then the elders' task is to determine certain "mitigating circumstances" about the homicide, which Westbrook suggests formed part of much earlier Near Eastern law codes (1992: 71). These likely included questions about degrees of intentionality or volition, which do enter other homicide disputes in Homer. So what the elders want to know from the plaintiff is: "Can he in good faith, before the gods and the assembled community, deny the killer's plea for peaceful resolution?" Moreover, Carawan continues, "The moral onus upon the plaintiff becomes all the more compelling, if . . . even his own kinsmen are willing to reconcile. Can he defy the overwhelming force of custom and community interests that even his kinsmen have acknowledged?" (1998: 66). If this reconstruction is correct, then the inquiry on the shield is not primarily aimed at the fact of guilt or innocence, or at debating community norms about reparation for homicide, but at probing states of mind – that of the killer and of a kinsman of the victim.

The inquiry thus aims to confront the "force of custom and community interests" – *themis*, in other words – with different ways the crime was experienced by two subjects who, in our modern view, have privileged access to their inner worlds. And its dynamics as a joint action apparently hinges on what has occurred and will occur in these inner worlds. The settlement certainly seems to be respecting the autonomy of two individuals, the killer and the victim's kinsman, as voluntarist and deliberative selves free to project goals, initiate projects, practice retrospection, and achieve self-reflexive distance vis-à-vis traditions,

---

[39] See Carawan 1998: 65–67, noting the Draconian code's concern for unanimity among kinsmen eligible to participate in disputes and concern over questions of volition; his interpretation builds on Gagarin 1981a, and is also endorsed by Sealey (1994: 103–4).

opinions, and pressure to conform. And, as suggested above, its communicative dynamics as a type of joint action does invite participants to explore the various subject positions of all three senses of a world. But by proposing and witnessing oaths, the winning elder will foreclose the possibility that these revelations might be worth debating according to universally acceptable reasons for and against. His oaths will impose on this recalcitrant plaintiff and perhaps on the killer or his family a temporal-spatial frame designed to trump the validity of any reasons that emerge from the two subjects' inner worlds. The oaths will short-circuit any chance that litigants and spectators intersubjectively comprehend the crime and the reasons for refusing customary reparation because they will use community memory and heroic tales to *divert* the attention of all present away from rationalizing the issues into debatable questions with defensible yes/no positions.

The oath succeeds as a "mode of proof" because it substitutes other reasons why nonviolent consensus should be achieved – reasons that are mythological and ultimately magical in nature. The *basileus* must "witness" the peace-bringing oath because he stands in as a human representative of the gods who will witness it, and specifically he imitates in this regard Zeus, who serves judicial *basileis* as a "model of mimesis" for all redistributive actions that reapportion *moirai* and *timai*. Once again Hesiod provides the prototypical scene (at *Th.*386–403), when Zeus recruited Styx to join his household as the prime witness for divine oaths. A more dramatically effective example, however, is the oath Agamemnon finally swears when he ends his dispute with Achilles (at *Il.*19.258–65) – in effect concluding the *dikê* Nestor tried to render as a judicial *basileus* (at *Il.*1.247ff.)

> *May Zeus now be my witness first, the highest and noblest of gods!*
> *Then Earth, the Sun, and the Furies who punish those men below the*
> *earth who've sworn a false oath: That I never laid a hand on the*

maiden Briseis nor ever used her for the sake of taking her to bed or for
anything else and that she remained inconspicuous in my camp. And if
any of this is falsely sworn, may the gods give me very many agonies – as
many as they give when someone sins against them when he swears
upon them. (19.258–65)

Note how the oath permits Agamemnon to avoid providing reasons why
he took Briseis, and that Achilles replies with an oath discouraging further inquiry into the reasons for his devastatingly angry reaction.[40]
Oath swearing under a *basileus'* supervision thus served prestate communities better than any other social device to reenact *themis* because it
mythologically and magically renewed what Carawan calls the "moral
burden" of litigants' claims, and, prior to the "coercive command of the
state," it "constrained [them] by social conscience" (1998: 68).

    Before we probe more into ways the oath can accomplish this, we
need to consider a final reason why Homer doesn't resolve the settlement
on the shield. This will help us understand how oaths might resemble
laws (*thesmoi*) as a means of resolving disputes by diverting or translating them ontologically into a trumping temporal-spatial frame. Some
scholars have noted how the scene on the shield serves as a paradigm
for typical attempts to resolve conflict; and so they believe Homer is
encouraging his audience to retroject the scene backwards toward the
poem's major unresolved conflict between Agamemnon and Achilles.[41]
If the recalcitrant kinsman is indeed the focus of the shield's dispute,

---

[40] 19.270–75. Agamemnon's reasons, when given at 9.116ff. and 19.86ff., match
Achilles' as mythological, magical explanations because they attribute errors in
moral decision-making to Zeus and other divinities. B. Williams sees Agamemnon's reasoning as one way Homeric individuals accept moral responsibility for
their decisions (1993: 52ff.).

[41] See Schein 1984: 141–42; Taplin traces verbal and thematic links between all the
scenes on the shield and the rest of the poem (1980: 1–21); see also Andersen 1976: 5–18.
See Wilson's careful delineation of *apoina* (forms of compensation such as ransom)

then his moral dilemma mirrors the one faced by Achilles vis-à-vis the Achaeans and, in Phoenix's speech to Achilles, by the earlier hero Meleager vis-à-vis his family and community (*Il.*9.524–605). Thus the shield's scene echoes not only Achilles' intransigence in Book 9[42] but also the conflict's outbreak in Book 1 and Meleager's dilemma as well. That outbreak and Meleager's dilemma both unfold as escalating, unpredictable joint actions concerning an individual's loss of *timê* (Agamemnon's at 1.106ff., then Achilles' at 1.163ff., and Meleager's at 9.524ff.).

In Book 1 and in Meleager's tale, attempts were made at resolution when an adjudicating elder (Nestor) or local *basileis* (the *gerontes Aitôlôn*, 9.574–75) used their wisdom to try to negotiate a "proper" (*kata moiran*, 1.286) apportionment of each man's *timê* (1.275–81).[43] In Book 9 the attempts at resolving the Achilles–Agamemnon dispute intensified when the offending party himself (Agamemnon) made a generous offer of compensation for damaged *timê* (a "compensation without limit," *apereisi' apoina*, 9.120–56), and when the Aetolean priests, acting by authority of the local *basileis*, offered Meleager the choicest land for a *temenos* (9.575–80). Both offers of compensation for damaged *timê* (cf. 9.155) are not unlike the *poinê* offered by the murderer or his kinsman on the shield.[44] In both Books 1 and 9, however, the litigants Achilles and Meleager exploited their autonomy to refuse (*anaineto*, 9.585) the restitution as insufficiently representative of their worth, and so prolonged the joint action.

---

and *poinê* (forms such as retribution or revenge) as distinct themes and types of exchange in the *Iliad*, which also may be "mixed" (2002: 16–17).

[42] See Schein (1984: 142) and Muellner (1976: 105–6), among others.

[43] Cf. Gagarin's emphasis on Nestor's role here as a judicial *basileus* (1992: 70).

[44] Note that Agamemnon offers Achilles a perhaps unconventional "compensation without any limit" (*apeiros' apoina*, 9.155), whereas the judicial elders on the shield are attempting to set a perhaps conventional limit (*peirar*) on the murderer's *poinê* (18.501).

Especially noteworthy is one reason Ajax gives Achilles to accept Agamemnon's offer: "Anyone will accept the compensation for a murdered brother or a child who is killed. And the killer remains in his district because he has paid out a lot, and he who receives compensation calms his heart and savage spirit" (9.632–36). Ajax's brief narrative provides a positive exemplum of dispute settlement over homicide because it foregrounds a neglected act in the script "rendering a *dikê*": *accepting* a *dikê*. It likens Achilles to the anonymous man on the shield in that both, along with Meleager, refuse to allow their self-worth to be negotiated through symbolic forms of wealth. By refusing a "straight" *dikê*, all three obstinately refuse unanimity with their kinsmen, prolong periods of social disorder, and suspend mutual acknowledgment of each other's social persona.[45]

If we contrast the anonymity of the men in Ajax's exemplum and on the shield, fixed in their stereotypical scripts, to the rich, complex detail of Achilles' dispute with Agamemnon, we come face to face with the productive, tense interplay between script and joint action. The act of accepting a *dikê* endorses custom or *themis* in Ajax's exemplum and in the scene on the shield with their promise or hope of a straight *dikê*. But Homer's audience has already seen Achilles reject custom once and has no assurance at this point that he will accept compensation from the Trojans for Patroclus' death. Because the scripts in Ajax's exemplum and on the shield are typical, they convey greater predictability and prescription as positive paradigms for ideal social behavior, while Meleager's refusal, an "old tale with nothing recent in it" (9.527), dramatizes a corresponding negative paradigm with proscriptive force. In

---

[45] In *Il.* 1 and 9, Achilles' critique of Agamemnon dismantles the latter's social persona as a competent chieftain; and his own refusal to fight or accept Agamemnon's offer nullifies his persona's ability to participate in the generalized reciprocity of chieftain exchange. See Gill 1996: 136–54, indebted on this point to Donlan 1982b and Claus 1975.

this regard, all three share an ambiguous ontology in relation to the present dilemma of Achilles' anger: hovering outside the *Iliad*'s main narrative, they are accessible only to the privileged sight of bard and *basileus*.

How Oaths, Exempla, and Similes Resemble Laws

Ajax's exemplum, the Meleager tale, the scene on the shield, and the oath as a mode of proof resemble the similes Homer scatters throughout his narrative – as Redfield puts it, the shield seems to function as a "kind of master simile" representing the wider world of productive life outside the "reduced" world of the Greeks fighting at Troy (1975: 187). Taplin too links the shield to the similes in their capacity to place the *Iliad*'s heroic world of war "in perspective within the world as a whole," somewhat the way a reproduction of a painting can place a detail "within a larger landscape."[46] In cognitive terms I'd describe the shield, the tale of Meleager, the homicide exemplum, and the similes as slices of the "shared lifeworld" of the Greeks from about 900–700, that is, as the "storehouse of unquestioned cultural givens from which those participating in communication draw agreed upon patterns of interpretation for use in their interpretive efforts" (Habermas 1990: 135). I'd also connect the ambiguous ontology and proscriptive force of these bits and chunks of ideal social behavior from the lifeworld to oath swearing and to the oral laws, called *thesmoi*, which the Greeks believed judicial *basileis* rendered for city-state communities in the seventh and sixth centuries.

As chunks of the lifeworld vividly preserved and scattered throughout Homer's poems, these oaths, similes, exempla, and so on, resemble

---

[46] Taplin 1980: 12. Taplin also connects the shield's *basileus* surveying his fertile agricultural precinct (*temenos*) (18.555–57) with the exemplum of the idealized *basileus* used by Odysseus to describe Penelope's renown at *Od*.19.109–14.

laws because they hypothesize scripts for an orderly life. And, like laws, they must closely reflect the scripts that play themselves out more or less predictably in the audience's everyday life – unlike the scripts in the poem's main narrative, which, as we saw, have a greater potential to develop into joint actions. In Habermas' terms heroic encounters that turn into joint actions "decenter" an understanding of the world because they "differentiate" the shared lifeworld from the world(s) that problematic agents like Achilles experience (1990: 138). And the more that lifeworld is decentered, the more coherence must be provided by "interpretive accomplishments of the participants themselves" (1984: 70). While these participants may include heroic agents, they surely include Homer's audience.

If the *Iliad* seems to anticipate later Greek statute law, it's because Homer endows it with multiple ontological dimensions whose scripts are played out in varying degrees of social order and disorder; and the poet, like a lawgiver, intends his listeners to navigate cognitively from one to another. Like the judicial *basileis* on the shield, when Homer confronts intractable dilemmas over *timê*, he has access to a cognitive resource his litigating characters and audience lack. The *basileis* possess oath formulae and, as we'll see, a community memory of paradigmatic crimes and the oaths that resolved them; Homer has his storehouse of oaths, exempla, similes, and old tales like Meleager's. But the difference between the *basileis* and Homer is this: Homer shares with his audience, and sometimes with his characters, the information in these ontologically other dimensions. With this information he demonstrates to his audience how "decentering" the moral behavior of an Agamemnon and Achilles is, and this prompts the audience to provide the "interpretive accomplishments" which, as Habermas suggests, are a kind of "risky (because rationally motivated) agreement" akin to communicative action (1984: 70).

Homer's ontological shifting, far from inhibiting the autonomy of his heroic litigants and his audience, inspires them to exercise it. In Chapter 4 I argue that early lawgivers, as performers of wisdom, did much the same when they supposedly fashioned *thesmoi* into law codes, for these required an interpretation that shuttled between the many contingencies of an alleged crime and each law's idealized script for achieving *dikê*. But since Homer offers his listeners not laws but alternative idealized scripts (oaths, similes, exempla, etc.), how does he cue them to the subtlety of these ontological shifts? Can his listeners recognize from his language the world into which he is taking them? In literary terms, whenever a poet develops scripts from within the lifeworld into artistic forms like the problematic joint actions of heroes, they appear as chronotopes. As we've seen in Chapter 1, for Bakhtin chronotopes are the dominant representations of time, space, and agency in verbal or visual artifacts; they define the parameters of physical and metaphysical reality as well as the logic enabling characters to interact with their environment and one another. Homer's chronotopes are scripts that have been elaborated into particular genres of storytelling: some emerge as similes and exempla, but others result in a thrilling version of heroes "on the battlefield," "at the war council," "on a sea voyage," "establishing guest-host relations with an enchantress," or "visiting the land of the dead."[47]

Since they are meant to entertain, surprise, evoke wonder and provoke reflection, chronotopes offer storytellers and listeners artistic portals through which the stereotypical knowledge contained in scripts can appear in one of two ways: as orderly, familiar narrative structures, such

---

[47] Griffin's comparison of Homeric epic with other poems in the epic cycle foregrounds these ontological and chronotopal differences, especially the use of "fantastic" elements typical of romance and the possibility of humans escaping mortality (1977: 39–43).

as similes and exempla, replete with the force of custom (*themis*) and cosmic apportionment;[48] or as defamiliarized, disorderly scripts "gone wrong," when unpredictable heroes enact extraordinary adventures. Either way, they help listeners to connect the remote heroic world to their everyday world as they transform the same data bank of cultural knowledge into markers of the distance between the heroic world and the audience's post-heroic existence.[49] So, to travel freely between the heroic and post-heroic worlds, the epic singer uses not so much scripts themselves, as Minchin (1992: 237) and Bakker (1997a: 76–80) claim, but chronotopes, sometimes uniting the two worlds and sometimes distancing them from one another.[50]

Homer's chronotopes thus cue his audience to recognize a joint action as a deviation from the right order of a simile, exemplum, or ideal scene on a shield, just as lawgivers will enable citizen jurors to refer the details of an alleged crime to a specific statute law. Since some of these ideal scenes will someday be replaced by statute law, they serve here as proto-laws, marshaling epic chronotopes to help with the work of what Havelock called the "oral storage" of information in non- or semi-literate cultures (1978: 42–43). Through them a listener can shuttle back and forth among different ontological registers – or "frames," as we've called them in Goffman's sense. These consist of interpretive contexts

---

[48] The shield's cosmic images are carefully structured: at its center the earth, sky, sea, sun, moon, and stars, with the river Ocean around its rim (see, e.g., Redfield 1975: 187–88; Taplin 1980: 5–11).

[49] For the shield's reference to realities outside its mythological world, see Schein 1984: 29–30; cf. Rheinhardt 1961: 405–6.

[50] E.g., a simile uses the everyday activity of harvesting to represent heroic warriors slaughtering one another (11.67–9, cited by Taplin 1980: 8). For Bakhtin chronotopes in epic and drama mix mythological, natural, and historical experiences of time: "In every aspect of his world the Greek saw a trace of mythological time; he saw in it a condensed mythological event that would unfold into a mythological scene or tableau" (1981: 104).

or codes for rendering meaningful a "raw strip" of activity (1974: 10–25). Any observer of such a strip can project different frames onto it, thereby "rekeying" or transforming its activity from, say, fighting to playing, tragic to comic action, sincere to sarcastic comment, and so on.[51] In this way a Homeric chronotope like "at the war council" provides a narrative bridge modeling conduct at everyday councils in a village society – and this might induce Homer's audience to rekey a heroic decision like Achilles' refusal to accept a *dikê* into an act that conforms with or violates what is *themis* in their own world.

RENDERING A *DIKÊ* WITH GIFTS, OATHS, AND SONGS

Our second major piece of evidence for legal disputes occurs during the funeral games for Patroclus in *Iliad* 23. Like the *ekphrasis* on Achilles' shield, the games describe scripts that are self-contained narrative digressions from the *Iliad*'s unresolved major conflicts, and by analogy the scenes on the shield and the games offer an ideal solution to the intractability of those conflicts. And so, like the shield's dispute scene, the chariot race's disputes also dramatize ways a *basileus* may perform a *dikê* consistent with *themis*. Unlike the shield scenes, however, Homer's narrative of all eight events in the games provides us

---

[51] See Goffman 1974: 39–44. Goffman defines a "key" as "the set of conventions by which a given activity, one already meaningful in terms of some primary framework, is transformed into something patterned on this activity but seen by the participants to be something quite else" (43–44). This accurately describes the effect on a Homeric audience when similes describing peaceful activity are used to represent heroic warfare, as at *Il*.11.67–69. The term "frame" is unfortunately confusing because its meanings vary so much, ranging from Goffman's "primary frameworks" or "schemata of interpretation" (1974: 21–30) that determine the ontological nature of "what is going on" (waking reality, dream, play, divine intervention, etc.) to simple linguistic "facts" like the word-concept "house" (Minsky 1975). Compounding the confusion, Bakker uses "frame" to indicate how Homeric narrative circumscribes a field of vision so an action can be outlined and its details described (1997a: 88ff.). I follow Goffman's sense of primary framework.

with rich details about each. Of no event is this more the case than the chariot race, whose narrative is more than ten times the average length of the others; and disputes over prizes in this race comprise a major portion – about 20 percent – of this lengthy account. So we are very well informed about how the disputes arose from circumstances before and during the race, the multiple attempts to resolve them, and the motives and arguments of the participants as they unfold.

We consequently stand to learn a great deal more than we could from the shield's dispute about an adjudicating *basileus'* role in achieving consensus. Specifically, we'll see how his virtuoso performance of cognitive and communicative acts orchestrates disputants and spectators in ways that inhibit both the disputants' individual exercise of autonomy and the collective autonomy of the group. More concretely than on the shield, we'll witness displays by *basileis* of ontological frame-switching that are tied to gift-giving, or the chief's economic function as a redistributive center. This will explain more clearly how the illocutionary force of the claim "*themis esti . . .*" sanctions the *basileus'* use of adjudication to construct personal authority at the expense of disputants and spectators who are not free or knowledgeable enough to represent themselves as equal participants in reaching a settlement.

Minchin clarifies how Homer narrates the chariot race by following a general script, the "contest," with internal variations for each event in the form of different "tracks" (2001: 42ff.; 1992: 238). In this way, she argues, Homer can rouse his audience's interest by interrupting the contest script's predictable outcome with unpredictable actions.[52] Minchin notes how this technique is particularly evident when Homer problematizes the "collection of prizes" in the chariot race, specifically the claim to second prize, but she doesn't notice that Homer inserts

[52]   Minchin 2001: 42ff., esp. 44–45; cf. 1992: 238.

the script "seeking/rendering a *dikê*" into the general script of the contest.[53]

In fact by the time all the prizes have been claimed, we find three *dikê* tracks in which a *basileus* has ingeniously negotiated the question of an individual's *timê*: Antilochus and Achilles square off in the first (23.541–54); Menelaus and Antilochus in the second (23.566–95); and in the third Nestor benefits from Achilles' respectful recognition of his past and present standing (23.615–50). Unlike the scene on Achilles' shield, Homer allows us to witness the race as a "raw strip" of activity, and so we have little need to hear each disputant's contradictory narrative claims and self-presentations. Instead, when the race goes wrong and like a lightning rod attracts quarrels among spectators about who's in the lead and among contestants about who deserves what prize, Homer highlights speech genres associated with status-assertion: threat, accusation, insult, invective, and challenge from the plaintiffs; concession, self-effacement, and conciliation from the defendants – genres that cut to the quick of litigants self-presentations in demanding that one's *timê* be recognized or another's diminished.[54]

All three *dikê* tracks wrestle with the knotty dilemma in a highly competitive society of the changing, multiple degrees of *timê* won and lost by individuals through personal mettle, rank, fortune, and the passage of time. In this way they problematize the action "collection of prizes" by asking: "How significant are such fluctuations in *timê*? Should some occasions for acquiring *timê* take precedence over others? Should these fluctuations require wholesale renegotiation of an

---

[53] However, Minchin does acknowledge that Homer, after problematizing the collection of prizes, presents a "model of an amicable dispute settlement" (2001: 65, 67–68).

[54] For Redfield these games are "an arena in which honor can be won" and "a stage upon which honor is recognized" (1975: 209).

individual's social standing and identity?"[55] According to Sealey's definition of Homeric *timê*, "Each man's *timê* is his inherent quality. It reflects his descent and it is reflected in his deeds and in the esteem that people accord him" (1994: 143). And "Homeric *timê* is the sum of a man's rights. Moreover each man's *timê* is distinctive. It inheres in him in consequence of his own quality, in which descent is one among several factors" (145). These claims to an "inherent" quality and to uniqueness in an individual's *timê* almost merge the Homeric concept with the characteristics of an autonomous modern self.[56] Nevertheless, there is little doubt that the questions Homer raises to problematize the collection of prizes speak directly to aspects of individual autonomy as Homeric elites could experience it, asking, "Do individuals establish a single self-identity biographically (throughout a lifetime), or multiple, changing identities through discrete eras of a life? And how consistent should an individual be in his actions over time?" In a more contemporary idiom, "Which dimensions of a hero's self dominate his performance of the self-determination responsible for reputation: voluntarist, cognitive, or deliberative?" (cf. Warren 2001: 63)

TRACK ONE: ACHILLES AND ANTILOCHUS

These issues come to the fore because the chariot race establishes a ludic frame in which each participant ambiguously enjoys two identities as he passes onto and off the playing field: his "normal," quotidian self with its social persona and *timê* intact, and a competitor temporarily stripped of that identity and equal to all others in his opportunity

---

[55] Thalmann sees the chariot race as intracommunal competition and violence revealing tension between personal excellence and one's ascribed position in a society where status depends more on lifelong achievement than on competitive display (1998: 136–37).

[56] As a corrective to this "modern liberalist" understanding of *timê*, cf. Gernet's emphasis on its fundamentally collective nature 2001: 281–302.

to win, place, show, or lose altogether, with a corresponding rise or fall in the *timê* symbolized by chariot racing. Here, then, Homer finds another ontological frame to alternate with the heroic narrative: this one imposes, as in ritual, a "liminal" identity on each competitor, making him both the same and not the same person.[57] When the race is over, disorder erupts when participants return to their everyday identities from their ludic counterparts. First, Achilles acknowledges Diomedes as the winner but decides, in an unexpected move, to award second prize to Eumelus, who finishes last. According to a ludic rationale – its special sense of time, space, and agency – this is not a logical move; but Homer tells us that Achilles performed it because he "felt compassion when he saw Eumelus" (*ton de idôn ôikteire*, 23.534).[58] As we've seen, compassion's rationality derives from understanding the subjective sense of a "world" to which Eumelus has privileged access. It emerges from a perception that is Eumelus' own, namely, that his excellence as a horseman prior to the race (noted at 23.289, 536, and 546) deserves recognition despite current results.

Now, Hammer stresses Achilles' capacity here for compassion as emblematic of "a process of public decision-making, in which contending claims are made and must be mediated" (2002: 140). And for him this characterizes the emergence of a new kind of public space typical of the city-state. Ideologically speaking, is Achilles' gesture consistent with the big man/chieftain redistribution of prestate communities or

[57] On liminality see Turner 1995: 95–130. Cf. Redfield's characterization of the funeral games as "midway between games and ritual" (1975: 262, n. 78) and his emphasis on how "conditioned" they were by rules, unlike combat (210).

[58] Achilles' unpredictable move, consistent with a joint action, is explained by cognitive psychology and discourse analysis as essential to good storytelling: of Achilles' decision to award Eumelus second prize, Minchin says, "It is the unpredictable element and the working out of its consequences that catches our interest" (2001: 65).

with the nascent city-state? Notice that it is Achilles who articulates this silent plea on Eumelus' behalf, validating the worth of the man's reputation, his consistent garnering of *timê* and his personal identity as a horseman over time. Curiously Homer quickly indicates that this judgment, although coming from Achilles, wins the consensus of all those present (539): in other words, as an adjudicating *basileus*, Achilles orchestrates the communicative action of an accolade by "ventrilo-quizing" Eumelus' self-presentation and co-opting his freedom to give his own reasons for deserving a prize. In so doing Achilles also short-circuits any chance at debate among spectators, who mimic through approval their leader's gesture.

A few moments earlier while the race was still in progress and its outcome very much unknown, Achilles had more dramatically com-promised the Achaean crowd's expression of opinion in judging the results. A spontaneous debate breaks out between Idomeneus and the lesser Ajax about the likely winner (448–87). Since it's conducted among the "Achaean leaders and counselors," who are addressed as *philoi* (457), the discussion approximates a *boulê* of the elite. Following the dynam-ics of a joint action, it quickly escalates to insults, which each man uses to impugn the other's rhetorical skills of thinking and reasoning until a full-blown physical confrontation (*eris*) is about to erupt (490). Achilles intervenes to upbraid both of them for such "unseemly" con-duct (493), and his rationale for stifling this expression of opinion by a group of peers derives once again from the intersubjective perspective he imposes on them: "You'd reproach someone else who behaved this way" (494). So in both instances it is the leader's superior intelligence which induces a healing emotion and good sense in his public: while the intersubjectivity may appeal to us as a civic virtue, the dynamic more resembles a chieftain's mode of consensus formation than a civic one.

Not surprisingly, Antilochus, who finished second, is quick to claim he's been cheated, and so he appeals for a *dikê* (542). He argues in effect that the rules of competition established by the ludic frame require that only he be awarded second prize; for Antilochus, reality outside the ludic frame is irrelevant and Achilles' compassion for Eumelus constitutes an "illegal" switch of ontological frames. Note, however, that in his protest he suggests a solution that draws upon another activity within the *basileus'* traditional repertoire of prestige-building interactions, gift-giving through redistribution:

> And at this point he would have given him [Eumelus] the horse – the
> Achaeans approved it – had Antilochus, son of great-hearted Nestor,
> not stood up to answer Achilles son of Peleus by calling for a dikê:
> "Achilles, I'll become very angry with you if you enforce what you say.
> You plan to take my prize away because you figure that, even though his
> chariot and swift horses did their damage, he himself is nevertheless a
> man of quality [esthlos]. . . .
> . . . But if you feel compassion for him and cherish him in your heart,
> your hut has plenty of gold, bronze and livestock as well as slave women
> and horses with solid hooves. So pick out from them some better prize to
> give him, either later or right away, so that the Achaeans will approve."
> (540–44; 548–52)

As the ultimate referee and judge Achilles defuses a potentially explosive joint action to produce the straightest *dikê* possible. He accepts Antilochus' claim to second prize as well as his suggestion that he find a new prize for Eumelus. In effect Achilles' judicial wisdom and authority enable him to occupy the subjective positions of both competitors, both inside and outside the ludic frame, outlining for Homer's audience an intersubjective link between them. He creates two second prizes to symbolize an equal measure of *timê* for both: Antilochus for today, Eumelus for the accumulated *timê* of past occasions. He thereby forges a consensual solution to the problem of whether an individual's social identity changes significantly due to fluctuations in *timê* by cornering all possible objective, normative and subjective perspectives on the question. Displaying cognitive and communicative versatility, he adumbrates a universal moral consciousness for the Achaean community – and in the process demonstrates how self-transformative the role of judicial *basileus* can be, for in his present capacity he hardly resembles the intransigent disputant of Books 1 and 9.

It's no coincidence, however, that Achilles achieves this through the economic transaction of gift-giving. The games themselves, for all their ludic, quasi-ritual organization, mask an important redistributive occasion: as Redfield underscored it, these games "use up property" (*aethloisi ktereize*, 23.646) by redistributing the dead man's goods as prizes in an organized set of reciprocal relations between the mourners (here Achilles) and the competitors (the Achaean elite) (1975: 205–6). From a functional perspective there is no difference between a winner's claim to a prize from Patroclus' treasure trove and Achilles' decision to give a gift from his hut as a supplementary prize; in both instances Achilles plays the center whose wealth creates prestige for himself and reasserts his position atop a hierarchy when he recognizes *timê* in others. A generous spirit in performing adjudication can thus bring lucrative rewards to all parties. So the rosy glow of social solidarity emanating from Antilochus' "prudent," conciliatory suggestion and from Achilles' "affectionate" acceptance camouflages two self-interested acts: Antilochus preserves his own new status as a winner, and the higher-ranking chief reasserts superiority over a younger colleague.[59] That this resolution, acceptable to all and conforming to tradition, enables both elites to achieve self-interested gains, tempers Hammer's overstatement that the disputes over this race illustrate a new "recognition" by leaders that they must operate "in a [public] space constituted by others" (2002: 143).

---

[59] On Antilochus' tact and prudence, see Minchin 2001: 66, and Redfield 1975: 208.

TRACK TWO: ANTILOCHUS AND MENELAUS

The major dispute and *dikê* over a prize in the chariot race, however, is the second. It erupts between Antilochus and the man he beats for second place, Menelaus. Here we learn crucial information about the dispute's genesis prior to the race, when old Nestor advises his son Antilochus to compensate for a slow team of horses and lack of driving experience by using cunning skill (*mêtis*) in his racing strategy. Applying this advice, Antilochus in a daring move cuts off Menelaus, almost forcing him off the track. At the collection of prizes, Menelaus is outraged and accuses Antilochus of winning unfairly through cunning (*dolos*, 585 and *mêtis*, 590) rather than true skill (*aretê*, 578):[60]

> *Antilochus, look what you've done, though until now you've shown good sense. You ruined my display of skill, you fouled my horses, you cut in front with your own – and they really are far inferior. Come now, Argive leaders and advisors, render a* dikê *openly and fairly. . . .*
>
> *. . . No, why don't I render the* dikê *myself, and I claim that none of the Danaans will challenge me on it: it will be straight. Come here then, Antilochus, descended from gods, this is according to* themis: *stand in front of the horses and chariot, take hold of the thin whip with your hands, the one you used to drive them forward, and grab onto the horses. Then swear by the god who holds and shakes the earth that you did not voluntarily use deceit to tie up my chariot.* (23.570–74; 579–85)

In this second *dikê* Menelaus' high rank precludes turning to Achilles as arbiter and judge; instead, he formally takes the symbol of authority, the staff (*skêptron*), and summons the Argive elite to engage publicly (and perhaps competitively) in a *dikê* between the two of them. In effect he draws on chiefly prerogative to convene an assembly on the spot, as indicated by his formulaic address, "Come now, Argive leaders

---

[60] See Gagarin's helpful discussion of this dispute (1992: 67–68).

and advisors, render a *dikê* openly and fairly. . . ." (574). This initiates a procedure for dispute settlement more or less resembling the one depicted on Achilles' shield. Menelaus launches his accusation sharply and succinctly, concerned that his claim to second prize *not* appear to rest on his past reputation for outstanding skill (*aretê*) and his chieftain's power (*biê*) prior to the race (578). In other words he seems to endorse the priority of the reality within the ludic frame.

Before the Argive leaders can even begin to hear Antilochus' self-defense, Menelaus, true to a joint action's unpredictability, suddenly scuttles the communal attempt at a *dikê* in favor of a personally engineered one: "No, why don't I render the *dikê* myself . . ." (*ei d'ag' egôn autos dikasô* . . . 579). This, he implies, will result in a swifter, more certain proof of his accusation and will indeed be recognized by all as the best possible solution (580), and consistent with age-old custom (*themis*, 581).[61] Menelaus challenges Antilochus to stand in front of his horses and chariot, touching the horses and his whip, and to swear an oath to Poseidon that he did not intentionally (*hekôn*) use deceptive tactics (*dolos*) to impede Menelaus (582–85). This oath raises a number of questions: Why does Menelaus substitute this personally constructed path to dispute settlement over the communal one? Why does the speech genre of the oath satisfy everyone as the perfect solution? Is there a substantial difference between the two solutions?

To answer the second question first, we should turn again to Thür's persuasive argument that in early Greece "magistrates" (*basileis* or elders) like those portrayed on Achilles' shield did not decide on the substantive issue of guilt or innocence but on the procedural issue of which party was to swear what sort of oath to which deity (1996: 61ff.). As

---

[61] Carawan sees Menelaus' insistence on rendering a *dikê* himself as the "right" of the top-ranking *basileus* there (1998: 52). Vos sees Menelaus' commandeering of legal procedure and oath challenge as privileges *themis* grants a *basileus* (1979: 8–9).

we've also seen, Sealey and Carawan endorse this reconstruction, with Sealey insisting that "a *dikê* is not a judgment" but a "mode of proof" (1994: 101). Likewise, in the dispute between Menelaus and Antilochus, Menelaus' original intention to convene the Argive leaders to render a *dikê* would also have produced a number of oath suggestions as well as discussion about which disputant would be challenged to swear it. In effect, then, there is no substantial difference between Menelaus' first and second paths to a settlement. He decides only that the case is clear enough (Thür 1996: 65), or his standing sufficiently superior (Sealey 1994: 93–94; Carawan 1998: 52) to skip group discussion and proceed directly to the foregone conclusion that he be the one to word an oath for his opponent. Thür says, ". . . the two *dikazein* in this text seem to harmonize best if we assume that the other leaders [would have] formulated oaths, too, as Menelaus did. An oath according to the *dikazein* sworn by one of the litigants would have settled the dispute" (1996: 66).

But how does cognitive virtuosity in the composition of an oath restore a proper reciprocal recognition of *timê* between litigants? We've recognized the oath as a speech genre built from three simpler speech genres, which in turn trigger a series of ontological switches. Each oath enacts a ritual imperative in a manner analogous to trial by ordeal or by combat.[62] Through its invocation an oath calls divine attention to human affairs; through its content ("I swear to . . .") and imprecation ("May *x* happen to me if I swear falsely") it invites its human participants to switch ontological frames by using chronotopes to see the circumstances of their mundane dispute through the lens of a heroic

---

[62] On Homeric oaths see Sealey 1994: 95–100; at 106–7 he draws the connection to trial by battle and by ordeal. See Gernet 1981: 190, where the oath and the ordeal are said to be "governed" by "the same mode of thought." Elsewhere he proposes that trial by battle and oath swearing preceded the use of voting to settle disputes: originally the number of combatants or oath swearers each side could produce determined the issue; later, oath swearing itself became a mode of proof (2001: 104–5).

world where divine agents regularly intervene in human affairs. As ritual, oaths reconfigure petty human disputes in cosmic and heroic terms because, when human efforts fail, they insist that the gods activate their superior capacity for proper apportionment.[63] That is why oaths provide a favored device for reenacting *themis*.

Cognitively speaking, then, and within the context of a joint action, oath challenges provide a performative "diversion" because, as Antilochus demonstrated in his dispute with Menelaus, the very prospect of using an oath to switch frames and embroil divine agents in human affairs can shift litigants away from a self-interested understanding of their dispute and toward its reevaluation.[64] Menelaus' challenge compels Antilochus to revise in at least three ways his understanding of the importance of the *timê* he has just won. As we've seen, the older chief seems to insist on the importance of his achievement in the current occasion rather than, as with Eumelus, on his accumulated reputation. Why? In his wording of the oath, the key word *hekôn* ("voluntarily") forces Antilochus to accept personal responsibility for his action in the race, admitting in effect that it was deceit and not chance which caused Menelaus' chariot to falter. This admission confirms Menelaus' skill in the race just run.[65]

---

[63] Gernet (1981) sees the oath as a ritual intended to: communicate with "the other world" (170); alter the participants' relationship "in the world beyond" (172); and send (as an ordeal) one or both "to another world, where their destinies are played out" 1981 [1968] (190).

[64] Gagarin sees dispute settlement in Hesiod as a "tactful diversion" designed to move litigants and spectators toward consensus (*paraiphamenoi* at *Th.* 90 and *paretrape*, 103), parallel to Homeric poetry as an "effective diversion" to please an audience (1992: 66).

[65] See Sealey on voluntary action in oaths (1994: 94–95), B. Williams on the importance of terms like *hekôn* and *aitios* for Greek notions of responsibility (1993: 50–74), and Rickert (1989; cited by Sealey) on Greek terms for voluntary and involuntary actions (1989). See also more general discussions by Gernet 2001: 350ff., and Cantarella 2003: 253–74.

But at the same time this admission of responsibility reminds Antilochus that this recent boost in his standing within a ludic frame cannot compare to a lifetime of such achievements by Menelaus. Again, like Achilles adjudicating the previous dispute over the same prize, both present and past acquisitions of *timê* are validated, both inside and outside the ludic frame, along with the continuity of Menelaus' social identity as an outstanding chief.[66] Lastly the oath offered to Antilochus invokes the horse god Poseidon to project a shadow over any number of future, horse-related actions the young man might undertake. As B. Williams suggests, when no specific cause is apparent for the outcome of human actions in Homer, divine interventions frequently "operate in place of those hidden causes" (1993: 32). Were he to swear falsely, Antilochus would acquire a lifetime of divine explanations for future mishaps "at Poseidon's hands."

In the world of Homer's audience oaths work as a conclusion to problematic joint actions because they enclose the dispute in a heroic time and space where divine and human agents interact. This ritual imperative to negotiate a *dikê* serves the human participants as a catalyst to form consensual understanding on the purely religious grounds that anyone should fear the prospect of retribution from superhuman agents as an explanation for his misfortunes. Oaths bind and constrain future human actions because they sustain the belief that heroic chronotopes from the poetic tradition can without warning absorb human agents engaged in real life scripts or chronotopes. Through an oath an individual permits his identity to acquire in effect a double ontological dimension, operating simultaneously within the frames of everyday reality and heroic tales. Oaths thus serve the judicial chief who wields them not only to resolve dangerous joint actions through consensual

---

[66] Again, contra Hammer (2002: 143), reconciliation confirms the elder *basileus'* status.

understanding but also to project this cognitive solution away from himself and the participants and onto divine agents.[67]

And so Antilochus quickly resolves the dispute by backing down from the challenge to swear an oath, blames himself for youthful impetuousness, and recognizes Menelaus' superior rank. He offers to give Menelaus the prize mare and then, as earlier with Achilles, tries to establish a gift-exchange relationship with Menelaus, this time casting himself as the giver to confirm his inferior status as a *basileus*-in-the-making:

> *Stop now – I'm far younger than you, Lord Menelaus, and you're older and more accomplished than I. You know what results when a young man's out of control. His mind runs away with him, but his wisdom is slim. So let your heart bear with me. I myself will give you a horse, this mare. And if you asked for something better, then I'd wish right away to give it to you, a man descended from gods, rather than fall from your favor ever after and be sinful in the eyes of spirits. (587–95)*

As did Achilles, Menelaus finds this offer impossible to refuse, and so he forgives Antilochus on account of his youth and his noble family, and then seals the harmony by reversing the suggested gift exchange so that he himself becomes the giver. He converts the prize mare into a gift for Antilochus, almost redundantly reasserting his superiority as a very high ranking *basileus*. Once again I suggest that Homer's narration sentimentalizes the gesture as a display of affection in order to deflect attention away from its economic, self-interested motivation.[68]

---

[67] I agree with Minchin on a literal level when she claims that this dispute is settled "without mediation and without divine intervention" (2001: 68), but the oath shows that it would not have been settled without the *threat* of divine intervention.

[68] Minchin characterizes the resolution as a display of why Menelaus is "so well-loved by the Achaeans" due to his "appreciation of the efforts on his behalf of other, more capable, men and his readiness to acknowledge in public his gratitude" (2001: 69).

This combination of an oath challenge accompanied by reciprocal and redistributive gift giving in rendering a *dikê* therefore conjures up a collective misapprehension among the actors and spectators of the performance. Through it the mythologically grounded lifeworld of a premodern society is able to preserve its norms and their narratively based rationales – its understanding of *themis*, in short. We are now in a better position to understand how fundamentally this preservation of *themis* relies on the judicial *basileus*' authority to structure the relations and ranks of others from his position at the pinnacle of a social hierarchy and at the center of a redistributive network. It is crucial to these two roles, moreover, that he resort to the diversion of ontological frame-switching in order to assume responsibility for – to hijack, really – the autonomy of both individuals and the community at large when producing consensus.

TRACK THREE: NESTOR AND ACHILLES

How closely is the *basileus*' authority to recognize the *timê* of others and function as the center of a redistributive exchange system linked to the bard's skill at epic storytelling? The third settlement of a dilemma at the "collection of prizes" after the chariot race provides an answer; it also returns us to Tandy's hypothesis that in the eighth century *basileis* and bards colluded in sharing a special kind of knowledge based on access to community memory. In Track One we see how deftly Achilles the judge faces the delicate question of recognizing Eumelus' and Antilochus' *timê* with a symbolic prize. But when one prize remains unclaimed, he graciously – and unexpectedly – extends this form of tribute to old Nestor, awarding him a prize not for competing but, in fact, because he can no longer compete (23.615–23).[69] The prize thus

---

[69] While this prize is not conferred as part of a *dikê* in the sense of resolving a dispute, it does constitute a *dikê* in the related sense of a privilege or right, a "portion"

recognizes and recalls to everyone the old man's athletic prowess in his younger days. Nestor gratefully accepts the award, but then, as though on cue, completes this joint action with Achilles and the spectators by performing verbally what the prize achieves silently: he tells a narrative recounting his successful competition two generations earlier at the funeral games the Epeians gave Amarynceus (23.624–50).

Nestor's excursus into this personal exploit permits him to present himself to other elites and to provoke them, through a sign, to recollect and recognize his athletic achievements and his standing.[70] It also resembles a short narrative that an accomplished poet might have incorporated into a fuller account of Nestor's heroic life – in Homeric diction, his *klea andrôn* (Nagy 1990: 202). More particularly it resembles an *oimê* (song) that a poet could, according to one etymology, stitch together in the manner of a rhapsode to form a longer epic narrative or, according to another etymology, embark on as a poetic path to a new theme. And so, just as judicial *basileis* were entrusted with establishing "strands" or "paths" of adjudication when disputes arose, so were bards (*aoidoi*) and rhapsodes entrusted with the task of demonstrating an individual's *timê* through songs (*oimai*) representing "strands" or "paths" of song. In both etymologies, the *oimê* triggers an ontological switch for poet and audience.[71]

---

someone deserves in his or her "proper place in the order of the universe" (Sealey 1994: 139–40). Gagarin (1992: 68) implies that Achilles confers this prize on Nestor because he was cheated of one years before in the chariot race at the games for Amarynceus (23.638–42).

[70] See Nagy's discussion of the term *sêma* in Homer as a cue to prompt recognition, including its use in Nestor's instructions to Antilochus just before the race and its connection to the poetic memory of his youthful achievement (1983: 40, 51); more broadly, see Barnouw 2004: 259–90 and 319–45. Gagarin sees a connection between poetry and adjudication in the speech act Nestor uses in Book 1's dispute between Achilles and Agamemnon, but he does not note the connection here.

[71] See Nagy 1996: 63–64, Ford 1992: 40–48, Bakker 1997a: 60–61, and Rubin 1995: 62.

What Are *Themistes* and *Thesmia*? How Are They Linked?

Epic poets encourage faith in the judicial *basileus*' ability to invoke the world of divine wrath and punishment when they locate mythological prototypes for this judicial figure in heroic narratives. In terms of cognitive discourse analysis, the poets evoke the script "rendering a *dikê*" within a fixed scenario that intermingles the divine, heroic, and everyday, human worlds. In addition to the figure of Minos (*Od*.11.568ff.), whom we'll discuss in Chapter 3, divine apportioners of *timê* in Homer and Hesiod haunt both the Olympian and chthonic otherworlds, always and everywhere on guard against the breaking of oaths.[72] Hesiod likewise believes that gods and the spirits of deceased humans served as "apportioners" (*daimones*) watching over humans, especially when disputes were settled (*dikai*) and evil deeds committed.[73] These poetically evoked scripts of divine retribution certainly make more rational the notion that the gods, inevitably and without warning, can inflict misery on humans, but Hesiod provides (at *WD* 121–26) a clue to how these "apportioners" may have originated in historical, everyday reality when he concludes his description of the men of the Golden Age:

---

[72] At *Il*.3.276–80 and 297–301 both elite leaders and common soldiers are very aware of punishment for breaking the oaths they are about to swear just before the duel between Menelaus and Paris, itself akin to trial by combat (Sealey 1994: 106–7). See also *Il*.19.258–65 for the Olympian and chthonic deities (the Erinyes) who punish forswearers. Hesiod sees similar deities or wicked humans wielding this retribution at *WD* 190–94, 219, 282–85, 803–4, and *Th*. 231–32.

[73] For the etymology linking *daimones* to apportionment (*daiomai*), see West 1978. See *WD* 267–69, where Zeus watches over *dikê*, a function West connects with guardianship over oaths (1978). At *WD* 121–26 Hesiod identifies the deceased men of the Golden Age as *daimones* guarding over men, and at 254–55 he warns the *basileis* who produce *dikai* that 30,000 immortals watch over the settling of *dikai*. Not coincidentally, when Antilochus comes to his senses and refuses to swear the oath Menelaus composed for him at *Il*.23.582–85, he claims he does not want to appear "sinful" to *daimones* (... *daimosi einai alitros*, 595).

> *And then when Earth in fact covered over that race, they ended up as*
> *holy spirits above ground, as noble protectors and guardians of mortal*
> *humans. They range over the land clothed in mist, watching over the*
> *settling of* dikai *and criminal activity and providing wealth. This is a*
> *special reward for* basileis.

Their nobility, an earthbound rather than celestial nature, a role as guardians of mortals, the capacity to bestow wealth (fertility), and judicial-moral supervision all characterize privileges granted the Early Iron Age's community elder or chief, his *geras basilêion*.[74] But why should only *basileis* among humans have access to divine knowledge about apportionment? I suggest it's because they alone possessed in each village community the accumulated experience of generations of dispute settlement; they alone therefore had the privilege of turning to these spirits of Golden Age humans as "models of mimesis" (in Nagy's sense) for settling disputes.[75] What the spirits "watch over" or "preserve" (*phulakes*, 123; *phulassein*, 124) is the community's memory of previous cases, decisions, and oath formulae, a treasure-trove of information thought in retrospect to be divine and external to the human agents who over time created it.

In a fixed script of judicial performance this privileged cognitive talent enabled these leaders to switch ontological frames, using chronotopes to glide among tales of gods and men, their community's memory of disputes, and the conflicting, dialogical positions of the dispute at hand. In effect this knowledge imparted to them a versatile, sophisticated bifocalism or trifocalism when examining complex human

---

[74] West attributes their supervision over justice (*dikai*) and criminal acts (vv. 124–25) to an interpolation from vv. 254–55 (1978).

[75] As mentioned above, according to Gagarin, "There is no indication . . . that in Hesiod's time the *basileis* have any other public function than that of judging" (1992: 63). Edwards also points out their "exclusively. . . judicial role" in Hesiod's world (2004: 64–66).

affairs.[76] While oaths were no doubt instrumental in deploying this multiple vision, we may wonder whether the Greeks had a name for the performative act itself when the *basileus* displayed this cognitive ability to conjure, probe, and navigate multiple realities and then return to the issue at hand with the "correct" oath solution. So far we've identified a number of speech genres in the performance of a *dikê*: the litigants' use of assertion, denial, threat, accusation, boast, and so on, and one major genre, the oath formulated by the *basileus*. There is one term, however, designating an exclusive possession of gods and *basileis*, which presumes the capacity to comprehend these minor genres and then trump them in rendering a *dikê* through whatever speech genres are needed to persuade others to accept it.

In Homer this term is *themistes*. It's most often translated broadly as the plural of *themis* to mean something like "traditional rules and customs" or more restrictedly as a "collection of *themis*" in the sense of rules or laws.[77] But its meaning is, I think, more complex, referring to what one does in order to see how to achieve "what is *themis*" (*hê themis esti*). The term occurs six times as a possession or privilege of the *basileus* bestowed by Zeus along with the staff (*skêptron*) that metonymically indicates its performance when rendering a *dikê*, providing counsel (*bouleuô, boulê*), or proffering an oath (*horkos*) in public assembly (*agora*).[78] Its absence strikes Homer four times as an index of cognitive

---

[76] Whether settling disputes in Homer or according to the Gortyn Law Code, the *basileus'* role, Carawan claims, was "to reconcile the hostile parties; each is to recognize the claims of the other, thus disavowing the cycle of vendetta that would inevitably arise if one side were faced with an unacceptable outcome" (1998: 61).

[77] See Gagarin (1992: 75) and Westbrook (1992: 66–67). Vos defines *themistes* as "not only rights and privileges belonging to a position but also the rules for legal proceedings, the unwritten laws [*Gesetze*]." They constitute a "'body of principles' for administering justice that were not sufficiently known to everyone" (1979: 9). Gernet calls them "divine decisions – inspired by Zeus – by the head of a *genos*" (2001: 24).

[78] *Themistes* + *skêptron* occurs at *Il.*1.238 (with *dikê* and *horkos*); 2.206 (with *bouleuô* and *agora*); 9.99 (with *bouleuô*); 9.156 and 298; and at *Od.*11.569 (with *dikê*). At *Il.*16.387,

inadequacy – either a personal lack of social sense when relating to others, or a people's inability to display public intelligence in assembly or with counsels.[79] But a particularly telling use occurs (at *Od*.16.403), when Homer describes Amphinomus, the only one of Penelope's suitors with redeemable moral qualities. When the suitors learn that Telemachus has returned safely from his journey to Pylos and Sparta, Antinous, their ringleader, proposes to assassinate the young chief-in-the-making. Amphinomus then rises to speak as "the man whose speaking [*muthoisi*] pleased Penelope the most because he possessed a noble frame of mind [*phresin . . . agathêsin*]." He addresses the suitors with good intentions [*euphroneôn*] (16.397–99):

> "Comrades, I have no desire to murder Telemachus. – it's a terrible thing
> to kill someone born of chieftain stock [genos basilêion]. First let's seek the
> gods' counsels [boulas]. If the themistes of mighty Zeus advise [ainêsôsi]
> it, I myself will murder him and urge on everyone else. But if the gods
> turn us from this course [apotrôpôsi], then I say hold back." (16.401–405)

Most of the semantic elements clustered around the *themistes* are present in this scene: their connection to Zeus, to public speaking and specifically to the speech genre of counsel, and their indication of proper, intelligent thinking. This script does not, however, concern an actual *dikê*, nor are the suitors engaged in the script "rendering a *dikê*." Zeus' *themistes* therefore are not restricted to judicial decisions. On what occasion(s) then may a *basileus* display or enact them in

---

"crooked" *themistes* (with *dikê* and *agora*) are produced by the judgment (*krinô*) of men who ignore the gods. Zeus' name appears in nine of the fifteen occurrences of *themistes*.

[79] At *Il*.5.761 Hera characterizes Ares as "senseless" (*aphrona*) and "knowing nothing" (*ou tina oide*) of *themistes*, while at *Od*.9.215 Polyphemus is said to be knowledgeable (*eidota*) neither of *dikê* nor *themistes*. The race of Cyclopes have no public assemblies (*agora*), counsels (*boulê*), or *themistes* (*Od*.9.112); each head of household administers his own family disputes (*themisteuei*), ignoring the other households (9.114).

performance? Homer himself tells us how they manifest themselves to humans through his use of the verb *aineô*. Following Nagy, this verb and its noun (*ainos*) designate in Greek poetics an "authoritative speech . . . an affirmation, a marked speech-act, made by and for a marked social group" (1990: 31). Among other characteristics, it creates a "social contract" between speaker (or poet) and listeners, for it functions as a code comprehensible only to those smart enough, refined enough, or allied closely enough, to understand it.[80]

These insights return us to the meanings of *themis* discussed earlier and explain further how one individual's vision of consensus can be embraced by all. The *basileus* who performs *themistes* receives and understands a coded message from the gods that potentially defines a morally upright community linking gods to humans. As a performer, his challenge must have been to make this coded message comprehensible and cogent to his listeners. Significantly Amphinomus' speech (*muthos*) does persuade the suitors, at least for the moment. More importantly, his use here of both *themistes* and *aineô* on a nonjudicial occasion foregrounds a key element that is only implicit in all the other Homeric references to *themistes:* by revealing to whoever exercises *themistes* the will or counsel of the gods, they are oracular. Like oracles *themistes* convey a *basileus'* mind to the gods' transcendent perspective, which includes past, present and future, and they inspire this *basileus*, also called an *istôr* on Achilles' shield (18.501) – "he who sees beyond what others see," in Nagy's phrase – to convince those who lack this second sight.[81]

---

[80] Nagy 1990: 148, and 1979: 237–41, where the word's links to intelligence (*phroneô*) are indicated. Despite his good sense, Amphinomus never follows up his suggestion that the suitors consult the gods, nor does he comprehend the *ainos* or riddle Odysseus, disguised as the old beggar, offers him to save himself from the impending slaughter (18.125–50).

[81] See Gernet on the oracular nature of *themis* (1981: 189–90). Vos explains *themistes* here as Zeus' way of expressing his will through "laws" (*Gesetze*) difficult for humans to know but which the god, as an *istôr*, can know (1979: 19). *Istôr*, derived from *oida*

Themistes may therefore be enacted at any human assembly deliberating the best course of action, and they are strictly performative or
illocutionary in the sense that to articulate them is to claim the authoritative utterance of a human who knows how to consult the gods to
discover how they understand a human interaction. As was suggested
in discussing *themis*, "what the gods know" is what will in retrospect
be evident to all as the most advantageous course for the community
to have taken. If we are on the right track, then the performance of
themistes in this general, deliberative, and illocutionary sense should be
more familiar to us than we may realize. Of their connection to "royal"
justice in Homer, Schofield observes that in a war story like the *Iliad*,
far from normal community life, "one would not expect to see [*basileis*]
at work administering the *themistes*." But if, as he insists, "the bare idea
of kings [*basileis*] using good judgement in the dispensation of justice"
was at home both in eighth-century society and in Homer's imaginary
heroic world, then *themistes* and *euboulia* ("good judgment," "excellent
counsel") should be everywhere inseparable in Homeric and Hesiodic
poetry (1986: 12).

   How can the meanings of these two terms be so intertwined? As
already noted, Schofield persuasively argues that *euboulia* is a "preeminent virtue of the Homeric chieftain" that may garner for him
almost as much *timê* as prowess in battle (9, 13–16). And even though
none of these six meetings formally enacts the script "seeking/rendering
a *dikê*," each provides an occasion where, as in a *dikê*, disputing

---

(I have seen, I know), literally means "the one who knows," and in the dispute on
Achilles' shield it designates either the *basileus* who actually settles the dispute or
one who sets its terms (Cantarella 2003: 286; cf. Thür 1996: 68–69). Nagy connects
his seeing with oracular vision (1990: 259–60), but the word can also designate the
basileus as "witness" to an oath or wager (Carawan 1998: 61–62). These two meanings
of *istôr* meet in the ability to switch ontological frames and see the here and now in
terms of a transcendent reality.

individuals compete for a redistribution of *timê* before their peers that is subject to the sanction of a dominant *basileus* whose display of *euboulia* forges consensus. In addition Schofield attributes to *euboulia* another quality, which we evoked earlier, and which now clarifies its link to *themistes*: the ability to understand a present situation in terms of both the past and the future, to introduce to deliberation a "point of view *external*" to the heroic code's fix on *aretê* and *timê* (16, emphasis in the original). This is what we see judicial *basileis* doing when they demonstrate through *themistes* an uncanny "oracular" knowledge to trump opposing arguments with a vision of how things will turn out for the best. A good counselor, Schofield says, must be able to manipulate both reason and the emotions to be persuasive, ". . . but at the same time he must usually be right. He must concentrate on what is to be done now, but this will involve drawing on past experience and thinking about the future" (16.) The "past" and "future" in question more often than not require switching frames temporally *and* ontologically, retrojecting elements of a current debate back into community memory and heroic myth and forward through prophetic insight into divine knowledge.

The third quality of *euboulia* that *themistes* incorporate likewise returns us to the disputes already discussed. We saw how the compassion Achilles felt for Eumelus when he performed poorly in the chariot race – unreasonable in the logic of competitive game-playing – did introduce a reason to honor him anyway because of past successes, a reason based on Eumelus' privileged access to a subjective reality. And the crowd's acclamation of this gesture confirmed an intersubjective relation linking competitors, judge, and spectators. In the same way, Schofield argues, a display of *euboulia* sometimes invites disputants to examine the conflict from their adversary's position – most notably in *Iliad* 1, when Nestor attempts to render a *dikê* for Agamemnon and Achilles: "Achilles and Agamemnon are invited to think not just of themselves and their own honour (*timê*), but of

the other man's point of view, and what *his* position or situation entitles *him* to expect."[82]

The reasonableness of *euboulia* and *themistes* are thus one and the
same in embracing objective, normative and subjective perspectives
in order to generate consensus in a communicative action. *Themistes*,
we might say, enact the abstract quality of *euboulia*, usually through a
basileus' performance of narrative speech genres that switch temporal
and ontological frames in search of a performative solution, sometimes
prompting him to compose the "right" oath to the "right" deity for the
"right" litigant to swear, and sometimes enabling him to recall from
community memory an event, exemplum or prophecy of paradigmatic
significance for the present dilemma. In all cases, before their performance, *themistes* offer the illocutionary, authoritative assurance based
on past experience that *euboulia* will emerge; after their performance,
they are recognized by the consensus of a successful communicative
action.[83]

When performing *themistes* includes the script "rendering a *dikê*,"
we can be more precise about the secret at the core of the *basileus'*
privileged, "oracular" knowledge of past and future, and his ability to
"hijack" the autonomy of litigants and spectators. As Thür suggested,
"To settle disputes, the authorities of the early polis must have kept
in their minds a considerable repertory of oath formulae" (1996: 69).

---

[82] 1986: 28; Schofield points to similar reasoning used by Odysseus when he attempts
to reconcile Agamemnon and Achilles at 19.181–83.

[83] At *Il*.9.155–56 we see harmony resulting when a *basileus'* judgment will in retrospect
be deemed "correct" by followers. Agamemnon promises Achilles seven communities who will "honor him [*timêsousin*] like a god and will fulfill [*teleousi*] the shining
themistes he performs with his scepter." That is, these followers will "bring to pass"
(*telousi*) Achilles' advice or judgment by carrying it out as a policy or settlement
with which all are in accord. Cf. the more usual interpretation that the followers
will carry out the "ordinances" in deference to a superior (e.g., Griffin 1995: 93 or
Vos 1979: 5).

This had to be a legal memory bank in the form of a complex speech genre preserving oral records of successful settlements in a community's past, not unlike the mini-narrative of Meleager embedded in *Iliad* 9 by Phoenix to persuade Achilles. We have no precise name for such a speech genre, but as oral records they would have been narratively reduced versions of litigants' self-presentations and status assertions, and they would have been organized through a mnemonics linking categories of crime (such as "themes," "scripts," strands or paths of song) to oath formulae.[84] Our knowledge of the prehistory of Greek legal procedure identifies the end product of such an oral speech genre in literate form as *thesmia*, which most scholars understand through Aristotle's use of the term (at *Ath.Pol.*3.4 and 16.10) to be, in Ostwald's words, "records of judicial proceedings, embodying either the decisions rendered in each case or the principles underlying particular decisions" (1969: 174–75).[85]

If this prehistory of *thesmia* is accurate, *basileis* produced them at the point where an oral, communal memory grounded in heroic chronotopes dovetailed with a more literate sort of memory containing

[84] For Havelock, "All types of information stored in the oral repertoire are thus likely to be cast in narrative form. . . ." Legal regulations provide the best example: "in order to frame a legal directive, a situation is conceived and stated, cast in the form of an event or an action by a given agent, not in the form of a general principle within which a given case might fall" (1978: 43). To me this describes the first step in constructing oral *thesmia*; but before achieving written form, a *thesmion's* action and agent should be narratively reduced in favor of an abstract interaction and principle. E.g., *Ath.Pol.*16.10 quotes or paraphrases a possibly Draconian law on tyranny: its preamble declares it one of "the *thesmia* and ancestral traditions of the Athenians." It states: "If any men rise up to attempt a tyranny, or if anyone cooperates in setting up a tyranny, he and his descent group shall be outlawed [*atimon*]." Cf. the probable *thesmion* at the Hesiodic *Catalogue of Women* 43(a).41–43, which will be discussed in Chapter 3.

[85] See also Ruzé 1992: 87; Gagarin 1981b: 71–72, who understands *thesmia* as "written notes or records of at least some . . . important decisions for use in future cases" (72); and Rhodes 1981, *ap.* 3.4, who is uncertain whether Aristotle understands the term this way.

chronotopes that were civic, post-heroic and (for us) more historically recoverable. As a result, *thesmia* seem to us to form a transitional
stage in the development of written laws (*thesmoi* and later *nomoi*). In a
community's orally transmitted memory, judicial *basileis* would have
recomposed and reorganized *thesmia* relevant to the dispute at hand
as they performed *themistes*.[86] The *thesmia* enabled them to reperform
memorable local judgments, "returning" the community to a past that
brought them closer to the heroic age; and this may have contributed
in no small part to the persuasiveness of their *dikê*. Their performance
also had a persuasive resource in models of mimesis, such as the 30,000
"immortals" (*athanatoi*, *WD* 250) and the Golden Age *basileis* Hesiod
calls *daimones* (*WD* 122). If, as suggested, these heroic avatars "watched
over" or "preserved" (*phulakes*, *WD* 123; *phulassein*, 124) the community's memory of important cases, decisions and oath formulae,
then Aristotle understood Athens' *thesmothetai* to perform precisely
this function before Draco's legal reforms (ca. 621/20) when he
claimed, ". . . in order that, by writing down the *thesmia*, they
might preserve or protect [*phulattôsi*] them for the settling of disputes"
(*Ath.Pol.*3.4).

What would an oral *thesmion* have sounded like? In the oral stage of
their development as a speech genre, *thesmia* would have resembled the
genres that serve as building blocks for longer narratives, such as the
epic. In addition to mini-narratives like Meleager's tale "with nothing
recent in it," the "list" and "catalogue" come to mind as similar short
chunks of information stored by memory in the epic singer's repertoire.
The catalogue may be especially pertinent for comparison with *thesmia*,
for it records items (e.g., personal and place names, ships and armies)

---

[86] Vos envisions a similar process – without tying it to *thesmia* – when he sees Hesiod's
reference at *WD* 221 to judges who perform *themistes* by "rendering crooked *dikai*"
as settlements where judges "choose from their '*Kodex*' legal requirements that are
not suitable for the concrete case" (1979: 10).

like a list but then narratively elaborates a little upon each, in effect transforming a spare script like "defeating the enemy in battle" into two or more chronotopes typical of the longer epic, like those that evoke a dying victim's family ties and homeland in time of peace. Like lists and catalogues, *thesmia* would have relied upon a "cognitive map" storing "first-level" information for retrieval (personal names and place names), and then "nesting" within them memorable acts that violated someone's *timê* and the nature of the *dikê* that redressed the imbalance.[87]

This link between oral *thesmia* and catalogues like Homer's extends even more strongly to a related poetic genre, genealogical poetry in hexameters, which is dominated by the catalogue structure. Despite its fragmentary survival under the names of Hesiod and later poets, we understand the organization and scope of this genre well enough for me to propose that poems such as the Hesiodic *Catalogue of Women* served as models on a grand scale for oral *thesmia*. We can even speculate that genealogical elements must have been included in the performance of *themistes*, for performing them and listening to genealogical songs about ancestors were both essential to the maintenance of a chieftain's authority and indispensable to his performance repertoire. So if Hesiod thought *basileis* had a special talent to "decide upon *themistes* by means of straight *dikai*," seeing analogies between the speech acts of *basileis* and bards, then the bard was necessary for a big man/chieftain to claim a heroic lineage in order to maintain his *timê* and surpass that of his rivals.[88] Both *themistes* and epic song draw on the same cognitive ability to switch ontological frames, receding by stages from the present everyday world into the recent and increasingly more remote past of heroes and gods. As West aptly said of Maori culture in this regard: "It was

[87] See Minchin's cognitive map of catalogues and lists in Homer (2001: 73–99, and 1996).

[88] On the link between genealogical poetry and a *basileus*' family status in the Late Geometric and Archaic periods, see West 1985: 8–9. Note how Nestor cites Achilles' divine genealogy to induce Agamemnon to reach a settlement (*Il*.1.280).

considered to be an essential part of the education of everyone having any pretensions to chiefdom to be able to recite his pedigree for at least 20 generations and to know the family alliances to remote degrees."[89]

As a script of early dispute settlement, "rendering a *dikê*" therefore placed a premium on the talents of the individual *basileus*, challenging him to orchestrate a suite of communicative and cognitive acts, some of which he himself performed and others which he induced litigants and supporters to perform. The tradition placed at his disposal quite a repertoire of speech genres and cognitive moves whose complexity I've tried to outline from our limited written sources. These include making authoritative, illocutionary claims to *themis*, remembering oath formulae and *thesmia*, ontological frame switching, ventriloquizing the subject positions of some participants, assuming the intersubjective perspectives of all concerned, and the ability to combine all this in a godlike display of knowledge and language called *themistes*. I've argued that such a virtuoso performance was consistent with other forms of chiefly authority and exchange upon which communities depended in the Formative period.

Now, despite the emergence in the *Iliad* of prototypical forms of citizen communication and cognition centered around Achilles, the poem's representations of dispute settlement do not really enact roles and procedures characteristic of citizen participation. Nevertheless, it is apparent that dispute settlement did undergo a transformation within a few generations of our *Iliad*'s completion, for the first written statute laws begin appearing around 640. Somehow civic magistrates and elite citizens of this age (and later) felt competent to reorganize the script "rendering a *dikê*" into arbitration proceedings and jury trials, providing themselves with the featured roles. In Chapters 3 and 4 we'll see how the virtuosity of the judicial *basileus* yielded its effectiveness to types of

---

[89] West 1985: 24. For this example West is quoting S. P. Smith 1921: 16–18.

deliberation and reasoning that reduced reliance on such techniques of consensus formation as personal claims to *themis*, ontological frame switching, oath formulae, ventriloquizing others' subject positions, and assuming the intersubjective perspective of all concerned. In Chapter 3, taking a key insight from Gernet (2001), we'll see how the script of dispute settlement could be reorganized into the jury trial only when all parties in an alleged crime understood the cognitive and moral dimensions of one type of individual's subjective, inner world: a person who is the object or victim of an injustice, specifically of the arch-crime called "hybris." Even more specifically, I'm speaking of Odysseus as the prototype for the individual citizen who suffers hybris at the hands of others – and who learns how to transform himself from a victim of injustice into an agent of justice.

3 SELF-TRANSFORMATION AND THE THERAPY OF JUSTICE IN THE *ODYSSEY*

◎▣◎

HOW WERE SCRIPTS AND AGENTS OF JUSTICE TRANSFORMED?

If the *basileus* served in the city-state's Formative period as the arch-performer of justice thanks to his privileged cognitive and communicative skills, could an ordinary citizen ever acquire these skills as an agent of justice? In Chapter 2 we saw that the *basileus*, not unlike an epic poet, demonstrated several virtuoso abilities: he put the dispute at hand into different temporal and ontological frames, one of which would trump the others; he marshaled the illocutionary force of *themis* when performing *themistes* and yoked such speech genres as the oath challenge, the exemplum, and the genealogical catalogue to the appropriate *thesmia* in community memory; he controlled the dispute as a potential joint action by hijacking the autonomy of litigants and spectators and representing to all present the subject positions of both litigants and of the community at large; and he achieved consensus by realigning the litigants' *timai* in a manner that left intact his own authority as a center of redistribution for the community. In this chapter and the next, we'll consider how, as the state's central authority grew after 700, these specialized talents of the *basileus* yielded the performance of justice to other citizen scripts and agents.

Chapter 4 will explore how lawgivers and statute law contributed to the development of the jury trial, but in this chapter I ask what sort of self the Greeks needed to imagine as the archetypal performer of these new roles and scripts of justice. It seems reasonable to infer that the judicial *basileus* of the Formative period had to undergo a self-transformation if his privileged knowledge and communicative skills were to be adapted to the capacities of citizens at large. What might such a self-transformation entail? And how would the possibility of this new self, whether real or hypothetical, enable judicial magistrates and jurors to exercise their cognitive abilities when performing the law court version of the script "rendering a *dikê*"? To replace the judicial *basileus*, magistrates and citizen juror-judges – hereafter called "jurors" – would have to retain an ability to consider a dispute under multiple temporal and ontological frames, although the nature of the frames, we'll see, had to change. Like the *basileus*, magistrates and jurors needed to speak and decide in accordance with *themis*, but instead of a virtuoso performance of *themistes* they had access to *themis* from *thesmoi*, the earliest civic laws. (These, as I will argue in Chapter 4, were the codified record of legal performances by their state's lawgiver – his most important real or imagined *themistes* and *thesmia* classified by category of offense and punishment.) Magistrates and jurors then faced the challenge of interpreting the dispute at hand in light of these abstract directives, whether written or unwritten.

Finally they had to confront the question of the litigants' autonomy. Unlike the judicial *basileus*, they did not have license to assume responsibility for the injured party's subject position as the dispute settlement unfolded. And while the jury trial, as a carefully arranged script of speech genres and subject positions, ultimately protected the autonomy of litigants and prevented the dispute from escalating out of control as a joint action, in the early Archaic period magistrates and jurors needed to enlarge their understanding of how much autonomy litigants, in particular the defendant, should exercise in thought and deed. They also had to ensure that the litigants remained within a consensual understanding of how one citizen's *timê* should relate to another's and to the community as a whole.

To provide a model for these future judicial roles and scripts, the self-transformation of the *basileus* thus required cognitive and moral changes elite citizens could comprehend, assent to, and imitate. Morally, they had to revise their understanding of human agency, especially the question of how responsible each citizen was for his own decisions and actions when he interacted with others, and what forces of luck or divine intervention lay outside his own control. This question was, as Nussbaum puts it, "central for the Greeks" throughout their tradition and remains relevant to us in our post-Kantian world (1986: 4–5). In particular, she links it to the Greeks' ethical quest to protect the self from luck or divine intervention (contingency) through a self-sufficiency grounded in rational evaluation and choice. To understand this quest, she suggests we compare how the Greeks related the ideal of autonomy to, on one hand, "external goods" like friendship, love, political action and possessions and, on the other hand, to "the more ungovernable parts of the human being's internal makeup," especially the "so-called 'irrational parts of the soul': appetites, feelings, emotions" (6–7). Self-transformation, she concludes, is crucial to this quest both for the Greeks and for ourselves: "We need to ask, then, whether a restructuring of the human being, a transformation or suppression of certain familiar parts of ourselves, could lead to greater rational control and self-sufficiency, and whether this would be the appropriate form of self-sufficiency for a rational human life" (7).

I propose that the *Odyssey* and the development of its central character Odysseus provided Greek audiences after 700 with the experience of self-transformation they needed to adopt the performance roles of judicial magistrates and jurors. But before we explore this possibility, we should consider how in recent years this same question of whether or not the self can transform itself has proven central to the debate among liberal, communitarian, and deliberative democratic notions of selfhood. As we saw in the Introduction, the crux of debate in all three theories of the autonomous self and its relation to others is this: Is the self prior to its ends and therefore free to choose them, or are its ends given by others and left to the self to discover and articulate? In his recent discussion of the liberal vs. communitarian notions of self, Kymlicka puts his finger on the sticking point: *it is a question of where we draw the boundaries of the self* (2002: 226–27). He observes that, if Rawls is correct, and the self is truly prior to its ends, then "its boundaries are fixed antecedently" (226). Since communitarians tend to see the self's ends contained in community traditions and communal senses of the good, it would appear that they too regard the self's boundaries as predetermined.

But what troubles Kymlicka is that some of the most influential communitarian thinkers (like Sandel and Taylor) argue for fluid boundaries when the self articulates its position as a person – much as Rawls argues when he describes the self's ability to revise rationally any ends it has chosen in the past. "At this point it is not clear," Kymlicka observes, "whether the distinction between the two views does not collapse"; for if the person is prior to his or her ends, then the disagreement is "over where, within the person, to draw the boundaries of the self" (226–27). In other words, Sandel's and Taylor's topographies of the self remain somewhat open, resembling hybrid entities enacting now liberal, now communitarian, scripts. Finally, deliberative democracy's view of the autonomous self is decidedly open as well. In addition to self-identity (the ability to recognize continuity in one's past, present, and future life), Habermas emphasizes even more our capacity for distancing that self-identity from the circumstances that define us, including traditions and communal values (Warren 2001: 63; 1995: 173). Most important to our autonomy, however, is the ability to exercise critical judgment about ourselves through reason-giving exchanges with others in some type of public discourse. As Warren puts it, "the autonomy of the self depends upon and requires participation in intersubjective processes of reason giving and response. Autonomy, in other words, implies communicative competencies that cannot exist as individual properties, but only as part of a shared fabric of communicative understandings and interactions" (2001: 64; cf. Habermas 1990: 199).

So whether contemporary theorists posit the self as prior to or constituted by its ends, all allow for degrees of self-transformation that shift the self's boundaries. Deliberative democracy actually allows for the self to acquire autonomy and to reset its boundaries through a therapeutic model, a kind of psychotherapy, that returns us to the Greeks, their ethical quest for rational self-sufficiency, and dispute settlement. Warren in particular has asked whether personality disorders that hamper individuals in their communicative interactions – and so prevent them from achieving recognition of their autonomy from others – might not benefit from engaging in the reason-giving exchanges posited by deliberative democracy. He asks: "Can persons who have relatively functional selves but who are nonetheless subject to internal blockages that disrupt group decision-making processes – insecurities, anxieties, overconfidence, and so on – become more autonomous if these groups are subject to democratization?" (1995: 188).

I will argue that, to take on a dominant role as the agent of justice, the Greek citizen at large required this sort of therapeutic self-transformation. But where in the culture of Archaic Greece could he find an appropriate therapeutic model and process? The answer lies in the same resource that provided the judicial *basileus* with his legal aid in the Formative period: the epic poet. I believe the *Odyssey* provided its audiences with the opportunity to experience a self-transformation whose trajectory outlined the cognitive and moral education needed to regard oneself as an agent of justice. In performing Odysseus' wanderings, homecoming, and vengeance on Penelope's suitors, the Homeric poet reenacts in the hero a personality transformation which he intends his audiences to share intersubjectively. Through this transformation, astute listeners could acquire the know-how to perform a *dikê* by assuming the multiple perspectives of different individuals, groups, and the community and by replacing ontological frame-switching with new frames to understand litigants' actions – especially the frames of voluntary vs. involuntary action and the notion of moral responsibility. This would enable these future judicial magistrates and jurors to offer individuals locked in dispute a more civic version of *themistes* and *thesmia* where they might entertain multiple visions of self leading to a self-interpretation consistent with community values rather than with "ends" dictated by individual or kin-group needs and desires. Ultimately the most innovative feature of this ability is the juror's presumption to determine for another the nature of his or her self and to persuade litigants and spectators to realign *timai* in the community's interest while also respecting the litigants' inner, subjective worlds.

To argue this hypothesis, I focus on two episodes of the *Odyssey* where I claim the hero does undergo self-transformation: his decision to leave the sea-nymph Calypso in Book 5, where Homer strategically decides to introduce his audience to the hero; and his visit to the underworld in Book 11 (the *Nekyia*), which occurs earlier in Odysseus' wanderings but which Homer's narrative nevertheless has the audience experience after the Calypso episode. Both episodes permit us to explore from perspectives both ancient and contemporary the process by which the hero transforms himself as a human agent, redefining himself as a person and reconfiguring his autonomy. They also evoke questions scholars have long debated about this extraordinary poem and its hero: Does the *Odyssey* dramatize a moral universe that is significantly different from the *Iliad*'s – one where human agents enjoy greater moral responsibility for their fates, succeeding or suffering not because of divine favor or enmity but due to their own moral decisions? Is Odysseus a new type of hero compared to his role in the *Iliad* and to his Iliadic predecessors like Achilles and Hector? If so, can we link this novelty to a new type of self? Does the character of Odysseus actually change throughout the poem? In particular, does his moral consciousness undergo development?

From a contemporary perspective Odysseus' decision to abandon Calypso provides Homer's audience (and us) with a blueprint for reordering the voluntarist, cognitive, and deliberative dimensions of the self, in effect instructing them and us how to reconfigure boundaries for each of these to form a citizen self for the state. Sandel's and Taylor's discussions of selfhood – with help from Habermas, Warren, and Kymlicka – will clarify for us the difference, already at work within Odysseus' character, between the self as an agent and a person, and the self as a relatively closed or relatively open performance of roles.

I am especially interested, however, in Odysseus' visit to the underworld in Book 11, where he and Homer's audience intersubjectively share the experience of what a judicial *basileus* performed by himself in the state's Formative period: the *themistes* and *thesmia* we discussed in Chapter 2. Borrowing Simon's suggestion that Homer embedded in his epic performance a form of psychotherapy for his audience (1978), I'll discuss in particular the final moments of Odysseus' visit to Hades, when he encounters Minos, who looks to me like a model of mimesis in the Greek tradition for performing *themistes* and *thesmia* (11.576–627). Here we'll understand how Odysseus begins to acquire a transformed autonomy when he experiences the *thesmia* of five heroic figures: Orion, Tityus, Tantalus, Sisyphus, and Heracles, all of whom I characterize as transgressors guilty of hybris. The psychoanalytic theory of Kohut's "self psychology" (1985, 1984, 1977) will offer us an intersubjective understanding of individual autonomy that is compatible with the Greek state's autonomy of citizen and self and with the debate over autonomy in liberal, communitarian, and deliberative democratic theories. We'll then examine key moments when Odysseus in fact performs as the agent of divine justice by judging and slaughtering the suitors – and when, I'll claim, he draws on the cognitive and moral understanding acquired when he visited Hades and decided to leave Calypso. Finally, we'll compare Odysseus' visit to Hades in Book 11 to the arrival in Hades of the suitors' ghosts in Book 24. By contrasting the justice he exacts from the suitors with the way Homer resolves Odysseus' subsequent dispute with the slaughtered suitors' kin, we'll answer the question, "Is the *Odyssey* itself the performance of a grand *thesmion* for Homer's audience?"

A Poetic Deliberation on Hybris and Justice

Few would argue that the *Odyssey* is a poem whose primary concern is that, with divine assistance, Odysseus obtain justice for himself, his family and his community. But this need not mean that its successful ending "satisfies the *natural* human desire to see justice done in the world and evildoers punished" (Rutherford 1992: 5; my emphasis). That is to say, the justice Odysseus seeks is not naturally but historically conditioned; and it must serve the interests of its audiences in state societies of *poleis* and *ethnê* from around 700 – a type of justice that we should therefore not expect to match that of the *Iliad*. Scholars have in fact long noted key differences in the two poems' conceptions of the gods (their "theology") and in the moral consequences for humans of relations between gods and mortals. Twentieth-century Homerists especially point to Zeus' "programmatic" comment at *Od.*1.32–43, where he refutes humans who blame their misfortunes on the gods: "No, they [mortals] themselves experience miseries beyond their usual fate due to their own moral stupidities" (*atasthaliêisin*, 34). This contention seems to stand in stark contrast to the insight we saw Achilles share with Priam at *Il.*24.525–51, where he imagines Zeus despotically allotting all humans portions of good and evil from two jars.

It therefore appears that human beings in the *Odyssey* are more morally responsible and to a degree more autonomous than in the *Iliad*.[1]

---

[1] See the following for comparisons of the two poems' alignment of gods, humans, and moral responsibility, with most scholars endorsing a greater degree of human

Historically speaking, we might even take this difference in each poem's worldview to suggest that Homeric society's "lifeworld" – its horizon of ancestrally grounded, implicit, unquestioned truths and validity claims – is not uniform, and that the presumably later poem's worldview "decenters," in Habermas' sense, moral elements of the presumably earlier poem's (cf. Habermas 1984: 70). If this sounds plausible, then the later poem's theology and profile of human responsibility provide reasons for and against the question of whether gods or mortals themselves constitute the proper cause of human fates. The *Odyssey* itself seems to debate this key point because it has struck scholars as contradictory or inconsistent, representing humans as to a degree morally autonomous but also as victims of unjustified, divinely inflicted miseries.

The poem's first 102 lines set up this contrast and open a polemic with the *Iliad*'s moral universe in a series of quick brushstrokes which, like *thesmia*, outline a string of crimes, their perpetrators, and fates. The Homeric narrator evokes the first crime, that of Odysseus' crew, "who perished because of their own moral stupidities [*atasthaliêisin*], the fools, when they ate the cattle of Hyperion the sun god" (1.6–9). Zeus describes the second and third crimes at an assembly attended by all the gods except Poseidon: these are Orestes' murder of Aegisthus in retaliation for Aegisthus' marriage to Clytemnestra and Aegisthus' murder of Agamemnon (29–30 and 35–43). These conjoined *thesmia* are what prompt Zeus' exasperated outburst about how mortals are responsible for their own "moral stupidities" (32–34) since, the father god points out, the gods had carefully warned Aegisthus against his actions (37–43). The fourth crime is Odysseus' blinding of the Cyclops,

responsibility in the *Odyssey*: Jaeger 1966: 83–84; Dodds 1951: 32; Fränkel 1975: 85–93; Rüter 1969: 69–82; Lloyd-Jones 1971: 28–32; Griffin 1980: 144–78; Clay 1983: 215ff; Kullmann 1985; Friedrich 1987: 375–78; Heubeck 1989: 22–23; Rutherford 1992: 3–7; Yamagata 1994: 32ff.; Cook 1995: 32–45; and Barnouw 2004: 46–49.

recalled by Zeus to remind Athena of why Odysseus has been delayed so long on his return: "Poseidon the earthshaker remains steadfastly angry at him on account of the Cyclops whose eye he blinded" (68–69). Athena recounts the last crime, which belongs to Penelope's suitors, for the goddess intends to instill enough strength and courage in Telemachus to call an assembly in Ithaca to "speak out against all the suitors, who are continually slaughtering [Odysseus'] swarming flocks and plodding, curved-horn cattle" (91–92).[2]

Why does Homer align in programmatic fashion these five abbreviated stories of crime and punishment? And does this alignment begin to telegraph to his audience a vision of justice, human responsibility and autonomy? To reiterate Nussbaum's formulation, do the *Odyssey*'s introductory one hundred lines adumbrate a kind of hero and self that might guide Greeks along an ethical quest to develop a self-sufficiency grounded in rational evaluation and choice, one that might protect the self from bad luck or divine intervention (1986: 4–7)? It's not possible here to summarize all the scholarly speculation on these questions in recent decades, but I join those who see Aegisthus' crimes as paradigmatic for the crimes of Odysseus' crew and the suitors, with all three groups of transgressors bearing full moral responsibility for their offenses.[3] In contrast, Odysseus' "crime" against the Cyclops lacks the

---

[2]   Among more recent scholars who see inconsistency or contradiction in these two conceptions of divine-human relations, see Fenik 1974: 211ff., Clay 1983: 219ff., Kullmann 1985, and Thalmann 1992: 32–34. Those seeing a compatibility include Friedrich 1987: 383, Segal 1994: 195–227, and Cook 1995: 45ff. (In my discussion of hybris in the *Nekyia*, I argue for the latter position.)

[3]   See, e.g., Cook 1995: 15–48, esp. 33–48, emphasizing the "paradigmatic" nature of Aegisthus' punishment (44–45), Segal 1994: 215–27, Friedrich 1987, and Kullmann 1985: 6–7. Barnouw sees the crew, Aegisthus, and the suitors as foils of recklessness for Odysseus' persistent use of a "practical intelligence" that considers contrasting impulses, ideas, and possible outcomes while heeding signs and warnings (2004: 37–49). (Friedrich argues that the crew's intent is not as willful as the suitors' and

fully knowledgeable, willful intent we see in the others; by these standards it is no real crime at all but an example of how gods can for selfish
reasons unjustly victimize humans. In Poseidon's case that reason stems
from a close kinship relation to his monstrous offspring, Polyphemus
the Cyclops, which Zeus details for us (1.71–73) and declares invalid as
an excuse for Odysseus' continued suffering (76–79).

Now the fact that this kind of divine rationale for inflicting woes
on mortals predominates in the *Iliad* does not necessarily mean that
its condemnation by Zeus in the *Odyssey* represents an evolutionary
advance in Greek moral reasoning.[4] But the later poem does devalue the
reasoning behind Poseidon's wrath and punishment against Odysseus
in favor of the reasoning that justifies the punishments of Aegisthus, the
crewmen and the suitors. Why? Because, its vision of justice is designed
to engage the minds of a state society rather than a prestate society, but
a state society whose political landscape is more articulated than that
faced by Achilles as a prototypical citizen in the *Iliad*. As a self Odysseus
confronts more clearly recognizable political challenges with resources
originating from a more articulated interior landscape, from a greater
depth of personhood, than Achilles. As for the later poem's vision
of justice, in Cook's succinct formulation, "In the *Odyssey*, Olympic
justice is civic justice."[5] However, behind this helpful formulation lies

so their guilt is not of the same degree.) For recent interpretations that do not find
the crew responsible for their fate, see Fenik 1974: 212–13, and Clay 1983: 35–36 and
230. Nagler sees the poem's opening lines as aligning these crimes with Odysseus'
"crime" as the agent of justice: he slaughters the suitors (his retainers) in his own
home (1990).

[4] See, e.g., Kullmann 1985: 14–20, Burkert 1985: 247–50, and Cook 1995: 42–45.

[5] 1995: 33. Jaeger first linked the *Odyssey*'s vision of justice to Solon's (1966); see also
Lloyd-Jones on justice in the *Odyssey*, Hesiod, and lyric poets (1971: 28–54), and
Havelock 1978: 150ff. Cook doesn't pursue his insight into the poem as a blueprint for
city-state justice because he sees Poseidon structurally as emblematic of the natural
rather than the prestate world, specifically the sea and the enchanted lands Odysseus

a problem: how to find a necessary link between justice as a political (state) dilemma and the personality of Odysseus. We find a path to such a link in what, as we saw in Chapter 1, first provoked Achilles to embark on his self-definition and self-transformation: the archetypal Greek crime, hybris.

Gernet reminds us that even though the *Iliad*'s major conflict between Agamemnon and Achilles erupts from an act of hybris (1.203), the *Odyssey* is the poem where hybris proliferates. This thematics testifies to a greater concern with the collapse of a society built on kin group social formations and their leadership (2001 [1917]: 24–25) and, in my opinion, makes this epic a poetic, narrative deliberation on hybris.[6] So when Homer evokes the fate of long-suffering Odysseus in the poem's opening 102 lines and ties this to crimes by the crewmen against the sun god, by Aegisthus against Agamemnon, and by the suitors against Odysseus, the poet's audience must confront both the objects (victims) and subjects (perpetrators) of acts that qualify as hybris.

All the gods but Poseidon certainly feel compassion for Odysseus as a victim (1.19–20) and are roused by Athena and Zeus to support his homecoming. Odysseus' crew and Aegisthus are without question subjects of hybris: they display the moral blindness designated by *atasthaliai* (1.7 and 34), whether this is provoked by a god or erupts from a person's inner, natural inclination, somewhat like a possession they carry with them (Gernet 2001: 26).[7] But, as subjects, the suitors nearly monopolize

visits. But he does associate Poseidon and the natural world through a hypothetical link between the *Odyssey* and Athenian civic cults to Erechtheus and Athena.

[6] The *Odyssey* has twenty-six of the thirty-one occurrences of hybris words in Homer (Fisher 1992: 151).

[7] For the link between hybris and *atasthalos*, see Gernet 2001: 26 and 54–55, Segal 1994: 200, Fisher 1992: 155–56, Clay 1983: 35–36, and Nagy 1979: 163. Hybris words are linked to *atasthalia* at *Od*.16.86 (*atasthalon hybrin* = 24.352), 17.588 (*hybrizontes atasthala* = 20.170), and 24.282 (*hybristai . . . kai atasthaloi*). (For the relative frequency of *atasthalos* and *atasthalia*, see Saïd 1979: 42, n. 2.) With Fenik 1974 and others Clay does not believe the

the poem's use of hybris words: nineteen times speakers – the Homeric narrator, Athena, Telemachus, Eumaeus, unnamed suitors, Penelope, Laertes and Odysseus in disguise – so incriminate them; in their mouths the word seems to resound with the illocutionary moral force of the *Iliad*'s "*ou themis esti*. . . ."[8]

This illocutionary force framing hybris words highlights the concept's often overlooked performative dimension: hybris is accusatory.[9]

crew's *atasthaliai* entail moral responsibility for their crime, but Friedrich refutes this argument (1987: 389–93). He does stumble though in claiming that the crew's transgression is "free of criminal intent" compared to the "hybristic crimes of the suitors" (397). Like the suitors, the crew ignore warnings and break religious and social customs to satisfy their appetites; Segal emphasizes the "carefully demarcated stages" through which the crew assume full responsibility for their decision (1994: 215–17). At 14.262 Odysseus uses hybris to describe the excess appetite for material goods of the *fictional* crewmen who disobey orders he gave them in Egypt. But this episode mirrors his actual crew's behavior at 9.44, when as "great fools" (*mega nepioi*) they refused to obey him among the Cicones and later in the land of the sun god, where their "proud spirit" (*thumos agênôr*, 12.324) leads them again to disobey him and break the oath they swore not to kill the cattle. These arguments refute Fisher's claim that the crew are not guilty of "straight hybris" because their folly and dishonoring of the sun god do not arise from a "blatant, fully intentional" motivation that is "seriously hybristic" (1992: 182). They also contradict Fisher's earlier contention that Homeric speakers allow for "varying degrees of heinousness" in hybris (166–67).

[8] The occurrences, speakers, and listeners are: Athena to the gods (1.227); Telemachus to the suitors, Nestor, Menelaus, and Eumaeus (1.368, 3.207, 4.321, 16.86); the Homeric narrator (4.627, 16.410, and 17.169); Eumaeus to the disguised Odysseus and Penelope (15.329, 17.581); Penelope to the suitors, Antinous, Eumaeus, and Eurycleia (16.418, 17.588, 23. 64); anonymous suitors to Antinous (17.487); Odysseus in disguise to Eumaeus, the suitor Eurymachus, and again Eumaeus (17.565, 18.381, 20.170); and Laertes to the disguised and then the recognized Odysseus (24.282 and 352). (These nineteen occurrences represent seventy-six percent of the poem's twenty-five occurrences of hybris words [Saïd 1979: 42, n. 2.]) As we shall see, Odysseus does not actually use hybris words when, in Book 22, he confronts the suitors as the agent of justice in his own person, though he does use the accompanying word *hyperbasiê* (64) in response to the suitor Eurymachus' self-incriminating use of *atasthala* (47).

[9] As MacDowell points out, "*hybris* is always bad. It is an evaluative word, not an objective one" (1976: 21). Fisher calls Hesiod's use of the word "one of the most powerful linguistic weapons" of the peasant class ca. 700 (1992: 198).

It enacts a righteous claim by its speaker that its subject X is inflicting dishonor on its object Y for selfish reasons, because X fails to recognize the correct limits of Y's *timê*. The speaker in effect says that X is failing to align him-, her- or themselves properly with Y's self, with the result that Y suffers harm to his or her social and perhaps physical well-being. In the eyes of the hybris speaker, X hasn't interiorized the position of the community's dominant social other vis-à-vis Y; as a result, Y is displaced from his, her or their collectively recognized status. This explains why hybris offends both individuals (or groups, if it is so directed) as well as the community at large; and this is why (as we'll see in more detail) the illocutionary force behind the hybris speakers's accusation is meant to arouse anger and indignation from the entire community (*nemesis*), not just from the individuals or groups most directly concerned.

So in this sense it is not true to claim, as MacDowell does, that there can be acts of hybris without a victim; for even where no individual or group is named or indicated as its object, hybris offends the dominant social other's ideological conception of society, adumbrating a virtual harm to social order.[10] Likewise, it's misleading to claim, as Fisher does (1992: 148), that a perpetrator of hybris must willfully intend to offend someone. As Cairns argues, hybris often designates a person's long-standing "subjective attitude" or "disposition" that consistently displays an "implicit affront" to the honor of others (1996: 10). From the perspective of the supposed perpetrator of hybris, as well as of

---

[10] See MacDowell 1976: 23–24; cf. Cairns on the need for at least an "implicit" victim of hybris (1996: 10, 32), and Cantarella on why hybris must have a victim (2003: 119). I think Gernet correctly opposes hybris and "correct social order" (*eunomiê*) at *Od*.17.487, no matter what circumstances surround the alleged act of hybris (2001: 21–22). I disagree when Fisher claims that Gernet's study contains "major flaws" for emphasizing the religious and communal dimensions of criminal concepts over the individual (1992: 5): *eunomiê* at 17.487 does not necessarily refer to individual conduct rather than a social condition (Fisher 1992: 173).

anyone listening to the accusation, a hybris word's illocutionary force also issues a warning. This discourages uses of moral autonomy that misalign one self with another or that cause someone to depart from a communally sanctioned code of conduct. It is perhaps for this reason that spatial concepts dominate the concept of hybris, and a heightened concern for boundaries, for the word is often linked – perhaps etymologically – to terms for "transgression" or "going beyond," such as *hyperbainô, hyperbasiê, hyperbios*.[11] Whether in its objective or subjective senses, then, throughout the Greek tradition hybris foregrounds the drawing of boundaries in people's minds that define the nature of social groups but that also foster attention to individuality, to what is at stake in both proper and improper ways of being an individual. From our contemporary perspective, hybris words indicate for both the Greeks and ourselves – and here we should paraphrase Kymlicka again – where to draw the boundaries of the self in relation to those groups (2002: 226–27).

CALYPSO, ODYSSEUS, AND THE UNENCUMBERED SELF

If the *Odyssey* intends to open a deliberation about hybris, including consideration of which individuals are its objects (victims) and subjects (perpetrators), then both its audience and its hero need to understand two sorts of moral agency and (in our sense) subjectivity: how does a person think and act if he or she is a victim of hybris? And if he or she is a perpetrator? More importantly, how *should* a person think and act in each position? And does a person better understand how to perform in each role if he or she understands the subjectivity of his or her antagonist? Odysseus is of course the poem's principal object of hybris

---

[11] See Gernet 2001: 27–28. In the *Odyssey, hyper* words are conjoined with hybris words at 1.227 (*hybrizontes hyperphialôs*), 368 (*hyperbion hybrin* = 4.321 = 16.410), 3.206–207 (*hyperbasiês . . . hybrizontes*), and 17.581 (*hybrin . . . andrôn hyperênoreontôn*). (On the relative frequency of these *hyper* words in the poem, see Saïd 1979: 42, n. 2.)

and the suitors its principal subject. But from the perspective of hybris and its grip on individuals, the poem opens with a curious dilemma. The hero is stranded on Calypso's isle, where his physical dependence and moral impotence do not permit him to assume actively the role of an object of hybris. Even though he already knows from Tiresias' prophecy in Hades that the suitors are behaving hybristically toward him, and that he *might* exact revenge on them were he to return (11.115–120), he cannot yet choose to act on or perform this role.

So Homer introduces us to Odysseus as an individual who both is and is not an object of hybris; and until he gives the lie to the suitors' contention that he is dead (2.96), they are not quite guilty as subjects of hybris either. As a moral dilemma, this question of where Odysseus locates himself within hybris relations provides an altered perspective on the traditional question of his ambiguous identity on Calypso's isle. But it's also a political dilemma in the late eighth century for communities struggling with statehood and with how autonomous individual households will be. I suggest that it challenges the poem's audience to reflect on an individual's moral and political capacity to draw the boundaries necessary for the criteria of citizenship and selfhood outlined in the Introduction: a measure of individual *timê* deserving sufficient recognition from others to maintain a positive public image; a qualified personal autonomy permitting exercise of the will in individual and family interest, so long as community welfare is ensured; and a set of deliberative freedoms, especially the freedom to participate with peers in assembly, speech and exchange of reason giving. We should note that these boundaries claim both personal connections to loved ones, to land and to property and also social and political roles – and from the perspective of the early state's "middling" ideology outlined by Morris (1996), all these boundaries invite violation by others. Because this boundary drawing links all these ends to individual personhood, before Odysseus can become an agent of justice he must choose to become once again a person. And this person looks to me like a "new man" in the same "middling" sense Achilles discovered in his great speech in *Iliad* 9.

I don't think we can separate Odysseus' moral mandate to recreate himself as a person from the inclination of some scholars to identify him as a "new man." By this I refer not only to a transformation of the predominant type of heroic self we find in the *Iliad*, where Odysseus' capacity for endurance, self-restraint and cunning intelligence (*mêtis*) displaces the *Iliad*'s preference for courage, martial prowess and displays of authority typical of aristocratic chiefs, but to a more articulated paradigm for personhood than the one outlined by Achilles in *Iliad* 9. We might see with Fränkel a "new kind of heroism" in Odysseus (1975: 87), one based on an enhanced moral responsibility that enables Homer's audience "to master life," which means "to know the world as it is constituted, to confront situations in the way that is most advantageous, and to come to grips with one's life, each with his own" (93). Or we might understand Odysseus' self in Pucci's sense of a "new hero" (1987: 44, 47) representing the consciousness of an "innermost self" through an internal voice that links language and intelligence so that it "mirrors or bespeaks what is immutable (essential) in man" (77, 76–80). Consistent with Pucci's recognition of Odysseus' ability to achieve "self-identity" through "depth" (79), Peradotto sees in the hero's many guises and turns of identity "a paradigm of human potential" offering a "broadened sense of self," one that again provides "a sense of self with depth" (1990: 169). Because the hero's character flirts over and again with anonymity and variation, for Peradotto it reveals a more dynamic, open, and "less deterministic" type of subjectivity (169).[12]

---

[12] Cf. Goldhill's discussion of how the opposition between Odysseus' anonymity and his proper name conditions the poem's thematics of recognition (1991: 4–5), involving not just the poem's characters but its audience in a "discourse of recognition" whose concern with norms and transgressions transforms it into an "ethical discourse" (27).

Segal too uses this notion of a new sort of "inner man" (and "deeper" man) as a key to Odysseus' character, especially because the hero passes from a state of suspended identity with Calypso to the land of the Phaeacians (1994: 15), where he will undergo "rebirth" and in books 9–12 will narrate his own fantastic adventures as a "voyage of the soul" (19–20). The chief virtue of Segal's study is that it identifies this process of rebirth and renewed self-formation with the poem's concern throughout Odysseus' experiences for "how a moral consciousness is shaped over the course of a lifetime of suffering and witnessing divinity's workings among mortals" (197) – and Segal sees this process as preparatory for administering justice (195–227). He also insists that Odysseus' character throughout the narrative remains a work-in-progress, changing cognitively because the hero learns from past experience, acquires self-restraint and endurance, and so "reestablishes" a former "state of being . . . on deeper foundations" (57–58). Barnouw argues cogently that Odysseus is a "new sort of hero" compared to the *Iliad*, because over and again he dramatizes through inner deliberation the operation of a "practical intelligence" whose "single-mindedness" consistently ponders contrasting impulses and courses of action, anticipates potentially positive and negative outcomes, and both infers the meaning of signs and prompts others to do the same (2004: 54) – all with the sole aim of "recovering" his former sense of self grounded in family relations and possessions.

Segal believes it may be "a difficult question" to determine whether Odysseus' character undergoes transformation (57; cf. Thalmann 1992: 70–71), but recent Odyssean scholarship offers sufficiently cogent arguments for us to concur with Segal that it does. Rutherford for one persuasively claims that the poem presents a "coherent . . . moral picture" of Odysseus' character development, not unlike Achilles', and that there are "stages" to this "process" of moral development (1986: 147 and 1992: 20–27). In addition he argues that the hero doesn't merely acquire a "psychological" complexity such as we perceive in living persons (cf. Griffin 1980: 51–52); rather Odysseus changes in order to teach the "moral lessons" of self-restraint, self-denial and endurance to a Homeric audience in whose eyes he is meant to acquire the "moral authority" necessary to the task of "testing and dealing out justice" (Rutherford 1986: 150, 160). In effect Rutherford portrays the hero's adventures as a moral trajectory passing from a subject of hybris to its object, for he remarks that Odysseus once roamed the seas as a "buccaneering hero" engaging in criminal behavior but ends up a "more sombre and authoritative figure" exacting "the punishment ordained by the gods for the suitors" (1992: 22).

These recent philosophical and moral discussions of Odysseus' self-transformation certainly help restore interest in the poem's central ethical concerns (long recognized by the ancients).[13] But they also return us to two questions: How should we connect a moral focus on Odysseus' personality with the historical dimensions of his identity and the justice he enacts? And how closely or distantly should we align ancient and modern concepts of self? Segal underscores the divide between Homeric and modern senses of self, somewhat along the lines of Gill's distinction between the "objectivist" and "subjective-individualist" models (Segal 1994: 5). This distinction links these two questions by reminding us that Odysseus' subjectivity, no matter what its novelties and peculiarities, must be related to historically determined boundaries and senses of justice – for example, to values particular to a social class and to early Archaic cultural development. Is it possible to see Odysseus enacting his changing character, which we've portrayed as a new moral

---

[13] See, e.g., Aristotle's well-known description of the *Odyssey* as, compared to the *Iliad*, "complex" due to its pervasive concern with the process of recognition. And so for Aristotle the poem is "character-based" (*êthikê*, *Poet.*1459b15), meaning that recognizing an individual's character depends on morally evaluating changing patterns in behavior. Rutherford gives other ancient references to the poem's moral nature (1986: 145, n. 1).

or philosophical paradigm of the self, within the historically circum-
scribed roles of an aristocratic leader and head of household in the early
state's age of colonization? This interconnecting of moral and historical selves, of a unique personality and a definite social type, has not
attracted much scholarly interest apart from the proponents of what
used to be called *Geistesgeschichte* – scholars like Snell, Dodds, Fränkel,
and Atkins, who in the mid-twentieth century believed Odysseus' novel
self marked the emergence in Archaic Greece of a new evolutionary
stage in Western consciousness.

But if we avoid this type of claim, how do we historicize Odysseus'
moral refashioning of self, his assumption of the object's role in hybris
relations, and his self-transformation into the agent of justice? We are
fortunate to have recent studies that clarify Odysseus' social role in a cultural or political sense. Some, such as Malkin (1998) and C. Dougherty
(2001), see him as a prototype of the Greek explorer in the western
Mediterranean or as a new kind of culture hero suited to the age of
colonization.[14] Others, Rose (1992) and Thalmann (1998), for example,
portray Odysseus as a political subject during the era of state formation
when Early Iron Age aristocratic interests are being contested by previously subaltern groups.[15] But if we wish to link Odysseus' moral profile

---

[14] Malkin equates Odysseus with protocolonial exploration of the Mediterranean
west of Greece from the ninth to mid-eighth centuries; he would even like to
locate the *Odyssey*'s composition in the ninth or tenth century (1998: 259–73). C.
Dougherty identifies Odysseus as a "culture hero for a new age" (2001: 175), the
age of colonization in the eighth century, where he acts as a mediator negotiating
differences in cultural and economic meanings between Greeks and non-Greeks.
She's particularly interested in his poetic role as interpreter of cultural differences
through narratives for a Greek audience. Neither study focuses on the poem's theme
of justice, but despite their differences both highlight the hero's role as founder (or
refounder) of Greek societies. They thus see him as a drawer of cultural rather than
political or moral boundaries between self and other.

[15] Rose sees the hero as a "composite character" who resists Homer's artistic attempt to
render him a "coherent, autonomous subject" because his colonizer's role combines

as a person to the social roles that are available for him to adopt or renounce, we need to return to his development of moral consciousness through a kind of cognitive performance that compares and evaluates the choices open to an agent, whether of colonization or of political interests.[16] These choices put into play key values that resonate positively for some (though not for all) members of the poem's audiences from the eighth to the sixth centuries.[17] And with help from moral philosophers like Taylor and political philosophers like Sandel, I'll

the values of various peasant and *déclassé* artistocratic groups (1992: 120–21). Thalmann sees Odysseus – especially as the agent of justice when he wins the archery contest – representing an embattled, late eighth-century aristocracy eager to impose its hierarchical vision of social order on a society in pursuit of more egalitarian ideologies. He claims that despite Homer's dramatization of alternative subject positions like those of slaves and free non-elites, the poem plays off these alternative values to present "the aristocratic male as suited by both nature and achievement to wield dominant authority in the well-ordered home and polity" (1998: 283). Cf. Saïd's conventional view of the hero as a "complex character" with military, intellectual, and moral virtues (1998: 214–26).

[16] We'll see that this involves recognizing different types of subjectivity in the poem's moral trajectory, including the nature of voluntary and involuntary actions and the parameters of moral responsibility; see, e.g., Cantarella 2003: 253–73. Barnouw's study of Odysseus focuses squarely on the hero as a cognitive agent, the initiator in the Western philosophical tradition of a "practical intelligence" we find from the Stoics to the moderns, including Hobbes, Leibniz, Kant, Schiller, Schopenhauer, and Dewey (2004). He also squarely confronts the scholars influenced by *Geistesgeschichte*, with its notions of the self's evolution (Snell, Fränkel, Adkins) (149–76). His examination of Odysseus' self is almost, however, ahistorical; he declares it "innocent of any pretension to expertise in the historical world behind Homer's text" (237).

[17] See Thalmann's nuanced discussion of how various groups identified by class may have responded in the eighth century and Archaic period to the poem's key values, choices, and outcomes (1998: 291–305). (I will return to this question when I consider the importance of Book 24 and the second *Nekyia*.) L. Dougherty explores the possibility of female audiences, both "internal" to the poem's narrative and "implied" or outside its narrative frame (1995). (Our discussion of justice will also return to this possibility.)

argue that the same choices can also resonate for the poem's audiences today.

Redfield most clearly describes how the *Odyssey* puts key values into play when he characterizes the poem as a communication between poet and audience that rests on "shared, normative values" (1983: 218). The hero's various adventures arouse interest because they put "ethical choices at play" and "dramatize values" as "thought-experiments" about the most pressing cultural questions during the age of colonization (ca. 770–550) (219). What emerges is another formulation of Odysseus as a new type of self, one whose cognitive and moral profile outlines an "economic ethic" that enacts a "specific kind of deliberation" (218). Redfield sees this deliberation as strictly a rational calculation, one inaugurating the desire for control over luck and divine intervention that Nussbaum posits as the ethical quest of the Greek philosophical tradition; for Odysseus time and again must compare the amount of pain and loss (physical and emotional) he will endure, in the face of hostile forces, with such "ordinary things" of value as family, home, and community (Redfield 1983: 230; cf. Nussbaum 1986: 6–7).

In our contemporary terms this calculation of "economic man" resonates as a version of the struggle between the liberal conception of self dominated by the voluntarist capacity to choose one's ends and the communitarian self's cognitive understanding of the ends with which others endow us – and to which we should own up.[18] Actually, today a communitarian thinker like Taylor would revise Redfield's "economic man" to see him less as an *agent* and more as a *person*. By this I mean

---

[18] Redfield adapts his "economic man" from the *homo oeconomicus* whose prototype Horkheimer and Adorno saw in Odysseus: the bourgeois, liberal self of capitalism who learns to practice reasonable self-sacrifice to advance his "atomistic interest" (1972: 61). For an informed, critical discussion of Redfield's and Horkheimer's and Adorno's Odysseus, see Barnouw 2004: 211–16.

understanding him not primarily as a subject of teleological or strategic action who calculates the costs of achieving one goal or another but
rather as someone open to a "struggle of self-interpretations" (Taylor
1985a: 23). This is an individual who ponders alternatives that amount to
"strong evaluations" because they require that individual to articulate
preferences "deep" enough to reveal plural visions of self, of different
ways to be a person (24–27). For Taylor we thus enact our personhood not
according to objective criteria others may evaluate by a "performance
criterion" (103–4) but as a "subject of significance": this is a peculiar
kind of agent who finds meanings in his or her own life (and in others'
lives) that are uniquely human because they concern emotions such
as "pride, shame, moral goodness, evil, dignity, the sense of worth, the
various forms of human love, and so on" (102).[19]

From the very moment Homer presents the character of Odysseus,
he takes pains to portray his hero as more a person in this sense than as a
successful or failed agent on a quest to return home. It is of course one of
the *Odyssey*'s salient narrative features that the protagonist and his fate
are focalized by many other characters before the poem's narrator permits us to encounter him directly in Book 5, isolated with the goddess
Calypso on her remote isle. We recall this episode's uniqueness in the

---

[19] While my focus on Odysseus' interior deliberations intersects in many ways with
Barnouw's hero of practical intelligence (2004), I argue that Odysseus ponders
different possible senses of self. Barnouw understands Odysseus' self as essentially
the same, and so not subject to transformation – though he believes the hero does
learn from experience as his character is molded (15). He sees Odysseus struggle to
"recover a sense of self" and "regain an identity" he once enjoyed (e.g. 5, 259). Like
Barnouw, I see the inner workings of Odysseus' thoughts and emotions as those of
a unified self possessing a will. See Barnouw's refutation of Snell's (1960) influential
arguments against Odysseus' display of a unified or true self (2004: 163–74). Cf.
Vernant's denial that the Greeks had a Cartesian agency of the "will" (1988) and
B. Williams' assertion that Odysseus has a genuine will in the modern sense (1993:
39). Taylor's concept of the person as a self-interpreter and "subject of significance"
builds on but distinguishes itself from a Cartesian sense of agency (1985a: 97–98).

poem's overall "extended narrative pattern": the hero not only fails to encounter here a strange society whose challenges elicit his characteristic talents of inner strength, endurance, and cunning, but his situation with Calypso on Ogygia also locks him in an ontologically ambiguous and liminal world "caught between two modes of existence."[20] Why in effect would Homer insist that audiences first encounter the hero suspended in such an isolated and "in-between" existence so different from more familiar circumstances? And why does Odysseus' relation to this powerful female – herself anomalous compared to the poem's other powerful females – seem so "intimate" and anchored in her "deep emotional investment" in him?[21]

If we infer that Homer crafted these and other details in the episode by design, one of its goals may be, as Simon has put it, to create a "poem of inwardness" intent on representing "certain mental processes" experienced by a hero "who is threatened by extinction and with the danger of being stripped of all that defines the Homeric hero as an individual" (1978: 64–65). And the recent scholarly descriptions by Pucci, Peradotto, and Segal (and others) of the hero as a new sort of "inner, deeper" man suggest that this intent strikes a responsive chord with modern and postmodern senses of self. The "threat of extinction" Simon evokes seems essential to the move of any ancient or modern self inward toward a meditation on identity. We might characterize many of the anomalies

---

[20] Here Crane compares Calypso's otherworldly realm (with its overtones of an "island of the blest" and the underworld) to the everyday realities of Ithaca (1988: 15). Louden indicates how intentionally different the Calypso episode appears in comparison with the poem's "extended narrative pattern" (1999: 2).

[21] Louden 1999: 110–11. While Calypso's similarities to other female figures (especially Circe) are often noted, Louden notes important differences (104ff.), pointing out that she doesn't conform very well to the Greek and Near Eastern stereotype of the "dread goddess who communicates with mortals" (114; for the stereotype, see Nagle 1996, esp. 141–49). For scholarship comparing Calypso and Circe, see Crane 1988: 31ff.

surrounding the Calypso episode as Homer's attempt to imagine, as in a thought experiment, a zero degree of self in the age of colonization. The poet achieves this by subtracting from his hero almost all those qualities this age considers essential to personhood, submitting Odysseus for seven years to a radical process of dispossession. In the end all that remains, as the hero's life force ebbs (5.151–53; 160–61), are one cognitive and one moral resource: the first is his ability to calculate the value of his life with Calypso – with its offer of an anonymous immortality no mortals will ever hear of – by comparing it to the struggles he must endure in hopes of recovering (to echo Nussbaum) "external goods" like friendship, love, political action, and possessions. Odysseus' second abiding resource, a moral one, is his will.[22]

This thought experiment of Odysseus on Ogygia looks to me like a Homeric version of a deontological self – more exactly, like Rawls' "unencumbered self" in its hypothetical "original position" (1971). It looks as though Homer was inviting his audience to engage in ontological frame-switching and imagine a heroic self lost in an ontological neverland, stripped of all material and social possessions that might link him to what he knew of humanity, a self constituted prior to any ends it might choose; only its faculties of rational deliberation and moral choice remain. Consistent with an unencumbered self in the original position, Odysseus seems caught in the dilemma of two possessive conceptions of selfhood, as outlined by Sandel: he is aware of a distance separating himself from the "external goods" he once possessed, and his self-knowledge on Ogygia indicates to him that his "essential" self can in fact exist without them.[23] But at the same

---

[22] Vernant emphasizes the anonymity of the immortality awaiting Odysseus on Ogygia, comparing it to that of the nameless dead evoked by Hesiod at *WD* 154, in his brief, lyrical meditation on the hero's identity (1996: 188, with n. 17).

[23] Sandel in fact chooses Odysseus (with help from Allen Grossman) as his prime example of a self enjoying an integrity and continuity generated by the knowledge

time his long sojourn with Calypso has compensated for this dispossession by providing a surfeit of substitute possessions (physical comforts, including sexual, and the goddess' nurturing care and companionship), and these have nearly smothered Odysseus the way an obsessive desire for *x* or *y* can rob someone of a sense of self.[24] Caught between these two versions of selfhood, Odysseus dramatizes a new transformation of the basic question linking decisions about justice to conceptions of self: "As I contemplate playing the agent of justice, what type of person must I become? And is this the person I *wish* to become?"

And so, according to Sandel, "possession is bound up with human agency and a sense of self-command" (1998: 56). Consequently, when the self experiences dispossession within either conception of possession, it's faced with the threat of disempowerment, and here we confront the question of the self's boundaries and personhood. The distance separating Odysseus from the ends he once possessed is both geographical – Ogygia is as remote as possible from human and divine habitation (1.50 and 5.100–2) – and cognitive, for Calypso intends to make her guest forget his homecoming (1.55–57) and vanish from the memory and esteem of mortals (1.235–43). Sandel's description of this first type of dispossession accurately captures the hero's dilemma as his former ends recede from him, nearly transforming him into a nobody:

> we gain when we distance ourselves from possessions. I see this as too simple an assessment of the hero's identity, for it supposes that his "self-knowledge" remains constant, and that "he was able to return home the same person who had left, familiar to Penelope, untransfigured by his journey, unlike Agamemnon, who returned a stranger to his household and met a different fate" (1998: 56).

[24] I borrow these two possessive conceptions of self from Sandel (1998: 56–59), who only applies one to Odysseus (see previous note). The smothering loss of self from the second conception adds yet another nuance to Calypso's function as one who "conceals" or "covers over" (*kaluptein*) the hero.

> *It becomes increasingly unclear in what sense this is my end rather than*
> *yours, or somebody else's, or no one's at all. The self is disempowered*
> *because dissociated from those ends and desires which, woven gradually*
> *together into a coherent whole, provide a fixity of purpose, form a plan of*
> *life, and so account for the continuity of the self with its ends. (1998: 57)*

But if the self is truly prior to its ends, and its boundaries permanently established, then why should it be vulnerable to the loss of
such external goods? One answer in the minds of Homeric audiences
might be: "Because then such a self would never need fear becoming
the object (victim) of hybris!" As we'll see, should Odysseus accept the
immortality Calypso offers, he would affirm for Homer's audience the
possibility of forever escaping the misalignment of selves in the net of
hybris relations, and for us he would affirm the value of such a radically
deontological, unencumbered self. At this moment Odysseus resembles
Achilles in *Iliad* 9, isolating the ability of the "I" to choose and rechoose
its objects and ends; and, like the earlier hero, he has entered an interior
landscape Homer identifies in the *Iliad* with evaluating the *psykhê*.

But also distressing is the second type of dispossession, the predicament of a self engulfed by desires and purposes such as those Calypso
showers on Odysseus and those that linger in his mind as the former
ends he longs to reclaim. Again Sandel evokes the hero's situation:

> *Crowded by the claims and pressures of various possible purposes and*
> *ends, all impinging indiscriminately on my identity, I am unable to sort*
> *them out, unable to mark out the limits or the boundaries of my self,*
> *incapable of saying where my identity ends and the world of attributes,*
> *aims, and desires begins. I am disempowered in the sense of lacking any*
> *clear grip on who, in particular, I am. (Sandel 1998: 57)*

The antidote to each type of disempowerment is an understanding of
human agency dominated either by a voluntarist exercise of the will

or a cognitive exercise in self-interpretation. The act of choosing new ends (or renewing old ones) can always assuage the self's alienation from previous ends and purposes, and it bolsters the self's sense that it stands outside and prior to these ends. In this way we can read Odysseus' solution as enacting the ethic of Redfield's "economic man" who plays the agent of rational calculation: having experienced both the pleasures of Ogygia and the responsibilities of Ithaca, he opts to recover the latter. He in other words affirms that the value of possessing x or y is greater than the risk of losing them to subjects (perpetrators) of hybris.

If we recall the discussion of Achilles in Chapter 1, that hero also rejected defining his life and *psykhê* in terms of values others might covet in traditional exchange circuits, but he too ultimately anchored the ability of his "I" to choose in the future act of expressing preference for a wife and household peculiar to his own nature and needs. Both heroes therefore enact a moral autonomy through their will, but in the *Odyssey* Homer has maneuvered his audience to focus carefully on this act by ontologically isolating it and its agent and by structuring his entire narrative around it. If this is indeed the "most highly wrought" episode in the poem (Louden 1999: 104), one reason is that here Homer elaborates a representation of the "inner" act of exercising the will. He takes pains to foreground this act by contrasting it with its opposite, Odysseus' state of passive bondage to Calypso, for even in lovemaking, "the goddess no longer gave him pleasure – he always slept with her at night in her hollow cave by necessity; she was willing, he was not" (5.154–55; cf. 5.14–15). And despite the gods' role in motivating Calypso to release him, our understanding of Homeric morality in the *Odyssey* indicates that Odysseus does in fact have a will and is responsible for his decision to leave.[25]

---

[25] See B. Williams against Snell's (1960) and Vernant's contentions (1988) that Homeric mortals lacked a will consistent with the modern understanding of this term (1993:

But Homer also encourages us to attribute this choice to Odysseus' cognitive effort at self-interpretation. In Taylor's terms the hero broods over multiple visions of himself as the husband, father, and leader in Ithaca, the erstwhile sacker of Troy, and the consort of a goddess. (Here let's recall how scholars such as Pucci isolate Odysseus' penchant for brooding and introspection as a key to his novel personality; how for Peradotto a key lies in the hero's ability to project himself into multiple personalities; and how Barnouw identifies Odysseus' character with inner deliberation through various cognitive and emotional acts.[26]) By exploring the "depth" (Taylor's word) in such a cluster of possible identities, Odysseus must weigh the options provided him by his social, communal attachments and by what Nussbaum terms "the more ungovernable parts of the human being's internal makeup" – the "so-called 'irrational parts of the soul': appetites, feelings, emotions" (1986: 7). In this reading the hero qualifies as a "strong evaluator" and

<hr />

29ff., and 38–39 for Odysseus). Hammer (1998) refines our sense of how cultural values color notions of agency, will, and chance when comparing Iliadic heroes to modern individuals. Cantarella returns to Gernet (2001: 349ff.) for Homeric terms indicating willful, voluntary action (*hekôn, ethelôn, boulesthai*, 2003: 257–59). Lloyd-Jones insists that Homer represents humans as genuinely exercising a will despite divine meddling (1971: 9–10), and, at 28ff., he discusses the "unquestionably different moral climate" of the *Iliad* and *Odyssey*: in the latter, the gods do not interfere with human decision making and even warn mortals against immoral acts (e.g., *Od.*1.32ff.). See Yamagata 1994: 32ff. on the moral responsibility the *Odyssey* attributes to humans for their decisions.

[26] See Pucci on the poem's scenes of introspection where the hero "ponders" contrary courses of action (*mermêrizein*) (1987: 75); these scenes "represent a deep tension in the innermost being of the character" (69). Peradotto locates Odysseus' deeper sense of identity paradoxically in his capacity for multiple identities and for anonymity – i.e., in his ability to identify himself as "no one," a zero-degree identity that refuses categorization, in this way expressing the only truly unique, autonomous type of self (1990: 152–55). Barnouw carefully distinguishes the various verbs of considering, pondering, and wondering about impulses (*memêrizein, hormainein, dokein, phainein, bouleuein*) (2004: 190–20), and he describes the dispersed sites of this "visceral thinking" within the depths of Odysseus' self (*thumos, phrenes*, etc.) (99–108).

"subject of significance" who grounds a sense of his personhood in several of the quintessentially human emotions of "pride, shame, moral goodness, evil, dignity, the sense of worth, the various forms of human love, and so on" (Taylor: 1985a: 102).

But why should Homer portray a hero open to two different types of self, one dominated by a voluntarist dimension and action, the other by a cognitive; one a self hypothetically constituted prior to its ends, the other constituted by those ends? We find an answer if we return to the notion of the Calypso episode, which is centered around this act of choice, as a thought experiment, an exercise in ontological frame-switching fashioned by Homer for his audience. By having hero and goddess enact the choice in dialogue form, Homer creates a performative attitude not only intended for Odysseus but for audience members as well, a way for him and them to "answer to" (in Bakhtin's sense) the prospects of human suffering and death on one hand and on the other anonymous immortality. First, Calypso's offer:

> "Son of Laertes, descended from gods, resourceful Odysseus, do you
> really wish to return right now to your precious native land? Well then,
> farewell it is. But if you only had the intelligence to know how many
> miseries were in store for you before you reach your native land, then
> you'd stay right here with me to watch over my house and to be
> immortal, even though you long to see your wife and pine for her every
> day . . ." (5.203–10)

Then Odysseus articulates his choice:

> ". . . But this is what I want [ethelô] and pine for every day: to go home
> and see my day of return. Even if some god shatters me on the
> wine-dark sea, I'll endure [tlêsomai] it because I have a spirit in my
> chest that endures pain [talapenthea]. I've certainly suffered a lot and
> sweated a lot at sea and at war. Let this be added to that." (5.219–24)

This offer and its refusal invite both hero and audience to at least glimpse the possibility of being a deontological, unencumbered self, in Rawls' sense, a self with no ends or purposes but to enjoy the supreme form of well-being humans can imagine: perfect *eudaimonia* in an age where most Greek citizens and noncitizens knew only scarcity and toil.[27] As Vernant claims, "The Kalypso episode presents, for the first time in our literary tradition, what might be called the heroic refusal of immortality" (1996: 188); but to echo Redfield, this refusal enacts a *devaluation* of the ambition to be a self prior to its ends. Instead, Odysseus' reply valorizes the risk I've associated with entering into the grip of hybris relations: the remarkable line 522 (just quoted) uses two words from the stem *tla-*, *tle-*, to capture the moment when the self (re)establishes itself by simultaneously assuming and endangering its own welfare. As Pucci reminds us, the stem can mean both "dare" and "endure," that is, "to take upon oneself" in the sense of "to assume responsibility for," but also in the sense of "to put up with [endure, support]" (1987: 46). As a prototypical citizen self, Odysseus models how destructive this not-quite-real, deontological life of obscure immortality is compared to a more dangerous but meaningful sense of self, for a life surfeited with needs, desires, and fulfillment blots out any true identity.[28]

What Homer invites his audience to learn as prospective judicial magistrates and jurors, I suggest, is not only that this sort of unencumbered personhood is worth less than a harsh human life but that we can understand this only if deliberation and moral choice take place within the self, in some temporary zone of retreat or concealment

---

[27] Cf. Redfield on prosperity and surfeit (*koros*) as the most difficult ethical problems in Odysseus' world (1983: 243–44), and Rose's discussion of hunger as a powerful motive for characters within the poem and in Homer's audience (1992: 106–12).

[28] As we shall see, figures like the lotus-eaters and, to some extent, Penelope's suitors themselves exemplify this undesirable possibility of articulating ones' personhood.

where the self's voluntarist and cognitive dimensions can be evoked and compared. Now this understanding may promise a special reward for those few citizens who are inclined toward a personal ethical quest and self-transformation as Nussbaum outlines it, but for most the benefit will emerge at a jury trial or arbitration, where a different sort of self-transformation might result when elite and at other times ordinary citizens perform justice. Here, as the primary performers, they will be called upon to envision, in a hypothetical thought experiment that must to some extent be deontological, how the litigants before them might embody alternative selves open to the self's competing voluntarist and cognitive dimensions. In rendering a *dikê*, these magistrates or jurors must determine for the litigants, who are fellow citizens, how they have chosen to enter the grip of hybris relations and how they might or should escape them, reconfiguring their boundaries of self in conformity with a consensual, communal understanding.

THE *ODYSSEY*'S AUDIENCES: COGNITIVE AND MORAL CHALLENGES

The Calypso episode offers important lessons in the Odyssean school of performing justice. In the first place it demonstrates the value of becoming a person who is an object (victim) of hybris. To put this another way, the episode suggests that one cannot actually be a person unless one risks misalignment with other selves by becoming an object of hybris. (If this sounds paradoxical, we should recall Gernet's insight that individualism begins with the socially injured party in a dispute, for he or she suddenly becomes an object of sympathy and collective concern over *eunomiê*; this individual also channels within his or her person the authority to apply the sanctions of justice, usually in a self-help action.[29]) And the Calypso episode also reveals that this

---

[29] 2001: 257–302; see how Cantarella elaborates this insight in connection with anthropological approaches to prestate law (2003: 274–79; cf. 1979: 217ff.).

process of becoming an object of hybris occurs as a self-transformation enacted by a heroic self who marshals his cognitive and moral resources in an act of contemplation (Homeric "brooding" [*mermêrizein*]). This brooding, moreover, explores "depths" within the self leading the hero on a temporary detour into a deontologized realm where voluntarist thinking enables him at least to imagine the self prior to its ends.

But as we saw in Chapter 2, the judicial *basileus* in the state's Formative period had several means in his repertoire to induce ontological frame-switching and alternative visions of self, among them *themistes* and *thesmia*. Does the *Odyssey* teach its listeners, as prospective magistrates and jurors, to perform these too? It's worth recalling that *themistes* probably consisted of short narratives from community memory and myth that the adjudicating *basileus* thought relevant to a dispute; they may have included exempla, similes, and genealogical information related to the disputants. *Thesmia* were short narratives of crimes in community memory that had achieved paradigmatic status and probably included oath formulae or other devices that produced a straight *dikê*.

Let's also recall Havelock's insight that the overarching narrative structures of both Homeric poems are variations on the script "seeking a *dikê* from a *basileus*," and that the *Odyssey's* basic narrative structure portrays Odysseus and his family consistently suffering injustices at the hands of morally reprehensible agents (1978: 150–51). So is it far-fetched to infer that Homer encouraged his audience to identify Odysseus, Telemachus, and Penelope as potential "plaintiffs" in a dispute settlement (like the one on Achilles' shield) with their enemies, particularly the suitors? In Book 2 the assembly of Ithacans publicly establishes that there is a dispute between the house of Odysseus and the suitors, but it also makes clear that the dispute will have to unfold as a self-help action. For despite Telemachus' impassioned pleas for assistance, the community can't or won't take collective action against the suitors on behalf of its absent (or deceased) chief's household. The principal antagonists in this dispute are Telemachus, representing the household, and Antinous, the suitors' ringleader. But who is the audience for this dispute, and as it unfolds what sort of performance role is assigned to them?

Answers to these questions are not unambiguous. One audience for the assembly – the "internal" audience addressed by characters within the narrative – consists of the Ithacans.[30] Homer identifies them as *laoi* (the "people," 2.13, 41, 81, and 252), a term with particular meanings in epic, where it refers to undifferentiated community members who are often subordinate to and dependent on a leader, and whose condition may be perilous.[31] The *laoi* at the Ithacan assembly meet this definition but are nevertheless represented dramatically by three authoritative, elite members of the community: Aegyptius, Halitherses, and Mentor, of whom the last two will join in prophecy and moral harangue to urge their fellow Ithacans to support Telemachus' arguments. While neither the Homeric narrator nor any of the participants uses the word *dikê* to describe the aim of this dispute, the arguments of the "plaintiffs" (members and partisans of Odysseus' household) indicate that their goal is for the Ithacans to produce a judgment between the interests of two antagonistic parties. This decision, the plaintiffs hope, will result in an intervention whose outcome will see the suitors cease their courting of Penelope and remove themselves from Odysseus' house – voluntarily, we must presume. By the standards of dispute settlement examined in Chapter 2 – let's recall the dispute depicted on Achilles' shield, where the *laoi* were conspicuous (18.497 and 502) – this would likely result when "elders" emerge from their seats to lead the people to take sides in deliberation and decision.

---

[30] For some of the *Odyssey*'s "internal" audiences, see L. Dougherty 1995: 19ff., adapting the term from Iser 1978. (Dougherty doesn't apply it to the Ithacans at this assembly.)

[31] For the term's Homeric meanings, see Haubold 2000: 1–46, esp. 1–3 and 12–13.

In fact Haubold's recent study of the *laoi* in Homer and the later tradition indicates that, while generally weak socially or politically, the people possess "conceptual strength" as a public to whom appeals are made to render justice, end transgressions, and decide matters of communal importance (2000: 157). In particular, he claims, the *Odyssey* always keeps the Ithacans in mind as the necessary "backdrop" for the story of Odysseus' struggle with the suitors in order to "invoke . . . , contest . . . and manipulate" their judgment.[32] This clarifies the cognitive role of the *laoi* as an internal audience for this assembly and for Odysseus' revenge, but it does not settle the question of their identity. As we've seen, the *laos* may be largely undifferentiated, but elite individuals like Aegyptius, Halitherses, and Mentor may emerge from them. I also think it's noteworthy that Aegyptius has four sons who claim membership in three groups internal to the narrative: one (Antiphus) accompanied Odysseus as a companion (crewmember) and was devoured by the Cyclops; one (Eurynomus) is a member of the suitors; and two others (whose names aren't given) remain members of the *laos* by devoting themselves to their family's household affairs (2.17–22). This otherwise non-essential information suggests that the identity of the *laoi* is fluid, and Haubold's recent study confirms that speakers within the poem make competing claims about the suitors' and companions' membership in the *laos*.[33]

But in addition to being both undifferentiated and individualized, and fluid in membership, the identity of the *laoi* has yet another

---

[32] Haubold 2000: 110. Somewhat incongruously, Haubold at times describes the Ithacan *laoi* as "a powerful third party" to the struggle between Odysseus and the suitors (114) and its "powerful judge" (118). Despite their conceptual importance as representatives of the common weal, the *laoi* in Homer do not possess such authority or power.

[33] 2000: 104–25, esp. 112–13 and 120–21. (Haubold doesn't note the multiple memberships of Aegyptius' sons in all three groups.)

dimension, for it reaches beyond the narrative to include the poem's "implied" audience. This describes the hypothetical listeners/readers addressed by the epic narrator and projected as the ultimate recipients of the tale (L. Dougherty 1995: 19ff.). Despite our lack of information about the nature of Homer's "original" audience for the poems as we have them, or even for his early audiences over the first few generations of performance, scholars in recent years have offered engaging arguments pointing to citizens of sixth-century Athens as a favored, historically identifiable recipient for the earliest standardized version, whether oral, written or both.[34] Cook, for example, finds intriguing similarities linking Odysseus' return to Ithaca with Athenian civic cults of the Archaic period dedicated to the hero Erechtheus, Athena and Poseidon (1995: 128–70). Closer to our interests, he (along with others) links the poem's emphasis on human responsibility for personal and social ruin to core themes of Draconian and Solonian justice (ca. 620–590) (Cook 1995: 33–34).

But in my opinion it's more useful to speculate about who constitute the *laoi* both inside and outside the poem's narrative, and what their performance role as audience members might be. Haubold's study identifies the *laoi* appearing in Archaic and Classical texts as a figure for a society's autochthonous people occupying a historical, civic community's time and space in the heroic world prior to the emergence of civic institutions. More importantly, these legendary inhabitants constitute a "founding people" who lay the groundwork for civic institutions; as aetiological folk, poets and historians evoke them to demonstrate how later institutions develop from embryonic, heroic prototypes (2000: 169–70). Most importantly, the ritual and early political gatherings of these *laoi* serve latter-day citizens and institutions as models of

[34] On an Athenian version of the poem, see Nagy 1996: 110–11, and S. West 1988: 36–40.

imperfect, often failed social actions which the latter-day city-state will bring to perfection (173ff.).

Haubold returns us to Archaic Athens as a privileged audience for the Odyssey by suggesting that Homer's *laoi* evoked in Athenian citizens a version of their ancestors, specifically at the Great Panathenaea Festival, which showcased performances of the *Iliad* and *Odyssey* from the mid-sixth century onward. Here the festival's ritual reenactment of Athens' founding offered a particularly potent opportunity for Athenian citizens to recognize the origins of their state and political institutions in the exploits of heroes like Erichthonius and Theseus – and perhaps in legendary *laoi* like those in Homer (183–96). In addition to rituals connected with the Panathanaea, Haubold points out that conspicuous among the Athenian civic institutions which legendary *laoi* establish and prefigure is a law court (171–72): Aeschylus attests to this in *Eumenides* when he has Athena announce to the *laos* on stage a new "law" (*thesmos*) establishing the homicide court of the Areopagus, whose first members she recruits from their number (681–84); and Euripides too evokes the *laos* of Argos as a first homicide law court convened there by Danaus (*Orestes* 871–73). If Haubold is correct to claim that the poetic tradition projects the initial, halting stages of judicial decision making onto legendary *laoi*, then it is not unreasonable to infer that the "internal" audience of the Ithacan *laos* in Odyssey 2 and throughout the poem assumed this function for early Homeric "implied" audiences in Athens and other locations where law courts emerged.

When the Ithacan *laos* fails to respond to the promptings of their leaders to take action against the suitors, are they inducing Homer's early audiences to see in their apathy or confusion a "typically" inadequate legendary performance of precivic justice? And if these Homeric audiences recognize in Ithaca's *laos* a primitive, imperfect prototype of themselves as juror-judges, is the poem recruiting them to compensate for their ancestors' cognitive and moral helplessness? If these questions merit consideration, we need to understand more exactly the nature of the Ithacans' cognitive and moral shortcomings – and why the dispute between Odysseus' household and the suitors fails to lead to a *dikê* – because these shortcomings will constitute the challenge Homer lays at the feet of the Ithacans' latter-day counterparts, the poem's implied audiences. Let's recall too that within the poem membership in the *laos* appears to be fluid: individuals may, like Aegyptius' sons, belong to the *laos* and then become companions (crewmembers) or suitors; and suitors may refer to themselves as *laoi* when it pleases them (e.g., 22.48–49). So the poem's performance may encourage Homer's audiences to identify themselves with the cognitive and moral profile of one of three groups: if so, the assembly scene challenges audience members to decide "Whose side are you on?"

As a leader, the young, inexperienced Telemachus is partially to blame for the failed *dikê* when he tries to jump-start the dispute settlement. But the demands he makes of the *laos* seem in principle appropriate, and he isolates the key cognitive and moral question, in effect asking both the internal and implied audiences: "Do you know hybris when you see it, and do you know how to respond properly to it?" Without using hybris words, he openly characterizes the suitors' behavior as hybristic (they violate norms of guest-host relations and of marriage customs, 2.48–58), as vicious enough to rouse the Ithacans to collective anger (*nemesis*, 64) and to provoke an individual sense of shame in each person before his or her neighbors (*aidôs*, 65), and as a threat to the community's welfare (angry gods will punish all, 66–69).[35] He

---

[35] Fisher notes that as soon as we see the suitors at 1.225–29 their offenses against Telemachus' hospitality "can readily be seen as acts of hybris against the house" (1992: 165; cf. 176, where the suitors' "deliberate and sustained assault on all the members of Odysseus' house" conforms to fifth-century Athenian criteria for hybris). Saïd offers a succinct portrayal of the suitors' vices (1998: 243–50) and a paraphrase and thematic breakdown of the Ithacan assembly's nine speeches (126–29).

also leaves the Ithacans (and, I suggest, Homer's audiences) no moral room to assume a neutral position – they must stand either for or against his house (73–74); and he holds the Ithacans themselves partially reponsible for the miseries he's enduring (79). When Antinous refutes his claims by shifting responsibility for their prolonged visit onto Penelope's devious delaying tactics, Telemachus' reasons lose whatever cogency they may have possessed for the crowd, and his cause begins to flag.

True elders, Halitherses and Mentor, must rise to bolster it, each using a different technique to jolt the *laos* into grasping a kind of knowledge that eludes them – and I would characterize each man's performance as consistent with the cognitive aims of *themistes* in dispute settlement. Halitherses prophecies by interpreting an ominous bird-sign to mean Odysseus will certainly return to destroy the suitors (161–76). Mentor, while not overlooking the suitors' haughty, violent, and morally ignorant ways (235–36), attacks the Ithacans more vigorously for failing to remember: that in judicial matters a *basileus* whose authority is legitimate possesses knowledge of how things should be properly apportioned (*phresin aisima eidôs*, 231); and that the *laos* has forgotten how Odysseus was such a *basileus* who cared for and protected them (233–34). To remedy this cognitive failure on their part, he performs for them the indignation and outrage (*nemesis*) they should all be feeling and points out an authoritative speech act all the Ithacans should be directing against the suitors: "Right now I feel indignation" (*nemesizomai*, 239), mentor says, not toward the suitors, "but toward the rest of our community's inhabitants [*allôi dêmôi*, 239] for the way you are all sitting there in silence and not at all using words to attack [*kathaptomenoi epeessi*, 240] and to rebuke [*katerukete*, 241] the suitors, even though you are many and they few." In this harangue Mentor effectively implies that the Ithacans are incapable of aligning themselves properly in relation to the suitors and to the values of the dominant social other; in other words, as Telemachus warned, they risk identifying themselves with the suitors and their hybris (cf. Haubold 2000: 112).[36]

Why are the Ithacans so resistant to these compelling reasons and admonitions? Since they outnumber the suitors, as Mentor reminds them, I don't find persuasive Fisher's contention that the *laos* lacks physical force and yields to a "realistic appraisal of the strength of the suitors' position" (1992: 166).[37] Their "apathy" (166) no doubt reflects a prolonged lack of effective leadership and, historically speaking, the relative weakness in pre- and early state societies of community institutions in relation to the interests of households and descent groups. But we should not overlook the possibility that the Ithacans' deficient response is both thematic and programmatic. By this I mean that it is motivated by the traditionally passive role of the *laoi* in epic; but I also mean that Homer needs to represent his *internal* audience as, in social terms, abjectly unaware of how needlessly pusillanimous they are in the face of displays of wealth and power and, in cognitive and moral terms, how disgracefully incapable they are of recognizing the suitors' hybris as insupportable and untenable. In this way Homer

---

[36] In Lévy's lucid analysis of Homeric *nemesis*, he demonstrates systematic links between this term and *aretê* (excellence), *timê*, and *aidôs* (an individual's sense of shame before others) in heroic, aristocratic values (1995). If Mentor models the performance of *nemesis* for the Ithacans, we might infer their imperfect grasp of aristocratic values or their endorsement of how the suitors perversely enact them. See also Barnouw's discussion of the assembly, also emphasizing *aidôs* and *nemesis* as expressions of community values and morality, and arguing against the influential readings of Adkins (1960, 1972) and M. I. Finley (1979). Edwards points to Aegyptius, Halitherses, and Mentor as "men of prestige and standing" who represent an "informal *gerousia*" (council of elders) in the absence of a community's *basileus*, or in villages too small to require an individual leader (2004: 121–22).

[37] I also disagree with Cantarella that at this assembly "force is the only logic [the people] seem to know" and that "royal power" and all social relations in Ithaca are based on force (2003: 123, 126). A few pages later she concedes, "While it's true that power rests on force . . . Homeric royalty rests just as firmly on popular consent" (129–30).

cues the *implied* audience in communities like Athens to see themselves as judges whose social, cognitive, and moral intelligence can and must answer challenges that surpass the competence of an epic *laos*.

THE JUDGMENT OF THE DEAD AS PSYCHOTHERAPY

For these reasons I believe Homer recruits his implied audiences to play the role of jurors for the dispute between Odysseus and the suitors. Through the Calypso episode the poet also summons his audiences to witness the uncertain question of how Odysseus will himself assume the role of the agent of justice – or, I should say, the role of a *person* who will become an autonomous agent of justice. Remember that audiences learn, upon encountering Odysseus directly in Book 5, that this would-be litigant undergoes a self-transformation and a self-interpretation by comparing multiple visions of himself. This is all Homer's audiences know about Odysseus' inner life when he leaves Calypso to founder at sea, until he reaches the land of the Phaeacians and, through them, Ithaca. But the cognitive and moral understanding they've acquired in Books 1 to 5 constitutes an important step toward assuming the role traditionally played by the judicial *basileus* because they now occupy all three of the dispute's perspectives: the judge's objective, third-person perspective, and the subjective positions of the plaintiffs Odysseus, Telemachus and (to a small degree so far) Penelope, and of their adversaries, the suitors. And I've also contended that in Book 2 the poet is challenging them in effect to "know hybris when they see it" before completing the *dikê* the Ithacan *laos* leaves unfinished.

An even deeper understanding of these perspectives and of the nature of hybris is of course needed for them to presume (as jurors) to define for each plaintiff on behalf of the community the boundaries of self, especially as defined by the voluntarist and cognitive dimensions. And from our discussion of the judicial *basileus'* talents, we know that an essential component of an enriched third-person, objective perspective is the ability to place the dispute at hand in different temporal and ontological frames, including past and future moments of everyday reality and more hypothetical, other-worldly realities characteristic of myth and other types of lore in community memory. This, I've claimed, is the essential task of *themistes*, often accompanied by *thesmia*. This offers us a fresh approach to Book 11 (the *Nekyia*), which recounts Odysseus' consultation at the mouth of Hades with a few souls of the deceased and his quasi-descent to its underworld realms to encounter more souls.

The narrative patchwork that constitutes this episode has raised innumerable problems for scholars and critics since antiquity, but its "ambitious organization" characterizes for me a grandiose performance of *themistes* climaxing in a string of *thesmia* devoted to varieties of hybris and its punishments.[38] The audiences for these *themistes* and *thesmia*, I propose, are internal (the hero himself) and implied (Homer's audiences in Athens and elsewhere in their capacity as prospective judicial magistrates and jurors). The *Nekyia* has five principal sections: first, the hero's consultation (*nekuomanteia*) with the recently deceased souls of his crewman Elpenor, the prophet Teiresias, and his mother Anticleia (11.51–224); second, the catalogue of famous women (wives, mothers, and daughters of heroes and gods) from previous generations whose souls Odysseus silently witnesses (225–332); third, a brief "intermezzo" returning Odysseus to the present time and place of Phaeacia, where he is narrating this adventure to his hosts (333–84); fourth, a *katabasis* (hero's descent into the underworld) where Odysseus first encounters and converses with the souls of his companions at Troy (Agamemnon, Achilles, and Ajax) (385–567); and then, fifth, his silent witnessing of the souls of the judicial *basileus* Minos and what I'll call four heroic perpetrators of hybris from previous generations (Orion, Tityus, Tantalus,

---

[38] See Tsagarakis 2000 and Crane 1988 for a summary of scholarly dispute and opinion.

Sisyphus), concluded by an encounter with the phantom of Heracles (568–626).

At a glance we can see how this episode consistently switches temporal and ontological frames, shuttling back and forth among the present (Odysseus' wanderings; the predicament of his household and community in his absence), the recent past (events at Troy and in Ithaca), and a deeper heroic past, roughly contemporaneous to the era of his grandfather Autolycus. This shifting has been noted by scholars such as Nagler, who divides the entire poem into two ontological "zones": the "here-and-now of Ithaca" and the "mantic space" of the amazing adventures Odysseus narrates to the Phaeacians (1990: 339). Nagler sees these adventures at the poem's center, including the underworld visit, as performing what I consider a primary cognitive function of *themistes*: they "hold a kind of ontological mirror up to the situation in Ithaca, a mirror in which we find the main features of the relatively 'real' society reflected in a complex system of inversions and parallels" (1996: 151; cf. 1990). I'd like to develop this idea somewhat differently by asking what cognitive function two of the "otherworldly" zones (the necromantic consultation with the first three souls and the vision of Minos and the four heroic perpetrators of hybris plus Heracles) has in relation to the "relatively 'real' society" of Ithaca.

Nagler's notion of ontological mirroring provides a clue. We can adapt it to propose that what Odysseus hears and sees in Hades mirrors back to him alternative visions of himself: in other words, as when a prescient judicial *basileus* performs *themistes*, these encounters with figures, times, and places that are no longer real hold out to Odysseus-the-litigant the prospect of self-transformation through self-interpretation. They reveal resources from his cultural tradition that can provide him with the inner "depth" we moderns associate with introspection and even with access to unconscious knowledge.[39] For this reason I propose that the self-transformation Odysseus enacts on Calypso's isle has its roots here in Hades. The hero's need to consult Teiresias in order to return home safely, often criticized by scholars as insufficiently motivated, does seem justified on both narrative and moral terms. For he needs to know he will indeed reach home under adverse conditions, and that he can and should wreak vengeance on the suitors (11.100–20), and he does profit from the warning that he and his crew are morally responsible for fatal consequences if they eat the forbidden cattle of the sun god.[40] But what necessity can we attribute to the rest of the hero's encounters amid these patches of discontinuous narrative?

[39] I contest B. Williams' assertion that Homeric mortals after all lack "innerness," an "inner life" of the sort that might harbor "secret motives" (1993: 46). Much of what Odysseus sees and learns in Hades imparts an understanding and resolve he cannot and should not share with others, even though we see him act on them when he decides to leave Calypso and arrives home. Griffin's discussion of the "psychology" of Homeric characters claims they possess distinctly individual personalities that respond to "hidden motives," revealing "complexity" and even "inscrutability" (1980: 50–80, esp. 51–52 and 76–78). On "depth" in Odysseus' self, and on the link between this psychological depth and the poem's use of obscure meanings that gradually come to light, see Barnouw 2004: 30 and 249–59. If it's plausible to regard Odysseus himself as unable to link *all* that he learns in Hades to his earlier or later experiences in everyday reality, then we can see Homer evoking here the concept (though not the word) of a personal unconscious (contra Segal 1994: 63).

[40] Tsagarakis similarly defends the need to consult Teiresias (2000: 48–49). In Rheinhardt's description, Teiresias' speech fulfills the key function of *themistes*: it facilitates the hero's achievement of a *dikê* by revealing to him and to Homer's audiences hidden connections from past and future time linking the Cyclops' episode, the cattle of the sun god, and revenge on the suitors. It also indicates which actions and agents in past and future are in the right and wrong, and it assures that in retrospect all will appear to be in accord with divine will (1996 [1942]: 110–14). Cf. Cook's description of the "thematic centrality" of the *Nekyia*, which, along with the tales of the Cyclops and the cattle of the sun god, comprise a "commentary" on the hero's return and revenge (1995: 11).

Earlier we suggested that the deliberative democrat notion of the self holds out the prospect of a therapeutic self-transformation when engaging in reason-giving dialogue with others in the effort to reach consensus – a process whose end result, if not whose means, resembles the judicial *basileus'* ability to induce litigants to redefine their social personae and realign *timai* in a therapeutic self-transformation through *themistes* and *thesmia*. If we see a mirroring of self in Odysseus' encounters with individual souls in Hades, then we might consider this dynamic too as part of a psychotherapy imparting a knowledge of self in relation to others that forms an essential part of reconfiguring the boundaries of the self. In his discussion of "Epic as Therapy" Simon proposes that the performance of Homeric and Hesiodic narratives encourages a "blurring of boundaries" that is "more characteristic of childhood thinking and dreams than of adult and waking thinking." And the poems, he adds, are "replete with the language of enlargement and expansion of the self" (1978: 86).

In particular, following Rohde, he sees the souls Odysseus encounters in Hades as doubles of the self, reflecting back to Odysseus the undesirable heroic quality of a non-autonomous agent who passively endures suffering rather than acts to overcome it (Simon 1978: 57). For Simon, such episodes as the *Nekyia* exemplify how epic serves as a form of psychotherapy, for it allows the poet and audience to experience, through Odysseus' communicative interactions with others, "transient and largely unconscious identifications" with social and familial roles other than their own. In this way poet, audience, and heroic character all "work through the [hero's] sorrow and distress" in a healing process that generates a "new integration" (75) of the heroic self, overcoming his problematic "dedifferentiation" (87).

One psychoanalytic model Simon mentions for the self's identification with others is Kohut's "selfobject" (Simon 1978: 86, n. 21). Kohut's "self psychology" redefines narcissism as our primary mode of interaction with others. Narcissism also provides a key to understanding that a psychological symbiosis built on intersubjectivity rather than autonomy is both inevitable and desirable for the self's emotional health (1984: 47, 52). "I-you" relationships, Kohut claims, are of two fundamental types: in the first, the "I" targets the "you" as an object of desire and love or of anger and aggression; in the second, the "I" experiences the you as a "selfobject" representing key figures in its environment – what Taylor might call "significant others" or (in my reworking of Mead) versions of the "dominant social other." These offer images of the cohesion, strength, and harmony the self needs if it is to thrive as a "unit in time and space, connected to [its] past and pointing meaningfully into a creative-productive future" (52). Selfobjects respond to three kinds of transference linking the self to an "empathic" other: the first seeks through empathy a confirmation and approval from a figure that mirrors back to it a "grandiose" image of its cohesion and strength, usually in a maternal relationship; the second type seeks the empathic response of a figure (often parental) who reflects the image of the self's idealized aspirations; the third transference looks to a selfobject capable of providing a reassuring likeness of its talents and skills, usually as a twin or alter ego (192–93; cf. 1977: 185).

Let's approach just a few of Odysseus' encounters in Hades as dramatizations of these three types of transference between self and selfobject. At the same time we can compare what these transferences teach us about the hero to a more classically Freudian understanding of his struggles – as, for example, in Rose's attempt at a historicized psychoanalytic discussion of the *Odyssey* (1992: 122–34). Rose suggests that Homer explores Odysseus' identity by evoking fears and desires typical of elite (or near-elite) males of the late eighth century (123–24). He sees Odysseus as "a loner among males" whose "identity is primarily explored in relation to women," in particular through very ambivalent attitudes toward a series of powerful females he encounters (124). These include Calypso, Nausicaa, Circe, the Sirens, Scylla, and Charybdis, all representing desires for sexual gratification, physical nourishment, and protection, or forbidden knowledge, but also fears of castration or incorporation, including physical engulfment.

As selfobjects, however, most of these figures acquire a significance that does not so much objectify Odysseus' fundamental drives (libido, aggression) as reflect cohesive and fragmentary states of self or idealized senses of self to which he aspires.[41] Thus Calypso's empathic, maternal protection and nourishment mirror back to the shipwrecked hero a sense of wholeness and plenitude bordering on the grandiose possibility of immortality. His seven-year sojourn with her certainly evokes the extended period of childhood security provided by the mother, but it also indicates how fatal a prolonged dependence on such an archaic form of transference can be to any hope of securing a more mature selfobject relationship – his connection to Penelope.[42] Nausicaa too offers Odysseus an opportunity for empathic transference, but her rescue of the shipwrecked hero provides an idealized image of the security and prosperity a marriage partner can provide the self, again to be realized with Penelope.[43]

---

[41] Kohut's self psychology rejects Freud's reliance on the primacy of drives as constitutive of the self; it looks rather to narcissistic relations with others.

[42] Cf. Rose's conclusion that "Abandoning [Calypso] is perceived as the hero's only route to survival – to having an identity as a dominant, independent male" (1992: 125).

[43] Odysseus himself suggests this link between Nausicaa and Penelope as selfobjects when, at 6.180–85, he wishes Nausicaa an ideal harmony of spirit (*homophrosunê*) between husband and wife. Many scholars concur that Homer intends us to draw the analogy between the two women here (e.g., Schein 1996: 27, Felson-Rubin 1996: 178, n. 36, and Segal 1996: 209). Homer reinforces Penelope as a selfobject for Odysseus when he compares the reunited couple to two shipwrecked swimmers reaching shore (23.233–40).

These two females stand in stark contrast to Odysseus' encounter in Hades with his mother Anticleia. Seen as a selfobject, she confronts her son with the withered remnant of a self that suffers because it has been abandoned or disconnected from a dominant other. Her pathetic, decomposed state in effect represents the condition of Odysseus' own sense of self – this is, she says, the "*dikê* of mortals, whenever someone dies: the sinews no longer hold flesh and bone together but the potent strength of a blazing fire subdues them just when the life force [*thumos*] leaves the white bones and the soul [*psykhê*] flits about, flying off like a dream" (218–22). And she evokes for him a similar selfobject with the equally pathetic image of his still-living father's disintegration due to the hero's absence (187–96). When answering her son's question about the cause of her own death, she flatly declares, "I too perished and met my fate in this way . . . . Longing for you and your concerned, gentle ways robbed me of my life force, sweet as honey" (197; 202–3). Through these mirroring self-images, Anticleia imparts to Odysseus a knowledge he cannot yet comprehend consciously: that he abandoned in Ithaca a sense of his own self whose ends, acquired from familial, social, and communal roles, nourished himself and others; and he opted instead to assume a warrior-self pursuing such ends as individual glory (*kleos*) at Troy and the destructive means it required.[44] Anticleia, like Calypso and Nausicaa, also reorients the hero toward Penelope as the selfobject capable of fully restoring his life-nourishing self (161, 224); but since the trip to Hades occurs early in his wanderings, he is years away from understanding how imperative this is.

Encounters with selfobjects in Hades also illuminate Odysseus' relations with male figures, belying Rose's contention that "Unlike the

---

[44] Rose links the punning sense of Anticleia's name (perhaps meaning both "competing for *kleos*" and "opposed to *kleos*") to the Odyssean theme that devalues the warrior's pursuit of glory in the *Iliad* (1992: 129, with n. 65).

typical war heroes of the *Iliad*, Odysseus does not seem to identify or bond primarily with other males" (124). This may be so at the manifest level of the poem's narrative, but in Hades the hero interacts with no less than ten significant male others who reflect different needs and possibilities for his self-development. Two of these, Teiresias and Minos, offer him idealized images of wise elders whose oracular and judicial knowledge can subject the present to temporal and ontological frame-switching. The other seven males all mirror back talents, skills, and actions that mark them as twin figures or alter egos – and in every case but one (Heracles) they provide a negative, "shadow" image of a self with which the hero, if he has any hope of self-transformation, should refuse to identify. In Agamemnon and Achilles, Odysseus empathically engages with selves who underscore the futility of skills and values essential to the Iliadic warrior's pursuit of *kleos* (martial leadership and prowess, the desire for glorious death in battle, the high esteem of one's peers). These come to nothing, Agamemnon and Achilles demonstrate, if the voluntarist dimension of the self chooses them at the cost of an identity based on a supportive, nurturing connection to others such as a wife and son: Agamemnon overtly contrasts Clytemnestra and Penelope; he and Achilles pine for news about sons now lost to them (Orestes and Neoptolemus, respectively), while Odysseus still might recover Telemachus. And in Ajax, who epitomizes the self-destructive shame ignited by the competition fueling a warrior culture, Odysseus sees a self so dispossessed of social qualities by a zeal for glory that it's no longer capable of empathic response. Once again we can infer that Odysseus learns something essential about himself from these encounters, though I would not call this knowledge in its Homeric or modern contexts "conscious."[45]

---

[45] Cf. Tsagarakis on the knowledge Odysseus acquires in Hades: "The hero listened to the dead and remembered events and people connected with them; he became

MINOS AND THE FIVE PERPETRATORS OF HYBRIS

The *Nekyia*'s final section (568–627) plunges farther back in time to generations of heroes long before the Trojan War. It also returns us to the script of dispute settlement, for here Odysseus encounters Minos, seated in a judicial pose, holding a golden staff and "performing *themistes*" (*themisteuonta*, 569). The nameless dead surround him: "both sitting and standing they were seeking *dikai*" (*dikas eironto*), a phrase that may have been formulaic in judicial procedure both before and after state formation (Gernet 1981: 212, n. 289). Homer then offers a brief catalogue of five heroic figures glimpsed by Odysseus: Orion, Tityus, Tantalus, Sisyphus, and Heracles. Each is named and then briefly described performing an action emblematic of a punishment or ultimate fate. While this section has struck many in antiquity and in the modern period as a later interpolation into the poem, it's now recognized as integral to Homer's composite vision of Hades as a selective combination of encounters and figures typical of the *katabasis* as a poetic tradition.[46]

There's much less consensus, though, about why Homer has selected these remaining six figures for his hero to see, exactly what action each is performing, and how those actions are related to Odysseus' situation. The Cretan king Minos was a proverbial judge of the dead in Hades, paired with his brother Rhadamanthys, who is mentioned at *Odyssey* 4.564 as dwelling in the paradise of Elysium, and much later at Pindar *Ol.* 2.75 as judging the virtuous dead in the islands of the blest.[47]

conscious of them, and that was important. A latent 'collective memory' in him, essential to his survival and the realization of his goal, comes to life." He then contrasts the "external forces" Odysseus faces in his journeys with an understanding that "in the *Nekyia* he deals, as it were, with his memories" (2000: 69).

[46] On the passage's disputed authenticity, see Heubeck 1989: 76–77; Crane 1988: 87–89; Sourvinou-Inwood 1995: 84–85; and Tsagarakis 2000: 11–13. On the *Nekyia* and the *katabasis* tradition, see Tsagarakis 2000: 26ff.; Crane 1988: 101ff.; and Clark 1978: 38ff.

[47] On Minos and Rhadamanthys as Minoan kings linked to a cult of the royal dead and as judges in the Greek afterlife, see Sourvinou-Inwood 1995: 34–36 and 55 (their

But Minos' appearance here from 11.568 raises an immediate question: What sort of *dikai* are the dead seeking from him? Are they asking him to render decisions about disputes they are having among themselves in the afterlife; or, as newly arrived *psykhai*, are they seeking a judgment about the particular fate each will enjoy or suffer in the afterlife?

Scholars are unfortunately divided on this question, and evidence for early Greek beliefs about eschatology from the eighth century through the Archaic period does not permit us to draw neatly coherent, consistent rules about what may or may not transpire in the afterlife.[48] A crucial sticking point concerns whether the dead experienced individual or collective fates after death. Homeric conceptions of the afterlife do envision punishment and reward for behavior on earth in the case of elite or heroic individuals, and this notion of a particular fate borrows from dispute settlement in everyday life the suppositions that: an eschatological *dikē* about a deceased person can determine virtuous or criminal behavior; and it can lead to transformation of the self in the afterlife in accordance with cosmic apportionment.[49] But if, as Sourvinou-Inwood argues, this does not apply to the "ordinary" dead until sometime in the seventh century, when grave monuments and epitaphs testify to it, then are the nameless souls who "were seeking *dikai*" from Minos simply protagonists from an ordinary but "lively,

---

individual status here in the afterlife). Minos appears as a judge of the dead at Plato *Apol.* 41a, *Gorg.* 5233–524a, *Minos* 318d–318e, and *Axiochus* 371b–c (Tsagarakis 2000: 116, n. 503).

[48] For debate about the Greeks' eschatological beliefs during this period, see the exchange between Sourvinou-Inwood (1981, 1983, and 1995: esp. 413–44) and Morris (1989a). Also see Gnoli and Vernant 1982, Garland 1985, and Vermeule 1979.

[49] On punishment after death in Homer, see *Il.*3.276–80 and 19.258–60, where the offense is swearing a false oath; on rewards, see *Od.*4.563–69, and the reference to an "asphodel meadow" at 11.539 and 573 (all cited by Tsagarakis 2000: 116–17, with notes). See also Sourvinou-Inwood 1995: 67, with n. 167.

quarrelsome dead" who get along with one another no better in death than they had in life?[50]

Given the spotty nature of the data available to us, we can't know with certainty how Odysseus or Homer's early audiences understood the goal of Minos' *themistes*. I suspect that the original intent was to portray Minos in Hades displaying the same status he had in life, that of a judicial *basileus* whose cognitive virtuosity benefited the community.[51] But the meaning of his official, hieratic posture here may have shifted for later audiences who came to anticipate that souls, heroic and otherwise, would upon entering Hades receive an individual moral judgment to determine their fate. Either way Minos stands as an icon for the performance tradition of dispensing *dikai* – somewhat like the model of

[50] 1995: 87 and 66–67; 1981: 22 and 38, though Sourvinou-Inwood admits that already in Homer we find the seeds of belief in a generalized experience of individual fate after death (1995: 66–67). On Minos as settling disputes arising among the dead in Hades, see Crane 1988: 89, with nn. 32 and 33. Heubeck, for example, supports this view (1989: 111); cf. Page 1976: 48, n. 6, and Rheinhardt 1996: 117. But Morris' account of the Homeric afterlife sees Minos passing judgment on the individual dead (1989a: 309–10). Crane too concludes that this entire final section of the *Nekyia* (568–627) gains more "consistency" if we understand that Minos represents "some discrete act or process [that] sorts out the psychai and determines their fate." He surmises that, even though fourth-century texts articulate Minos' judgment of the dead more clearly, belief in an individual fate may be "appropriate to the eighth as well" (1988: 104); Tsagarakis agrees (2000: 116, n. 503). In relating the myth of Er in the *Republic*, Plato wanted readers to recall what Odysseus saw in Hades as an alternative to his own anonymous jurors (*dikastai*) judging (*diadikaseian*) the fate of each soul (*Rep.* 614b and 614c).

[51] Sourvinou-Inwood plausibly suggests that Minos continues to judge in the afterlife just as Achilles, a leader of great authority while alive, continues to rule over the dead (11.485 and 491) (1995: 87). She speculates that Minos represents here a transformed version of a Minoan funerary cult at which the ruler presided (34–36, 45, 55, 87–88). But it seems unlikely to me, as Cantarella argues, that in performing *themistes* Minos preserves a genuinely Mycenaean legal practice of royal judgment (2003: 281–83). His actions, set in a thoroughly heroized conception of the underworld, look to me consistent with the role of the judicial *basileus* in the Early Iron Age, including the early state period.

mimesis Nagy (1996) identifies in the poetic tradition: he models for all successive judicial *basileis*, and later for any citizen in the position of a magistrate or juror, the cognitive virtuosity required to reach a straight *dikê* when settling disputes and meting out punishment. And, as suggested, he serves Odysseus as a selfobject representing an ideal performance as an agent of justice.

But what is the connection between the tableau of Minos rendering *dikai* for the dead at 568–71 and the catalogue of heroic figures that follows? Is there a discontinuity here, as most commentators believe, with Odysseus at one moment seeing Minos adjudicating and in a subsequent moment passing on to witness in turn the heroic figures and their individual fates (see e.g., Sourvinou-Inwood 1995: 88)? Or is the catalogue a logical extension of that adjudication by exemplifying a few well-known cases of Minos' judgments – some receiving a good fate (Orion and Heracles), others bad (Tityus, Tantalus, and Sisyphus) (Crane 1988: 104)? Or in a similar way does the catalogue foreground cases that were "famous" and whose "severity" impressed Odysseus (Tsagarakis 2000: 111)? I believe that the sequence of figures gains in consistency if we speculate a bit and see it as illustrating Minos' very performance of *themistes*, specifically his use of *thesmia* from a panhellenic memory bank to settle disputes or determine fates for the nameless dead seeking *dikai*. Let's recall from Chapter 2 our reconstruction of *thesmia* as a speech genre preserving records of successful settlements in the narratively reduced form of the catalogue, probably arranged mnemonically by category of crime. If the catalogue of heroes follows directly the description of Minos adjudicating for the nameless dead, is this because these heroic fates constitute paradigmatic cases preserved or guarded by the arch-adjudicator as the most useful for rendering "straight" decisions? The nameless dead sit and stand at assembly like a *laos* of Hades, not unlike the community members in the dispute scene on Achilles' shield (*Il.*18.497–508) or at the Ithacan assembly (*Od.*2.13ff.).

What they "seek" (*eironto*, 2.570) is, to paraphrase Mentor's idealized evocation, that this "wise, soothing and kind sceptered *basileus*" bestow on them his knowledge of how things should be properly apportioned (*phresin aisima eidôs*, 2.231). Each hopes, I maintain, to see in at least one of Minos' *thesmia* a selfobject mirroring back a crucial act in his or her own past behavior. In the fate of a heroic figure each of the dead would likewise see a blueprint for a transformed sense of self, which is the cognitive goal of a justly rendered *dikê* or a justly apportioned afterlife.[52]

At the same time, keeping in mind Nagler's suggestion that episodes like the *Nekyia* provide an "ontological mirror" of what is happening in the everyday world of Ithaca, we should remember that each heroic figure is seen through Odysseus' eyes. Are they therefore meant to provide him a "second sight" concerning himself and others in both the recent past and the near future? That is, can they mirror back to him the condition of his own self, and also what has been (and will be) happening to his crew during their adventures at sea, as well as the behavior of the suitors in Ithaca? In this way they will evoke for him what Teiresias outlined in his warning (11.100–20) about the crew's possible fate before reaching Ithaca and the condition of Odysseus' household and the suitors when he alone arrives there.[53] As selfobjects catalogued in the form of *thesmia*, these five heroic figures would then prepare not only the nameless dead but also Odysseus and members of Homer's audience who are prospective citizen jurors (and litigants)

---

[52] Rohde characterizes the presentation of Tityus, Tantalus, and Sisyphus in terms that implicitly outline *thesmia* in the sense I propose: "Probably these three are selected as examples out of a much larger collection of such pictures" (1925; rpt. 1987: 40).

[53] Here, using Kohut, I'm suggesting what's implicit in Nagler's notion of ontological mirroring: the crewmen and suitors are selfobjects for Odysseus because they reflect the shadow side of the self-control and moral autonomy he strives for.

for an eventual cognitive and moral self-transformation into agents of *dikê*.

Since, as we've seen, the scripts "seeking a *dikê* from a *basileus*" and "suffering injustice at the hands of others" provide overarching themes for the poem's narrative, the lessons Odysseus learns from the figures in these *thesmia* should instruct him how to avoid the flawed moral and cognitive perspective of parties in dispute who yield to *atasthalia* (moral stupidity) and *atê* (blind delusion) because, in Nagler's words, they instead "ignore the claims of other actors, lose awareness of larger consequences, and make disastrous decisions."[54] This, it seems to me, describes the moral profile of someone in the grip of hybris, and in what follows I will argue that each figure appears in a *thesmion* as a *hybristês* exemplifying a variety of hybris. So the spectacle of Minos' *thesmia* should induce Odysseus, and Homer's implied audiences, as well as the nameless dead, to prepare their roles as agents of justice by recognizing hybristic behavior in others as well as in themselves and by assigning either positive or negative moral roles to the crew, the suitors, members of Odysseus' household, and so on.[55]

I'll also argue that, as paradigms of hybris, the five figures the hero is about to encounter bridge universal and particular fates if we recognize

---

[54] 1990: 352, discussing the flawed perspectives that prevent disputants like the suitors from abiding by traditional means of conflict resolution like oath swearing or a contest.

[55] Heubeck refers to the crimes of Tityus, Tantalus, and Sisyphus as "hybris which encroached on the privilege of the gods" (1989: 113.) Plato draws on these three figures as paradigms of criminality in his scene of eschatological judgment at *Gorg.* 523a–526d (esp. 525e and 526c–d), where Rhadamanthys, Aeacus, and Minos preside. Socrates claims that the most wicked, incurable souls are hung on display in Hades as "examples" (*paradeigmata*), "spectacles" (*theamata*), and "warnings" (*nouthetêmata*) to others (525c–d). These were for the most part kings (*basileis*), tyrants, and rulers who abused their power: the most typical crimes Socrates mentions are abuse of authority (*exousia*), self-indulgent excess (*truphê*), and hybris (525a).

each as a transitional stage in the development of moral consciousness according to the deliberative democrat notion of self. As such each can contribute to Odysseus' psychotherapy by returning him to scenes of conflict, punishment and obedience in the panhellenic storytelling tradition that happen to characterize Kohlberg's "preconventional level," where reciprocal relations dominate our interactions with specific others (usually powerful authority figures in a familial setting) and where our notion of right induces us to obey their rules and authority so as to avoid punishment (cf. Habermas 1990: 123). By recognizing himself (actually or potentially) in figures who remain fixed at this first stage, or who anticipate the second and third "conventional" and "postconventional" levels, Odysseus will then grasp the fundamentals of a moral reasoning capable of recognizing that the authoritative will of persons in our own lives actually partakes of a will that I identify with the dominant social other because it is suprapersonal and collective (153–54).

When internalized, it is this will that ensures our conformity to moral norms or, as the Greeks would put it, to *themis*. Finally, these heroic figures can serve as selfobjects for Homer's audience of potential jurors because, in dramatizing a stage in the development of moral consciousness, each figure will introduce listeners to increasingly complex types of what later ages will call a "criminal mentality." In effect this section of the *Nekyia* provides astute listeners with at least an intuitive understanding of the criminal mentality in Archaic Greece – an introduction to a psychology and psychotherapy of the criminal mind that should be indispensable for assuming the role of an agent of justice. In Gernet's terms, these souls dramatize the subject or perpetrator of hybris for a hero who will at a future moment on Calypso's isle decide to assume the role of the object or victim of hybris. And, to tweak Gernet's thesis a bit, they demonstrate how early Greek moral and legal thought could explore the individual behavior of those who perpetrate hybris as well as those who suffer its effects.

Sociologically speaking, it's not coincidental either that these heroes for the most part exemplify *basileis* of generations past whose crimes draw on excess appetites in an attempt to manipulate exchange relations with superiors and encroach on their *timê*. In her structural analysis of Tityus, Tantalus, and Sisyphus, Sourvinou-Inwood deftly demonstrates how each violates a code of behavior governing the cosmic alignment of humans and gods in relation to sex, food, and death (1986 and 1995: 67–70).[56] While I draw on her study's insights and reinforce its identification of boundary crossing as an overarching theme, I will supplement her abstract, cosmic understanding of criminal behavior by foregrounding hybris in its cognitive, moral, and social contexts as the archetypal offense in the development of Greek adjudication.

1. Orion. The first figure emerges from the deep mythological past: gigantic Orion, the hunter destroyed by Artemis, either for his slaughter of wild animals or (as Calypso claimed) because Artemis was jealous when he became enthralled to an insatiable lover, the goddess Dawn (5.121–24).[57] This is how Odysseus describes him: "And after Minos I noticed gigantic Orion rounding up wild beasts through the asphodel meadow, beasts he himself had slaughtered in the mountains of solitude. He held in his hands a club all of bronze, forever indestructible." (572–75). It's customary to explain this tableau as an example of how Homer describes the dead performing in the afterlife the activity they habitually performed when alive, and so Orion appears to be enjoying a pleasant fate hunting.[58] But is this fate meant to be, as

---

[56] Cf. Cantarella's discussion of these three sinners, whose crimes she characterizes primarily as a defiance of divinity and an unwillingness to recognize the distance between gods and humans (2003: 223–26). She does not link these crimes to hybris or discuss Sourvinou-Inwood's interpretations.

[57] For a summary of surviving versions of the Orion myth, see Fontenrose 1981: 6–21.

[58] See, e.g., Sourvinou-Inwood 1995: 88; Heubeck 1989: 111; Crane 1988: 103, Burkert 1985: 196; J. Finley 1978: 126; and Rohde 1925: 39.

most commentators understand it, a morally neutral one? If so, then it contrasts sharply with the harsh punishments meted out to Tityus, Tantalus, and Sisyphus, whom modern scholars have invariably called "sinners."[59] A closer look at Orion's roles in the mythological tradition (both pre- and post-Homeric) suggests that he was always associated with morally reprehensible, hybristic actions; and when we try to square his activity as an archetypal hunter with possible meanings he might have as a selfobject for Odysseus, we likewise find a morally negative judgment. Orion, in other words, also looks to me like a hybristic "sinner."

As an archetypal hunter, Orion incarnates in the tradition a violence against other creatures (including humans and gods) without the civilizing restraint that comes with recognizing the need for reciprocal exchange (Schnapp 1997: 33–34). And indeed the tradition contains multiple examples of Orion's lack of restraint, not only in using violence to hunt but in his sexual and oral appetites as well. For example, in the Hesiodic tradition (fr. 148aMW; also Parthenios [20]), he was a grandson of Minos and a son of Poseidon who cleared Chios of its wild beasts in hopes of winning Merope from her father Oenopion ("Wine-face"). When Oenopion procrastinated, Orion got drunk, sexually assaulted Merope, and was blinded by her father (in one version Minos himself was Orion's host and Minos' daughter his victim).[60] These acts categorically illustrate scenarios from the script "committing hybris," especially when the agent enjoys youthful impetuousness and the advantage of great physical strength.

---

[59] On these three as "sinners" see Sourvinou-Inwood 1986 and 1995: 67–70; for a bibliography on all three, see 1986: 37, n. 1; for Tityus, 37, n. 3; for Tantalus, 40, n. 17; for Sisyphus, 47, n. 52.

[60] See Fontenrose 1981: 6ff., with references, including Apollod.1.4.3. Orion is also said to have competed with Artemis and to have sexually assaulted her (Aratos *Astr.*2.34) or another maiden, Opis (Apollod.1.4.5).

If, as Schnapp claims, Orion "incarnates uncontrolled violence more than any other hunter" (1997: 453), and if an overview of his myth reveals a hybristic character that is "impetuous, violent, reckless . . . [and] lacking in self-control" (Fontenrose 1981: 18), then he mirrors back to Odysseus an alter ego from a psychologically archaic stage of development, when the self is incapable of practicing self-control in exchange for approval from dominant others. As an object of Dawn's erotic interest and Artemis' anger or jealousy, he serves as an analogue for Odysseus himself, enthralled by Calypso, for the crew as well, enthralled by the "dread goddess" Circe, and even for the suitors, enthralled by Penelope's erotic appeal.[61] Orion's indiscriminate slaughter of the wild beasts (sacred to Artemis) also parallels the crew's slaughter of the cattle of the sun god, and their ironic transformation from unlawful sacrificers into victims, just as the suitors indiscriminately slaughtered Odysseus' herds and were victimized in turn by him. As we'll see, Odysseus too is implicated in this parallel of the lawless hunter because of his impure slaughter of the suitors.[62]

So Orion's emergence in Hades may be more laden with meanings than most scholars suppose. But what of his ultimate fate? Most sources, including Homer, acknowledge that Zeus honored him after death by transforming him into the constellation that still bears his name, but he is imagined in Hades as a hunter continuously driving before him, through a meadow (*leimôna*, 573), all the wild animals he has slain in the isolated mountains, holding in his hands the instrument of their

---

[61] On the "dread goddesses" and their male victims, see Nagler 1996: 142–53.

[62] Odysseus will encounter in Heracles a stronger analogue than Orion of the unlawful hunter. For parallels between the crew and the suitors due to the perverted sacrificing of forbidden cattle (which is also linked to Odysseus' impure slaughter of the suitors), see Nagler 1990: 339–42. Sourvinou-Inwood only links Orion and Odysseus as hunters through Odysseus' "lawful" shooting of a stag on Circe's island at 10.156–73 (1995: 88).

death, his bronze club. However, it seems to me that the text indicates that he is *manifestly no longer hunting*, or performing in the afterlife the act he so loved during life, because these beasts have already been slain (*katepephnen*, 574) in the mountains. What, then, is he doing and what significance does this action have? His career as a hunter emphasizes an excess of force in destroying all the beasts of a land (Chios and Crete are mentioned), and this excess causes one version of his death because of Earth's anger (Hes. fr. 148aMW.15–17). If in the afterlife he is "driving together" or "rounding up" (*homou eileunta*, 573) the beasts he has killed in the mountains when alive – there are no mountains in the landscape of Hades – then a self-transformation has occurred: Orion the hunter is reassembling after death the ghostly evidence of his excessive appetite in life, and now he ironically appears more like a shepherd herding animals through a pasture.[63] More than a privileged repetition of an honorable activity enjoyed during life, this fate looks to me like reparation after death – in short, a punishment.

2. Tityus. The next heroic figure is the even more gigantic Tityus, whose description provides all the essential narrative elements for a complete

---

[63] For *homou eileunta* as "drive together, round up," see Heubeck 1989: 112. Because of Orion's hybristic, criminal personality, I disagree with Heubeck and others that here we see the principle of "iteration" by which a soul in Hades repeats his lifetime's primary activity (111, citing Nilsson 1967: 454). Rather, here the hero herds the souls of the dead beasts he excessively slaughtered; not unlike the sun god's cattle, these creatures are thought in some sense to be immortal (cf. Vidal-Naquet 1986a: 24). As a prototype for the hunter and a figure of transformation, Orion represents, from a structuralist perspective on city-state ideology, the passage from savage to civilized life and from an unjust, greedy consumption of meat without sacrifice to the just partitioning of resources with others; see Schnapp 1997: 35–36. In his youthful beauty – linked at *Od*.11.308–10 with the giants Otus and Ephialtes – Orion resembles later ephebic figures like Melanion and Hippolytus; see Vidal-Naquet 1986a: 118–19, citing Oppian *Kyn*.2.28–2

thesmion: his name, genealogy, his violation against divine *timê*, the divinity he offended, and his punishment:

> *And I saw Tityus, son of glorious Earth, lying on the ground. He lay*
> *spread over nine acres and a vulture on either side of him tore at his*
> *liver, penetrating his innards; his hands could offer no defense. This is*
> *because he raped Leto, Zeus' famous bed-mate, when she was passing*
> *through lovely Panopeus on her way to Pytho. (576–80)*

Tityus' crime is the overtly sexual one of desiring the Skygod's mate.[64] Both he and his fellow giant Orion suffer the fate of those who could not control the unbridled *thumos*, where powerful feelings and appetites originate, characteristic of the broods of monstrous and gigantic offspring (including the Titans) produced by Earth and Sky before the Olympians' birth (cf. Hesiod, *Th.*126ff).[65] But Tityus' injustice against Zeus arises more pointedly from lust, with its particular seat in the liver. According to Sourvinou-Inwood's structural analysis, he transgresses against "the sexual code which helps articulate the universe" because he violates divine-human boundaries; his punishment then turns the sexual aggression he directed upward towards a goddess and Zeus' honor downward toward his own "organ of sexual desire" (1986: 38).

But I would add that, together with Orion's, Tityus' *thesmion* makes clear to Odysseus and to Homer's audience where, and with what moral elements, one who is *hybristês* must reconfigure the self's boundaries

---

[64] See Caldwell's psychoanalytic discussion of Tityus' crime and punishment, linking them to crimes and punishments by other canonical sinners the tradition placed in Hades (1989: 134–40). Caldwell links the child's curiosity about parental sexuality (32ff.) to Teiresias and Sisyphus in the underworld (37–39), with direct links to later myths (cf. Apollod.1.4.3). But both Orion's and Tityus' adventures reflect various oedipal anxieties of the son, the former including powerlessness before the phallic mother (the goddess Dawn; Artemis) (cf. Caldwell 1989: 33).

[65] Cf. Teiresias' warning to Odysseus that he and his men will return home "if you are willing to restrain your *thumos* (apetite) and your companions'" (11.105).

in order to become an agent of justice: in the "ungovernable parts of the soul" and with the voluntarist capacity of the will. And while Tityus was said to be a wicked king living in Euboeia (*Od.*7.321–24) or Phocis – his burial mound was still pointed out in Pausanias' day (10.4.4) – like Orion his physical stature was enormous. As a self-object, he too suggests to the hero and to Homer's audience that we suffer if we linger too long in that archaic stage of childhood where we bask in self-affirming exhibitionism and grandiosity (Kohut 1977: 185). Most importantly, Tityus dramatizes to Odysseus how the will can use sexual desire and aggression to exercise a misguided autonomy in determining ends and objects the self must possess.[66] This imparts to him a knowledge that is at best only partially conscious, intimating two of the four major injustices the suitors will perpetrate against him: their sexual violation of his household women and their insistence on courting Penelope while he still might be alive.[67]

3. Tantalus. Tantalus is the third heroic criminal Odysseus meets:

> *And I actually looked upon Tantalos suffering terrible pains: he was standing in a pond of water up to his chin. He had a thirsty look but couldn't manage to drink, for whenever this esteemed man* [ho gerôn] *bent his head down to drink, the water vanished, sucked down so that*

[66] Sourvinou-Inwood emphasizes ways in which Tityus, Tantalus, and Sisyphus differ from Odysseus rather than resemble him: as offenders against the gods, the three are "comparable" to Odysseus because he offends Poseidon and to his crew because they offend the sun god (1995: 88). With the trickster Sisyphus, however, she draws closer parallels to Odysseus' personality (88–89).

[67] Yamagata identifies these as two of the suitors' four principal injustices; the others are their nonreciprocal consumption of Odysseus' property and their refusal to fear the gods or the *nemesis* of men. In addition, they are prepared to murder Telemachus and Odysseus, should he return (1994: 28–31). But as Saïd indicates, most of the suitors' offenses against Odysseus' household concern feasting (eating and drinking) (1979: 10).

dark earth surrounded his feet – a god dried it up! Above his head trees
with tall branches spread out their fruit – pears, pomegranates,
shimmering apples, sweet figs and flourishing olive trees. But whenever
the esteemed man attempted to take some in his hands, the wind tossed
them up toward the shadowy clouds. (582–92)

In this fragmentary *thesmion* no crime is described, but there's little doubt from the nature of the punishment and from the earliest surviving fragments of the Tantalus story that he transgressed against an "alimentary code," as Sourvinou-Inwood puts it (1986: 42), and against norms of reciprocity in divine-human relations concerning feasting. Her extended discussion convincingly argues that Tantalus' original crime – one Homer decides not to describe here – is cannibalism: Tantalus murdered his son Pelops and attempted to serve the boy's body at a banquet for the gods (Sourvinou-Inwood 1986: 40–47). Since in Greek eyes cannibalism transforms humans or gods into beasts, Tantalus' crime hybristically inflicts dishonor on the Olympians because it threatens "to make the very guarantors of the cosmic order transgress one of the fundamental rules which helps articulate the cosmos" (42). We'll see too that the theme of cannibalism, for the Greeks the most virulent form of "improper eating," makes Tantalus an effective alter ego or selfobject for the suitors and for Odysseus' crew.

The meaning of Tantalus' crime, however, does not reside solely in cannibalism but in the social network of culinary exchange relations in which it occurs. The theme of commensality with the gods persists in alternative versions of the story that replace cannibalism with the hero's attempts to steal the food of the gods or divulge secrets learned at their table.[68] The epic *Nostoi (Returns of the Heroes)* describes

---

[68] See Pindar *Ol.* 1.60–64 and Euripides *Or.* 8–10, respectively, with Sourvinou-Inwood's discussion, which contains additional variants (1986: 44–46). Cantarella is mostly interested in the scholiast's variant (*schol.Od.*11.582) which has Tantalus

Tantalus' unbridled appetite for pleasures reserved to the gods, which he shared thanks to Zeus' generosity. Zeus offered Tantalus whatever he desired; exploiting this lavish offer, the hero greedily chose the pleasures of being served at table by the gods themselves and to live their way of life. Obliged to keep his promise, Zeus complied but placed a stone over Tantalus' head, short-circuiting the hero's ability to enjoy the bounty before him (fr. 3 West = fr. 10 Allen).[69] This specificity of feasting as a cultural context for criminal behavior suggests to me that Tantalus' hybristic crime, which like Orion's and Tityus' springs from excessive appetite, originates from a moral reasoning different from the sort employed by the two giants – that is, from a more complex stage in the development of moral consciousness. When Orion and Tityus interact with authority figures, they enact the preconventional stage where the ego's behavior remains "context-bound" by its own intentions and those of its adversary. Whether out of an aggressive desire for killing beasts or a need for sexual gratification, the ego directly expresses its will in spite of its adversary's position and seemingly in ignorance of any generalized will representing social expectations and norms (Habermas 1990: 153–54). When the ego's adversary turns out to be more powerful than anticipated, the ego suffers the direct consequences of inevitable punishment, as is often the case in the child-parent relations the stories of Orion and Tityus appear to illustrate.

suspended on a mountain with his hands tied: this enables her to link him to Prometheus and to the form of punishment, attested later in Athens, of "crucifixion" (*atympanismos*)(2003: 226–30). But this has little to do, I think, with the Tantalus we see here in Homer.

[69] Gernet links Tantalus to the *eranos* or feast given by a *basileus* to recruit followers; these followers were in turn obliged to reciprocate the chief's gifts. Gernet sees this early relationship of debt and obligation developing into a "veritable category of moral thought" in the forms of social contract and the law (1981: 151–59, esp. 157–58).

To put it another way, these giants don't seem able to achieve an objective position toward their own actions that might represent to them the system of reciprocal relations outside their particular encounters with authority figures. When Tantalus sets out to exploit Zeus' generosity, however, he clearly does grasp the position of an impartial observer of the reciprocal system governing guest-host relations. Because he uses strategic reasoning to try to outwit his divine exchange partner, he must see the interchangeability of their roles and the collective will of the dominant social other behind them (Habermas 1990: 154). By resorting to ruse, he nevertheless refuses to subordinate his own will to this objective, generalized position. His crime and subsequent punishment therefore demonstrate to observers how much more intelligent and powerful the impartial, suprapersonal authority of exchange relations can be: in effect it controls every "move" within the system, and even a divine player like Zeus is constrained to follow its dictates since he must after all keep his lavish promise to Tantalus.

What then does Tantalus mirror back as a selfobject for Odysseus and members of Homer's audience? Thematically we've seen that his original attempt to perpetrate cannibalism upon the gods violates the alimentary code, and he compounds that violation by performing it within the sociological network of reciprocal feasting between guests and hosts. Like him the suitors' hybris also unfolds within the context of guest-host relations and feasting; in particular they fail to reciprocate their host's generosity, and Homer describes their manner of devouring Odysseus' herds and improperly sacrificing and cooking the meat in terms that evoke cannibalism.[70] Tantalus also mirrors back to Odysseus the hybris of his crew's inability to control their appetites when they devour the sun god's cattle. In killing these beasts, the crew

---

[70] See Saïd 1979: 24–41, and Vidal-Naquet 1986a: 25.

pervert the proper form of sacrifice in a scenario of "improper eating" that also plunges them back into a savage past.[71]

Just as importantly, however, Tantalus displays for Odysseus and Homer's audiences a more subtle type of criminal mentality than Orion or Tityus because, with superior cognitive abilities, he's more aware of reciprocity's subjective positions of self and other and its objective role of a third-person observer. He's also more conscious not only of his deception but of his *intent* to deceive – and so he's more morally autonomous and responsible for his act. At the same time, despite his intelligence, he mirrors back to Odysseus and Homer's audience a fatal blindness I'd equate with *atasthalia* and *atê* since he seriously underestimates what his divine exchange partner can see and know. In this regard he provides a foil for Odysseus' crew members, who fail to understand, despite a warning, that the all-seeing sun god will observe and punish their theft of his cattle. The suitors too find themselves reflected cognitively and morally in Tantalus' crime and punishment since they also disregard warnings about their unjust consumption of Odysseus' livestock. Like Tantalus they too will find themselves as ironical guests at one last feast – this one in Odysseus' home, when he slaughters them in a simulation of the wedding feast each hoped to celebrate as Penelope's new husband (23.141–51).

4. Sisyphus. Sisyphus appears next, eternally rolling his rock up a slope, a figure of almost overdetermined significance for both Odysseus and the suitors, for his cognitive abilities and criminal mind are marked by even stronger degrees of conscious intent to deceive and manipulate than are Tantalus':

> *And I actually looked upon Sisyphus suffering terrible pains: he was sizing up a gigantic rock with both his hands. Bracing himself with*

---

[71] See Cook 1995: 56, and Vidal-Naquet 1986a: 23–24.

> *hands and feet, he pushed the rock up a hill, but whenever he was about*
> *to get it over the top, its overwhelming weight tilted it back, and so the*
> *pitiless rock rolled back down to the bottom again. And then, exerting*
> *himself, he pushed it back, sweat pouring from his arms and legs and*
> *dust rising about his head.* (593–600)

In Homer, Sisyphus was already proverbial for his cunning, and his appearance in the Hesiodic *Catalogue of Women* in fact identifies him as a judicial *basileus* in Corinth, one of the Aeolidae, "*basileis* who perform *themistes*" (*themistopoloi basilêes*, fr. 10.1).[72] As a son of Aeolus, the catalogue makes him Odysseus' ancestor in the Deucalid genealogy (West 1985: 176), though we'll see that an alternative tradition makes Sisyphus, and not Laertes, Odysseus' true father. Sisyphus emerges from these early traditions as a consummate trickster, and so it's not surprising that his criminal mentality surpasses Tantalus' in its intent to deceive and outwit the various systems of norms and obligations that restrain the selfish desires of humans. If he functions here as a selfobject for Odysseus, the suitors, and prospective jurors (and litigants) in Homer's audience, two of his exploits in particular point to the moral lessons he can offer.

His presence in the *Nekyia* is perhaps directly connected to his principal trickster feat: the use of cunning speech to cheat death itself. From sources like Theognis, Alcaeus, and Pherecydes, and probably in Aeschylean and Sophoclean dramas too, we know that Sisyphus undertook a *katabasis* to the underworld, "illegally" crossing the ontological

---

[72] See *Il.*6.153–54, where he is described as *kerdistos egenet' andrôn* ("he was born the slyest of men"), Hes. fr. 43 (a) 41ff., *Theognis* 697–718, where he possesses *poluidrêiai*, "very smart ways" (703), and *poluphrosunai*, "lots of shrewdness" (712), and Alc. 38a5– 10 (*andrôn pleista noêsamenos*, "most cunning of men," 38a6), and a possible pun on his patronymic in the *Catalogue of Women* (*aiolomêtês*, 10.2). For references to Sisyphus in Archaic and Classical authors, see Sourvinou-Inwood 1986: 47–49.

boundary separating human life from death (Sourvinou-Inwood 1986: 47–48). Relying on his wits, he was like Odysseus a master of deceptive, cajoling words (*haimulioisi logois*, Theognis 704), and with this talent he entered the underworld and won over its dread goddess, Persephone, much as Odysseus won over the dread goddesses Circe, who gave him passage to the underworld, and Calypso, who offered him immortality. Or in Pherecydes' tale, when Zeus sent Death to punish Sisyphus, he lay in ambush and tied it up, preventing Death from taking any human life.[73]

But as we saw with Tantalus, Sisyphus' crime does not consist solely of violating the boundaries of cosmic categories like divine-human-animal or life-death. He too dishonors deities by out-thinking them within the net of a cultural system to which all subscribe – in this case, funerary ritual and beliefs about the afterlife. For, when compelled to die and enter Hades, this trickster told his wife not to perform the customary funeral rites (*ta nenomismena*) so that he could persuade Hades to send him back to chastise her; once on earth again, he lived out his life to old age.[74] Like Tantalus, Sisyphus' wit enables him to

---

[73] Pherecydes fr. 78 (= *schol. Il.*6.153), partially preserved in Apollodorus 1.9.3. Since Sisyphus didn't use persuasion to foil Death, we needn't conclude that he used force, as Sourvinou-Inwood claims (1986: 48): the scholiast implies that Sisyphus' ability to note and anticipate Death's approach was the key to tying up his adversary (*aisthonomos tên ephodon . . .*) – perhaps a combination of *mêtis* (cunning) and *biê* (force).

[74] Sourvinou-Inwood distinguishes rigidly between a Homeric belief that souls could not enter Hades prior to burial and a post-Homeric belief that they could. She then infers that in the tale's original version Sisyphus enters Hades after burial but cajoles Hades to allow his return to earth to request something else in the funeral rite that was due the dead. In subsequent versions, she claims, he enters Hades before burial and so returns to request burial itself (1986: 50–51). But can we draw rigid distinctions for Greek funerary practices and beliefs based on Homeric vs. post-Homeric sources? Cf. Morris' critique (1989a) of Sourvinou-Inwood's methods and her reply (1995: 413–44).

stand outside the exchange relations of funerary ritual while anticipating all the subject positions (the deceased, the burying group, Hades himself) and the obligations of each. But, again like Tantalus, he learns that the divinity he dared dupe and dishonor, Hades, represents and enacts the funerary exchange system's ultimate control over its participants. Sisyphus' punishment of rolling the stone upward and witnessing its inevitable descent therefore enforces on him the inescapability not only of death itself but of the system's eternal circuit of roles interconnecting the living and the dead.[75]

I suspect that Sisyphus' *thesmion* here in the *Nekyia* calls to mind for Odysseus and the poem's audiences a second exploit, one which unfolds within the reciprocal relations of another exchange system, bride exchange, and reveals how even here on earth an arch-trickster can himself be duped. In a fragmentary, unclear narrative from the Hesiodic *Catalogue of Women*, we find that Sisyphus paid many cattle to Aethon to obtain his daughter Mestra as a bride for Sisyphus' son Glaucus (fr. 43[a]). But when Mestra returned to her father as a runaway bride, Sisyphus demanded back his payment (and perhaps the bride as well). Athena likely adjudicated the case and produced the following *thesmion*. Note how it depersonalizes and narratively reduces the dispute's details to formulate a suprapersonal law about more generalized reciprocal exchange. Not only does this resolution anticipate the transition from the *thesmion* as an individual resolution of dispute to the *thesmos* as an orally formulated law, it also displays the switch in cognitive and moral perspectives from Kholberg's preconventional to conventional levels. Athena decreed: "Whenever someone demands to get back property in return for its purchase-price, it is absolutely necessary to...concerning the purchase-price....the value [of the object?]...

---

[75] Sourvinou-Inwood's insightful reading of the punishment focuses on its repetition of the cosmic upward-downward movement of Sisyphus' crime itself (1986: 52–53).

Once someone has paid in the first place, [the object? the payment?] cannot in fact be handed back" (fr. 43 [a]41–43).[76]

It looks as though Sisyphus was duped by Mestra (and her father) so that she could strengthen the economic fortune of her paternal *oikos*. As a pair of swindlers, this father-daughter team anticipates the team of Penelope and Odysseus (at 18.274–80), when Penelope dupes the suitors by upbraiding them for violating the reciprocal responsibilities of bride exchange because, so she claimed, their lack of bridal gifts constituted an abuse of their host's generosity and ignorance of the proper role (*dikê*) of suitors. In this way she uses her own *mêtis* to trick them into giving her lavish bridal gifts for a marriage she hoped would never take place, all the while secretly winning the approval of her husband, who stands by silently laughing in his old beggar's disguise. In broader terms Sisyphus' escapade in the Hesiodic *Catalogue* matches the injustice the suitors commit in courting Penelope while her husband is still alive, for the moral-legal offense at issue here seems to be a male's illicit desire to obtain for his household a woman whom the head of her household (father or husband) has no obligation to relinquish.

As a selfobject, therefore, Sisyphus reflects a shadow figure for anyone who pretends to exercise a *basileus'* superior cognitive abilities and privileges. I've argued that his appearance in Hades evokes his attempts to abuse such talents and privileges within two exchange systems, but we need not rule out a third if we consider that dispute settlement by a judicial *basileus* was based on exchange also, as we saw on Achilles' shield and in Hesiod's bitter experience. Unlike the previous three heroes, Sisyphus' appetite has few physical qualities but expresses itself through an intelligence and a will to misalign the self with others by expanding its boundaries cognitively, morally, and ontologically. I've tried to show in Chapter 2 how the judicial *basileus'* talent

---

[76] Gagarin discusses and renders the passage a bit differently (1986: 56, n. 16, and 35–36).

uses ontological frame-switching as an indispensable part of performing *themistes*, and this suggests to me that Sisyphus dramatizes ways a *basileus* may, as a "trickster-*basileus*," turn his cognitive virtuosity into a *mêtis* capable of crossing such boundaries as life and death, human and divine, and the obedience to and evasion of rules. Unlike the first two sinners, but like Tantalus, Sisyphus' mature intelligence assures us that he knows these rules and knows too the roles assigned to all parties when they contract obligations to one another.

Sisyphean hybris thus operates at the conventional and even anticipates postconventional levels of moral consciousness, where individuals wrestle with conflicts between the values and interests of one's own group and the universal, impartial values and interests secured through a social contract (Habermas 1990: 123–24). This dilemma of course becomes Odysseus' own once he returns to Ithaca, where he must use *mêtis* combined with *biê* to perform justice. Endowed with the sympathy and authority of the object of hybris, he will after all bypass relying on a judicial *basileus* to reach a *dikê* with the suitors; assuming the complex role of a trickster-*basileus*, he will launch a self-help action and conduct his own judicial deliberation to determine the guilt or innocence of his offenders. Sisyphus' rise and fall should then strike Odysseus as an apt warning for what lies ahead since he will indeed violate the reciprocal guest-host relation when he deceives and then slaughters the suitors in the interests of his household and chieftain authority. This potential for abusing the trickster-*basileus*' social and cognitive superiority over others perhaps explains why an apparently non-Homeric tradition regarded Sisyphus rather than Laertes as Odysseus' true father.[77]

---

[77] Athenian tragedy reviles Odysseus as "the offspring of Sisyphus who is beyond hope" (Soph. *Ajax* 189) and "the seed of Sisyphus" (Eurip. *Iph. Aul.* 524). Sophocles has Philoctetes identify Sisyphus as Odysseus' father at 417, 449, and 624–25,

5. Heracles. At the culmination of the *thesmia* evoked by Minos, Odysseus meets the hero Heracles – or, as Homer explains, his phantom only:[78] "And after Sisyphus, I noticed mighty Heracles, or just his phantom – he himself enjoys feasts in the company of the immortal gods and has the lovely-ankled Hebe for a wife, the daughter of Zeus and golden-sandaled Hera" (601–602). To understand why Homer places this figure last, we need to recall that the four previous figures dramatize a hybristic self, prone to *atasthalia* (recklessness) and *atê* (delusion) because it cannot subordinate its excessive appetite (whether physical or intellectual) to a suprapersonal authority, and so it violates rules typical of the preconventional, conventional and (at least embryonically) postconventional levels of moral consciousness. The ironic punishment each suffers suggests that while alive each of these selves remained fixed, arrested within one of these stages. In other words each was in life incapable of the self-transformation we posited as the goal of Odysseus' visit to Hades. If Heracles appears in this series as the climactic self-object for Odysseus and for Homer's audience, I suggest it's because in his mythological tradition he recapitulated the hybristic recklessness

including a reference to the tale that Autolycus allowed Sisyphus to impregnate Anticleia before accepting Laertes' bride-price for her (417). While we cannot date this tale with certainty, it suggests that Odysseus' grandfather was a trickster-*basileus* who manipulated multiple exchange systems, bride-exchange in addition to the thievery and (presumably) false oaths he devised to settle disputes in his favor (*Od.*19.396). Some believe this Sisyphean paternity originated with Aeschylus' lost play on the contest between Odysseus and Ajax over Achilles' armor (Stanford 1963: 103, 114, and 261, n. 4), but this tradition may have originated in the sort of genealogical poetry prominent in *Od.* 11. For a detailed discussion of Odysseus' Autolycan legacy, see Clay 1983: 68–89. Barnouw wants to see the *Odyssey's* Odysseus as a sort of "reformed" trickster who no longer merits the name because his ruses are not gratuitously deployed but always carefully aimed at advancing his self-interest to achieve the goal of return and recognition (2004: 23ff.).

[78] See M. L. West for the argument that Heracles' divinity points to a date after 600 for the composition of the Hesiodic *Catalogue of Women* (1985: 134), where it is a "firm article of the . . . poet's belief" at fr. 1.22, 25.26–33, and 229.6–13 (130).

and blindness of the previous four – and then atoned for committing these injustices by undergoing a self-transformation, before his death, from a hero prone to displaying hybris to one who devotes his talents to squelching hybristic behavior in others.[79]

First of all, Heracles returns us to Orion the hunter because, as Schnapp points out, more than any other hero Heracles incarnates in the Greek anthropological imagination the hunt's savage violence, when humans had not yet undergone the tempering influence of reciprocal exchange relations with gods or rules of combat with other men (1997: 34). Unlike the hoplite of the Archaic and Classical periods, he employed the club and the bow, tracking his prey through ruse and the long-range strike (35). As he emerges in the *Nekyia* he in fact appears to Odysseus in a posture of unbridled aggression, holding his bow drawn, ready to shoot, advancing menacingly through Hades, scattering frightened souls like birds; and on his belt are figured terrifying emblems of violence against nature and humankind. Heracles also recalls Orion's propensity for enthrallment (both literally and figuratively) to powerful females (e.g., Hera and Omphale); in connection with this, he too, like the giants Orion and Tityus, had little control over his sexual appetite and like them was punished for this by an authoritative father figure (he was blinded Zeus [*Il*.19.95–125]). And like Tantalus his proverbial appetite for food surpassed the norm of ordinary mortals.

But Heracles departs from the giants in sharing with Tantalus and Sisyphus the aspiration to a more than corporeal expansion of the self's boundaries, for he also crossed ontological boundaries by conquering death. Like Tantalus he sought immortality as a guest of the gods on Olympus (cf. Slater 1968: 387–88). More famously than Sisyphus, he

---

[79] Fisher uses the Heracles of Classical Athenian culture as an ironic example of a culture hero whose own appetites and violence often display the very hybris he attempts to "quell" in the savage, barbarian behavior of others (1992: 121).

experienced a *katabasis* when he traveled to and returned from the underworld.[80] This adventure, more than any other, probably motivated Homer to choose Heracles for Odysseus' final encounter because it marked Heracles' destiny as unique – at least up to this point in Greek storytelling: he was the first human to violate the norms of humanity's physical, ontological, and moral boundaries and survive the ensuing punishment to emerge transformed into a figure of justice.[81] In other words, unlike Tantalus and Sisyphus, he "evolved" morally to win the prizes they sought, revising illicit human yearnings into legitimate aspirations. This seems to explain why Homer focuses, in the few words Heracles speaks to Odysseus, on the punishment of the "misery without end" (*oizun . . . apeiresiên*, 620–21) which the older hero had to endure to win his achievements:

> . . . *Heracles recognized me right away when he laid eyes on me, and he moaned as he sent words on wings to me. "Son of Laertes descended from gods, Odysseus full of tricks, how awful that you too must lead a wretched fate like the one I endured up in the world of sunshine! Even though I was a son of Zeus, Cronus' son, I bore misery without end. I was made subject to a man by far my inferior, and he forced harsh trials on me. He once sent me right here to fetch a dog – no trial harsher than this could he devise for me. But I carted off that dog and took him out of Hades, with Hermes and gray-eyed Athena as my escorts." (617–26)*

As an alter ego, Heracles therefore offers a vision of self that passes from indulgence in his own unjust exploits to a long period of painful service that enables him to achieve a moral state of absolute justice in the afterlife. And while it's clear that his suffering atoned for the

---

[80] In the epic poem *Minyas*; see Tsagarakis 2000: 26ff.

[81] Cf. Schnapp's observation that Heracles served Greeks of the Archaic and Classical periods as a model of the transformation from an unjust to a just man (1997: 36).

recklessness (*atasthalia*) and delusion (*atê*) that arise when appetites within the voluntarist dimension of self become excessive, he owes his self-transformation to changes that are more cognitive than voluntarist. That is, in complete contrast to the previous four heroes, he seems to have achieved a new self-understanding, a revised conception of his own identity. It is this, I suggest, that enables him to induce a far more effective psychotherapy or cure in the souls of Odysseus and Homer's audience than the first four heroes.

Certainly, as the hunter given to excess, Heracles reminds Odysseus and his crew that in their wanderings they must sometimes resort to hunting for survival. We can even say that, as a figure of voluntarist excess, he foreshadows the crew's self-destruction on the island of the sun god where they will "regress culturally" by attacking and consuming the sun god's cattle as hunters rather than proper sacrificers of meat.[82] And there is no question, as scholars have long recognized, that Heracles the hunter appears here as an analogue for the violent crime Odysseus will commit against the sanctity of the guest-host relation when he slaughters the suitors in his own home. A material object constitutes the link between the two heroes as savage hunters: the bow Heracles displays (at 607–8) which foreshadows the bow Odysseus will use as his instrument of justice against the suitors.[83]

As a symbol of the transference between the two heroes, this object connects different temporal and ontological frames for Odysseus and Homer's listeners, linking the deep heroic past to Odysseus' past and future adventures. But more importantly Heracles' bow and Odysseus' bow function in this regard as a *thesmion* to recall a paradigmatic crime,

---

[82] Schnapp 1997: 58–61, following Vidal-Naquet 1986a. Cook sees Heracles' raid on Geryon's cattle as the "mirror opposite" to the cattle of the sun god episode – and even as a sort of *katabasis* in its own right (1995: 85–86).

[83] On the affinities between Heracles and Odysseus, and the bow as a symbolic link between them, see Thalmann 1998: 175–77 and Clay 1983: 93–96.

its criminal and his punishment. When (at 21.2ff.) Penelope sets up the archery contest, forcing Odysseus to reveal his true identity to the suitors, she retrieves the nearly forgotten weapon from a far corner of the storeroom (*thalamonde . . . eskhaton*, 8–9). At the sight of it, the poet recalls its history as a guest-gift the young Odysseus received from Iphitus in Messenia where both had come to settle separate cases of negative reciprocity (the theft of livestock). Odysseus apparently resolved his mission successfully, but Iphitus met his "murder and his fate" (*phonos kai moira*, 24) when he asked Heracles to help him recover some stolen mares, for the great hero "killed him even though he was his guest in his own house, the stubborn fool [*skhetlios*] – he had no respect for the gaze of the gods or the host's table, the very table he provided Iphitus. Despite that, he killed him while he himself kept the strong-hoofed mares in his halls" (21.27–30).[84]

As a selfobject Heracles, like Sisyphus, offers Odysseus a sobering lesson from the conventional and postconventional stages of moral consciousness about the prospects of playing the agent of justice in Ithaca: asserting one's individual will – even in the interests of one's own people or household – runs the risk of violating universal norms of reciprocity and paying a terrible price to a suprapersonal authority. And so Odysseus will have to answer to his community (specifically to the suitors' kin) for slaughtering his guests. Nevertheless, Heracles offers another lesson whose cure for the soul promises much more than a warning about the limits of personal volition in social interactions. In Kohut's terms the older hero opens a "path of empathy" for the younger that is capable of replacing the self's "bondage" to archaic (in the ontogenetic sense) selfobjects like those represented by Orion and

---

[84] At *Il.*5.392–404 Heracles is also called *skhetlios* (403) for using his bow to attack Olympians like Hera and Hades. According to Apollodorus (2.6.1–2), Heracles may have killed Iphitus out of revenge for feeling cheated by Iphitus' father at an archery bride-contest; this revenge may have also motivated his theft of the mares.

Tityus and to the more ontogenetically developed selfobjects Tantalus and Sisyphus (1984: 65–66). He points ahead, I suggest, to the complex moral decision Odysseus makes when he refuses the comforts, security, and immortality offered by Calypso in Book 5. As we saw there, the hero rejected an empathic relation with a maternal selfobject who reflected back to him a grandiose self that nevertheless felt powerless and infantile. In its place he chose to suffer punishments in hope of a qualified autonomy through alignment with a more mature selfobject in the person of Penelope.

This painful path to a cure through a redefinition of self constitutes Heracles' essential message; and, as with Calypso, Anticleia and Teiresias, Homer gestures to an essential component of this self-transformation: the qualified autonomy the self enjoys in the relation of husband and wife. When the two heroes recognize one another (at 601–2), Odysseus identifies Heracles not only as a man who enjoys the gods' immortal pleasures but as a husband reunited with his wife. As an analogue to Penelope, Hebe offers Heracles an empathic relation with a mature selfobject providing the self with a basic "intuneness" that will realistically mirror its coherence and reflect back to it a realizable ideal image of its achievement (Kohut 1984: 70).[85]

AGENCY AND PERSONHOOD IN ODYSSEAN JUSTICE

Do these five perpetrators of hybris impart knowledge that is vital to Odysseus' self-transformation on Calypso's isle and to his performance in Ithaca as the agent of justice? Do they prepare him to serve future

---

[85] Thalmann too notes this relation between each hero and his wife (1998: 175–76). He expands on the analogy between Heracles and Odysseus by placing the archery contest and Odysseus' use of violence in his own house within a broader sociological and anthropological context: elite male competition in prestate societies over the exchange of women like Penelope, who symbolize wealth, prestige, and power (181–206).

judicial magistrates, jurors and litigants as a model or prototype? His roles as an agent of justice and as a prototype for deciding questions of justice constitute two separate questions. In Ithaca Odysseus understands from his experiences in Hades how important it is to assume, through empathy, the subject positions of those who perpetrate hybris and those who suffer from it. The Calypso episode dramatized for us his decision, years after visiting Hades, to assume the painful role of the object (victim) of the suitors' hybris by returning home to reclaim his household and his personal authority. But that decision also propelled him into another role: the need to play the trickster-*basileus* whose *mêtis* will outwit the suitors by manipulating, in the guise of an old beggar-guest, the rules of guest-host relations. In addition to balancing these subject positions and roles, Odysseus also learns from Minos' *thesmia* that a *hybristês* may demonstrate degrees of guilt based on his awareness of multiple roles within systems of exchange and thus on his intent to deceive. This, as previously explained, can only be determined if one assumes the objective, suprapersonal perspective of the system itself – basically, the perspective of Zeus and Hades (and possibly Minos) as judges and punishers of Tantalus and Sisyphus.

When, in Book 22, Odysseus displays the thoughts and actions needed to perform justice, he assumes this position of judge and punisher. Or we should say he simultaneously holds two positions, that of the "plaintiff," the object of the suitors' hybris, who remains within the system of exchange relations, and that of the suprapersonal, divine judge and punisher who stands outside it. This ambiguity will prove problematic when we consider whether Odysseus may serve citizens as a prototype for a judicial magistrate or juror, and we cannot dissociate it from the lesson of Heracles' troubled career as a culture hero. In fact at the start of Book 22 Odysseus reveals himself as the avenging agent of justice by striking the same menacing, violent posture he saw Heracles assume in Hades. At 22.1–4 he reveals his *mêtis* by dropping his beggar's rags and leaping onto the threshold of his hall, holding his bow and quiver full of arrows. If, as Nagler claims, this moment on the threshold announces a boundary crossing, this is not just because the hero is about to unleash violence in his own home against the suitors who are his "retainers," jumping from the ritual archery contest to ritualized murder (1990: 348–51 and 354). He also announces that he is switching cognitive, moral, and ontological perspectives. Now, he asserts to the suitors, I stand outside our dispute and claim a divine understanding that the actions I am about to perform unmistakably constitute a straight *dikê*. "This competition" (*aethlos*), he says, "has truly turned out to be *aatos*" (22.5).

The perplexing word *aatos* has been taken to mean "unerring" or "unprecedented" and may refer to the fatal shot he is about to direct at Antinous (22.6ff.). It also may refer to a competition (here and at 21.91) or an oath (at *Il*.14.271) that brings unerring resolution to a conflict (Nagler 1990: 351–52). But as Nagler and others emphasize, its etymology suggests that it also means a "competition whose results do not bring *atê*," or the sort of disaster that usually follows upon someone's *atasthalia* (moral recklessness or stupidity). Nagler glosses this as a "loss of perspective" that causes antagonists ". . . to ignore the claims of others actors, lose awareness of larger consequences, and make disastrous decisions."[86] But the ambiguous syntax of the next line (6) suggests that Odysseus may depart from this certain knowledge of the rightness and justice of his revenge as he announces his first shot with the bow. He either says, "Now, *finally* [*nun aute*], I'll aim at another target [instead of the axeheads] at which no man has yet shot, and if I'm lucky may Apollo grant me glory" or "Now, *however*, I'll aim at another target. . . ."[87] By one

---

[86] Nagler 1990: 352; see also Fernández-Galiano 1992: 157.

[87] 22.6–7. For the line's syntactical ambiguity, see Fernández-Galiano 1992: 219 and Nagler 1990: 351, n. 50. Barnouw argues against interpreting the *aatos* of 22.5 with

reading the hero sees the slaughter as an extension or completion of the archery contest, by the other a contradiction of its rightness and justice. In other words Odysseus may see his slaughter as a descent into the sort of struggle that often *does* rise from recklessness and generate *atê*. So, at this one moment, *aatos* and Homeric syntax capture the ambiguity of an event that unfolds as a version of the scripts "seeking and rendering a *dikê*" and as bloody combat. Odysseus will thus assume the subject position of the plaintiff in his conflict with the suitors, the more objective, impersonal position of a divinity whose judgment and punishment will turn out to benefit the community, and the perpetrator of a new cycle of hybristic violence.

After slaughtering Antinous, the hero continues to switch back and forth among the roles of avenger, adjudicating judge, and violent warrior. Note how he elides one position with another through a skein of reason giving based on a justice grounded in the values of his household. For example, in keeping with the scripts "seeking and rendering a *dikê*," he formally recites his list of five accusations against the suitors: you depleted my household; you sexually assaulted its women; you courted my wife while I was still alive; you had no fear of the gods; you did not fear the righteous indignation (*nemesis*) of humans (22.35–41). But in the next breath he assumes the role of cosmic apportioner when he declares, "Now the boundary lines [*peirat'*, 41] of destruction are fastened upon all of you."[88] One of the suitors, Eurymachus, does acknowledge

---

an uncontrollable, reckless violence unleashed on the suitors by Odysseus; here he sees the hero working well within the control of his habitual "anticipation and foresight" (2004: 89–91).

[88] For *peirata* here, see Fernández-Galiano 1992: 226; for *olethrou peirat'*, Bergren 1975: 35–40, esp. 38–40. In this proclamation, Odysseus echoes the Homeric narrator, who earlier declares how unintelligent the suitors were not to see that, even after Antinous' death, "the boundary lines of destruction had been fastened upon them all" (32–33).

the hero's judicial skill in "saying things that are properly apportioned" (*tauta . . . aisima*, 46); and, consistent with the script of a *dikê*, he introduces in self-defense the notion of relative degrees of guilt for the suitors' parade of offenses. He fingers Antinous as the wholly guilty or responsible individual (*aitios . . . pantôn*, 48) on the basis of human will, accusing the dead man of "plotting" (*alla phroneôn*, 51) to manipulate bride-exchange in courting Penelope since he was not really looking for a wife but wished to rule as *basileus* in place of Odysseus.[89] Eurymachus then proposes a compromise to reach a *dikê* supportive of Odysseus' household: he portrays the suitors as members of Odysseus' *laos* and promises to make restitution for the loss of Odysseus' property (54–59).

To counter these claims, the hero must slip back into his plaintiff's role. Not unlike Achilles rejecting Agamemnon's generous offer of compromise and restitution in *Iliad* 9, Odysseus scorns even boundless restitution as inadequate (61–62). The only viable payback (*apotisai*) he accepts is violent combat likely to cause death (64–69). Now at this point we need to observe that in administering justice Odysseus will indeed slay every one of the suitors, even though (as Eurymachus argues) some participated in hybris more willfully and vigorously than others. The hero will, however, spare some members of his household while destroying others. As Cantarella claims, are we in fact looking at two different "logics" behind the administration of a "public" justice to the suitors and a "household" justice to family members and dependents (2003: 250; 236–53)? We've just seen that, in his desperate move to reach a settlement with the hero, Eurymachus does introduce a human standard to determine innocence or guilt on the basis

---

[89] 22.45–59. Eurymachus also accuses Antinous of plotting Telemachus' murder (53). Thalmann explains the strict link in these lines between marriage to Penelope and the position of the *basileus* in a community like Ithaca (1998: 187–88). Foley (2001: 126–43) and Cantarella (2003: 85–104) offer portraits of Penelope that stress her ambivalence in embracing this role while at times subverting it.

of intent or will. Cantarella believes, however, that Odysseus approaches public justice (vengeance) with no interest in the "mental dispositions" or "subjective states" of his enemies: facts, not intentions, are what matter. When deliberating the fate of household members, Odysseus will nevertheless admit questions of voluntary/involuntary action and moral responsibility (25). The act of pardoning, she adds, does not concern the offender's "psychic disposition" but only the inclinations of the offended party's personality (252).

While it's true that none of the suitors is spared, not even the morally sensitive Amphinomus and Leodes, Odysseus' reasoning does not support Cantarella's contention. When Leodes the soothsayer supplicates the hero, begging for respect and compassion, Odysseus uses an argument based on likelihood in concluding that, by virtue of his profession, the man "must no doubt often have prayed" (*arêmenai*) for Odysseus' death and his own marriage to Penelope (321–25): in other words, the man's inner hopes and desires likely matched the suitors' wishes – and for this reason he must die.[90] The bard Phemius enjoys a better fate: he supplicates Odysseus with the same words as Leodes but, unlike the soothsayer, he can cite an influential witness, Telemachus, to testify that he sang unwillingly, without desiring it (*ou ti hekôn ... ou khatizôn*, 351), and under compulsion (*anagkêi*, 353). And Telemachus, claiming to understand Phemius' inner thoughts, does designate him "innocent" or "not responsible" (*anaitios*, 356). The herald Medon too is spared, but here the personal memory of his past conduct in rendering family service and doing good deeds (*euergesiê*, 374) testifies to his long-standing intentions.

---

[90] Homer implies that judgments like Odysseus' about Leodes' "inner life" are morally complex, for earlier Leodes was the only one among the suitors' entourage who regarded their moral stupidity (*atasthaliai*) as repugnant (21.146–47). Just the same, as Cook points out, this man is called the son of Oenops ("Wine-face") and habitually sits by the mixing bowl (144–45), which identifies him with the suitors' hybristic ways (1995: 151).

If all the suitors perish, it is primarily because they heed Eury-machus' rallying cry (and later that of Agelaus and others) to join in aggressive resistance against the hero (22.70–78ff.; 241ff.). It's true that a hierarchy dominates the way punishment is meted out: the suitors die heroically in postures of battle whereas some of the householders (most noticeably Melanthius and the servant girls) die ignominiously.[91] But in his acts of judgment and punishment of both suitors and householders, Odysseus deliberates – with help from witnesses, his co-avengers – and makes evaluations and decisions based on a likely understanding of each defendant's inner intentions over a long period of time. Not only does this foreground a very human rather than divine perspective within the net of hybris relations, it also reaches a *dikê* by abandoning the ways a judicial *basileus* used ontological frame-switching (through myths, *thesmia*, and oaths) in favor of cog-nitive and moral frames for human behavior, including determining whether an act is voluntary or involuntary, involves inner consent or desire, and the agent is morally responsible or not. Nevertheless, while Odysseus does demonstrate to Homer's audiences that an indi-vidual victim of hybris may act and think on his own (with help from supporters) when deciding justice, once the judging and punish-ing of the suitors are complete, he does again stand back to assume the divine perspective of fate. In reporting the slaughter to the nurse Eurycleia, he disavows much of his own responsibility and claims that "a fate sent by the gods [*moir'... theôn*] and their own monstrous deeds destroyed them" (413). He grimly concludes, "Through their own moral stupidity [*atasthaliêisin*] they pursued a shameful destiny" (*aeikea potmon*, 416).

---

[91] Cantarella discusses the "female" punishment of the servant girls in connection with traditions about ritual modes of death (2003: 240–47) and Melanthius' torture and death as a form of early state "crucifixion," *atympanismos* (247–50).

Earlier I suggested that Odysseus' encounter with Heracles illustrated the irony that those who use violence to prevent acts of hybris in others run the risk of inflicting dishonor on their victims; they break the very rules of the exchange systems within which they must operate and so violate boundaries they intend to protect. Despite his adeptness at switching roles, at frame-switching from human to divine perspectives, and at applying cognitive and moral frames, Odysseus cannot escape the consequences of his violent performance of "household" justice. Book 24 of the *Odyssey* is designed to accommodate this unsavory consequence – and also to answer the question, "Can Odysseus serve future magistrates, jurors, and litigants as a prototypical performer of state justice?" Long debate among scholars hasn't yet determined whether this book was composed as an integral part of the rest of the poem or whether it was added later, perhaps under the influence of Athenian civic notions of justice and performance at the Panathenaea.[92] I believe it was composed with the ideals of state justice in mind, and specifically to devalue reasons for the household-driven pursuit of justice.

The book's most remarkable compositional feature is its duplication of two scenes earlier in the poem: a second *Nekyia*, this one depicting the flight of the suitors' souls to the underworld, where they meet the ghosts of Agamemnon and Achilles (24.1–204); and a second Ithacan assembly, this one attempting to reach a *dikê* in the new dispute between the suitors' kin and Odysseus (420–66). I suggested earlier that the first *Nekyia* in Book 11 functioned as a grand performance of *themistes* designed cognitively and morally to prepare Odysseus, the poem's internal audience of Ithacans, and Homer's implied audiences, for the hero's

---

[92] For a brief overview of the controversy, see Heubeck 1992: 353–55, with references. I agree with recent discussions by S. West 1989, Seaford 1994: 38–42, and Sourvinou-Inwood 1995: 94–106, who see Book 24 as the work of a "continuator" who integrated its themes well with the rest of the poem to achieve a closure more suited to civic notions of justice, probably in the late seventh or sixth centuries, and in Athens.

return to Ithaca. The *Nekyia* of Book 24 likewise prepares Odysseus and these other audiences for a performance of justice – but instead of originating in personal decision making by partisans of a household, this second performance emerges from the objective, suprapersonal authority of Zeus and Athena, who set it down as a *thesmos* or orally decreed law for the community. The first *Nekyia* prepared the hero to see how his impending *aethlos* (contest) with the suitors could become more comprehensible and meaningful in light of paradigmatic crimes of hybris from the heroic past: the *thesmia* of Minos in this way used stories of the deep past to justify Odysseus' personal acts of judgment and punishment in the near future. The second *Nekyia*, however, prepares the hero for Zeus' justice by framing and commenting differently on Odysseus' just-completed revenge. When Agamemnon learns in Hades from one of the suitors' ghosts that Odysseus has returned to slay them, he erupts in praise for his former companion and for Penelope, predicting a particular *kleos* (fame) for her (192–202). These words justify the very recently completed slaughter by folding it into epic stories of the Trojan past and especially by foretelling a future of *kleos* tales about the event and its glorious agents.

Nevertheless, the narrative does not permit this judgment of Agamemnon to stand unqualified. For when the second Ithacan assembly fails to produce a *dikê*, and the suitors' kin and Odysseus' household cohort resort to violence, Athena delivers to the Ithacans the judgment Zeus earlier rendered to her on Olympus (at 481–86). Her abrupt command is: "Ithacans! Stop your harsh conflict! Split apart without bloodshed!" (531–32). This implements Zeus' earlier directive to her when he said, "But I will tell you what would be proper: since Odysseus has taken revenge on the suitors, let them swear oaths and have him rule always as *basileus*. Yet we shall decree [we shall impose, *theômen*, 485] that there be a forgetting [*eklêsis*], of the slaughter of sons and kinsmen. Let them be *philoi* to one another as before, and let there be prosperity and peace aplenty" (481–86). This *eklêsis* amounts to an amnesty in the true sense of the word: a public ordinance by divine *thesmos* (what is imposed) that officially bans the remembering and retelling of events which no one in Ithaca will likely forget for some time.[93]

The ban's meaning, however, differs for the poem's two audiences, internal and implied, in a highly significant way. For the fictional Ithacans it likely prohibits public discussion and debate in assembly about the murders and also public performance of songs in praise of the avenger or in lamentation for the slain. But what about its meaning for Homer's implied audiences? They of course hear Zeus' judgment and decree within the *Odyssey*, a poem in praise of the way Odysseus, Penelope, and their supporters exact household justice from the suitors. And, as I've been maintaining, the poet certainly wants his implied audiences to debate and discuss the means and reason giving Odysseus uses to implement that justice. In this regard, for Homer's implied audiences the *Mnêsterophonia* ("Slaughter of the Suitors") constitutes a grandiose *thesmion* about the crime and punishment of the suitors. Yet we've just seen that divine decree forbids the *laos* of Ithaca to remember or retell this tale. For them it therefore cannot become a *thesmion*, and Odysseus' heroic *dikê* is never to be replicated.

This contradiction between the meaning of Odysseus' justice for each audience prompts the following question: "Of what use is a heroic agent of justice whose own people must not remember, retell or imitate his achievement?" We find an answer in the minds of Homer's implied audiences as they ponder the divide separating them from the imperfect world of the Ithacan *laos*. They (and we) may wonder, "Is justice a question of how Odysseus and we *act*, or of how he and we *think*?" To put it another way, returning to Odysseus' debate within himself over Calypso's offer of immortality, they and we may ask, "Is justice an affair

---

[93] On this unusual word (a neologism?), occurring only here, see Heubeck 1992: 413.

between agents or persons? Is it a matter of achieving ends that suit the interests of one party or a matter of reaching mutual understandings with one another about who we are?"

Let's recall from the discussion of Odysseus on Ogygia the different meanings of agency and personhood. Agents embody strategic reasoning and actions that succeed or fail to accomplish particular ends: in Odysseus' case this meant returning to sea on a perilous voyage home, where he knew he needed to adapt his *mêtis* to the role of a trickster-*basileus* who would turn violent warrior against his own guests. This agency of justice is what Zeus enjoins the Ithacans from ever duplicating again; and so they may not convert the tale into a *thesmion*. But we saw that as a person Odysseus learned from his inner debate on Calypso's isle and from his encounters in Hades that the self could be transformed through a self-interpretation. It could evoke and evaluate multiple versions of self defined by contrasting moral positions that enact proper or hybristic alignment with others, and it could determine different degrees of responsibility or guilt in itself and others. And we saw that Odysseus applied this cognitive and moral understanding of self and others in Ithaca when juggling his roles as avenger, judge, and punisher. And so while Zeus' ban forecloses for the Ithacans an imitation of Odysseus' violent actions in a vengeful agency of justice, it opens to Homer's implied audiences and to us the task of imitating not the hero's achievement of justice in the imperfect, atavistic world of epic *laoi* but his understanding of justice as an inquiry into and realignment of persons.

Cantarella trumpets the "birth of [Greek] law" (*diritto, droit*) at the end of the *Odyssey* because an injured party (Odysseus) applies punitive sanctions by force and because elsewhere Homeric society recognizes the specialized, adjudicating role of *basileis* like Minos or the judges on Achilles' shield (2003: 274–91). But it seems to me that, if Greek law arrives by the poem's end, it occurs through the sudden, outside intervention of Athena and Zeus. They warn both parties of quarreling elites to check pursuits of self-interest and pursue instead the interest of community peace and prosperity – and they back this warning up with Zeus' terrifying threat of force (24.39–40). And they insist that the traditional cognitive acts and emotions on which revenge feeds – especially remembering, retelling, and re-experiencing – be jettisoned along with the sort of force Odysseus used to slaughter the suitors. If such a divine decree really does qualify as a *thesmos*, then Athena's sudden arrival uses the traditional epic figure of a divine messenger who issues a warning – but her warning carries with it a cognitive break with the past. She prepares the Ithacans to assume moral and political responsibility for achieving not the gratification of victory over one another but an understanding of what lies in the interests of all.

As outside agents of justice, she and Zeus intervene amid the quarreling Ithacans the way arbitrators (*diallaktai*) and lawgivers (*nomothetai*) were said to have appeared during the seventh and sixth centuries in city-states throughout the Greek world, especially in communities approaching civil war (*stasis*). We'll see in Chapter 4 that these individuals provided citizens with a new instrument and a script of justice to replace the storytelling and lamentation Zeus ordained the Ithacans to forget: I'm speaking of written, statute laws and the jury trial. We'll also see that at least one of them, Solon of Athens, played the multiple roles of arbitrator, lawgiver, and poet. I'll explain why this one individual combined these roles and enforced the notion that citizens could best act as agents of justice *and* persons by using statute law and the script of the jury trial. For this new instrument and script would enable them to separate Odysseus' bloody force as a revenger from his cognitive skills as a thinker and judge, permitting them to probe the inner self (*psykhê*) of litigants as persons caught in the roles of objects (victims) and subjects (perpetrators) of hybris and other crimes.

4 PERFORMING THE LAW: THE LAWGIVER, STATUTE LAW, AND THE JURY TRIAL

⊙▣⊙

SO FAR WE'VE EXAMINED HOMER'S TWO FICTIVE HEROES AS prototypes for ways the *basileus* of the Formative period (ca. 900–760) and early state (to ca. 700) transformed himself into a new kind of social role and a new kind of self. I've proposed that Homer dramatizes Achilles' and Odysseus' struggles to assume this traditional role as the agent of justice, and that as they struggle to "render a *dikê*" they open to Homer's audiences the possibility of theorizing about the self. Each hero is temporarily isolated from his peers and inferiors, experiencing a version of individuation that enhances his moral autonomy. This takes the form of a shelter in which he chooses performatively to redefine and realign himself with the dominant social other, whom I identify with the corps of elite citizens in the nascent state. In contemporary terms each hero enacts an autonomy that briefly conjures up the image of an "unencumbered" self – but then chooses to "re-encumber" himself with a cluster of intersubjectively constituted social roles. This re-encumbering, we saw, enables Achilles to resolve disputes among peers and reconcile with an arch-enemy; it enables Odysseus to undergo a self-transformation in order to punish peers who threaten his individual status (*timê*) and his household's welfare. For Achilles this led to acknowledging that his fate was in some way interchangeable with the fates of others in his community; for Odysseus it led to understanding that achieving justice means realigning the objects (victims) and subjects (perpetrators) of a crime as persons rather than mere agents.

But during the ensuing seventh and sixth centuries, what sort of agent, and what kinds of cognitive and communicative talents, came to dominate the performance of justice in states? Our knowledge of Greek legal practices in this period remains sketchy, but it is clear that the judicial *basileus* eventually yielded his prominent role in dispute settlement to groups of elite citizens in oligarchic states and eventually (by the mid-fifth century) to common citizens in democratic communities like Athens. It's clear too that the script "seeking/rendering a *dikê*" underwent major revisions to accommodate this shift, resulting in the script we recognize as the jury trial in a civic law court. In this chapter I reconstruct key moments and figures in this script's development. In the first section I focus on the contribution of a new kind of speech genre, statute law, which ultimately enabled the jury trial to replace the *thesmia* and *themistes* of judicial *basileis*. I ask what sort of ontological frame (in Goffman's sense) statute law provided for the allegedly criminal behavior recounted in jury trials, and whether it enabled citizens at large, when deciding lawsuits as jurors in court, to assume a civic version of the *basileis'* authority and cognitive virtuosity. My inquiry also returns to the questions of what sort of self the Greeks imagined as the performer of justice in creating the scripts of the jury trial and statute law, and how this self, whether real or hypothetical, enabled jurors to exercise cognitive abilities when performing the law court version of "rendering a *dikê*."

Statute law emerged in the middle decades of the seventh century in the form of written laws inscribed on surfaces like stone (on temple walls and *stelai*) and wood (on boards or panels); and these inscribed laws were always displayed in the state's most public spaces.[1] Accompanying

---

[1] For evidence of the earliest written laws, see Gagarin 1986: 15 and 51–52; for their display in public spaces, see R. Thomas 1996: 28–29 and 2005, and Detienne 1992: 33; for the transition from oral to written laws, see R. Thomas 1996 and 2005, Camassa 1992, Maffi 1992a, and Ruzé 1992; for the political context of early law-writing, see Hölkeskamp 1999: 11–27, Gehrke 1995, Maffi 1992b, and (for Athens) Humphreys 1988.

this innovation – at least in the minds of later Greeks – was a conspicuous display of legal wisdom on the part of extraordinary individuals, the so-called lawgivers (*nomothetai*). Starting in the mid-fourth century and continuing into the Hellenistic era, philosophers and historians looked back at least three hundred years to around 650, providing names like Zaleucus, Charondas, Diocles, Andromadas, and Philolaus, along with the better known Lycurgus, Draco, Solon and Pittacus, as writers of law codes for the colonial city-states of Italy, Sicily, and Thrace, as well as Corinth, Sparta, Athens, and Mytilene, respectively.[2] We also find, not long after the mid-seventh century, evidence for the first citizen juries in connection with these laws.[3]

---

[2] In the mid-fourth century the historian Ephorus said that Zaleucus was the first to write laws for a city-state (Locri in southern Italy) (*FGrHist* 70F 139), and his activity is traditionally dated to the mid-seventh century, but the earliest surviving mention of him is either in Ephorus or in Aristotle (*Pol.* 1274a20) (cf. Van Compernolle 1981: 761). Plato mentions Charondas in passing at *Rep.* 599e; and Aristotle also discusses the lawmaking of Charondas along with Philolaus, Draco, Pittacus, and Andro-damas (1274a20–1274b25). We owe our fullest surviving account of Charondas (and Zaleucus) to Diodorus Siculus ([ca. 40–30] 12.11.3–12.21.3). Hölkeskamp discusses the significance of these relatively late sources (1992: 88) and traces the theme of the lawgiver in Plato, Aristotle, and their sources (1999: 28–59).

[3] I refer to the fifty-one *ephetai* mentioned in line 17 of Draco's homicide law. (For the text of the law, see Stroud 1968). "In effect," Gagarin claims, "the Ephetai were the jury who decided the case." (1981a: 47), and Carawan observes: "[These] justices would appear to be the earliest trial jury, in the sense of a representative body constituted specifically for the task of deciding disputes by majority vote" (1998: 80). This law distinguishes the authority of certain *basileis* (l. 12) in cases of unintentional homicide to render a *dikê* (*dikazein*, ll. 11–12) from the authority of the *ephetai* to "decide" (*diagnônai*, l. 13; cf. l. 29) the case. I follow Carawan in identifying these *basileis* with Athens' tribal chiefs and in understanding their act of *dikazein* as essentially the same as that of the judicial *basileus* in the Formative period: to shepherd both parties in a dispute to a consensual resolution. The *ephetai* decide the case only if no consensus is possible (1998: 69–72), and their cognitive task (*diagnônai*) is to find for either the plaintiff or the defendant (71–83); cf. Gagarin 1981a: 47–48). See also Humphreys 1983: 236–38.

There is a historical link in Athens between the lawgivers Draco and Solon and the emergence of the jury trial, though the information is so slight that we are left to speculate about how newly written laws empowered and instructed citizens to master the trial as a new script for dispute settlement. I use the concept of performance to link the lawgiver and citizen juror, and I argue that the figure of a lawgiver writing laws for a citizen body willing to accept them provides state ideology with a performance tradition capable of recruiting anonymous citizens – ultimately the "anybody who" (*ho boulomenos*) of Athenian democracy – to perform justice according to the new script. But I also suggest that an important mediating role was played by poets in the epic tradition's hexameter verse (Hesiod) and by elegiac poets from the aristocratic symposium (Solon and Theognis). For while poets were largely – with Solon the important exception – unsuccessful at revising scripts of adjudication for the state, the reputation for wisdom in their performance tradition and form of mimesis provided a prestige lawgivers and their law writing sorely lacked. Ultimately, as latter-day *nomothetai*, citizen jurors in the fourth century would be encouraged to see themselves as apprentices to a repertoire of legal wisdom initiated by a Draco or Solon, a Zeleucus or Charondas, a repertoire whose mimesis induced them to believe they were exercising the abilities of a cognitive superman, the lawgiver as a heroic agent of justice.

In the second section, I propose that this apprenticeship, and the type of reasoning together it induced jurors to practice, went hand in glove with the ideology of "the sovereignty of law" which appealed to Athenians from the very end of the fifth and through the fourth century. This ideology saw the lawgiver's gift of the law code as a version of the social contract suited to this age. But earlier, for much of the fifth century, the jury trial flourished under an ideology of "popular sovereignty," and in this era the lawgiver was, as a figure of the self, not yet essential for performing justice. One of the earliest surviving courtroom speeches, Antiphon's *On the Murder of Herodes* (ca. 420), demonstrates how the use of arguments based on reasoned likelihood (*to eikos*) provided jurors with a hypothetical experience of self that induced them to reason together in a more egalitarian manner consistent with popular sovereignty. And in Antiphon we'll find a link to the origins of social contract theory.

In the third section I try to understand why, ideologically speaking, the lawgiver could only re-emerge in later speechwriters like Aeschines and Demosthenes as a cognitive model for jurors after several shocks – surrender to Sparta in the Peloponnesian War and the oligarchic coups of 411 and 403 – had rocked both the democracy and its faith in the wisdom imparted by deliberation among equals. One thread of my argument about changes in this legal performance tradition from the seventh to fourth century explores its competition with the better known traditions of poetic wisdom, which, as Nagy argues, imagined their origins in a master performer ("model of mimesis"): Hesiod, Theognis, and Solon the poet exemplify this poetic wisdom and its overlap with the pursuit of judicial wisdom. Of course the mimesis jurors would perform certainly differed from that of poets, but whether they used arguments based on likelihood to speculate about a hypothetical self, or imitated the legal intelligence of a Solon and Draco, the jurors' cognitive mimesis taught them how to perform justice by switching ontological frames as the judicial *basileis* had done before them (through *themistes* and *thesmia*) and as poets habitually did. Only now, as I suggested when discussing the end of the *Odyssey*, statute law would provide entry into a hypothetical reality and sense of self quite different from the narrative, mythological realities and selves to which judicial *basileis* and poets had privileged access.

Looking back to the Formative period, I believe we can link the jury trial's speculation about the self to Homer's experiments with selfhood in Achilles' and Odysseus' scenarios of individuation. This will require isolating two cognitive acts for jurors to perform, one suited to fifth-century trials and the other to the fourth century's, and a key illocutionary statement to accompany each act. Both pairs of statement and act will in ideologically different ways permit each juror to conclude, "I can imagine myself as another," thereby performing in a novel way the interchangeability of fates and the realignment of persons enacted in the *Iliad* and *Odyssey*. Our discussion concludes with a look at how the fifth- and fourth-century speculations about the self can be paralleled to the speculative thinking and to a shadowy individual appearing in today's dominant script for performing justice: the "arbitrator" in Rawls' "original position."

I Revising the Script of Justice: Lawgivers and Statute Law

Who Were the Lawgivers?

It's true that the Greeks of the Archaic and Classical periods often attributed the earliest administration of human justice, and sometimes the law itself, to divine or heroic figures in their mythological traditions. We've seen that Hesiod identified the spirits of Golden Age men as anonymous "guardians over dispute settlements [*dikas*] and criminal acts" (*WD* 124; cf. 253–55),[4] and the Minos we observed performing *themistes* in Hades with his repertoire of *thesmia* (*Od.*11.568ff.) clearly appeared there as a mythological prototype for dispensing justice. During the first half of the fourth century, Plato names him not only one of Zeus' three sons appointed to judge the dead (*Gorg.* 523e–524a) but also a true lawgiver to humankind who received his laws directly from Zeus (*Laws* 624b). A bit later Aristotle even knew of a community in Crete that claimed it still used Minos' original law code, adopting it from previous inhabitants (*Pol.* 1271b29–30). Other lawgivers were also

---

[4] In *Laws* 713d–e Plato describes a race of *daimones* in the age of Cronus who perform essentially the same functions as Hesiod's; cf. *Statesman* 271d–272d.

reported to have received their laws from gods: Lycurgus from Apollo and Zaleucus from Athena.[5]

But for the most part the Greeks of the Classical period attributed the early laws of states to human beings. By the fourth century the lawgivers' names formed an associative grouping or series, a sort of lawgivers' club, resembling another club whose members reportedly lived about the same time, the Seven Sages; anecdotes and legends clustered around the various figures of both groups, often with parallel themes.[6] Due to the authority of Plato and Aristotle, modern scholars have usually accepted – even though at times hesitantly – a core of historical reality for the more celebrated lawgivers (Solon and Pittacus certainly; Zaleucus and Charondas probably).[7] However, it's recently been argued that we should deny almost completely the historical likelihood that figures such as Zaleucus or Charondas ever existed – one scholar has gone so far as to characterize the figure of the early lawgiver as a "pseudo-historical invention" rooted in the fifth and especially fourth centuries, a "philosophical and ideological smokescreen"

[5] For Lycurgus and Apollo, see Plutarch's *Life of Lycurgus* 31.2; for Zaleucus, Aristotle fr. 548, and Plut. *De laude sua* 543a, Clement of Alexandria *Stromates* 1.26.152 (the last two sources are cited by Bertrand 1999: 82, n. 317).

[6] For themes within the narrative tradition of the lawgivers, see Hölkeskamp 1999: 44–59 and Szegedy-Maszak 1978; for the Seven Sages, see Martin 1994. Two names, Solon and Pittacus, appear in both groups, and one of the Sages, Bias of Priene, was noted for his ability to reach settlements (*dikazein*) (Hipponax fr. 123W, quoted in Diog. Laert. 1.84). Diogenes tells anecdotes about Bias' death while arguing a case (1.84) and his advice that it's better to render decisions (*dikazein*) in disputes between one's enemies rather than one's friends (1.87). For all the sources on Bias, see Hölkeskamp 1999: 232–33 and Martin 1994: 110–11 and 125, n. 10.

[7] See, e.g., G. Smith 1922; Adcock 1927; Bonner and Smith 1930: 67–82. For more recent considerations that hesitate but seem ultimately to endorse the tradition (or parts of it), see Fine 1983: 102ff.; Gagarin 1986: 51–53; Camassa 1992; Sealey 1994: 25–29; Bertrand 1999: 68–69. Note in particular Sealey's speculations on whether Syracuse's lawgiver Diocles was a historical or heroic (imaginary) figure (1994: 26–28); cf. Hölkeskamp 1999: 242–46.

obscuring the historical realities of early city-state leadership.[8] He has also argued that we should reassess the likelihood that full-blown law codes could have emerged in the seventh or sixth centuries. The nature of the earliest written laws do seem to preclude the possibility of an individual writing a systematic law code in this era. And in fact the earliest laws respond concretely to particular contingencies (actual and feared) that threatened early states: they look like "single enactments, independent, complete and self-contained statutes . . . . individually framed to meet particular needs."[9]

If there is reason to doubt the historicity of the lawgivers and their achievement, can we identify the purposes these perhaps largely hypothetical figures served for Greeks of the fifth, fourth and later centuries? For one, lawgivers like Draco and Solon in Athens lent credibility to appeals politicians and forensic orators made in the late fifth and fourth centuries when they spoke of restoring an imagined "ancestral constitution" (*patrios politeia*).[10] Somehow latter-day Athenians

---

[8] Hölkeskamp 1992: 89, and 1999: 11–27 and (in summary) 60. He concludes his review of all the sources on Zaleucus as lawgiver of western Locri (1999: 187–98) by suggesting that "Zaleucus and his *nomothesia* – a fundamental support for the idea of a panhellenic wave of lawgiving – are and remain extremely shadowy." Of Charondas and his achievement (130–44) he claims, "Like the figure of Charondas itself, his great *nomothesia* is ultimately not discernible as a genuinely historical phenomenon." See however, Osborne's critique of such arguments (1997).

[9] Hölkeskamp 1992: 91, and 1993: 59–65; cf. 1999: 14–21, where it's admitted that the laws of Gortyn (Crete) do conform to the modern notion of a code (17).

[10] For an overview of Athenian appeals to an ancestral constitution, see Hansen 1991: 296–300. Among political and forensic orators in the late fifth and fourth centuries who invoke it, the earliest (ca. 411) may be Thrasymachus fr. 1 (in the mouth of an unknown Assembly speaker). Of speakers who invoke it using the lawgivers Draco, Solon, and/or Cleisthenes, see the report in *Ath.Pol.*29.3 of Cleitophon's rider to a decree of 411; the decree of Teisamenus (404) to launch a wholesale revision and republication of Athenian laws (Andoc. 1.83); and also: Dem. 22.30–31; 24.153; 26.23; Isoc. 7.15–16; Aesch. 3.257. Finley 1975: 34–59 puts Athenian appeals to an ancestral constitution in a comparative and modern perspective.

needed to connect a few extraordinary individuals like Draco, Solon or Cleisthenes with the act of writing laws and with the possibility that succeeding generations could imitate or repeat this act for the city-state's benefit – although we'll see that latter-day lawmaking could also at times be defamed as irresponsible citizen behavior detrimental to the community. In other words lawgiving seems to have functioned for political leaders and speechwriters as a citizen script open to success-ful and unsuccessful performances by ordinary folk. And the lawgivers themselves, it appears, were thought to have inaugurated this script as a performance tradition whose initial daring and innovation, and whose cognitive virtuosity, could be domesticated when transferred from its original scenario to citizen jurors sitting in a law court.

What was lawgiving's original scenario?
The legendary anecdotes about lawgivers identify this original script as a crisis of *anomia* or "lawlessness" in the early history of a state; it's usually provoked by factional disputes (*stasis*) or the challenge of establishing a strong, centralized state authority over a heterogeneous population.[11] The citizens invariably choose the lawgiver as an arbi-trator because of his reputation for wisdom, and he offers remedies for their predicament in the form of a law code and a new "con-stitution" (*politeia*) (usually a reorganization of the citizen body and its various privileges and powers). What results is harmonious "law and order" (*eunomia*).[12] This script contains so many stock motifs that we should certainly question its historicity, and we've seen that it's not too difficult to question the historical certainty that a Zaleucus

---

[11] See Hölkeskamp 1999: 48–50, and Szegedy-Maszak 1978: 201–6, with sources.
[12] See Raaflaub's discussion of Archaic lawgivers and the central importance of *eunomia* to early Greek political thought (2000: 42–48, esp. 46).

or Charondas actually performed these functions.[13] (Scholars remain divided about the existence and possible achievements of Lycurgus in Sparta.)

Nevertheless we cannot easily dismiss the historical likelihood of an extraordinary individual's exerting a profound influence on a state's welfare. Even an otherwise obscure figure like Damonax of Mantinea surely did perform the role of arbitrator (*katartistêr*) when the citizens of Cyrene invited him in the mid-sixth century to end civil strife: he redivided the citizens into new tribes and redistributed political and juridical power and religious privileges.[14] Still earlier a tyrant like Cleisthenes of Sicyon (ca. 596–560s) was thought to have enacted a similar sweeping reorganization of the citizen body (Her. 5.68), and Herodotus is quite explicit when he claims that this tyrant's grandson, Cleisthenes of Athens, "mimicked" him (*emimeeto*, 5.67.1) by reorganizing the Athenians into ten new tribes so that democracy might emerge from a political crisis there in 508. So we must conclude that elements of a lawgiver's (or arbitrator's) script are grounded in historical crises of city-state reorganization and reconciliation among citizens during the seventh and sixth centuries. And there is one canonical lawgiver whose performance of this script is never doubted: Solon. There may remain questions about just which reforms and laws Solon actually introduced to Athens early in the sixth century, but he is far more

[13] As I suggested at the end of Chapter 3, the failed Ithacan assembly in *Od.* 24 and the bloody confrontation between Odysseus' faction and the suitors' kin match the first part of this script. Athena's sudden intervention, bringing Zeus' "*thesmos*," looks to me like an epic version of the supposedly historical lawgiver's appearance.

[14] The principal ancient sources for Damonax's reforms are Her. 4.161–162 and Diod. 8.30. The best modern account of this and other developments in Cyrene's history remains Chamoux 1953: 138ff.; for a more recent discussion see Hölkeskamp 1999: 165–72.

strongly anchored in our sense of historical reality than a Zaleucus or Lycurgus.[15]

Writing the Law and Establishing a Performance Tradition

Why did the state's earliest statute laws have to be written? There are many reasons why Greek citizens may have seen advantages, at around 650, to adapting the relatively new technology of writing to resolving legal disputes and recording decrees by various citizen assemblies and councils. To take this last function first, a written law could preserve for future generations any number of important state decisions: as Bertrand puts it, each law constitutes a brief "historical narrative" that records, "The following pleased the citizens of Gortyn" (Crete), or "This is how the city-state decided" at Dreros (Crete).[16] An assemblage of such narratives therefore provides citizens at any present moment in a state's history with a tangible, visible demonstration that even the most remote moments of their past could endure and influence citizen behavior into the foreseeable future (Bertrand 1999: 82). Since laws were inscribed on temple walls and other public buildings and on *stelai* in the state's most public spaces, this demonstration in fact takes the form of a monument to state sovereignty and longevity.[17]

Bertrand suggests that ultimately laws like these joined two ontological realms, the everyday reality of a present here-and-now and a primordial time when ancestors, assisted by the gods, founded the state

---

[15] For a detailed discussion of the laws attributed to Solon, see Ruschenbusch 1966; see also Mossé 2004. For a recent review of ancient and modern scholarly debates about Solon's reforms, see Almeida 2003: 1–69.

[16] See Bertrand 1999: 55–56, where these two examples are chosen from van Effenterre and Ruzé 1994 (I.16 and I.81, respectively).

[17] On the possibility that the public display of inscribed laws in the seventh and sixth centuries was intended as a monument to city-state authority in general, to the concept of law itself, or to elites who controlled judicial practice, see Detienne 1992: 31–33; Hölkeskamp 1992: 99–101, and 1999: 278–79, 284; and Whitley 1997: 660.

and managed in moments of crisis to preserve it – often thanks to the lawgiver – when they produced, again with divine aid, *eunomia*.[18] In the earliest written laws the legal wisdom of the *nomothetês* himself could be detached from its creator in the time of origins to be made available for future citizens to imitate. In this sense, too, written law establishes a mimetic tradition whose performance by citizens guarantees civic order.[19] And so, as mini-narratives of successful decision making, and as kernels of divine wisdom made accessible to the present, laws fulfill some of the same functions as the oral *thesmia* retrieved from community memory by the Formative period's judicial *basileis* when they performed a *dikê*. Only now the medium of writing on stone or wood renders those memories automatically accessible to any citizen who can read or listen: when written, the law enjoys a performative autonomy challenging the uniqueness of the judicial *basileus'* creative recall.[20]

Many (if not most) early written laws are preoccupied with the procedures of dispute settlement rather than with recording political decisions or addressing substantive legal questions. It is sometimes pointed out that they are particularly concerned to control abuses by magistrates who inherited the judicial role of the *basileis*; Humphreys succinctly designates the principal intent behind Solon's law writing as

---

[18] As Bertrand indicates, Zaleucus was said to have received his laws from Athena (Plut. *On Self-Praise* 543a; Clement of Alexandria *Stromates* 1.26.152), Lycurgus from Apollo (Ephorus in Strabo 10.4.19), and Minos from Zeus (Plato *Laws* 634a) (1999: 39, with nn. 125 and 126). On this theme see also Szegedy-Maszak 1978: 204–5.

[19] Maffi points out how early Greek laws issue an "impersonal command" even when they're attributed to an individual lawgiver (1992b: 425). Bertrand's reference for this mimetic nature of the law is Plato's *Laws*, where the Athenian Stranger tells of a community in the age of Cronus that serves as a model (*mimêma*, 713b) for the best contemporary states because guardian spirits (*daimones*, 713d) administered justice there. The tale's moral is that, in contemporary city-states ruled by humans, all should imitate (*mimeisthai*, 713e) the Cronian model (Bertrand 1999: 85).

[20] On the autonomy of writing and written law, see Detienne 1992: 31 and 49.

"preventing the abuse of the powers which had been given to magis-trates and were still wielded by local landlords (1983: 237).[21] Here too, then, early laws address the question of performance by those who hold judicial office; they seek to control its privileges, issue prohibi-tions, and define its risks and temporal limits in ways that begin to transform the nature of dispute settlement's agents, actions, and time-space dimensions. As Humphreys suggests, "Written law is itself a way of distancing the judge from the judgment in which he 'applies' it." Or, when a law limits a judicial magistrate to a fixed term by appoint-ment or election, it likewise distances him from his local connections and interests (232). Laws even provide instructions on cognitive issues in the decision making leading to a *dikê*: for example, they dictate the nature of proofs an official could use; they define the speech genres judi-cial officials, litigants, and their supporters had to use to communicate with one another; and they arranged these speech genres into a proper sequence to assure that the process of settlement would unfold in a well controlled "joint action," a predictable set of carefully spaced-out performance pieces.[22]

[21] On the procedural nature of early written law, see Gagarin 1986: 8–15 and 2005a; on its intent to curtail possible abuses by judicial magistrates, Gagarin 1986: 85–86, and Humphreys 1988: 466–73. Others maintain that elites used written laws to curtail political gains by common citizens (R. Thomas 1996: 10) or, in a city-state like Gortyn, to regulate competition among a small number of families for a key civic office like the *kosmos* (Whitley 1997: 660).

[22] Maffi describes the lawmaker's cognitive ability to form a mental picture of a legal procedure that is sufficiently clear and orderly so as to lend the procedure or trial a "life of its own" (1992b: 428). At Dreros (Crete) ca. 650–600 a man could hold a post called the *kosmos* ("arranger") only at intervals of ten years. Should someone ignore this, it nullified his settlements, imposed on him a fine double that of any settlement fee he should assign a litigant, and barred him for life either from future office or from citizenship (Meiggs and Lewis 1969, n. 2). On Chios (575–550) penalties were levied on both the demarch ("community leader") and *basileus* for taking bribes, and a double fine imposed if anyone was harmed while on trial in the demarch's court; a popular council was also set up as a court of appeals. In

Particularly conspicuous in these laws are stipulations about the use of oaths. As we saw in Chapters 1 and 2, oath taking situated a judicial procedure within a mythological or heroic chronotope when administered at its beginning and end. The laws from Dreros and Chios probably enabled the state to compel officials to take oaths placing themselves under divine scrutiny when fulfilling duties, which was certainly the case later at Athens (*Ath.Pol.*55.5), but the law at Dreros may have required the use of oaths when a *kosmos* himself was tried for breaking its provisions (Gagarin 1986: 82–85). The surviving inscriptions seem more concerned, however, to dictate when an official may or must administer an oath to a litigant. At Eretria (550–525) oaths had to be administered before a *dikê* could be rendered; and at Gortyn conditions for settlement by oath are specified in disputes involving slaves. Laws might also determine not only who should administer oaths to whom but might even provide details about composing an oath.[23]

Because written laws deal with procedures for reaching a *dikê* and with other political actions citizens practice individually and collectively, they guarantee the performativity of the most vital civic acts. By this I mean they make it virtually certain that someone – so long as that person is entitled – will enact the correct procedure, punishment, or payment needed to maintain the civic "glue" connecting citizens to their institutions, offices and norms. And written laws both prescribe and predict that various civic bodies (assemblies, councils,

---

Eretria (550–525) an official (*archos* or "leader") who did not enforce payment of a citizen's fine must pay it himself, as must the *kosmos* at Gortyn on Crete. See the discussions of these laws by Gagarin (1986: 86–96) and Gehrke (1995: 16–18). Also at Gortyn (sixth to fifth centuries), various laws specified when judicial officials had to follow established procedures in settling cases and when they could use (in Sealey's phrase) "discretionary authority" (1994: 41).

[23] At Eleutherna (Crete) in the late sixth century, provisions are made to administer oaths to *allopollitai* (outsiders to the community?), though it's not certain the context is dispute settlement (*IC* II, 148, cited in van Effenterre and Ruzé 1994).

boards of magistrates) will act and speak on the proper occasion with one mind and voice. What is more, the laws' injunctions to make decisions, reconcile with enemies, or punish wrongdoers are divorced from any unique moment when a *basileus* displays his cognitive virtuosity: the acts they prescribe are by their nature routine, standard, and infinitely repeatable.

Written laws about legal procedure thus provide citizens with a trove of "scripts" in our ordinary sense of a predetermined sequence of words and actions open to performance by an "anybody who," so long as the citizen meets the stated qualifications. From the long perspective of a state's history, each year its written laws automatically set about recruiting anonymous performers for these scripts; and they operate autonomously of any individual citizen's likes or dislikes to ensure the state's survival. On the other hand laws concerned with punishing criminal acts or the consequences of ordinary events in a citizen's life (e.g., the head of a household dies and leaves no heirs) frame "scripts" in the more restricted sense of stereotypical bits and chunks of cultural knowledge. As Maffi expresses it, the lawgiver's extraordinary cognitive talents enable him to delineate these scripts of citizen life: "lawgiving thus means knowing how to reduce the variety and complexity of human behaviors to foreseeable schemas that will endure (*schemi di previsione duraturi*)" (1992b: 425).

In addition to his cognitive talents, the law's detachability from the lawgiver who writes it confers on him an ambiguous sort of individuality. The legends sometimes represent him as an outsider to the community, or one who removes himself to receive laws from a deity, or one who must absent himself from the community once he has bestowed his laws on it.[24] In any event he is an uncommon, if not

---

[24] Lawgivers are often wide travellers who acquire their wisdom abroad (e.g., Lycurgus [Plut. *Lyc.* 4]; Solon [Plut. *Solon* 2.1]; Zaleucus [Ephorus in Strabo 6.1.8]). As we've

unique, citizen, definitely not one just like the others. Nevertheless, as Bertrand insists, the lawgiver doesn't exist prior to the state and must serve its needs; he can never rule over it as its master (1999: 42, 46).[25] (For example, one of the most colorful anecdotes about early lawgivers dramatically ascribes Charondas' death to a moment of weakness when he inadvertently broke a law of his own and inflicted its punishment – death – upon himself.[26]) Why do the legends juxtapose these contradictory themes of the lawgiver's freedom from and dependence on his community? As Solon dramatizes for us, the first theme imagines him as radically individual and autonomous in his ability to create or receive laws and live apart from fellow citizens. The second provides a strongly negative response to this proposition: it domesticates this hypothetical autonomy by re-embedding him in his community, dramatizing his need to subject himself to his own laws, just like any other citizen.[27]

Mimesis and Justice in Poetry and Law

From the perspective of performance, written laws initiate and control a kind of civic mimesis. By this I mean that they constitute an

seen (n. 18) some leave home to receive the laws from a deity. Among those who removed themselves from their communities are Solon (Aristotle *Ath. Pol.* 11; Plut. *Solon* 25–28) and Lycurgus (Plut. *Lyc.* 29). On this last theme see Szegedy-Maszak 1978: 206–8.

[25] McGlew overlooks this point in the parallels he draws between archaic tyrants and lawgivers (1993: 87–123). When a tyrant performs justice as a man "who sets straight" the immoral behavior of citizens (63–67), he acts as an autocrat above or beyond the law, which is not true of lawgivers. See now Dewald's discussion of Herodotus' use of eastern, non-Greek autocracy as a "despotic template" for Greek tyranny (2003: 27–32).

[26] The best version of this anecdote is found in Diod. 12.19.1–2, who says the same tale was told of Diocles in Syracuse.

[27] Contrast this thematic opposition between the lawgivers' autonomy and dependence to the more individualistic behavior of sixth-century Greek tyrants, at least as Herodotus describes them (Dewald 2003: 40–47).

authoritative repertoire of actions, words and roles for citizens to reenact in the future: in a phrase Nagy borrows from Kierkegaard, this repetition "recollects forward" the state's most vital scripts (1996: 52). In this regard the Greeks seem to have applied the new technology of writing to the traditionally religious and poetic nature of mimesis, which Nagy understands as the ritual reenactment and repetition "forward" of an archetypal action or figure (56). Its most conspicuous occurrence in the Archaic city-state, he suggests, was in choral lyric – particularly those repertoires whose goal was to offer a divinity or hero the honors (*timai*) due him or her while at the same time transforming adolescent boys and girls into mature male and female citizens. Each year, under the supervision of a chorus leader, these choruses repeated the songs and dances of archetypal performers who appear in the songs themselves as its original players or "models of mimesis."[28]

Could written laws have borrowed this performance dynamic to ensure that mature citizens would properly reenact their obligations to the community and to one another – and so maintain their relative *timai* in correct proportions? If so, then a performance tradition of statute law might have borrowed another feature from mimetic traditions like those "recollected forward" in the various genres of poetry. Nagy describes this as the need within each tradition to retroject backward in time the figure of a "proto-creator" (1996: 76) or "model of mimesis" whom future performers will imitate as they "recompose" the original song or text. Nagy proposes that this retrojection of a model performer – who may or may not have been a historical figure – accounts for the self we identify with a Homer, Hesiod, Archilochus,

---

[28] E.g., in Alcman's *Maiden Song* (ca. 600) the original chorus leader within the poem, Hagesichora, and her young companion, Agido, are impersonated by all future performers. Likewise future performers of the *Homeric Hymn to Apollo* impersonate the Delian Maidens who present themselves as its first performers (Nagy 1996: 56–57; 73).

and so on. Law writing too would have then retrojected backward in time the figure of the lawgiver as the model of mimesis whose declarations and intentions citizens imitate when they obey or apply the law.[29]

And I suggest that the term *thesmos*, meaning statute law, designates an oral or written legal declaration attributed to a lawgiver who is supposed to be its original speaker or writer and model of mimesis for future citizens. In addition to religious and political statutes, Ostwald understands the term to designate "the establishment of a fundamental institution," as well as the ordinance used to establish it and the obligation to obey various cultural regulations and practices (1969: 12–19). All these senses convey the need to "recollect forward" an original command by repeated performance of its injunctions. If one of its original contexts concerned dispute settlement, could *thesmos* have been coined to draw a distinction with *thesmion* (pl. *thesmia*)? I have suggested that the latter term represents the orally pronounced and stored case of an intractable dispute, with its decisions and solution (e.g., through oath formulae or punishment), and whose performance constituted one of the principal privileges of *basileis*. As such, a *thesmion* could not be reproduced by just anyone, for it bore the virtuoso signature of an individual *basileus*: it tended to "recollect backward" toward the past in community memory and the heroic age and not, like *thesmoi*, project forward through citizens' mimetic reenactment.

---

[29] Nagy suggests that the tradition of the lawmakers conforms to this mimetic pattern (1996: 76), and we'll see how he develops this parallel in the case of the poet Theognis in Megara (1985). In a similar way most scholars associate the importance of the early lawgiver to the fifth- and fourth-century intellectual habit of designating one individual as the "founder" of major institutions (e.g., Hansen 1990: 82; Szegedy-Maszak 1978: 208). The basic study of this intellectual habit remains Kleingunther 1933.

Hesiod's Poetic Justice

Before the script of law writing emerged, with its version of "rendering a *dikê*" through statute law, at least one tradition of poetic performance tried to revise the script of adjudication dominated by the judicial *basileis* discussed in Chapter 2. There the similarities in the cognitive and communicative talents of epic poets and judicial *basileis* during the Formative period were noted, and I suggested that these two figures colluded to bolster the authority of the *basileus* in a village-based society. I also pointed out how Hesiod (ca. 700) paralleled their use of language at *Theogony* 79–104. Armed with this understanding, the same poet in *Works and Days* offers a poetic performance designed to supplant a poor performance by judicial *basileis* of the script "rendering a *dikê*." The occasion (whether real or imagined) is a dispute over inheritance in the village of Ascra (Boeotia), where the *basileis'* initial judgment favored Hesiod's brother Perses.[30] By framing his poetic performance as the script "obtaining a *dikê*," the poet tries to demonstrate a superior cognitive and communicative virtuosity suited to a more just verdict than that delivered by the "bribe-eating" judges. But it's important to note how his repertoire of speech genres and cognitive acts relies almost entirely on "recollecting backward" into community memory; without statute law, a poet in search of justice has no other devices.

---

[30] Morris discusses Hesiod as the principal early spokesperson for the "middling ideology" of Greek citizenship – i.e., the belief that all citizens were basically moral and social equals, and that a moderate life of hard work and moral rectitude best exemplified that underlying equality (1996: 28–31). He too links Hesiod to Solon with the observation, "The core of Hesiod's ideal persona recurs in elegy, despite a major change in audience" (30). See Millett's argument that in *WD* Hesiod fundamentally displays a peasant society and its characteristic values (1984); but Edwards has since argued persuasively that Hesiod's Ascra was a community "more primitive and more autonomous than a peasantry" (2004: 5, and *passim*). On Hesiod's poetic persona in the poem, see M. Griffith 1983: 55–63. On his dispute with his brother, see Gagarin 1974 and Edwards 2004: 38–44, 176–84.

Hesiod first describes how one goddess of Strife (Eris) motivates humans to fight destructively while another Strife motivates them to compete productively, and then addresses his brother:

> *Perses, take these things to heart: don't let the Strife that enjoys*
> *wickedness keep your mind from work when you gape and get involved*
> *with disputes in the marketplace. There's little time for marketplace*
> *disputes when someone hasn't got a year's supply of harvest stored up – I*
> *mean what earth produces, Demeter's wheat. Only if your barn's full*
> *should you attend to disputes and quarrel over other people's goods. And*
> *you won't do to me again what you once did – no, let's decide our own*
> *dispute right here and now with straight agreements* [dikêisi]: *these are*
> *from Zeus, the best kind. We already divided up our inheritance, but you*
> *carted off most of it, grabbing it from me by flattering the bribe-eating*
> basileis – *the kind who are eager to settle this sort of case* [dikên]. *The*
> *idiots! They don't know how having half of something can be better than*
> *all of it, or how precious mallows and asphodel can be. (WD 27–41)*

To strengthen his analogy between dispute settlement and epic song, Hesiod minimizes his narrative of self-presentation and deftly inserts its few details within the speech genre of wise counsel or instruction that dominates the poem. In advising his brother not to waste time participating in judgments about strangers' property claims in the agora, the poet recalls their own dispute when a perhaps desperately needy Perses used bribery to influence the elders to redivide the inheritance, bestowing on Perses more than his fair share. Or perhaps their dispute has not yet been adjudicated (Edwards 2004: 39). So, Hesiod sets about either to right a past wrong or to dissuade his brother from taking their case to the judges. He proposes, much as Menelaus did with Antilochus, that he and Perses themselves negotiate a proper *dikê*. This must be achieved by a cognitive act capable of defusing the animosity in their ongoing joint action – an act we would call a "recognition," as when

Antilochus acknowledged his relative lack of standing vis-à-vis the older Menelaus, or the assembled Argives in *Iliad* 18 recognized Nestor's bygone days. In Antilochus' case, the prospect of frame-switching by swearing a false oath brought the younger man to his senses; here Hesiod, more like Nestor, counts on his own poetic performance to open Perses' eyes.

The script of poetic singing therefore constitutes Hesiod's self-presentation, with little need for storytelling and only occasionally for speech genres of status assertion. Because of his privileged access to the moral wisdom stored in cultural memory, Hesiod is confident he can make Perses concur about a proper measure of *timê* for each. He evidently believes his epic performance is just as effective as an oath in prompting listeners like his brother to switch cognitive perspectives from mundane, everyday reality to a mythological-heroic world; and in this respect Hesiod's poetic arsenal contains weapons not unlike Homer's exempla, ecphrastic devices, and similes. But at the same time its grounding in the very real and (to Hesiod) pressing question of righting or preventing an injustice by powerful members of his community anticipates by about two generations the script of the jury trial. Only here the "jurors" are members of the poet's audience and the "defendant" is Perses. In procedural terms, the poem pleads for what Solon, at around 590, would call *ephesis* or "removal," an "appeal," from one level of justice (before a magistrate) to another (the court of the citizen assembly).[31]

But what in Hesiod's performance takes the place of the written statute laws that in about 650 made the jury trial possible? In Chapter 2

---

[31] Van Groningen proposes that Hesiod, in hopes of reversing the judges' decision, did indeed publicly perform the poem in place of a legal speech (1957). Edwards may be closer to the mark in proposing that the villagers of Ascra were the poem's original audience (2004: 183–84).

I noted Gagarin's argument that for the early Greeks the judicial and poetic uses of speech acts were parallel in origin, effect, and function. At *Theogony* 80–103, he suggests, Hesiod spells out these parallels in terms of verbal skills that are divinely bestowed, pleasing to humans, and quick to remedy the disorder occasioned by social quarrels or griefs. In my terminology both poets and judicial *basileis* accomplish this by inducing a switch of ontological frames or narrative chronotopes – only the poet describes this effect as a possibly deceitful persuading (*paraiphamenoi, Th.* 90) or "diverting" (*paratrape*, 103) of his listeners from their conscious thoughts (Gagarin 1992: 61–64). So Hesiod's early poetic performance of justice in *Works and Days* shuttles his listeners back and forth between two realities: on one hand the mundane concerns around 700 of agricultural work, creating and raising a family, relations between neighbors, and so on, as they relate to Perses' unjust behavior; and on the other hand kernels of moral wisdom scattered through the poem as snippets from poetic lore: mythological fragments about the gods, the origins and development of human communities, beast fable, and a swarm of axioms and proverbs on moral, social, and religious questions. These, I maintain, serve the same function for Perses and Hesiod's "jurors" as the written laws and the testimony of witnesses that would eventually punctuate the script of the jury trial. In the mature jury trial both these kinds of performance are sporadically and strategically inserted into the speeches given by prosecutors and defendants so that jurors can switch ontological frames away from mundane details of the litigants' narratives and pleas and toward the law's relatively denarrativized account of ideal, eternally just human behavior; and the testimony of witnesses confirms that the litigants' claims conform to community standards of accuracy or truth.

Without question the dominant theme and concern of Hesiod's *Works and Days* is justice (*dikê*), and he dedicates a "poem within a poem" of seventy-three lines (213–85) to a particularly dense compendium of the moral principles behind just and unjust behavior. These generally evoke the occasions where humans and gods either succeed or fail to resolve disputes through proper settlement.[32] Like statute laws, they tend to be relatively denarrativized accounts – scripts, really – abstractly sketched as positive or negative paradigms of justice or injustice. Havelock finds a series of cogent parallels between most of these scripts and the fully developed narratives of specific episodes and characters in Homeric epic – and he suggests that Hesiod composed them with the help of writing (1978: 193ff.). For example, Hesiod at one point in his poem within a poem personifies justice as a woman seized and dragged off by rapacious men: "And a commotion arises whenever Justice is grabbed and bribe-eating men haul her away, and they render decision in their *themistes* by means of crooked settlements" (*skholiêis . . . dikêis*, *WD* 220–21).

The "bribe-eating" men of course recall the "bribe-eating *basileis*" who decided or may decide in favor of Perses; and their *themistes* here recall the argument made in Chapter 2 that by performing *themistes* judicial *basileis* decided cases on the basis of paradigmatic crimes in community memory that were successfully resolved through oath formulae.[33] The woman whose victimization symbolizes injustice, Havelock argues, suggests Homer's Chryseis in *Iliad* 1 or Andromache

---

[32] See Havelock's extended discussion of this "poem within a poem," where he connects Hesiod's rather abstract occasions and scripts with Homeric episodes where disputes unfold and settlements are at stake (1978: 193–217). Also see Gagarin's general discussion of *dikê* in this poem (1973) and Lloyd-Jones' comparison of Hesiodic justice to justice in Homer and the lyric poets (1971: 32–52).

[33] Two lines earlier at 219, Hesiod personifies Oath in two other scripts, a journey on which the traveler Justice passes another (Arrogance), and then a race where the competitor Justice reaches the finish line before Arrogance (216–19). Oath then takes the place of Justice as a victorious competitor against crooked judges: "And see how Oath runs neck-and-neck (*hama*) with crooked settlements." For this reading see Havelock 1978: 196.

at *Iliad* 6.454–60. If Havelock is correct, then Hesiod alludes to these two episodes as panhellenic *thesmia*, from whose concrete details he has abstracted what is not quite yet a law (*thesmos*).

Was Hesiod's poetic attempt at producing a new *dikê* successful? We of course have no idea how Perses (if he ever existed) responded. But despite Hesiod's influence on the Archaic and Classical poetic tradition, his poetic script of justice seems more to end a performance tradition than to establish a new one. His peculiar repertoire in *Works and Days* of axioms, proverbs, fables, mythological snippets and *thesmia* reflects an idiosyncratic virtuosity tailor-made for the village world of Ascra – and not intended to recruit "anybody who" to repeat its performance or adapt it to new circumstances. In this sense it recollects only backward toward the tradition; without recollecting forward (cf. Nagy 1996: 52), Hesiod's is a performance of justice citizens cannot imitate.

Solon: Making Citizens, Singing Songs, Writing Laws

Solon provides the most compelling evidence for the possibility that by around 600 traditions of legal and poetic mimesis could be inter-twined in novel ways that both broke with the performance tradition of judicial *basileis* and provided citizens with formulas for a state script of dispute settlement. Homer and Hesiod demonstrate how effectively the epic tradition could sustain the earliest Greek judicial and political reflections, but the ending of the *Odyssey* and Hesiod's idiosyncratic attempt to right or prevent a "personal" wrong indicate the limits of that tradition for state justice.[34] But when, in poem 36, Solon proclaims, "I have written laws . . ." (*thesmous . . . egrapsa*, 18–20), he inaugurates a distinctly different performance tradition that establishes law writing as an archetypal act of citizenship and himself as its creator.

---

[34] See Raaflaub's review of Homer's and Hesiod's contributions to early Greek political "reflection" (2000: 26–37).

We know of course that his civic achievement included more than the script of lawgiving, for in 594 he was appointed to arbitrate a social and political crisis in an Athens bordering on civil war. Our ancient sources (primarily the Aristotelian *Ath. Pol.* 5–13.1 and Plutarch's biography) describe his dramatic cancellation of debts to resolve the immediate crisis of debt-slavery, his reorganization of the citizen body into four classes, and his issuing of a new law code to replace Draco's, among other reforms. Presumably he issued his laws, usually dated around 592–91, in an attempt to ensure the longevity of the just settlement he achieved as arbitrator (*diallaktês*), thereby recollecting it forward in perpetuity.[35] But Solon was also innovative at a kind of perfomance whose dynamics offer interesting parallels to lawgiving: poetic song in elegiac, iambic, and trochaic verses composed for the symposium (drinking-party).[36] Traditionally classicists and ancient historians haven't had much success in understanding Solon's poetry in relation to his arbitration and lawgiving, but this has begun to change.[37] Solon combines – and

[35] In addition to Almeida's recent detailed summary of ancient and modern historians' conflicting accounts and assessments of Solon's political career (2003: 1–69), see Foxhall 1997, Mitchell 1997, Wallace 1997. Balot 2001: 73–79, and Mülke 2002: 13–16.

[36] I assume that all of Solon's surviving verses, including the elegies, were performed for sympotic audiences of some kind; see Tedeschi 1982 and Mülke 2002: 11. On the symposium as a near-universal institutional context for monodic (solo) performances, see Pellizer 1990: 177, with reference to Rossi 1983: 44. In the past most scholars assumed that a poem's extra-sympotic dramatic setting, such as the agora of Solon's poem 1, actually described the locale of its performance. E.g., Herington (1985: 33ff.) believes that such overtly "political" poems could be performed at "public gatherings." Bowie (1986: 18–20) (contra West 1974: 12) favors the poem's sympotic performance, as does Anhalt (1993: 122); see Mülke's comprehensive discussion (2002: 73–75).

[37] Almeida attempts to juxtapose the work of historians on the reforms to the work of literary scholars on some of the political poems (2003: 70–118). But he limits his literary discussion principally to L'Homme-Wéry 1996, Blaise 1995 and Manuwald 1989, omitting studies such as Anhalt 1993, Loraux 1992, and Balot 2001: 58–98, which help mediate the approaches and concerns of both types of scholar.

confuses – his political, legal, and poetic roles into an agency of justice that depends on a peculiarly self-conscious act of self-fashioning.
Like Achilles in *Iliad* 9 and Odysseus in *Odyssey* 5, this self emerges
from an exercise at self-valorization; and like the epic heroes, it reflects
hypothetically on the link between individual and community. It's an
unencumbered self also, but unlike theirs Solon's self insists it is beyond
reconciliation with the new community he defines.

We can start with an insight by Loraux, who points out that in
poem 36 the speaker of Solon's poetry equates writing laws with the
most important political action (*ergon*) an individual can perform in a
city-state, and this action is the crucial event from the lawgiver's script
which restores order after a crisis of *anomia* (1992: 95; 115–16). In a few
bold strokes the first-person speaker summarizes the key achievements
of Solon's reforms: the cancellation of debts and the ransoming back
to Attica of debt-ridden citizens sold abroad into slavery (36.1–12). The
speaker then declares (13–20):

> *And those who possessed shameful slavery right here, by now trembling
> in fear of their masters, I made [ethêka, 15] free. I achieved this
> [tauta . . . erexa, 15–17] by fashioning a joint [xunarmosas, 16] with my
> power [kratei, 15] that links both force [biên] and just settlement
> [dikên, 16] alike – and I went through to the end as I promised. In the
> same way I wrote [egrapsa, 20] laws [thesmous, 18] for both the wicked
> and the righteous by fashioning a joint [harmosas, 19] made of straight
> settlement [eutheian . . . dikên, 19] for each person.*

Why does Solon align these two actions, "making [citizens] free" and
writing laws?[38] We might describe the first as the gesture of a man who
arrogates to himself the supreme political act: he (re)ordains citizens

---

[38] See also the discussions of these parallel actions by Blaise 1995: 27, and Almeida
2003: 229–30.

by rescuing them from enslavement. He assumes in his own person the citizen body's sovereignty to confer or refuse recognition to others as equals in status. This single gesture also enacts a just settlement in dispute (*dikê*) by compressing a man's thought and speech into one historical action (*erexa*, 17), and this is the political deliberation and decision making normally practiced by many mouths and minds. Its parallel or twin action, the speaker claims, is the writing of laws, for which he claims the same authority and sovereignty. Note that both actions are constructive in nature: they amalgamate formerly separate entities into one, the way a carpenter "fashions a joint" (*ksunarmosas*, 16 and *harmosas*, 19) to build a ship or table – or (to use a more modern metaphor) the way a welder solders one metal to another. He who writes laws is therefore imagined to be a master joiner.[39]

Solon apparently cherished this image of carpentry, an art of "harmony" that joins or articulates different elements into a single structure,

---

[39] Cf. *Od.*5.247–50, where Odysseus constructs his raft by "fashioning joints" to connect planks together (*kai hêrmosen allêloisi*, 247) and then "hammers them with pins and bands" (*harmoniêisin*, 248) like a "man well skilled in carpentry" (*anêr...eu eidôs tektosunaôn*, 249–50). In discussing the construction of the raft, C. Dougherty (2001: 28–29)(following Casson 1971 and 1994) distinguishes between traditional shipbuilding techniques and a new technique in the eighth century that more resembles cabinetry than carpentry, because it joins planks by inserting wooden tabs ("tenons") into slots ("mortises"). Both techniques, she argues, serve as metaphors for song-making in archaic poetry (C. Dougherty 2001: 29–37). For Nagy carpentry serves as a metaphor for poetic composition in the Indo-European tradition along with weaving. If we distinguish between the carpenter (*tektôn*), who directly constructs objects out of wood, and the joiner (root *ar-*), who assembles already constructed pieces into a new object, we can then parallel the two metaphors by distinguishing the weaver, who creates new cloth, from the stitcher, who combines pieces of cloth into a new garment. And so "the *carpenter* of song is to the *joiner* of song as the one who *weaves* the song is to the one who *sews together* or *stitches* the song, that is, the *rhapsôidos*" (Nagy 1996: 74–76). Fränkel (1975: 138) sees the figure of the carpenter in archaic poetry as a type of community member who is honest, conscientious, and industrious (e.g., *Il.*3.60–63, where Paris compares Hector's badgering personality to an indefatigable shipwright). To this Morris (1996: 35) adds Archilochus' Charon, the carpenter in fr. 19; I would add Solon, the political deliberator and law writer.

as the key to a new city-state understanding of justice (*dikê*). Throughout the poems this image serves him as an architectonic device explaining the just organization of a citizen body, a citizen mind, and a well-wrought poem.[40] Like the judicial *basileus*, justice for Solon is a question of seeing, but his vision does not locate it as Hesiod and Homer do in ontologically different frames that privilege myth and community memory over everyday senses of reality; nor does he resolve disputes through a repertoire of *thesmia* with their oath formulae and canonical punishments. Justice for him relies on a cognitive joinery that seeks out multiple points of connection, all of them open to human observation and rational understanding.[41] Some points reveal how to define the opposing political interests of elites and commoners.[42] Others show links of cause and effect deriving the disastrous political behavior of individual citizens and groups not from divine will but

[40] See L'Homme-Wéry's (1996) discussion of ways Solon uses this image to represent poetic skill and, as a lawgiver, political wisdom; in particular see her note on the etymology of words like *harmazô* and *artios* (145, n. 1). On 36.15–20 see also Blaise 1995: 26–27.

[41] Cf. Jaeger's influential essay "Solon's *Eunomia*," where Solon's goal is to help Athenians "to understand the universal laws that govern the living relationship of men in their city by making them recognize the essential connection between the social behavior of the citizens and the city's welfare" (1966: 90). See also Vlastos on the "intelligibility" of Solon's civic justice: it operates "through the observable consequences of human acts" (1995: 32). Mülke's critique of this influential modern interpretation of Solonian justice is not convincing (2002: 93–95). Raaflaub characterizes this as a thinking that is "empirical and political" (2000: 40). Almeida emphasizes the role of *nous* (understanding, intelligence) in Solonian justice, especially the opposition between a *nous* that is "unjust" (*adikos*, 4.7) and a *nous* that is "well-fitted" (*artios*, 6.4) (2003: 191–92, 194, 203); cf. Mülke 2002: 112–13 and 200, and Anhalt 1993: 68–69. Solon apparently coins a word, *gnômosunê*, to indicate a faculty that permits one to distinguish (*noêsai*) the limits of all things (fr. 16; L'Homme-Wéry 1996: 150). J. Lewis foregrounds Solon's awareness of the cognitive limits of *nous* when trying to understand the fortunes of individual human lives (2001: 126–35).

[42] E.g., in poems 4, 5, 6, 36, and 37. On this theme see Almeida 2003: 190–91: and Balot 2001 : 80–86.

from willful mismanagement of voluntarist elements within the self –
most dangerously manifest as hybris.[43] Still other points represent citizens' different perspectives and subject positions as these emerge in
political deliberation.[44] Then there are points revealing how citizen
lives can be analyzed as predictable patterns – "foreseeable schemes
that will endure" (Maffi 1992b: 425) – just as one can recognize political
patterns connecting a community's past, present, and future.[45] Finally,
as we saw at 36.18–20, written laws serve as points of connection permitting citizens to render a "straight" judgment, by which Solon means a
ruling uniquely suited to each case.[46]

[43]   On human responsibility for political disaster, see poems 4, 9, and 11, with Jaeger
(1966: 83) pointing out the similarity to Zeus' speech at *Od.*1.32ff; cf., for example,
Anhalt 1993: 70–71. On hybris in Solon see poems 4.8 and 4.34, 13.11 and 13.16, and
6.3, with Fisher 1992: 69–76 and 210–12, including his argument that the Athenian
law against hybris (*graphê hybreôs*) may well be Solonian in origin (76–82). See also
Balot 2001: 90–94; Mülke 2002: 113 and 198–99, Almeida 2003: 191–95 and 198, and
Anhalt 1993: 82–91, all discussing hybris in relation to *koros* (a penchant for excess) in
Archaic poetry. Helm indicates how in poems 6 and 13 Solon invents a genealogical
metaphor tracing the origins of hybris and moral ruin (*atê*) to prosperity (*olbos*) and
surfeit (*koros*) (2004: 26–27).

[44]   E.g., poem 33, where Solon portrays the voice of critics who publicly berate him
for not seizing a tyranny, and 34, where he describes citizens' political aspirations
antithetical to his own. On poem 33, see L'Homme-Wéry 1996: 152, Anhalt 1993:
104–5, Balot 2001; 95–96, and Mülke 2002; 338–40.

[45]   In poem 27 Solon categorizes a typical citizen's life into ten stages of seven years.
Poem 13 offers a portrait gallery describing the moral postures that characterize
the "inner life" of various anonymous citizens responding to their good and bad
fortunes in life (on this poem see Manuwald 1989 and Mülke 2002: 232–43). For
Vlastos (1995), Solon attributes the justice of good or bad fortune in a person's life
(one's *moira*) to divine will rather than rational cause and effect, but J. Lewis (2001)
tempers this view. When Solon personifies *Dikê* as a goddess at 4.14, Almeida speaks
of her "cognitive ability" to understand the present through knowledge of the past
(2003: 212); and at 36.3 and 13.8 a personified *Dikê* for the same reason likewise has
"an active and cognitive force" (202).

[46]   Havelock suggests that Solon's written laws produce a "straight" *dikê* through an
oral-written sort of joinery: each judgment, though based on a written law, is oral and
contingent on particularities of the case. It thus engages in "a process of adjustment,
of negotiation . . . . [b]ecause the measurements made are proportionate, are relative

This last sort of cognitive joinery – writing a law, then understanding it and how to apply it – is what interests me most. Of the three distinct types of action Solon isolates in poem 36 – poetic singing, political thinking/speaking (deliberation), and law writing – the last is too new to enjoy a cultural pedigree and prestige. How can citizens be persuaded to embrace and practice it? Solon's poetic solution is not only to parallel political deliberation and writing laws but to splice the one into the other, fashioning a poetic joint for them when he uses *tithêmi* ("I put, place, set") in its simple past tense (*ethêka*) to describe the political act of liberating or refashioning citizens. And yet the same verb is also used to designate the action of lawgiving (as in *thesmothetês*).[47] A listener who makes this connection may therefore wonder, "Are the two actions essentially the same?" But in fact Solon the poet uses the simple past of *graphô* ("I write") to take the place of *tithêmi* when designating lawgiving (*thesmous...egrapsa*, 18–20). He seems to believe that an ambiguity or play between the similarity and the distinction of the two actions, setting citizens free and writing laws for them, is worth maintaining.

As Loraux suggests, it looks as though Solon wishes to frame the writing of laws as an efficacious political action: if Plutarch is accurate in quoting him at *Solon* 25.6, he referred to his written laws as *ergata megala*, "great political achievements" (poem 7) (1992: 122). But he apparently also wished to frame his laws as songs, for Plutarch also reports that some claim Solon set his laws into a poem in epic hexameters beginning with the words, "First let us pray to Zeus son of Cronos, our leader, to grant fame and fair fortune to the following laws (*thesmois*

---

to status and circumstances; they have to be 'fitted' individually" (1978: 253). Blaise seems to borrow and endorse this interpretation (1995: 30). Cf. Almeida 2003: 226.

[47] Presumably the Athenian office of *thesmothetês* and the term itself were current in Solon's time: Aristotle (*Ath.Pol.* 3.4) assumes this, along with Plutarch (*Sol.* 25). Rhodes suggests that etymologically "*thesmothetês* ought to be a lawgiver" and assumes that the office was created before Solon (1981: 102). See also Ostwald 1969: 12–20.

toisde)" (poem 31). What purpose might Solon have had in deliberately maintaining a distinction *as well as* a confusion among writing laws, singing songs, and taking political action?[48] I believe the answer lies in a need at about 590 to establish law writing immediately as a distinct performance tradition in its own right – but one capable of creating citizens in a manner just as wise and authoritative as the performance traditions of sympotic song and political deliberation.

Solon's solution to the problem of garnering prestige for what is not yet a performance tradition uses two strategies: one uses laws to "recollect justice forward," the other epic storytelling to recollect backward to Odyssean justice. But both strategies depend on Solon's claim that all three actions are one because of the effect they produce: *eunomia*. The word literally refers to the most appropriate way to distribute privileges and goods, but in poem 4 it reveals itself to be a carpenter's structure of well-ordered and interconnected parts (*eukosma kai artia pant'*, 4.32). Almost miraculously, Solon claims, the erecting of such a structure shackles the unjust citizens, suppresses their penchant for a life of excess (*koros*), and puts an end to their hybris (4.32–34). Since *eunomia* also straightens crooked judgments (*dikas*, 4.36), its miraculous impact matches the straight judgments the law induces in poem 36 for elite and low-born alike (36.18–20). In other words, by imitating the lawgiver and fitting his *thesmoi* to each case when they render judgment, citizens automatically produce a proper alignment of citizen interests. And the justice traditionally attributed to Zeus becomes, as Blaise puts it, "auto-produit" (1995: 30 and 32); or we might say it enacts the "performative autonomy of law" discussed above (Detienne 1992: 31 and 49).

---

[48] There is some evidence that laws were sung in oral performances in Archaic and Classical Greece, including the role of a "lawsinger" (*nomôidos*); see Bertrand 1999: 98–100, R. Thomas 1996: 14–15 and Camassa 1992: 144.

Solon's second strategy returns us to Book 24 of the *Odyssey* and the sudden intervention of Athena at 24.529–32. There she delivers to the quarreling Ithacans the *dikê* Zeus pronounced at 24.481–86, which enjoins the suitors' families to cease their bloody conflict, permit Odysseus' acts of vengeance to stand, swear oaths of reconciliation, ban recollection of their kinsmen's death, and permit peace and prosperity to follow. Now if, as just suggested, Solon's favorite image of justice as a carpenter's construction evokes for his audiences the cognitive skills of Odysseus the carpenter and avenger, can we link these skills to the goals of Solonian justice? We've seen that one principal goal in the poems is to provoke a wisdom rooted in the ability to overcome hybristic, self-interested pursuits and to embrace communal welfare, which in poem 4 Solon calls *eunomia*. Interestingly, *eunomia* only appears once in the *Odyssey*, when a suitor wonders if the disguised Odysseus might be one of those gods who goes about in human form, "watching over [*ephorôntes*] both the hybris and the proper social behavior [*eunomiên*] of men" (17.487). In poem 4 Solon seems to flesh out this watchful divinity in the person of Athena the "guardian" (*episkopos*, 4.3), and what she sees are anonymous citizens bearing a passing resemblance to Homer's suitors: their stupidities (*aphradîeisin*, 4.5) lead them to value riches; their leaders have an intelligence lacking a sense of justice (*adikos noos*, 4.7); they will soon suffer because of their hybris (4.8); and they don't know how to control a penchant for excess (*koros*) or remain orderly when enjoying themselves at feasts (4.9–10).[49]

---

[49] Almeida also connects the hybris of poem 4 to the suitors' hybris and to their cognitive deficiencies; he links the suitors' lack of wisdom (*pinutos*, *Od.*1.229) to *pinuta* (at 4.39), where this word describes *eunomia's* effects: a well-ordered city-state (*eukosma*, 4.32) where everything is well interconnected (*artia*, 4.39) and "rational" (*pinuta*). Anhalt also briefly links this Solonian hybris to the suitors (1993: 80) in discussing the thematics of *koros* in Archaic poetry (82–91). She sees Solon's image of Athena *episkopos* as a Homeric transformation but does not connect it to *Od.*17.487.

Just as Zeus in the *Odyssey* insisted that the hero's vengeance prevail over the suitors and their kin, Solon too sees his kind of *dikê* as an avenger which will ultimately, inevitably prevail (4.15–16, 13.8ff., and 36.3). And he does not shirk from insisting that his vengeful *dikê* wields genuine force, for in exercising political authority (*kratei*, 36.15) as arbitrator, his joinery links "force and just settlement alike" (*homou biên te kai dikên ksunarmosas*, 16). If the actions of liberating citizens and writing laws are really one, then the physical compulsion behind the one applies to the other as well. While it's true that *dikê* and *biê* are sometimes antithetical, as in Hesiod (*WD* 274ff.), Solon need not be breaking with tradition here, for the *Odyssey* too grapples with the dilemma of how violence should serve justice.[50] As observed, Zeus condones Odysseus' use of *biê* against the suitors, but he simultaneously forbids citizens to "recollect it forward": he will not permit the establishment in Ithaca of any precedent for a statute law of vendetta through a self-help action. But at the same time the god punctuates this decree, which I likened to a *thesmos*, with his traditional display of *biê* in the form of a thunderbolt (*Od.*24.539). As Blaise succinctly puts it, "As lawgiver, Solon is Zeus in a space, the city-state, where he alone [as a human being] is responsible. And so in putting himself, through his action and the principles it engages, at the level of the king of the Olympians, he places himself at the foundation of the law" (1995: 33).

This violence at the origins of statute law returns us to the problematic individuality of the lawgiver and to questions about Solon's

---

Balot discusses the "cycle" of *koros* ("greed" and "satiety") and hybris in Solon's thought (2001: 91–93).

[50] See Almeida's discussion of the meanings here of *kratos, dikê* and *biê*. He argues for Solon's absolute innovation in breaking down the antithesis between *dikê*, and *biê* (2003: 225–30). Blaise doesn't see the two terms as necessarily antithetical, and she recognizes in Zeus' exercise of *kratos* a legitimate use of violence, which Solon tries to assimilate to his understanding of justice and law (1995: 28–30 and 32–33); cf. Mülke 2002: 385–87. Balot puts Solon's concern over power and justice in the wider context of subsequent Athenian political thought (2001: 97–98).

own individuality. In legend the lawgiver often arrives at a community as an outsider, or removes himself to receive the laws from a
divinity, or absents himself once he has provided his laws – but let's
recall that he does not precede his community or stand over it as
its master (Bertrand 1999: 42. 46). Solon's poems certainly evoke this
script of lawgiving, but they primarily dramatize the moral challenges and pitfalls a poet-citizen faces in light of the various roles
he chooses to play in his community's political and legal life. Actually, I would say that in the poems the persona of a citizen-poet asks
himself and his listeners, "Is the role of citizen compatible with the
roles of arbitrator and lawgiver, or is it mutually exclusive to these
two?" This option of mulitiple roles lies at the heart of our difficulties in understanding Solon's "creative individuality." The phrase is
Jaeger's, and he attributes it to a "unique fusion" of "supra-personal
elements," by which he means our objective, historical understanding
of Solon's political roles as arbitrator and lawgiver (1966: 98). Jaeger
doesn't find problematic the notion that Solon gathers these multiple
roles "in a personal pattern of unity" through the voice speaking in his
poems.

   In my discussion, however, I try to keep distinct the multiple roles
Solon plays as arbitrator, lawgiver, would-be tyrant, poet, and citizen –
roles that at times we can distinguish from the historical Solon and
at times cannot – because I believe that Solon's poetic persona (or personae) tends to confuse them and even undermine the primacy of any
one over the others. McGlew's valuable discussion of Solon as arbitrator, lawgiver, and poet illustrates the need but also the difficulty
we face when we refer to these multiple roles and Solon's tendency to
interplay them. He claims Solon used poetry for a "self-representation"
that "cultivated the image of himself as embattled, unpopular" (1993:
102; cf. 104), calling this a "poetic invention of [Solon's] political *persona*" (104; my emphasis), a "*persona*" he "molded" himself (107; my
emphasis). For McGlew this results, for example, in Solon's taking on

"a tyrant's *persona*" as mediator and agent of justice (111; my emphasis) only to "alienate that power from *himself*" (107; my emphasis) when he renounces tyranny. But if "Solon's achievement was . . . essentially dramatic: he acted out in *his own person* solutions to the political dilemmas he saw in Athens" (106; my emphasis), the natures of this *self*, *persona*, and *person* remain to me unclear.

Generally McGlew distinguishes Solon's "poetic self-representation" from the self biographers like Plutarch create when they comment on his "story" (107), an opposition between poetic and historical selves that more or less matches Almeida's distinction between the Solon that historians, ancient and modern, struggle to understand and the poetic Solon that modern "literary critics" grapple with (2003: 1–118). We can improve on these distinctions about selfhood if we admit that: Solon the historical agent chooses to speak and sing in the poems in the guise of various poetic personae crafted by the traditions of elegiac and iambic performance; and that these poetic personae evoke actions and decisions made by Solon the historical agent when he plays various political roles (arbitrator, lawgiver, would-be tyrant, citizen). (And as we've seen, some of these roles – especially lawgiver and tyrant – themselves have scripts and performance traditions that were developing in the seventh to sixth centuries.)

I believe we can best capture Solon's elusive individuality by pointing to moments in the poems when the poetic persona isolates "inner" moral debates and decisions. These moments are dramatic in that they engage voluntarist, deliberative and cognitive dimensions of a self, whether it's "merely" a self in performance (a persona) or a historical agent playing a political role (another kind of persona). In all cases this dramatic kind of self-engagement can provoke the "I" in Mead's sense to examine and evaluate the various "me" roles it can, must, or should adopt. Solon the singer isolates in some of the poems two decisions where, like Achilles and Odysseus, he is compelled to confront what I call the programmatic questions of Greek selfhood: "What sort of person must I become in order to decide a question of justice?" And: "Is this the sort of person I *wish* to become?"

The first decision concerns the unprecedented authority (*kratos*) Solon enjoyed as arbitrator and then lawgiver, when he found himself in possession of nearly unlimited powers whose potent force (*biê*) he wished to harness for citizen performance.[51] These included liberating citizens who had been enslaved through debt-slavery, possibly reorganizing the citizen body into classes with proportionately different privileges, and fashioning new laws to guide the citizen judgments that would secure these new relationships for the future. In the iambic tetrameter poems, Solon dramatizes his dilemma through the questions, "Who should a citizen on the brink of omnipotence desire to be? And how should he evaluate his options – and himself?" These questions should recall Odysseus' inner struggle on Calypso's isle, where the hero must choose between what Sandel calls different "possessive" senses of self, each threatening a kind of dispossession or loss of self: one promises as many "external goods" (in Nussbaum's sense) as he might desire, smothering an understanding of what the self's true ends might be. The other sense of self rejects reliance on these possessions, becomes "unencumbered" of them, but is confused over where to find a stable, continuous version of self.

Solon stages possible answers in the form of a dialogic exchange running through the tetrameter poems, an exchange with fellow citizens who urge or expect him to seize a tyranny in Athens. Their voices articulate for him an expectation about the sort of "me" role (in Mead's sense) a "reasonable" citizen in his situation might choose: around 600 this role is the tyrant's, the Greek version of an autocrat.

---

[51] For scholarly debate on whether Solon's role as arbitrator predated his appointment as lawgiver, see Almeida 2003: 20–26; cf. McGlew 1993: 94–95.

But Solon rejects this "wisdom" from the dominant social other. "I am not ashamed because I spared my country, didn't grab for tyranny and brute force (*biê*), besmirching and disgracing my reputation (*kleos*)!" (32.1–4). Instead he defines his goals in terms of an alternative vision of power and selfhood: "For this way I think I'll score more victories over many people" (*pleon gar hôde nikêsein dokeô pantas anthrôpous*," 32.4–5). This is a self based on renouncing any sort of social *biê* that is personally enacted in self-interest. Solon the iambic singer devalues this way of valorizing the self by imagining in poem 33 a mocking citizen berating Solon the arbitrator's lack of craftiness, foresight, tenacity, guts, and his all-round stupidity in not taking a tyranny from god's hand (33.1–4) – and this from a citizen so smart he'd trade his life and family's welfare to live just one day as tyrant of Athens! (33.5–7).[52]

But Solon's rejection of tyranny only answers part of the question about what sort of self he must be – and wishes to be – as the agent of justice. It rejects what are essentially offers others make to him – fellow citizens – and opportunities provided by his extraordinary political roles: appropriately, as we just saw, its autonomy rests on its refusal to feel shame (*ouden aideomai*, 32.4). Yet once he has rejected *their* sense of his self based on a surfeit of possessions, how can and should he define himself in relation to others? In other words, once the dominant social other's various "me" roles have been dismissed, how does the "I" reorient personal choice to choose an alternative, superior "me" role? Here

[52] In poem 34 Solon again links tyranny to *biê*, which characterizes the desires and hopes of others but "does not gratify me"; he seems to equate a tyrant's power with forcefully redistributing land equally among elites and low-born (34.7–8). In 36 the tyrant champions the commoners (*dêmos*) and, unlike Solon, would have "goaded" them on without restraining them (36.20–22). In 37 Solon rejects partnership with those whose force (*biê*) makes them high and mighty; here too he knows how to hold back the *dêmos*. On the image of the "goad" (*kentron*), see Anhalt 1993: 122–24, Blaise 1995: 33, and Mülke 2002: 390–91.

Solon's poetic imagination visualizes himself suspended in a posture of isolation as a hypothetical, "deontological" or unencumbered sort of self – and one from which his citizenship cannot be redeemed. He stands apart from his arbitrator's role and portrays that type of self as a point of connection between contending parties: "I took my stand in between them like a boundary stone" (37.9–10). Or he reworks a heroic image to portray himself as a warrior who "stood holding my shield over both parties, not allowing either one to score a victory" (*nikan*, 5.5–6).[53] Lastly, his most dramatic self-representation again twists epic imagery into a warrior both heroically and unheroically defending himself against disputing factions "like a wolf keeping dogs at bay" (36.26–27).[54]

In these images Solon's poetic persona isolates its "I" as an unattached, floundering ego unable to secure itself to personal ends that are viable within his community. Like Achilles' in *Iliad* 9 and Odysseus' in *Odyssey* 5, he demonstrates degrees of moral autonomy in rejecting ends valued by others. But unlike them he experiences difficulty reconfirming himself as a "subject of possession" (Sandel 1998: 54) because the end his political personae have passionately embraced amounts to a vision of

[53] This image occurs not in an iambic poem but in poem 5, an elegy. While the content of elegiac and iambic poetry may overlap, generally iambic speakers engage in more aggressive forms of invective and insult, employing more impersonation in portraying self, enemies and friends. See M. West 1974: 22–39, esp. 32–33; Gentili 1988: 33–36 and 108–10; Pellizer 1983 and 1981. Just the same, Solon's self-image in poem 37 as a *horos* stone impersonates the "voice" of an inscribed boundary marker; see Ober's discussion of the link between Solon and this artifact which can establish just and unjust sorts of differentiation capable of making and unmaking citizens (1995: 103–5); also see Mülke's discussion of the image (2002: 407–9). For Balot, Solon's poetry enacts "multiple ideological stances" and "cannot easily be pinned down as 'elitist' or 'egalitarian'. . . " (2001: 79–80) but he does not link this protean political identity to Solon's variations in poetic genres and personae.

[54] See Anhalt's discussion of this simile's Homeric and un-Homeric qualities (1993: 125–34); cf. Blaise 1995: 33–35, and Mülke 2002: 394–97.

city-state justice – what I call "cognitive joinery": an end that does not yet exist and that his fellow citizens do not yet grasp. What is more, Solon's joiner, unlike Homer's, Archilochus', or (as we'll see below) Theognis', must wield an *impersonal* force (*biê*) in making judgments, for this is a force that no individual self can appropriately possess or use in self-interest unless it desires to be tyrant. As a result Solon's joiner remains unstable, always in between factions and caught in the gap between a renunciation and reacquisition of ends shared and endorsed by others. This self remains a subject of dispossession, too unencumbered, an extra-social creature generated by the "I."[55]

Despite the impasse Solon the poet experiences when he permits his "I" to reflect on his political personae and role as citizen, a solution does emerge, one glimpsed in Chapter 1 in the discussion of the compassion of Achilles for Priam in *Iliad* 24. When the "I" finds no "me" role to embrace, no one in society to reflect back its own estimation of itself, it can imagine a different social order, ideal and universal, developing out of an "intelligence" latent in the present. Mead describes this as "a commonwealth of rational beings" (1964: 404), and I suggest that this utopian community corresponds to Solon's vision of a city-state ruled by his sort of cognitive joinery. In his poems – especially in the iambic trimeter fragments – his poetic personae appeal to audiences to recognize not only the value of this transcendent social vision and the intelligence required to pursue it but especially the worth of the citizen who sacrifices self-interest when wielding the force that constructs and maintains it. But how can a poetic performer of Archaic poetry call upon his listeners to value an individual who remains an unstable subject of dispossession?

---

[55] Recall from Chapter 1 that Mead understands the "I" as our ego in the form of a speaking subject spontaneously (and ephemerally) evaluating which "me" roles serve our individual self-interest (1934: 173–86, and 1964: 138–41 and 142–45).

The answer lies in the last of the poetic self-representations just discussed, where Solon defends himself against disputing factions "like a wolf keeping dogs at bay" (36.26–27). Critics are accurate, I believe, to identify the ritual gesture of scapegoating in Solon's self-image as a wolf, since this figure captures well what it means in Archaic Greece to be potentially everyone in one's community and yet no one, and to save one's community while remaining an extra-social creature.[56] Its appearance in this poem seems to emerge from the performative attitude of a speaker bereft of meaningful "me" roles to play and actually intent on sacrificing his own citizenship to the hope for a future social order. As we've seen, the new self of this order must be impersonal: in recollecting forward the authority of the laws, it should not, as Solon the arbitrator did when acting as agent of justice, use force (*biê*) or even authority (*kratos*) in self-interest. In other words this new self should not be anybody in particular: a justice sustained by cognitive joinery needs to depend on anonymous subjects like the "anyone who wishes" (*ho boulomenos*) who will direct the Athenian democracy one hundred years hence. Solon's self-portrait as a scapegoat gives birth to this complex notion that the agent of justice and social salvation should be both everyone and no one, both encumbered and unencumbered.

It's important to emphasize that Solon enacts this self-sacrifice poetically, in the play-world of iambic and elegiac verse, where his various personae may be interchanged and confused at will. As a historical

---

[56] See Anhalt 1993: 134 and 138–39. On the wolf as a figure of the outsider in Greek culture, see Svenbro and Detienne 1979, who refer to "*le loup nomothète*" (*apud* Aesop fable 229) (218–21) and "*le loup légiférant*" (225). While they relate this figure to sacrifice and the establishment of social order, they do not connect it to Solon. Cf. from Chapter 3 Peradotto's claim that the paradoxical key to Odysseus' identity as a new type of man was his ability to be "no one" by constantly changing identities (i.e., by being everyone). For Peradotto this constitutes a truly unique, autonomous self (1990: 152–55).

agent, he may or may not have enacted it through the ten-year self-imposed exile historians and biographers attribute to him. He may also, as McGlew suggests, have borrowed this gesture of self-exclusion from scripts about lawgivers who disappear from their communities in various ways (1993: 107–9). But what matters most, I believe, is that he dramatizes this inner reflection on the sort of hypothetical individuation or rebirth a citizen must undergo when he assumes the adjudicator's role in new civic scripts of arbitration and the jury trial. In effect he says to future citizens: "When you become a juror, you are no longer yourself: you're nobody – and everybody." Balot seems to grasp this injunction when he claims that Solon the lawgiver extends his own responsibility for civic justice to each citizen by stressing "that each citizen is responsible for incorporating a sense of justice into his own self-image" (2001: 86). Such a "re-fashioning" of self (94, 97) is no easy task, for it requires the individual Athenian to forget momentarily the justice of his own lot in life (*moira*) – and that of his fellows – in order to visualize their just relations as citizens in the civic sphere (cf. Vlastos 1995 and J. Lewis 2001). The most far-reaching accomplishment of Solon's self-sacrifice was the establishment and proliferation of citizen juries that were at least in principle resistant to an individual's manipulation or inimitable display of judicial wisdom. And while Draco's homicide law demonstrates that in Athens around 620 a citizen jury of fifty-one juror-judges called *ephetai* was to decide certain homicide cases,[57] it's Solon who seems to have established jury trials as the

---

[57] See Carawan's discussion of the alternate theory that the Council of the Areopagus, consisting of former archons (magistrates), was Athens' original homicide court (1998: 8–13). I find persuasive his conclusion that a court of *ephetai* preceded the Council of the Areopagus, and that its function was to resolve the question of liability in homicide cases only when the families of the victim and defendant, in dispute settlement before "tribal kings" (traditional judicial *basileis*, as in the Formative period), failed to produce a consensual resolution. These *ephetai* would

ultimate authority in dispute settlement. Two of his reforms permitted the law to recruit a far wider spectrum of citizen jurors than Draco's *ephetai*: in the first the law granted "anyone who wishes" the right to initiate a legal suit (*graphê*) accusing any other citizen of wrongdoing when the injured party was unable to do so.[58] In one stroke the law offered each citizen, even the weakest, the hope of initiating the civic script of dispute settlement against any other citizen, even the most powerful.

But Solon's second reform was more consequential for the development of juries: it permitted "removal" (*ephesis*) of a case from one judicial level, presumably an archon's (magistrate's) individual judgment, to a new court called the *hêliaia* – and this court was most likely the entire citizen Assembly.[59] With this right of appeal, the judicial archon (magistrate), equivalent to the judicial *basileus* of old, no longer had the authority of a final decision: that power belonged to the citizen body as a whole. As Ostwald claims of this reform, "It made the people the court of last resort" (1986: 15; cf. Vlastos 1995: 41).

Eventually, by the late fifth to the fourth century, the Athenian judicial system comprised *ephetai* serving at five different homicide courts; several "people's courts" (*dikastêria*) with juries numbering from 201 to 2501 drawn from a pool of about 6000 who registered each year for jury service; courts on occasion consisting of the citizen Assembly and

---

have been an elite group of representatives from the four citizen tribes plus the three chief archons (79–83 and 133–35).

[58] Our most important sources for this reform are *Ath.Pol.*9.1 and Plutarch *Solon* 18.6–7. For debate about its details, see Rhodes 1981: 159–60, and Ostwald 1986: 9. Christ discusses Solon's intentions in introducing the principle of "volunteer prosecution" (1998: 120–22); Osborne examines the practical legal consequences of this option to prosecute a fellow citizen through a *dikê* or *graphê* (1985).

[59] Our most important sources for this reform are again *Ath.Pol.*9.1 and Plutarch *Solon* 18.2–3, with Lys. 10.16. and Dem. 24.105. For discussion see Rhodes 1981: 160, and Ostwald 1986: 9–15.

the Council of 500; and courts for different boards of magistrates.[60] Through the script of the jury trial, from the mid-seventh to the fourth century courts and court procedures proliferated in Athens and elsewhere, surely working profound changes in a citizen's experience of himself, his relation to other citizens and noncitizens, and his understanding of the civic world they all inhabited. But before discussing these changes, we should return to the parallels Solon drew between writing laws, acting politically, and performing songs. While, as discussed, at times in his poetry he wishes to equate or merge these three activities and at times keep them distinct, one of his aims might be to garner for the new technique of writing laws the same prestige which political deliberation and poetic singing enjoyed when they transformed individuals into citizens.

Theognis: How to Fail as a Poetic Lawgiver

Hesiod was not the only poet who anticipated the lawgiver's creation of written statute law; nor was he alone in insisting that sometimes performances of justice by elite individuals require "removal" to a more popular court of appeal. Closer to Solon's own poetic repertoire, the elegiac poets of Megara (ca. 640–470), known collectively as "Theognis," also lay claim to performing justice in their city-state. And they too took their need for justice to their version of a court of appeal. This link between the lawmakers of the seventh and sixth centuries and monodic poets like Theognis (and Solon too of course) has not gone unnoticed. But the Theognid corpus demonstrates to us that not all elegiac singers of this period anticipate the lawgiver's written statutes or the "removal" of unjust decisions to a more popular judicial body. By these criteria

---

[60] For an overview of the various kinds of courts and their jurisdictions, see A. Harrison 1971b: 36–64; on the people's courts, see Hansen 1991: 178–99. For recent speculation on the development of the five homicide courts, see Carawan 1998: 84–125.

the Theognis poet's performance of justice is misleading. Compared to Solon, the poet in this elegiac tradition makes a false claim to the lawgiver's status, and Morris' contention, that "The core of Hesiod's ideal persona recurs in elegy, despite a major change in audience" (1996: 30), is not universally true for all elegists. To be sure, as Nagy argues (1985: 31ff.), the Theognis persona presents himself in ways that parallel the achievements of such lawgivers as Lycurgus and Solon: he speaks out at a time of civic crisis (Theognis 39–52; 773–82), claims a lawgiver's moral authority, points to the Delphic oracle as a source of his wisdom (805–10), and claims to render straight judgments equitable to all (543–46). Like Hesiod he even has a quarrel (*neikos*) with one who is an intimate (a *philos*) (1082c–1084).

Despite these claims, the Theognis poet doesn't fashion his moral precepts and positions into a densely compiled set of universally acceptable injunctions all citizens can agree to imitate in perpetuity. He does, however, assume postures similar to Solon's, as when representing himself as a fair-minded settler of disputes, complete with carpenter's tools and skills:

> *I must settle this dispute* [tênde dikassai ... dikên], *Cyrnus, with carpenter's rule and square, to provide equally for both parties, and use prophecies, bird auguries and sacrificial offerings so that I can escape the shameful reproach that results from making an error* [amplakiês].
> (543–46)

If we follow Nagy (1985: 37–38) in comparing Theognis' adjudicating carpenter to Solon's joiner in poem 36, we can notice key differences in addition to the similarities Nagy indicates. In poem 36 we heard Solon proclaim, "I wrote laws by fashioning a joint made of straight settlements for each person," and it is no exaggeration to understand this as a confident boast about unquestionably successful action in the public arena: the speaker is certain that he in no way fell short of his goals (36.1–2), that his decisions will stand the test of time and divinity (36.3–5), and that no other individual could have achieved this (36.20–25). It's at this point he offers his self-portrait as a wolf keeping dogs at bay (36.26–27).

Theognis may utilize the same figure of a carpenter scrupulously calculating the "straightness" of his decision so that both parties receive their proper share, but he immediately enlists supernatural signs of divine approval to avoid the "dogs" of reproach from one party or the other. It's clear as well that Solon's political actions and law writing comprise multiple steps and decisions whereas the Theognis speaks here of just one particular case (*tênde . . . dikên*, 543–44): as we'll see, this may well refer, as in Hesiod, to his own unjust treatment at the hands of others. When Theognis' adjudicating carpenter reappears (at 805–10), his skill again owes its precision to a divine, oracular source, and he confides that the secret to avoiding error (*amplakiên*, 810) will be to depart not the slightest bit from divine guidance. In contrast to Solon's poetry, permeated by human responsibility for actions and a strong sense of personal agency, why does the Theognis poet lack confidence in his own ability to act politically?[61] Throughout the corpus he consistently presents a bipolar vision of Megarian society split between "worthless men" (*kakoi, deiloi*) prone to hybris and "upstanding men" (*agathoi, esthloi*) (e.g., 39–52; 667–82). At times it's the poverty and ignorance of social upstarts that renders men worthless, while at other times they are elites corrupted by a moral worthlessness.[62]

Either way, unlike Solon the Theognis poet identifies himself with the true *agathoi/esthloi*, and unlike Solon he does not envision an

---

[61] Anhalt notes Solon's emphasis in poems 13, 4, and especially 36 on "human responsibility for human actions" (as opposed to divine) and his emphasis in 36 on personal responsibility for his political actions (1993: 117; 142–44).

[62] On these oppositions and ways their terms can reverse themselves, see Cobb-Stevens 1985.

acceptable political remedy for either type of *kakoi* through some process of adjudication. To the contrary, he depicts himself as a victim who has lost his property and status to the greed of *kakoi* – and who lacks a viable political recourse to recover his goods and status. He can only imagine the supernatural, folkloric remedy of returning from the grave as an avenging spirit, a hell-hound (341–50); or he identifies a model agent of justice in the avenging Odysseus returning from Hades to kill the suitors (1123–28). Seeking justice through this sort of ontological frame-switching resembles the traditional cognitive solutions of a judicial *basileus* or a poet who plumbs a community's memory bank of mythological narratives more than it resembles a lawgiver's use of written statute law. Nagy traces a compelling set of parallels between the Theognis poet and Odysseus (1985: 74–81), but I suggest that the intelligence (*noos*, 350, 650) and craftiness (*polupou ... poluplokou*, 215) the two share derive from different sources: the Theognis poet develops his intelligence within the restricted circle of the symposium, where in principle only social and moral equals gather.

Although he can imagine the symposium's cognitive and communicative dynamics as a utopian rehearsal for ideal interactions among citizens in the city-state at large (e.g., 31–38; 467–96; 563–66), the symposium cannot generate the sort of deliberation and evaluation suitable for civic discourses, especially concerning justice, because its institutional purpose is to breed factional rather than universal modes of communication and behavior.[63] One could hardly imagine a social space less congenial to the development of statute law: whatever laws the symposium relies upon adhere more to the ritual and ludic spheres than

---

[63] On the symposium as a microcosm for the city-state in Theognis, see Levine 1985; but note Donlan's (1985b) important qualification: "As a descriptive and prescriptive analogue of the *polis*, the symposium is not perfectly satisfactory; moreover it fails to cohere precisely at the crucial juncture beween what ought to be and what is. The *polis* should be like a well-ordered symposium ... but it is not" (238).

the political.[64] From this perspective the riddling formulations dear to sympotic groups – their production of a coded language (*ainos*) only initiates can decipher – constitutes the greatest divide between Solon and the Theognis poet: the latter notoriously tests his fellow symposiasts with camouflaged meanings (e.g., 667; 949–54; 959), whereas Solon's songs go against the grain of sympotic tradition in speaking a language that not only embraces all citizen groups but maintains stable, public meanings in its key terms.[65] In this way Solon aims to transform the symposium into a reasonable facsimile of the Assembly, and his songs emerge as a surprising form of political deliberation in verse – an analogue to the written laws he translated into hexameters (see poem 31).[66] In purpose and meaning, if not in form, Solon's three kinds of

---

[64] Dupont attempts to draw analogies between civic law and the ludic rules governing the symposium and its pursuit of pleasure, particularly in relation to Solon as legislator and sympotic poet (1977: 21–39). Despite her many evocative associations linking civic and ludic order, I do not find the parallels she draws between written law and sympotic law, and between the symposium and the citizen Assembly, persuasive (25).

[65] In her discussion of Solon's poem 13, Anhalt emphasizes his break with the sympotic tradition of coded speech: "Solon seeks not to appeal only to a small segment of his society, but to unify the *polis* as a whole" (1993: 21). In discussing poem 4 she explicitly contrasts Theognis' attempts to portray the symposium as a microcosm of the city-state with Solon's rejection of this analogy (81–82; 101), and she indicates how in this poem Solon endows words with specific meanings comprehensible to all (68; 94–95). Balot also contrasts Solon's and Theognis' use of the symposium (2001: 88–89), though he underrepresents differences in the political ideologies endorsed by each poet (e.g., 80, 83–85, 90).

[66] Dupont sees the symposium's elegiac songs as a medium permitting one to speak about political matters at the banquet or in the agora before prose discourse emerged as a vehicle for political deliberation (1977: 26). Loraux points to a difference in the meanings Theognis and Solon give to the word *epos*, which traditionally designates poetry's reference to itself. Both poets use it in this sense and also to designate speech in general. Theognis uses the word to express either meaning, but for Solon *epos* as "speech" refers to the sort of deceptive political deliberation Peisistratus used (11.7–8) and which he seeks to replace with a *logos* conducive to a more democratic discourse (Loraux 1992: 120–21).

action – political deliberation, law writing, and sympotic singing – all turn out again to be versions of one another.

Small wonder then that the Theognis poet often loses his nerve in the properly political sphere. I've mentioned at least one moment (at 543–46) when he strikes the lawgiver's pose, drawn to the joiner's art; another occurs at 945–46 when he claims, "I walk the straight path following the chalk-line [*stathmên*, 945], and I don't swerve to either side because I must think about how everything joins together" (*artia panta noein*, 946). He can even promise, "I shall set our country in order [*kosmêsô*, 947], a shining city-state, but without turning toward the common citizens [*dêmôi*, 947] or trusting unjust men."[67] But more often the public sphere appears as a nearly hopeless, dystopic arena where no truly just man can achieve justice from either men or gods, and where no one trusts in oaths or knows how to perform *themistes* (1135–50; cf. 734–52). In his more despondent moments the poet even rejects the script of political deliberation as a secure occasion for citizen interaction: in contrast to Solon's proclamations in poem 36, he advises the young Cyrnus, "Do not ever boast when speaking in public [*agorasthai epos mega*], for no human knows what a night and a day will in the end do for a man" (159–60). Committed to a partisan perspective, he is no lawmaker for he cannot recognize anything of his own intelligence and consciousness in the minds of fellow citizens. And so his wise pronouncements have no chance to establish through a performance tradition a repertoire of just actions all the citizens can imitate and "recollect forward":

> *The rays of sunshine that fall upon humankind look upon no man over*
> *whom blame doesn't hover: I cannot understand what sort of mind*

[67] While *kosmeô* is probably used here in the political sense of putting a city-state in order (cf. Her. 1. 59, describing Peisistratus' successful administration in Athens), it can have the more ambiguous, ludic meaning of "decorate," "adorn," which is how M. West renders it (1993: 144). In that case the distich might also refer to Theognis' poetic, sympotic art.

[noos] *the citizens possess, for I don't please them whether I treat them nicely or poorly. The majority blame me, the worthless as well as the upstanding. But not one of the citizens can imitate* [mimeisthai] *me. (1183–84 + 1184a–1184b [= 367–68] + 369–70)*

II THE JURY TRIAL AND ITS FRAMES

Earlier I suggested that the influence of statute law on the establishment and proliferation of jury trials must have provoked a number of changes in a citizen's experience of self, his relations to other citizens and noncitizens, and his understanding of how the self and others sustained the civic world they all inhabited. By controlling the components of traditional dispute settlement (e.g., oaths, other speech genres and their sequencing) and by transferring authority from individual judges to anonymous jurors, the law enabled citizens to perform multiple roles in a new script, the jury trial, as a transformed version of dispute settlement. This new version in effect required them to redefine the ontological frame (in Goffman's sense) surrounding the interaction that one litigant (the prosecutor) alleged to be unjust, criminal, or otherwise unlawful.[68] By this I mean that the jury trial, because it often (though not always) controlled self-help action on the part of litigants and insisted on an impartial state solution, compelled its practitioners to engage in a complex procedure designed to rework – in Goffman's term, to "key" – the allegedly unjust interaction into a kind of spectacle with clearly defined roles for each litigant and for the citizen jurors.[69]

---

[68] Goffman 1974: 21–25. Ultimately this framework was the state's "cosmology" or lifeworld – a concept Goffman adapts from Schutz (Goffman 1974: 3, n. 6.).

[69] See Johnstone 1999: 4–6 on the "transformations" the jury trial imposed on litigants' social roles and on the dispute that brought them to court. (These transformations will be discussed in greater detail in Chapter 6.)

In Athens' private and public cases (technically called *dikai* and *graphai*, respectively), this required the prosecuting citizen to suspend the "primary framework" of civic life (the state's "lifeworld") that induced him to think the defendant had wronged him (or the state) and to replay it, this time not as a certain reality, but as a set of arguments and demonstrations, using speeches, witnesses, other types of evidence, oath challenges, and so on. In this way what Goffman calls a raw "strip" of experience – let's say it's an intentional homicide – was removed from its primary framework in social life and was replayed or "keyed" in a revised, transcribed version for the scrutiny first of a magistrate in a preliminary hearing and then, if the case went to trial, for fellow citizens.[70] Honest jurors, at least in principle, would then consider the prosecutor's display within the frame of a *hypothetical* reality, and also the defendant's contrary display of arguments and demonstrations, and then perform a number of cognitive actions. By these actions they would fundamentally decide or judge: which hypothetical version of the alleged injustice fit more closely within the primary framework's communal standards of truth and whether the version they judged more truthful fit into the category of a violation when they examined it within the frame of a specific Athenian law.[71]

As a complex script, the jury trial therefore induces a complex series of frame switches or "keyings" on the part of its role players. Each switch puts at stake a particular sense of reality and the different frames that determine how to interpret what was real. For example, jurors had constantly to be alert to the possibility that the frame of lying dominated

---

[70] See Goffman's definition of the "strip" (1974: 10) and its "transcription" (44).

[71] Maffi identifies written law's "metaphysical" quality in juridical discourse's ability to "infuse meaning" (*semantizza*) into the generalized norms of social life when a judge sees a correspondence (*riscontro*) between key verified events and a law's particular pronouncement (*enunciato*) of those norms (1992b: 426–27).

the claims and testimony of one litigant or the other (or his witnesses);[72] or the frame of delusion might also move them to deny credibility to what a litigant or witness said. Once they had considered these frames (and a number of others), the jurors finally had to set their preferred version of "what really happened" alongside the frame of an Athenian law which described ideally just actions and ways to remedy injustice through punishment. Note how each of these cognitive actions, occurring in response to a spectacle of largely oral and written communicative acts, calls for jurors to fit information within ontological frames and to "frame-switch."[73] Ontologically and rationally speaking, the script of the jury trial thereby calls for each juror to play the joiner's role that was once the privilege of the judicial *basileus* and the lawgiver.[74]

But does this theoretical, schematic account of the judicial process conform to actual practice in an Athenian court under the democracy? Does it accurately explain how and why jurors decided a particular defendant was guilty and worthy of punishment? Or does it attribute too controlling an influence in judicial procedure and decision making to what I call the frame of the law? If this were the case, we would have to claim that the script of law writing alone guided and determined the

---

[72] Hesk discusses in detail how self-conscious Athenian forensic oratory was of the various techniques and counter-techniques orators used to deceive jurors (2000: 202–41).

[73] E.g., at Dem. 25.3 (delivered 338–324) the prosecutor describes a trial's cognitive tasks as: (1) for jurors, "to learn [*mathêsomenoi*] from the prosecutor and defendant the case [*to pragma*, the matter] about which you will have to vote"; (2) for each litigant, "to show that the legality [*ta onta . . . dikaia*] of the laws is on his side."

[74] The juror's cognitive task of "joining" cultural assumptions about human behavior, the alleged interaction between litigants, and the frame of the law was more extensive than a modern juror's. Greek law's generality left many "gaps" in the law code between the law itself and the particularities of a case, and these gaps required interpretation. On the "theory of gaps" in Greek law, see Sealey 1994: 51–56; see also Harris (1994: 138–39, and 2000) on Greek law's "open texture," correcting Osborne 1985: 43–44 and Ober 1989: 144–45.

performance of justice. The realities of Athenian litigation were considerably more complex. An appreciation of the underlying motives driving many Athenians into litigation reveals that an exclusive concern for law writing and the frame of the law was an ideologically driven democratic fiction, for this only partially controlled judicial procedure. We find confirmation of this complexity in a few recent studies that identify a number of underlying motives and rationales outside the law proper for the prosecutions we know about in the Athenian legal system in around 420–320. David Cohen points to the practice of "feuding" as anthropologists understand it to explain many cases of criminal prosecution: this describes ways an elite Athenian citizen and his family could exploit the courts to carry on campaigns of social warfare against rival individuals and families, sometimes throughout an individual's adult life and into the next generation (1995a). From Cohen's perspective the frame of the law serves largely as a pretext for generating social disgrace (loss of *timê*), and this diminishes the aura of the law's authority over citizens.

In a similar vein Matthew Christ focuses on the Athenians' ambivalent attitudes toward their legal system's excesses and its vulnerability to abuse; in particular he suggests that the courts served as an arena to play out cultural contradictions between the appropriate use of aggression against fellow citizens and ideals mandating cooperative behavior between them (1998: 12; 160–90). Danielle Allen uncovers an Athenian social psychology permitting the controlled use of aggression and anger (*orgê*) as justifications for punishing fellow citizens (2000). Here the real drama behind the spectacle of a given prosecution is a tactical game in which one citizen tries to redress violation of the ideal reciprocity Athenians thought should govern citizen interactions. The prosecutor achieves this by skillfully orchestrating social memory, unstated "rules of engagement" governing the negotiation of desert, and the sovereignty of public opinion. Legal procedure and the law itself provide a necessary camouflage to conceal this complex social dynamic of perceptions, democratic ideology, and the social expression of emotions like aggression, anger, eros, and compassion. And statute law itself does not govern the motives or procedures behind prosecution. Instead it functions as a kind of social memory and opinion whose validity jurors had the option of ratifying or denying: in effect the law was subject to the citizens' sovereign opinion and not vice-versa (175–79).

These three interpretations of the Athenian legal system provide a necessary corrective to the blanket assumption that Athenian democracy was ruled by the sovereignty of law.[75] They uncover a deeper, more occluded dynamics that complicates the relation of statute law to a prosecutor's experience of "obtaining justice" from a defendant (*lambanein dikên*) or a defendant's experience of suffering conviction and "giving justice" (*didonai dikên*) to a prosecutor. In effect litigants (or their speechwriters) and jurors tried to bend the law to harness its authority as a proof of innocence or guilt because the courts served as an acknowledged, acceptable arena for playing out real-life dramas of social enmity and political interest.[76] Nevertheless, this occluded dynamics is ideologically driven as well, for it depends on sustaining belief that written law was and still can be authoritatively performed.

---

[75] For the historical background of the transition to a democratic ideology based on the sovereignty of law, see Ostwald 1986: 497–524. For a counterview see Sealey 1987, and Todd's comparison of the two (1993: 299–300); cf. Hansen 1991: 299–304.

[76] In D. Cohen's summary view, "Prosecution[s] for offenses against statutes were brought before the *demos* in their capacity as lay judges [jurors], and they reached judgment by considering whether or not the accused had violated the communal sense of right and wrong whose contours were only vaguely sketched out by the written statutes (*nomoi*)" (1995b: 244; see also 1995a: 34ff, and the more complex argument in 2005). Cf. Allen 2000: 179–90, but also, for her prior discussion of law as proof, the typical arguments used to subject the law to social opinion, and the uselessness of equity in Athenian legal decisions (174–78). On using the law to pursue personal and political enmity, see also Rhodes 1998, esp. 156–60.

If we emphasize exclusively how the law was instrumentalized to serve particular social or political interests, we slight the importance in courtroom procedures, decision making and especially in forensic rhetoric of *maintaining the fiction* that jurors somehow need to participate in the script of law writing (i.e., somehow engage with both the law writer and the act of writing law) in order to render a *dikê*.[77] it seems clear that to serve on an Athenian jury in the late fifth or fourth century meant participating in law writing as a performance tradition, and that this tradition required jurors to practice a kind of mimesis not unlike poetic mimesis. To demonstrate this, we have to reconstruct the cognitive flow of a jury trial, to examine how jurors acted as "joiners" when they connected the litigants' courtroom spectacle to the various ontological frames that proliferated in courtroom procedures and arguments. We also need to see how litigants (or their speechwriters) tried to connect this act of "joining" to the figure of the lawmaker and his defining act.

Mimesis and the Frame of Reasoned Likelihood
As discussed in Chapter 2, the goal of early Greek dispute settlement was never to establish the truth of "what really happened" or "who really did or said this." It was instead to produce a mutually satisfactory res-

---

[77] Asking why it was important to maintain the fiction that the laws themselves were sovereign (*kurioi*) helps reconceive the question of the jurors' relationship to the laws. As D. Cohen (1995a; 1996b) and Allen (2000) argue, we may owe the notion of the law's supremacy to Platonic and Aristotelian theory, but it is grounded in state traditions of performance. For other perspectives, see Todd, for whom the laws are primarily persuasive and not binding on jurors (1993: 60); Ober (1989: 299–304), suggesting that Athenians themselves wouldn't have seen the contradiction between popular sovereignty and the sovereignty of law (1989: 299–304); and Carey (1996: 33–34), who distinguishes between the primary function of citing a law in a given case, to determine guilt or innocence, and its ancillary function, to persuade, prejudice or cajole jurors. The essays in Harris and Rubinstein 2004 address various aspects of the rule of law inside and outside of Athens.

olution by aligning conflicting accounts of "what really happened" or "who really did or said this" with two or more ontological frames (e.g., the frame of everyday reality; the frame of community memory where *thesmia* resided; the frame of mythological or heroic narratives that anchored oath formulae). Each frame controlled a certain interpretation or understanding of the relative *timai* of each litigant, and ultimately dispute settlement was a question of deciding which of two or more competing frames could generate a significance that trumped the other(s) in the minds of adjudicators, litigants, and spectators. As the jury trial developed, this goal with its dynamics of competing frames did not change, but the nature of the frames did. In particular the frame most susceptible to transformation was the one I've identified as the generator of a hypothetical sense of time, space, and agency that could be "joined" or connected to everyday reality. (Recall the speech genre of imprecation that typically concludes an oath with a hypothesis, such as the one Agamemnon uses to establish formal settlement of his dispute with Achilles: "If I've perjured myself concerning any detail in my words, may the gods grant me many pains . . . ." [*Il*.19.264–65].)

In those early disputes the adjudicating *basileus*, in a display of cognitive virtuosity, often co-opted the autonomy of one or both litigants when he assumed the perspective of their subjective, inner worlds and incorporated it into the third-person, objective perspective of a public settlement in everyone's interest (e.g., Achilles assumes the positions of both Antilochus and Eumelus in *Iliad* 23). As the jury trial develops, this need to replicate these multiple perspectives and "key" them in competing frames persists – only now it is the jurors who must play that role and display that cognitive virtuosity. They are induced to achieve this by a new citizen script whose goal is to have them *reason together*. This reasoning together took different forms at different moments in the democracy's history, and 403, the year the democracy was restored after the second oligarchic coup in eight years, marks an important transition from one form of reasoning together to another. But both before and after 403, the jurors' cognitive challenge was to recreate the mental and emotional states of several individuals, each of whom might ultimately serve the individual juror as a "selfobject" in Kohut's sense.

At some point between 460 and 420, jurors achieved this by becoming adept at imposing a frame of hypothesis on the intention or premeditation (*pronoia*) of the alleged wrongdoer; they had to acknowledge the prosecutor's anger or desire for compensation; and they also had to compare these states of mind and feeling to the frame of a relevant, written statute law.[78] But after 403 a new kind of individual entered into this cognitive task, and the jurors were induced to recreate his "inner self." And at this point their judgment would take on the more formal appearance of participating in a performance tradition based on mimesis. In effect they were now challenged to reason together in order to replicate the "original" intention a mighty lawgiver such as Solon or Draco had in writing the law relevant to the case.

What evidence do we have that early jury trials aimed to recover the intention of one or more litigants? Carawan's *Rhetoric and the Law of Draco* (1998) helps answer this question by reviewing long-standing scholarly debates and reaching some cogent if provocative conclusions about Draco's homicide law and Solon's subsequent contributions to Athenian procedures in homicide cases. In a nutshell he argues that Draco's law submitted homicide disputes to public inquiry only when very special circumstances obtained. I previously discussed Carawan's

---

[78] Gernet reminds us that *pronoia* ("premeditation") serves as a synonym for an "intent" (*hekôn, hekousios*), covering many ways to commit a crime voluntarily, consciously, willfully. In this regard it's the opposite of a crime committed "unintentionally" (*akôn, akousios*) in a variety of ways: through accident, negligence, or even momentary passion (2001 : 352–54). Vernant clarifies how the first type of crime was socially "reprehensible," the second socially "excusable" (1988: 61).

claim that during the seventh century, when self-help resolution failed, normally the litigants in a homicide case would resolve their dispute much like the trial scene on Achilles' shield – that is, by consensual resolution through the swearing of oaths brokered by tribal *basileis* (64–72). But where the parties could not agree – let's say the murderer admitted involvement but claimed the act was unintentional, justifiably provoked, or accidental – and there were no surviving kin of the victim to demand compensation, Carawan believes that from about 620 Draco authorized the *ephetai* of fifty-one jurors to determine not whether the murderer acted with intent to kill – that was an issue left up to the victim's kin – but whether he was liable (*aitios*). According to Carawan, liability (guilt) does not ask these jurors "to decide a state of mind *per se*" (72) but only to reconstruct a causal chain of events identifying the defendant as the instigator of the murder (72–79).

It was Solon, he claims, who isolated and submitted to public inquiry the question of the murderer's intent (*pronoia*). For, in addition to his law permitting "removal" (*ephesis*) of a case from a magistrate's authority to a court of the citizen assembly (*hêliaia*), from about 590 Solon constituted (or reconstituted) the Council of the Areopagus as a homicide jury. In this way "he [Solon] took the question of the killer's intent out of the hands of the families involved and put it to the council" (384). It is here that we can begin to see how this jury of elite citizens approached the task of reasoning together in order to reconstruct the murderer's motives. Carawan immediately points to their need for a new frame (in Goffman's sense), a frame capable of generating hypotheses to resolve the "inscrutable question of the killer's intentions." That frame was reasoned likelihood (384). The jurors had to construct it around an imagined moment of *pronoia* in one individual's mind and actions, choosing from any number of available scripts in citizen life the one most likely to "join" or connect to the known facts and statuses of the litigants – and in such a way as to rekey the raw strip of allegedly unjust citizen interaction into certain identification of the defendant as the murderer.

From the moment the verdict in a jury trial turned on the jurors' ability to fashion this "joint," we can say that statute law induced jurors to perform cognitively the reenactment of a critical moment of a fellow citizen's life. In this regard they exercised the authority, as Solon the political reformer and law writer had done, to (re)confirm a person's citizenship or to revoke it through exile or death. But exactly what sort of mimesis did this require them to enact? At this point Carawan's cogent reconstruction of changes in judicial procedure stumbles a bit, for he claims that the criterion for intentionality from the sixth down to the fifth centuries was "not so much a measure of the [killer's] inner conscience as a reflex of the outward acts," and that the jurors did not need to investigate "the more elusive factors of probable motive (personal desires, intentions)" (385). Apparently, Carawan believes, they only needed to establish that the defendant's actions – for example, that he was seen carrying a weapon near, quarreling with, or waiting in ambush for the victim – conformed to a reasonably likely version of the script "one citizen murders another without just cause." It was, he adds, an external pattern of "calculated enmity" the jurors sought to uncover and not the "inner logic" behind the crime (385).

Even though, technically speaking, the law did not demand from jurors an account of the defendant's "inner conscience" or "inner logic," how could they divorce questions about an individual's external deeds from their culture's belief that certain intellectual and emotional states habitually accompanied particular crimes like murder, theft, embezzlement, and so on?[79] Or, in terms of Habermas' action theory, how could

---

[79] Dover illustrates from fifth- and fourth-century texts popular notions of behavior and "psychology" about understanding, moral responsibility, pain, grief, fear, aggression, compassion, friendliness, and enmity, etc. (1974: 116ff.). Cf. Allen's more

jurors on one hand judge actions teleologically (actions successfully or unsuccessfully achieve their ends) and normatively (actions conform or deviate from standards of what is proper, lawful, etc.) without on the other hand necessarily understanding these same actions as true or false expressions of an agent's inner world? Surely no culture that heroizes a crafty Odysseus can be ignorant of how such a "dramaturgical" dimension may stalk every individual's outward behavior. If we turn to our earliest surviving law court speeches for homicide, we find that defendants are very keen to draw jurors into an "inner logic" that explains how unlikely a motive they had for the crime. These earliest surviving speeches belong to two trials whose defendants hired the speechwriter and sophist Antiphon to write for them, and they are dated to just before and after 420. Carawan states that "murder trials in the age of Antiphon were still preoccupied with outward acts of planning and largely unconcerned with motives" (385). I believe the speeches indicate otherwise.[80]

In the more complex and accomplished of these speeches, *On the Murder of Herodes* (ca. 420), the defendant Euxitheus is at a disadvantage in several ways. First, he is not an Athenian citizen but an elite citizen of Mytilene, an allied city-state subject to Athenian law, and he is on

---

recent discussion of the notion of "desert" in Athens and her analysis of anger (*orgê*) in the Athenian cultural mentality (2000: 36–38 and 50–59).

[80] Before this, Carawan concedes, "Of course, this conception of forethought clearly prefigures reasoning from probabilities of means and motive, and it may seem to us a very short step from the outward demonstration of malice [*pronoia*] to the inner intent" (1998: 385). In Antiphon's earlier speech, *Against the Stepmother for Poisoning* (before 420), the prosecutor portrays the alleged murderer as a woman whose husband has "wronged" her (*adikoito*, 1.15), presumably through infidelity (see Gagarin 1997: 114–15). So he encourages jurors to infer that the outward acts indicating her *pronoia* and willingness (*hekousiôs*) to kill (1.5–6) were motivated by the jealous anger of a familiar citizen script. He then locates the origin of her guilt (*aitia*) in the "inner" act of "deliberating over it in her heart" (*enthumêtheisa*) and then "carrying it out" (*kheirourgêsasa*, 1.20).

trial for killing an Athenian, Herodes. Second, he strongly protests that he is being illegally prosecuted under the wrong law (in other words, he wishes to reject the frame of the law the prosecutor has chosen and the judicial magistrates approved). Third, the chief witness for his defense, a slave, gave conflicting accounts about Euxitheus' involvement in the crime when the prosecutors tortured him for testimony – and then they killed him. And fourth, the presumably murdered man simply vanished in the night: his corpse was never found.

Since all the evidence in the case is circumstantial, part of Euxitheus' defense is to argue on the basis of reasoned likelihood [*to eikos*] that he had no motive for the crime.[81] In other words the raw strip of allegedly unjust interaction between him and Herodes is defective: it has critical lacunae that prevent certain knowledge of key events. To fill in these blanks, reasoned likelihood appeals to typical citizen scripts and to a culture's notion of which emotional responses and cognitive states (such as friendship or anger, awareness or ignorance) are likely in different situations. With this information it induces the jurors to rekey the known facts (*ta genomena*) within a hypothetical frame accommodating both known and likely facts (*ta eikota*, Ant. 5.25). But, moments before, Euxitheus clearly prepares the jurors for this by inviting them to speculate about his own intention (*pronoia*, 5.21): this, he implies, will serve as a guide to rekey both established events and likely events, along with emotions, thoughts, and so on. Cognitively speaking, the jurors cannot be invited to replay a sequence of known and likely events without privileged access to motives (or lack of motives) in Euxitheus' subjective "inner world."

Antiphon uses this interplay between reasoned likelihood and one individual's intention so he might stage in the jurors' minds a

---

[81] For recent discussion of the strategy behind Euxitheus' arguments, see Gagarin 2002: 152–60 and 164–69, and Carawan 1998: 314–54.

performance of his client's innocent interaction with Herodes. Since Euxitheus and Herodes had spent a good part of the night drinking, he prompts the jurors to imagine the Athenian stumbling off into the dark, out of control, and prey to any sort of misadventure (5.26). And he suggests likely reasons for deciding which statement in the dead slave's testimony is likely to be true: his identification of Euxitheus as the murderer or his later denial that Euxitheus was involved (5.37). Antiphon even has his client dress up reasoned likelihood in the honorable – even heroic? – guise of a military script when he has him declare, "For indeed, reasoned likelihood [*to eikos*] is my comrade-at-arms" (*symmakhon*, 5.43).

But Antiphon's most telling use of *to eikos* occurs in a less conspicuous passage which describes how it initiates a relation of intersubjectivity between defendant and jurors. After completing his version of events within the frame of likelihood, Euxitheus declares that he has demonstrated his innocence as best he can. He adds:

> Now the prosecution employs as their strongest argument the fact that the man [Herodes] has vanished – and you desire just as strongly to hear about this very fact. But if for this reason I'm obliged to engage in reasoned likelihood [eikazein], you can do this just as well as I, for neither you nor I am guilty of the crime. (*5.64, my emphasis*)

With these words Euxitheus envelops the jurors in a shared cognitive capacity to reason together if they will join him in erecting a hypothetical frame of likelihood around a raw strip of narrative about Herodes' death. In this simple way Euxitheus, a foreigner and an ally subject to Athenian sovereignty, establishes his equality with the Athenian jurors. He even evokes the interchangeability of their fates: they are innocent men all around. What is more, Antiphon has Euxitheus insert the jurors into the cognitive dilemma he himself faces in light of Herodes' disappearance: what are the possibilities of knowledge when we lack certain key information? Regarding his use of arguments based on reasoned likelihood, he claims,

> *I believe that each of you, if someone asked you something you happened not to know, would speak in this sort of way and say that you did not know. And if someone asked you to say more, I gather you'd be in a lot of difficulty. Therefore don't present me with this difficulty which you yourselves would not be able to escape.* (*5.65–66*)[82]

But Euxitheus then insists that the best criterion for the jurors' judgment is *not* an argument based on reasoned likelihood. He requests, "If I do a good job of using reasoned likelihood (*eu eikazô*), don't think I should be acquitted in this way" (5.66). He instead insists that the gold standard for determining his innocence is for the jurors to understand not how Herodes met his end but how he, Euxitheus, possessed no motive ("I had no involvement that would lead me to kill him," [5.66]). While he marshals all sorts of external signs of his and others' actions in order to convince the jurors that his guilt is unlikely, Euxitheus' final proof is the jurors' ability and willingness to mimic his train of thought, his state of mind, and the "inner logic" behind his behavior. Should they do so, he will succeed in establishing an intersubjective link with them that conforms to the model of the "selfobject" we saw in Odysseus' encounters with the arch-criminals in Hades. In this case each juror who votes for acquittal will see in Euxitheus a version of self who is like a "twin," someone essentially similar to oneself who provides reassurance that one can overcome shared human limitations (Kohut 1984: 193). This sort of transference, we should recall, resembles Odysseus' recognition

---

[82] Here Antiphon may be exploiting a problem Protagoras raised in discussing the limits of human knowledge. The cognitive dilemma Euxitheus presents the jurors recalls Protagoras' reconstructed fr. 3: "To you who are present, I appear to be sitting; to someone not present I don't appear to be sitting: it is unclear whether I am sitting or not sitting" (Farrar 1988: 52–53, with n. 32).

of Heracles as a fellow sufferer, a relatively powerless victim who must endure circumstances imposed by fate. This is why Euxitheus begins to erect the hypothetical frame of reasoned likelihood by encouraging the jurors "to consider these circumstances" of his casual acquaintance with Herodes "from the start – they came about not by intent (*pronoiai*) but by chance" (*tukhêi*, 5.21).[83]

In all three of his surviving courtroom speeches, Antiphon succeeds in transforming a lack of definitive proof, and the limitations this places on knowing the truth, into his client's asset. In each case he transforms cognitive uncertainty into an opportunity to immerse jurors in a particularly democratic experience of hypothetical time, space, and agency that is far removed from settling disputes by relying on the acumen of an Achilles, Menelaus, or other *basileis*. For arguments based on *to eikos*, this means fashioning mental simulacra of the defendant's and prosecutor's selves based on known and likely facts and the citizen scripts they suggest. Here Mead's distinction between the "me" roles constituting the self and the peculiar agency of the "I" is again helpful. From their reconstructions of what likely happened on the night Herodes disappeared, the jurors must arrive at what they believe to be a reasonably good approximation of Euxitheus' "me" roles: an elite Mytilenean, a faithful subject ally of Athens, a dutiful son, and so forth. And they

---

[83] In his summation Euxitheus tells the jurors that, if they judge him incorrectly, they are just as prone to moral error (*hamartia*) as the prosecutor (5.89). He then claims that mistakes we commit involuntarily (*ta . . . akousia*) are excusable, deserving "fellow feeling" or compassion (*syngnômê*) because they are due to chance (*tykhê*), whereas a voluntary mistake (*hamartêma*) is due to a reasoned judgment (*gnômê*, 5.92). Gernet claims that by the mid-fifth century *tychê* becomes an abstract, universal force that causes human error, appearing as a new concept, *physis* or human nature (2001: 335–36). In Chapter 6 I will argue that *physis* as human nature also means for Antiphon an individual's self-interest, especially when used to form reasoned judgment (*gnômê*). On appeals to compassion (pity) and "fellow feeling" in Greek law, see Konstan 2000.

must weigh their assessment of this against a similar approximation of the prosecution's "me" roles. But Antiphon has Euxitheus shepherd the jurors through this task by coaxing them to reenact several times those cognitive acts which his "I" must have used to make decisions based on criteria of morality and self-interest – in sum, his "inner" intentions.

Euxitheus' bid to persuade the jurors to stage a version of his *pronoia* prompts them to do more than use reasoned likelihood to speculate about what happened the night Herodes disappeared. It induces them to replay the likely critical, moral evaluations his "I" enacted when it weighed the demands of socially prescribed behavior against self-interest prior to, during, and after that night. He invites them, in Taylor's sense (1985a), to reconstruct his moral dimensions as a person. He of course reminds them of his thoughts and actions as a "subject of strategic action" seeking certain goals: he'd befriended Herodes at some point in the past (5.57–63); the morning after Herodes disappeared he participated in the search party (5.23); and without question he seeks to exonerate himself because his very life depends on the jurors' ability to "judge correctly" (5.46). But he also bids the jurors to portray him as a "subject of significance" – that is as an individual who evaluates the choices open to him according to standards of behavior that are colored by his own emotional response to them. When, for example, he runs through a checklist of his possible motives for the crime, he denies any "hostile feeling" (*ekhthra*) between him and Herodes; he rejects as morally repugnant the suggestion that he committed the crime as a favor for a friend; he claims he never feared Herodes might murder him; and he rejects as absurd the notion that he, a wealthy man, would have murdered for money a man who had none (5.57–58).[84] The key to

---

[84] Even if Euxitheus lies about or distorts certain facts and his emotional responses, his defense rests on the subjective terrain of a personhood he induces the jurors to

his defense therefore rests on the jurors' willingness to perform a version of Euxitheus' personhood which reveals a great improbability: that he could have used his *will* to commit the murder.[85] They're invited on their own authority to reach this conclusion by mimicking, cognitively and morally, crucial evaluations in the inner life of a would-be peer, the equivalent of a fellow citizen.

This is why Euxitheus' plea ultimately asks the jurors to use reasoned likelihood (*to eikos*) to produce two cognitive acts: a reasoned judgment (*gnômê*) uncontaminated by haste, anger, or prejudice (5.71–72), and the emotional act of compassion (*eleos*) (*eleêthênai*, 5.73). If they succeed in imitating his will (being his *lack* thereof) on the night Herodes disappeared, they will understand that "mistakes committed without intent [*ta men akousia*] deserve fellow-feeling [*syngnômên*], those committed through intent [*ta de hekousia*] do not" (5.92). With this request, imitating a person's *pronoia* (intention, premeditation) and imitating that person's misfortune through compassion converge in a single deliberative act. And Antiphon has Euxitheus immediately spell this out when he claims, "For a mistake committed without intent happens by chance [*tês tykhês*], but one committed through intent happens by reasoned judgment" (*tês gnômês*, 5.92) – which I've argued is equivalent to exercising one's will. If Gernet is right to link chance and human nature (*physis*) in mid-fifth century thought (2001 [1917]: 337–38), then

---

imagine. On his possible misrepresentations, see Carawan 1998: 322, and Gagarin 1997: 174–75.

[85] This cognitive mimesis concerns Euxitheus' exercise of a will in our modern sense, contra Vernant's contention that Classical Greeks were not autonomous enough to separate inclinations, desires, and intellectualized notions of the good from the "center" of their moral agency. I believe Euxitheus' self-examination and rejection of possible motives for killing Herodes make it reasonable to infer that, by the criterion of "his own action of willing . . . the true source of his actions," he had no reason to commit the crime (cf. Vernant 1988: 67). His plight as a foreigner and fatherless son in a hostile Athenian court may well contribute to his need to hypothesize so readily about his inner life (cf. Vernant 1988: 82).

compassion lends this judgment an affective dimension linking a foreign client's *physis* to each juror's individual experience of the same. In its simplest form Antiphon's argument to the jurors revises Solon's cognitive joinery in the following way: to be yourselves, you must be nobody and anybody – and you must try to become Euxitheus.

Popular Sovereignty and the Athenian Social Contract

This cognitive mimesis of Euxitheus which Antiphon induces in the jurors makes common cause with Athens' reliance between about 460 and 411 on various expressions of popular sovereignty through *nomos* (written statute law) and *psêphismata* (decrees of the citizen assembly). More than the Assembly, however, the law courts were the surest platform for exercising this popular sovereignty, in all likelihood ever since Ephialtes' reforms of 462 and Pericles' policies in the 450s helped create and staff the proliferation of popular courts beyond the *hêliaia* (the citizen Assembly serving as a court of appeal) (Ostwald 1986: 5; 78–82). Of all the early sophists, Protagoras was the political theorist who most clearly provided rational arguments to legitimate this ideology. His epistemology in particular validated only knowledge based on the individual's personal experience, or, as Farrar describes it, "the development of beliefs in the interaction of persons as they experience themselves in the world" (1988: 47). Because this interaction both shaped citizens and was controlled by them as they pursued social harmony (77–78), popular sovereignty emerges in Protagorean thought and in Periclean policies as the surest expression of human nature.

But Antiphon too was a political theorist, one whose intelligence seems to have been ignited by the bombshell of Protagoras' arrival in Athens around 460–450 (or a bit later).[86] He appears to have both

---

[86] For the relation of Antiphon's theories to Protagoras', see Gagarin 2002: 84–85, 106, 172, 179; Pendrick 2002: 247–48, 266, 271, 292, 321, 353–54 (largely citing – and

contested and furthered a Protagorean understanding of politics and human nature by explicitly describing – so far as we know, for the first time in Western thought – a social contract theory. We catch a glimpse of this in his essay *On Truth* when he uses the antithesis of *nomos/physis* (law vs. nature) to claim: "For the activities arising from a city-state's laws [*nomoi*] are superficially imposed [*epitheta*] [on a citizen] while those arising from nature [*physis*] are unavoidable. The activities arising from the laws, since they are agreed upon [*homologêthenta*], are not natural products, whereas activities arising from nature, since they are natural products, are not agreed upon" (B44[a]I.23–II.1).[87]

I devote a good part of Chapter 6 to a discussion of Antiphon's paradigm for citizenship and selfhood in Periclean and post-Periclean Athens, but for now I suggest that we see Antiphon's notion of the social contract at work in the agreement (using the verb *homologein*) Euxitheus proposes to the jurors when he asks them to use reasoned

---

dismissing – other scholars' opinions); Farrar 1988: 113–20; and Decleva Caizzi 1986: 297.

[87] Ostwald sees in these lines the "earliest explicit statement of a contract theory from the Greeks" (1990: 298), agreeing with Decleva Caizzi (1986: 296), along with Kahn (1981: 95, with nn. 3 and 5; and 102, n. 17). Guthrie (1971) sees a social "compact" theory implicit in Protagoras and explicit in Antiphon but Kerferd (1981: 147–48). strongly disagrees about Protagoras. He cites several fifth- and fourth-century sources for contract theory yet omits these lines (148–50). Farrar finds a social contract in Protagorean teaching (1988: 91–95) and believes that in these lines Antiphon acknowledges a social contract but attacks contemporary versions like Protagoras' as harmful to the individual (116–17). Pendrick's facile dismissal of any reference to social contract theory in these lines – he believes scholars "read [it] into" Antiphon – does not seem to me justified; he interprets the notion of "contract" too literally (2002: 325). Kahn suggests the concept is present where "political union" is described "in terms of a contract or mutual agreement" (1981: 94), and Kerferd where "political obligation flows from actual or implied contractual agreement" (1981: 147). Rose summarizes sophistic thinking about a social contract as the second of three stages in an anthropological understanding of human development (1992: 275–76).

likelihood to imitate his state of mind prior to and following Herodes' disappearance. The agreement in question is, as described above, cognitive and moral, and it requires the jurors to align three ontological frames: Euxitheus' hypothetical reconstruction of his likely thoughts and deeds; the prosecution's alleged raw strip of activity (their version of the murder); and the law on wrongdoing (*kakourgia*). They must then eliminate one of the first two frames and join the other to the frame of the law. Such reasoning together with one another, and with either Euxitheus or the prosecution, enacts citizenship by persuading citizens to perform critical moments in one another's lives – to agree to *become* one another. This is the core experience in social contract theory and in the interchangeability of fates resulting from it.[88]

III RAISING THE LAWGIVER FROM THE DEAD

After the debacle of the Sicilian invasion (415–413) and the first oligarchic revolution, which briefly toppled the democracy in 411, institutional expressions of popular sovereignty and its forms of reasoning together began to lose their proud and privileged status as the foundation and bulwark of the Athenian state. Soon after 411, and more quickly after Athens' conclusive defeat by Sparta in 404 and the second oligarchic coup of 403, Athenian ideologues (political leaders

---

[88] In Antiphon's *On the Chorus Boy's Murder* the defendant demonstrates how agreement among citizens can result from this aligning of frames when he notes how the testimony of witnesses at the alleged crime scene corroborates his version of "what really happened" and not the prosecution's: "I, however, am presenting reasonable [*eikotas*] accounts to you, witnesses who agree [*homologountas*] with these accounts, activities that agree with the witnesses, and arguments based on the activities themselves . . ." (6.31). At the start of Antiphon's *Second Tetralogy*, the prosecutor generally observes, "Disputes in which everyone agrees on the facts [*ta homologoumena . . . tôn pragmatôn*] are settled in advance by the law and by decrees of the Assembly, which are sovereign over all aspects of city-state life" (3.1). (A minority of scholars disputes the authorship of the *Tetralogies*; see, e.g., Carawan 1998: 171–92, and Sealey 1984).

and speechwriters) started transforming the way they conceptualized the sources of authority in the Athenian state. In one sense they depersonalized that authority by identifying it with the abstract sovereignty of the city-state's "laws" (*nomoi*) rather than with a trajectory of popular decision making under the influence of leaders from Themistocles, Cimon and Pericles to Cleon, Nicias and Alcibiades. As we mentioned earlier, they conceived a pressing need and nostalgia for "the condition of our city-state as the ancestors believed it should be," a circumlocution of mine that captures the sense of *patrios politeia* better than the literal "ancestral constitution." But this appeal to the abstract authority of the laws also had an association with past leaders and their personalities: Solon and Draco now loomed large as the lawgivers responsible for the powerful democracy that emerged from their political wisdom.[89]

When the democracy was first restored in 410, this need and nostalgia manifested itself in an effort to clarify the existing law code by collecting and publishing all the laws, but especially those of Draco and Solon.[90] When the democracy was again restored in 403, the Athenians made a more concerted attempt to codify their laws by reviewing, revising, and republishing the laws attributed to their two canonical lawmakers. This task, however, did not fall to the citizen Assembly but to a composite body of specially elected and appointed *nomothetai* or "lawmakers," numbering at this time between 510 and 560 members.[91] How did this new nostalgia and reverence for law, the

---

[89] On Solon as a model for lawgiving after 411 and 403, see Ostwald 1986: 370–72, 415, and 511–14. For Solon's even greater prestige in the fourth century as the "founder" of the democracy, see Hansen 1990: 78ff. and Mossé 2004.

[90] On this attempt to revise the law code, see Hansen 1991: 162, and Ostwald 1986: 369ff. On where different laws were publicly displayed and how readily they could be consulted, see Sickinger 2004.

[91] On the *nomothetai*, see Ostwald 1986: 512–13 and Munn 2000: 264–72. From Demosthenes we learn that in the fourth century they were chosen from the jury pool of 6,000 citizens on days when changes in legislation had to be debated (24.20–23).

act of lawmaking, and the figure of the lawmaker manifest itself in the courts? Not surprisingly, we find in the surviving speeches from around 400 through the mid-fourth century a constellation of references evoking the authority of both Draco and Solon and casting the lawmaker's role as the most pivotal to civic well-being. And here we see that the Athenian jurors' ability to perform justice had to accommodate the recent ideological shift to the sovereignty of law.[92]

To meet this need speechwriters worked elements of the new ideology of law into the semblance of a performance tradition. The act of mimesis at its heart was cognitive and looked to each of the two lawgivers – but especially to Solon – to be a "model of mimesis" whose wisdom jurors could imitate as latter-day lawgivers. This fabrication of a performance tradition bears interesting analogies to changes that had also been occurring in the poetic tradition from the sixth down to the fourth centuries. The two attempts to codify Draco's and Solon's corpus of original laws – including of course many laws these two men could never have composed – resemble efforts made in Athens to revise and edit the scripts or performance texts of such poets as Homer and the three great Athenian tragedians.[93] The tragedians' works were

---

Hansen believes their numbers fluctuated from 501 to perhaps more than 1501 (1991: 167–68).

[92] Johnstone discusses the use speechwriters made of the lawgiver in fourth-century forensic rhetoric as a "trope" and "interpretive protocol" leading to a form of "legal reasoning" that permits a speechwriter to authorize a non-literal interpretation of a law; an interpretation of a law conforming to other laws in a systematic code; and an interpretation of a law confirming its fundamentally "democratic" nature (1999: 25–33). I focus on ways this "trope" legitimates a mimetic and cognitive performance tradition for legal decision making consistent with the ideological transition from popular sovereignty to the sovereignty of law. See also Yunis 2005: 201–7.

[93] Nagy proposes five periods in the transmission of Homeric poetry. My analogy of the revised law code with a performance text corresponds to the latter stage of period 3, centered in Athens from the mid-sixth century to the later fourth century (1996: 110).

already assuming canonical form by the end of the fifth century, and in the fourth Athenians made concerted efforts to establish official texts of their plays for continuing reperformance in the development of an Athenian state theater.[94] Aristophanes' *Frogs* (405) clearly demonstrates the community's desire in the period between the two oligarchic coups to recollect backward to the moral and political guidance contained in authoritative poetic performances, although his comic retrieval from Hades of the spirits of Aeschylus, Sophocles, and Euripides was not an original bit of stagecraft. In 412 a rival, Eupolis, in his play *Dêmoi*, brought back to life the spirits of such leaders as Miltiades, Pericles, Aristides – and perhaps Solon as well.[95]

This nostalgic need in the theater toward the end of the fifth century to revive authorities from the past certainly appears consistent with the turn in political ideology away from confidence in popular sovereignty and toward recovery of a *patrios politeia*. And just as Athenians felt impelled to retrieve, through the medium of writing, the "authentic" words of master poets, they likewise sought in writing the "true" *thesmoi* of Draco and *nomoi* of Solon in order more faithfully to perform the lawmakers' judgments. But would the evocation of Solon and Draco in the law courts make sense to Athenians in the same way as the appearance on the comic stage of great poets and politicians from the past? To bring the great tragedians back to Athens, Aristophanes spoofed the

---

[94] Sometime between 350 and 325 the Athenian politician Lycurgus developed an official "state script" of the three tragedians and had bronze statues of each erected (Pseudo-Plut. *Lives of the Ten Orators* 841ff., cited in Nagy 1996: 174–76 and 201). These reforms were extended by Demetrius of Phaleron in the last quarter of the century when the state took over the sponsorship of tragedy from private citizens (Nagy 1996: 156–57).

[95] For the political context of Eupolis' play, see Ostwald 1986: 341–42; Edmonds suggests a reconstruction of its plot (1957: 978–94). In the Periclean age the comic playwright Cratinus may have brought Solon back from the dead in *Chirones* (fr. 246–68, Kassel and Austin 1983). See Vickers on this comic tradition of *idolopoeia* (1997: 7, w. n. 34).

epic tradition of *katabasis*, the hero's descent into Hades, and the function of the *psykhagôgos*, a wizard who enabled the living to consult the dead or who put troubled ghosts at peace.[96] And as I have explained, his predecessor Eupolis (and Cratinus too) used elements of necromancy to retrieve the souls of political leaders.[97] What succeeds as silly hocuspocus in comedy, however, would certainly be out of place in court.

Just the same, in 414 Aristophanes (at *Birds* 1553–64) ridicules Socrates' efforts to improve the souls of his fellow Athenians by having him practice the shady trade of a *psykhagôgos* who "leads souls" from the underworld to converse with the living. Evidently Aristophanes believed the script of necromantic consultation and temporary "reviving" of the dead would strike Athenians as a facsimile – however silly – of Socrates' serious intent to help his fellow citizens attain wisdom through some sort of cognitive transformation. So it is perhaps not so surprising that for over seventy years speechwriters resorted to a rhetorical sort of necromancy to revive Solon and Draco in the minds of jurors before they decided a case. In 330, for example, Aeschines concludes his lengthy attack on Ctesiphon (and Demosthenes) by conjuring up for the jury Solon's ghostly image, to be followed by the image of Aristides:

> And when he [Ctesiphon] concludes his speech by summoning those
> colleagues who all shared with him in taking bribes, imagine
> /hypolambanete/ that you see up on the rostrum, where I myself now
> stand as I speak, our state's champions drawn up in formation against
> the lawlessness of these men: Solon, who set our democracy in order
> with his most wonderful laws, a man who was a philosopher and noble
> lawgiver, begging you calmly, as befit him, in no way to have more

---

[96] On the *psykhagôgos* and its connection to necromancy, see Ogden 2001: 95ff.

[97] Ogden places these comic efforts within the cultural context of necromancy (2001: 263).

> *regard for Demosthenes' words than for your oaths and laws. And*
> *Aristides . . . (3.257–58)*

Earlier (in 345) Aeschines employed a somewhat more graphic visual aid to evoke Solon's ghost; and as a former actor he no doubt prided himself on his understanding of performance skills. When attacking Demosthenes' colleague Timarchus for an immoral and indecent life, and in particular for his vulgar way of speaking in public, Aeschines recalls the decorous comportment of statesmen like Pericles, Themistocles, and Aristides. All these men, he claims, observed Solon's law about how to speak in public. But his most powerful piece of evidence (*semêion*) for how to perform in public is a Solonian spectacle familiar to all the jurors, a sort of three-dimensional written law, and he describes it with particular emphasis on its function as a model of mimesis:

> *I know very well that all of you have sailed out to Salamis and have*
> *seen the statue of Solon. You yourselves can testify that Solon is set up in*
> *the markeplace of Salamis with his hand inside his cloak. This,*
> *gentlemen of Athens, is a reminder and a portrayal /mimêma/ of*
> *Solon's stance and of the way he himself used to address the people of*
> *Athens. (1.25)*

Not to be outdone as an expert on this Solonian performance tradition, Demosthenes soon found occasion to trump Aeschines' use of the statue as a "paradigm of moderation" for public orators in the past. In 443 he succeeded in bringing suit against Aeschines for committing treason as an ambassador in negotiations with Philip of Macedon. Demosthenes' aim is to discredit his rival's credentials as a rhetorical *psykhagôgos* of Solon, and he delivers his first blow on what we would call historical grounds.[98] He points out that Solon's statue in Salamis

---

[98] This contest in forensic necromancy between the two orators fits into their broader exchange about mimesis within true and deceptive uses of rhetoric, which Hesk

has only been standing there for fifty years; since the lawmaker lived two hundred forty years before, the sculptor who crafted his image could never have known what Solon's stance looked like (Dem. 19.251). But in the context of a performance tradition, Demosthenes' critique is not so much historical as cognitive, for he impugns Aeschines' ability to "see" or know the true nature of his model of mimesis. Like a poet telling a variant of a myth that is irreconcilable with a rival's, like a competing rhapsode who impersonates a contrasting version of Homer, or like an adjudicating *basileus* on Achilles' shield whose competitive performance of *themistes* departs radically from his peers', Demosthenes strikes at Aeschines' cognitive virtuosity when it comes to frame-switching between the ontological registers of community memory and the here-and-now. He complains that Aeschines, despite his ignorance of Solon's signature stance, "nevertheless spoke of it to the jurors and imitated it" (*emimêsato*, 19.252).

More importantly, in this attack Demosthenes also points to the presumed goal of proper participation in the Solonian performance tradition: this is the necromancer's ability to "see the soul" of the deceased so that he or she might speak once more:

> "Yet the part of this stance [skhêma] that's much more beneficial to the state is the ability to see Solon's soul [psykhên] and his degree of understanding [dianoian]. And this he [Aeschines] did not imitate – all to the contrary!" (19.252).

At this point Demosthenes cannot resist finishing off his rival with a few virtuoso moves of his own. To display his own credentials as a more authoritative expert in this performance tradition, he evokes the dramatic moment in Solon's career when the Athenians voted to ban public discussion of Salamis' recent revolt from their hegemony. He

analyzes from Aeschines' speeches about the embassy to Philip and the crown for Demosthenes (2000: 231–39).

reminds the jurors of the great personal risk Solon took to circumvent that ban when, according to the anecdote, he disguised himself as a herald, entered the agora, and recited elegiac verses in place of a political speech. And then Demosthenes transforms the law court into a stage, and he proceeds to impersonate Solon by performing another of Solon's elegies, poem 4, as an instance where political action, song, and a vision of justice coincide in one extraordinary individual's degree of understanding.

As he intones, "Our state will never be destroyed because Zeus alloted that fate or because the immortal gods so intended . . ." (Solon 4.1–2), Demosthenes momentarily embodies or impersonates Solon the way Nagy claims rhapsodes impersonated Homer in "reperformance" (1996: 59ff.). How much more clearly could Demosthenes illustrate that Solon is a poetic *and* cognitive performance role to which jurors must repair if they are to decide a case correctly? Aeschines, by contrast, merely replicated a Solonian stance or posture copied from an untrustworthy memory, the recently erected statue in Salamis. This amounts to a failed mimesis of the model, and Demosthenes drives home the point by declaring, "He [Aeschines] can't bring Solon back to mind" (*memnêsthai*, 19.253). He then derides his rival's failure to perform Solon's stance accurately by comparing the lawgiver's decorous posture to the charge of bribery he has been hurling at Aeschines: "It's not necessary for you to speak with your hand inside your cloak – but to act like an ambassador with your hand inside your cloak" (19.255).

Mimesis, it appears, has the capacity to convey a poet's or lawgiver's soul from the past, where it lies inert in death, to the present, where a listener or spectator can reanimate it.[99] And it is the quality of that great

---

[99] Fourth-century sculptors and painters certainly attempted to capture and communicate the individual ethos and the *psykhê* of their subjects. And the wizardry of the *psykhagôgos* described their art. In *Mem.* 3.10.3 Xenophon has Socrates ask the painter Parrhesius whether the "character of the soul" (*tês psykhês ethos*) can be imitated (*mimêton*); and he puts a similar question to the sculptor Cleiton (possibly

individual's thought (*dianoia*) and, as we'll see, his "intention" (*pronoia*, sometimes *dianoia*) in writing a law that the jurors are enjoined to revive, as they participate silently in courtroom deliberation, by imitating him as latter-day lawgivers. We've seen that in an age where belief in popular sovereignty thrived, speechwriters like Antiphon could induce jurors to imitate the intentions of a fellow citizen when they reconstruct his inner life through arguments based on reasoned likelihood. But for an age invested in the sovereignty of law, reasoning together is thought to require another sort of mimetic performance from jurors, one that may well induce them first to imitate a defendant's intention to commit an injustice but ultimately asks them to revive the lawgiver's intention in writing the law. Before discussing that intention, however, we should ask whether fourth-century speechwriters like Demosthenes recognized a genuinely cognitive dimension in this second kind of mimesis.

In one of his earliest speeches (355), Demosthenes pleads with the jurors' not to accept and live by a recent law proposed (written) by the defendant Leptines and passed by the Assembly. This law, he claims, is disgraceful and will only encourage envy and rivalry among citizens: "He who wrote the law [Leptines] may be intent on these sorts of things, but it isn't appropriate for you to imitate [*mimeisthai*] such things nor

---

a pseudonym for Polycleitus). On the pleasurable effects of Cleiton's art, he asks, "How do you work into your statues that which captures people's souls [*psykhagôgei*] when they look, that ability to make something appear lifelike?" He suggests that the key lies in the sculptor's ability to find simulacra in his artistic figure for "the activities of the soul" [*ta tês psykhês erga*]. Elsewhere he imagines a statue of his friend Cratylus that would possess the man's "way of moving [*kinêsin*], his soul [*psykhên*], and his way of thinking [*phronêsin*]" (*Crat.* 432b–c). In Steiner's discussion of these passages (2001: 32–35; 69–70) she characterizes Archaic and Classical sculpture's ability "to reenact an earlier performance," sometimes to "promote contacts between the living and the absent or dead" when representing "the 'core' nature and qualities of an absent individual." And when such statues are erected in public places from the fifth century on, they enable individual spectators "to define themselves as citizens . . ." (31–32). On mimesis in the passage from Xenophon, cf. Stewart 1990: 83.

appear to entertain thoughts [*phronountas*] unworthy of yourselves"
(20. 157). And as a positive counter-example to this inadvisable kind
of mimesis, he immediately contrasts the benefits Athenians derive
from following the directives in Draco's homicide laws (19.158). In the
speech discussed above in which he attacks Aeschines, Demosthenes
also pleads with jurors to render a proper judgment through a cognitive
sort of imitation that is equivalent to imitating actions. He urges them to
turn to their ancestral, Athenian models of virtuous men and "to imitate
[*mimeisthai*] them through action," even though the jurors live in a time
of peace and cannot score great military victories. But he claims they
can perform such a mimetic action when "you imitate [*mimeisthe*] the
way the ancestors thought clearly" (*to eu phronein*, 19.269), for "nothing
is more tedious or troublesome than having a poor opinion of excellent
thinking" (*to kalôs phronein*, 19.270).[100]

In these passages of Demosthenes and Aeschines, the cognitive
dimension of mimesis helps jurors to settle a dispute through the art
of "joining" as Solon and Theognis conceived it. Generally speaking,
Greeks from the sixth century onward regarded mimesis as the ability
to link two distinctly different categories of being or ontological orders
– whether a human copied the movements or sounds of an animal, or a
Greek copied the accent of a foreigner or another Greek, or whether one
citizen simply copied the demeanor of a neighbor.[101] To put it another
way, the most essential quality of mimesis appears to be its ability to
join, in an act performed here and now, two different entities separated

---

[100] The topos of "imitating the ancestors" occurs sporadically in the speechwriters
(e.g., Dem. 22.78 and 24.186 (*idem*); Aesch. 2. 138 and 171; Lycurgus 20.110 and 123), but
it usually refers to imitating their deeds. Aeschines does, however, specify the need
to call the ancestors to mind (*memnêsthai*) by imitating (*mimeisthai*) their capacity
for good judgment in deliberation (*tas euboulias*, 2.75).

[101] See, e.g., Else's (1958) discussion of sixth- and fifth-century occurrences of *mimeisthai*
and its derivatives in his review of Koller 1954.

by categories of being, space, and time. In this regard the use of mimesis to render a judicial decision amounts to the sort of frame-switching we attributed to the cognitive virtuosity of the formative period's judicial *basileis* when they rendered a *dikê*. Their recall of *thesmia* from community memory (paradigmatic crimes and their successful resolutions) now yields to a democratic judicial mimesis in which "anyone who" can engage in forensic deliberation when he enacts a kind of necromancy summoning the lawgiver of the past to "join" his law to the raw strip of alleged injustice in some present circumstance.[102] Of course the lawgiver's "appearance" in the courtroom clearly takes the form of jurors who imitate his act of *nomothesia* when they understand how to apply his law.

As suggested above, that quality of the lawgiver's soul the jurors need most to imitate is his intention (*pronoia*) in writing the law. How can they grasp this? Just as the jurors in Antiphon's speeches need to enter a hypothetical sense of time, space, and agency when they imitate or recreate the defendant's inner life, here too hypothesis guides their mimetic efforts. To repeat Aeschines' words, they must "imagine" (*hypolambanete*, 3.257) not only Solon's ghostly presence but his state of mind when framing the law in question. In a tone often bordering on harangue, Aeschines asks jurors to reflect on how much *pronoia* (intention, forethought) Solon, Draco, and other lawgivers of their time invested in legislation concerning a citizen's moral need for self-control (*sôphrosynê*, 1.6–7). Demosthenes too urges jurors to "examine" (*eksetasai*) Solon's *pronoia* as the key to his lawmaker's character (*êthos*, 22.30), and when he repeats the verb "he knew that . . . he knew

---

[102] See Nagy 1990: 42–44, where his definition of mimesis as "the reenactment, through ritual, of the events of myth" (42) conforms to my sense of ontological frame-switching and the activity of judicial *basileis* in the Formative period plumbing community memory to reproduce solutions for crimes committed in the here and now.

that . . ." to demonstrate Solon's intent or forethought (*êidei gar êidei*, 22.31), he emphasizes the lawmaker's ability to understand in advance the needs of a democratic society. As Johnstone points out, this appeal to the lawgiver's intention enables speechwriters to bend and twist their interpretation of a given law to suit their client's needs.[103] In fact Solon's name frequently inspires a constellation of nouns and verbs indicating the cognitive acts of knowing, understanding, thinking, distinguishing between matters, and showing intellectual concern for a need.[104]

Imagining, recovering, and imitating this sort of intention or forethought differ considerably from recreating a defendant's intention in

---

[103] Johnstone describes this rhetorical strategy as an attempt "to hone the law" in order to permit "the deduction of implicit meanings" (1999: 26–27). As examples he cites: Lycurgus 1.9, and 31.27, Dem. 22.11, 36.27, 58.11, Aesch. 3.11, and Isaeus 2.13. (The lawmaker is not named in any of these passages.) Cf. Yunis 2005: 201–7.

[104] The same verb, *êidei* (from *oida*, to know), recurs at Dem. 22.25 along with *hegeisthai* (to think, to suppose) to describe Solon's cognitive talents in a passage where Demosthenes exhorts the jurors to "learn" (*mathein*) what sort of lawmaker Solon was – particularly in his prescient ability to understand the varying levels of citizen intelligence. *Hegeisthai* again describes these talents at Dem. 21.45 and 24.213; at 23.54 it refers to either Solon or Draco; at Lysias 1.31–32 to either Draco or Solon; and at Isocrates 20.3 to an unnamed lawgiver; and it occurs with *nomizein* (to think) and *gignôskein* (to know) at Dem. 36.27. (At 3.11 Aeschines praises an anonymous lawgiver for "nicely anticipating" [*eu prokateilêphotos*] some leaders' attempts to manipulate their required audit at the end of office, while Lysias excuses a lawgiver's inability to "anticipate" [*elpizein*] a citizen committing an unimaginable offense of desertion [31.27]). *Nomizein* appears again in connection with Solon at 22.31; *diorizein* (to distinguish) at Dem. 42.1; *diairein* (to divide) at Dem. 23.54 (of Solon or Draco); *oiesthai* (to suppose or think) at Dem. 18.6, 20.89–90, 21.46, 24.115, 24 148, 22.11 (of an unnamed lawgiver), and Aesch. 3.175; *epimeleisthai* (to concern oneself with) at Dem. 48.56 and Aesch. 3.38; and *spoudazein* (to be anxious about) at Dem. 43.62 and Isocrates 20.2 (of unnamed lawgivers). Solon's *gnômê* (intelligence, understanding) is cited at Dem. 20.104 and the same word occurs in the sense of a "motion" Solon put up for a vote (Aesch. 3.108) (see Dover 1994: 123–24 for discussion of the differences in meaning of *gignôskein, gnômê, and dianoia*). At 1.46 Aeschines praises a lawgiver (probably Solon) as *sophos* (wise). At 20.102 Demosthenes claims Leptines doesn't read or understand (*sunienai*) Solon's laws.

committing a crime. And while fourth-century speechwriters certainly encouraged jurors to concern themselves with the criminal intentions of their fellow citizens, just as Antiphon had done, we still need to account for this new emphasis in deliberation on hypothetical thinking as reasoning together. The rhetorical necromancy described earlier, and Johnstone's "interpretive protocol" only partially account for this as a shared vision of the great man's intellect; when evoked, it only prepares the way for a final cognitive act on the jurors' part: *to see themselves as the lawgiver*. What did it mean for a citizen to assume a lawmaker's identity or be described as such by a speechwriter?

In Antiphon's *On the Murder of Herodes*, the defendant Euxitheus angrily labels his prosecutor a *nomothetês* for changing the law to suit his own interests (5.15). Here the appellation is clearly derogatory and, as Gagarin says, "scornful," implying that his opponent thought himself the equal of a Draco or Solon (1997: 184). Demosthenes too scornfully labels defendants like Androtion (22.25) and Timocrates (24.103, 106 and 113) "lawmakers" in a perverse sense and explicitly compares them to the paragon, Solon. However, the jurors themselves are sometimes called "lawmakers" in a very positive sense. This might occur under special circumstances: Lysias, for example, reminds jurors in 395 that they are trying a case for military desertion and refusal of service for the first time since the democracy has been restored (and the new codification of laws completed). As a result, he claims, "in deciding this case here and now you are not only jurors (*dikastas*) but lawmakers" (*nomothetas*, 14.4). In a speech delivered after 323, Demosthenes (or whoever authored it) reminds the jurors in a case involving default on a shipping loan that "even though you are deciding a single case here and now, you are making law [*nomotheite*] for the entire port" (56.48); earlier, in 330, Lycurgus also urged jurors to act as lawgivers by applying a wide interpretation of a law (1.9). But since the courts were, in Hansen's words, "a political organ on a par with the Assembly" and sometimes were "even described as the highest organ of state" (1991: 180), speechwriters could remind jurors that they were lawmakers simply because their decisions wielded ultimate authority over the Assembly, Council of 500, and so on, as well as all politicians (179–80).

The most dramatic of these reminders occurs in a speech delivered in the third quarter of the fourth century and attributed (very doubtfully) to Demosthenes. To drive home to the jurors their need to exercise "intelligence" (*nous*) in rendering a decision, the speaker utilizes the topos of "imitating the ancestors" and recalls to mind, as Aeschines and Demosthenes had done in the 340s, a statue of Solon, this one in bronze, standing in the Athenian agora:

> It is just terrible that your ancestors had the daring to die so the laws wouldn't be destroyed while you won't punish men who sin against them, and that you erect in the agora a bronze statue of Solon, the man who wrote them, and yet appear to belittle the laws themselves for which he happened to receive such boundless esteem. (26.23–24)

As a rhetorical device the statue certainly enables the speaker to contrast the mass of citizens to the single great individual, but it also suggests to the jurors that when they gaze on that image they ought to see themselves reflected in it, especially when deliberating silently in court:

> How doesn't it turn out absurd if as lawmakers you become angry at wicked men but when you catch them in the act you let them go untouched? And if the lawgiver, a single person, makes enemies of all the riff-raff while you yourselves won't even show that you despise wicked men but let yourselves be bettered by just one? (26.24)

Once again I suggest that the performance of justice requires its agent to see in another individual a "selfobject," one that in this case reflects back to the agent not a twin, a true alter ego, but an idealized, grandiose

image of self (Kohut 1984: 192–94; 1977: 185).[105] The speechwriters, it
seems, evoke these either mental or plastic images of the great lawgiver
so that jurors might have access to his extraordinary cognitive actions
and, through an idealizing transference, form an empathic connection to his performance of them. Antiphon on the other hand hoped
Euxitheus would provide the jurors a "selfobject" in the form of an
alter ego whose cognitive abilities and emotional inclinations matched
their own. Both types of intersubjective relationship emerge through a
cognitive sort of mimesis that joins a hypothetical experience of time,
space, and agency – in particular a hypothetical self – to matters and
persons in the present. Both also seem capable of empowering ordinary citizens to assume democratically the role of the agent of justice,
for both generate a reasoning together accessible to a legally qualified
"anyone who." However, the difference between them as recruitment
strategies for performing justice marks the divide between the ideologies of popular sovereignty and the sovereignty of law. In the former,
citizen jurors are asked to perform one another when their deliberation and reasoning together lead them to imitate the personhood of
the defendant or plaintiff. They find a coherent sense of self through a
judicial deliberation that relies on cognitive acts they share under their
own authority. Under the sovereignty of law, citizens are also asked to
perform one another, but they must derive their authority to do so by
detouring into a reasoning together that resembles a mass possession
by the soul of an ancestral cognitive giant.

   To put it another way, in the fourth century jurors are thought
competent to perform justice and engage in the interchangeability
of fates only when they conjure up the imagined intelligence of a

---

[105] When Socrates evokes *psykhagôgia* to describe the effect Cleiton's statues have on
viewers, he seems to be describing the transference typical of a selfobject: the statues
"capture people's souls" by imitating "the activities of the soul" (Xen. *Mem.* 3.10.8).

lawgiver – and seek shelter as an individual agent of justice under his cognitive shadow. In this regard we might say that forensic speech-writers are pushing a social contract that differs significantly from those explicit or implicit in the teachings of Protagoras and Antiphon. It more closely resembles a Platonic version in which ordinary citizens defer to the wisdom of "great-souled" leaders whose ability to frame-switch returns the Greeks to a reliance on the cognitive virtuosity of extraordinary individuals like the Formative period's *basileis*.

Yet at the same time our predominant contemporary model for a social contract, Rawls' original position, also imagines the need for a "lawgiver" to broker consensus among citizens as they decide questions of justice. Under the hypothetical veil of ignorance about our own and others' concrete social identities, Rawls suggests we think of the original position not as an actual assembly of persons but as a "guide to intuition" whose perspective we may conjure up at any moment irregardless of circumstances. But when we and our like-minded fellows achieve a certain conception of justice on an issue, how are we to communicate and argue this with absent parties of fellow citizens who are doing likewise? And how will consensus rather than faction emerge from this abstract convocation? Rawls' solution is to conjure up a hypothetical individual: "imagine that the parties are required to communicate with one another through a referee as intermediary." He or she forms a cognitive relay over groups dispersed in time and space, explains all parties' reasons and arguments for their positions, forbids coalition formation, and then announces when understanding has been reached (1971: 120).

This referee, it seems to me, performs cognitive and communicative functions in Rawls' script of deliberation similar to the lawgiver's in the Greek historical and political imagination. Like ghosts, both inhabit a people's political and legal tradition, embody superhuman capaci-ties for memory, represent the perspectives of groups dispersed socially and temporally, know how to speak for and to these groups, and most importantly ensure that civic unrest (*stasis*) will not prevail over consensus. Of course we might wonder why the citizens of a given era in our contemporary or in ancient Greek society can't exercise sovereignty by performing these functions for themselves. In the next chapter we will examine the pitfalls citizens and selves faced in Athens when the ideology of popular sovereignty was just taking hold – and when citizens and leaders had to decide questions of justice on their own, without a lawgiver's or referee's metaphysical guidance.

5 CITIZENSHIP BY DEGREES: EPHEBES AND DEMAGOGUES IN DEMOCRATIC ATHENS, 465–460

◎▣◎

I CITIZENSHIP AND MANHOOD

In Book 3 of his *History*, Thucydides describes a civil war gripping the city-state of Corcyra in 427, but this event inspires him to sketch out a portrait of factional strife between democrats and oligarchs everywhere in Greece where Athenian–Spartan hostilities provoked "the same human nature" (3.82.2) to acts of hostility and brutality (82.1, 82.3 and 83.1).[1] His portrait highlights several variations on the basic script "how citizens deliberate," and the cumulative effect of this script's several tracks dramatizes how citizens individually and in factions can assume performative attitudes toward one another which produce (in Taylor's terms) "webs of interlocution" and a "for-us" public space that is actually degenerative to city-state community. By this I mean that, in these quickly sketched variations, deliberating citizens believe they are following a familiar script to achieve the consensus necessary for *dikê* and *nomos*, but in reality their deliberations sabotage the goals of the script in question and push their communities beneath the threshold of statehood. The tracks include: "forming an alliance" (82.1–3); "interpreting the habitual meanings of language" (82.3–4); "evaluating the deliberator" (82.5–6); and "how to achieve consensus" (82.6–7).

---

[1] Hornblower recognizes the description as panhellenic: "After all, the phrase 'in the cities' occurs at intervals . . . in paras. 2, 3 and 8, and it might be better to see it all as an analysis of stasis in Greek cities, punctuated by universal remarks . . . and prompted by Corcyra, which is never quite lost sight of . . . ." (1991: 479).

If it is true that these citizens show how a city-state can fall beneath the threshold of statehood when they depart from the goals of deliberation, then it's reasonable to ask whether as deliberators they push themselves beneath the threshold of citizenship itself. What might it mean to regress from the ability to speak, think, and respond like a citizen? And what sort of self resides on the nether side of citizenship's threshold? We find one answer in the track that undermines "interpreting the habitual meanings of language" (82.3–4), for it suggests that citizens with impaired cognitive and communicative abilities not only misunderstand the proper performance of key civic virtues but in the process become something less than men. We can paraphrase the scrambling of civic virtues within this track into six propositions. First, the reckless abandonment of deliberative reason (*alogistos*) suddenly looks like the sort of manhood (*andreia*) that links comrades to one another (*philetairos*). Second, a prudent concern for future events looks like cowardice (*deilia*) with a handsome face. Third, moderation (*to sôphron*) is called a screen for lack of manhood (*tou anandrou*). Fourth, displaying intelligence looks like laziness. Fifth, senseless anger looks like the definition of a real man (*andros moirai*). Sixth, long-term deliberation for security's sake resembles a well-phrased excuse for doing nothing (82.4).[2]

According to these perverse interpretations of civic virtues, achieving recognition as a citizen and a man involves more than passing a

---

[2] These six propositions are a catalogue of civic virtues whose contextual rather than literal meanings change when consensus is formed in a factionalized city-state. Thucydides refers to this as an "extreme in ways new meanings [*tas dianoias*] were invented" (3.82.3). Hornblower clarifies, "The point . . . is not that the *meanings* of words acually changed . . . but that the use which people made of the available descriptions changed as their evaluation of the relevant action changed" (1991: 483; emphasis in the original). See M. F. Williams' chart of the changed meanings of these virtues and their moral valences (1998: 24–32, esp. Table 1) and Edmunds' similar chart (1975: 77, Table 1).

political and biological muster: somehow one must display the know-how to play the moral role of a kind of deliberator, or assume the kind of subject position and performative attitude proper to the autonomy of citizens who are "real men." Moments before, Thucydides designates this know-how as a capacity for intelligent judgment (*gnômê*) that was hopelessly impaired by faction (82.2.6), and we may take it as his hallmark for the ideal cognitive achievement of the mature citizen.[3] In the Introduction we glimpsed how for Athenian males the question of becoming a citizen evokes their transformation from boys to men, in particular the ephebe's (apprentice citizen's) awkward experience, including the illocutionary act of the ephebic oath that launched each speaking subject into the city-state's "webs of interlocution." In time of civil war, would falling back beneath this threshold therefore return a citizen to a version of the ephebic experience, when adolescent moral traits of recklessness, anger, and fear had not yet come under control, and discursive traits of reasoned argument, prudence, moderate response, and a capacity for intelligent decision making (*gnômê*) had not yet been acquired? If so, as a general script we might describe "behaving like an ephebe" as both a formative phase in aspiring to citizenship and a potentially degenerative phase in losing it.

To put it another way, Thucydides' dystopic portrait of the city-state (at 3.82–83) suggests that, when civil war begins to unravel the deliberative protocols and reason giving that sustain deliberation, each citizen is haunted by images of an ephebe – either an early, incompetent version of his mature self or a future version of the citizen he will no

---

[3] For Farrar,*gnômê* is "Thucydides' term of art for the intellectual quality, judgment…" that often restrains *orgê* (anger and all impulsive behaviors) (1988: 156). See also Luginbill on Thucydidean *gnômê* and *orgê* (1999: 24ff.), defining the former as the "perceptual, evaluative side of human nature" (*physis*) (26).

longer deserve to be.⁴ And "behaving like an ephebe" hovers over the performance of citizenship like a potential catastrophe threatening to collapse the borders of selfhood and citizenship, in particular at that point where an individual succeeds or fails to form the crucial alliance with the dominant social other conferring recognition as a citizen. In this chapter I examine the passage from noncitizen to mature citizen status as an attempt to align oneself properly with others; and I ask how this alliance formation transforms an individual's personality from a radical autonomy outside citizenship into the tempered autonomy of a political creature. At the same time we'll see that the prospect of civil war (or an equivalent civic calamity) threatens to disintegrate an individual's citizenship not only into the characteristics of the pre-citizen ephebe but also into elements of more alien types of identity. These are the foreigner and the female, along with their more domesticated counterparts: the ally, the metic (resident alien), and the citizen wife.

It's my hypothesis that the anxiety of civic collapse triggers refraction in an individual's experience of citizenship, splitting and scattering its component parts into a spectrum of noncitizen elements. This may occur especially when a citizen faces the prospect of civic collapse and must simultaneously confront questions of justice. What results is a radical form of the programmatic question about citizenship and selfhood, one that provokes a citizen to ponder his citizenship as a question of degrees of selfhood and otherness: "In deciding this question of justice, to what degree must I experience otherness within myself as

---

⁴ The prosecutor in Dem.25.6 (ca. 338–324) challenges jurors with this prospect, warning that their decision in the case risks their reputation as citizens. The defendant may be on trial, he says, "But *you're* undergoing scrutiny [*dokimazesthe*]," referring to the *dokimasia* (ceremony of inquiry) an ephebe had to pass to gain citizenship or that a citizen had to pass to hold state office. For A. M. Bowie, Aristophanes' comic hypothesis in *Clouds* (423) and *Wasps* (422) is "*ephêbeia* in reverse," where an old citizen's craziness causes him to behave like a reckless ephebe (1993: 78–133).

an ephebe, a foreigner, a female?" I suspect that Greek citizens would have answered this question in various ways at various times and locations. I think Athenians in the 460s would have wondered whether the key to successful democratic citizenship lay in alliance formation with citizen leaders and with noncitizens, including the noncitizen elements within themselves.

The figure of the ephebe strikes me as particularly apt if we're looking for a portal within mature citizens that opens onto experiences of noncitizenship; and among the many scripts of citizen life a script called *dokimasia* emerges as the most useful for recalling the liminal experience when an individual wavered between noncitizen and citizen status. For each citizen had to play out this script prior to swearing the ephebic oath, when a boy took the most important step toward recognition by asking to approach the "illocutionary threshold" of speaking and being spoken to like a citizen. Athenian cultural myths about the ephebe – about Theseus in particular – portray him in our contemporary terms as a voluntarist self endowed with a hyper-autonomy that freely expresses itself through hybristic acts and the devious intelligence of *mêtis*. The civic script of the *dokimasia*, however, will tame this wild, impetuous youth within each ephebe by provoking in him an anxiety and performative attitude more suited to a hypo-autonomous self, one whose cognitive and deliberative abilities are inadequate and socially invisible – so unacceptable as to make him appear unnatural and unmanly – just like a foreigner and just like a woman.

Nowhere in Athens but on the tragic and comic stages could individuals so freely and outrageously express themselves at one moment in one script and then be judged inadequate by the civic norms of other scripts. There Athenians and their foreign guests encountered dramatic selves displaying voluntarist, cognitive, and deliberative dimensions out of all proportion. Tragic selves in particular often sought justice and recognition from one another and from the spectators; and they usually appeared as mythological characters modeling behavior we can reasonably identify as ephebic, foreign, and female. One play in particular, Aeschylus' *Suppliants* (ca. 463–461), portrays an attempt by a foreign, female protagonist to cross the threshold of Greek citizenship in ways that I believe evoke the ephebe at the *dokimasia*.[5] Our understanding of the play has changed over the past fifteen years due to a series of strong political and cultural readings by scholars such as Meier (1991 [1988]), Farrar (1988), Zeitlin (1996), Rohweder (1998), Gödde (2000), C. Turner (2001), and Föllinger (2003); when supplemented by studies by Sicherl (1986), Rösler (1993) and Sommerstein (1995, 1997), we can now read this play, along with the two missing dramas joined with it in the Danaid trilogy, as pitting a foreign, feminized, ephebic protagonist against two types of the mature, elite citizen leader ("demagogues" in the broad sense). At the same time this play invites us to scrutinize the recent trend to interpret tragic characters and situations in terms peculiar to the Athenian democracy's political types, dilemmas, and ideological norms.[6] As Rhodes suggests, shouldn't we broaden our interpretive context to focus on meanings that are not "distinctively democratic" but prevalent in "a wider Greek intellectual context" (2003b: 115)?[7] Or as

---

[5] Scullion's attempt to redate the play to 475–470 only succeeds in reminding us that most dates for Aeschylean and Sophoclean plays are precarious (2002). His stylistic and structural reasons – ring-composition, frequency of "postponed *de*," the chorus' central role, lack of a prologue – are less convincing than the arguments based on the "political assumptions" and "historical allusions" he dismisses because they have "varied widely" (99).

[6] See the essays in Winkler and Zeitlin 1990, esp. Goldhill 1990 and Winkler 1990, with roots in studies like Vernant and Vidal-Naquet 1988, Vidal-Naquet 1986, and Meier 1991; see also Euben 1990, Seaford 1994, and the essays in Goff 1995. More recently, see Goldhill 2000, the essays in Pelling 1997, and in Easterling 1997, and Connor 1996.

[7] Rhodes rejects "distinctively democratic" readings because: contra Goldhill 2000 and 1990, ceremonies in the City Dionysia Festival don't necessarily support a democratic ideology (2003b: 106–13); and key themes in the plays reflect general city-state concerns, not specifically democratic ones (113–19). He admits that some plays (e.g.,

Loraux argues more radically, don't we need to recognize in tragic characters, discourses, and music forms of discourse, reasoning and memory that are "antipolitical" or noncivic – and that challenge *eunomia*, the ideal of peaceful harmony in the city-state's political ideology?[8]

Our discussion of the play pursues meanings that are at times "antipolitical" in Loraux's sense, at times political in senses relevant to all city-states, and at times specifically tied to contexts of Athenian politics in the 460s. While I give prominence to the scripts "behaving like an ephebe" and the *dokimasia*, they are constantly intersected and displaced by other scripts that run more deeply in Greek social life: religious suppliance; "seeking/rendering a *dikê*," especially where a litigant claims to be a victim (object) of hybris; the jury trial; and particular tracks of "how citizens deliberate," especially where an oligarchic versus democratic dynamics of leadership is at stake. Just as conspicuous are the political scripts of alliance formation between states and of reconciliation between factions within a state. Finally, the script of marriage, of proper relations between men and women, looms large over the trilogy. But ultimately I hope to demonstrate how a tragedy in the 460s can provoke citizens and noncitizens to reflect on what I call citizenship's "refracted" nature. This is the disquieting thought that

Aeschylus' *Suppliants* and *Eumenides*) do "allude to" democracy (105, 113). Somewhat differently, Griffin upholds specifically "literary" as opposed to political meanings in the plays (1999 and 1998).

[8] Loraux understands the "antipolitical" as "any behavior that diverts, rejects, or threatens, consciously or not, the obligations and prohibitions constituting the ideology of the city-state." This ideology's essential injunctions are that the city-state remain united and at peace with itself, and that citizens forget past conflicts and suppress an understanding that politics are "inherently conflictual" (2002b: 26). Within tragedy she focuses on female characters, especially lamenters, as challengers to this ideology (2002b, 1998, 1987). Her more broadly conceived *The Divided City* (2002a) traces the politics of reconciliation and forgetting after civil war in several Archaic and Classical city-states, with a strong focus on democratic Athens.

each citizen self, and the collective citizen body, relies for its apparent autonomy and its harmony on a network of alliances with nonciti-zen others. This trilogy speaks of alliances that need to be negotiated in multiple senses of reality: in the everyday world of political life where treaties link states – the 460s did see the dawning of an "age of autonomy" in Greek political history; in cultural life where marriage conferred autonomy on a male citizen and his household, though at the cost of a woman's freedom; and in that "inner" world of thoughts and emotions each individual citizen might, soon after 460, call his *psykhê*.[9]

The Ephebe's Performative Attitude and Subject Position

The Athenian ephebe's status has received its share of scholarly atten-tion over the years, but this has mostly clarified the term's meaning in two senses, one narrow and one broad, both distinct from the per-formative sense I'm suggesting. The narrow sense refers to the legally defined, state-organized and financed program of compulsory mili-tary and moral training between the ages of eighteen and twenty, after which young adult males joined the ranks of citizens proper as *neoi*, the youngest age group in the hoplite phalanx. While the Athenian ephebate in this strict sense can only be surely dated from the mid-fourth century, most scholars infer that elements of it existed earlier, perhaps originating in the early years or decades of the democracy

---

[9] There are numerous parallels between the Danaid trilogy and the *Oresteia*, produced some 3–5 years later in 458. For Goldhill the latter serves as "the paradigmatic tragedy for ... educating the citizen into citizenship" (2000: 48), and he argues against Meier that we must include the trilogy's gender politics in this notion of tragedy as political education. "For what boundaries should there be to the construction of the self as political subject?" he asks (48–49). My discussion of the Danaid trilogy poses the same question – but adds the adjective "antipolitical." As I've argued in previous chapters, when the Greeks hypothesize about the self they can temporarily shelter it, as a version of the unencumbered self, from political subjectivity.

itself.[10] But scholars also speak of ephebes in the longer-standing and broader cultural sense of a period of late adolescence in Greek states, beginning with the appearance of certain physical signs of sexual maturity, ending with acceptance into the ranks of the hoplite *neoi*, and characterized by experiences and values typical of initiation rituals in many cultures.[11]

Elements from both the narrow and broad senses of what it meant to be an ephebe permit us to identify a characteristic performative attitude and deliberative role – and to outline a specific script that launches the would-be citizen on a trajectory eventually leading him to swear the ephebic oath. This attitude and role are decidedly problematic, forming a cluster of traits from myths, ritual acts, and details of the fourth-century ephebic program that lend the general script "behaving like an ephebe" a negative cultural valence. In short, the negativity results from the ephebe's display of an undesirable autonomy, either the hypo-autonomy of a self whose cognitive and deliberative shortcomings make him incapable of acting or speaking on his own behalf before citizens, or the hyper-autonomy of a voluntarist self driven by self-promotion through actions and words offensive to citizen norms. Among hypo-autonomous traits are: his physical and

---

[10] For the *ephêbeia* in this sense, see pseudo-Aristotle's *Ath.Pol.*42, with Rhodes' commentary (1981: 497ff.) and Pélékides 1962. On epigraphical grounds Reinmuth suggests an origin for the ephebate as a separate military unit in the first half of the fifth century, perhaps 478–477 under Aristides or Themistocles (1971: 136–38); but this has been challenged (Siewert 1977: nn. 1 and 3). Ridley reviews the literary evidence (1979: 531ff.), seeing some kind of ephebic training in the fifth century (534).

[11] See, e.g., Vidal-Naquet 1986a, 1986b, and Winkler 1990. Fisher helps us see a sense of "ephebic" between the narrow, mid-fourth century meaning and this broader context. He builds on Ridley 1979 to suggest hoplite training as the goal of state-sponsored (through liturgies) athletic training of boys and young men for festivals like the Panathenaea over a major part of the fifth and fourth centuries, including non-elite citizens (1998: 84–104). Cf. A. M. Bowie's reasonable conjectures (1993: 50–51).

communicative isolation from the general population; his geographic marginality through movement out in the borderlands of state territory, much like a wandering foreigner; his association with a less civilized economic activity such as hunting rather than agriculture or hoplite warfare; and an ambiguous gender identity connected to feminine places and activities.[12] His hyper-autonomous traits complement this marginality by taking the form of violent actions, both in combat and sexually, and deceptive acts typical of trickster behavior, all of which make him the precocious subject of the archetypal Greek crime, hybris.[13]

Early in the democracy, for example, the figure of Theseus, the "archetype of the ephebes," comes to the fore in Athenian myth, poetry, and iconography.[14] One cycle of stories clusters around his status as a foreigner, a youthful wanderer across the Saronic gulf toward Athens, a heroic actor accomplishing exploits of hybris and *mêtis*, and a son demonstrating to his father Aegeus in Athens' city center the true signs of their father-son relationship. Another cycle recounts his sea voyage to Crete to outwit Minos, defeat the Minotaur, steal away Ariadne, seduce and then abandon her, seek his undersea "father," Poseidon, and then return to Athens to cause, inadvertently, Aegeus' death.[15]

---

[12] For these traits see Vidal-Naquet 1986a and 1986b.

[13] Hesk sees ephebic deceptiveness as a foil in democratic ideology for the Athenian hoplite's openness compared to his Spartan counterpart (2000: 29–40).

[14] For Theseus' popularity in literature, iconography, and political life before the mid-fifth century, see Walker 1995: 35–111; Calame 1990: 397ff.; Mills 1997: 1–42; Castriota 1992: 33ff. and Shapiro 1989: 143ff. On his role as an archetype of the ephebe, see Walker 1995: 94–96; Strauss 1993: 105–6; A. M. Bowie 1993: 51–52; and Calame 1990: 188–195; reinforcing Jeanmaire's earlier equation of the Theseus myth with the Athenian ephebate (1939: 245). Walker links Theseus the ephebe to the antisocial, ethically marginal behavior in crosscultural initiation rituals (1995: 101–4, with references).

[15] The earliest extant literary accounts of Theseus' exploits are Bacchylides' dithyrambs 17 and 18 (470s); the fullest narrative account is Plutarch's *Theseus* 6–23.

Theseus' ephebic experiences also appear in cultic form, integrated into such Athenian festivals as the Oschophoria and Apatouria.

Ephebes in the narrower, military sense acted out these mythological roles of outsider and wanderer as *peripoloi* when they took their obligatory tour of religious shrines and border forts throughout Athens' territory; and during this period of mobility they were consigned to silence as legal or political subjects because they were barred from court proceedings.[16] In addition to military training, their two-year stint had moral dimensions as well that recall the unacceptable, hybristic autonomy of mythological ephebes like Theseus and the "black hunter": one title among their adult supervisors or trainers was *sôphronistês* – literally a "moderator" – and another *kosmêtês* ("one who keeps order"). But ephebes in this narrow sense also experienced a carefully scripted moment that seems designed to have them experience performatively the recognition scene of a hero like Theseus before his father Aegeus.[17] This inaugural script of citizenship was the *dokimasia* – a "welcoming" (*dekhesthai*) after scrutiny of credentials – and was indeed a moment for passing muster, a scene of self-presentation and testing by the community's dominant social other, in effect the first plea for recognition of citizen *timê*.

Walker discusses the dithyrambs in light of ephebic experience (1995: 83–104). On the cycle of myths associated with an epic *Theseid* and its possible date, see Mills 1997: 19–25, with references, and Calame 1990: 397–406. Calame links the land-based stories with the first year of ephebic service and the maritime tales with the second year (1990: 190–91).

[16] Except in extraordinary circumstances; see *Ath. Pol.* 42.5. Thucydides refers to the military duty of the *peripoloi* as early as 458 (1.105.4), later at 2.13.7, 4.67.2, and 8.92.2; see A. M. Bowie 1993: 51, n. 24, and Ridley 1979: 531.

[17] Theseus' name was derived from key acts in a recognition scene: Aegeus "putting down" (*thesis*) tokens of identity under a rock to prove his paternity, or his later acknowledging (*themenon*) of Theseus when the young man displayed these at Athens (Plut. *Theseus* 4).

Dokimasia occurred at the end of an adolescent's eighteenth year, when his father, acting as a *kurios* (legal master and guardian), presented him for citizenship early in the political year to the assembly of their deme at a special meeting convened for this purpose.[18] This neighborhood *dokimasia* had two objectives: to ascertain that the candidate had completed his eighteenth year; and to determine that he was freeborn and from two Athenian parents. The deme members then voted under oath on the two issues of age and parentage. Contested decisions could be referred to a jury court, and later in the year, at the state level, the Council of 500 performed its own *dokimasia* to ratify the deme's vote on each ephebe. The deme *dokimasia* was no minor event since, along with actually registering the names of citizens as demesmen, this scrutiny comprised one of the two "most fundamental elements" of the deme's administrative functions, and it may have been instituted soon after the democracy was formed.[19] But it was in effect the last in a series of presentations a *kurios* made to his community peers of a child and adolescent in his care: in all likelihood, a boy was presented first in infancy during the festival of Apatouria to his father's phratry (a fraternity probably based on descent) and then again around the age

---

[18] I base my reconstruction on *Ath. Pol.* 42, with Rhodes' commentary (1981: 493–510), and on Pélékides 1962: 88ff., Harrison 1971a: 73–96, and Whitehead 1986: 97–104, with their sources. Whitehead calls the deme's control of its membership "the most crucial of the functions of a deme assembly" (97). For Strauss, "An important ceremony of great legal and psychological significance, deme registration was a milestone of the boy's continuing integration into the community of citizens" (1993: 95). *Dokimasia* also meant scrutinizing the credentials of new state officials, naturalized citizens, and rhetors who spoke in the Assembly; see Harrison 1971b: 200–7, and Adeleye 1983. For examples of speeches written for state officials' *dokimasia*, see Lysias 16, 25, 26 and 31.

[19] Whitehead 1986: 35 and 98–99. Registration and enrollment were crucial functions since the deme's written register of its members constituted the state's only listing of its citizens (34 and 97). (Aristophanes' joke about the *dokimasia* at *Wasps* 578 indicates it was a familiar procedure by 423.)

of sixteen. He might also be enrolled as a member of other groups to which family members belonged.[20] It's clear from *Ath. Pol.* 42.1–2 that the *dokimasia* itself climaxed with the demesmen's vote, or its subsequent legal appeal, and then required confirmation by the Council of 500. But can we reach a clearer understanding about how the ceremony unfolded, what its principal roles were, and what sort of speech genres it entailed?

Despite a fair number of passing references in forensic oratory to the *dokimasia* for admission to citizenship, whether conducted by the deme or the Council of 500, no concrete facts emerge about the ceremony's cognitive or communicative dynamics at the deme level.[21] Unfortunately, the two most detailed references we have to a deme's *dokimasia* do not describe the typical ceremony for an eighteen-year-old candidate but one for older adult males in unusual circumstances who would already have established (legally or not) a public persona.[22] What

[20] The first ceremony, the *meion*, included a sacrifice, as did the second, called the *koureion*. The phratry might also have had its own sort of *dokimasia*. On these ceremonies and their relation to the deme's *dokimasia*, see Lambert 1993: 161–78. A father might enroll his son in religious organizations like the *oregeones*, as Isaeus 2.14 attests.

[21] It's not always clear whether forensic references to a *dokimasia* indicate the deme's or Council's decision. We find clear references to the deme's *dokimasia* at Demosthenes 39.5 and 29; 44.35–37 and 41; 57.9–14; 59.122; Isaeus 2.14 and 7.28. References to the Council's state-ratified *dokimasia* likely occur at Lysias 21.1; 10.31; 32.9; Demosthenes 27.5, 30.6 and 15.

[22] At Demosthenes 57.9–14 the speaker Euxitheus appeals in court his removal from the deme's register of citizens, probably after the law of 346 purging all deme lists. So the *dokimasia* he describes is not his original scrutiny for citizenship but one related to or subsequent to the purge. (Whitehead emphasizes how "atypical" this particular deme meeting was [1986: 93].) Euxitheus also claims, prior to this (presumably second) *dokimasia*, that he has delivered damaging testimony against his rival Euboulides: he is therefore already an adult male authorized and accustomed to speaking in public. Demosthenes 39.5 and 29 also involve the *dokimasia* of a citizen well beyond eighteen. In a speech over whether the speaker Mantitheus or his half-brother Boeotus is older, it's generally agreed that the jury recognized the

can we reasonably infer about the standard procedure for eighteen year olds? It seems reasonable to assume that the dialogical format of question and answer was used. The demarch (deme leader) would likely have asked the prospective ephebe, his father, or other guardian (*kurios*), for details or descriptions concerning the candidate's birth and parentage, and he must have anticipated corroboration from deme members, who may previously have been informed about the candidates' names by some sort of public posting.[23]

It seems to me that a key question was whether the would-be ephebe himself responded to these questions or whether he remained silent while his father or other guardian spoke for him.[24] In other words, standing on the threshold of his legal majority, was he for the first time a participant in a dialogical exchange with a representative of the dominant social other? And was he permitted to assume responsibility for representing his own status (*timê*) in a first-person narrative about

---

half-brother to be two to five years older (Carey and Reid put birth dates at 387–382 for Boeotus and Mantitheus at 382–380 [1985: 163ff.]). Mantitheus claims his father registered his half-brother with his phratry (probably at the *koureion* around 16), but that after his father's death (by 357) the half-brother stole Mantitheus' name and "registered himself with the demesmen under the name 'Mantitheus'..." (39.5). So Boeotus was 25–30, a fully adult male, when he "registered himself." Therefore neither Demosthenes 57 or 39 describes the standard *dokimasia* of an eighteen year old.

[23] Pélékides 1962: 93. The requirement that both parents be of Athenian birth would have originated with Pericles' citizenship law of 451–450. As for deme convocations in general, E. Cohen argues that these may have been limited to one per year, were often (or usually) not held in the deme territory but in the city, and that quorums for conducting official business were minimal (2000: 112–18). But our evidence for all deme meetings is spotty, and his best example is the unusual meeting of Euxitheus' deme in Demosthenes 57.

[24] Pélékides suggests, "the demarch probably gave the floor to the candidate's father or tutor, or perhaps to the candidate himself, to speak of his birth and to justify his claims to citizenship; if no one objected, they went immediately to a vote..." (1962: 93–94).

his birth and genealogy? Or, not yet summoned across that threshold, was he forced to remain a passive, dumb spectator to this brief narrative as it unfolded through the mouths of others? If court proceedings offer a valid parallel, he likely needed to remain silent until he had in fact been registered in the deme, for minors had to be represented by their fathers or guardians and could not enter into contracts or other legal business (A. R. W. Harrison 1971a: 73). Here the ephebic candidate's situation paralleled that of the household's women, who relied on their *kurios* for legal representation since they couldn't appear in court or offer testimony on their own behalf, and at least partially that of metics and foreigners.[25] In fact our sources suggest that the moment a young man passed his *dokimasia*, he could – and sometimes should – cease his life of legal silence and passivity and spring to action as an autonomous public person.[26]

If the would-be ephebe couldn't speak but had his *kurios* speak for him, the local *dokimasia* was designed to keep him on the nether side of an illocutionary threshold – and this would strengthen the claim that swearing the ephebic oath loomed as his first performance of a citizen's speech genre. As a recognition scene, the deme's *dokimasia* would then have unfolded while he silently listened to others' illocutionary statements, something to the effect of his father saying, "I assure you

---

[25] On women's legal silence in Athens, see McClure 1999: 19–24, and Just's extended discussion of women's legal capabilities (1989: 26–39). Metics likely needed a patron (*prostatês*) to represent them legally, at least up to the early fourth century (A. R. W. Harrison 1971a: 192–93); a foreigner's situation depended on treaty relations between Athens and his home state (A. R. W. Harrison 1971b: 84). Patterson reconsiders metic status in Athens, examining court cases involving metics (2000, esp. 102–10, using Whitehead 1977).

[26] E.g., at Lysias 10.31 the speaker boasts that "as soon as I passed my *dokimasia*, I indicted the Thirty at the court of the Areopagus." At Lysias 32.9, an uncle tells the eldest of several orphans that, "Since you've passed your *dokimasia* and become a man, from now on you yourself must take care of your usual needs." Demosthenes boasts that, as soon as he left the ranks of boys (*ek paidôn*) and passed his *dokimasia*, he equipped a war ship and performed multiple public services (21.154–57).

that it is commonly known throughout the deme … that my son … was born during the archonship of … of a union between my wife … daughter of … and myself … son of … of this deme. Many will also recall that I presented him two years ago to the phratry … on the occasion of the Koureôtis."[27] If this scenario is accurate, note that the would-be ephebe's performative attitude would *not* have been that of a speaking subject but of a subject embedded in a performance by others of narratives concerning *their* habitation, marriage, genealogy, and child-rearing. His subject position would have remained latent as a third-person referent – although a privileged one – in these narratives, as a spectator to a drama about himself, consigned to silence and inaction while his life unfolded through the words of others, or like a boy listening to a story about parental courtship, marriage and struggles with child-rearing "back then" when he was anything but an autonomous agent in the family saga.

If these were the communicative dynamics of a local *dokimasia*, the ceremony enforced a hypo-autonomy on the candidate by insisting he play spectator and listener to the discourse of others. Through his father's or guardian's statements – whose truth value the demesmen would shortly determine by a vote – the young man witnessed the elements of his *timê* emerging as the intersubjective core of *their* understanding of who he was, of who *they* recognized him to be. It is even possible to argue that the candidate at *dokimasia* presented a passive physical spectacle to elders whose "subjective" gaze objectified him when they examined his naked body to determine whether he had reached the sexual maturity necessary for citizenship.[28] As dumb

---

[27] As indicated in note 14, the *koureion* ceremony was in effect a dress-rehearsal for the *dokimasia*; see Parke's description (1977: 89–91). I base my suggested wording of the *kurios*' claims on the ephebe's behalf on the questions "Aristotle" says were asked at the *dokimasia* of archons-elect (*Ath.Pol.*55.3–4).

[28] B. Robertson (2000) tries to reconstruct the *dokimasia* using the long-debated wisecrack in Aristophanes' *Wasps* 578 (in 422), where old Philocleon declares that one of

spectator or dumb spectacle (or both), the candidate found himself during the ceremony transformed into the adult version of the self Mead called the "me" and that Taylor pointed to as the dialogical rather than monological discovery of who we are.

In cognitive and moral terms the would-be ephebe is forced to adopt a new perspective by seeing himself as both the citizen subject and object others take him to be. What he gains from the silence and passivity imposed by the ceremony is an ability to see himself as both a self and an other, or as a "recognized" participant in citizen interpersonal relations. Habermas suggests that adolescents typically acquire such a cognitive perspective when they learn to move from an observer's perspective into the performative attitude of a participant in interaction. Note how learning this new attitude depends on playing the role of a witness who listens or views: "[This] performative attitude," he continues, "is coupled with the neutral attitude of a person who is present but remains uninvolved ... the attitude of a person who witnesses an interactive event in the role of a listener or viewer" (1990: 146). We will shortly see the implications the ephebe's role as listener or viewer might have for Athenian theater.

And so the *dokimasia* looks like a communicative event designed to fashion a new self out of an old: a citizen self emerged essentially

---

the powerful privileges of being a juror is "to look at the genitals of boys undergoing the *dokimasia*!" This obviously refers to disputed decisions about age which come from the local *dokimasia* and go to a jury court for settlement. Robertson establishes the likelihood that age determinations were not calculated chronologically (i.e., at eighteen years) but "subjectively" through communal opinion about who has reached sexual maturity. But he doesn't prove that all candidates at the local *dokimasia* had to be examined naked by the demesmen, especially since Philocleon's joke refers to disputed cases that went to court. It's more likely that only candidates with apparent signs of sexual immaturity (e.g., lack of facial hair or skeletal/muscular development, a high-pitched voice, etc.) would be required to pass the more decisive test of genital scrutiny. This is consistent with Whitehead 1986: 100–1, with n. 76, and Rhodes 1981: 500.

aligned with others and was intersubjectively constituted by its relations to them where previously stood a non- or pre-citizen self not (yet) interconnected with others in a politically meaningful way. From our contemporary perspective this new self resembles, not surprisingly, the communitarian self outlined in Sandel's critique of Rawls' liberal self and in Taylor's work, for it emerges from the ephebe's capacity to recognize himself in the third-person referent of a narrative carried on in a dialogue between representatives of the dominant social other. The non- or pre-citizen self appears to be voluntarist in Sandel's sense, an immature self whose ends are acquired through a force of will that tolerates no encroachment from others – hence, as suggested above, the ephebe's sometime hyper-autonomy expresses a hybristic, untamed will to define himself as a radical individual.

The *dokimasia* ceremony, interestingly enough, seems calculated, first, to evoke for the ephebe the expectation that he'll be recognized as a "person" in Taylor's sense, which is "a being who can be addressed, and who can reply ... a 'respondent'" (1985a: 97); and second, if I am correct, immediately to frustrate that hope when silence is imposed on him. If the ephebe must remain silent, it's because others will not yet permit him to answer for his emergent personhood by saying "I" to a "you"; in such a subject position, he cannot yet be accountable to the demesmen for himself. For Sandel the ephebe at this stage is challenged to achieve a "cognitive" sense of self because his ends are given in advance by others, and his task is therefore to achieve "self-command ... by reflecting on [him]self and inquiring into [his] constituent nature, discerning laws and imperatives, and [ultimately] acknowledging [his] purposes as [his] own" (1998: 58).

The autonomy of the deliberative self shares this ideal of participation in reciprocal, I-you relations but holds out a further challenge: the ability to achieve what Habermas calls an "ethical self-understanding" *outside* of an I-you relationship, which would permit a citizen to know, before self and others, who he or she is and who he or she wants to be (1992: 168–69). Such individuality may at first strike us as unattainable for any Greek citizen, but it consists not in mere self-invention or pure singularity; it can only be achieved performatively in dialogue with others. So the *dokimasia*, in staging the ephebe's desire to respond on his own behalf to the "ends" others give to him, at least opens the possibility for him to understand that:

> *The self of an ethical self-understanding is dependent upon recognition by addressees because it generates itself as a response to the demands of an other in the first place. Because others attribute accountability to me, I gradually make myself into the one who I have become in living together with others. (170)*

We'll see to what extent this self-fashioning may even entail a self-reflection that permits the democratic citizen at some point to distance himself from his particular circumstances and traditions, not unlike Achilles, Odysseus, and the lawgiver Solon, all of whom hypothesize over an autonomous selfhood apart from others. In this way he might at some point, as Warren puts it, engage in an "intersubjective fabric of reason giving" where appeals can be made to universal reasons divorced from those particular circumstances and traditions (1995: 172–73). Ultimately, if it's possible anywhere, this is where participation in democratic deliberation promises an autonomy won through self-transformation.

It is I think significant that this first call to accountability as a citizen may have meant learning to be a silent listener to a dialogue by others while recognizing oneself as a third-person referent in their deliberation. In practical terms the ephebe is being trained to assume a role essential to a society where the key citizen privileges of *isêgoria* (freedom to speak in a public forum) and *parrhêsia* (freedom to speak one's mind) first demanded a willingness to listen without interrupting and to interpret what is said in light of individual and communal self-interest.²⁹ And so to pass one's local *dokimasia* successfully, one had to demonstrate a willingness and ability to occupy what to us looks like the minimal subject position on citizenship's threshold: the passive listener and spectator. Clever politicians and playwrights could even caricature democratic Athenians with the "topos of the passive spectator" when they believed citizens were playing the silent listener's role irresponsibly or unintelligently – as though regressing back to pre-ephebic status.³⁰ By implication, then, silent listening and self-recognition in the discourse of others formed at least the first of several performative steps leading up to and across the threshold of citizen subjectivity.³¹

---

²⁹ Citizens at the Assembly or Council of 500 were enjoined to listen to speakers without interrupting them (Stockton 1990: 76, extrapolating from Aeschines 1.35). On the relation of *isêgoria* and *parrhêsia* to freedom (*eleutheria*), see recent discussions in Monoson 2000: 51–63, Henderson 1998, and Wallace 1996.

³⁰ In 427 the demagogue Cleon chided citizens in the Assembly for acting like "spectators of speeches" infatuated with the entertainment value of competitive speech-making and unable to understand where self-interest lay (Thuc.3.38). A few years later Aristophanes' Philocleon yearns to serve on a jury where the defendant, a tragic actor, will feel inspired to incorporate into his defense lines from his piteous portrayal of Niobe (*Wasps* 580). See McClure for these and other examples of the topos (1999: 14–16).

³¹ Some scholars of today's Athenian democracy studies explain citizen communication by using the notion of a passive, mostly silent spectator who recognizes himself in others' discourse. For Ober, common citizens and elite leaders form an implied contract: elites receive commoners' support and maintain their class privileges so long as their rhetoric represents them in the "fictional" guise of an average citizen *recognizable to the* dêmos *as such* (1989: 304–309). Others propose that ordinary citizens in the theater understand the behavior of tragedy's heroic characters by constructing multiple meanings out of the gap between their own familiar social interactions and the "counterfactual" world of heroic legend. Like ephebes at a *dokimasia*, the tragic audience was *in theory* passive, mostly silent and challenged to interpret a heroic world in which they could not intervene (see Easterling 1990, esp. 90, and Ober and Strauss 1990). Jurors in a courtroom were likewise *in theory* passive spectators trying to recognize patterns of citizen life in the litigants' presentations,

Is the Ephebe the Ideal Subject of Tragedy?

As a citizen script the deme's *dokimasia* was malleable: it could be enacted in various guises in democratic institutions other than the deme assembly or Council of 500. The tragic and comic stages in particular could draw on this script to condition audience response in a variety of ways. Some scholars since the 1990s have suggested we identify the ephebe as the notional subject of tragedy: as its ideal spectator, as the analogue in everyday Athenian citizen life for the tragic protagonist on stage, and perhaps literally as a tragic performer, if ephebes constituted the chorus.[32] If the pageantry, ritual and theater at the City Dionysia festival were in fact "focused" on each year's new cohort of ephebes, as Winkler, Goldhill, and others maintain, then we should identify them, and not the mature citizen, as the festival's cognitive subject. Could it be that this three-day event celebrated what it meant to speak, think, and respond like a citizen by reenacting the emergence of the formative, ephebic phase of citizen consciousness? In particular, tragedy appears to address not the military or even strictly political training of ephebes but their moral curriculum, one of whose primary goals (at least in the fourth century) was to instill the moderation (*sôphrosynê*) essential to exercising a citizen's judgment (*gnômê*). If, as Goldhill has suggested, tragedy's plots and characters deliberately problematized the civic norms of democratic Athens, then as a "didactic and questioning medium" it would have immersed its ideal ephebic spectator, sitting passively among his comrades, with the emotional and cognitive

---

though their often noisy reactions permitted them more intervention than theater spectators enjoyed (see, e.g., Hall 1995: 43–44).

[32] See Vidal-Naquet 1986a, 1986b, and 1997; Winkler 1990; Segal 1998 and 1999; Bassi 1998: 215ff. Rhodes limits his critique of Winkler to observing that the argument would succeed better if one claimed it was "appropriate" rather than "it actually happened" (2003b: 109). A. M. Bowie assumes Aristophanes' spectators recognize the Sausage-Seller of *Knights* as an ephebe, with at 178–93 a parody of the *dokimasia* (1993: 52–58). We've already pointed out Bowie's belief that the comic hypotheses of *Wasps* and *Clouds* are structured around a "reverse *ephêbeia*" (78–133).

challenges proper to "the duties and obligations of a citizen" (1990: 125). The script "being a tragic spectator" thus would have returned him to the threshold experience of the *dokimasia* he thought he had recently navigated with success.

There's no question that the plots, character types and moral dilemmas of numerous surviving tragedies echo ephebic themes and situations, most of them identified by scholars attentive to structural categories of Greek cultural and social life (e.g., oppositions linking boundary and center, movement and stasis, hunting and hoplite warfare, foreignness and native birth, female and male, deceit and honesty, hybris and moderation, etc.).[33] Verbal echoes of the ephebic oath also continue to be found in fifth-century tragedy, comedy, and prose.[34] In a broad sense, then, tragedies presented Athenians with mythological and ritual scripts from the heroic past to which, as Easterling (1990) and others suggest, citizens could compare their own scripts of everyday life. But if tragic performances at the City Dionysia evoked for audiences the cognitive, emotional, and communicative dynamics of becoming an ephebe, of approaching the threshold of citizenship in some version of *dokimasia*, how might surviving tragedies dramatize the ephebe's performative attitude and subject position – namely his self-presentation to significant others and his request for recognition of citizen *timê* and personhood? And what might they tell us about the nascent citizen self, refracted into noncitizen elements and displayed in the ephebe's hypo- and hyper-autonomy? Lastly, might the tragic version of ephebic self-presentation contain elements Loraux would identify as "antipolitical," introducing thoughts, emotions, and especially

---

[33] In addition to studies mentioned in note 32, see Zeitlin 1996, Bérard et al. 1989, Segal 1982, and Goldhill 1990. Loraux indicts such "anthropological" studies of the Greeks for emphasizing timeless cultural patterns, types, and iconography that "censor" the conflictual, changing nature of Greek political life (2002a: 45–62).

[34] For echoes in authors like Aeschylus, Sophocles, Aristophanes, and Thucydides, see Siewert 1977: 104–7, and Winkler 1990: 29–30, with nn. 22–26.

memories that run counter to the city-state's citizen ideals of peaceful coexistence and nonconflict?

With help from Vidal-Naquet, we need to return to the plot lines and character types of the surviving tragedies. Vidal-Naquet remarks that, from the thirty-three surviving plays (thirty-two tragedies plus Euripides' satyr play *Cyclopes*), "there is not a single play in which the opposition between Greeks and barbarians, or between citizens and aliens, does not play a significant role" (1997: 112). In emphasizing how fundamental the ephebe is for tragedy, he also defines this figure as "a temporary alien" and "a temporary woman" because of its association in myth and ritual with foreignness and the feminine sphere (116). As playwrights develop these oppositions in story form, their most prevalent plot, he observes, is not the exile or estrangement of a native youth from his city (Hippolytus) but the reverse process "in which a man arrives as a stranger in a city and then reveals it to be his homeland" (Oedipus and Orestes). Essential to this dramatic progression is the young man's performance of a "disquieting strangeness" in speech or dress (often a disguise), which Vidal-Naquet names "one of the principal moving forces in tragic action," if not "the *main* moving force" (118). Here he characterizes the confrontation between Dionysus and Pentheus in Euripides' *Bacchae* as a variant of the ephebic master-plot he sketches for tragedy: "A foreigner at the head of a foreign band, Asiatic, effeminate, masked . . . Dionysus of the *Bacchae* will in fact turn out to be a Theban, first cousin to King Pentheus, who goes on to imprison him in the name of the masculine and warlike values of the hoplite" (118).

II SCRUTINIZING CITIZENS IN AESCHYLUS' *SUPPLIANTS*

The Danaids: From Foreigners and Females to Ephebes, Metics, and Wives
Some elements in this description of plot and protagonist from the last surviving tragedy (ca. 406) bear a striking resemblance to the plot and protagonist in two of our earliest surviving plays, Aeschylus' *Persians*

(472) and *Suppliants* (ca. 463–61). In fact, for the latter play we need only transform the "man" who "arrives as a stranger in a city and then reveals it to be his homeland" into a "foreign band" of Asiatic (Egyptian) young women who suddenly appear on the borders of Argos – a polis frequently chosen on the tragic stage as a figure of Athens.[35] These women constitute the play's chorus and collective protagonist; they are emotionally distraught maidens, daughters of the leader Danaus, who have fled Egypt to escape unwanted marriages to the sons of their father's brother, who are in hot pursuit. Because their female ancestor, Io, was a woman of Argos who fled to Egypt to escape an unwanted union with Zeus, the Danaids hope to persuade the Argives to recognize them as legitimate members of the community and grant them the privileges of full protection under Argive law – a female equivalent to citizenship. In the course of the play the Argives, guided by their leader Pelasgus, in an apparently democratic deliberation, decide to confer on them the status not of citizens but of metics (resident aliens) – in fact, at lines 609 and 994 we find two of the earliest occurrences of this term (*metoikein* and *metoikôi*).

As I have already suggested, this play simultaneously stages multiple scripts from Greek social life, complex and simple, anthropologically "timeless," but also heroic and contemporary to Athens in the 460s. A few, such as suppliance and lamentation, do intrude on the others to thrust troublesome questions in the minds of Argive citizens and the play's spectators (Athenians, metics, and foreigners) about the roles of women as potential wives and as daughters, and about hybristic male violence against them. To link them all, we should ask whether one

---

[35] For contrasting perspectives on tragic representations of Argos on the Athenian stage, see Zeitlin 1990: 145–47, and Saïd 1990. For Aeschylus' use in this play of Egypt and Egyptians as foils of otherness to define the Greek male self, see Vasunia 2001: 33–58.

admittedly generalized script – let's call it "alignment with another" or "constructing a relation between self (same) and other (different)" – recurs time and again to provoke an anxiety over selfhood, autonomy, and harmony in both public and private life. Is this script being played out when the dramatic action and characterization call to mind for spectators an ephebe seeking recognition by mature citizens, a demagogue leading citizens to a decision, one state concluding alliance with another, and – not least importantly for this trilogy – a woman and man joining in marriage?

The proliferation of scripts in *Suppliants* achieves a kaleidoscopic pace early in the play that deliberately blurs one into another, creating a discursive confusion we should link to the question that has preoccupied modern scholars as the play's central concern: the character of the Danaids themselves, or the nature of the Danaid self, especially as revealed in their reason for refusing to marry the sons of Aegyptus.[36] This modern preoccupation arises from our imperfect knowledge about the other two plays with which *Suppliants* formed a trilogy (probably entitled *Aigyptioi* [*The Egyptians*] and *Danaïdes* [*Children of Danaos*]).[37] What is certain is that these maidens appear on stage not only as foreigners to Argos in a cultural and legal sense but as strangers to the discursive protocols regulating Greek interactions between one citizen and another and between citizens and foreigners. And if the Danaids sound discursively inept, it's because of the ambiguous hypo- and

---

[36] See Garvie 1969: 212–13, Winnington-Ingram 1983: 59–60, Sicherl 1986: 82ff., Seaford 1987: 110 and 117–18, Fisher 1992: 267, Sommerstein 1995: 121ff, C. Turner 2001: 28, and Föllinger 2003: 194–204.

[37] For reconstructions of the trilogy and each play's place in it, see Garvie 1969: 180ff., and Winnington-Ingram 1983: 53–72, but Rösler (1993: 7ff.) and Sommerstein (1995: 121–30) are now more persuasive; cf. Föllinger 2003: 188 and 201. Without question, we need a dose of "ingenuity" to reconstruct the nature and sequence of the trilogy (Winnington-Ingram 1983: 55).

hyper-autonomy they enact as speaking subjects, consistent with the ephebe's performative attitude and subject position.

In other words their kaleidoscopic mix of scripts stages an essential question for any Athenian approaching the threshold of citizenship: What type of self, and what degree of autonomy, must I perform to obtain recognition of citizen *timê* from the dominant social other? In the Danaids we find what looks like an overdeveloped voluntarist self, a cognitive self with a diminished capacity for intersubjective relations, and a deliberative self immured in its own circumstances, irresolutely adhering to the "wrong" sort of reason giving, and unaccountable to others for its position. True to the cultural profile of the ephebe, the Danaids are foreign in origin, speech, and dress; they journey from abroad to the borders of the city-state; they're sponsored by a paternal *kurios* (their father Danaus), who instructs them how to speak and act in accordance with Argive customs (especially moderation in their comportment); they present themselves to the local community's leader (the Argive chief Pelasgus); and they resort to a ruse (*mêtis*) to compel this community to deliberate their plea. But their ephebic status rests more fundamentally on moral and cognitive shortcomings as a self ill-prepared for the citizenship they so brazenly claim, with an autonomy at once overdeveloped and underdeveloped. Despite their claim to a kind of citizenship, they present themselves as "untamed," apolitical, irrational creatures motivated solely by a personal, even perverse, aversion to male domination in marriage.[38] And so, because they defy

---

[38] Zeitlin sees their defense of virginity as an argument for the virginal body as a "whole unto itself, a sign of the self's integrity that resists encroachment on any of its boundaries, any admixture or compromise to contaminate its pure state of being" (1996: 131). On their status as potential brides who resist "taming" by men, see Seaford 1987: 111 and Gödde 2000: 2, 7–8 and 215 – 48. Cf. Föllinger's critique of this scholarly focus on sexuality and sexual roles (2003: 191–92). Rohweder understands the Danaid's aversion to marriage as a refusal to accept the subordinate role in a

authority (Egyptian traditions) and misunderstand authority (demanding recognition from an ancestral Argos they know little about), their behavior shares a morally outrageous character with the ephebe of myth. For us it might also recall the recalcitrant adolescent's fierce claim to a radical autonomy that is socially unacceptable because it refuses to assume a subject position in an appropriately reciprocal I-you relation.

The play therefore *seems* to invite Athenians to reflect on the citizen's individual autonomy vis-à-vis the state's collective autonomy – which is how both Farrar and Zeitlin read it, seeing the maidens' refusal to accept political authority as an inability to understand how political discourse may transform the noncitizen's problematic autonomy into the citizen's self-control.[39] But this political reading is accurate only up to a point, for it sums up only the maidens' performance in this play of a radical, voluntarist subjectivity whose autonomy *appears* aberrant, unnatural, and unsuited to types of alignment that are politically valid. These include not only an ephebe's relation to the mature citizen, but the proper way for a demagogue to align himself with the *dêmos*, for a citizen faction to align itself with the state, and a state itself to form alliances with other states. In all these political scripts the nature of the self and its autonomy, both individual and collective, are put at

power relationship. She denies the need for any further, more "practical," reasons and interprets this refusal in terms of Athenian politics in the 460s (1998: 111–13, 117–18).

[39] Farrar sees in the play a "vision of democratic interaction as in principle reconcilable with – indeed, essential to – personal autonomy" (1988: 34). With the *Oresteia* (458) she regards it as an early contribution to a democratic theory that sought to reconcile "a self-conscious sense of [individual] agency" with democratic social order (1988: 15). Zeitlin sees the power of persuasion, both erotic and political, as the key to the Danaid resistance to state authority: in both spheres persuasion enjoins two subjects to modify their autonomy in a reciprocal relationship (1996: 136–43). For Rohweder, the Danaids reject marriage because they equate the wife's role with slavery in an "asymmetrical" power relationship (1998: 105–11, 181).

risk in performance; and these risks were very much on the minds of Athenians when the trilogy was produced sometime between 463 and 461, for this decade has been identified as the gestationary period for the very concept and word *autonomia*.[40] Nevertheless, these women deliver an unwelcome message to Pelasgus and the Argives that challenges their notions of political relationships, reason giving, and identity. Against all appearances they insist that they are not foreigners but natives, and that their dilemma as objects of hybris is now the Argives' dilemma. Incredibly, their message is: "We are (one of) you. And in order for you Argives to remain yourselves, you must acknowledge us as (one of) you."[41] To paraphrase Mead, "You must be others if you are to be yourselves."[42]

Autonomy, Lament, and Self-Evaluation

Interestingly, this play stages the Danaid script of self-presentation *three* times: first when the women are alone (in their entrance song

[40] For the concept's origin ca. 468–456, see Ostwald 1982: 40. He restricts the meaning of *autonomia* to political relationships between independent states where one is clearly more powerful than the other, as in Athens' relations with allies in the Delian League. Farrar argues that in the mid-fifth century it refers to relations between citizen groups and the state and between the individual and the state (1988: 103–6).

[41] For Loraux, tragedy's preference for plots drawn from myth rather than from recent political events enabled playwrights to create fictional worlds where "the other becomes surprisingly close." As a result traditional conceptions about self and other "... did not fit easily into fifth-century Athens" (2002b: 49). By confusing self-other relationships in the theater, tragedy thus confounds civic ideology's strict division between citizen men and barbarian others: "Nothing could be more alien to this [civic] construct," she concludes, "than the statement 'the other is native...'" (51).

[42] Vasunia reads the play's conflict between Greeks (Athenian democrats) and others (autocratic Egyptians) as a "model of how to incorporate otherness into the very heart of the Greek polis." Adapting Goldhill's perspective on tragedy (1990, 2000), he suggests that the trilogy concludes with a "controlled integration of the other" (Vasunia 2001: 70–71). In C. Turner's reading of the play, the Danaids confuse the clear Greek-barbarian polarity of the 470s (2001).

or parodos and first choral ode, 1–175); then with an interlocutor, the Argive chief, Pelasgus (234ff.); and then indirectly when Danaus reports onstage Pelasgus' off-stage presentation to the Argives of the women's plea (600ff.). The Athenian audience is thus afforded three occasions to evaluate, and so to compare, their demand for recognition of citizen *timê*: once in an unmediated exposure to the women, once focalized through the eyes of an elite leader, and finally re-focalized through Danaus' report of how Pelasgus interacted rhetorically with his *dêmos*. Early in the play, I expect that the audience would have seen these maidens as poor players of their script, as candidates illegitimately trying to establish themselves as legitimate speaking subjects. From their first moments on stage the Danaids consistently offend citizen protocol in a number of ways, but especially by: speaking out of place and turn; jumbling specific citizen scripts together; and confusing speech genres from the public and private, and male and female, spheres. These scripts and speech genres include supplication, *dokimasia*, oath swearing, seeking a *dikê*, praying, cursing, and lamenting – a torrent of speech and emotion that mocks the hypothetical silence I attributed to ephebes at a geniune *dokimasia*.

At lines 1–18 the maidens utter a quick prayer to Zeus for protection, and then, with no invitation from anyone to speak and possessing no authoritative status to sanction their speech, they emit short, quick, anapestic bursts of information appropriate to a typical *dokimasia:* they sketch out their origins and journey, identify their paternal *kurios* by name and role, and then blurt out their genealogical claim to descent from an Argive ancestor. This is not typical behavior for young women either in heroic narratives or in later civic discourse, challenging the cultural rule about female silence, especially in public spaces. And while the Danaids do properly name their father as their "advisor" (*boularkhos*, 11), in the same breath they call him the leader of a faction (*stasiarkhos*) and a "chess player" (*pessonomôn*), splicing into their would-be *dokimasia* a jarring script about political refugees of factional strife in Egypt who now seek alliance with Argos; and into this they quickly interject the script of suppliance (19–39).[43]

Aeschylus makes it appear that these brazen declarations are fueled by the Danaids' sense of an individual autonomy separating them from both the Egyptian state and their suitors, and that its source is a flamboyant voluntarist subjectivity: "We've fled the sacred land bordering Syria, not because we were condemned to banishment for murder by a state vote, but because of our own *self-motivated* aversion to marriage" (*autogenê phuxanorian*, 8).[44] And they will soon categorically insist that the proposed marriage to their Egyptian cousins violates the sacred custom (*themis*) governing relations between father's brother's kin because it would have permitted these young men "to mount *unwilling [aekontôn]* beds" (39). But we later learn that this marriage between cousins is in accord with Egyptian law, and that the Danaids refuse any subjection to males in marriage (387–95). What therefore motivates this aversion, and in what sense is it "self-motivated"? Modern scholars see in these questions a key to understanding the play, identifying the cause of the aversion either as "a supposed moral or social principle" (such as their stated fear of incest) or a "motivation purely in their own character" (Garvie 1969: 221), perhaps an adamant refusal to have their "will violated" (Fisher 1992: 267).[45]

---

[43] For the ominous overtones of *stasiarkhos*, see Friis Johansen and Whittle 1980, vol. 2: 16–17. *Pessonomôn* refers to *pessoi*, a board game whose strategic moves may have symbolized for fifth-century Athenians ways of playing at citizenship in a game called *polis*; see Kurke 1999: 254–73, esp. 260–61. Since alliance formation is crucial to civic autonomy (cf. Thuc.3.82ff.), by hoping for citizen status the Danaids already threaten Argos' autonomy.

[44] On possible meanings of the unusual adjective *autogenê*, see Friis Johansen and Whittle 1980, vol. 2: 13–15.

[45] Zeitlin opts for Garvie's "supposed…social principle," seeing the girls as a paradigm for the timeless Greek virgin who resists brutal possession by male eros yet aspires to

What scholars actually seek to determine with this question of motivation is the nature of the Danaids as a self. They are asking, in Sandel's terms, how the Danaid self "comes by its ends." Are these ends given in advance to them by the dominant social other, or are they struggling for the freedom to choose these ends for themselves (1998: 58)? In Gill's terms, do the Danaids exhibit an "objective-participant" model of the self or a "subjective-individualist" one (1996: 11–12)? Before choosing between these alternatives, let's observe that the Danaids' self-presentation insists that all the maidens are victims (objects) of hybris. This term occurs more frequently – ten times – in this play than elsewhere in Aeschylus' extant work, always refers to the sons of Aegyptus' desire to force marriage on the Danaids, and the maidens themselves hurl this accusation on all but one occurrence.[46] In Chapter 3 we saw that Odysseus' act of individuation and

a sexual union mediated by persuasion and charm (1996: 153–59). Seaford too pursues this logic, arguing that they fear the enforced isolation of a new bride from her own kin, especially a bride lacking a dowry (1987: 110 and 117–18); Vasunia concurs (2001: 55–56), and Gödde expands this thematics of marriage (2000: 215ff). Farrar opts for a "motivation purely in their own character" (again Garvie 1969: 221), seeing in *autogenê phunaxorian* the hallmark of a "subjective-individualist" self motivated by "the actions and feelings of the Danaids themselves, their 'self-will'" (1988: 31). Meier too sees their motive as "to make their own will prevail" (1991: 119). Rohweder believes their reasons form part of an "obscure prehistory" that is "irrelevant" to understanding the power struggle at the heart of the play's dramatic conflict (1998: 118). Ireland argues that their motivation is too "ambivalent" to accommodate a "unified approach" to identifying it (1974).

[46] See Fisher 1992: 267–70. Hybris words occur at: 30, 81, 104, 426, 487, 528, 817, 845, 880–81. Only at 487 does someone other than the maidens, Pelasgus, use the term. According to Helm, hybris occupies the middle position in a "negative genealogy" of five vices leading to moral ruin (*atê*) in Aeschylus' *Persians* and *Oresteia*. *Sôphrosynê* occupies an analogous position in a corresponding "positive genealogy" (2004: 29–52). In *Suppliants* these contrasting genealogies seem to crystallize around the relation between the Danaids and sons of Aegyptus, with help from Pelasgus, especially in the last third of the play (e.g., lines 762–1038). With more knowledge of the trilogy, we might also find Danaus implicated in these genealogies.

self-definition, and his self-transformation throughout the poem depend heavily on his decision to assume the role of the object of hybris. And, following Gernet, we identified becoming an object of hybris with the earlier of two cognitive paths by which the Greeks developed concern and respect for the individual in their moral tradition (2001 [1917]: 45–48). Gernet links this concern for the object of hybris to the kind of reasoning that prompts a "generalized and spontaneous religious sympathy" for a suppliant presenting him or herself as the victim of a crime (*adikêma*, injustice) – and *Suppliants* is his prime example (97–98).

From their very first moment on stage, then, the Danaids compel the spectators – and later will compel Pelasgus and the Argives – to respond to a kind of self, to emotions (shame, respect, fear, and compassion), and to reason giving that challenge civic discourse, identity, and harmony. And yet like ephebes at a *dokimasia* they increasingly demand that Pelasgus and the Argives translate their appeals into questions of citizenship and civic welfare. With Pelasgus as their "ally in justice," they in fact succeed in having the citizens translate their dangerous plea for suppliance into the ultimate democratic discourse: a law in the form of a unanimous vocal vote (*psêphos*). These demands in effect impose on the play's implied and internal audiences a bind between two logics.[47] It seems as though the nature of the Danaid self is undecidedly cast between extra-political and political senses of identity. We might almost agree with Winnington-Ingram in concluding that, concerning their aversion to marriage, "This obscurity must be deliberate" (1983: 60; cf. Rohweder 1998: 118).

---

[47] I therefore disagree with Fisher, who claims of the Danaids, "at no stage do they state their case rationally, and they certainly do not come over at all sympathetically" (1992: 269–70). I argue that they provoke antipathy for violating the norms of civic discourse but sympathy for their appeals as suppliants and lamenters.

We can, however, illuminate this obscurity somewhat by remembering that these women – as the Athenian spectators well knew – in
the course of the trilogy turn from being objects of hybris into subjects
(perpetrators) of violence when they murder their Egyptian husbands
on their wedding night, as Fisher and others observe (1992: 270). I find
Sicherl's (1986), Rösler's (1993), and Sommerstein's (1995) arguments convincing when they claim, building on a scholiast's comment to l. 37, that
Suppliants' Athenian audience would have understood what motivated
the Danaids' aversion to marriage: in the bitter rivalry between Danaus
and his brother Aegyptus for control of Egypt, an oracle prophesied
Danaus' death at the hands of a son-in-law. (Rösler and Sommerstein
take *Suppliants* as the trilogy's *second* play and see the oracle established
in the first play, *Aigyptioi*.) Consequently, the maidens' aversion to marriage with their cousins arises out of the filial duty every daughter owes
her father. While it appears extreme, such motivation could hardly
be more traditional – in fact, as an "objective-participant" self, their
"ends" are so given in advance that they are dictated by their father's
wish to prevail in his struggle for power as a faction leader. And prevail
he does, for in the trilogy's final play, *Danaïdes*, war breaks out between
Argos and the sons of Aegyptus, and Danaus replaces the slain Pelasgus
as tyrant of Argos. What are the Danaids then but mere instruments
of their father's tyrannical will?[48] And what do they lead Pelasgus and

---

[48] Sommerstein calls them "pawns" in their father's political gamesmanship, building
on their reference to Danaus as a "chess player" (*pessanomôn*, 12) (1995: 116). He also
raises a question. Did the Danaids themselves know about the oracle, or did Danaus
not trust them with this information and simply raise them to feel unnaturally
repelled by the prospect of marriage (ibid. 119)? I assume (like the scholiast to l. 37)
that they did know about the oracle: this would have placed greater moral constraint
on them to obey Danaus' order to murder their husbands on their wedding night.
This way, in sparing her husband Lynceus, Hypermestra is more culpable as an
accomplice to parricide. While some scholars balk at accepting the hypothesis about
the oracle (e.g., Conacher 1996: 109–10) or remain unsure (Latacz 1993: 141), others

the Argives to do but democratically admit oriental tyranny and *stasis* into their city-state's public sphere and female violence into its private households?

As performers, however, the maidens adeptly disguise their motivation before Pelasgus and the Argives. They assume a radically voluntarist selfhood that rejects both human custom and the "natural" law of male-female sexual desire and female submission to the male in marriage. With the phrase *autogenê phuxanorian* ("self-motivated aversion to marriage"), they therefore announce to the spectators an autonomous self that is two-faced: in one sense it's a mirage, a subterfuge, to conceal subservience to their father's ambition, but in another sense it's very real because it introduces the non-civic performative attitude and subject position they will assume with Pelasgus. Because Aeschylus embeds their deceptive performance of autonomy within a poorly played ephebic script of *dokimasia*, he encourages his spectators to judge the women's voluntarist autonomy negatively, as ideologically unacceptable according to criteria for citizen behavior. But at the same time Aeschylus orchestrates for them ritual actions, storytelling, and lamentation whose emotionally compelling logic, while different from the logic of politics (Loraux 2002b: 87–88), the theater spectators and Argives cannot necessarily reject as insincere. For just as they appear, they announce themselves as suppliants (20–39) with "proof" of Argive identity: the painful memory of sexual violence against their female ancestor, Io.

As we saw in our discussion of Achilles' relationship to Priam in *Iliad* 24, the ritual script of suppliance stages a public confrontation between

endorse it strongly (C. Turner 2001: 27–28; Föllinger 2003: 199–200, 209 and 234). Gödde's general thesis suffers for neglecting to consider it seriously (2000: 18–19, n. 47), and Rohweder's dismissal of the hypothesis of the oracle does not seem well founded (1998: 112–13).

a relatively powerless outsider and a powerful, authoritative agent who holds the key to social integration.[49] By performing one or two actions from a limited repertoire of gestures – throwing oneself on the ground, clasping behind the knees, kissing the hands, bearing branches – the powerless agent unleashes before spectators and the authoritative figure a threat packing strong emotions to accompany a verbal plea for physical protection and social acceptance. The predominant emotion is shame and respect (*aidôs*), accompanied by the fear of reprisal or reproach from the dominant social other, usually figured as "Zeus protector of suppliants."[50] But suppliants sometimes try to provoke compassion (*eleos, oiktos*) as well, and here, too, fear is provoked, though of a different sort.[51] Again, from the earlier discussion of Achilles and

---

[49] On suppliance in ancient Greek society, see Gödde 2000, Giordano 1999, and Gould 1973; in Homer, see Crotty 1994, Thornton 1984 and Pedrick 1982. In different ways, C. Turner (2001), Naiden (2004), and Gödde (2000) demonstrate how ineptly the Danaids perform their supplication. Although the maidens present themselves to their Argive protectors as victims of persecution, they will soon threaten the well-being of all Argives (C. Turner 2001: 27–39). Their supplication is also "troubling" and riddled with "peculiarities" not only due to an improper formal presentation but because, in light of Classical Athenian religious and legal practices, they misunderstand that a local political authority must judge the legal and moral grounds for their appeal (Naiden 2004: 83–88). Gödde also explores ways the Danaids transform the ritual of supplication into a craftily wrought "rhetoric" of self-interested "transgressions" (2000: esp. 177ff.).

[50] At 345, after they drape suppliants' wreaths around altars of the gods, they beg of Pelasgus, "Feel shame/respect [*aidou*] before the ship of state's prow, crowned in this way." He immediately responds with fear (*pephrika*, "I'm trembling," 346), soon after will cry out that "fear grips my mind ..." (*phobos m'ekhei phrenas*, 379), and they warn him about the profundity of Zeus' anger as protector of suppliants (347). (This anger, they soon point out at 386, is impervious to pleas for compassion [*oiktois*]). Pelasgus himself will wrestle with the need to fear/respect this anger (*aidesthai*, 478), calling this the "height of fear" for mortals (*hypistos ... phobos*, 479).

[51] At 211 the Danaids directly appeal to Zeus for compassion (*oiktire ...*) so they may not perish at the Egyptians' hands, and at 639 they celebrate the Argives' decision to admit them by saying "... they felt compassion for us" (*ôiktisan hêmas*). When they begin lamenting their fate at 57ff., they evoke the nightingale "worthy of

Priam, we saw how in the fourth century Aristotle defined compassion (*eleos*) as "a kind of pain" aroused by the sight of another suffering undeserved miseries – miseries one might expect oneself or one's intimates to suffer at some time (*Rhet.* 2.8.2). In other words, to feel compassion for another we need to determine that we ourselves are vulnerable to the other's misfortune, or that our well-being is somehow linked to theirs because we share similar "goals and ends" (Nussbaum 2001: 319). So while the Danaids may behave like pawns in their father's civic struggle against his brother, they perform their role in his scheme by splicing into their attempt at civic discourse appeals to reasoning based on shame and fear, and, when they switch to lament, on compassion with its fear of suffering a calamity akin to what they anticipate from the Egyptians.

Caught between two logics, the spectators would have first used performative criteria from the protocol of different citizen scripts to apprehend the Danaids' seeming autonomy. When Danaus enters at 176,[52] he will advise the women not to be too hasty or too slow in speaking (200); but when they're on their own in the parodos, their speaking out of turn and mixing of scripts continue. At 23–39 they launch into a prayer that combines elements of a key citizen oath – one faintly echoing, I believe, the ephebic oath. But no sooner does the oath begin to crystallize when they transform it into another speech

compassion" (*oiktras*, 61) as a self-image and characterize its song as *oiktos* (59, 64), a word meaning both lament and the compassion it tries to elicit. After hearing the Danaids' plea, Pelasgus speaks of his confidence that all the citizens will detest the Egyptians' hybris and feel compassion for the young women (*oiktisas*, 486). Conversely, when near the play's end the Egyptian herald threatens to drag the women away, he says their robes will be torn "with no compassion" (*ou katoiktiei*, 904). On this mixture of fear and compassion aroused by their plea, see Gödde 2000: 178.

[52] Danaus likely enters at this point (Friis Johansen and Whittle 1980, vol. 2: 4), though Taplin suggests he stands silently beside his daughters as soon as they appear on stage (1977: 193–94).

genre, a curse on the Egyptian cousins pursuing them. Their prayer (23–39) invokes the sacred powers of this land – those nameable as divinities and those that don't take human form. These include an unnamed Olympian host (*hypatoi . . theoi*, l. 24), chthonic divinities of fertility, and the tombs of local heroes (*thêkas*), all presiding over the city-state, the land itself and its rivers (23–25). So, if the Danaids have already cued the Athenian audience to recognize the script of suppliance as an inappropriate *dokimasia*, this particular invocation may trigger associations with the ephebic oath's invocation, normally administered one year after the *dokimasia*, where the divinities and heroes of the land, Olympian and chthonic, were named as witnesses as well as the land itself and its borders.[53]

If the promissory intent of the ephebic oath is to secure the hoplite's loyalty to the comrade "standing alongside" (*parastatên*) him in the phalanx, then the Danaids perversely transform that promise into a female curse upon the men forcing the alliance of marriage upon them. Their words conjure up images of the traditional "bad death" of ship-wreck that was antithetical to the hoplite's "beautiful death," holding his orderly position in rank:

> *Send the arrogant, male-choked swarm born of Aegyptus, along with their fast-rowed ship, down into the sea before they land a foot in this muddy swamp. And there may they perish battling against* [antêsantes, 36] *the tide in wind-storm, thunder, lightning, and savage, rain-swept gales, before they ever violate what sacred custom forbids, selfishly abusing the right of father's brother's kin by mounting unwilling beds.*
> (29–39)

---

[53] Possible echoes of the ephebic oath's sound and sense at 19–27 include: *euphrona* (19), echoing the oath's marked repetition of *euphronôs* at 12 and 14; *barutimous . . . thêkas* (24–25), echoing the oath's *timêsô hiera ta patria* at 16; and *Zeus . . . oikophulax hosiôn andrôn* (26–27), echoing *amunô . . . hyper hierôn kai hosiôn* at 8–9.

Once the Danaids have begun to speak autonomously, they cannot control their script-switching and elision of one speech genre into another, but overall I believe the cognitive framework of the *dokimasia* prevails. Their first choral ode (40–175) expands their invocations to include Io and snippets of genealogical narrative about ancestors in the female line. Here they boldly promise to show the citizens of Argos "pieces of evidence [*tekmêria*] that are trustworthy [*pista*], even if they seem surprising to the natives here" (54–55), and they are confident of the recognition this evidence will provoke in the Argives when they expound it fully (*gnôsetai de logou tis en makei*) (56). Tokens of recognition were of course what each ephebe hoped to demonstrate to the deme, and we saw how they play a crucial role when the arch-ephebe Theseus encounters his father Aegeus.[54] But at the same time the presentation of *tekmêria* as evidence or proofs to community members evokes another citizen-script, "seeking a *dikê*," which by the fifth century meant a jury trial or arbitration.[55]

Up to this point the maidens only hint at such a script, but once they breathe the word *dikê* in some form at 79 (*to dikaion*) to refer to their plea, it will recur repeatedly (twenty-five times) throughout the play, leaving no doubt that, as objects of hybris, they place their demand for proper recognition of their *timê* within the framework of dispute settlement.[56]

---

[54] *Tekmêria* can indicate proofs of identity in the form of words or objects: Pelasgus uses the term to refer to the verbal evidence he gives identifying himself as chief of Argos (271), and Plutarch uses it for the objects and narrative information that proves the ephebic Theseus' relation to Aegeus (*Thes.* 4). But *tekmêria* can also indicate arguments and objects presented as evidence at jury trials, arbitrations, and preliminary hearings.

[55] Private arbitration would have been used before 399; see Gernet 1955: 103ff., and MacDowell 1978: 204.

[56] On the play's references to divine and human justice, see Kaufmann-Bühler 1955: 38–50. Naiden clarifies that supplication always intertwined "divine and human elements," mixing religious laws with civic laws (2004: 12). This was especially true

Like Achilles and Odysseus, this posture and demand seem to require them to assume a radical, extra-social autonomy, and like the heroes they will back up their demand with a violent threat. Knowledge of the entire trilogy is again essential here, for there is good evidence that the final play climaxed with a jury trial. Since their Egyptian suitors were victorious against the Argives, the Danaids were compelled to marry them after all. As extensions of their father's tyrannical will, however, they heeded his command to murder their husbands on their wedding night – all but one, Hypermestra, who spared her husband because she had fallen in love with him.[57] It's likely that in the final play, Danaus took her to trial, charging her with disobeying his proclamation as her father and tyrant of Argos, endangering his life (in light of the oracle), and making his deadly proclamation and her sisters' complicity seem more blameworthy.[58]

---

in its final phase, when "an act of judgment" was rendered on the plea – in Athens, usually by the Council of 500 and sometimes the Assembly as well (75–83).

[57] For speculation about the trilogy's final play, see Garvie 1969: 204–33, now in my opinion surpassed by Sicherl (1986), Rösler (1993) and Sommerstein (1995). Rösler (1993: 16–21) argues most cogently for the hypothesis of a jury trial at the climax of the final play, with evidence from Pausanias (2.19.6) and strong parallels to *Eumenides*. Despite his ingenious reconstruction of the final play, Sommerstein's reasons for dismissing the trial fall flat, especially the "serious drawback" he finds in the thought that a trial scene in *Danaïdes* "would have greatly reduced the impact" of the trial in *Eumenides* several years later. "It is most unlikely that Aeschylus tamely repeated himself in this way," he concludes (124). This supposes that Aeschylus knew in the late 460s that he would compose *Eumenides* in 458 or that an artist of such genius had to display stark originality in each play we happen to possess. Most recent scholarship accepts the likelihood of a trial in the final play (Latacz 1993: 146, Föllinger 2003: 188), though some, like Conacher, remain sceptical (1996: 106).

[58] The key evidence for details about the trial comes from Pausanias 2.19.6; see Rösler's discussion (1993: 16ff.) and Sicherl's (1986: 102ff.). Their most persuasive evidence that Hypermestra's trial occurred in *Danaïdes* is this: at 2.19.7, a few lines after describing the trial, Pausanias makes clear reference to Aeschylus' *Seven Against Thebes*, indicating that he's using the playwright as an authoritative source for early Argive history.

Because Hypermestra rejects paternal and civic authority in favor of love, and submits to the reason-giving deliberation of a jury trial, she opens the possibility that by the trilogy's end the Danaid self might be redefined and transformed through democratic deliberation. But for now such therapy is not in sight: we only see that the maidens are intent on presenting credentials for female citizenship, as at a *dokimasia*. But they present these credentials, the "trustworthy tokens" of their identity, as a maternal memory (*matros . . . mnasamena*, 50–51) of Io and the child, a calf named Epaphus ("Caress"), sired by Zeus' touch. They pour this memory forth in the form of another genre, lament, the quintessential female, noncivic discourse for expressing uncontrolled emotion over the loss of a family member (57–76). Engineered by their voluntarist self, a discursive autonomy – in its root sense of "self-legislation" – now leads them to speak of death, a particularly female death that brings self-destruction. Through lament the maidens present themselves as agents who have lost control of their own destiny, as creatures given to self-consumption out of a grief that turns a woman aggressively against herself or her own family. They equate themselves here with the archetypal lament performer (Nagy's "model of mimesis") who first sang the nightingale's song; usually called Procne, they rename her "Mêtis worthy of compassion" (*Mêtidos oiktras*, 61).[59] When the barbarian Tereus, husband of Procne/Mêtis, raped her sister Philomela, the two women took revenge, murdering his son; Mêtis was transformed into the nightingale and Tereus into a hoopoe or hawk.

With the unusual name Mêtis, the Danaids not only continue to echo ephebic characteristics, but for a second time they splice the citizen-script of *stasis* into their self-presentation, suggesting their readiness

[59] See Loraux's exploration of why the myth of the maternal nightingale appeals to such tragic maidens as the Danaids, Cassandra, Antigone, and Electra (1998: 57–65).

to use deadly cunning deceit (*mêtis*) in their plea for help from the gods and the Argives. Mêtis may also employ a "dramatic irony" by referring to the Danaids' future plot to assassinate their Egyptian suitors on their wedding night (Friis Johansen and Whittle 1980 vol. 2: 56); but it surely has a plurality of referents, including their self-interested use of suppliance, their upcoming threat of suicide, the harm they bring to Argos, and their eventual murder of their Egyptian spouses.[60] As the nightingale, the Danaids explicitly equate performing autonomy with a deadly peril to themselves and anyone they claim as their own, for they characterize Mêtis' murder of her own child as *autophonôs* (65), which can mean slaying oneself or one's kin. While here it refers to the latter, they will in a few moments issue a suicidal threat to hang themselves on the trees in a border sanctuary by the Argive shore (159–61).[61] As they see it, if the gods do not move the Argives to welcome them, they will simply extend the script of suppliance by performing it in the underworld.

This is the moment when an isomorphic link emerges between *autophonia* and *autonomia*. About twenty years after Aeschylus' *Suppliants*, we find the earliest surviving use of *autonomia*, and it occurs as a personal and not a political characteristic. It comments on this same tragic situation of a maiden willing to descend to Hades because she

---

[60] On this last possibility, see Rohweder 1998: 122–24. Mêtis can also refer to their inventive discursive autonomy. They pointedly refer to the nightingale as a performer who "composes [*ksuntithêsi*, 65] her lament [*oikton*, 64] about her child's fate in grief over exile from her native haunts along lush riverbanks," using *suntithêmi* to mean assembling a verbal account from disparate parts – and even mixing speech genres inappropriately. (See Liddell, Scott, and Jones II.b, with citations and Friis Johansen and Whittle 1980, vol. 2: 62–63, with citations). Cf. Nagy on the nightingale's song as a paradigm for oral composition displaying the "capacity to maintain continuity through variety" (1996: 59).

[61] The word may signify both meanings depending on context; see Friis Johansen and Whittle 1980, vol. 2: 63.

refuses to obey a community law she judged harsh. At *Antigone* 821–22, Sophocles has the chorus taunt Antigone:

> *Without glory, without praise, off you go to the deep region of the dead.*
> *You weren't stricken with wasting disease, nor did fate reward you with*
> *a sword-thrust: because you determine for yourself what is law*
> [autonomos], *only you among mortals will go down to Hades while*
> *still alive.*[62]

Again, at 875, they berate her:

> *Your pious action [burying her brother] may achieve some sort of piety,*
> *but you can never pit your own power against he who is entrusted with*
> *power. Your uncontrolled temperament* [orga], *because it acquires*
> *knowledge by itself* [autognôtos], *has destroyed you.* (872–75)

The Danaids do not actually use the term *autonomia* to describe themselves, even though, as I suggested earlier, the word may have been coined during the decade in which the play was produced (Ostwald 1982: 40). But that doesn't mean they don't proclaim their *autonomia* in a manner of speaking, especially given their peculiar discursive habits. Just as this play contains the earliest surviving expression of the concept "democracy" without quite uttering the word *dêmokratia*,[63] the

---

[62] Farrar argues that these two Sophoclean passages express *autonomia* as a "personal quality and achievement" (1988: 105). On suicide as a nonheroic, feminine death assimilated to murdering one's kin and to *mêtis*, see Loraux 1987: 8–11, with 71, n. 6.

[63] See the circumlocutions at 604 (". . . where the people's show of hands rules by majority count," *dêmou kratousa kheir hopêi plêthunetai*) and 699 ("May the community of the people keep their privileges safe and rule over the city-state," *phulassoi t'asphaleis timas to damion, to ptolin kratunei*). For 604 see Friis Johansen and Whittle 1980, vol. 2: 491; for the link in both passages to *dêmokratia*, see Pelling 1997: 75. In addition, see 942–43 ("such a single, people-wrought vote was fashioned from the city-state," *toiade dêmopraktos ek poleôs mia psêphos kekrantai*). On Aeschylus' wordplay in *Suppliants* with key democratic terms like these, see Musti 1995: 19–53.

Danaids stake a claim to *autonomia* through a circumlocution they fashion by exploiting the female prerogative to perform lamentation. Ostwald contends that the word originated in interstate politics, soon after Athens established the Delian League, out of a "plea" by Athens' weaker allies for "recognition" of their traditional privileges of independent self-rule, and that Athenians first used the term grudgingly and with disapproval, as suggested by the chorus in *Antigone* (1982: 7–9).[64] A *plea* for independence by the weaker party in a dialogue, and a *reproach* by the stronger for claiming independence: *autonomia* arises historically from the performative use of two illocutionary speech acts contesting the nature of self-legislation.

Here, in the throes of uncontrolled lamentation, the maidens utter a startling self-description that vaunts self-legislation free of dialogic interference from anyone; they couch their vaunt in terms consistent with the language of lament but stretch its resources. Note especially how their self-description inverts the citizen script of *timê*, where third-person spectators evaluate a citizen's standing on the basis of a self-presentation, because the Danaids perform a *self-evaluation* as speaking subjects with no need of any such observer:

> *My way of speaking* (legô) *is to shriek out miserable pains like these;*
> *they are sharp and deep and make tears fall,*
> *ai! ai! how they stand out as dirges!*
> *Though still alive I use my cries of lamentation to determine my own*
>   timê
> [zôsa goois me timô]. *(112–16)*

With remarkable succinctness they adapt the protocols of lamentation to assume simultaneously the roles of the deceased and of the female

---

[64] Ostwald says that, at *Ant.* 821, "*autonomos* here is a quality 'objectively' predicated by others; it is not a quality 'subjectively' claimed by an individual" (1982: 11).

kin who traditionally keened praise for the deceased and blame for his or her enemies.[65] Discursively, this means they monopolize two subject positions, the first-person speaker and the third person who is evaluated; and here, as we've indicated, there is no second-person interlocutor.[66] In Chapter 1 we saw Achilles inappropriately adopt lament's two roles and subject positions (the lamenter's and the deceased's) in order to perform an autonomous self-evaluation, first before Thetis in Book 1 and then his peers in the Greek embassy in Book 9: the Danaids now repeat that performance in the Athenian theater, with the spectators playing the role of the absent interlocutor. Achilles' peers certainly expressed dismay in Book 9 when he spliced the script of lament into "how leaders deliberate." Will the Athenian spectators do likewise, anticipating by about twenty years the disparaging terms *autonomos* and *autognôtos* uttered by Sophocles' chorus in 441?

The Danaids most violate linguistic usage when they transform the normally transitive sense of the verb *timan* into a reflexive one: and this grammatical hapax points clearly to a botched script of *timê* in which

---

[65] We saw in Chapter 1 that the *goos* mentioned here was originally an improvised series of spoken cries, perhaps narrative in form, opposing the fate of the deceased to that of the mourners and his or her enemies. See Alexiou 1974: 165–84 and Derderian 2001: 31ff. While it's true that these oppositions enable the mourning woman to call attention to her own plight, Loraux exaggerates in claiming that epic *goos* "is primarily a song of self-lamentation for women" (2002b: 109, n. 35).

[66] We find lamenting for oneself while still alive in two other Aeschylean plays: *Ag.* 1322–23, where Cassandra, about to go to her death, responds to the chorus' expression of compassion for her fate by saying, "I want to speak once more a speech or rather a lament, one that would be my own" (*hapax et'eipein rhêsin ê thrênon thelô emon ton autês*). At *Libation Bearers* 926, Clytemnestra, about to be slain by Orestes, remarks, "I feel like someone who, while alive [*zôsa*], laments [*thrênein*] in vain upon a tomb." For another echo of the Danaids' line, see Aeschylus' *Niobe*, where the mourning mother is described: "Sitting for three days, she, still alive [*zôsa*], broods like a hen over these burial rites for her dead children" (fr. 6–7 Diggle). For tragedy's use of *timan* to refer to honors for the dead, see the references in Friis Johansen and Whittle 1980, vol. 2: 103.

a subject arrogates to itself one of the dominant social other's primary functions in a society dominated by an "objectivist-participant" concept of the self.[67] But why should mid-fifth century tragedy connect *autonomia* as individual self-legislation to behavior that is female and funerary? Loraux argues that the city-state long suppressed women's "antipolitical" mourning behavior because it unleashed family passions leading to civic conflict (*stasis*).[68] She emphasizes too how tragedy's grieving women, as partisans of their family's cause, use lamentation "for their own purposes and on their own behalf"; figures like Cassandra, Antigone, Helen, and Iphigeneia "will borrow a song that was intended for the dead, a deceased other, and apply it to themselves, the living." And she cites as a paradigm of this female "reappropriation" of lament the Danaids' shrieks that climax with, "Though still alive I use my cries of lamentation (*goois*) to determine my own *timê*" (2002b: 58–59).

These maidens therefore manipulate lament as Achilles did to emerge as extra-social creatures clamoring for justice and claiming they are near to death. They will nevertheless not kill themselves but succeed in weaving their antipolitical discourse into the Argives' political deliberation, persuading (or is it finagling?) Pelasgus and the citizens to respond with shame (*aidôs*) and compassion, each with its component of fear, and produce a democratic vote welcoming them into the community. In other words, theirs is a frightening autonomy.[69] But

[67] See, e.g., the general discussion of *timê* in Gernet 2001: 281–302, with special reference to what is due the dead (289); recall the discussions of Homeric *timê* in Adkins 1972: 14–18, Sealey 1994: 142–45 and 150–52, and Yamagata 1994: 121–31.

[68] See 2002b: 20ff., 2002a: 31–44, and 1998.

[69] From our contemporary perspective, their moral consciousness remains fixed at Kohlberg's "preconventional" level of moral consciousness, blind to the realization that only the dominant social other should determine their worth or virtue. Habermas claims that agents at this level make moral judgments dominated by strategic reasoning and passion: they will use threats, weapons, or enticements to

while I believe Aeschylus orchestrates their self-presentation to arouse antipathy among his spectators according to the logic of citizenship, I suggest he also calculates it to provoke sympathy for the women as objects of hybris and bonafide suppliants. Not unlike Achilles with Priam, they evoke membership in a broader human community where self and other can hypothetically cohabit.[70]

Why would Aeschylus deliberately bind his audience up in contradictory claims by a voice of citizenship ("These maidens could and should never be one of us!") and a voice of shame and compassion ("I must respect age-old custom, and I can see myself suffering their distress!")? Let's first consider the end result of the Argives' democratic vote, which was engineered by Pelasgus' rhetorical skill: calamity for Argos and its leader, an Asiatic tyrant installed in his place, and a bridal bloodbath. Somehow the Argives fail to deliberate carefully enough in weighing two imperatives: their need as humans to identify with the maidens' distress by yielding to a compassion in which they each see their own *individual* well-being implicated in the maidens' well-being, and their need as citizens to safeguard their *collective* well-being as a community. Aeschylus is foregrounding for his play's implied audience how necessary it is for them as individuals to set aside the norms of citizenship in order to assent to *aidôs* and *oiktos* – but also how necessary

influence their opponents' definition of the moral situation (1990: 133). To paraphrase one liberal theorist of moral autonomy, agents like these who lack a cognitive ability to see the alternatives open to them are "moral idiots" (Kekes 1997: 32). In Athenian terms, the Danaids' moral autonomy perverts their supplication (C. Turner 2001), refuses to recognize that an authoritative political group must evaluate their status (Naiden 2004), and transforms their ritual behavior into a deadly rhetorical strategy (Gödde 2000).

[70] See Loraux's discussion of tragic catharsis as a mixture of pity (compassion) and fear that the spectator experienced primarily as an individual, or as a member of a human community that "transcended his membership in the civic community" (2002b: 88–93).

it is for them as a collectivity to deliberate and reason well about the expediency of these feelings. For after all these are powerful emotions which, in binding us to others, may render us vulnerable to their otherness.[71]

It isn't clear whether the Danaids willingly terminate their first scene of self-presentation with these outcries, or whether their father Danaus, entering to hear these last threats, has simply heard enough. At any rate, he silences them with a direct admonition: "Girls, you must come to your senses!" (*paides, phronein khrê*, 176). Immediately his paternal authority as *kurios* provides the third-person perspective that's been missing from their discursive performance. And immediately they share in his magisterial know-how when he describes from a lookout post the arriving Argives and instructs them about performing a ritually correct act of suppliance. A quick pedagogical exchange with their father prepares them to encounter Pelasgus and, through him, the Argive citizens; it also forms a bridge between their two scenes of self-presentation. But most importantly it recalls for the audience their ephebic subject position. Danaus reminds them of their helplessness, their foreignness, their need to display appropriate and modest behavior, and he instructs them to invoke gods whose images adorn this border sanctuary on the shore.[72] Now forewarned with paternal advice and

---

[71] Here, I'm indebted to the exchange between Alford (1993) and Schwartz (1993), where Alford argues for tragedy as a "civilizing" education (*paideia*) in compassion and Schwartz for tragedy as an invitation to "take one step back" from compassion so that audiences find a "deliberative space" to compare their interests and passions (Schwartz 1993: 283). From the perspective of Athenian religious and legal practices, Naiden notes the Argives' mistake in not exercising their "right" to examine closely the Danaids' character and to consider rejecting their plea (2004: 87).

[72] It's long been thought that Aeschylus was here evoking the Altar of the Twelve Gods in the Athenian agora, where suppliants sometimes sought refuge (Friis Johansen and Whittle 1980, vol. 2: 166–67), but it also recalls the ephebe's religious education and tour of Attica's major sanctuaries, and his invocation to divinities, Olympian and local, in the ephebic oath.

forearmed with a modicum of cultural knowledge, like most ephebes
they're reasonably well prepared for the role of respondents to questions posed by the leader of a community to whose membership they
feel entitled. Their impersonation of an ephebe at his *dokimasia* should
therefore improve upon their earlier, untutored rehearsal at 1–175. Their
signs of foreignness, however, couldn't be more apparent – dark skin
(154–55), Egyptian dress, thick accent (118–19), and unkempt appearance
(from self-laceration, 120–21).[73] If they strike us as hardly resembling
an ephebe confronting a demarch at this ceremony, it's worth recalling
Vidal-Naquet's characterization of the ephebe as a "*temporary* alien" and
"a *temporary* woman" (1997: 119; my emphasis). Very much marked with
otherness, then, the Danaids insist on assuming the subject position
and performative attitude of the outsider seeking an intersubjective
relation with Argives through language.

Dokimasia *as Dialogue*

What unfolds, however, is a dialogue; and we should understand how
their appearance presents a challenge to Pelasgus as well. If his role in
this encounter really does resemble the demarch's at a *dokimasia*, his
response to these bizarre female and foreign ephebes will model for
the audience the mentality of leadership that must assume the performative attitude appropriate to evaluate their *timê* on native grounds.
Pelasgus is confronted with a hermeneutic challenge to decipher this
thoroughly foreign spectacle that nevertheless shows "ritually correct"
(*kata nomous*, 242) signs of suppliance, and a moral challenge to comprehend the spectacle of a person who, despite a thoroughly foreign

---

[73] Blackface is an attested version of the blackness in the ephebe's appearance; see Ma's
discussion of the "black hunter" Damon in Plutarch's *Cimon* (1–2) (1994: 50–51 and
62; cf. Vidal-Naquet 1988: 112). For symbolic associations of the Danaids' black skin
(and of Egypt in general) with death, see Vasunia 2001: 47–53; cf. Seaford 1987: 112,
n. 70.

appearance, claims to be Argive.[74] What he first models for the audience, though, is cognitive confusion. The Danaids too are not sure to whom they are speaking, and when they ask Pelasgus to identify himself by social position ("Would I be speaking to a private citizen, a temple warden, or a community leader?" 247–48), a precarious dialogue emerges from mutual confusion: somehow two strangers must create an intersubjective relation in which each shares in the other's subjective world.

Pelasgus responds to their naive question by rooting himself squarely at the origins of Argos' narrative history. As "pieces of evidence" or "proofs" (*tekmêria*, 271) of his identity, he presents his personal genealogy, his role as the community's founder, Argos' prehistory, and the geographical extent and borders of its territory (250–74). In ephebic terms, he establishes the community narrative into which each candidate (or his *kurios*) must insert himself – and the maidens are very quick to pick up the cue. They immediately perform a solemn declaration of their Argive origin – "We publicly profess to be Argive by descent" (*Argeiai genos exeukhometha*, 274–75) – and they formally assure him they will confirm "the whole truth" of their claim through what they are about to relate (276).

But Pelasgus cannot yet permit them to proceed. He remains too confused about the authenticity of their claim to be Argive women, stymied by their foreign appearance and by a set of stereotypical images or scripts used by Greeks to identify barbarian women. He catalogues four such scripts that are not too difficult for us to understand; he wonders whether they are: Libyan women (279–80); creatures nourished

---

[74] Cf. Loraux on the problems faced by Clytemnestra and the Argive chorus in *Agamemnon* when they try to decipher Cassandra's appearance and speech (2002b: 75–80).

in Egypt by the prodigiously fertile Nile (281); Indian nomadic women like those who ride side-saddle on camels and live near the Ethiopians (284–86); or meat-eating, bow-wielding Amazons who live without men (287–89). At 282–83, however, Pelasgus inserts a fifth script in the middle of the other four, one that has been considerably more difficult to comprehend: "And a Cyprian imprint [*kharactêr*] is similarly stamped on female matrixes [*gynakeiois typois*] by male craftsmen."

Much of the difficulty scholars face in grappling with this complex image results from misunderstanding its context. Sandwiched between the first two stereotypical scripts of Asiatic women and the last two, it describes not an additional stereotype but the cognitive process itself by which a patriarchal culture like Greece's uses gender stereotypes to make sense out of something – a person, a spectacle, a material of some sort – that is indistinct or difficult to identify.[75] Zeitlin's and Loraux's readings of this passage help clarify its blend of sexual and artistic metaphor,[76] and Loraux in particular intuits a connection between the engraver's *typos* (mold or matrix) and the Platonic *khôra* as a kind of nature that is "halfway between perceptible and intelligible." She calls it a "receptacle and nurse ... which receives all bodies, impression-carrier for everything, cut into figures by the objects that enter it and imprint themselves" (1998: 74). But Kurke's reading comes closest to seeing how Pelasgus is describing his own cognitive struggle to use stereotypical

---

[75] Friis Johansen and Whittle suggest excising this passage, but their philological and cultural reasons aren't convincing (1980, vol. 2: 223–26). They're puzzled about why a passage filled with non-Greek names includes Cyprus, a "quasi-Greek place" in the fifth century where Greek and non-Greek cultural characteristics mingled (224–25), but Cyprus' culturally mixed connotation suits the Danaids (and Pelasgus' impression of them) perfectly. They miss entirely the more important erotic connotation linking Cyprus to Aphrodite.

[76] Zeitlin 1996: 153–54, and Loraux 1998: 73–74, where Cyprus' erotic connotation is fundamental to both.

bits of knowledge to "stamp" or "engrave" these ambivalent, mixed-up creatures with a definite form and identity. And she equates him with *dokimasia* of another sort: the state inspection of currency to test its inner "nature" (*physis*). So "Pelasgos struggles to gauge inner nature from outward signs."[77] In a more modern idiom, I would say he finds their claims "incredible" (*apista*, 277), observing, "My male intelligence is trying to penetrate the resistant surface of your appearance by projecting [i.e., stamping or engraving] stereotypical images or scripts upon you."[78]

The dialogue between these two perplexed subjects might have ended here had Pelasgus not declared himself willing "to be instructed (*didakhtheis*) so he might know more" about their claim (289). Now the maidens have a formal invitation to reprise the story of their ancestor Io before a community leader – the same tale they spontaneously poured out earlier in fits and starts before no one. This time, however, their narrative performance will not be an uncontrolled monologue inappropriately mixing such scripts and speech genres as genealogy, prayer, oath swearing, and lament. Rather, Aeschylus has them – their chorus leader, actually – recite the tale in dialogical tandem with Pelasgus himself, each speaker contributing a "mytheme" in appropriate narrative sequence through the rapid-fire format of tragic stichomythia (291–324). Note how the Danaids provide the first piece of information early in Io's story, and how Pelasgus confirms the tale's identity as a *phasis* and *logos* in the Argive repertoire of narratives. From that point on, the story unfolds through question and answer, with Pelasgus

---

[77] Kurke 1999: 321. Kurke links the *dokimasiai* of Athenian coins and citizens (309–16).

[78] In sketching out this catalogue of scripts (279–289), Pelasgus' initial and concluding words make clear that it emerges from his subjective, cognitive effort to draw comparisons and inferences: he starts by saying the Danaids "more resemble" (*empher-esterai*, 279) Libyan women and ends by saying, "I should surely have thought [*kart'an êikasa*, 288] you were . . . Amazons had you been archers" (287–88).

asking all the questions and the Danaid chorus leader providing all the responses:[79]

> *Chorus*:   They say that Io was once a priestess at Hera's temple here in this Argive land.
>
> *Pelasgus*:   That's certainly true; the tale [*phatis*] is widely held. And according to one account [*logos*], didn't Zeus sleep with a mortal woman?
>
> *Chorus*:   Yes, but those embraces were hidden from Hera.
>
> *Pelasgus*:   And how did this dispute between Lord and Lady turn out?
>
> *Chorus*:   The patron goddess of Argos changed the woman into a cow.
>
> *Pelasgus*:   And so did Zeus actually get close to the lovely-horned cow?
>
> *Chorus*:   What they say is that he took on the form of a bull to impregnate a cow.
>
> *Pelasgus*:   What then did Zeus' mighty wife do in response to this? (291–302)

In this way Pelasgus and the maidens construct a shared social world, a reality "for-us," through proofs that are linguistic, consisting of *mythos*, *phatis*, and *logos*. As these two interlocutors reassemble them, the bits and pieces of Io's tale even take on the material reality of a *symbolon* binding them together.[80] The narrative unfolds simultaneously as a

---

[79] Despite the play's notorious textual difficulties, most editors assign the questions to Pelasgus and the responses to the Danaids, beginning with l. 295 (Friis Johansen and Whittle 1980: vol. 2: 232–33).

[80] The dialogue seems to enact verbally the silent gestures used in Archaic Greece when a *symbolon* reunited elite participants in a guest-host, political, or commercial partnership. This was a physical token representing the original alliance, often a ring but sometimes a coin or clay object broken in half so that at a future date the

drama in which an elder examines a novice in elements of community
lore – an idealized performance of an ephebe's *dokimasia*. And just a
few lines later the Danaids have the perfect opportunity to turn this
questioning about the general tale of Io into the story of their own
genealogy: like an ideal ephebe, they effortlessly insert the story of
their own lineage into the community narrative.

Pelasgus:	Who then proclaims himself the cow's calf by Zeus?
Chorus:	Epaphus, truly named "prize-taker."
[*Pelasgus*:	And who was born from him? (a line is missing here)]
Chorus:	Libya, she who reaps the most of any land.
Pelasgus:	Whom do you name then as her offshoot?
Chorus:	Belus with two sons, one of whom was the father of my father here.
Pelasgus:	Tell me this man's most distinguished name.
Chorus:	Danaus, and his brother had fifty sons.
Pelasgus:	Also disclose that man's name directly.
Chorus:	Aegyptus. Now that you know my ancient lineage, would you take action to protect this band of Argives? (314–24)

III   THE DEMAGOGIC SELF: DELIBERATION AND AUTONOMY IN ATHENS, 465–460

With this exchange, the Danaids successfully cross the threshold of
a quasi-citizenship (*metoikein*, 609, and *metoikôi*, 994) and undergo
a transformation from a self dominated by voluntarist elements to

---

parties to the pact (or their delegates or descendants) might prove their membership
in the relationship by reuniting each half (Gauthier 1976; Shell 1978: 32–36). As the
Danaids remark to Pelasgus halfway through the genealogical tale's performance,
"All you've said glues together with what I've said" (*kai taut' elexas panta sugkollôs
emoi*, 310).

a predominantly cognitive self whose ends will now seemingly be defined by its dominant Argive others. But as soon as the Danaid chorus leader blurts out the hated name of their pursuers' father (Aegyptus), and abruptly challenges Pelasgus to take action as a result of the scrutiny they have just undergone, the play's moral and cognitive focus shifts to the performative attitude of a mature, elite, citizen leader. More specifically, Pelasgus' cognitive skills and moral autonomy come under scrutiny in a crisis where the community's collective autonomy is at stake. With increasing detail he will focalize for the spectators the challenges that emerge when scripts coincide: mythological and ritual scripts like Io's tale and suppliance, and scripts from political life governing deliberation and decision making among elite leaders and citizens.

These scripts of citizen deliberation are of course not Argive but Athenian in nature, and I assume that, if the spectators are to find them meaningful, the scripts on stage match scripts enacted in Athens in the 470s and 460s. Aeschylean scholarship has always been willing to accommodate "political readings" of the plays – and in recent years has begun to identify the nature of democratic leadership from the 470s to 450s as one of the playwright's predominant concerns.[81] *Suppliants* in

---

[81] "The Aeschylean hero, then, and the *polis* he rules, are shown in a crisis of leadership and, although the problem is cast in a mythical age, it really reflects a situation made familiar to Aeschylus' audience by contemporary Athenian history" (Podlecki 1986: 96). See Sommerstein 1997, and Podlecki 1990 and 1986. Podlecki discusses Xerxes (*Persians*), Pelasgus (*Suppliants*), Eteocles (*Seven Against Thebes*), and Orestes (*Oresteia*) in terms of "a new set of problems which the Athenians – leaders and followers alike – were having to face" in the early decades of the democracy (1990: 55). While Podlecki doesn't connect these dramatic leaders to actual political figures, Meier does, suggesting that in *Suppliants* Aeschylus reflects Ephialtes' belief that any individual leader or faction must be weak and ineffective compared to the sovereignty of the citizen body (1991: 120–26). Burian identifies Pelasgus' dramatic situation as the "dilemma of a statesman" but rejects identifying him with any historical leader (1974: 10). In Rohweder's reading, the play is a plea, prior to Ephialtes'

particular has struck some scholars as Aeschylus' conscious attempt to explore, through heroic characters and situations, "very real," contemporary Athenian questions concerning the deliberative autonomy of ordinary and elite citizens. As Podlecki puts these questions: "how are decisions arrived at in matters when it is crucial to have the support of a whole citizen body? What, in short, is the nature of effective leadership in a society of free, and often independent-minded, individuals?" (1986: 86).

But scholars produce no consensus on how to associate heroic characters in tragedy with leadership types or individual leaders in Athenian political life. We'll see in fact that scholars can directly contradict one another in identifying a tragic character like Pelasgus with political leaders in the late 460s such as Ephialtes and Cimon, who were bitter factional rivals. In the matter of leadership the trilogy's full scope has also been overlooked, for Pelasgus' performance as a leader can be more clearly understood within the context of the bitter fraternal and factional rivalry between Danaus and Aegyptus in what I take to be the first play and the tyranny Danaus establishes over Argos in what I take to be the last.[82] We might even want to rephrase the second question Podlecki attributes to Aeschylus as: "What sort of *self*, in short, provides the most effective leadership in a society of free, and often independent-minded, individuals?" For the reconstructed trilogy and Athenian politics of the 460s suggest that citizen leaders (and not just ephebes) exhibited degrees of voluntarist, cognitive, and deliberative

revolution, for the traditional aristocratic leadership to share its control of the political process with common citizens. She suggests that it also pleads with commoners to accept their traditionally "asymmetrical" relationship with an elite leadership (1998: 184–86).

[82] Sommerstein suggests that, from the trilogy's perspective, we revise our understanding of its major character to be Danaus, not his daughters; and he sees tyrannical vs. demagogic leadership as its second most important theme, after marriage (1995: 131).

selfhood in the performative attitudes and subject positions they assumed vis-à-vis citizens. Perhaps we can rephrase the question on Aeschylus' mind once more as a version for leaders of deliberative democracy's program: "What must we demand of a leader's self if we wish our political life to be governed by talk rather than coercion...or blind consensus?" (cf. Warren 1995: 194).

To interpret tragic leaders politically, I suggest we reject any direct identification of heroic characters on stage with individual politicians, living or dead. Instead we're better off isolating particular performative attitudes and types of autonomy that tragic characters display when they deliberate, and then identifying these with performative attitudes and types of autonomy we can reconstruct using reasonable inference about debates in the Athenian Assembly or elsewhere.[83] As a focalizer in *Suppliants*, what Pelasgus increasingly enacts is cognitive distress over choosing between two competing types of autonomy open to a leader. One is archaic and assumes responsibility for (and compromises) the community's collective autonomy, and the other is a novel form grounded in denying oneself such a privilege so that citizens' collective autonomy may determine its own character. And while his cognitive distress explodes in the familiar accents of a tragic protagonist ("I am without solutions; fear grips my mind about acting or not acting and choosing success!" 379–80), Pelasgus' dilemma, as Meier and Rohweder express it, is particular to the democracy's first few decades, especially the 460s: how to evaluate actions according to traditional morality and belief on one hand and according to political exigency and consequences on the other (Meier 1991: 119–120; Rohweder 1998: 143–53).

---

[83] In Chapter 7 I'll compare this way of linking characters on stage to historical figures with Vickers' notion of "polymorphic characterization," where different stage characters reflect "different facets of the same [historical] individual" (1997: 15).

Small wonder, then, at how weak and paradoxical a figure Pelasgus cuts as an agent caught in such a bind: he's a democratic chief (a *basileus*) who "rules" over an Argos that anachronistically combines features of a prestate chiefdom and a mature, democratic city-state. In cognitive terms this means discovering reasons for and against each type of autonomy and then performing a devaluative shift from one to the other. Aeschylus splices into his dramatic character a struggle among competing elements of a voluntarist self who, like his foreign counterpart Danaus, chooses domination over rivals as his end, a cognitive self whose ends are dictated by the traditional privileges of a Greek *basileus*, and a deliberative self who might through self-reflection distance himself from tradition and prevailing opinions to find universal reasons to make a decision for which he'll be accountable.

Because Pelasgus has just established a "web of interlocution" with the Danaids, they mark him as the sole Argive privileged to renew their long-suppressed link to his community – and they naturally assume their suppliance will reattach them to Argos through alliance with his household (348–53; 359–64). But Pelasgus responds by rejecting out of hand the possibility of a privately negotiated alliance. Thinking like a democrat, he immediately considers the impact on the city-state and people as a whole of welcoming the Danaids (356–8; 365–69). Unlike the tyrannical Danaus, he certainly denies himself a voluntarist autonomy of personal interest in deciding about an alliance, but at the same time he rejects the more communitarian understanding of the archaic leader as a cognitive self entitled to think and act on the community's behalf. The Danaids nonetheless insist that he play this role and plead their case as though they were litigants in a dispute seeking a *dikê*: "Take Just Settlement [*Dikê*] as your ally and make the judgment that is righteous before the gods" (395–96; cf. 343). Pelasgus responds, not by rejecting the script "seeking a *dikê*," but by refusing a key role traditionally assigned to *basileis* in Greek society. As discussed in Chapter 2, in the prestate and early state periods these leaders adjudicated disputes by drawing upon a cognitive virtuosity based on their privileged access to community memory and myth.[84]

Pelasgus instead assumes the subject position of one who renounces all judicial authority and even competence: "This isn't an easy judgment – don't choose me as its judge!" (397). Earlier we saw the Danaids interact with Pelasgus as though he were the demarch at an ephebe's *dokimasia*. Here, when they switch scripts to dispute settlement, the Danaids attribute an autonomous judicial authority to him consistent with their assumption that he *was* the city-state itself, incarnating its collective will (*to dêmion*), a ruler above the judgment of others (*prytanis akritos*) (370–75). Some might assume the maidens are projecting an Asiatic script and notion of judicial authority onto a Greek community, but the sort of dispute settlement and judge they have in mind probably evokes for the spectators associations closer to home in Athens. Despite our spotty understanding of Athenian judicial reforms from around 600–450, we have enough evidence to conclude that local disputes in demes were traditionally settled by individual judges – possibly demarchs themselves – whose autonomy was strong enough to represent state authority.[85]

---

[84] In Chapter 2 I noted Gagarin's emphatic claim about *basileis* in Hesiod: "every *basileus* who is part of Hesiod's contemporary world is a judge or is addressed in terms of his judicial role. There is no indication, in other words, that in Hesiod's time the *basileês* have any other public function than that of judging" (1992: 63). We saw Carawan too emphasizing how, in the Archaic period, "in procedures before kings and councils of elders . . . justice was to be found in the wisdom or inspiration of the judges themselves" (1998: 5); cf. Cantarella 2003: 279–81.

[85] According to *Ath.Pol.*16.5, the tyrant Peisistratus set up judges in demes and often himself went into the countryside to settle disputes. Cleisthenes too may have used demarchs to settle minor disputes (see *Ath.Pol.*21.5, with Dem. Phal. 228 F31; cf. Rhodes 1981: 257); and by 453 local judges were "once again" (*palin*) settling disputes in demes (*Ath.Pol.*26.3; cf. Rhodes 1981: 331). Whitehead endorses the notion that demarchs "acted as local justices in their demes" from Cleisthenes to 453 (1986:

But why should Pelasgus, who at times acknowledges his considerable authority, believe himself incompetent to render a decision about alliance?[86] Could his reticence amount to more than rejecting tyrannical ambition and the *basileus'* traditional authority? Could it point to a cognitive deficiency in *any* leader's exercise of individual autonomy in political decision making? If we recall Thucydides' portrait of *stasis* in Corcyra and other city-states in 427, the track "forming an alliance" from the script "how citizens deliberate" marks the first step citizens take in time of war down the path to civic ruin (3.82.1–3). Let's recall too that the remedy for this and the other tracks of the script "how citizens deliberate" was a form of deliberative intelligence Thucydides calls *gnômê* – the hallmark, I'll maintain, of a deliberative self.

Aeschylus' Pelasgus anticipates by a full generation this Thucydidean conclusion. The track of alliance formation was certainly an Athenian preoccupation in the late 460s, when the democracy endured a precarious phase in its development. Domestic tensions between elites and commoners over state sovereignty were building toward the Ephialtic revolution of radical democrats, which climaxed in 462 with Ephialtes' victory over the conservative Council of the Areopagus and his own assassination. Internationally, starting with the victories over Persia in 480–79 and the Delian League's formation in 478, the tensions of empire building embroiling Athens with other Greek states and Persia foregrounded a cluster of questions surrounding the choice

---

37). At the state level, Sealey suggests that in the early democracy a long-standing practice from Solon's age, whereby individual archons settled disputes, yielded to popular courts because individual archons feared their decisions would offend powerful interests (1976: 259–60).

[86] Right after begging, "don't choose me as its judge," Pelasgus adds, "As I said before, I don't wish to carry out political actions without consulting the people, even though I have power over them" (. . . *oude per kratôn* . . . 399). Podlecki notes Pelasgus' other claims to absolute rule at 252, 255, and 259 (1986: 83).

of allies. As we've already seen, these same years from the late 460s to the early 450s provided the matrix from which *autonomia* emerged. Despite scholarly consensus that *autonomia* referred primarily to the independence of a weaker city-state vis-à-vis a more powerful ally, Athens' most pressing concern at this time focused on the degree of *individual* sovereignty elite leaders of extraordinary talent should exercise in matters that put the community's welfare at risk, especially outright warfare and the making or breaking of alliances.

Put simply, that concern gravitated around how autonomously an individual citizen should act in the public interest and how as a deliberator he should exercise cognitive and linguistic autonomy in ways that would encourage rather than stifle citizens' collective autonomy. In democratic Athens he would of course have to be a mature citizen and "all man" – in Zeitlin's description, one who incarnates a "civic definition of masculinity: the political master who is master of *logos* in debate" (1996: 142). Such a figure can most accurately be described with a neutral sense of the word "demagogue." As M. I. Finley claims, this type of leader was a necessary "structural element" in the democracy; and the word was "equally applicable to all leaders, regardless of class or point of view," who would be judged "individually not by their manners or methods, but by their performance" (1985b: 69). Finley in effect redefines the demagogue as a deliberative agent whose individual autonomy ideally facilitated political action by citizens. In this expanded sense he therefore describes as demagogues all prominent Athenian leaders from Themistocles, Aristides, Pericles, and Cimon, to Cleon, Nicias, and Alcibiades (61).

Cimon and Ephialtes as Demagogues and Deliberators

But what about Pelasgus? Can we assimilate his performance as a deliberative agent to that of a contemporary Athenian leader in the 460s, and will that performance be demagogic as well? Podlecki thinks his political sentiments sound Ephialtic, and he categorizes Pelasgus as "something like a *dêmagôgos* in the technical sense, a political leader who has to put his ideas across by compellingly persuasive rhetoric" (1986: 84–85). From the mid-470s to 460 we know that Athens' elite leaders walked a tightrope in pursuing a policy of alignment with one ally in particular, Sparta; first Cimon and Themistocles, then Cimon and Ephialtes led opposing factions over cooperation or hostility with the Spartans. By the late 460s Ephialtes and his faction were promoting Argos itself as the preferred alternative to alliance with Sparta – Themistocles had been welcomed there as a suppliant – and Athens had concluded a treaty with Argos by 460.[87] It's no exaggeration to say that the major deliberators in these debates risked their citizenship itself since Themistocles likely suffered ostracism over this question in or around 472 and Cimon in 461.[88]

Sommerstein has observed how in the 470s and 460s "the theatre seems to have been something of a political battleground," adding that at this time the citizens in the theater and Assembly shared the same balance of opinion found in the public at large (1997: 69–70). Since *Suppliants* was produced sometime in the mid- to late 460s, it's reasonable to consider whether Aeschylus was replaying in the theater a script of alliance formation similar to one that was animating Assembly debates. Sommerstein remarks on how "extraordinarily similar" the play's plot and character motivations are to events of one particular year, 462, when Cimon's political career and the Ephialtic revolution were on a

---

[87] For Themistocles in Argos, see Thuc.1.135.3 and Plut. *Themistocles* 23.1. For Athens' treaty with Argos, see Thuc.1.102.4; Hornblower gives the date of 460 (1983: 37). C. Turner sees a somewhat different link to alliance formation and the Delian league in the play's thematic oppositions between Greek-barbarian and citizen-foreigner (2001: 46–48).

[88] For these ostracisms, see Plutarch *Themistocles* 22 and *Cimon* 17; cf. Meier 1991: 105–11 and Fine 1983: 344–45.

collision course (76). But we'll achieve more insight if we suppose that Aeschylus had his mythological, ritual, and political scripts coincide in order to enact a split between two performative attitudes, one archaic and one novel, over how much deliberative autonomy a leader should exercise in allying the community with outsiders – and Pelasgus is the moral agent incarnating the difference between them.

Pelasgus has already shown how each of these performative attitudes combines the voluntarist, cognitive, and deliberative elements of selfhood to different degrees, but the historical debates of the 460s reveal how each element has a different capacity to understand an event as an "action concept" with its corresponding type of rationality criteria. Through the debates each element and capacity for understanding take the form of a mentality expressing itself in deliberation through rhetoric, which in this play becomes an index to appropriate vs. inappropriate uses of individual autonomy. One Aeschylean question underlying a demagogue's deliberative performance is therefore: How can an individual leader deliberate to exert a just influence over collective autonomy by promoting rational analysis, and how can a leader also unjustly curtail that autonomy by confusing and deceiving?

In the early 460s Athenians were unsure about taking a fateful turn in the precarious alliance with Sparta they had maintained since defeating Persia in 479. In 465–64 a helot revolt threatened Sparta following an earthquake, and the Spartans sought military assistance from Athens (Thuc. 1.101–103). More than a generation later, around 412, Athenians still publicly remembered how this request included the dramatic gesture of the Spartan Pericleidas, who crossed the scripts of ritual and politics by approaching Athenian altars as a helpless suppliant "begging for an army."[89] They also remembered this event in connection with

---

[89] See Aristophanes *Lys.* 1137–44: "Pericleidas the Spartan once came here as a suppliant to the Athenians and sat at these altars, pale in his scarlet cloak, begging

performances at an Assembly deliberation, where the radical democrat Ephialtes protested against the "proposal" (*to phronêma*) to restore
Athens' "rival" (*antipalos*), while the conservative democrat Cimon
"considered what benefited the Spartans more important than his own
country's increased stature." Cimon won this debate over whether to
restore Spartan autonomy or augment Athens' autonomy at Spartan
expense by "persuading" or "misleading" – *anapeithein* can mean both –
the *dêmos* to send a large hoplite force under his command to Sparta.[90]

How did he do it? Also remembered was the rhetorical move that
clinched Cimon's victory that day. According to Ion of Chios, a poet and
thinker visiting Athens as Cimon's houseguest, Cimon combined two
metaphors to depict the Athenian-Spartan alliance and the need to preserve it. Note how each translates into respectable martial imagery the
pathetic ritual gesture of the suppliant Pericleidas. "Cimon encouraged
[*parakalôn*] [the Athenians] not to let Greece go lame and not to overlook
the needs of the city-state that had become their yoke-mate" (*tên polin
heterozugon*).[91] It's clear enough from the first metaphor that Cimon
regarded alliance with Sparta as essential to Athens' (and Greece's) well-
being in light of persistent Persian threats. But it also implies that
Athens' expediency lay in continuing to regard its own autonomy as
partial, necessarily compromised by ties to other states, rather than
complete, determined strictly by its own interests. Ephialtes' argument
struck cleanly at this suggestion in pleading with the Athenians to

---

for an army . . . and Cimon went with four thousand hoplites and saved all of
Lacedaemonia."

[90] See Plutarch *Cimon*.16.9. Plutarch attributes part or all of this memory about
the debate to Critias: the passage may be read, "Critias says that, when Ephialtes
objected and protested . . . Cimon considered what lay in Sparta's interest. . . ."
Alternately, the phrase "Critias says . . ." may govern only "Cimon considered. . . ."

[91] Plutarch *Cimon* 16.10; for a fuller reconstruction of these events, with sources and
historiographic issues, see Fine 1983: 347–48.

consider Athens' strategic interests alone and to identify their own individual interest with the state's. Cimon's "yoke-fellow" parries Ephialtes' characterization of Sparta as a rival in wrestling (*antipa-los*) and vividly asserts that Athens should in no way conceive of its autonomy as absolute vis-à-vis Sparta.

But it also confuses the issue for the Assembly with a double sleight-of-hand. It first substitutes the traditional figure of the hoplite soldier for Athens itself, interchanging a citizen's individual autonomy for communal. Cimon thereby argues that Athens should assume as much responsibility for Sparta's welfare as the hoplite traditionally did for the neighbor (often a family member) to his right in the phalanx.[92] (This responsibility, it's worth recalling, is the second one to which each ephebe swore in his oath.) But once he has confused the question of what sort of autonomy is at issue, individual or communal, he uses the image of a pair of Athenian and Spartan hoplites to mask the long-standing practice of elite Athenian leaders like himself who cultivated ties of *philia* and *proxenia* with elites of other states, Greek and non-Greek, as sources of personal prestige and wealth.[93] Sparta was of course preeminent among these foreign states.

Cimon thus encouraged the citizens to translate their collective identity and decision making into the mentality of an individual whose cognitive elements compromise his autonomy by emotional ties to a Spartan counterpart: he was pleading with Athenians to own up to ends they shared with Spartans – in short, to feel a compassion for Spartans with its fear that one might suffer the other's sad fate. This hoplite image of Athens agonizing over ties to a yoke-mate substitutes

---

[92] On the bond between hoplites in the same line in the phalanx, see Hanson 1989: 119–25.

[93] Sealey summarizes what we can reconstruct of Cimon's rivalry with Ephialtes (1976: 261–64 and 267 n. 8). On Greek elites' friendship with foreigners, see Herman 1987; for friendship in Athens' elite politics at this time, see Connor 1992: 35ff.

traditional feelings of loyalty and comradeship for the more pressing cognitive challenge: how to evaluate rationally the most expedient
course of action. Cimon's rhetoric thus prevents the Athenians from
"stepping back" to deliberate wisely and weigh their individual fellow
feeling with Spartans against their collective welfare as Athenians. At
the same time it conceals the voluntarist, self-interested motives behind
the decision making of elite leaders such as himself. Most importantly,
this image allowed Cimon to arrogate to himself a cognitive task that
Ephialtes urged the citizens to assume for themselves.

Judging expedience calls for an evaluator to reflect on competing
courses of action that are "teleological" in the sense that they will or
won't achieve certain ends in an objectively determined world. An
evaluator's rational criteria for choosing among alternative actions will
depend on how closely these approach the "true" conditions or how
effective they are likely to be. The Spartan suppliant's plea, however,
and Cimon's substitution of the hoplite agonizing over his yoke-mate
frame the situation in moral or "normative" terms of what the evaluator *ought* to do in order to comply with social norms (here religious,
familial, and civic). A third frame emerges when the evaluator considers the suppliant's plea and the injured Spartan yoke-mate as subjective
(or "dramaturgical") acts of self-presentation expressing a performer's
subjective world, a world to which he has privileged access. Here rationality criteria will try to determine whether the performance is sincere
or duplicitous, or whether the evaluator can plausibly see himself in
the performer's situation – and so respond with fear and compassion.[94]

---

[94] For these three action concepts and their corresponding criteria for rationality, see
Habermas 1984: 85–100, where the actions are described as "teleological," "normative," and "dramaturgical," respectively. Naiden emphasizes in Athenian terms the
key evaluations a deliberative body must make in response to a suppliant's plea: Is
he or she "worthy" (*axios*)? Is his or her plea "legitimate/legal" (*ennomos*)? (2004:
82–86).

The multiple perspectives of action concepts enable us to see more clearly how Cimon's skillful rhetoric suppresses objective criteria in favor of normative and subjective criteria, and how it discourages citizens from considering the question under all three types of action. The normative and subjective criteria magnify the I-you subject positions of selves locked in an intersubjective tie, and they obscure the perspective of an objective, third-person observer. In terms of speech act theory, Cimon's performative attitude before the Assembly embeds his double metaphor in an illocutionary exhortation, something to the effect that "*It is not just or proper for you to allow* Greece to go lame and to overlook the needs of the city-state that has become your yoke-mate."[95] Framing the debate this way deflects the citizens' attention away from ascertaining the objective truth value of such perlocutionary propositions as "Athens' autonomy cannot be divorced from Sparta's." In effect it robs the citizens of their collective cognitive autonomy, encouraging them to undervalue Athenian autonomy as the greatest good in their deliberation. It also likens them to the sort of citizens the Danaids hope to find in Argos: compassionate members of a kin group who fear the plight of a kinsman in distress.

How accurately do Aeschylus and his troupe, when they enact Pelasgus squaring off with the Danaids, capture the performative attitudes of Ephialtes and Cimon? Pelasgus is well aware that welcoming the Danaids is a teleological action that will put Argos at risk of attack by their Egyptian pursuers. From the perspective of normative action, he knows too that he should grant asylum since they are under the protection of the gods. He must also evaluate their bizarre

---

[95] This reading is strengthened if we understand *parakalôn* in its sense of "demanding" or "requiring," which reinforces the speaker's moral superiority to his audience. Cf. Liddell, Scott, and Jones 1940 *s.v.* IV; cf. *ta parakaloumena* (Demosth. 18.166, Polybius 4.29.3).

self-presentation as a dramaturgical action, which may not be sincere (it may be a ruse) or may not be a reasonable subjective response with which others can identify. His task is complicated by the fact that the Danaids' self-presentation simultaneously interweaves all three action concepts, defying any simple attempt to disentangle each action for separate analysis. For, to a ritual performance of suppliance, the Danaids add the threat of mass suicide by hanging if they are refused asylum (457–67), and the resulting religious pollution, in the Greek mentality, would promise devastating consequences for Argos.

So while Pelasgus' dilemma sounds the familiar distress call of the tragic protagonist ("I am without solutions; fear grips my mind about acting or not acting and choosing success," 379–80), his need to juggle the multiple perspectives of these three action concepts lends more complexity to his struggle. Aeschylus leaves no doubt that the true source of Pelasgus' distress is cognitive: the *basileus* exclaims (at 452–54), "I'm at a terrible loss over this dispute! I wish I were a know-nothing [*aidris*] instead of an expert [*sophos*] about these miseries! If only, contrary to how I understand it now [*para gnômên emên*], this would turn out well!" In effect each time the Danaids try to invoke their kin-based understanding of justice and their emotional plight, Pelasgus counters with an autocritique of his *gnômê*, his individual capacity for decision making. He understands that it is impossible for one autonomous individual to evaluate the rationality criteria of all three action concepts activated by the Danaids' self-presentation. To his thinking literally no one is competent to judge this issue.

This explains why, as a demagogic self, Pelasgus seems inherently weak and confused; it even suggests that *all* demagogues of no matter what ideological stripe are weak vis-à-vis the *dêmos*. If he pleads, "This isn't an easy judgment – don't choose me its judge!" (397), it's because he believes a new type of self must evaluate the maidens' *timê*. He can already hear that self's voice as a third-person objective observer accusing him, "By recognizing the *timê* of foreigners, you've destroyed the city-state!" (*epêludas timôn apôlesas polin*, 401). Clearly this self is democratic, collective and irreducibly plural; it shares with Ephialtes a concern for collective autonomy; and that autonomy moves from a plurality of opinions to consensus by deliberating reasons for and against, not by merely voting approval of measures its moral superiors advise it to adopt.[96] It's also a self Pelasgus fears for its fickleness – it criticizes rulers but detests hybris and feels compassion for those less fortunate than itself (483–88).[97] In other words it *can* accommodate into its civic discourse the individually experienced "fear and respect" (*aidôs*) and the "compassion and fear" (*oiktos*) demanded by supplication as both a normative and dramaturgical action. It appears, though, to subject these powerful emotions to an overriding concern for collective well-being and autonomy. But will this plural, democratic, citizen self be able to avoid the inevitable vulnerability to others embedded within these feelings?

In short, this plural self does have the cognitive capacity to embrace all three subject positions and understand all three action concepts with their respective rationality criteria. When the Danaids learn of the citizens' decision, they immediately understand how the Argives responded with shame/respect (*aidôs*) and compassion (*oiktos*), each with its component of fear, even though they predicated their supplication on a terrible maternal memory and awkwardly articulated it

---

[96] Meier emphasizes how this consensus cannot be achieved through the kind of consultation Cimon and other Areopagites engineered when they expected the citizens to "participate by voting"; it had to be a "decision ... they themselves take" (1991: 122). Rohweder draws a parallel between Pelasgus' refusal here to decide by himself so important and difficult an issue and Athena's insistence at *Eumenides* 470ff. that Athenian jurors, rather than she alone, decide the fate of Orestes the suppliant (1998: 148).

[97] See Podlecki's discussion of these lines (1990: 74–76).

in civic terms as a *dokimasia*. But they also understand how the citizens transform these emotions into the perfect expression of a civic discourse, a unanimous vocal vote. And so they now pray for peace and fertility in Argos and exclaim: "This is why they felt compassion for us [*ôiktisan hêmas*] and cast a vote [*psêphon*] of kindness; this is why they showed shame/respect [*aidountai*] for Zeus' suppliants, miserable flock that we are" (639–42). Of course, Pelasgus and the Danaids have some difficulty naming the citizens' cognitive capacity, but through circumlocutions for *dêmokratia* and by twisting traditional terms into new meanings, they succeed in describing a "popular sovereignty that rules the city-state." They hope it "may with steady hand protect [citizens'] *timai* as a form of rule [*arkha*] endowed with foreknowledge and the skilled intelligence to produce the common interest" (*eukoinomêtis*, 698–700).[98]

Ideally speaking, what this subject performs is a fourth action concept Habermas calls "communicative action." This kind of action evaluates opposing subject positions and the senses of the world each articulates, negotiates the different meanings each employs, and produces a common understanding or consensus for coordinated action (1984: 100–1). Communicative action doesn't, however, emerge spontaneously from deliberation; it relies on deliberative agents who display or conceal, encourage or suppress, the sort of autonomy participants need to generate it. And, as Cimon demonstrated, a demagogue's attempt to master a debate by relying on voluntarist and cognitive elements of selfhood

---

[98] Some of these traditional terms are *polis* (357, 358, 366), *xenêi laos* (367), *astoi pantes* (369), and *dêmos* (398). Meier points out (1991: 123–24) that a new linguistic coinage enters the dialogue when Pelasgus tries to explain to them a social reality they have no knowledge of, the principle of popular sovereignty: *to dêmion* (370). Ironically, Aeschylus has the Danaids first pronounce it as they try to reject the very notion: "But *you* are the city-state [*polis*], *you* are popular sovereignty [*to dêmion*]; and as a ruler beyond judgment you control the altar and hearth of the land . . ." (369–72). They reiterate the term later as *to damion* at 699 (an occurrence Meier doesn't discuss) to express astonishment over the citizens' decision to welcome them.

may contribute to a communicative action that falls far short of the ideal – like the decision in 465–64 to aid the Spartans. But the demagogue still seems inherently weak vis-à-vis the *dêmos* when it acts as a collective deliberative self, for in 462–61 Cimon again persuaded the Athenians to help Sparta by sending 4,000 hoplites to oust the helots from their citadel at Ithome.⁹⁹ Only this time his role in generating a communicative action would lead to his undoing. He and his men were disgraced when the Spartans grew nervous about their presence and sent them home; and in Cimon's absence Ephialtes and his faction (perhaps with Pericles' participation) staged their revolution by persuading the *dêmos* to remove many members of the Council of the Areopagus. When Cimon returned to Athens and tried to reverse this development, he was ostracized.

Sommerstein points out how closely these events of 462–61 parallel *Suppliants'* plot and characters, especially in light of the trilogy as a whole: like Cimon vis-à-vis the Athenians, Pelasgus persuades the Argives to help a foreign ally, the Danaids and Danaus, only to have the Egyptians attack, defeat the Argive army, kill him, and make Danaus tyrant of Argos.¹⁰⁰ So is Pelasgus' performance Ephialtic or Cimonian? Deliberatively and cognitively speaking, it displays demagogic elements common to *both* Ephialtes and Cimon. When Pelasgus insists that the *dêmos* decide whether to accept the Danaids, he strikes an Ephialtic pose against privileged kinship ties and elite, kin-based alliances with foreigners and in favor of the deliberatively democratic notion that the citizens enjoy autonomy in determining the question.

---

⁹⁹ For the ancient sources, see Thuc.1.102, Aristoph. *Lysistrata* 1141–44, Plutarch *Cimon* 17.2, and a passing reference at Xenophon *Hellenika* 6.5.33.

¹⁰⁰ Sommerstein 1997: 76–77. As Sommerstein suggests, Cimon's ostracism in 461 may have been predicated on the belief that his policy of compromising Athenian autonomy vis-à-vis Spartan would soon render the Athenians subject to their rivals (77).

But when Danaus paraphrases for his daughters Pelasgus' actual address to the citizens (at 615–20), we find, as Sommerstein suggests, that the Argive leader strikes a Cimonian performative attitude in confusing the issues and compromising the citizens' cognitive and deliberative autonomy.

Pelasgus appears to conceal crucial information from them concerning the well-being of Argos – namely, that the Danaids' Egyptian suitors are in pursuit, and in its place he substitutes solely the religious fear of reprisal from Zeus, the Protector of Suppliants, and of pollution from the maidens' possible suicide.[101] In terms of action concepts and rationality criteria, then, Pelasgus resembles Cimon in preventing the citizens from seeing the prospect of alliance with foreigners as a teleological action in all its dimensions, including grave consequences for Argive autonomy. And like Cimon he emphasizes the normative aspects of their request, using an illocutionary speech act to strike a pose of moral superiority in an I-you relation: he "warns" (*prophônôn*, 617) them about what they *ought* to do to avoid divine reprisal. Knowing they are already prone as individuals to hate hybris and feel compassion (486–87), he now focuses his appeals on their individual capacity for the fear experienced in *aidôs* (shame/respect). And so, like Cimon, he "was persuasive by delivering this sort of speech" (*toiande epeithe rhêsin . . . legôn*, 615); and, like Cimon, that speech relied on rhetorical manipulation. As Danaus puts it, "And the Pelasgian *dêmos* heeded the orator's highly persuasive moves" (*eupeithês strophês*, 623–24).[102]

---

[101] Friis Johansen and Whittle 1980, vol. 2 believe mention of "pollution [*miasma*] before the city" must refer to the maidens' suicide threat at the border sanctuary. They claim, "The King does not repeat the awful threat of [line] 465 before the assembly in so many words . . ." but that "pollution before the city" indicates this is definitely "what he has in mind" (508).

[102] It's possible that Pelasgus did inform the Argives of the Egyptian military threat, and that Danaus withheld this information from his daughters and the spectators.

These "moves" mark the traces of a virtuoso's performance before an appreciative audience that acknowledges his talents.[103] As a description of the rhetor's art, they describe a performative autonomy and skill that reflect an expert's superior cognitive abilities before listeners of ordinary intelligence. So despite his earlier disclaimer, "I'm at a terrible loss over this dispute! I wish I were a know-nothing [*aidris*] instead of an expert [*sophos*] about these miseries! If only, contrary to how I understand it now [*para gnômên emên*], this would turn out well!" (452–54), Pelasgus does accept his role as a *sophos*, exercise *gnômê*, and lead the *dêmos* through deliberation to a decision. Only the "moves" of his performative autonomy, despite democratically correct intentions, *do* limit the citizens' collective autonomy, bringing them to a unanimous vote that, as a communicative action, fails to grasp all action concepts and rationality criteria vital to their welfare. As a result they unwittingly introduce war, foreign tyranny, and female violence into the marriage beds of the new tyrant's family.

Must every demagogue's individual autonomy contaminate to one degree or another the citizens' expression of collective autonomy in an ideal communicative action? Pelasgus seems to have intuited as much in feeling cognitively inadequate before the *dêmos*. This new self is a collective, third-person, objective observer, largely plural, but fickle in criticizing leaders and yielding to its individual need to feel compassion for the less fortunate. When Finley declares the demagogue a "structural element" in the democracy, he gestures to a cruel necessity motivating the leader to speak. Whether we think of Themistocles,

---

By having Danaus focalize the speech for us, its contents are filtered through two demagogic selves, one (Pelasgus) driven by deliberative elements, the other (Danaus) voluntarist.

[103] *Strôphês* connotes the "turns" of a horseman or charioteer (Friis Johansen and Whittle 1980, vol. 2: 510) but also a wrestler's twists and turns, a musician's melodic movements, or a dancer's (Liddell, Scott, and Jones 1940).

Cimon, Ephialtes, Pericles, or their later counterparts, each *risks* his individual autonomy as a citizen whenever he comes forward to facilitate the deliberations through which the citizens realize collective autonomy. And this is because his expert *gnômê* and advice cannot possibly embrace all perspectives and all outcomes that a plural self like the *dêmos* might foresee in articulating a communicative action – or that might eventually transform the demagogue's fate when that action has run its course. Themistocles and Cimon lost their individual citizen autonomy through ostracisms in around 472 and 461, respectively; Ephialtes lost his life to a political assassin in 462; Pelasgus lost his life defending Argos against foreign invasion. The other leader in *Suppliants*, Danaus, profits most from Pelasgus' risk through his transformation into tyrant of Argos, which in democracy is the ultimate expression of how one individual's autonomy can devour the autonomy of all. At the same time, however, when the demagogue risks his own individuality he puts the *dêmos* at risk collectively by launching rhetorical appeals to each individual citizen's emotional needs.

Ephebe and Citizen in Love: Performing Justice and Tyrannicide
And so I do not believe Aeschylus expected his spectators to pair the mythological and historical leaders evoked in this play with one another in an exclusive, one-to-one identification. Pelasgus is not necessarily Ephialtes or Cimon, nor is Danaus, though both heroic figures model aspects of demagogy that invite spectators to reflect on scripts of political confrontation witnessed in recent memory and feared in the near future. Through performance Aeschylus manages to split demagogy into multiple selves, all somehow relevant to the education of ephebes – who, I suggested, might constitute the cognitive subject of tragedy. Zeitlin captures this neatly when she identifies Pelasgus and Danaus as alternative "figures of masculine authority to the Danaids" who are each open to judgment; and she delineates

contrasting cognitive profiles of each leader (1996: 143–44). Whereas Pelasgus lacks confidence in his political intelligence (*gnômê*), Danaus is "shrewd, practical, confident, and decisive," with an "instrumental" intelligence (*phronêsis*) that is "oriented toward *technê* (skill) and *mêchanê* (devising)" (143). Each leader also prefers a distinctly different cognitive habitat: Danaus is a superlative navigator and sea captain, whereas Pelasgus, born of an autochthonous ancestor, expresses cognitive distress through metaphors of impending shipwreck: "I've truly reflected on this, and see how I've run aground!" (438), and "I've embarked on this sea of disaster, bottomless, impassable, nowhere any haven from miseries!" (471–72).[104]

Such a splitting of demagogy's cognitive profiles and elements must have resonated strongly for Athenian spectators in the late 460s, demonstrating how citizenship required degrees of self-fashioning and self-transformation for both ephebes and leaders. As we've seen, each type of self could combine voluntarist, cognitive, and deliberative elements with varying success as it negotiated its identity with the dominant social other. For the ephebe that negotiation began at the *dokimasia*, for the demagogue every time the Assembly convened. The trilogy's final play, *Danaïdes*, no doubt drove this point home more forcefully than *Suppliants* alone, for it dramatized the reversal of Danaus' apparent triumph as a tyrannical, voluntarist self and the final transformation of the Danaids from ephebic outlaws into proper citizen wives. The catalyst for this reversal and transformation was that performance of

---

[104] Zeitlin cites the shipwreck metaphor at 438–42 but not 471–72; she also cites Pelasgus' maritime metaphor at 407–10 of the "clear-sighted diver" whose "steady eye unclouded by wine" must "see sharply" if he is to obtain "deep understanding bringing salvation" for Argos and himself (1996: 144). We can assimilate both leadership profiles to Rohweder's reading (1998) if we see them representing a spectrum of elite leaders in the decades between the democracy's origins (508–507) and the late 460s.

justice in which the *dêmos* acted collectively as a deliberative self: the jury trial.

Danaus' charges against Hypermestra – disobedience, endangering his life, and intensifying culpability for the murdered Egyptian husbands – try to perpetuate the traditional privileges of the *basileus* and father in his most virulent form, the tyrant.[105] Through a gesture of refusal Hypermestra claims autonomy from the dominant social other's attempts to dictate to the self its ends in advance: she tries, like our contemporary deliberative self, to control her own life history by distancing herself from traditions and prevailing belief. But apparently she alone can't engage in an "intersubjective fabric of reason giving" that makes her accountable for her decision. She can only achieve this if she passes through a form of scrutiny which, like an ephebe's *dokimasia* or a demagogue's interaction with the Assembly, confirms or denies her attempt at self-definition and transformation. Through what must have been divine intervention, Hypermestra will have the Argive *dêmos* determine her *timê* in a jury trial.

In *Suppliants* she and her sisters once brazenly cried, "Though still alive I use my cries of lamentation to determine my own *timê*" (*zôsa goois me timô*) (112–16). Now the scholarly hypothesis of a climactic jury trial in *Danaïdes* encourages us to see this script as civic therapy for her paradoxical hyper-autonomy and enslavement to Danaus' tyrannical will. All we know of this trial are seven lines from the argument of Aphrodite, pleading on Hypermestra's behalf. But it's clear that

---

[105] These are the charges reported by Pausanias in his account of the trial (2.19.6). Unlike Sommerstein (1995: 123), I believe they do constitute crimes that are sufficiently serious to warrant Hypermestra's arrest and trial, not unlike Creon's accusations against Antigone and her motivation for disobeying his tyrannical edict. But Sommerstein's reconstruction of Lynceus' possible role in the final play helps us see how he and Hypermestra together constitute the moral agent restoring political and moral order. Föllinger's reading of the play sees this conflict of interests between generations – and the "conflict of decision making" it provokes – as the play's central concern (2003 : 226–34, esp. 227).

this plea was anchored in the universally legitimate power of love (*erôs*) and the sexual union (*gamos*) of male and female, from which all fertility flows – "and for these things," Aphrodite concluded, "am I responsible" (*paraitios*, fr. 7, Diggle 1998). When acquitted, Hypermestra emerges from the citizens' judgment as a self cleansed of submission to her tyrannical father and of association with her violent sisters. The Argives recognize in her a moral and deliberative agent who refuses ends Danaus gave her in advance and who exercises her will in allying herself with a husband.

And what of Danaus and the other forty-nine Danaids? If an oracle did foretell Danaus' death at the hands of a son-in-law, then Lynceus, acting with and on behalf of Hypermestra, likely took revenge for his brothers and struck the tyrant down.[106] In marriage he and Hypermestra join forces – she a reformed foreigner and female, once an "ephebe," then a "metic," and now a wife, he a newly minted citizen husband. Are they together a pair of tyrannicides restoring Argos to its formerly democratic regime? And if *Danaïdes* concluded with this erotic union between ephebe and mature citizen, would the play's implied audience in the theater have recognized in them the "founding myth" of Athenian democracy: the "just love" (*dikaios eros*) that joined Harmodius and Aristogeiton and motivated them in 514 to kill the tyrant Hipparchus?[107] The other forty-nine Danaids may have

---

[106] See Sommerstein 1995: 125. Since Sommerstein rejects the hypothesis of a trial for Hypermestra, he sees Aphrodite's speech as a divine exoneration of the forty-nine Danaids: they should be excused for murdering their husbands because their father perverted their minds against the cosmic principle of sexual union. On the likelihood that Lynceus murdered Danaus, see C. Turner 2001: 28–29, n. 9.

[107] Monoson 2000, Ludwig 2002, and Wohl 2002 point to this erotic bond as a peculiarly Athenian paradigm linking the individual citizen to the citizen body in the age of Pericles (460–ca. 429) and after. Wohl in particular discusses the tyrannicides' relation as a "just love," borrowing the phrase from Aeschines 1.136 (2002: 3–10 and 20–29). C. Turner also suggests identifying Lynceus and Hypermestra with Harmodius and Aristogeiton (2001: 47). Cf. Rohweder's argument that the

been purified of their crime and remarried to Argives or other Greeks, although one tradition sees them eternally punished in Hades.[108] Reconciliation with Argos through marriage does, however, seem more likely on thematic and dramatic grounds, especially since Herodotus reports that these maidens brought Demeter's panhellenic ritual of female citizen fertility, the Thesmophoria, from Egypt, teaching it to the original inhabitants of the Peloponnesus, the "Pelasgians" (2.171).[109]

If *Suppliants* seems dominated by scripts concerning the passage from noncitizen to citizen status, and alliance formation between citizens and noncitizens and the *dêmos* and its leaders, then it's hard to resist seeing the trilogy conclude with an end to *stasis* through marriage, tyrannicide and a general reconciliation between self and other that ensures collective well-being. But this need not mean that Aeschylus enfolds these solutions within the "recuperative, reassimilating power of an ideological frame" (Goldhill 2000: 47). I think he has tried to expose the illusion that an individual or a community can enjoy autonomy as a harmonious relation between homogenous, component parts of oneself. By evoking female memories and laments about men's violent hybris, by exposing ways demagogues and women use deceitful *mêtis* to provoke shame, respect, compassion, and fear in the stoutest hearts of democratic citizens, he rouses in both citizens and foreigners the

asymmetrical marriage bond between husband and wife serves in the play as a "model" for the political relationship in Athens between elite and common citizens (1998: 180–86).

[108] Apollodorus relates that Hermes and Athena purified them at Zeus' command; they then married new husbands who won their hands as victors in a foot-race (2.1.5). On their punishment in Hades – to carry water in a sieve – see Garvie 1969: 234–35.

[109] D. S. Robertson (1924) first suggested this link between Herodotus and the trilogy's ending. It appeals to many scholars, not the least because it parallels the cult established for the Furies in Athens at the end of *Eumenides*; see, e.g., Zeitlin 1996: 164–69, and Conacher 1996: 107. Föllinger, however, rejects it (2003: 190).

specter of the ephebe as a portal to a dangerous memory: that a pre- and noncitizen other resides within the self. He also refracts the citizenship of Athenian spectators into component parts whose instability underscores the necessity and pitfalls of alliance formation between emotions that bind in the interest of individual well-being and deliberations that ensure the interest of collective well-being.

6 THE NATURALIZATION OF CITIZEN AND SELF IN DEMOCRATIC ATHENS, 450–411

⊙▣⊙

IN OUR DISCUSSION OF AESCHYLUS' *SUPPLIANTS* WE'VE SEEN THAT tragedy invites its spectators to deliberate as both citizens and as non-civic members of a wider, more hypothetical community, the human race. We've seen too that the trilogy prompts spectators to reason differently as members of each community. Citizen deliberation favors a reason giving that uses shared teleological and normative criteria to determine collective self-interest, often by separating the citizen self from others. Reasoning as a human being, however, relies more on an individual's ability to evaluate subjective (or "dramaturgical") criteria by withdrawing into the self, making cognitive use of such powerful emotions as compassion, shame/respect, and fear, and temporarily identifying with others. And in an age when popular sovereignty was beginning to flex its ideological muscle (470s–60s), the Danaid trilogy seems to suggest that a community's well-being may depend on how wisely citizens, guided by their leaders, oscillate between these two deliberative experiences. Apparently, in the age of popular sovereignty some Athenians like Aeschylus sensed that, when citizens experience emotions individually and use them to reason about public affairs, they may be blinded to what lies in the city-state's interest.

In Chapter 4 I noted a similar anxiety about how citizens make decisions during the script of the jury trial. In the 420s, with faith in popular sovereignty waning but still intact, a speechwriter like Antiphon in *On the Murder of Herodes* entrusted jurors to identify with a foreigner by keeping their compassion (and its component of fear) well under control, calibrating it according to a customary civic formula: show positive reciprocity (compassion, forgiveness) toward moral agents whose misfortune is due to unintentional or accidental actions, and show negative reciprocity (anger, aggression) toward those whose intentional acts cause suffering. I noted that from 403 to the 320s, however, the ideology of the sovereignty of law prompted forensic orators to temper individual jurors' decision making; orators now encouraged jurors to decide justice within a performance tradition based on imitating a legendary lawgiver's cognitive talents. This chapter returns us to the heyday of the democracy's commitment to popular sovereignty and to the anxiety that an individual citizen's idiosyncratic experience of moral agency (including both reason and emotion) could arouse. It examines a citizenship paradigm engineered in the 450s–420s by the sophist Protagoras and the political leader Pericles, one designed to inoculate each Athenian's performance of citizenship from susceptibility to the voluntarist dimensions of the inner life. But we'll contrast this model of the citizen to another paradigm that emerged in response to it in around 430–411, engineered by another sophist and reluctant political leader, Antiphon the speechwriter, and designed to insulate a citizen's inner life from the unwise decision making characteristic of citizen scripts and norms.

CITIZEN AND SELF ACCORDING TO PROTAGORAS AND PERICLES

After Cleisthenes brokered the democracy's emergence in 508–507, the Athenians probably began using the umbrella term *nomos* for statute law and the decrees of the Assembly. This replaced the term *thesmos*, which referred to statutes created by lawgivers such as Solon and Draco. In so doing they lent a stricter, political sense to *nomos*, extending its general sense of social custom to designate the innovative deliberative procedures and outcomes of the new regime (Ostwald 1969: 158–60). In the Periclean age (460–427) the prestige of *nomos* in this narrower sense soared, for it designated the preferred form of reasoning together in institutional settings like the citizen Assembly and the Council of 500 in addition to the law courts.

Here we can credit the sophist Protagoras, who probably resided in Athens on and off from the 450s to about 421, with conferring intellectual legitimacy on *nomos* and the ideology of popular sovereignty. He believed that reasoning together produces optimal advantages for a society when its inhabitants enjoy an autonomous, well-ordered use of practical reason grounded in the realities of day-to-day experience. Only in this way, he thought, would the Athenians fulfill their highest potential as individuals, citizens, and human beings.[1] It's ironic that Protagoras reportedly answered Pericles' call to serve as lawgiver for the colony Athens organized at Thurii in southern Italy (444–443), but his teachings nevertheless provided an ideological cornerstone for the democracy's political ideal of collective lawmaking. His own career therefore embraced both the historically older sense of statute law as an individual's virtuoso display of judicial wisdom – a *thesmos* like those of the canonical lawgivers – and the new democratic sense of a cooperative creation by citizens, an act of *nomos*.

We can identify Protagoras – together with Pericles – as the architect of a new kind of citizen self, one defined by the sort of "nomological knowledge" that was described in Chapter 5. Meier understands this Weberian term as a generalized, normative knowledge permitting Athenian citizens to order their thoughts, actions, and experiences according to shared notions of what was true or false, and just or unjust, within political and also religious and cosmic contexts (1991: 47–49). And, Meier adds, this knowledge was not simply a collective expression but was individually experienced by each citizen (48–49). But how

---

[1] On Protagoras' visits to Athens, see Kerferd 1981: 42–43, with sources. For the connection between his teachings and the ideology of popular sovereignty, see Farrar 1988: 44ff., esp. 91–98.

compatible was this new nomological citizen self with an individual's capacity for enacting personhood through the reflection and interpretation that Taylor says characterizes us as subjects of significance? To what degree could this nomological self receive the modern individual's need for recognition from the dominant social other? Because little survives of Protagoras' words and teachings, these questions are not easy to answer. But we can argue that he opened the individual citizen to a novel cognitive and moral autonomy through his epistemological dismissal of the gods and divine knowledge[2] and through his famous maxim, "An individual human being [*anthrôpos*] is the measuring stick of all things – of the things that exist, that they exist, and of the things that don't exist, that they do not" (DK 80 B 2). Most importantly, he held that it was an individual's personal experience that held the key to his or her capacity for knowledge. As Farrar puts it, "All the scraps of Protagorean theory that remain to us suggest that the Sophist opposed theories or approaches to understanding not grounded in personal experience."[3]

And we can even extrapolate from such a grounding of knowledge in personal perception and reasoning to claim with Mansfeld that Protagoras' *anthrôpos* or individual human subject is equivalent to our modern sense of a "person," a being with a single identity persisting over time, distinguishing him or her from all others, and presenting options he or she confronts with an intelligence conditioned by a personal

[2] Fr. 80 B 4: "As for the gods, I cannot know whether they exist or not, or what sorts of form they take, for there are many obstacles to such knowledge, among them its lack of clarity and the shortness of human life."

[3] 1988: 50. Cf. the fragment culled from a papyrus containing works by Didymus the Blind: "To you who are present, I appear to be sitting; to someone not present I don't appear to be sitting: it is unclear whether I am sitting or not sitting." See Mansfeld's discussion, where he understands the fragment's concern to be "the cognitive status of an experienced state of affairs: 'I am sitting'" and what this tells us about "personal knowledge – at a moment of time *t* . . ." (1981: 51–52); Farrar's interpretation concurs (1988: 52–53).

history (1981: 45–46). But does this sort of individual person encounter limits to his or her cognitive and moral autonomy? Farrar's extended discussion of the Protagorean subject makes it clear that the *anthrôpos* in question in the "man-measure" doctrine is "man *qua* citizen, not man *qua* man," and that he functions as "the measure" only "through intersubjective interactions with others and with experience in a changing world" (1988: 98). But since the citizen experiences his autonomy and cognitive independence through primarily political interactions (94), Farrar's qualification indicates to me that the Protagorean person's "genuine autonomy and freedom" (95) is not entire because it is necessarily tempered by *nomos*. In Mead's terms, because this *anthrôpos* consists primarily of "me" roles provided by the community's dominant social other it's difficult to see where the *anthrôpos* might enact the agency of the "I" that evaluates such roles in light of self-interest – and so at times resist convention. In Taylor's sense the Protagorean person doesn't seem to be a subject of significance seeking recognition for its idiosyncratic qualities, feelings, and choices.

PERICLES AND THE SHADOW CITIZEN

As the ideology of popular sovereignty came under increasing attack in the 430s, it had to account for differences in the way the citizenry and the individual citizen experienced and understood the changes worked by the democracy on the Athenian lifeworld.[4] Within the age of popular sovereignty there is no more influential document

---

[4] Already in 441 Sophocles in *Antigone* could critique an individual's radical use of *nomos* in the political sense with open appeals to the superiority of religious custom (*nomima*). In 438 Pericles and his colleague Pheidias were charged with embezzling funds, with Pheidias imprisoned or exiled; soon after, Pericles' mentor Anaxagoras and his companion Aspasia were charged and tried for impiety (Plutarch *Pericles* 31.2–32.6). For discussion of the historical accuracy of these charges and trials, see Stadter 1989: 284–304; for their political context, see Ostwald 1986: 148–61 and 191–98.

on the differences between collective and individual experiences of both citizenship and selfhood than Thucydides' version of Pericles' Funeral Oration in 430 (2.35–46). Let's briefly turn to it to determine whether at this stage of the democracy Athens' nomological knowledge could extend recognition to Athenians not only as citizens but as persons who are subjects of significance. There's little question that the speech itself is structured around the antithesis between Athenian public life and its citizens' willingness to order their individual lives in ways that assured their participation in that public life. As Ober characterizes the speech, it "addresses the issue of the inverse relationship between acting in narrowly individual self-interest and polis greatness" (1998: 84).[5] But it remains to be seen how both the Thucydidean Pericles and recent commentators understand the nature of the individuality that a citizen expresses through self-interest, and whether that individuality refers to the idiosyncratic moral choices characteristic of the modern person.

Early in the speech, Pericles programs its goals when he claims that, before praising the war dead, he will first describe "from what sort of adherence to customary practices [epitêdeusis] we have arrived at our recent great achievements [i.e., acquisition of the empire, defeat of the Persians], and what sort of political organization for our city-state [politeia] and ways of life [tropoi] accompanied this" (2.36.4). While the reference to politeia clearly alludes to the rich civic life open to

---

[5] Hornblower suggests that we should not insist on this "distinction between Athenian life in its public and private aspects" because the two were not so separate for Thucydides (1991: 296), but Yunis is perhaps more accurate in pointing out that the speech is focused on a perennial political question in the ancient world: "the nature of the obligation owed by individual citizens to the community as a whole, particularly in an exemplary polis" (1996: 79–80). For McGlew, the speech "dramatizes a radical division and ranking of private interests and public responsibilities, duties, and rewards" (2002: 27).

the citizens as a whole, it is less clear whether the terms *epitêdeusis* and *tropoi* refer to social roles prescribed for citizens irregardless of personal preferences – what Mead calls "me" roles – or to activities that reflect individual moral choices – where Mead sees the agency of the "I" evaluating choices in light of self-interest. We might compare this "map" of citizen activity to another, occurring a few moments later, where Pericles famously outlines three life-long pursuits typical of Athenians:

> *For we love beauty* [philokaloumen] *within reasonable means, and we love wisdom* [philosophoumen] *without going soft, and we make use of wealth* [ploutos] *more for seizing opportunity than as a boastful topic of conversation. And being poor is not associated with anyone's shame – though not acting to escape it is rather shameful. The same citizens have concern for their private affairs and for affairs of state* [ta politika], *and others who are concerned with their occupations still have adequate judgment in affairs of state. (2.40)*

Rusten demonstrates how neatly the triptych of citizen activities in these lines corresponds to a familiar topos in ancient thought, the three alternative kinds of life (*bioi*): one devoted to the pursuits of philosophy or "higher education" (love of what is *kalos* and of *sophia*); another to politics (concern for *ta politika*); and the third to wealth (concern for *ploutos* and an energetic avoidance of poverty). Rusten then links these three with the earlier references at 2.36 to *epitêdeusis* ("adherence to customary practices"), *politeia* ("political organization of our city-state") and *tropoi* ("ways of life"). The first two of these, he claims, concern the citizenry as a whole, while *tropoi* characterize the preferences of individual citizens (1985: 17).

Each of the three *bioi* Pericles adumbrates at 2.36 and 2.40 requires some degree of moral choice on the part of the citizen who pursues them, and Pericles arrays them in what appears to be a taxonomy without hierarchy. Rusten is generally correct to distinguish the socially sanctioned activities of philosophy, politics, and economic gain (or survival) from citizens' more individualistic and nebulous "ways of life." Devotion to learning, politics, and accumulation of wealth all embed citizens in "me" roles constituting socially determined (and approved) paths. We might call each a "vocation," but I prefer MacIntyre's term, "practice," which is "any coherent and complex form of socially established cooperative human activity" that enables an individual to achieve "goods internal to that form of activity" as he or she pursues its "standards of excellence" (1984: 187). MacIntyre certainly sees selecting a practice and applying oneself to it as a moral choice an individual makes, and one that confers a sense of identity; but this can only be achieved by "subject[ing] my own attitudes, choices, preferences and tastes to the standards which currently and partially define the practice" (190). A practice is therefore predominantly a "me" role, although an individual's "I" may scrutinize his or her commitment to it before choosing. Just the same, a practice does not fundamentally provide an individual with choices and standards that are likely to deviate from *nomos* in both the broad sense of social custom and the narrow sense of what is politically sanctioned.

By including *tropoi* among possible citizen pursuits, Pericles gestures to a moral arena where an individual's choices may not concur with prevailing social or political norms. We've seen that such choices often originate in the self's voluntarist elements of appetite, desire, and love. But Pericles'confidence in the transformative power of *nomos* usually leads him to leave in shadow most of these possible choices. He prefers to see *nomos* as a remedy for socially disruptive individual behavior or behavior providing a citizen unfair advantage over the less fortunate or miring him in poverty. That is, he believes Athenian state culture and law will successfully enable each citizen to negotiate the translation of voluntarist senses of the good into cognitive senses of who and what one ought to be. And so while conceding that Athenians are divided into the favored few and the not so fortunate many, he is sure the law will impose equal status on those engaged in "private disputes"; provide social recognition solely on the basis of individual merit, not class or faction (*apo merous*), to any citizen who enjoys a fine reputation;[6] and enable even a citizen of low status to make a valuable political contribution (2.37). When he again considers the idiosyncratic behavior enabling a citizen to articulate the self's voluntarist elements, he finds that freedom (*eleutheria*) and tolerance defuse its socially disruptive potential, for "Not only do we conduct state business freely, but we also act freely toward one another when it comes to suspicion over daily habits [*epitêdeumata*]. And we don't get angry at our neighbor if he does something just for his own pleasure [*hêdonên*], nor do we wear annoyed expressions which, though not harmful, are not pleasant to see" (2.37).[7]

---

[6] I follow Pope (and others) in understanding this troublesome expression to refer to groups within the citizen body from which an individual may emerge to enjoy prestige (Pope 1988: 292). This is a less politically specialized sense of the expression than "due to rotation in office-holding," and it logically develops the distinction Pericles has just drawn between the tendentious relationship in a democracy between "the few" and "the many." (Cf. Ober's interpretation of the ambiguity behind Pericles' mention of the divide between these two groups [1998: 86–87]).

[7] My distinction between *epitêdeusis* ("adherence to social custom") and *epitêdeumata* ("daily habits") tries to capture a degree of moral choice in the more abstract first term as opposed to the rather automatic behavior connoted by the second. (On this distinction, see Hornblower 1991: 298). Loraux elicits the connotation in *epitêdeusis* at 2.36.4 of a "*force* that animates behavior" and of an activity's "*exercise*" (1986: 407–408, n. 11; emphasis in the original), whereas I'm calling attention to the moral quality of that force and exercise. Cf. Thucydides' use of *epitêdeusis* to indicate moral choice when he uses it at 7.86 in his eulogy of Nicias, claiming that he of all Greeks least deserved execution by the Syracusans "on account of the complete commitment [*epitêdeusin*] he regulated [*nenomismenen*] according to virtue [*aretên*]." But here too this is not a moral commitment idiosyncratic to Nicias but a practice in MacIntyre's sense and a "me" role in Mead's: the pursuit of excellence in public service as a political leader (*rhêtor*) and military commander (*strategos*). Westlake translates *epitêdeusis* here as embracing "the basic beliefs on which a man's way of life [*epitêdeumata* . . .] was

In this fleeting reference to self-interested pleasure (*hêdonê*), Pericles allows us to glimpse the nature of an individual's truly subjective choices outside social custom, the law, or a practice (in MacIntyre's sense). The private pursuit of pleasure, it seems, possesses neither "internal goods" nor "standards of excellence" in Pericles' version of the Athenian cultural tradition. He sanctions the personal experience of delight (*terpsis*) on a daily basis only within the scope of a citizen's *tropos* (his way of life or "lifestyle" in our contemporary sense) when exercising taste in his private surroundings – but this plays second fiddle to the more proper, regulated delight citizens experience publicly through a state calendar of festival games and sacrificial meals (2.38). When Thucydides describes the plague right after he recreates the Funeral Oration, he paints in darkest colors this self-interested pursuit of pleasure outside *nomos*, for certain individuals (*tis*) contributed to "a greater lawlessness [*anomia*] in the city-state" by publicly sporting a personal pleasure-seeking (*kath'êdonên*) and delight (*to terpnon*) centered around the body and worldly goods (2.53.1–3).[8]

This helps to explain why, when Pericles outlines the three practices of higher education, politics, and economic gain (or survival), he indicts the citizen who chooses not to combine politics with either of the other two, not just as a man who opts for solitude or keeps to himself (*apragmona*), but as someone "useless" (*akhreion*) to his fellow

---

founded" (1968: 209). Note how Nicias' pursuit of *aretê*, unlike Alcibiades', is literally tempered by *nomos* (*nenomismenen*).

[8] Thucydides returns to the theme of the citizens' private vs. public pursuit of pleasure when he evaluates Pericles' leadership at 2.65: citizens publicly supported Periclean policies early in the war but privately mourned such deprivations as loss of luxurious estates and furnishings (2.65.2); they later failed to stay the Periclean course because they sought personal ambitions and advantages (*kata tas idias philotimias kai idia kerdê*, 2.65.7). One key to Pericles' success was his refusal to say anything in order to please the citizens (*pros hêdonên ti legein*, 2.65.8), while his demagogic successors entrusted public affairs to the pleasures of the demos (*kath'êdonas*, 2.65.10).

citizens (2.40). This sort of man, bereft of the meaningful relationships into which a practice would insert him, is indeed hardly a
citizen: the term "shadow citizen" might suit him best. Such a do-
nothing refuses to find suitable "me" roles for the self's voluntarist
dictates; cognitive elements of its self refuse to own up to them; and
deliberative elements avoid the sort of interactions that forge collective senses of the good. What results is a citizen and self practicing a
"useless" moral autonomy that will not risk putting its understanding of "what I want" and "what kind of person I wish to be" to the
test in the arena of *nomos*. As this first part of the speech reaches its
crescendo, Pericles implicitly opposes such a man's useless autonomy
to the autonomy an individual citizen enjoys *on account of* his relationships to others rather than in spite of them: "To sum up then, I say
that as a whole our city-state offers a lesson for Greece, and in my opinion each individual among us could show himself personally [*to sôma*]
self-sufficient [*autarkes*] in a great many ways, and with versatility and
charm" (2.41).

In acknowledging but denigrating the individual citizen's "I," the
speech certainly withholds recognition in Taylor's and Habermas'
senses from individuals whose moral evaluations and pursuits project
them outside *nomos*. In effect Pericles denies recognition to any citizen who leans toward the shadow side of citizenship because such a
citizen cannot function as a deliberative self in both its ancient and contemporary contexts. Immediately after dismissing the unattached citizen as "useless," Pericles elaborates on his positive counterpart, the
collective body of Athenians: even though within this body an individual citizen's choice of a practice or way of life may leave him unpre-
pared for "straightforward reflection" (*enthymoumetha orthôs*) on policy
formation, he and his kind nevertheless prove their worth because
they do know how to make final decisions (*krinomen*) about policy

(2.40.2).[9] Through this commitment to deliberation in the pursuit of a "democratic knowledge," any Athenian can display a minimal practice and minimal "me" role for participation in the city-state.[10] That is why Thucydides recognizes individual self-worth only when the individual in question acts in concert with others as a corporate entity, a collectivity, and in the interests of all. Otherwise he characterizes forms of acting in a self-interest that does not coincide with others as, in Ober's words, the "pathological extreme" of "hyperindividualism."[11]

From this perspective we can reevaluate Pericles' famous injunction to the citizens that "you must every day gaze upon our city-state's power and become its lovers, and whenever it seems to you great, you must reflect that it was bold men, knowing what needed to be done and feeling responsibility for their actions, who accomplished this" (2.43.1).

---

[9] See Hornblower's discussion of translating this phrase (1991: 305–6, with sources). According to McGlew, an implicit premise of Pericles' rhetoric in this speech is that "the first and greatest duty of democratic citizens is to perform an ongoing autopsy on their own lives and pleasures" (2002: 43–4) – an autopsy that will reveal "the impossibility of an independent private life" resulting in virtue (aretê) (40).

[10] Cf. Ober's discussion of "democratic knowledge" in connection with this passage (1998: 88) and Pope's more general discussion of the way Thucydides attributes the authority of all city-states, democratic and oligarchic, to citizens in their capacity as deliberative agents (1988: 279–81).

[11] These terms are Ober's (1998: 68–69). Pope observes that "for Thucydides decision-making takes place among equals" and is usually preceded by " 'deliberation' or 'putting heads together'. . . ." For this reason in Thucydides "no individual non-Greek, king or satrap, ever makes a decision" (1988: 281). Scholars sometimes observe that the History's first half (up to 5.24) shows little interest in individuals' "personal feelings or aspirations" (Westlake 1968: 308; cf. Cogan 1981: 241), whereas its second half, where public deliberation fades, highlights individuals and their personalities through private conversation and consultation (Westlake 1968: 311–18; cf. Cogan 1981: 242). Later in this chapter I will argue that – with the important exception of Alcibiades – this is not the case for our contemporary sense of moral individualism.

In an age where gender studies have transformed the way we look at the world, present and past, much attention has been paid to Pericles' striking image urging citizens to perform citizenship by enacting an erotic script, "playing the elite game of love." In this game an active lover pursues a younger, passive loved one, selflessly sacrificing his all through gifts and ardor to win a reciprocal sign of affection from his blooming love object. Scholars have traced this image's genealogy to the love bond between Harmodius and Aristogeiton, which in 514 transformed their private passion into a public gesture of freedom from tyranny for all Athenians – and in the process cost them their lives.[12] But it's worth pointing out that there is *nothing erotic* about the advice Pericles gives his listeners here: his plea in effect is for them to set aside any personal erotic relationships and to "overcode" these libidinal longings with patriotic fervor.

The desire Pericles tries to arouse here does not partake of the same sort of pleasure (*hêdonê, terpsis*) evoked earlier in the speech to characterize a citizen whose "I" chooses to pursue self-interests inconsistent with *nomos*. Ludwig clarifies well the kind of substitution of affection and zeal Pericles has in mind: citizens are urged to climb a Socratic ladder of love by abandoning a debased love for whatever is "one's own" and by ascending toward more noble (and bloodless) objects such as civic honor and beauty (2002: 320ff.). If they seek these superior ends or goods, Pericles advises, they will first use *philotimia*, a love of honor, to risk their very lives for their lover, the state – and the state will reciprocally recognize such "other-directed" generosity with rewards like those the Funeral Oration metes out to the fallen warriors that day. As Ludwig indicates (328), Pericles promises that this pursuit of *timê* (*to philotimon*) will yield an end or good (being honored, *to timasthai*) they

---

[12] I'm thinking of recent discussions by Wohl 2002: 31–72, Ludwig 2002: 140–69, and Monoson 2000: 64–89.McGlew reads the image somewhat differently (2002: 41–2).

will in time find more lasting and pleasurable (*mallon terpei* . . .) than mere material acquisition (*to kerdainein*, 2.44.4).

In offering this erotic image and promise to citizens, over what is Pericles negotiating? Over citizen lives, to be sure, for he wants them to sacrifice themselves for the state; but he's bargaining for another part of them that is equally precious. As discussed in Chapters 1 and 3 Achilles and Odysseus demonstrate how powerfully the language of erotic preference in the Greek poetic tradition could channel the preferences of a citizen's "I" into hypothetical senses of self. And from these interior deliberations new kinds of self and social orders could develop. Pericles' clarion call in 430 for a citizen lover tries to forestall anything like Achilles' attempt in *Iliad* 9 to stake his autonomy on preference for a sexual partner – or similar expressions by an Archilochus or Sappho. Instead his call insists that each Athenian bring eros out of the shadows so it might help him better play the "me" role of a patriot.

As a result the citizen subject in this speech (and elsewhere in Thucydides) appears to be not a corporeal individual but an intersubjective creature who is plural and decorporealized. Public discourse and deliberation, the building blocks of *nomos*, sustain this collective entity. The payoff for entering this transaction with Pericles is grand: by ditching private interest – the still relatively unexplored realm of *physis* – for the public good, an individual citizen ultimately gains access to a vision of beauty. Whether in life or death he can anticipate merging himself with the spectacle of that beauty and its power (*dynamis*, 41.2, 43.1). This may of course, as Ludwig suggests, refer to the physical spectacle of Athenian monuments, but its more accurate referent is hallucinatory. It conjures up the imaginary spectacle of the collective freedoms of all Athenians, which culminate in an imperial vision of omnipotence. But, (as will be seen more clearly in Chapter 7) this vision is also narcissistic, for Pericles beckons the individual citizen to gaze upon a vision of the collective self. In Ludwig's words, "He contemplates himself when he contemplates Athens" (2002: 334).

The anxiety of Pericles – and I think of Thucydides – over the extra-social, antipolitical nature of the "I" means that we don't find in the *History* any truly individual subjects or "persons" in our modern moral sense, with the glaring exception of shadow citizens, who audaciously project the private pursuit of self-interest and pleasure into the public glare. I'm thinking especially of Alcibiades. While he will be discussed in Chapter 7, we can at least say here that the *History* contains no modern sense of a "person" who merits Athenian recognition. So when we encounter individual citizens interacting in Thucydides, we should distinguish their subjectivity as an amalgam of other-directed, other-dominated "me" roles, not unlike the self favored by some contemporary communitarians, and rather unlike the self-fashioned, self-interested subject of the modern liberal tradition or the hybrid communitarian-liberal individual of Taylor and Habermas.[13]

Modern Thucydidean scholars largely ignore this distinction when they speak of the "individual" in the *History*; they tend to assume Thucydides' bias for recognizing only the nomologically sanctioned citizen in his "me" roles. In their purview the shadow citizen remains undeserving of tolerance, acceptance, compassion, or recognition as a uniquely constituted, intersubjective subject. From our contemporary

---

[13] In her reading of the Funeral Oration, Wohl plausibly claims that it "constructs a specific citizen subjectivity" through an aristocratic "ideal ego" reflected back to the Athenians (2002: 33). But it isn't clear to me whether this "citizen subject" and its "individual subjectivity" correspond to a moral subject in our modern sense. I doubt whether the speech's Athenian audience in the Ceramicus cemetery would have "arrive[d] as individuals" and left as "the Athenian demos" (37–39), if we understand their individuality according to the concept of a "person" outlined by Taylor (1985a), for in arriving these individuals would already have been dominated by the multiple "me" roles they had to assume.

moral perspective, they join Thucydides in describing individuals who, because they lack any positive agency of the "I," are incomplete selves. Not surprisingly, a recent study of ethics in Thucydides finds that "determining just precisely where individual character leaves off and state character begins is problematic" (M. F. Williams 1998: 3–4). It's also not surprising that this same scholar thinks Adcock's discussion of a citizen's "private" life in Thucydides (as opposed to a citizen's "individual" life) is confusing because the category of the private can less easily be elided into the almost exclusively public nature of Thucydidean man.[14]

PHYSIS: THE NATURE OF THE CITIZEN AND THE SELF

Thucydides does not hesitate to identify the motivation that can turn a genuine citizen into his shadow counterpart: it's what he calls "human nature" (*hê anthrôpeia physis*) or "the capacity to be human" (*to anthrôpinon, to anthrôpeion*).[15] For the most part the historian understands this motivating force to operate within a collective subject, usually a citizen body, since it describes a mass psychology that renders the

---

[14] To resolve this confusion, M. F. Williams advises her reader, "Accordingly, when I speak of individual character, I generally mean public character," and she believes that in Thucydides "presumably the private life of a virtuous individual . . . need not be commented upon because there exists no impending greater threat to the community at large from such an individual . . ." (1998: 10–11). Williams disclaims that she has any "preconceived theories or biases" regarding Thucydides' notion of virtuous behavior, or that she wishes to make "any statement either about what modern conceptions of virtue are or should be, or about modern political practice and its relationship to ethical theory" (12). Most earlier studies contain no such disclaimers, but they likewise duplicate Thucydides' nomological notion of individuality (e.g., Westlake 1968, Pouncey 1980, Cogan 1981).

[15] The term *hê anthrôpeia physis* occurs at 2.50.1 and the similar *hê physis anthrôpôn* at 3.82.2. A variant like *ho anthrôpeios tropos* also occurs (1.76.2), as well as expressions using the verb *pephukenai* at 3.45.3 and, with *to anthrôpeion* as its subject, at 4.61.5. We find *to anthrôpinon* at 1.22.4 and *to anthrôpeion* at 5.68.2 and, with *physis*, at 5.105.2. Cf. 4.108.3.

decisions of deliberators almost predictable.[16] This is not the case, however, with his indictment of the pleasure-seeking individuals during the plague's onslaught, where this shocking development exemplifies his earlier statement at 2.50.1 that the virulence of the disease "afflicted each person [*hekastôi*] too severely for his or her human nature to withstand."[17] At 3.45.3 we find a precise observation about how human nature can reveal itself in both individual (private) and collective (public) manifestations – and how in both cases it seems to defy *nomos*. In advising the Assembly about the crisis in Mytilene in 427, Diodotus remarks, "And it is in everyone's nature, both individually [*idiai*] and collectively [*dêmosiai*], to make mistakes, and there is no law [*nomos*] which will prevent this." Likewise, at 3.82.2, the historian also explicitly claims that human nature prompts individuals (*hoi idiôtai*) and collective citizen bodies (*hai poleis*) to respond alike, given similar circumstances.[18]

---

[16] As collective tendencies influencing deliberation, human nature and the capacity to be human are evident at 1.22.4, 1.76.2, 3.82.2, 4.61.5, 5.68.2, and 5.105.2.

[17] Cf. Ober's (1998: 68) and Farrar's (1988: 136–37) emphases on how human nature in this passage reveals itself in ways particular to individuals. At 1.138.3 Thucydides uses *physis* to describe the innate intelligence and judgment (*sunesis* and *gnômê*) of an extraordinary individual, Themistocles. We'll see that this use of the word to indicate an individual's singular character becomes increasingly common in the fifth century's final decades.

[18] In reading this passage Farrar emphasizes this point and indicates other passages where the historian makes similar observations (1.82.6, 1.124.1, 1.144.3, 2.8.4, 2.64.6, and 4.61.2) (1988: 156, with n. 58); cf. Hornblower's endorsement of this point (1991: 478 and 482). Cogan is, I believe, mistaken to claim on one hand that Thucydides uses *hê anthrôpeia physis* to refer to "intensely personal actions" grounded in human biology or behavior motivated by physical needs and on the other hand that *to anthrôpinon* refers to the collective "social actions" of states interacting with one another (1981: 186–89). Cogan's (like Crane's [1998: 300]) purely biological understanding of Thucydides' use of *physis* strikes me as reductive, and the historian makes it quite clear at 3.82.2 that the *anthrôpeia physis* of citizens like the Corcyreans manifests itself both in individual and in collective, shared ways. Cogan misunderstands Diodotus' claim at 3.45.3 that "everyone" (*hapantes*) makes mistakes both individually and collectively because he mistranslates the word as "all things" (1991: 190). Luginbill too

While Thucydides considers "human nature" and "the capacity to be human" frequently predictable when they induce citizens as individuals and groups to stray from their nomological selves – nowhere more clearly than in the penchant for factional strife in Greek city-states like Corcyra (3.82.2) – the effects of human nature are not constant but variable. For human nature describes a "psychological structure" dominated by the tension between reasoned judgment (*gnômê*) and powerful emotions (*orgê*): a terrain inviting both individuals and citizen bodies to engage primarily in moral reflection and deliberation. Farrar observes, "Human nature for Thucydides is not a fixed set of characteristics, neither basic, instinctual drives nor what man is at his best, but rather a psychological structure which underlies man's experience of the constant interaction of reason and desire. This interaction tends to be affected in regular ways by events" (1988: 135).[19] By understanding the concept in this way, we can regard the *History* as a stage on which Thucydides translates the epistemological dilemmas resolved by Protagoras' man-measure doctrine into moral ones. Both thinkers, however, insist that citizens only confront these epistemological and moral dilemmas through types of human agency, whether individual or collective, appropriate to scripts sanctioned by *nomos*.

Of the citizen scripts considered in this study, including the pre-citizen funerary ritual, epic deliberation and seeking/rendering a *dikê*,

---

insists on the fundamentally biological nature of *physis* for Thucydides (1999: 22). In addition to being reductive, these biological readings of the concept occlude or devalue its moral dimensions for both ancient and modern readers.

[19] Cf. Ober 1998: 67–69. Luginbill also discusses this psychological matrix (1999: 25–28), though I don't believe the historian sometimes uses *gnômê* and *orgê* synonymously, as at 3.82.2 (25). Crane sees human nature in Thucydides as "unchanging" (1998: 296), even "stable and transcendent" – a claim Thucydides himself invalidates when he describes the variability of human nature at 3.82.2. (Crane finds this passage "problematic" for his contention but not contradictory [300]).

and the real or imagined scripts of lawgiving and the symposium's poetic justice, the jury trial surpasses all in its self-conscious intent to erect the frame of *nomos* at each stage of the judicial process on litigants, magistrates, and jurors alike. In its late fifth- and fourth-century forms, the preparatory stages potential litigants had to pass through – the "summoning" (*prosklêsis*), the acceptance of the indictment, and the preliminary hearing (*anakrisis*) – began to rekey the raw strip of alleged injust interaction into carefully defined arguments and evidence that could be dialogically arranged into two conflicting accounts of the litigants' actions and careers. And the litigants began to see their own social personae straightjacketed by these accounts and by *nomos* in the form of the statute law that was supposedly violated and the social values that were at stake. The trial itself (or the arbitration hearing) then unleashed the full force of *nomos* to fix in the community's future memory the "true" natures of the interaction, accounts, evidence, and personae. In Johnstone's characterization, this script exerted a transformative power to "impose specialized roles" on disputants and to "simplify the complexities of social life" (1999: 4–5).

While the Athenians may have designed the jury trial to produce a more predictable "joint action" compared to earlier forms of dispute settlement, the script also introduced new kinds of uncertainty to the deliberation and judgment of ordinary citizens. We saw in Chapter 4 how the jury trial acknowledged an ontological shift to accommodate a hybrid sense of reality that mixed unproblematic states of knowledge about facts and persons with hypothetical ones, particularly knowledge and arguments based on reasoned likelihood. Through the summoning, acceptance of the indictment, and preliminary hearing, some of the raw strip's facts emerged uncontested while others were clearly marked as uncertain but of pivotal importance. And while some aspects of the participants' identities were clearly made known, the paramount question about the relative worth of their respective *timai* left the nature of their social personae yet to be determined. Dispute settlement in a rigorously imposed nomological frame therefore served as an epistemological laboratory to oppose different types of knowledge: what was absolutely the case (*alêtheia*), what was apparently the case (*doxa*), and their opposites, varying degrees of falsehood and deceit.[20] And of course jurors had to become adept at differentiating the two if they were to prefer one litigant's version of the strip. But how could ordinary citizens acquire this cognitive skill?

To navigate between different kinds of knowledge, in addition to reasoned probability they needed access to another frame for understanding and interpreting human experience. This additional frame had to be aligned with the others for comparative purposes, permitting the knower to switch back and forth among several frames, and in particular to align what the litigants claimed in court with alternate criteria for explaining the motives and choices behind their behavior. For if a litigant's behavior hadn't unfolded normatively or nomologically as it should have, what reasons might explain how and why it actually or probably did unfold? This new frame offered a higher order of organization than *nomos* since it embraced all the possibilities for human conduct that could render a litigant's behavior feasible and (to a juror) comprehensible, whether reasonable or unreasonable, both inside the frame of *nomos* – if the defendant violated no law or key community value – and outside *nomos* if the defendant did. It had to account for nomological questions connected to a litigant's class, past history of feuding, association with shifting relations among political leaders, family groups or political clubs, and so on. But more importantly it had

---

[20] Hesk examines how self-conscious Athenian speechwriters were of deceptive techniques in forensic rhetoric and of the strategies they devised to exploit them (2000: 202–41).

to include an understanding of how forces that were not only external but also internal to agents could motivate them and provoke them to make moral choices. Ultimately this super frame established a reference for human behavior that struck Athenians as not local, relative, and contingent to their own city-state but as universal and fundamental to any human being.

While in the 420s–410s Thucydides described a particular version of this frame in his *History*, calling it "human nature" or "the capacity to be human," this frame generally emerged as *physis* in the period after 450, when Athens' ideology of popular sovereignty and its democratic forensic culture were beginning to hit their stride. While the term once referred to the source and dynamics of all natural phenomena, it now designated "all those qualities which are physiologically and genetically ingrained in all mankind."[21] It projected an epistemological point from which jurors could stand both inside and outside experiences prescribed by their own social world and its scripts. And so while this split between *nomos* and *physis* provided alternating frames for understanding the same raw strip of human activity, it also suggested that the more certain type of knowledge (*alêtheia*) and the less certain type based on reasoned likelihood (*to eikos*) might rest outside custom and the law. The ability to oscillate in one's thinking between *nomos* and *physis* brought into both these types of reasonably dependable knowledge much that previously remained inscrutable or had been ascribed to divine intervention or accident (*tychê*). It permitted jurors to make alternative sense of the fact that litigants sometimes acted out of motives and choices that were not reducible to or commensurate with human behavior according to Athenian law and custom. In particular they could now clarify

---

[21] Ostwald 1990: 299. For a history of the word's changing meanings, see Heinimann 1945 and Naddaf 2005.

through universal human emotions the obscure promptings from a litigant's interior life.[22]

CITIZEN AND SELF ACCORDING TO ANTIPHON

Just as Protagoras and Pericles taught Athenians how to think and feel in innovative ways as democratic citizens in a society dominated by *nomos*, *physis* too had its master theoretician, though he preferred to perform in shadow rather than publicly. We met him briefly in Chapter 4 as the sophist and speechwriter Antiphon who composed *On the Murder of Herodes* for Euxitheus. In his sophistic essays *On Truth* and *On Harmony*, he wrote the earliest surviving documents exploring what is at stake for the self in the switch from the frame of *nomos* to that of *physis*, and he was said to be the first Athenian to write and publish speeches for others to deliver in the law courts and Assembly.[23] In the absence of contradictory evidence, it appears that Antiphon taught elite and ordinary Athenians how to acquire the cognitive virtuosity required to frame reality in multiple ways,

[22] As for the Athenians' ability to contrast *nomos* and *physis*, Ostwald suggests that "we may profitably assume that it was already in the air by the late 430s and early 420s…" (1986: 262). In 423 Aristophanes' *Clouds* (1075–78) presumes widespread familiarity with it. See also Guthrie's general discussion of the *nomos/physis* opposition (1971: 55ff.), and of *physis* in relation to Antiphon's "antinomian" concept of justice (107–16).

[23] As Ostwald claims, Antiphon was "the most explicit exponent of the *nomos-phusis* controversy which emerged in Athens in the 420s . . ." (1990: 293). There has been a long and still active scholarly debate on whether the Antiphon who wrote the sophistic essays and Antiphon the speechwriter (who was definitely an Athenian citizen from the deme of Rhamnus) are one and the same person – despite the fact that no ancient writer raised this question until the second century AD. Nowadays most scholars believe the two authors are one and the same person; Gagarin has recently been the most articulate spokesperson for this view (2002: 37–52, and 1990). Pendrick has recently been the most vociferous partisan of two different Antiphons (2002: 1–26, 1987 and 1993). As my discussion makes clear, I find the ancient evidence (both external and internal to Antiphon's writings) and modern arguments overwhelmingly in favor of one Antiphon.

first by recognizing *nomos* as a frame and understanding how to step outside it, and then by evaluating it from the perspective of a superior frame, *physis*. In addition to encouraging citizens to theorize about the dialogical relation between *nomos* and *physis*, he also taught them, as previously discussed, to manage arguments based on the frame of reasoned probability.[24] Finally, despite his reluctance to engage openly in public life, according to Thucydides late in life Antiphon took his faith in *physis*, which he'd forged as a fulcrum to destabilize democratic *nomos*, and put it to strategic use in hatching the oligarchic coup of 411 (with help from Peisander, Phrynichus, and Theramenes). And for this he was tried, convicted, and executed in that year (Thuc. 8.68).[25]

Speculation about Antiphon's role in the intellectual life of Athens from the 430s through the 410s has been heating up in recent years, and he is emerging from his preferred shelter in the shadows to become one of the democracy's more highly innovative and influential thinkers.[26] Gagarin's recent attempt at a global assessment of Antiphon's extant writings and career strikes me as cogent and enlightening in its outlines and conclusions about Antiphon's originality and versatility (2002), but my perspectives on citizenship, individual moral autonomy, and the performance of justice will lead us to an altered appreciation of Antiphon's career-long practice (in MacIntyre's sense) as an intellectual, speechwriter, advisor, and reluctant politician.

---

[24] See references and cross-references in Morrison 1972: 126–27.

[25] As my argument will make clear, I believe that in general Antiphon's understanding of *nomos* does not equate it, as Luginbill claims (1997), with the democratic regime. I suggest that only in the final, politically active phase of his career might Antiphon have taken the phrase in this narrow sense.

[26] In his recent commentary on Antiphon's sophistic writings, Pendrick offers a major counterpoint to this recent re-estimation of Antiphon. He consistently – and misleadingly, in my opinion – characterizes Antiphon's statements about justice and the law as conventional to traditional Greek thought and typical of sophistic discourse in general (2002: 57–59; 319ff.).

We can best understand Antiphon's practice as an extended attempt to define a paradigm for democratic citizenship that Athenians (and other Greeks) might consider a reasonable alternative to the Protagorean-Periclean model grounded in the ideology of popular sovereignty. Antiphon's project seems to me designed to cast a brighter light over the shadow citizen of Pericles' Funeral Oration, a citizen Thucydides dismissed because his pursuit of self-interest (especially pleasure) and his ensuing moral choices projected a darker side of human nature outside *nomos*. Through *On Truth* Antiphon tries to clear a moral ground for an autonomous individual more compatible with some of our contemporary versions of self: he pleads for a self that is qualified to weigh the necessities of *nomos* against the promptings of a person's morally legitimate and individual human nature – especially where this human nature acts out of an idiosyncratic self-interest. In discussing Antiphon's notion of the individual self, I identify its core with Mead's "I" and suggest that as a theoretician Antiphon isolates the "I" as that peculiar agency within the self that is responsible for switching frames between *nomos* and *physis*. This is especially the case when *nomos* immerses the self in the jury trial's performance of justice. For here the self, in trying to decide between each frame's values, finds its sole resource in its capacity to engage in an interior deliberation resulting in a reasoned judgment which Antiphon calls *gnômê* (understanding). I maintain that in exercising *gnômê*, Antiphon's individual seeks a moral recognition that is both outside citizenship and yet potentially consistent with it: a recognition not unlike the sort Taylor claims we modern individuals seek.

In *On Harmony* Antiphon addresses the problem of how a morally autonomous individual should enact democratic citizenship within its cluster of "me" roles, where the frame of *nomos* has the upper hand over a *physis* grounded in individual self-interest. Here I propose that the dilemma and its solution pivot around practical rather than theoretical issues, and that Antiphon provides ordinary citizens with familiar citizen scripts elaborated in unexpected ways. (For example, to merge selfhood with citizenship successfully, and so achieve recognition from the dominant social other, he proposes scripts such as "leading a married life" and "lending money to a needy citizen.") My final point is that Antiphon proposed a viable mode of performing selfhood and citizenship democratically and that it provided Greek political and moral theory with a social contract significantly different from that of Protagoras and other sophists.

ANTIPHON'S *ON TRUTH*: HOW TO NATURALIZE A CITIZEN

In the first comprehensible passage from the fragments of *On Truth*, we find Antiphon engaged in clearing a space for individual autonomy by destabilizing the powerful frame of *nomos* and conferring intellectual and moral legitimacy on *physis*. Like Thucydides he sometimes places a collective agent within each frame and sometimes an individual – but to very different effect. In fragment 44(A2) Antiphon lays bare one way *nomos* induces communities to understand themselves and their lifeworld in relation to the members and lifeworlds of other communities: the inhabitants of communities do this by generating graduated differences in their perception of others – what we would call varying degrees of "otherness." He claims, "<the customs> of nearby communities we know and respect, while <the customs> of faraway communities we neither know nor respect."[27] This observation suggests that, as a frame claiming to represent what is real, *nomos* has predictable epistemological limitations based on geography, and these affect a community's cognitive capacity to comprehend and judge others.

---

[27] For the text of Antiphon's sophistic fragments I rely largely on Decleva Caizzi 1989 and Pendrick 2002. Pendrick's edition reverses the order of frs. 44(A) and 44(B); see 2002: 316–17.

Antiphon immediately extends this destabilization of *nomos* to question the very capacity of a communal self to know or possess a stable identity of its own, and this deduction permits him to point to an alternate frame, *physis*, which promises to be more epistemologically and cognitively reliable: "In this regard we treat each other like foreigners, for we are all, whether Greeks or foreigners, at least by nature similarly developed [*pephukamen*] in every way." Here *physis* undoubtedly refers to universal human nature, much as in Thucydides; and Antiphon sees different communities, Greek and non-Greek, using their cultural traditions (*nomoi*) to introduce artificial distinctions which – I would add – often led to war in fifth-century Greece.[28] So *nomos* induces all human communities, including Greek city-states, to regard one another to some degree as foreigners.[29] Antiphon then refines the meaning of *physis* when he urges his reader or listener to examine "the activities required by nature" (*ta tôn physêi [ontôn anagkai]a*):

> Now we can examine the activities that are required by nature for all human beings and that are available to all to the same capacities. And in light of these considerations not one of us can be distinguished as either foreigner or Greek. For we all breathe out into the air through the mouth and the nose; we laugh when our mind is pleased and cry when distressed; and we take in sounds through our hearing and through light rays we see with our vision. We work with our hands and walk with our feet . . ." (*44[A]2.1–[A]3.12*)

---

[28] On the sense of *physis* here as universal human nature, see most recently Gagarin 2002: 67 and Pendrick 2002: 352–56; see also Ostwald 1990: 298–99.

[29] While in the case of Greeks vs. Persians Antiphon's listeners or readers may find this claim self-evident, they may be startled by its application to intra-Hellenic relations. Cf. Thucydides' dramatization of the epistemological and cognitive static resulting from the debate at Sparta in 432 where the Corinthians, Athenians, Spartans, and other Greeks struggle to understand one another's national characters in connection with recent Athenian aggression (1.66–87).

Most commentators on this and subsequent passages understand the "activities required by nature" to be the biological or physiological ground of human existence.[30] But Antiphon is precise in including a spectrum of human capacities under the umbrella of *physis*: he not only isolates one key physical apparatus for survival (the respiratory system) but demonstrates how this supports our psychological capacity to respond emotionally to stimuli with pleasure or pain; our cognitive and communicative capacities to comprehend what we hear and see; and our productive capacity to transform our bodies and minds into devices for labor and locomotion. Farrar is closer to the mark than most when she describes Antiphon's notion of *physis* as eudaimonistic, as "a standard of well being" for all humans (1988: 113).

But this passage makes it clear that, while this standard applies to all human beings, it operates primarily at the level of the *individual's* physiological, psychological and cognitive functions.[31] And here, it claims, the fact that we all have these same natural "capacities" (*dynameis*) renders us equals: we experience a zero degree of otherness. The essay's surviving fragments contain no explicit references to compassion, but Antiphon's examples in this passage include experiencing joy (*khairontes*) and pain (*lypoumenoi*). Interestingly, he locates the source of these emotions not in our capacity for naked emotion, in pure feeling, but in our capacity for conscious thought and comprehension (*nous*), which I've translated as "our mind." This suggests to me a cognitive use of the emotions not unlike that of the tragic spectator when he or she contemplates the suffering of others (especially foreigners) in a play like

---

[30] See, e. g., Gagarin 2002: 65, 68.

[31] Gagarin's insightful discussion tends to overlook Antiphon's oscillation between *physis* as universal human nature and as the idiosyncratic nature of one individual (e.g., 2002: 71–73). Luginbill's discussion entirely misses Antiphon's fundamental use of *physis* to refer to individual well-being (1999: 22–24).

Suppliants, detects a sort of kinship with them, and decides to imitate their pain.[32]

It looks as though an individual's emotions serve as a more cognitively reliable frame for understanding others than does *nomos*. In the next fragment (44[B1]) Antiphon concludes that justice itself, since it emerges from the somewhat unreliable frame of *nomos*, is entirely contextual, dependent on local laws and customs: "And so the practice of justice [*dikaiosynê*] consists of not violating the laws of the city-state where one happens to play the role of citizen [*politeutêitai*]."[33] By shrinking the stature of *nomos* in this way, Antiphon not only enables an individual human being (*anthrôpos*) to step outside it to deliberate or act, he also raises the possibility that an individual might manipulate this frame in his own self-interest (44[B1.12–16]). The key consideration, it turns out, has to do with the presence or absence of witnesses to acts that violate the law. But why should witnesses prove so pivotal to an individual citizen's ability to master the frame that traditionally mastered him?

Mead would answer that a citizen comes by his or her "me" roles thanks to the dominant social other and its institutions, and that the "I" cannot help but regard these sources of authority as alien to itself. Antiphon seems to concur: he declares that "the activities arising from a city-state's laws" (*nomoi*) are "superficially imposed [*epitheta*] [on an individual] while those arising from nature [*physis*] are unavoidable" (44[B1.22–27]). But as we saw when discussing this passage in Chapter 4, the requirements law and custom "superimpose" on a citizen are

---

[32] Cf. *On the Murder of Herodes*, where at the outset Euxitheus begs the jurors for "fellow-feeling" (*syngnômê*) if he should make a mistake in speaking (5.5). Gagarin suggests that this may refer not only to a defendant's familiar self-representation as inexperienced in courtroom rhetoric (5.3) but also to a mark of foreignness, the Lesbian dialect that is Euxitheus' native tongue (1997: 179).

[33] On the translation of *dikaiosynê* as "the practice of justice," see Gagarin 2002: 73–74.

"agreed upon" and so form part of the social contract that erects the frame of *nomos* in the first place. And this contract enables others to form an opinion (*doxa*) about a fellow citizen that may stray far from the truth (*alêtheia*) of his natural condition or well-being (44[B2]21–23). In fact it may disadvantage him with "shame and punishment" if others see him violating the law, while on the other hand a lack of witnesses to an illegal deed has no harmful consequences within the frame of *physis* (44[B2]7–20). Mead would say that here Antiphon's use of *doxa* refers to a citizen's "me" roles, which are determined by society's dominant other and are split off from another part of the self, closer to a personal truth (*alêtheia*) that is accessible only to one's native capacity to evaluate what constitutes self-interest and well-being. The justice of *nomos*, however, usually cares nothing for this recessed, inner part of the self: its quarry remains the standing of one citizen's social persona in relation to another's – in short, a citizen's *timê*.

Here is where witnesses become paramount. It is they who are the architects of an individual's "me" roles or social self, and it is they who "know" this self's identity when they use privileged senses like sight and hearing to reconstruct cognitively a fellow citizen's external behavior. In Goffman's terms the presence of witnesses "keys" or "rekeys" a raw strip of activity from the frame of *physis*, where the individual's "I" determines its significance for his or her own well-being, to that of *nomos*, where the dominant social other fixes its meaning. It is thus only before these witnesses that one can "play the role of citizen" (*politeutêitai tis*, 44[B1] 9–10); as Cassin describes the witnesses, they "initiate a chain of injustices" against the self by "introducing the public eye into the breach of privacy" (*dans l'échappée du privé*) (1995: 166).

And Antiphon, more than any Athenian, understood that nowhere did this operate more clearly than in the law courts when litigants and jurors engaged one another in performing justice. In fragment 44(B1) he in fact analyzes that strange process of transformation or defamiliarization which litigants (especially defendants) must have experienced once they found themselves inserted into the script of the jury trial. On such occasions a litigant had no choice but to present to jurors his cluster of "me" roles as a socialized, public version of his inner life. And when a litigant recounted his own narrative about the raw strip of allegedly unjust activity, he understood how thoroughly all his physiological and psychological faculties became subject to the moral and civic codes of *nomos*. These included not only the faculties witnesses might easily construe as components of his "me" but even those which his "I" found most vital to living a meaningful inner life: in short, when caught within the frame of *nomos*, the "I" fears that even its core elements might be legislated into a "me":

> *For legislation has been enacted* [nomothetêtai] *for the eyes concerning what they should and shouldn't see; for the ears concerning what they should and shouldn't hear; for the tongue concerning what it should and shouldn't say; for the hands concerning what they should and shouldn't do; for the feet concerning where they should and shouldn't go; and for the mind* [nous] *concerning what it should and shouldn't desire* [epithumein]. (*44[B2]31–[B3]17*)

It is I think no accident that the rhetorical expansion Antiphon uses to describe the grip of *nomos* on our body parts and functions moves from what is most easily observed by others to what is most hidden from them: our capacity for understanding (*nous*), which inclines us toward emotional responses like desire (*epithumein*).[34] And it is this last faculty that provides the "I" with the possibility of autonomous moral deliberation leading to decision making. We've seen that Antiphon

---

[34] For discussion of the rhetorical figure of *amplificatio* as Antiphon applies it to these various organs and functions, including the meanings of *nous* and *epithumein*, see Pendrick 2002: 328–31.

uses *nous* to designate how we process emotions cognitively; here that takes the form of our ability as persons to form those "second order" desires (desires that evaluate other desires), which Taylor identifies as fundamental to a modern sense of self (1985a: 15–44). In drawing this distinction between desiring on the one hand and on the other a capacity combining both understanding and judgment, Antiphon describes *nous* as an instrument bridging the voluntarist elements of self with the cognitive and deliberative. Here it's a faculty within the self that is indispensable to Mead's "I," that peculiar agent whose decisions shape our sense of who and what we are and inaugurate the process of autonomous moral deliberation.[35]

While we cannot say whether these two fragments, 44(A) and (B), are representative of the essay as a whole, they appear to isolate increasingly that particular kind of deliberation we've only glimpsed from time to time in traditional Greek culture: the autonomous effort of individuals to shelter themselves from the dominant social other in order to achieve self-definition or individuation. Not surprisingly, Antiphon encourages Athenians to understand this deliberative script as liberation from a sort of bondage imposed by *nomos*. But it's important to note that Antiphon doesn't see this deliberation as a facile calculation between the evils of *nomos* and the benefits of *physis*. He never suggests that we can actually escape the wide, loosely defined frame of *nomos*, and he alludes to certain of its social advantages.[36] But when viewed within

---

[35] Cf. Farrar's association of Antiphon's concept of *physis* with moral autonomy: "It is the demands of nature, stringent and inescapable, which express man's autonomy and interests, while law is both contingent and coercive" (1988: 115).

[36] Gagarin's discussion of these fragments recognizes the ambivalence Antiphon attributes to both *nomos* and *physis*, depending on one's cognitive perspective (2002: 70–73). Moulton too makes this point, inferring that Antiphon recognized "the reality of compromise" between the two frames (1972: 334). The notion of compromise, I'll suggest, looms large in Antiphon's paradigm of democratic citizenship and selfhood.

the frame of *physis*, these advantages become "chains" (*desmoi*) upon our self-interest while the advantages of our human nature remain "free" (*eleuthera*) (44[B4.5–7]). Ostwald summarizes this point succinctly as "to enjoy the advantages provided by the laws we have to sacrifice something of our human nature."[37] That "something" we sacrifice, I submit, is what Antiphon's inquiry (*skepsis*, 44[B2.25–26]) seems to encourage a citizen to recognize within himself, to nourish, and to protect from the reach of *nomos*: the ability to orchestrate the voluntarist, cognitive, and deliberative elements of self in performing an autonomous moral deliberation that switches frames from *nomos* to *physis* and back again in order to calculate the advantages and disadvantages of each.[38] Here I maintain (contra Vernant, 1988: 58–59) that Antiphon permits enlightened Athenians to exercise their will in our modern sense. First he enjoins them to distinguish that part of themselves that desires from a part that subjects desires to reasoned comprehension (the *nous*). Then he urges a form of interior deliberation under the competing frames of *nomos* and *physis* in order to determine alternative ends or senses of the good. Nowhere in this process need a person passively yield to ends urged by emotion or to senses of the good dictated by a necessity he or she cannot subject to personal evaluation.

[37] Ostwald 1990: 300. See Raaflaub (1983: 528ff.) for ways oligarchs appropriated the adjective "free" (*eleutherios*) after about 435 by connecting it not with a democratic political status but with personal qualities of birth, wealth, and education.

[38] Cassin captures this cognitive oscillation between the two frames when she observes, "For Antiphon, as for Protagoras and Gorgias, we are first rational-political beings, and only then, *once again or in another way*, physical animals" (1995: 171; my emphasis). But I disagree with the conclusions she draws about the ethical implications of this frame-switching, namely, that "the best way to respect the law is to have nothing to do with it, to not put oneself in a position to have to testify, to stay within the secret space of privacy, a position the law assigns to nature" (169). As my discussion of *On Harmony* indicates, Antiphon's ethical mandate to Athenians enjoined them to participate fully in social and political life – so long as they deliberated autonomously about potential gains and losses before moving forward.

In Chapter 4 we saw in *On the Murder of Herodes* a more dramatic set of circumstances where this moral, deliberative core of the self tried to assert itself. There Antiphon encouraged his client Euxitheus to foreground through arguments based on reasoned likelihood his inner capacity to respond to the events surrounding the missing man's disappearance. We suggested that Euxitheus not only hoped to induce the jurors to recognize the legitimacy of his inner deliberations but also to imitate these deliberations as part of their own determination of his guilt or innocence – and on that basis to feel compassion for him (5.73, 5.92). Is it possible that Antiphon's practice (in MacIntyre's sense) as sophist and speechwriter revolved around fostering the ability of the "I" to inaugurate such frame-switching in the interests of its various "me" roles? Did his ghost writer's talent in provoking this deliberation – and leading others to recognize its moral legitimacy – provide his clients an antidote to the vice-like grip *nomos* exerts throughout those deliberative scripts performed in the Assembly, Council, and especially the law court – scripts which sometimes proved (literally) fatal to individuals?

The alarm Antiphon sounds concerning the harm *nomos* sometimes inflicts on individual citizens alerts them to ways it inevitably and irresistibly transforms, and even betrays, the self. Because the proportions of *nomos* vary so widely, ranging from the most general customs to specific statute laws, it can pack a double punch of injustice, ensnaring a citizen in a double bind of conflicting imperatives. In the form of custom, *nomos* begins transforming a citizen's self in each and every citizen script; but as statute law, especially at work in the jury trial, it completes its work of alienating a citizen from his true nature.[39]

---

[39] Cf. Moulton's observations (1972: 333) on Antiphon's use of *nomos* in this essay to mean sometimes "moral customs" and sometimes "statutory law" without marking the difference for his listener/reader. Commenting on Antiphon's use of *ta nomima*

When citizens practice social habits without reflection, *nomos* encourages them to interact with and understand others solely in terms of their "me" roles. They are thus led to expect that, if all perform these socially prescribed "me" roles, a traditional justice based on generalized reciprocity, both positive and negative, will prevail: they are enjoined to treat friends well, enemies badly, and to anticipate the same.[40]

Antiphon claims, however, that citizens have an escape route from such nomological behavior when within the frame of *physis* a particular citizen's "I" introduces a moral calculus about individual self-interest into his or her interactions with others. Some citizens who are victimized by others' aggression, for example, will be induced to rely on self-defense rather than aggressive retaliation; some children mistreated by their parents will be encouraged to treat their parents well anyway; and some litigants will allow opponents the legal advantage of swearing to a false oath without availing themselves of the same strategy (44[B4.32–B5.13]). (In *On Harmony* we learn why some individuals decide their ultimate self-interest lies in a nonaggressive response.)

Despite the possibility of such escape hatches, when *nomos* takes the narrower contours of specific statutory laws, it completes its harmful transformation of one's own nature and self-interest. Prior to a lawsuit, the law doesn't always motivate citizens to interact in a just manner, nor does it always reverse unjust behavior when one hopes for a straight *dikê* in court. In effect Antiphon recognizes that the state's laws inadequately influence or correct citizen behavior because for the most part their justice comprehends only the behavior of "me" roles rather than thoughts and actions a citizen's "I" might subject to autonomous moral

---

(44[B1.5]), Decleva Caizzi identifies the spectrum of meanings to include, in addition to written law, "the entirety of norms, rules, and customs which the political community provides for itself and accepts" (1989: 203).

[40] Cf. Allen on the role such reciprocity played in the logic of Athenian legal punishment (2000: 62–65 and *passim*).

evaluation. Laws certainly cannot prevent what Goffman calls the raw strip of allegedly unjust interaction from occurring: as Antiphon puts it, "justice in accordance with law [*to ek nomou dikaion*] . . . permits the victim to suffer and the perpetrator to act. . . ." (44[B6.3–13]). Even worse, once litigants enter into a jury trial proper, *nomos* cannot guarantee that justice in the form of a proper adjustment of *timê* (a punishment, *timôria*) will prevail because the trial's agonistic, dialogic structure permits each litigant equal opportunity to persuade or deceive the jurors about the nature of his opponent's "me" (44[B6.14–30]).

Once again, witnessing looms as potentially catastrophic for the morally autonomous individual. The "customarily . . . just" (*dikaion nomizetai*) courtroom practice requiring a witness to testify truthfully is sure to trigger an offense against the self-interest of a litigant who has never harmed the witness, for the "truth" that emerges concerns only the litigant's "me" roles. When the testimony is rekeyed within the frame of the litigant's human nature (*physis*), the witness's testimony will violate that axiom of the wider sense of *nomos* which enjoins positive reciprocity between citizens; and the witness will then be open to retaliation from the injured litigant, who now becomes an enemy for life (44[C1.–C2.12]). Antiphon in fact attributes inevitably unjust outcomes not only for giving testimony (*martyrein*) but for a spectrum of cognitive acts performed within the frame of *nomos*: rendering a *dikê* (*dikazein*), producing a verdict (*krinein*), and arbitrating (*diaitan*) (44[C2.26–30]). In a paradoxical and exasperating manner, then, all senses of *nomos* as a frame conflict internally with themselves as well as with *physis* to generate a cycle of interactions oscillating hopelessly between behavior that is regarded as just (*dikaios*) and unjust (*adikaios*):

> For it is not possible that these wrongdoings [the injustices suffered by a truthful witness] are just and that the injunction not to wrong anyone or be wronged oneself is also just. Rather it is necessary that either one of these be just or that they both be unjust. And it is clear that rendering a

dikê (to dikazein), *making a judgment* (to krinein), *and providing arbitration* (to diaitan), *however they turn out, are not just since helping some people hurts others.* (*44[C2.17–30]*)

Since the essay is fragmentary, Antiphon's goal in *On Truth* remains elusive.[41] But if the major surviving fragments contribute in a fundamental way to the essay's aims, Antiphon appears intent on provoking his audience to reflect on the possibility of performing a special sort of calculation. As outlined above, this calculation prompts an individual citizen to weigh the advantages and disadvantages of a life that must be lived simultaneously within the frames of both *nomos* and *physis*, and then in a given moment to choose between enacting two different social identities: the first created by the *doxa* of others' opinions and the second a personal identity truer to his or her self-interest. It looks as though this essentially moral deliberation permitted Antiphon to put his peculiar stamp upon a favorite sophistic term, *gnômê*. Two of the essay's more important shorter fragments (DK 1 and 2) designate this cognitive faculty as one of intellect: but while it may originate in the senses (especially sight), it operates independently (DK 1) and in all human beings must dominate the senses as the "leader" (*hêgeitai*) of the body "when it comes to health, sickness and everything else" (DK 2). Coupled with observations in fragment 44(B2)30–(B3)15 about how legislated our bodily organs and functions are, including our understanding (*nous*) and desire (*epithumein*), the leadership of *gnômê* seems to have the final say in how one's *nous* evaluates desires. It takes responsibility for rendering in a permanent, reasoned formulation the "I"'s spontaneous ability to accept or reject various components of its possible "me" roles. *Gnômê* in other words is our will, fortified to provoke Athenians

---

[41] See Pendrick's survey of modern commentators' efforts to characterize the entire essay's contents and identify its unified theme (2002: 35–38).

to ask: "What sort of person am I *compelled* to become when decisions about justice are made within *nomos* about or by me? And what sort of alternative person might I *choose* to become within *physis*?"

ANTIPHON'S *ON HARMONY* AND THE GAME OF CITIZENSHIP

Judging from these fragments, and from Aristophanes' parody of argumentation based on the *nomos/physis* opposition in *Clouds* 1075–78 (performed in 423), it looks as though most Athenians would have found the prospect of this sort of deliberation and calculation daunting and a bit mystifying, as befits a sophistic performance in the Protagorean tradition.[42] Citizens might have felt more comfortable, however, with appeals to the superiority of *physis* and dramatizations of the *nomos/physis* opposition in Euripidean and Sophoclean tragedies.[43] Antiphon himself nevertheless provides an alternative performance for the public in his essay *On Harmony* (*Peri homonoias*). In both style and content this essay differs significantly from *On Truth*, and scholars continue to debate the relationship between them; but Gagarin plausibly suggests that Antiphon intended *On Truth* for an intellectual audience of readers and *On Harmony* for oral performance before a more popular gathering.[44] I disagree, however, that Antiphon arranged his two essays

---

[42] Moulton argues against earlier attempts to claim that *Clouds* parodies Antiphon's *On Truth*; Pendrick concurs (2002: 38). On Antiphon's essay as a rebuttal to Protagorean theories, see Farrar (1988: 113–19).

[43] See Ostwald on *physis* in Euripides, the "foremost Athenian exponent" of a "social criticism" based on this concept (266), and for references to *nomos/physis* in plays like *Trojan Women, Hecuba, Orestes, Hippolytus, Antiope*, and fr. 920 (1986: 260ff.). On Sophocles' use of *physis* in *Philoctetes* (409 BC), see Nussbaum 1976–77. Moulton sees a direct influence by Antiphon on Euripides' critique of the Athenian legal process in several plays (1972: 350–57). Guthrie also links *physis* in Euripides to Antiphon's "antinomian view" (1971: 113–14).

[44] For scholars' attempts to understand the relationship between the two essays, see Pendrick 2002: 54–56. On the essays' different styles and possibly different audiences, Gagarin suggests, "[*On Harmony*] is more rhetorical and less intensely

in the sophistic fashion of opposed *logoi* (Gagarin 2002: 96): on the contrary, *On Harmony* more resembles an attempt to encourage citizens to exercise "applied *gnômê*" – that is, to recognize in familiar scripts of citizen life a variety of readily comprehensible occasions for practicing the abstract deliberations outlined in *On Truth*.[45]

The question of the two essays' relation to one another is not trivial, for in the absence of more complete evidence it determines our understanding of Antiphon's position within the arena of Athenian social and political ideologies from around 440 to the oligarchic coup he presumably engineered in 411. For example, despite her insightful discussion of Antiphon, Farrar is, I think, wrong to claim, "Unlike Protagoras, Antiphon believes that man's interests are asocial" (1988: 117). This conclusion follows from her incomplete understanding of Antiphon's notion of the good as "from the point of view of social order, purely negative and essentially personal" (119). Luginbill also misinterprets Antiphon as an oligarchic, antidemocratic thinker bent on discrediting *nomos* in the strictly political sense of the democratic regime from Pericles to the 410s (1997). In both cases short shrift is given to *On Harmony's* injunctions to immerse oneself in citizen life. Gagarin too misrepresents *On Harmony* as a palliative to *On Truth's* critique of *nomos*; he sees it as a corrective reinforcing traditional morality (2002: 96–97).

---

analytical; its sentiments are more readily comprehensible; and it addresses popular issues and concerns rather than the concerns of contemporary intellectuals" (2002: 97–98).

[45] Despite his suggestion that we consider the two essays as "a pair of opposed *logoi*," Gagarin does link them as part of the same intellectual project. Of frs. 48, 52, 55, 63, and 65 from *On Harmony*, he says, "...it is possible that Antiphon's criticism formed the starting point for more positive advice urging people to use their intelligence more. In other words, these fragments are consistent with the view of *Truth* that by using their intellect, people can attain a better understanding, though many do not go beyond the information they receive through their senses" (2002: 95). Romilly claims that the two essays exhibit "*une éclatante unité*" (1988: 248).

From the existing fragments we can identify the intellectual and ethical thrust of the second essay; and we can characterize it as a sophistic variation on the performance tradition of the seven sages and other purveyors of wisdom.[46] This intellectual and ethical thrust takes the form of an imperative to citizens to employ the frame-switching *gnômê* outlined in *On Truth* whenever they contemplate interaction with peers. This notion of interaction, along with the idea of mixing or intermingling, in fact strikes me as paramount to this essay, for Antiphon consistently evokes the interaction and intermingling of persons, thoughts, evaluations, and emotions in various citizen scripts. On the whole these flesh out and render familiar the rather cold, stringent summons in *On Truth* to contemplate the simultaneous presence in both *nomos* and *physis* of advantages and disadvantages. They dramatize ways a citizen should use the self's cognitive and deliberative elements to temper the basic, voluntarist appetites enabling one to survive and thrive: desires for food, shelter, and a need to connect oneself to others through eros and friendship. And the goal is apparently for the individual citizen to reach a more precise understanding of how to achieve some measure of recognition from peers while minimizing the costs and maximizing the benefits to self-interest.

On Harmony's longest surviving fragment (fr. 49) concerns the script "living a married life" and offers advice apparently to a young man contemplating this move. However, when the speaker (presumably Antiphon) observes, "For marriage is a mighty contest [*agôn*] for a human being" (49.3–4), it's soon clear that the relationship of husband

---

[46] Reconstructing the essay's major themes relies on much guesswork since ancient authors only explicitly assigned fourteen fragments to the essay; modern scholars assign the other fifteen on the basis of content (Pendrick 2002: 39–40 and Gagarin 2002: 93–95). Pendrick believes the essay may have no underlying unity, consisting of "never much more than a string of sententious utterances on diverse topics of ethical interest" (2002: 45).

and wife stands for one of the many uncertain contests a citizen may enter. The *agôn* in this fragment almost assumes the status of a master citizen script absorbing many others that immerse an individual in interactions with others whenever he desires (*epithumêsatô*, 49.2) to gain happiness, well-being or success.[47] When observed within the frame of *physis*, contests motivate the individual's "I" to consider enacting whatever "me" role the frame of *nomos* dictates for a particular type of contest. MacIntyre is again helpful when he identifies the *agôn* in fifth-century Athens – and especially in the age of the sophists – as "an instrument of the individual will in grasping after success in satisfying its desires" (1984: 137). And indeed Antiphon's interest in such citizen scripts as marriage pivots around the moral choices an individual faces as the contest unfolds.

Like marriage, each competitive encounter opens the prospect of "a new destiny, a new fate" for the individual (fr. 49.2–3), one over which the citizen cannot expect to exercise genuine control. In marriage, what if a wife proves "unsuitable"? Is divorce a wise recourse if one wishes to regain personal happiness and well-being? Here, just as the jury trial in *On Truth* could force a person to testify truthfully against a fellow citizen and harm someone who had never harmed him or her, *nomos* dictates rules of divorce that will likely transform into enemies family members with whom one enjoyed warm relations of generalized reciprocity (4–7). Or from the perspective of *physis*, is the alternative preferable: to endure a married life in which pains replace the anticipated pleasures (7–8)? Even if marriage to a compatible spouse brings pleasures, Antiphon continues, "pleasures don't travel [*emporeuontai*] by

---

[47] This young man's dilemma resembles, though far less dramatically, the dilemma Aeschylus' *Suppliants* puts to its internal audience of Argives and its implied audience in the theater: whether or not to engage in the script of alliance formation with Danaus and his daughters – an alliance that harms their community's well-being and leads to a highly antagonistic marriage script.

themselves, but pains and hard effort accompany them" (13–14). Switching metaphors, Antiphon evokes another type of *agôn*, the panhellenic games at Olympia and Delphi, where pleasurable victories come only at the cost of great pains (14–17). The nub of the matter in any worthwhile contest, it seems, is the individual's ability to calculate the ratio of pleasure to pain these endeavors entail – and perhaps often conceal. For social standing or recognition (*timai*) and awards (*athla*) – benefits of one's "me" roles – appear like enticements, traps or pieces of bait (*deleata*, 17) which the gods set within the frame of *nomos* to motivate humans. But many individuals, the fragment implies, do not switch in advance into the frame of *physis* to see how much they will have to sacrifice of their individual well-being if they wish to obtain these social goods.

At this point the speaker of fragment 49 changes from the third to first person to provide a personal illustration of the sort of inner deliberation and calculation he has in mind. This switch appears unexpectedly: Antiphon (if he is the speaker) now places himself in the position of the man contemplating marriage so that he might perform the younger man's dilemma as though it were his own. Note how in this performance Antiphon the deliberator first hypothetically splits or duplicates himself in order to observe himself expending efforts, within the frame of *physis*, to ensure his physical survival and well-being and, within the frame of *nomos*, to achieve all the virtues his society dangles before a man of talent. Then note how this second self becomes, when applied to the prospective husband "in real life," a person different from the speaker:

> For if I possessed a second self [sôma heteron] *like the one I am for*
> *myself, I would not survive* [zên] *since I give myself so much trouble on*
> *behalf of my health and the daily livelihood I scrape together, and on*
> *behalf of the opinion I create of myself* [doxa], *my self-control, my honor*

[eukleia], *and my good reputation. What then if I possessed such a second self to look after in this way? It's not clear that a wife, even if she is compatible with her husband, gives him no fewer intimate pleasures and pains than he gives himself on behalf of the health of two bodies and of scraping together their livelihood and achieving [for both of them] self-control and honor.* (49.19–29)

Who is this first, speaking self who observes the second self? We can say that the first self hypothetically creates the second, and in order to place the second, as a simulacrum or image of itself, within the frames of *physis* and then *nomos*. It then observes this self-image as though it were a double, both familiar and alien, a someone else going about his daily life, fulfilling "me" roles just like the ones the speaker is contemplating. This first, reflexive self is ephemeral too, existing only in the speech act and in the hypothetical moment of this thought experiment. Here Antiphon captures beautifully the operation of Mead's "I" as it evaluates, in a performative attitude that is also a burst of self-consciousness, the conventional roles from which the "me" must choose if it wishes not merely to survive but to achieve recognition from the dominant social other. The goal of this thought experiment seems clear: to tally up the efforts expended verses the benefits gained in managing life in both frames. This is *nous* (mind) in action, serving the cause of rendering a *gnômê* (judgment) by imagining itself, to paraphrase Mead again, to be another (1964: 292). It's significant, though, that this first self, the "I," looks to *physis* when applying the decisive criterion of self-interest to determine how worthwhile it would be to maintain oneself and a double, and that criterion is the ability to survive (*zên*, 20).[48]

---

[48] This dramatization of a temporary retreat into the self exemplifies the "*sagesse toute intérieure*" and "*paix intérieure*" Romilly attributes to the essay (1988: 246, 247).

So we can understand Antiphon's deliberation here as a performance that hypothetically mimics a younger citizen's dilemma as he contemplates taking on the "me" role of husband, head of household and pater familias; for society dictates that such a citizen assume responsibility for the physical welfare and social reputation of his family members. The second self clearly turns out, after it emerges in the initial abstract hypothesis (19–20), to represent these family dependents (29–30). And the final tally does not look appealing: "Now everything is full of worries, the young man's sprightliness is gone from his judgment [*gnômê*], and his face no longer looks the same" (30–32).[49] Over time, the young husband's need to replicate himself within his household has altogether banished the prospect of pleasure, deprived him of the intellectual agility required to make the key calculation Antiphon is scrutinizing here, and even rendered him unrecognizable to his former self. Unfortunately the fragment ends here: should we infer that Antiphon's advice is to skip the nuptials?

Hardly. There is nothing in the fragments to indicate that Antiphon opposed participation in so fundamental an institution as marriage, or in any other social or political institutions. To the contrary, the remaining fragments counsel citizens to engage themselves in exchanges with one another, both social and commercial; but they are warned about the mixing of pleasure and pain, and of fortunate and unfortunate outcomes, which these exchanges inevitably bring. In one fragment Antiphon even tells a fable to criticize the citizen who in a miserly fashion hoards his money and refuses to lend it to another in need (fr. 54). By not putting commercial assets to social use, their value shrinks to

---

[49] *Gnômê* seems to have the same sense here as in *On Truth*, where it designates the cognitive ability to engage in comparisons and calculations preparatory to taking decisive action, after the senses have gathered information and one's understanding (*nous*) has rendered this comprehensible and signaled initial inclinations or desires. Pendrick takes *gnômê* here as "nearly synonymous with *psukhê*" (2002: 388); for him the relation in Antiphon's psychology between *gnômê* and *nous* is "obscure" (251).

THE NATURALIZATION OF CITIZEN AND SELF   467

that of a mere stone (54.13–16). We should even regard "making use of" (*khrêsthai*) one's assets, putting them to the test, as essential to Antiphon's moral imperative to fellow citizens, for only then can the true value of these assets and of a citizen's cluster of "me" roles emerge. Along the same lines, other fragments explore the challenges to know and choose genuine rather than false friends (frs. 64 and 65); another notes how interaction with our closest friend reduces the difference between self and other: we become "such as him" in our personal characteristics (*tropoi*) (fr. 62).

So instead of critiquing institutions and the demands of *nomos*, *On Harmony* tries to foster a cognitive ability that may well lead to a mixture of success and failure in social life – but more importantly will foster in an individual citizen a moral autonomy capable of seeking recognition from peers while acting in self-interest to protect vital physical and psychological needs. The key is to reason well (*to phronein kalôs*, 54.19) when understanding civic participation's costs and benefits to one's well-being. *Sôphrosynê* (sef-control, prudence, temperance) is a cardinal virtue, and for several reasons. It protects one from unrealistic hopes about all of life's contests and interactions, which may appear grandiose but are always "mixed with great pains" (51.3–4). Sober thinking also promotes reasonable calculations, optimizing the chance to maintain inner composure while contemplating the battlefield that is citizen life.[50]

---

[50] *Sôphrosynê* had political connotations for elite Athenians in the 420s and 410s, in particular those associated with the political clubs (*hetaireiai*) linked after 415 to anxieties about an oligarchic coup. Antiphon himself may have been active in one of these clubs (Andocides 1.35). (On *sôphrosynê* in general, see North 1966 and Donlan 1980; on its link to elite political clubs in the 410s, see McGlew 2002:125–32.) From this perspective the "harmony" (*homonoia*) in the title of Antiphon's essay may refer to the social concord that results when citizens of opposing interests find compromise and reconciliation. It may also refer to, in Romilly's words again, a state of "*sagesse toute intérieure*" and "*paix intérieure*" (1988: 246, 247), with the implication that each individual's psychic harmony contributes to social concord. Pendrick

Fragment 58 in fact defines *sôphrosynê* as the ability to use a tactician's cognitive delay – what we call "thinking twice" – to suppress the inner urge to gratify oneself by harming one's neighbor. It's prudent, Antiphon says, to wonder whether harming our neighbor might lead to things we don't want (58.1–2). This wondering provokes a "fear" (*deimainei*, 2) that within the frame of *physis* is salutary for our self-interest, especially in a society where *nomos* guarantees that our neighbor will retaliate for any harm we do him. This fear has a cognitive effect: it prompts our mind (*nous*, 3) to understand that by delaying we can undo our misguided wishes but not our actions (2–5), and so we'll reject "hopes" as a path to well-being. As in fragment 49, when describing the climactic moment of insight Antiphon splits the hypothetical individual he's discussing into two; once again it's a question of recognizing oneself in another. "No one can more accurately judge [*kriseien*] the *sôphrosynê* of another man than someone who himself blockades [*emphrassei*] the momentary pleasures [*hêdonais*] of his heart [*thymos*]" (8–10). Continuing the military metaphor, Antiphon describes such a self as one capable of "both exercising sovereignty over himself [*heauton kratein*] and conquering himself [*nikan . . . heauton*]" (10). Any wish for "momentary gratification" (*kharisthasthai . . . parakhrêma*) within the seat of pure emotion (the heart or *thymos*) is in effect a wish to harm oneself (10–11).

The scripts of battle and the contest were for Antiphon no idle metaphors for the varied scripts of citizen life. Fragment 52, explicitly assigned in antiquity to *On Harmony*, advises, "It isn't possible to take back your life like a piece in a game of *pessoi*." Thanks to Kurke's recent

summarizes scholarly debate on the title's possible meanings (2002: 41–42). (I don't find convincing his philological argument that it's implausible to take *homonoia* here as a reference to psychic harmony.) Farrar suggests that the title refers to psychic harmony in a manner similar to Sophocles' use of *autonomia* to refer to a personal characteristic in *Antigone* (821, 875) (1988: 119).

discussion of board games and Greek citizenship, we can recognize this fragment's reference to the "symbolic activity" of *pessoi* or *petteia*, a generic name for a board game played with tokens and sometimes with dice.[51] Kurke demonstrates how Archaic and Classical Greeks understood the game as a propaedeutic for citizenship, particularly in the form of a game called *polis*, which used tokens and was played in Athens in the second half of the fifth century (1999: 260–61). *Polis* used many tokens of equal status, and its goal, according to Pollux (*Onom.* 9.98), was to surround and capture an opponent's token with two of one's own. For this reason Kurke categorizes it as a "battle game" symbolic of citizenship in a democratic city-state (261, 265). We have good reason, therefore, to suppose that Antiphon was referring to this particular form of *pessoi* as an *agôn* whose "moves" required a *gnômê* forged out of careful thought and strategizing. In this regard we can take the advice on playing the game in fragment 52 as representative of the essay's overall attempt to impart to citizens – perhaps to the young citizen (*neos*) recently emerged from the ephebes' ranks – an understanding of the cognitive tools and practices necessary to score a victory in citizen life – or at least to avoid a fatal defeat.[52]

---

[51] Kurke 1999: 253–74; see 254 for the particular games *pessoi* (*petteia*) might designate. (In her discussion Kurke doesn't refer to Antiphon's fragment.)

[52] Antiphon appears to be following some sort of philosophical tradition in using this game to symbolize scripts of citizenship. Kurke cites Heraclitus fr. B 52 DK ("One's lifetime [*aiôn*] is a boy playing *pessoi*; the kingship is his"; my trans.) as a reference to a version of *pessoi* symbolic of competition in oligarchic city-states (1999: 263). She also cites (267–68) the anecdote in Diogenes Laertius which describes Heraclitus' refusal to write laws for Ephesus and his preference instead for playing knucklebones with boys. In angry riposte to the Ephesians' startled stares, he asks, "Isn't it better to be doing this than to be participating in citizen life?" (*politeuesthai*, 9.2–3). Cf. this use of *politeuesthai* with Antiphon's at 44(B1) 9–10. Commenting on Antiphon's fr. 52, Pendrick points to Stobaeus' claim that Socrates said, "Life is like a version of *petteia* [*petteiai tini*]: you must make the best move possible, for it is not possible to throw [the dice] again or to take back your piece" (4.56.39) (2002: 392–93).

This game player, engaged in inner deliberation about the wisdom of his next move, most clearly represents Antiphon's conception of the citizen and self. The player's need to strategize likewise makes Antiphon's ethical mandate clear: when the player accepts his opponent's invitation to play, he immerses himself in the liminal playworld of the game's *nomos*. He must keep in mind all the rules of *pessoi* (or *polis*) and obey them; and if he is adept he will reflect not only on all his possible moves at a given moment but also project his own understanding of the game onto all his opponent's possible moves. This totality of possible moves – both his own and his opponents' – comprises the composite perspective of Mead's dominant social other, and the citizen player only achieves this by intersubjectively putting himself in his opponent's place. Antiphon would, I think, insist that the *nomos* of *pessoi* or *polis* does not dictate the player's decision to move his piece this way rather than that, or compel him to keep on playing rather than quit for lunch or concede. Instead the player's *nous* evaluates his situation after each move by the opponent, and his "I" autonomously chooses his next move as the best possible one at the moment. Now it must of course be a legal move consistent with the rules, but in choosing it freely the cognitive elements of self own up to it as a personal response to the dominant social other. It's clear, though, that he would never have selected this move without first considering it in the frame of *physis*, whose criterion illuminates the path to self-interest.

7 DEMOCRACY'S NARCISSISTIC CITIZENS: ALCIBIADES AND SOCRATES

◎▣◎

I JUDGING ALCIBIADES

Antiphon's contribution to Athenian intellectual life legitimized the frame of *physis* as a temporary shelter or retreat where each citizen could perform a certain kind of moral deliberation with himself and rationally calculate his self-interest. Once an individual completed this deliberation and calculation, however, Antiphon advised him to seek recognition by returning to the contest in question, abiding by its rules, and risking a rise or fall in self-interest at the hands of opponents or fortune. But from the 420s onward, other Athenian minds responded differently to the lure of calculations forged within the crucible of *physis* – and to the intellectual and moral legitimacy with which Antiphon endowed these calculations. Because it maximized the freedoms *nomos* conferred on Athenians, this paradigm of citizenship and selfhood almost invited them to exploit its breakthrough and devise other strategies for a citizen's life – especially strategies reflecting a more radical attachment to self-interest. What sort of strategy would emerge, for example, if a citizen disregarded the need to return wholeheartedly to the frame of *nomos* and risk the moves prompted by *physis* and self-interest? What if, in returning to citizen life within the frame of *nomos*, he held the autonomy conferred by *physis* as a nonnegotiable value? What if he could play the *polis* game by sometimes confusing opponents about the rules of the game, or persuading them that his novel – and illegal – moves were permissable, even desirable, for communal well-being?

Most Athenians in the age of Antiphon wouldn't have seen such a player as a "nomological" self in the sense we used earlier. "Para-nomological" might more accurately characterize this individual as a rule-breaker who only sometimes followed the rules, or who pretended to follow them but bent them to his advantage before an opponent could spot the infringements. *Paranomia*, "rule-breaking," is the word Thucydides uses to summarize the performance of citizenship and selfhood by Alcibiades, Antiphon's younger contemporary by about thirty years (6.15.4). This term for transgression is a loaded one, inviting and igniting readers, ancient and modern, to assign Alcibiades' behavior according to various moral, legal, and (by today's lights) theoretical categories. Are his transgressions (social, political, and sexual) just aberrations, or do they willfully and strategically contest Athenian standards of citizen conduct? Or are they "perversions" of Athenian norms, as Wohl calls them, arising from those norms according to two possible logics? One sees them (à la Foucault) spring from norms and excite a desire that only serves to reinforce them, the other sees them (à la Judith Butler) generated by norms and exciting a desire that exceeds or contests them (2002: 124–27). Which of these models best accounts for Alcibiades' performance as citizen and self?

To decide, we need to identify the subject in question. By that I mean we need to choose whether the subject of Alcibiades' *paranomia* is primarily a historically located *system* of norms and transgressions whose logic plays out its strategic permutations by manipulating human agents, or whether the subject is primarily a historically identifiable, individual human agent who evaluates these norms and makes choices based on will – a *person* in Taylor's sense.[1] Throughout this study I opt

---

[1] On these options see Taylor's "Foucault on Freedom and Truth" (1985b: 152–84), "What is Human Agency?" (1985a: 15–44) and "The Concept of a Person" (1985a: 97–14). Ludwig's thematic study *Eros and Polis* (2002) generally avoids theoretical

for the second possibility. I would even say that in the 420s, thanks to the climate fostered by sophistic theorizing, "perversions" in personal conduct no longer exist for certain elite citizens: Antiphon for one argues that reasoned deliberation may induce an individual to determine that self-interest (*physis*) has moral parity with, if not priority over, the dictates of *nomos*. So confounding categories based on *nomos* – the promiscuity of mixing roles like democrat and tyrant, Athenian and foreign, masculine and feminine, active lover and passive loved one (cf. Wohl 2002: 136, 143) – may to certain individual subjects appear justified.

If this is the case, then we can ask how others, especially non-elites, might comprehend the sort of deliberation motivating such a subject's paranomological behavior. Alcibiades appears some thirty-two times in the *History*, between the years 420 and 411, and most often engaged in the script of citizen deliberation. These deliberations may be eminently public events, such as addressing the Athenian Assembly (e.g., 6.16–18), or semi-public occasions, such as serving as Athenian ambassador (5.61) and advising the leadership of other Greek states (6.88–92) and foreign powers (8.46–47).[2] But Thucydides also alludes briefly to areas of Alcibiades' life that are decidedly personal and private, primarily to underscore the impact these more shadowy deliberative moments have on Alcibiades' public life. At these moments the historian shines a bit of light on Alcibiades' peculiar performance of that shadow citizenship Pericles touched upon in the Funeral Oration.

---

models, but it slips into Foucauldian mode when discussing the erotic fantasy of human-divine sex: "Eros as transgression, the antinomianism of desire, proves that such eros is nomothetical at its very core. Only the presence of the boundary piques the desire" (357).

[2] Gribble attributes Alcibiades' influence in Book 8 to his talents for advising and persuading (1999: 198), but we find these skills wherever Alcibiades appears in the *History*.

Just when Thucydides is about to dramatize Alcibiades' passionate speech to the Assembly in 415 urging the expedition to conquer Sicily, he steps back to profile this leader's previous and current standing as a citizen. After noting the younger man's political rivalry with the older Nicias, and his ambition to command the expedition and conquer both Sicily and Carthage, Thucydides turns to the question of Alcibiades' personal desires. He actually focuses not so much on those desires themselves as on the citizens' efforts to understand and evaluate what they can witness of Alcibiades' external behavior and accomplishments.[3] Note how the resulting sketch oscillates between private pursuits and public performance, and how it reflects a leader-follower dynamics that amounts to something less than a coherent, consistent judgment about Alcibiades' public image and private self:[4]

> ... and he [Alcibiades] especially desired [epithumôn] and hoped that
> in this way he would conquer both Sicily and Carthage, and that if
> successful he would increase his private resources [ta idia] in both
> wealth [chrêmasi] and reputation [doxêi]. And because the citizens
> esteemed [axiômati] him for these things, he entertained desires
> [epithumiais] greater than his actual means for horse-breeding and
> other expenses. It was this which to no small extent later destroyed the
> Athenian city-state. For most citizens became frightened at the enormity

---

[3] Cf. Gribble on the "remarkable historical effects" Alcibiades produces through "his behaviour, his character, and the reaction it aroused in the Athenians" (1999: 184). Wohl rightly sees that our challenge is to account for the ambiguities and outright contradictions in the citizens' reactions (2002: 128, 144–54), but I believe the cognitive scope of these reactions goes beyond their "perverse love" for him. Erotic response does, however, form a fundamental thematics of the "Alcibiades effect," as Ludwig (2002) and Monoson (2000) also see, but Gribble underestimates (1999: 73–80).

[4] Despite this passage Forde claims that "Thucydides never gives us a synopsis of Alcibiades' career and character in the History as it stands" (apart from a few general, "notoriously ambivalent" remarks) (1989: 176).

of his rule-breaking [paranomia] *at a personal level* [kata to heautou
sôma] *regarding his lifestyle and at the enormity of his intent* [dianoias]
*in each one of the things he might achieve. This made them hostile to
him as though he were a man desiring* [epithumounti] *to be tyrant;
and even though in his public life* [dêmosiai] *he directed warfare
superbly, each citizen was privately* [idiai] *upset with his habits*
[epitêdeusin], *and so they turned to other leaders and in no time ruined
the city-state.* (6.15.2–4)

In these few lines Thucydides echoes key themes and terms from
the Funeral Oration Pericles delivered in 430 – only here the portrayal
of the individual citizen and the response he elicits from the masses is
shot through with dystopic rather than utopian consequences. We saw
in Chapter 6 how at 2.36.4 Pericles first separates citizen pursuits into
the categories of "adherence to customary practices" (*epitêdeusis*), participation in the "political organization of the city-state" (*politeia*), and
individually chosen "ways of life" (*tropoi*). The last of these, I claimed,
evokes an arena where an individual's moral choices might not concur
with *nomos* in the sense of prevailing social norms. And of all the goods
citizens might pursue in their "way of life," Pericles singles out personal
pleasure (*hêdonê*) as potentially problematic (2.37.2). But he is quick to
point to the Athenians' collective social and cultural practices (*nomos*) as
an effective antidote to the harm an individual's self-interested moral
choices might inflict on the city-state: widespread freedom and tolerance defuse suspicions over someone's daily habits (*epitêdeumata*, 2.37.2),
and Athenians don't put on annoyed expressions (*akhthêdonas*) at one
person's pursuit of pleasure. At this point Pericles draws a distinction
between typical Athenian behavior in personal affairs (*ta idia*), where
they interact without causing problems, and public matters (*ta dêmosia*),
where "we do not break the rules" (*ou paranoumen*) due to fear of those
in authority and especially of the laws themselves (2.37.3).

Much seems to have changed in Athenian *nomos* between 430 and 415 – and perhaps in Athenian cultural life because of thinkers like Antiphon. Alcibiades evidently presented citizens with a strategy for performing citizenship and selfhood which bedeviled Pericles' idealistic notion that citizens could certainly negotiate peaceful interactions beneficial to the state as they shuttled back and forth between private and public life. He insisted that an Athenian individual could easily manage both spheres, only chastising the do-nothing who avoided that shuttle (2.40.2). And to the do-nothing's "useless" autonomy from public life he contrasted the typical citizen's "versatile and charming" personal self-sufficiency (*autarkes*, 2.41.1).[5] But in Thucydides' profile of Alcibiades as citizen and self at 6.15, these patterns of civic life no longer obtain. Gribble reminds us how the historian's eulogistic assessment of Pericles' leadership at 2.65, together with his critique of the so-called demagogues who followed Pericles, marks the transition to a new pattern and era in Athenian politics, one in which leaders engage in "personal feuding" (*idias diabolas*, 2.65.11) to lead the demos and cater to its pleasures (*hêdonas*, 2.65.10) (1999: 169–70). As Gribble suggests, now both leaders and ordinary citizens resemble one another in pursuing self-interest rather than the civic good, and Thucydides increasingly attributes Athens' eventual ruin to this new age of individualism (175).

Yet despite the mimetic effect of leaders imitating ordinary citizens in this way, the Athenians cannot really comprehend or respond

---

[5] Gribble too links Alcibiades' individualism to these optimistic lines from the Funeral Oration endorsing a national culture's ability to curb each citizen's autonomous behavior. Of the figure I call Pericles' shadow citizen, he asks, "But what is to stop the citizen's quest for honour and for independence . . . developing in an uncivic direction?" (1999: 172, w. n. 44) – a question whose pertinence grows in light of Antiphon's reasons for grounding the self in *physis*. Cf. Forde on Pericles' attempts to control negative effects of the citizens' unparalleled individual freedoms (1989: 28–30) and McGlew on Pericles' rhetorical attempt to establish "public life's domination over the hopes and pleasures of private life" (2002: 31).

consistently to the individual impulses which prompt Alcibiades' "I" to select "me" roles in public life that (he calculates) will reward his self-interest. At one point they show esteem (*axiôma*, 6.15.3) for his personal resources of wealth and reputation: here their behavior is consistent with Pericles' boast that, despite the legal equality of all citizens, an individual can win good reputation (*eudokimêi*) and the esteem (*axiôsis*) of citizens who will recognize his talent for public service (2.37.1). They seem to understand perfectly how Alcibiades' ambition for public honor (*philotimia*) is motivated by a desire for something more pleasurable than material rewards, something "ageless," just as Pericles said (2.44.4). A bit later in Alcibiades' career, however, it is these same personal resources and talents that inspire fear over his penchant for breaking the rules – and Thucydides is precise in reporting the citizens' anxiety not only over Alcibiades' desires but over that instrument linking cognition and volition, the will, which expresses itself in a person's intentions (*dianoia*, 6.15.4). I suggest that what the citizens fear is Alcibiades' moral autonomy, which like a mysterious crucible generates his golden achievements. What is more, by 415 Athenians are expressing hostility even when he succeeds brilliantly in his "me" roles because each individual citizen harbors the same sort of private annoyance (*idiai . . . akhthêsthentes*) at Alcibiades' personal habits (*epitêdeumasi*, 6.15.4) that in 430 Pericles claimed did *not* inspire citizens to grow annoyed (*akhthêdonas*) at another's pursuit of self-interested pleasure through daily habits (*epitêdeumatôn*, 2.37.2).

Antiphon might have said that the Athenians are struggling to make informal judgments about the way Alcibiades retreats into the frame of *physis* as a temporary shelter from the frame of *nomos*. To be more exact, they have problems understanding how his public performance within *nomos* can be traced back to a comprehensible sort of inner moral deliberation within *physis*: in a word the citizens aren't very adept at frame-switching. If something specific in Alcibiades' performance of citizen

and self confuses them, it is the secret of what goes on when he deliberates within the crucible of *physis*. It's as though that shelter not only
enables him to identify a strong cluster of voluntarist goods that further
his self-interest, but also to discover a way to avoid negotiating these
personal goods into a stable, coherent practice (in MacIntyre's sense)
that, in keeping with *philotimia*, also pursues social goods. The citizens
perceive a disconnection, it seems, between his incessant emphasis on
self-interest and his persistent success as a military strategist. Instead
of following Antiphon's ethical prescription in *On Harmony* – that a
citizen in search of recognition must calculate the costs and benefits to
self-interest and then risk all at the hands of peers and fortune – Alcibiades up to 415 appears to have projected his voluntarist goods wholesale
into public life without permitting the dominant social other to redefine them. Devoted to and invested in what *physis* reveals, he's a nature
boy whose identity is grounded in that frame: he looks like the first
historically identifiable Greek individual whose unique personality
could be designated by the term *physis* alone.[6]

The final point in Thucydides' profile of Alcibiades emerges from
two almost parenthetical observations about the causes of Athens' ruin.
At 6.15.3 he claims with some emphasis that "It was *this* (*hôper*) which to
no small extent later destroyed the Athenian state." But the antecedent
to "this" does not in my opinion refer simply to Alcibiades' impru-
dent spending beyond his means; rather it refers to the leader-follower

---

[6] The word occurs in this sense ca. 424 in Euripides' *Hecuba* 598; in 422 in Aristophanes'
Wasps 1458; in 409 in Sophocles' *Philoctetes* 79, 88–89; in 408 in Euripides' *Orestes* 126;
after 406 in *Iphigenia at Aulis* 558–59; and 409–401 in Sophocles' *Oedipus at Colonus*
270. For its meaning in *Hecuba*, see Nussbaum 1986: 505–6, n. 8; for *Philoctetes* see
Nussbaum 1976–77: 32–33. See Dover on its use in other plays and fragments and
references to fourth-century writers, especially orators (1994: 88–92). (In the Platonic
Alcibiades 1, Alcibiades uses *physis* to account for his innate superiority over other
politicians [119b9–c1]).

dynamics permitting the citizens' high opinion of his public ambitions and personal resources to spur Alcibiades to an even greater desire for more esteem. The second observation likewise focuses on leader-follower dynamics when it links the citizens' private annoyance at Alcibiades' personal habits to their fickle switching of allegiance to other leaders. This strikes me as more than cycles in a love/hate relationship with him and his *paranomia*. These two observations at least imply that this prodigiously talented leader was prevented from assisting – even saving – Athens by a cognitive flaw in the citizens: their inability to understand the particularities of his *physis*, specifically, the inner, moral deliberations propelling him into the competitive fray of citizen life and, in addition, the magnitude of his "desires" and "intentions" in citizen life. The key questions Athenians faced about Alcibiades' performance as citizen and self appear to be: What is this man's *physis* (individual nature)? And how does it motivate and control his *paranomia?*

Narcissism and the Paranoid Position

If, as suggested in Chapter 6, thinkers like Antiphon and tragedians like Sophocles and Euripides helped fuel interest in *physis* as an individual's true character or personality, Athenians in the 420s and after must have begun to recognize the possibility and legitimacy of achieving self-sufficiency in ways for which the Protagorean–Periclean paradigm could not account. (And the comic and tragic playwrights did invite them to scrutinize this question in an Alcibiadean register.) Sagan calls this self-sufficiency in Athens the psychosocial manifestation of "radical individualism" prompted by radical democracy; he suggests that this autonomy generated an Athenian version of a narcissistic personality type – and that Alcibiades was its most conspicuous performer (1991: 208ff.). To pursue this suggestion we need to link the new legitimacy of *physis* as individual nature with the psychodynamics of

narcissism. Among modern theorists of the self, Alford for one identifies the "possessive individualism" of the modern liberal self with
a "paranoid anxiety" which assumes that others will determine our
standing in society and deprive us of livelihood and self-respect. From
this anxiety we experience our "most primitive fears of, and defenses
against, narcissistic injury."[7]

But on what grounds in Athens of the 420s (and after) could such a
narcissistic personality seem like a reasonable performance of citizenship and selfhood? Returning to the arguments Antiphon used in *On
Truth* to destabilize and devalue *nomos*, we find that the supplementary
rather than essential nature of *nomos*, and its inevitably harmful effect
on the self, help sow the seeds of a narcissistic personality. Both points
seem to articulate an anxiety over the possibility that the self and its
vital functions – breathing, seeing, hearing, talking, working, walking –
will be contaminated by *nomos* and its values. We should recall too that
witnesses to the self's external behavior were particularly powerful
agents of *nomos* capable of inflicting shame and punishment. What is
more, Antiphon proposes that the self recognize the true components
of its well-being within its own physical and psychological nature, that
is, within the psychosomatic boundaries of the self.

This anxiety over the integrity of the self, over its possible dissolution
or fragmentation, coupled with the notion that it should provide itself
with all the resources it needs to survive and thrive, corresponds to the
transition from primary to secondary narcissism. In the first state the

---

[7] 1991: 142–44. Alford sees Rawls develop the original position and its veil of ignorance
as fictions to mitigate this paranoid anxiety. The "difference principle," which leads
us to permit social inequalities only if they benefit the least favored social groups,
works toward this end. So does the "maximum solution," where we hypothetically
choose for ourselves and others the maximum resources society allots its least favored
group – i.e., we choose the maximum allocation our worst enemy could choose for
us (Rawls 1971: 65ff. and 132–39; cf. Kymlicka 2002: 60–70).

infantile self cannot establish clear boundaries between self and other and consequently provides itself with a notion of its own grandiosity and self-sufficiency. A secondary narcissism results when the self has grown aware of its separation from others, turns to them for confirmation of its omnipotent self-image, and is inevitably disappointed at their inadequate response. One particularly conspicuous defense mechanism against both paranoia and the inadequacy of others, Sagan points out, is an insatiable and ultimately self-destructive greed (1991: 29–30) – and he characterizes Thucydides' *History* and the role of Alcibiades as a chronicle of such self-destructive greed and grandiosity (364–66).[8] Kohut would say that the narcissistic self fails to establish with others relationships based on empathic transference, and so it cannot recognize in them adequate selfobjects to mirror back the admiration, strength, and alter ego it seeks.[9] The resulting "chronic narcissistic rage" will eventually take the form of anxieties about a hostile environment and lead to enacting the "paranoid position."[10] It seems to me that when Antiphon in *On Truth* destabilizes and devalues *nomos*, he lays the groundwork for enacting this position; and he expresses the narcissist's anxiety over the boundary between self and other through a sophist's discourse about the superiority of *physis* over *nomos*.

In *On Harmony*, however, Antiphon tempers this anxiety over both sets of boundaries by insisting that a citizen must not only recognize

---

[8] For a historian's view of greed as a "key ideological weapon in public debate" after 431 and an "individual motivation" for Alcibiades and others, see Balot 2001: 166–72.

[9] See Kohut 1977: 103–19, 171–91, and 1984: 192–94. In Alcibiades' personality Sagan sees primary narcissism in terms of two hypothetical speech acts: "I am beautiful because *I* say so. I need only the mirror to confirm that I am alluring and powerful." Secondary narcissism, where the self turns to others to mirror back this self-image, is "more problematic" because the self claims, "I am only beautiful if *you* say so" (1991: 217).

[10] See Kohut 1977: 121, borrowing the phrase from Melanie Klein. On the paranoid position in relation to democratic societies ancient and modern, see Sagan 1991: 13–33.

them but respect them – that is, he must interact with others within the frame of *nomos* because, if we choose well our friends and allies, these others can serve as more or less adequate mirrors of our self worth. In effect this essay upholds the legitimacy of a boundary between *physis* and *nomos*, however challenged the citizen may be to decide just where that boundary should lie. In particular it seems to point to the importance of recognizing true friends as selfobjects capable of resembling the self and of reflecting back to it a reasonably accurate sense of its social value or usefulness.[11]

The life of Alcibiades on the other hand rejects this essay's ethical mandate. From what the Athenians observe as witnesses to this life, Alcibiades often ignores the boundary between *physis* and *nomos*: he sometimes acts as though witnesses weren't present and as though *nomos* were of no account. And when he does note witnesses, he demands that they mirror back to him the omnipotent self-image his *physis* "reveals" to him, which denies their own autonomy and sees them as mere indexes to his inner life. In refusing to acknowledge the boundary mark of *nomos*, he demands that its values be translated into the self-interested values of his *physis* rather than the other way round. As Wohl sees the spatial metaphor in Alcibiades' *paranomia*, he brings what is "beyond" the law – what I equate with *physis* – "and settles it alongside (*para*) the normative. He brings what should be marginal to the center of Athenian political life . . . and sullies the center" (2002: 144).

The problematics of witnessing for a narcissistic personality makes more plausible my suggestion that most Athenians faced cognitive problems in understanding how to evaluate Alcibiades' *physis* and the *paranomia* it induced in him. The more astute among them might have

[11] Fr. 62 aptly describes a close friend as a selfobject: "Of necessity the self's character (*tous tropous*) becomes like the person with whom he spends most of the day." Cf. fr. 65 on our inability to recognize true friends because we prefer flatterers.

been able to diagnose, if they had such a term, a "personality disorder" likely to lead to personal ruin and, should the populace continue to support him as a leader, to the sort of public ruin Thucydides adumbrates. Is there a necessary link, as Sagan proposes, between radical individualism and social catastrophe? And between the narcissistic personality's "intrapsychic conflicts" and social displays of power and aggression in addition to greed (1991: 208–9)? For an answer I prefer to see the motive and dynamics of Alcibiades' *paranomia* as the unique historical effect of a narcissistic personality disorder that blurs the boundaries of self and other and *physis* and *nomos* – rather than as the inevitable manifestation of a systemic sexual code (Wohl) or as the boldly exaggerated political enactment of Pericles' injunction that each citizen long to possess Athens (and its power) as an active lover (*erastês*) (Ludwig 2002: 331).

In Chapter 6 we looked at Pericles' attempt in the Funeral Oration to transform the performance of citizenship into what Ludwig calls a politicized version of eros, a sublimated eros in which a citizen substitutes the self-regarding love of what is one's own for the higher pleasures of an other-regarding passion for civic honor and beauty. And we suggested that, if Pericles reminded citizens of the way Harmodius and Aristogeiton transferred their private passion for one another into a love of freedom for Athenians, it was because he wished to short-circuit that potential of erotic scripts in the Greek tradition to provide individuals with shelters where the "I" might experiment with moral autonomy outside socially defined "me" roles. His model of citizenship and selfhood therefore relied on recoding into the virtue of *nomos* whatever virtues a private erotic relationship might generate. What happens, though, if a citizen's narcissism interferes with this recoding? Does this change the nature of the eros he experiences and his ability to recode it?

Thucydides' profile of Alcibiades as citizen and self clearly serves as a prelude to his dramatization of the inconsistent, incoherent leader-follower dynamics linking Alcibiades to the majority of citizens. Alcibiades' passionate speech in 415 in favor of the Sicilian expedition, and the citizens' wildly enthusiastic response to the debate it provokes, demonstrates how the narcissistic personality triggers a distinctive sort of communication with others. In the speech's first rhetorical tactic Alcibiades resembles a gameplayer at *pessoi* or *polis* intent on confusing his opponent and any spectators about the rules. He needs to rebut Nicias' charge that he has broken the rules of good citizenship by caring only about himself (*to heautou monon*) and endangering the state just so he might win admiration (*thaumasthêi*) for his personal resources and "shine out" as an individual (6.12.2). How better to achieve this than to claim that in his case there can be no distinction between personal gain and public benefit, between self-interest and civic interest (6.16.1)? Or that a "brilliant" citizen may inspire in all who know him envy while alive but in death will become everyone's kin and be equated with the fatherland (6.16.4)?

Once Alcibiades has broached the possibility that his own *physis* may be equated with the collective well-being of Athens, and that its secret crucible will forge the city-state's success, he has persuaded the citizens to look upon him as a selfobject. He draws each of them into an empathic transference through which they see mirrored back to themselves their own confirmation of a grandiose-exhibitionist self. As a result he infects them with his primary narcissistic vision of a self needing no reliance on others. And at this point he is prepared to persuade them to experience the delusions appropriate to secondary narcissism, namely, to take up the "paranoid position" or to pull "out all the paranoid stops" as Sagan puts it (1991: 220). This generates a scatter-shot volley of enthymemes tenuously related to the realities of Greek interstate warfare: mere defense against a superior power is no match for preemptive, offensive action; by not continuing to increase our rule over others we are sure to be ruled by them; our citizen body can only exert power if it unites old and young; military idleness leads to civic deterioration (6.18).

The "lust" (eros) for the expedition that falls upon all the citizens in equal measure after this assault, and after Nicias misguidedly conjures up a grandiose and exhibitionist checklist of resources the Athenians would need to muster for a successful invasion, hardly resembles the sublimated eros Pericles counseled the citizens to adopt in 430 in imitation of the tyrant slayers. Nor is it, strictly speaking, a collective expression of mass hysteria. It is, rather, a libidinal attachment to Alcibiades, which each individual citizen constructs according to the self-interested values of his own *physis:* in effect the secret deliberations of Alcibiades' *physis* serve as a model of mimesis for each citizen to perform in his own way. And each directs his eros toward the expedition through Alcibiades himself in an empathic transference to him as a grandiose exhibitionist selfobject. Each Athenian then enacts in a public limelight the inner moral deliberation of Pericles' shadow citizen – and a new *nomos* (a state decree, law) emerges when each, after retreating into *physis*, publicly registers his vote.

The *dêmos*' "love" for Alcibiades therefore looks to me like a vicarious recognition within themselves of the legitimacy he proclaims for his own *physis* when he shares its deliberative techniques. If they love him "not in spite of those *hybrismata* [outrageous acts] so feared by his rivals but precisely because of them" (Wohl 2002: 145), it's because at moments like this those hybristic ends no longer appear to them as his but as ends they've come by on their own. As Ludwig suggests, eros arises in the citizens when they contemplate the vast resources for their impossible mission at least partly "out of a narcissistic exultation" eros can induce each of us to feel in our "physical prowess" (2002: 165). Secondary narcissism also helps explain the "infinite expansion" the object of desire undergoes once the self decides to own the fantasy: it's not just Syracuse but all of Sicily, later all of Italy,

Carthage, the Peloponnesus, and the entire Greek world (Wohl 2002: 189). Sagan calls this defense against the narcissist's anxiety of self-disintegration the "paranoidia of greed, the attempt to eat up the whole world" (1991: 29).

Narcissism and Personality Cult

In the script "how citizens deliberate" Alcibiades has changed the rules, but most of the participants and spectators have hardly noticed. He has succeeded in forging a collective *nomos* out of many individual expressions of *physis* – all of which, however, are modeled after his own *physis*. As a leader transformed into a selfobject, he has violated the boundaries of private and public, self and other, *physis* and *nomos*. And the secret motive behind this violation is a narcissistic anxiety, even rage, which he – and then each citizen – experiences when the self feels vulnerable to weakness or fragmentation because its omnipotence cannot be confirmed. Despite its secret nature, Thucydides lays bare this fear or rather records its enactment two or three months later in the confused time and space of an anonymous act committed partly in public, partly in private, by gangs of shadow citizens who perform under cover of darkness: I'm referring to the nighttime mutilation of the sacred statues or "herms" that marked boundaries between public and private spaces within the city (6.27). These schematic representations of the male body, whose features were reduced to head, column, and erect phallus, literally became fragmented when, according to the historian, their faces were smashed (6.27.1) and according to Aristophanes (*Lysistrata* 1093–94) their *phalloi* were knocked off.

Why did some citizens link Alcibiades with this sacrilege, as well as the drunken vandalism of other statues (6.27)? We find a global explanation in the narcissistic symptom of anxiety over the fragmentation of the ego, symbolized for the individual citizen by the defacing and castration of the herms and for the collective citizen body by an oligarchic or tyrannical dissolution of the democracy. More locally, fragments from lost comedies by Aristophanes before and after 415 indicate that phallic jokes were in the air when Alcibiades' name popped up: "he was born when Phallenius was archon" (fr. 244); he appeared thinly disguised in *Triphales* ("Triple-Big Phallus").[12] And the reasoning citizens used to formulate their accusation against Alcibiades and other suspected perpetrators, which soon assumed the legal formality of a motion in the Council for impeachment (*eisangellein*, Andoc.1.37, 43), did not conform to the same sort of cognitive acts the citizens habitually used when they evaluated (*axiôsis, axiôma*) Alcibiades' *physis:* from the descriptions by Thucydides, Andocides, and Plutarch, it's clear that the authorities launched a witchhunt to find the perpetrators, one of the classic ways a community collectively and universally enacts the paranoid position.

But we find more precise manifestations of narcissistic rage and paranoid defensiveness in the second scandal that some citizens immediately linked to the mutilation of the herms. This was the charge that Alcibiades and others profaned key ritual roles, actions, and words from the sacred state mystery cult, the Eleusinian Mysteries.[13] Munn is, I think, correct to argue that we not limit our understanding of this

---

[12] Munn suggests why Alcibiades "may have come to mind as the Athenians contemplated this outrage" by adducing comic fragments associating Alcibiades' nature with the phallus itself (2000: 104 and 382, n. 20, with references). Munn also links the mutilation with the crowd of herms standing around the agora's "stoa of the herms" (= *stoa basileios*), in front of which also rested the sacred stone on which the dismembered genitals of sacrificed animals (*tomia*) were traditionally placed for officials to stand on when they swore loyalty oaths. And to this he adds Plutarch's association of the mutilated herms with the "omen" of a man who castrated himself in the agora at the altar of the twelve gods, apparently in imitation of the ritual performed by male servants of the Mother Goddess Cybele (104 and 382, n. 21; 384, n. 35). Cf. Wohl 2002: 154–55, and McGlew 2002: 132–37.

[13] The key sources are Thuc.6.28.1–2, 6.53, and 6.60–61, and Plut. *Alcibiades* 19–20 and 22.3–4, along with Andocides I (*On the Mysteries*).

event to the few occasions cited in existing sources, and certainly not to Alcibiades and his friends alone, but that we identify it with a pattern of aristocratic behavior consistent with the habit of clustering into political clubs and symposia under a faction leader (2000: 106–10). He is perhaps also on the mark in supposing that Alcibiades' offense was not to mock or parody elements of the mystery cult but to *enact* them in an attempt to consolidate his personal aura of omnipotence: as he puts it, Alcibiades wished to "personal[ize] and sanctify[ ] the quality of his leadership" by "push[ing] the boundary between personal loyalties and the paramount loyalty to the state" (108–9). As a result, he "imitated" – *apomoumenos*, as Plutarch claims from the official indictment (*eisangelia, Alc.*22.3) – elements of the cult of Demeter and Persephone in order to initiate followers into his "communion," not with the Mother Goddess and Daughter, but with an alternative, his patron divinity, Eros.[14] My question is: in addition to dressing in the high priest's robe, assigning his comrades other ritual roles, and addressing those present as initiates, what "sacred things" (*ta hiera, Alc.* 22.3) did he reveal in imitation of the Eleusinian cult? And might this revelation tell us more about the inner or secret *physis* of the narcissistic personality – and also about a leader's ability to serve followers as a selfobject for their own narcissistic aspirations and fears?

Burkert tells us that Greek mystery religions seem to lead "beyond" the city-state by providing their initiates with opportunities to exercise their individuality in ways not prescribed by civic culture. They do so through their personal decision to enter the mysteries, to confront the problem of a personal death and afterlife, and to reach the "peak" of "the autonomy of the individual" by embracing a cult whose "rules are

---

[14] On Alcibiades' "communion with Eros," see Munn 2000: 111, with references. On the link between the various political clubs (including Alcibiades') and the mutilation of the herms, see McGlew 2002: 129–38.

set for a life on one's own responsibility" (1985: 278). Now the most sacred moments of Demeter's cult appear to have involved the revelation of objects contained in a sacred basket with a snake, and these objects probably communicated in symbolic form the interaction of cosmic forces of fertility (Burkert 1983: 266–74). Interpretations and evidence about the symbolism of these objects and the basket vary: did they symbolize the intercourse of male and female genitals (270–71)? Or the sexually sublimated action of mortar and pestle grinding wheat for cakes and a sacred beverage (272–73)?

Either way it's clear that the cult's ritual roles, symbols, and actions could readily be adapted to a cult of Eros, and in a way not too far removed from our sense of a "personality cult." Alcibiades would have encouraged prospective members to exercise their individual autonomy by choosing to join a micro-community centered around him as an alternative to the community formed by civic cults. In particular, if we understand eros as libidinal attachment, whether in the narrow sexual or the broader emotional sense, we can surmise that Alcibiades adapted the Eleusinian Mysteries to recruit or bind followers into a conspiratorial group led by him as its high priest and focused on communion with the power of Eros. Like the Eleusinian rites, this would have involved a manipulation of isolated objects, food, and drink to symbolize a connecting of fragmented body parts or natural substances, and an incorporation of the isolated individuals playing the "initiates" into a newly integrated, collective body. (Given the association Athenians formed linking the mutilation of the herms, Alcibiades' prodigious sexuality, and his imitation of the Mysteries, it would not be surprising if one of the symbolic objects he manipulated was a rendering of the phallus.)[15]

---

[15] Burkert points to traditions in Dionysiac mysteries that the god's dismembered phallus was hidden in a basket or revealed in a winnowing fan, and that the

If we are on the right track, Alcibiades' performance at these private parties or rites would have evoked in his conspirators the same powerful psychic response experienced by the initiates at Eleusis. Only in the case of Alcibiades and Eros, the ritual dramatization would have revealed to them the answer to the question the Athenians had been struggling to find for at least a decade: What was going on in the crucible of the great man's character or *physis*? If the secret of his *physis*, as I've outlined it above, is the psychic dynamics behind primary and secondary narcissism, then his performance illustrates the self's passage from the experience of disintegration or fragmentation to attempts to compensate for this weakness by imagining grandiose and omnipotent forms of selfhood – that is, the confederation of followers or conspirators united around the leader who serves them as a grandiose exhibitionist self-object. Since secondary narcissism turns to such compensatory psychic mechanisms as the paranoid position, it's not surprising that its dynamics finds and enacts boundary violations everywhere: and this, I believe, accounts well for Alcibiades' persistent *paranomia*. But, in keeping with the nature of mystery religions as Burkert outlines them, this bizarre ritual performance of citizenship and selfhood also demonstrates to followers how to enact a radical individuality and moral autonomy beyond what Antiphon or most Athenians would tolerate. In other words, the same dynamics of boundary violation and imagined grandiosity apply here: in an act of self-liberation, the morally autonomous individual violates with impunity the boundaries of traditional belief systems, all in hopes of achieving an imagined, greater integration of self.

---

dismembered genitals of Cybele's male servants were kept in recesses or receptacles (*thalamai*) (1983: 271, with n. 23 and references). We should also recall the possible link between the mutilated herms and the sacrificial victim's dismembered genitals (testicles) used in swearing oaths, civic as well as "private" or conspiratorial.

Gernet's notion of hybris as the archetypal Greek crime helps explain why the nexus linking Alcibiades, individual self-interest, eros, greed, and boundary violation generated a religious awe for his followers and revulsion for most everyone else. By the fifth century, Gernet claims, Greeks hadn't developed a psychology of the criminal mentality applicable to common criminals such as the *kakourgos* (malefactor), but they had begun to understand the mentality of the subject or perpetrator of hybris (the *hybrizôn*). This individual incarnated the subjective and intellectual principle behind crimes committed through a premeditated intent to commit evil "for its own sake." For while hybristic crimes may involve sexual aggression or material gain, they are not in principle motivated by desire for pleasure or profit or by uncontrolled emotions like anger: they're motivated instead by an individual's cool, calculating will to express evil as a power or superiority over others, a power that threatens city-state unity (2001 [1917]: 390–94). This "pure" concept of hybris, Gernet continues, may become increasingly "interiorized" for Athenians in the age of tragedy (399), linking the perpetrator of hybris to the concept of *physis* (430), but hybris still retains its traditional sense of religious violation through profanation or blasphemy – the same original sense of violation we find in *paranomia*, a term close to hybris (397–98), along with *pleonexia* (excessive greed). This explains why for Gernet Alcibiades is "the *hybrizôn* par excellence, the living synthesis, so to speak, of hybris in all its forms" (419).

Alcibiades' Autonomy: Comic and Tragic Stages

By 414 the Sicilian expedition was in progress, and Alcibiades had escaped to Sparta to avoid arrest for the mutilation of the herms and profanation of the Eleusinian Mysteries. That spring Aristophanes presented his comedy *Birds* at the City Dionysia Festival. Its hero Peisetaerus ("Persuades Comrades") and his sidekick Euelpides ("Has

Lofty Hopes") have quit Athens in search of a tranquil or "do-nothing" life (*apragmona*, 44) free from embroilment in the city-state's debt-ridden network of legal institutions. They venture into the disorganized, airy world of birds, where Pcisetaerus quickly spots an opportunity. He'll persuade these feathery folk, now ignorant, scattered, and battered, to establish a new community, an avian city-state, destined to recover the worldwide hegemony birds once enjoyed before Zeus and the Olympian gods came to power. Once this idea hits him, Peisetaerus is unstoppable: in a knock'em dead speech and debate with the chorus of birds (465–626), he traces their once glorious roles as world rulers, their decline into a subaltern race, and the even more glorious future they'll have when they become educated and "energetic busybodies" (*polypragmôn*, 471).

Scholars have interpreted this play widely, some claiming its highly imaginative plot has nothing to do with Athenian politics, but most admitting a probable connection to contemporary issues of political leadership, the influence of sophistic education and rhetoric on political deliberation, and the Sicilian expedition, which in 414 still looked rosy to most Athenians.[16] This cautious inclination toward "probable" topical references sees the play as a broad satire or utopian fantasy about the Athenian democracy, empire, and national character but rejects it as an allegory that systematically equates details of plot, characterization and language with specific political events, leaders, and decrees.[17] More

---

[16] E.g., for Whitman the play is "free of political concerns" (1964: 173), while others emphasize its escapist, fantastical elements (e.g., Sommerstein 1987: 1ff.); see additional references in Hubbard 1997: 42, n. 20. Dunbar's skepticism about references in the play to Alcibiades and the Sicilian expedition typifies scholarly conservatism on the issue. She calls "unconvincing" claims that Peisetaerus has Alcibiadean characteristics (1995: 3); see also MacDowell 1995: 21ff. and Craik 1987: 33.

[17] On the play as a political fantasy, see Arrowsmith 1973 and more recently A. M. Bowie 1993: 166–77; as a fantastic utopia, see the essays by Dobrov, Henderson, Hubbard, and Konstan in Dobrov 1998a. Katz 1976 previews the possibilities for the

recently, however, the readings of Vickers (1997), Henderson (1998b and 2003), and Munn (2000) have altered the landscape of *Birds* criticism on this issue.

These scholars argue that the extraordinary Peisetaerus, especially his grandiose, imperialistic vision, the intellectual and rhetorical talents he deploys, and the impact these have on his avian followers, point in allegorical fashion to Alcibiades.[18] While Peisetaerus may, as Henderson points out, share a vigorous "personal autonomy" with other Aristophanic heroes, he is nevertheless "atypical," a "complex composite" of elite characteristics (social and intellectual) who jumps radically from a life outside politics to political supremacy as tyrant of a new-found city-state empire (1997: 138–39). Vicker's concept too of "polymorphic characterization," in which different dimensions of one individual may be represented by several different characters on stage (1997: xxvi, 15), also challenges conventional notions of identity, as demonstrated in Chapter 5's discussion of the historical Cimon and Ephialtes in light of Aeschylus' tragic Pelasgus and Danaus. But we can narrow our focus on the question of Peisetaerus as a representation of Alcibiades by looking at the comic hero's performance of self and his followers' ability to comprehend the nature of his talents – and their desire to imitate them. This may shed light on how the play's implied audience in the theater of Dionysus understood both the comic hero and Alcibiades as agents of self-transformation.

Early in the play the birds reasonably ask what circumstance (*tychê*) has brought the two human intruders into their territory (410–11). The

more detailed "allegorical" links to Alcibiades in Vickers 1997, Munn 2000, and Henderson 1998b.

[18] See Vickers on the tradition for and against allegorizing Aristophanes and *Birds* (1997: xix–xxxiv and 154–60). Compare his list of parallels between Peisetaerus and Alcibiades (161–63) to Henderson's (1998b: 139–40 and 2003: 171–72) and Munn's (2000: 125–26).

answer they receive is unequivocal: "Passion (erôs) for the ways you make your livelihood and live your life [biou diaitês te . . .] and to dwell with you and always be with you" (412–14). Understandably the birds suspect that these Athenians have come for the typically partisan, self-interested goal of gaining an advantage (kerdos, 417) over some enemy or helping some friend.[19] But as soon as they hear that Peisetaerus promises a "prosperity that is indescribable and unbelievable," and that "he'll win you over by saying it'll be here, there and everywhere for you," the bird chorus' curiosity is piqued. "Is he raving mad?" they ask. "No, he's unspeakably smart," they're told. "Does he have some kind of wisdom in his brain?" they ask. "He's a very shrewd fox," they're informed, "all cleverness [sophisma], a swindler, an old pro, an intricate piece of work" (431). Now even though these birds know that "a human being [anthrôpos] is by nature tricky all the time in every way" (451–52), they plead for a public declaration so he might persuade them of his proposition (gnômên, 460). And their gullibility is boundless, for once Peisetaerus launches into a sophistic, anthropological explanation of their lost cosmic supremacy, they declare him their "savior [sôtêr] either by providence [kata daimona] or by some lucky chance [<tina> syntykhian]." As a result they declare, "I'm ready to settle myself down by entrusting my nests to you" (544–47).[20]

The birds, it appears, see in Peisetaerus' intellect the intervention of a specifically religious force (kata daimona) or a more abstract cosmic power (tykhê). They're astonished at how quickly his point of view (gnômê) has transformed him from an enemy to a "dearest friend" (627–28). But this transformation in him clearly transforms them as well,

[19] Cf. Nicias' charge against Alcibiades in 415 that he wished to invade Sicily for his personal gain and glory (Thuc. 6.15.2–3; Plutarch Nicias 12.4). This suspicion returns later in the play when Poseidon disclaims he's come to Cloudcuckooland for personal profit (kerdainomen, 1591). See Vickers 1997: xxx.

[20] For textual problems in these lines, see Dunbar 1995: 371–73.

and right on the spot they pass from inert, helpless creatures into a diplomatically and militarily mobilized threat:

> *"Bursting with confidence from your words, I warn and do solemnly*
> *swear that if you've come to establish conditions compatible with mine*
> *that are just, honest, pious and hostile to the gods, I'm completely*
> *like-minded that the gods won't for long be diddling around with our*
> *sceptres! Now* we're *in battle formation to do whatever brute strength*
> *needs to do; as for what intelligent planning* [gnômêi ... bouleuein]
> *needs to do – all that's entrusted to* you." (629–37)[21]

They are next urged "to do what needs doing" and "not delay by Nicias-ing around" (*oude mellonikian*, 639–40). This jab at the Sicilian expedi-tion's current leader, who was also Alcibiades' chief rival in the famous debate the previous summer (recreated by Thucydides at 6.7.3ff.), imme-diately calls the audience's attention to their leadership's contrasting types of deliberation and to leader-follower dynamics. The reference to Alcibiades as Peisetaerus' alter ego is unmistakable here.[22] But is there something specifically Alcibiadean in Peisetaerus' interaction with the birds and in the way his rhetorical skill and *gnômê* transform them?

Vickers argues that behind Peisetaerus' visit with the birds we should see Alcibiades' stay in Sparta, where in the months before and at the time *Birds* was performed he was enjoying refuge from the Athenian attempt to arrest him in Sicily for profaning the Mysteries and mutilating the herms. Vickers even sees a parallel between the comic hero persuading the birds to establish Cloudcuckooland to defy the gods and Alcibiades persuading the Spartans to establish a fortress within Athenian territory at Decelea to harass the Athenians (1997: 157–58 and 163–68.). Thucydides

---

[21] On military terms and alliance formation in these lines, see Dunbar 1995: 411–12.

[22] Earlier in the play Nicias is named for his clever military strategy (363).

reports that at a Spartan assembly Alcibiades "incited" (*parôxune*) and "roused up" (*exôrmêse*, 6.88.10) the Spartans (Vickers 1997: 167); and right after the speech he tells us they "felt a lot more strength return" (*pollôi ... eperrôsthêsan*) now that they'd heard from "the man with the surest knowledge" (6.93.1). So this proposed Spartan setting seems to document historically an "Alcibiades effect" in which a transfer of knowledge reinvigorates listeners, and the play's comic description of Peisetaerus' effect on the birds, their instantaneous mobilization, parallels this. But let's move backward to a moment before Peisetaerus gives his speech, when he declares his intention to reveal his *gnômê* to the birds. They insist he address them publicly, as though at an assembly or council meeting:

> "For perhaps you might happen to expound on something worthwhile
> you notice in me, or some greater power [dynamis] my stupid brain has
> overlooked. So do speak publicly [leg' eis koinon], for if you do see
> something brave [agathon] in me, it should be made public [koinon]."
> (453–59)

Peisetaerus, however, presents his speech as a kind of meal. "By Zeus," he declares impatiently, "I'm bursting with desire [*orgô*] for a certain discourse [*logos*] that's already been kneaded, but you're preventing me from mixing the ingredients together" (462–63). He then calls for a garland, tells everyone to lie down, and asks for water to wash his hands. It isn't at first clear just what sort of meal this speech will be, for the context is both sympotic and sacrificial. "Are we about to have dinner?" Euelpides inquires. But Peisetaerus only says, "By Zeus I've long been eager for a big, fattened-up speech [*epos*], one that will trample [*thrausei*] their soul" (*psykhên*, 465–66).[23] In place of a public

---

[23] Dunbar discusses the food images, the confusing sympotic/sacrificial context, and the final image of the speech as a "massive bull or ox charging and smashing the hearers' minds ..." (1995: 318–23). She sees the kneaded concoction as a barley-cake

deliberation, Peisetaerus' wonder-working rhetoric takes the form of a mixed symposium and sacrificial meal at which one man serves both a kneaded dish (a barley-cake?) and meat (a bull or ox?). Each guest, he hopes, will experience this meal as a mind-shattering experience – and we've just seen (at 629–37) how this "meal of words" indeed transforms his listeners into a threatening, aggressive force.

Because Aristophanes replaces the anticipated public deliberation with a discourse mixing the sacred (sacrificial) and profane (sympotic), as well as public and private, Peisetaerus is guilty of *paranomia* in Gernet's cultural and religious sense. As a sacrificial sharing of nourishment, the speech draws on the religious power to bind community members together and spiritually invigorate them; but as a sympotic occasion, it also invites them to indulge in personal pleasure. Now why does this inappropriate mixing, which constitutes a political deliberation as well, prompt Aristophanes to recall (at 638–39) the contrast between Alcibiades' and Nicias' leadership? We can legitimately infer that here the playwright draws on the most dramatic instance of *paranomia* in recent community memory: the profanation of the Eleusinian Mysteries, where at a private symposium Alcibiades re-enacted the role of high priest and manipulated sacred objects associated with Demeter's cult.[24] I've already speculated that Alcibiades

---

(319) and remarks that this "meal of words" "is now a sumptuous meat-dinner such as normally happened only after sacrificing an animal to a god" (323). Since the play's opening, Peisetaerus and his side-kick have been carrying sacrificial implements with them (a basket, cooking pot, and myrtle branches, 43; see Dunbar 151). Craik connects these plausibly to a parody of the Anthesteria festival (1987: 31).

[24] Earlier in the play, at 147, Euelpides worries about the state warship, the Salaminia, coming to fetch them: nine months earlier it had gone to Sicily to arrest Alcibiades and others on charges related to mutilating the Herms and profaning the Mysteries. Vickers sees Aristophanes covertly alluding to the profanation in what he reads as a parody of the Spartan ritual Hyacinthia at 685–72. He and others detect additional references to the profanation at 489–91 and 1553–64 (1997: 188). Ruck sees the necromancy Socrates performs with Peisander and Caerephon at 1553–64 as a clear reference to widespread aristocratic parodying of the Mysteries under Socratic

put Eros in place of the goddess and replaced the Eleusinian sacred objects, food, and drink with a different set centered on himself and symbolizing a combination of body parts or natural substances.[25] In *Birds* Peisetaerus gives a similar discourse, at first centering it on his own appetites for speech and political power, then aiming it at satisfying his listeners' individual appetites for food and drink, and then somehow "transubstantiating" these into an intelligence they'll equate with his power and theirs (*dynamis*, 455 and 163). So in place of deliberation and the reason giving of *nomos*, Peisetaerus substitutes acts whose value lie in the frame of *physis*.

All the play's critics recognize the sophistic opposition of *nomos/physis* as one key to its thematics, but not all take Aristophanes' use of *physis* to mean individual self-interest.[26] But if Peisetaerus looks like "the prince of physis" (Arrowsmith 1973: 159), it's because he himself persistently enacts self-interest as the greatest good – and inspires others to imitate that performance within themselves. His performance bears, though,

---

influence (1986: 152–60). Craik argues persuasively that the play largely parodies the Anthesteria festival and, by extension, echoes the profanation of the Mysteries (1987, esp. 34). Munn too sees a general reference to the profanation in the self-imposed exile of Peisetaerus and Euelpides from Athens and in wordplay around the *epops* (hoopoe bird) (2000: 125, w. 387, n. 66, and reference to Hubbard 1991: 159–82).

[25] The god Eros appears twice in the play, as a primordial deity and progenitor of the birds in the elaborate cosmogony Peisetaerus spins for them (696) and more conspicuously at the triumphant conclusion, where he appears driving the wedding chariot of Zeus and Hera as Zeus' "best man" (Dunbar 1995: 751ff.).

[26] Arrowsmith discusses at length *nomos/physis* in the play (1973: 157–64), emphasizing the more traditional meaning of *physis* as the power of nature, human nature, and national character made manifest within individuals. While noting that some like Peisetaerus act "selfishly" (159), on the whole he disregards the moral sense Antiphon gives the term and which I believe Aristophanes dramatizes in the play. Others recognize that the play dramatizes the "radical subjectivism" of the sophists (Hubbard 1998: 29) or the "ambitious individualism associated with the sophistic conception of human nature" (Konstan 1998: 16), but they don't link this explicitly to *physis*.

a particularly Alcibiadean signature, for the eros or passion that motivates him to live the life of the birds and "to dwell with you and always be with you" (412–14) is not primarily an appetite for food but for sex.[27] More specifically, as Arrowsmith plainly demonstrated, it is the power of the erect or "winged" phallus (1973: 135ff.). The most dramatic impact Peisetaerus has on individuals within the play is not to pique their appetite for food but to instill a desire for wings so they may emigrate to Cloudcuckooland. Now it's true that the chorus touts the advantages of wings to the audience for reasons sexual and otherwise: wings, they claim, endow us with an instantaneous mobility ensuring individual emotional, physical, and social well-being.[28] And Peisetaerus himself argues that words themselves are wings for the mind (nous), elevating the individual human being.[29]

But the play's dominant association of wings, flying, and birds celebrates the phallus. More than any other self-interested body part or action, for Aristophanes the phallus and its "elevation" liberate the self from what Antiphon terms the "chains" (desmoi) imposed by nomos on our body parts (eyes, hands, feet, etc.) and on our desire (44[B4.5–7]). But how does Alcibiades use the individual's self-interested use of the phallus within physis to break the chains of nomos? Again we need to return to the "Alcibiades effect" on those who hear his speeches or observe his religious acts. Xenophon describes a speech Alcibiades delivered to the

---

[27] Dunbar suggests in these expressions a sexual double entendre; cf. 324 (1995: 295).

[28] At 785 the chorus claims, "There's nothing better or sweeter than to be by nature winged [physai ptera]." Having wings promotes physis as individual well-being because: you can fly home for lunch when bored by the tragedies and return in time for the comedies; you can fly off to shit when you urgently need to and avoid embarrassment; you can fly off to have sex with the wife of a government official you see in the audience; you can strike it rich and acquire upward social mobility (786–800).

[29] "By words is our mind elevated and a human being raised up," he assures the sycophant, an occupation that uses language to foment social strife (1448–49).

Council and Assembly upon his triumphant return to Athens in 407, where he was named complete military authority (*hêgemôn autokratôr*) and savior of Athens' former power (*Hellenika* 1.4.20). Plutarch details the response of both the army and the uneducated masses to his next act, which was to guard the processional route to Eleusis from Spartan military interference for the first time since the enemy occupied the fortress of Decelea in 413. He tells us that: first, Alcibiades' own spirit (*phronêma*) "was uplifted" (*êrthê*) by this achievement; second, "he lifted" (i.e., inspired) (*epêren*) his soldiers to feel that they were "unbeatable and invincible as long as he was commander"; third, "he was so popular with the downtrodden and poor that they felt a wondrous passion [*eran erôta thaumaston*] to make him tyrant over them"; fourth, they hoped he'd "become mightier than the power of envy"; and finally, they hoped he'd "get rid of the decrees and laws and spreaders of nonsense who were destroying the state" (*Alcibiades* 34.7).

In this five-step, intersubjective progression we can pinpoint the dynamics of grandiosity – communicative, cognitive, and psychological – through a peculiarly Alcibiadean and phallic *physis*. It starts with an inner swelling or elevation experienced by Alcibiades himself, which is immediately mirrored by those closest to him, his troops. They experience this as a kind of hallucination: as long as they are under his command – that is, as long as their identity merges with his – they're invincible to the Spartans troops watching them parade by. Those at greatest social distance to Alcibiades, the poorest citizens, experience a swelling or elevation in overwhelming emotion combining sexual passion and religious awe (both eros and *thauma*). Like the soldiers, they too are mysteriously absorbed into the great man, but as his slaves, for he is now in their eyes a figure of absolute power, the tyrant. And their hope is that he will become more powerful still if he is "stronger than envy," which means that no other man could imagine himself a rival to Alcibiades. At this point of hallucination the great man achieves a truly grandiose omnipotence: he ceases to function for others as a mirror reflecting back to them any qualities they might recognize within themselves. He becomes, like a god, morally inimitable.[30]

Plutarch is precise in describing the political implications of tyranny, namely that one man, like a Creon, can sweep aside the community's decrees and laws and replace them with his own. Commenting on this passage, Munn observes that Alcibiades didn't need such absolute political authority: "Rather, he sought to channel popular support so that the laws and decrees of Athens were identified with his own will" (2000: 171). This magical ability to turn one's own will into law strikes me as an apt description of the secondary narcissism I've already discussed as a key to Alcibiades' personality. This results when the self realizes it must turn to others for confirmation of the infantile, omnipotent self-image it can no longer sustain. Once again Plutarch is precise when he traces the origins of Alcibiades' achievement in an intra-psychic dynamics that carefully plans the five-step, intersubjective process of grandiosity I just outlined. At *Alcibiades* 34.3–5 we learn that all matters are proceeding according to Alcibiades' intent (*gnômê*) and that "a sort of strong, not ignoble desire for *timê*" (*philotimia tis ouk agennês*, 34.3) swoops down and takes possession of him like a kind of religious inspiration. Once inside his psyche, "it [the procession to Eleusis] seemed a fine thing (*kalon*) to Alcibiades in light of reverence before the gods and reputation among people" (34.5).

With these observations Plutarch recreates how self-interested *physis* originates in a need for witnesses (divine or human) to mirror back to the self the mirage of its own autonomous omnipotence. I described

---

[30] Cf. Wohl 2002: 150–52, seeing here an illustration of the *dêmos'* "passive" love and "politically masochistic desire" for Alcibiades. Henderson sees Peisetaerus as an "ideal tyrant" for Athens and reads the play as "a fantasy of what might have happened had the demos in fact united behind Alcibiades" (2003: 172).

this earlier as "a refusal to acknowledge the boundary mark of *nomos*," and identified it as a key to understanding Alcibiades' penchant for *paranomia*. When individual will replaces law, self-interested *physis* has become *nomos* and vice-versa: there is no longer any meaningful distinction between them. In Mead's terms a narcissistic individual doesn't submit the evaluation by the "I" of the self within the frame of *physis* to the dominant social other for recognition in the frame of *nomos*, usually in the form of an acceptable "me" role. Instead the individual induces others to see in the untested self-evaluation by the "I" a mirror reflecting back to them a hallucinatory self-image, usually in the form of a godlike, grandiose omnipotence that is beyond testing or questioning – for a Greek, the image of a tyrant or god will do just fine.

For both Alcibiades and Peisetaerus, Eros is that godlike ability that causes swelling and elevation within the self and which others can so readily imitate. Metaphorically and iconographically, it's also feathery and birdlike and self-transformative. It certainly rejuvenates the graying Peisetaerus at the play's finale, when he wins for a bride the princess Basileia, a figure imagined to be Zeus' daughter and the "steward" of his phallic thunderbolt (1536–38). With a name that puns on "princess" and "sovereignty," she seems to be Aristophanes' sheer invention, but as a bride she symbolizes the sexual, political, and economic jackpot for a once down-at-the-heels elite like Peisetaerus. She's custodian of more than the thunderbolt, including "a whole bunch of other stuff: Good Advice [*euboulia*], Good Government [*eunomia*], Self-control [*sôphronsynê*], the dockyards, political mud-slinging, the state treasurer" and his bounty, the three-obol pay for daily jury service (1539–41). Such a royal lady was most certainly a hallucinatory object worthy of Alcibiades' *philotimia* in 414 and of hallucinatory imitation by all Athenians. And yet she was also an object he reportedly pursued in the flesh during the very months surrounding *Birds*' performance.

For, as Vickers reminds us, in the autumn of 413 and spring of 414 Alcibiades was said to have seduced the Spartan queen Timaea ("She Who is Worthy of *Timê*)," wife of King Agis.[31] And she bore a princeling he hoped would ever after disseminate his Alcibidean ego into the revered lineage of Spartan kings (Plut. *Alcib.*23).

In the play's final scene these predominant images of Alcibiades' psyche appear onstage: the god Eros is driving a wedding chariot carrying Zeus and Hera; Peisetaerus, now recognized as "tyrant" of the birds (1708), holds the thunderbolt; thunder reverberates amid the music; and in preparation for their nuptials the winged Peisetaerus approaches his bride Basileia.[32] Not surprisingly, he offers to elevate her on his wings: "Give your hand, blessed one, to take hold of my wings and dance with me. Lifting you up, I'll make you feel light as a feather!" (1760–61). At the play's conclusion the chorus shouts a victory chant to the hero as "the highest of gods" (*ô daimonôn hypertate*, 1765). I cannot disagree with Munn: "Peisetaerus is the perfect ruler. He is Eros incarnate, and, like that all-powerful deity, 'supreme of all *daimones*,' emblazoned on Alcibiades' shield and praised in the play's closing line, he is Alcibiades" (2000: 126).[33]

---

[31] Vickers 1997: 168–71, using Plutarch *Alcibiades* 23 and *Ages.* 3.1–2, where Vickers passes on the historian Duris' claim that Alcibiades admitted his objective here was *philotimia* (*philotimoumenon*). Vickers sees several references to Timaea in the Nightingale who appears as the hoopoe-bird's wife in *Birds*.

[32] Following Craik, I think we witness here a parody of the Anthesteria festival, which climaxed with the sexual union of the Basilinna, the wife of Athens' *archôn basileus* and someone impersonating Dionysus: Craik notes that Peisetaerus is called the *archôn* of the birds (1123) as well as their tyrant (1987, esp. 27).

[33] Cf. Ludwig 2002: 352–57: he doesn't connect Alcibiades with the play, but at its end he does see in the hero a narcissistic violator of divine-human sexual boundaries: "The imperial eros of Peisetaerus wishes to transgress all norms; he finds a beauty in transgression. The beauty he contemplates is his own, a vision of Peisetaerus transformed into an Olympian god" (357).

There's a strong likelihood that the Athenian fascination with Alcibiades, who may seem to us appropriately represented on the comic
stage as an erotic hero, extended to the tragic stage as well. I have
already noted Gernet's insight that hybris in tragedy frequently takes
the form of an individual committing a religious offense or blasphemy
(2001: 45, 399). In 409 Sophocles produced *Philoctetes*, a drama whose
protagonist violated the precinct of the goddess Chryse on her island
near Lemnos while en route to Troy. He was immediately punished
by a snake bite inflicting a wound so painful and nauseating that his
comrades felt they had no choice but to abandon him there if they
were to reach Troy. Ten years later a prophecy informs them they will
never take Troy without the willing participation of Philoctetes and
his bow (*Philoctetes* 610–13). The play's dilemma is therefore how the
Greeks – specifically the veteran warrior Odysseus and Achilles' inexperienced son Neoptolemus, on the cusp of manhood – might persuade
the banished, dishonored Philoctetes to join them to save their cause at
Troy. For several years after 415 the Athenians wrestled with a similar
dilemma over the banished Alcibiades, who was formally cursed for his
religious violations. But they finally recalled him in 411 and, as we've
seen, placed their hopes for the next few years in his military genius.

Mainstream Sophoclean scholarship has never favored an
Alcibiadean reading of this play, but A. M. Bowie's "allegorical" identification of Alcibiadean qualities in the play's three major characters
(1997) bolsters previous attempts by Vickers (1987) and others to establish
the likelihood that Alcibiades haunts the play's language and dramatic
"structure."[34] While I cannot discuss the play in much detail here, I
believe Sophocles presents his spectators with an Alcibiadean conundrum about individual autonomy and communal well-being; he also

---

[34] Unlike Bowie and Vickers, political readings by Calder 1971 and Jameson 1956 reject
identifying Philoctetes with Alcibiades.

invites them to ponder conflicts with which Antiphon wrestled, conflicts between values we perceive within the frame of *physis* and those we perceive within *nomos*. This question of frame-switching becomes, I think, the most useful key to explain the play's cruelest dilemmas and choices. As I've been arguing, it also accounts for the perplexity Athenians generally faced when trying to understand the mystery of Alcibiades' narcissistic personality, his intelligence and his knack for success – in short, his *physis*. For when we place each character and dramatic situation in the play within one frame and then the other, we appreciate how confusing and contradictory a set of cognitive and moral perspectives Athenians could draw on when comparing the importance of an individual's autonomy as a person to his citizenship.

The perspective of *physis* in all its senses seems to engulf Philoctetes completely: he has descended to a life of savagery, reduced to a near bestial subsistence on prey he shoots with his bow.[35] But to *physis* as the natural world Sophocles adds the more meaningful, moral sense of a person's "inner" self or character, a person's "nature" as expressed through the way an individual negotiates the difference between ancestral breeding and the unique personality which emerges from decisions about whether or not to own up to that heritage.[36] Because of his physical isolation and his hatred for the Greeks who dishonored him, Philoctetes knows only the world of *physis*, refusing to lay aside anger and rejoin his former comrades. In this regard Bowie suggests that he and Alcibiades share an "almost Achillean self-regard and insistence that they get what they think are their just deserts."[37] I think that his

[35] Rose discusses Philoctetes' psychological and moral isolation as an expression of sophistic ideas about human origins and evolution (1992: 282–88).

[36] *Physis* and its cognates are used at: 79, 87, 164, 903, 1052, and 1310. We find the concept if not the word referred to at 1284 and 1370.

[37] A. M. Bowie 1997: 57, referring to Philoctetes' interest in his reputation at 255ff., and 1348ff.; see also Hesk 2000: 195 (with n. 170), who remarks that "the whole play can

wound too persistently reminds him and us that it is has become his nature to live as an "extra-social" creature. In Nussbaum's description, "Philoctetes comes to light as the completely apolitical man, obsessed with self-interested and subjective concerns." Nearly a beast himself, he has no "social or other-related concerns" but lives in "solitary bitterness and a self-centered world" (1976–77: 40, 41; cf. Rose 1992: 323). The wound symbolizes this fractured capacity for other-relatedness, the fragmented self-image of a narcissistic personality. But the bow too offers a narcissistic self-image: Philoctetes recognizes in it the sole source of all his strength – and in fact the prophecy magnifies this to a strength of hallucinatory proportion, the omnipotence that can save the Greek cause at Troy.

The Greeks, and especially Odysseus, see Philoctetes solely within the frame of *nomos*. From this perspective his person and his bow harbor within them a mysterious, magical force they do not comprehend but that promises to remedy their military stalement at Troy. As Nussbaum describes Odysseus, he "accords ultimate value to states of affairs . . . which seem to represent the greatest possible good of all citizens" (1976–77: 30). A utilitarian in the modern sense, he "devalu[es] personal natures" and has no "fixed nature" himself (35). While he prefers to think of other humans solely as agents rather than persons, unfortunately for him Philoctetes and his bow cannot be separated because the prophecy at 610 specifies that the Greeks must *persuade* the man through speech (*tonde peisantes logôi*) to return with them (Hesk 2000: 192ff.). In other words Philoctetes and his bow are welded together as agent and person through the moral capacity of his will. For Odysseus the only recourse is to spin a version of the "noble lie" and deceive Philoctetes through some verbal ruse, in effect snaring Philoctetes' pursuit of self-interest within the frame of *nomos* and sacrificing personal autonomy along

be read as a reworking of the Iliadic embassy to Achilles," adding a reference to Beye 1970.

with it. As Hesk observes, "this approach leaves little room for respecting what we might call 'the rights' and 'integrity' of the individual. Odysseus' utilitarian lie undeniably undermines notions of individual freedom and dissent" (197).

Bowie reminds us that Neoptolemus, like Philoctetes (and Achilles and Alcibiades), is also driven by self-interest and concern for reputation.[38] He is after all fundamentally an ephebe facing his first citizenship test in this mission to persuade or deceive Philoctetes.[39] Because of his desire to please Odysseus and win recognition from the Greek leadership, he initially agrees to play the agent of *nomos* and implement the noble lie, even though such tactics run contrary to his own *physis*.[40] Like Philoctetes, he too cherishes the inner moral ground of *physis*, and it is this compatibility within the frame of *physis* that evokes compassion in him when he first sees the older man suffer horribly from his wound.[41] As an ephebe, it's as though he can still easily recognize within himself Philoctetes' bestial, extra-social otherness: in Nussbaum's words, the scene of pain makes "Neoptolemus conscious of the individuality and humanity of his purposed victim" (45). For his part Philoctetes sees in this young man a possibility to rehabilitate his narcissistic extrasociability, a self which, like his own, now wrestles with negotiating the transition from a personal life centered on *physis* to a citizen life centered on *nomos*. Kohut would say that the older and younger man offer one another the empathic relationship provided by a selfobject in

---

[38] A. M. Bowie 1997: 59. Calder's reading tries – without success, I think – to establish Neoptolemus as a thoroughly deceitful liar from start to finish (1971) – a reading particularly unable to account for the young man's display of compassion for the suffering Philoctetes (730 ff.).

[39] On Neoptolemus as an ephebe, see Vidal-Naquet 1988 and Vickers 1987: 174. Goldhill expresses doubts (1990: 118–23, esp. 122–23).

[40] "For by nature I wasn't born to perform any act motivated by evil trickery" (88). See Nussbaum 1976–77: 43ff., and Hesk 2000: 196.

[41] On Neoptolemus' compassion see Nussbaum 1976–77: 40.

the form of a healing alter ego, one whose likeness reassures us that we can survive our sense of limited capacities (1984: 193–94).

In this hope of transforming and healing the self, Sophocles dramatizes in heroic terms the historical dilemma faced by Alcibiades and the Athenians. How can a paranomological, hybristic creature centered on *physis* possibly negotiate a return to citizen status that is acceptable to his own self-interest and to community well-being? Can democratic citizens remain narcissistic, or must they first be cured through reestablishing empathic relations with others? The play poses these questions to its spectators but dramatizes no solution the parties themselves are able to negotiate. The necessity of community well-being intervenes as a deus ex machina, Heracles, who appears onstage to compel Philoctetes to bring his bow to Troy. If we recall how he appeared to Odysseus in Hades as a fellow sufferer who had undergone the "cure" of surviving pain to achieve self-transformation, we will not be surprised by his advice (*bouleumata*, 1415) urging Philoctetes to abandon pain and accept the glory awaiting him in Troy. We might also recognize that he does not permit this solution to sacrifice the values of self-interest perceived in the frame of *physis*, for he promises the older man rich personal rewards, fame, and a cure for his wound. He does, however, insist that the older and younger man cooperate as a twin hero, anointing them, as it were, selfobjects for one another: "I give you [Neoptolemus] the following advice: you are not strong enough to take Troy without him, nor he without you. The two of you must protect one another like lions sharing a hunting ground" (1433–37). This advice is of course Sophocles' too, given to the Athenians, especially to their elite leadership (cf. Nussbaum 1976–77: 48). For theirs was the task of learning how to admit their "lion," Alcibiades, and yet find leaders to help contain his range.[42]

---

[42] Plutarch claims that the young Alcibiades called himself a lion to vindicate his aggressive tenacity and desire to win at all costs (*Alcibiades* 2); cf. Thuc.5.43.2.

And the challenge to Alcibiades? To accept among his fellow citizens an alter ego whose likeness to himself might heal a damaged sense of self.

The Citizenship Game and its Magister Ludi

There was a tradition in antiquity that Antiphon composed a speech or speeches against Alcibiades in the form of invectives (*loidariai*). While the work is sometimes dismissed as spurious, the surviving fragments conform to the general tendency among ancient and modern writers to paint Alcibiades' *paranomia* with the broad strokes of polymorphous sexual behavior and self-indulgent lifestyle. Thucydides may have rendered these charges succinctly and modestly as "the enormity of his rule-breaking [*paranomia*] at a personal level [*kata to heautou sôma*] regarding his lifestyle [*diaitan*]" (6.15.2), where *kata to heautou sôma* literally means "in connection with his own body." And later he likewise vaguely refers to Alcibiades' "rule-breaking [*paranomian*] in personal habits [*epitêdeumata*] that was inconsistent with the democracy" (*ou demotikên*, 6.28.2).[43]

> Plutarch also refers to the way Aristophanes in *Frogs* (in 405) had Aeschylus describe Alcibiades: "You shouldn't raise a lion cub in a city-state; but if someone wants to care for one, he should be a slave to the ways it behaves" (1431–32). Cf. Vickers 1987: 186. In 1909 Croiset suggested that this expresses Aristophanes' own opinion (1973: 159–60).

[43] A list of scholars headed by Wilamowitz wishes to identify a work of Antiphon's entitled *Invectives against Alcibiades* with an essay attributed to him under the title *The Politician* (*Politikos*). Pendrick summarizes the sources and the arguments for and against this identification (2002: 47–49). Plutarch certainly believed Antiphon composed invectives, gives two examples of accusations, but sees them as untrustworthy because of Antiphon's personal admission of hostility toward Alcibiades (*Alc.*3). Gribble discusses the invectives in the context of other ancient sources about Alcibiades' scurrilous sexual escapades (1999: 74–80; 151–53). Munn accepts the invectives as a genuine work and plausibly suggests they constituted a written effort by Antiphon to destroy Alcibiades' character prior to his projected trial for violating the Mysteries (2000: 112–14).

But I noted previously how Thucydides at 6.15 probes a bit more deeply into Alcibiades' rule-breaking when he refers to the Athenians' concern about "the enormity of his intent [*dianoias*] in each one of the things he might achieve." So too in the one fragment of the *Invectives* that survives verbatim, Antiphon critiques Alcibiades' overt sexual behavior but pinpoints the nature of Alcibiades' *paranomia* in the cognitive realm of misguided *gnômê*:

> When you had passed your dokimasia *under your guardians'*
> *sponsorship, you took your inheritance from them and went sailing off to*
> *Abydos – but not to collect a personal debt or in order to be a foreign*
> *representative* [proxenias] *there. It was due to your rule-breaking*
> [paranomia] *and lack of self-control when it comes to judgment*
> [gnômê] *that you went to learn from the women of Abydos activities of*
> *that sort so that you could draw on them for the rest of your life.*
> (*Antiphon fr. C.1 [Maidment] = Athenaeus 525b*)

If Antiphon did compose this accusation, we can recognize in it his concern from *On Harmony* that a citizen learn to practice self-control (*sôphrosynê*), especially a new citizen whose recent ephebic training, as discussed in Chapter 5, was probably geared to instilling that virtue above all others. But Antiphon identifies Alcibiades' poor judgment as a *neos* (young citizen) to be the underlying cause of his inability to abide by the rules and typical behavioral patterns in this first stage of citizen life: from this perspective Alcibiades looks like the negative version, the shadow citizen, of the *neos* who may have been the ideal audience for *On Harmony*.

How did Alcibiades' *gnômê* differ from what Antiphon would have prescribed? And how might it have served to his advantage – at least for a while – in public and private life? Thucydides' *History*, we've noted, tends to dramatize Alcibiades' performances in public and semi-public deliberations with the Athenians, Spartans, other Greeks like the Argives, and with the Persians. So we can characterize his talents in this arena as those of a master player in the script "how citizens deliberate" – or even of a master player at a floating game of *pessoi* that begins in Athens but moves from state to state, eventually crossing into the Persian Empire. In fragment 52 Antiphon suggested that an adept player at *pessoi* needed to anticipate all the legal moves he could possibly make (and his opponent's as well) before changing his position on the board. We described his strategy as a kind of frame-switching between *nomos* (the rules of the game and all its legitimate moves) and *physis* (the player's self-interested desire to win).

In Alcibiades' case, however, the cognitive challenge seems exponentially more complex since in his public life from 415 to 406 he simultaneously, or in quick succession, played several different games of *pessoi*. He certainly mastered the Athenian game, probably the democratic version called *polis*, and he apparently learned the version of *polis* in democratic Argos as well, where in 420 he engineered a treaty with Athens and served as ambassador (Thuc.6.45–46, 61 and 84). But of course to achieve this, and to continue his public life successfully, he had to learn and master a form of *pessoi* suitable for oligarchic Sparta (6.88–92; 7.18; 8.6, 12 and 45). Kurke suggests that the game called *pente grammai* ("five lines") best symbolizes citizen life in oligarchies: it has far fewer pieces than *polis*, and one piece, possibly called the *basileus*, achieves the supreme position (1999: 261–65). And Alcibiades might have adapted this same game, or a royal version of it, when dealing with the Persian satrap Tissaphernes and the king himself (8.46–48 and 52).[44]

The complexity facing Alcibiades in his game-playing lies of course in his need to understand the rules of multiple versions of *pessoi*, and

---

[44] When discussing this period of Alcibiades' career, it's difficult to avoid the metaphor of game-playing. Gribble observes, "Certainly, Alcibiades is playing his own game, and aims to benefit no one other than himself" (1999: 202).

to contemplate his possible moves (and all his opponents' moves) in anywhere from two to four (or more) games that are underway simultaneously. The totality of ongoing games with their different sets of rules might encourage us to imagine Aegean domestic and interstate politics at around 420–406 as an international tournament of *pessoi*, and more than any other individual Alcibiades defined his *physis* as a champion's cognitive effort to advance his self-interest by weaving in and out of each important game in progress within the tournament. In 411, for example, he turns his deliberative talents to advising Tissaphernes and the king how best to advance their position at the expense of both the Athenians and Spartans. In a single sentence Thucydides' narration captures Alcibiades' inner deliberations, mixing into one cognitive stew a sequence of subjective thoughts in the form of judgments, intentions, projections of likely outcomes, calculations, and attempts to persuade:

> *Alcibiades gave this advice to both Tissaphernes and the King while he was with them not only because he thought it was the best advice but also because he was working on being restored to his country. For he knew that, if he didn't spoil this, it would at some point be possible for him to persuade [his fellow citizens] and return. And he thought he could best persuade them if it were to seem as though Tissaphernes were his personal friend* [epitêdeios]. *(8.47.1–2)*

We can best glimpse Alcibiades' inner deliberation as a game player's contemplation of each move open to him, as well as each of his opponents' moves, if we remove the frame of Thucydides' illocutionary statements ("he thought that," "he knew that," etc.) to suggest the original speech acts unfolding within Alcibiades' *physis*. Each move Alcibiades considers might then resemble the following stream of statements, some addressed to other persons or put into their mouths, but most unfolding in a sort of dialogue between his "I" and "me" roles, between his self-perceptions and self-evaluations and how he supposed others might perceive and evaluate him:

> *"Your Majesty and Tissaphernes, I advise you to ..."*
>
> *"This really is the best advice I can give them."*
>
> *"This action just might restore me to Athens."*
>
> *"I'd better not spoil this attempt."*
>
> *"At some point I might persuade the Athenians to let me return."*
>
> *"My best chance to persuade would result if I could hear them saying: 'Alcibiades and Tissaphernes are personal friends.'"*

I believe the difficulty of tracking the flow of this interior conversation stymied the Athenians' efforts to understand what went on in the shelter or crucible of the great man's *physis*. So far as we know, Alcibiades, more than any of his contemporaries, understood that achieving moral autonomy meant enacting Mead's dictum, "We must be others if we are to be ourselves" (1964: 292). Thucydides confirms that he succeeded in this instance by offering a coda to this particular interior conversation: "And this in fact is what happened" (8.47.2). Not long after this, Alcibiades launched a scheme (*eidos*) that set into motion an even more dizzying kaleidoscope of real and imagined intentions and speech acts. Because he wasn't sure of Tissaphernes' plans regarding the Spartans, or whether Tissaphernes wished to form an agreement with the Athenians, Alcibiades tried to sabotage any such agreement by having the Persian make excessive demands on the Athenians. But he wanted the Athenians to think that, although he had primed Tissaphernes to accept an agreement, they weren't conceding enough to the Persian for a deal to be made. Somehow he managed to script in his own mind the scenario of each party's intentions, fears, and likely responses, and then he staged a meeting where in Tissaphernes' presence he spoke to the Athenians on the Persian's behalf. They played out the role he had scripted for them, the agreement fell through, and only later, enraged, did the Athenians figure out what he had done (8.56). Along with us, Thucydides supposes that only the liminal frame of game-playing could have enabled Alcibiades to mastermind the cognitive pyrotechnics of four different subject positions.[45] As the historian earlier observed Alcibiades going to work on Tissaphernes: "And Alcibiades, *like someone competing [agônizomenos] for a great prize*, was enthusiastically fawning all over Tissaphernes" (8.52.15–17, my emphasis).

Whatever adversarial relation Antiphon may or may not have had with Alcibiades, the sophist's and speechwriter's teachings seem to have established a useful, key cognitive insight for the game-playing statesman to the effect that each game of *pessoi* with its rules, each type of society with its *nomos*, produced its own version of justice. As Antiphon expressed it, "And so the practice of justice [*dikaiosynê*] consists of not violating the laws of the city-state where one happens to play the role of citizen [*politeutêitai*]" (*On Truth* 44[B1]6–11). In Antiphon the statesman may also have found the legitimacy he sought for his refusal to submit the precious capacities of the "I" for self-perception and self-evaluation to the bondage of any one of the many sets of *nomos* he had mastered. The very suggestion that "legislation has been enacted [*nomothetetai*]" to regulate what our eyes, ears, tongue, hands, feet, understanding (*nous*), and desire (*epithumia*) should and shouldn't attempt (44[B2]31–44[B3]17) must have sounded a challenge to the radical individual within Alcibiades' narcissistic personality. In his exercise of moral autonomy there was no room for negotiation when it came to the needs of *physis* and the

---

[45] Romilly poses the obvious question in the minds of Thucydides, his readers and ourselves as we all try to puzzle out this *"étrange histoire"*: *"Comment expliquer l'attitude d'Alcibiade?"* Not surprisingly, as Romilly suggests, the best explanations we can find turn out to be *"purement hypothétique"* (1995: 170).

demands of *nomos*. If, as Ostwald observed, Antiphon conceded that "to be able to enjoy the advantages provided by the laws we have to sacrifice something of our nature" (1990: 300), Alcibiades' response would have been: "When it comes to the self, sacrifice nothing!"

II SOCRATES, THE INIMITABLE CITIZEN AND SELF

In addition to Antiphon and Alcibiades, Athenians knew another shadow citizen who was active in the years from 440 to the end of the century; and like them he too performed his citizenship as an outstanding partisan of *physis* in the sense of the individual self. Socrates was roughly Antiphon's contemporary and has of course been portrayed as Alcibiades' teacher and sometime lover.[46] Unlike Antiphon he did not base his faith in *physis* on the universal well-being of every person's psycho-physiological self, and he certainly did not share Alcibiades' pursuit of personal pleasure, material gain, and political success. He sought the shelter of *physis* elsewhere, in a private part of the self he considered the most essential to us as individuals and human beings: the *psykhê*. By this he meant our faculties to deliberate and reason as well as to experience emotions and desires. Above all Socrates thought of himself and each individual as a moral agent capable of withdrawing into the *psykhê*, where he or she necessarily distanced the self from the city-state's social and political institutions. Momentarily sheltered from the din of public opinion, he or she could reflect critically on the dominant values and practices of *nomos* and then choose a correct path

---

[46] By "Socrates" I refer to the historical individual whose arguments we can reconstruct from the early to intermediate Platonic dialogues; for the purpose of my discussion these are the *Apology, Crito,* and *Gorgias.* See Vlastos 1991: 45–80, for an appreciation of how many different Socratic minds we may retrieve from the full spectrum of Plato's work, and Nehamas 1999: 3–107. On Socrates' amorous relationship with Alcibiades, see *Symposium* 215a6–222b, where Alcibiades describes his interactions with Socrates, and *Protagoras* 309c12–13, where Socrates admits that love of wisdom is even more attractive to him than Alcibiades.

of belief or action that respected and nourished, rather than harmed, both the welfare of fellow citizens and one's own *psykhê*. As a result he legitimately appears to be the western tradition's "inventor of moral individualism" (Villa 2001: 1).

Socrates did resemble Antiphon and Alcibiades in performing his citizenship as a master deliberator, but he purposely avoided such arenas of public deliberation as the law courts, Assembly and Council in favor of two alternative types of deliberation, one semi-public and dependent on interaction with others, the other a wholly private and seemingly autonomous deliberation. The former we call the *elenkhos*, and it took the form of dialogue with one or several interlocutors, sometimes in the presence of silent witnesses; and we can legitimately consider it Socrates' method or *technê* for recognizing, respecting, and nourishing the needs of the *psykhê*.[47] The second type of deliberation was solitary and wholly interior to the person – a fact whose influence on later ancient and modern notions of the self cannot be underestimated.[48]

As a shelter of *physis*, the hidden recess of Socrates' *psykhê* must have struck Athenians as a mysterious, uncertain place and process, not unlike Antiphon's autonomous moral deliberation and the inner deliberations and choices behind Alcibiades' uncanny success and ultimate failure. It is indeed difficult to exaggerate the "strangeness" of Socrates' behavior and discourse to the Athenians. Like Alcibiades, Socrates shows up on the comic stage in connection with his intelligence. His

---

[47] On Socrates' abstention from and unfamiliarity with political deliberation, see *Apology* 31c4–e1, *Gorgias* 473e6–474a1, and 522b3–c3, where he also claims that his *elenkhos* constitutes the only true craft of politics (521d6–e1). See Yunis on how Socrates distinguishes his deliberating from public deliberations by erasing the distinction (1996: 153–61).

[48] For Taylor, Socrates is the first avatar of the "ideal of detachment" from community that constitutes one-half of our modern identity (1989: 36–37). He discusses this "inwardness" in the "moral topography" of the *psykhê* (which we will discuss) (111–14), linking it to Plato's concept of the soul in the *Republic* (120–24).

preoccupation with the soul and otherworldly realities transforms him in the popular imagination into a mumbo-jumbo wizard or magician (*goês*) – as we've seen in *Birds*, a necromancer raising Spartan-loving spirits from the dead.[49] But when earlier he appears in Aristophanes' *Clouds* (first produced in 423) as master of a school, called something like a "Think-atorium" or "Brain-iversity" (*phrontistêrion*), running it like a private mystery cult whose knowledge is open only to initiates like Chaerephon (*Clouds* 140–43), we cannot miss the implication that this business isn't harmless. By 405 (*Frogs*) his philosophizing still looks clownish – he sits around all day with friends, jabbering away over worthless nonsense, "a man out of his mind" (*paraphronountos andros*, 1499) – but again he does so ominously, using "high and holy discourses" (*semnoisin logoisi*) to produce his useless curriculum (1496–98).

In the *Symposium* Plato has Alcibiades exclaim about Socrates, "There are many other amazing things for which you might praise Socrates. But although you might say as much about any one of his customary practices [*epitêdeumata*], what most merits amazement is that he is unlike any other human being, either in the past or now living" (221c3–8).[50] There is no question that Socrates' *psykhê* incubates this strangeness, which emanates outward from an interior moral topography that was

[49] On Socrates as a comic *goês*, see A. M. Bowie 1993: 112–24. Munn links Socrates' comic image, his implied profanation of the Mysteries, his inner daimonic guide, and the charges brought against him in 399 by Meletus, to suspicions about Alcibiades as profaner of the Mysteries and to Antiphon as a "covert mastermind" of the oligarchic coup in 411 (2000: 286–91, with n. 30, 425).

[50] See Vlastos on how this strangeness is fundamental to understanding Socrates' identity and discourse (1991: 1), and on the way Alcibiades characterizes Socrates' uniqueness at *Symp.* 215a6–222b and the need to "open him up" in order to experience its effects (1991: 33–41, esp. 37, with n. 59). See also Nussbaum on the enticing prospect of opening up Socrates like a "toy" – the Silenus-box as a metaphor for sexual and epistemic knowledge (1986: 189–90). Villa attributes Socrates' strangeness to his willingness to abandon any belief, comparing the Socratic self to an unencumbered self (2001: 23).

difficult to describe without resorting to metaphor, for when it bubbled to the surface it made the man *atopos*, "impossible to place," among his fellow citizens.[51] Alcibiades can only describe this *psykhê*'s interior and powerfully therapeutic effects on other *psykhai* by reverting to the simile of a certain kind of box which is carved in the unappealing form of the piping satyr Silenus but contains within it miniature statues of divinities. He reports, "But when it [the box] is opened up *inside*, believe me, my fellow drinkers, how full of self-control [*sôphrosynê*] it is!" (216d7–9). Alcibiades then describes how, once within this inner sanctum, he marveled at the "statues *inside* . . . divine, golden, thoroughly lovely, amazing..." at which point he promptly (and ironically) surrendered to Socrates his own self-control and habitual inclination to make choices in self-interest (216e7–217a3).[52]

Like Antiphon and Alcibiades, Socrates protected his *psykhê* as a shelter of *physis* and believed in fundamental principles to ensure its health, and in this respect he too pursued a commitment to self-interest. These principles were just two in number, and they are both negative injunctions that monitor how the self behaves within its shelter of *physis*. One concerns relations with others, the other relations with the self. They are: to avoid at all cost committing an injustice against another person; and to avoid at all cost self-contradiction in one's own reasoning and the actions resulting from it.[53] So Socrates, like Antiphon

---

[51] At *Symposium* 221d3–4 Alcibiades claims, "But this is the sort of person [*anthrôpos*] who evades categorization [*gegone tên atopian*], both in his own person [*autos*] and in his discourse . . .)." At *Gorgias* 994d1 Callicles exclaims, "But how impossible you are to categorize, and how uncouth a deliberator!" See Vlastos 1991: 1, with n. 1.

[52] Examples such as these suggest that (contra Taylor) Plato does use the "inside/outside dichotomy" to account for how the virtuous individual chooses a good that may run counter to the community's goods (see Taylor 1989: 121 and 536–37, n. 7).

[53] On not committing an injustice, see, e.g., *Apology* 29b6–9, 32d1–4, 37a6–7 and b2–5; *Crito* 48b10–c1 and 49b8; *Gorgias* 469b8–10, 477e3–6 and 482b2–4. On not contradicting oneself, see, e.g., *Crito* 46b4–6 and *Gorgias* 482b7–11. For recent discussions

and Alcibiades, also values the self's well-being above all else, and his morality finds its motives in a species of eudaimonism. His practice of moral autonomy does seem rooted in egoism – and not surprisingly an egoism that is *atopos*, impossible or at least very difficult to categorize.[54] Irwin tackles the assumption that for Socrates (and Plato) "the final good promoted by virtue is always the good of the agent" (1977: 254) and distinguishes two types of egoism: morally "solipsistic," where I pursue virtue with concern about others' good *only if* it contributes to mine; and morally "egocentric," where I pursue virtue because it leads to *some* end I value as part of my own good – though it's an end I might possibly share with others (255). The key question turns out to be: When an individual pursues virtue because it benefits his or her *psykhê*, are those virtues necessarily "self-regarding," or might some of them be "other-regarding"? (225).

Since Irwin shows that a wider range of Socratic dialogues contains evidence for both types of egoism, it's difficult to answer the question definitively for the historical Socrates we are discussing. For example, when in the *Apology* Socrates tells the jurors he will never stop practicing his philosophy and playing the gadfly no matter what the consequences, is he motivated more by a need to improve their *psykhai* or to protect his own from committing an injustice and contradicting its principles? To put it another way, must his care for the *psykhê* necessarily cause him to pursue "other-regarding" as well as "self-regarding"

---

of these two injunctions see Villa 2001: 13–50, Wallach 2001: 92–119, 178–211, and Nehamas 1999: 63–69.

[54] Vlastos stresses how basic this autonomy is to Socratic morality, even though we find no explicit terms for it: "The concept of moral autonomy never surfaces in Plato's Socratic dialogues – which does not keep it from being the deepest thing in their Socrates, the strongest of his moral concerns" (1991: 44). Cf. Farrar on the Socratic project as in part "an attempt to establish man's capacity for genuine autonomy" (1988: 122).

virtues? Even more simply: must Socrates engage with others within the shelter of his *physis*? By performing the *elenkhos* in semi-public settings, Socrates surely finds others essential to pursuing virtue, and his injunction against doing anyone injustice raises this "other-concern" to a cardinal principle.

But there remains the question of his "strangeness" as Alcibiades describes it. The interior of the Socratic box, the inside of his moral treasure chest, does not seem to echo with interpersonal conversation. If there is an "other" here, it too appears in figural form: in the *Apology* Socrates calls this "my certain godlike and spiritual force" (*moi theion ti kai daimonion*), whose voice only he hears (31c8–d1); he also refers to it as "my habitual prophecy from a spiritual force" (*hê eiôthuia moi mantikê hê tou daimoniou*, 40a4). But even though it lacks dialogue, the echo of this private oracle speaks to Socrates in the form of a deliberative speech act, a warning, whose negative advice commands him to avoid morally incorrect behavior (40a6). And he states unequivocally, "I know that commiting an injustice and disobeying a superior being, whether a god or a human being, is wicked and shameful" (29b5–6).

This divine force, through "some sort of voice" (*tis phonê*, 31d3), represents the only kind of other who co-habits Socrates's *psykhê*. Where does it in fact originate, and what is its actual nature? Most Socratic commentators take the voice at face value or equate it with the modern notion of a conscience. I propose instead that it is Socrates' peculiar way of figuring that part of the *psykhê* that commands all its other faculties – what Antiphon calls *gnômê* (the capacity for reasoned judgment) and takes to be the "leader" (*hêgeitai*, *On Truth* fr. 2) of the other cognitive and volitional faculties (perception and the senses, understanding [*nous*], desire [*epithumia*], and the will). The mantic nature of Socrates' divine force clearly casts it as an anomalous private oracle, an inner seat of authority restricted to one auditor. In this regard it recalls the Delphic oracle whose authority motivated Socrates to inaugurate his life-long practice (in MacIntyre's sense) of philosophy – only now this external and public source of truth, which issues him a positive injunction, has been internalized as a strictly private index to moral truth.[55] Just as his discourse crosses the boundary between private and public when he claims that through the *elenkhos* only he practices the true science of politics (*Gorgias* 521d6–8), so does he confuse the boundary between public and private when he identifies the inner "divine force" as the source of the deliberation behind his moral authority. Earlier we characterized Alcibiades' *paranomia* as a crossing of similiar boundaries between the private and public, the self and the city-state, and we attributed this sort of transgression to the dynamics of his narcissistic personality.

Does Socrates' eudaimonistic egoism enact a "paranomological" citizenship and reflect a narcissistic personality as well? We can begin to answer this question by repeating Ober's observation that in the *Apology* Socrates' pursuit of virtue or wisdom through the *elenkhos* does not conform to the cultural pattern of the Seven Sages (1998: 173, n.33). As suggested in Chapter 4, these sages, not unlike archaic lawgivers and poets, functioned as masters of mimesis who established through their public performances a performance tradition which their followers kept alive through the art of mimesis as reperformance.[56] If the actual source of Socrates' wisdom lies in the *to daimonion* or divine force that inaugurated or legitimized his performance of the *elenkhos*, then Socrates' wisdom originates unseen within the shelter of *physis*, within his *psykhê*. This invisible performance – the source likewise of his strangeness or *atopia* – must therefore be unique to him as a person; consequently, it is

---

[55] See Brickhouse and Smith on the oracle's meaning (and Socrates' interpretation of it) in relation to his practice of philosophy (1989: 88–100); cf. Reeve 1989: 21–32.

[56] In Xenophon's *Apology* Socrates tells the jury he was no Lycurgus: while the Delphic oracle wasn't sure if the Spartan lawgiver was a god or a human, it referred to Socrates as a human (15–16).

inimitable.[57] To compare him with the lawgivers, the warnings issued by his divine force resemble a series of private laws or *thesmoi* uniquely framed for Socrates – but actually framed *by* Socrates.[58] And so when he "receives" a warning on a given occasion, and then acts accordingly to prevent committing an injustice, he enacts his own version of performing justice through cognitive frame-switching. (Instead of calling it *autonomia* we might more accurately call it *autothesmia*.) And as with Antiphon and Alcibiades, the frames in question are *physis* and *nomos*.[59]

If Socrates performs justice autonomously, and in a manner so idiosyncratic that strictly speaking others cannot imitate it, then his teaching can only encourage them to fashion inner divinities and voices of their own. Yet we hear of no such divinities echoing in the *psykhai* of his successors. Is his *to daimonion* so mysterious that it both imitated no one and defied replication in others? Was it in this regard "other-proof"? The Socratic self, it appears, nowhere finds a selfobject in ordinary human form capable of mirroring back to it an adequate image of its wholeness, its "grandiosity" (in Kohut's sense) and achievement.[60] Among mortals only Achilles strikes Socrates as an adequate

---

[57] In *Alcibiades 1*, Plato has Socrates imagine a god (*theos*) speaking to the young Alcibiades, offering him the moral choice of living a life content with all he currently possesses – or of dropping dead then and there if he weren't able to acquire more (105a3–5). Here too the divine voice figuratively represents inner moral deliberation prior to exercising one's *gnômê* in the act of choice.

[58] Athenians could explicitly liken Solon's legal authority to Delphi's (Demosthenes 43.66–67).

[59] Plutarch (*Alcibiades* 33.2) and Diogenes Laertius (13.69) say that Alcibiades also claimed a personal divine force which influenced his fate. Only his was an "envious spirit" (*phthoneros daimôn*) operating not within his own *psykhe* but in others' – it motivated their attacks on him. But of course this "spirit" very much inhabited Alcibiades' narcissistic *psykhê* as a paranoid fantasy exculpating him from responsibility for his own fate. Munn compares these Socratic and Alcibiadean divinities (2000: 290, 168).

[60] In the first of three conversations Xenophon imagines between Socrates and Antiphon, Antiphon reproaches Socrates for his inimitability, claiming that, since

self-image – and Socrates evokes the hero for the jurors just at the moment when Thetis prophesizes to her son about his choice between two possible fates (28c–d). As we saw in Chapter 1, it's this privileged knowledge that propels Achilles beyond the limits of a normal human life, opening his way into "second-order" reasoning about the justice of fighting at Troy and into hypothesizing about the person he wishes to become (*Il.*9.393–416). Like Achilles, Socrates claims that a disregard for death liberates him from any concern with shame (*to aiskhron*, 28c3) – within his *physis* there resides no internalized other. He locates a selfobject solely in the figures of Delphic Apollo, in his own private, interior oracle, or in Diotima, the priestess who, Socrates claims in the *Symposium*, reveals to him the nature of love. There Alcibiades tried to articulate Socrates' strangeness and uniqueness by asserting, "Someone like Achilles you may compare to Brasidas [the Spartan general] and others, and someone like Pericles to Nestor and Antenor, along with others. And you might compare other men in this way. But a man such as this evades categorization…" (221c8–d4). If Socrates has no ordinary human selfobjects to mirror back to him an integrated, "grandiose" sense of self capable of achievement, he likewise finds no citizens as selfobjects to embody the idealized aspirations of his philosophical practice. For these he must use the hypothesis or fantasy of the *psykhê*'s immortality and its practically unattainable moral perfection; he can only imagine, he tells the jurors, that in the afterlife he will deliberate with the shades of heroic wise men such as Homer, Hesiod, Orpheus, or Musaeus (*Symp.* 41a5–6).[61]

> Socrates' habits (*diaitasthai*) are so impoverished, no pupils would wish to imitate him as they do other teachers. Antiphon concludes that Socrates wants to lead others not to well-being (*eudaimonia*) but to misery (*kakodaimonia*) (*Mem.*1.6.2–3). We'll link this inimitability to Socrates' refusal to charge a fee for his company and the wisdom it imparts.
>
> [61] He adds that he'll meet heroic figures who serve as ironic selfobjects for the jurors and himself: the judges Minos and Rhadamanthys reveal how poorly the jurors

Can the Socratic Self Perform Citizenship?

In Antiphon's courtroom strategy for his client Euxitheus in *On Herodes' Murder*, he induced the jurors to use reasoned likelihood to imitate the man's evaluations and intentions, the work of his "I." Socrates' strategy in the *Apology* also attempts to induce the jurors to imitate the evaluations and intentions of his "I," but his speech records their collective failure to tie their own identities as individuals to a freely chosen, particular conception of the good that is largely non-negotiable – no matter how difficult (and dangerous) it may be for an individual to articulate for others the precise nature of this good.[62] The Socratic "I" in effect fails to achieve recognition from Athens' dominant social other because the jurors cannot "categorize" that "I" into one of the citizen "me" roles sanctioned by *nomos*. In bolder terms, we need to ask, "Can an 'inimitable' self function as a citizen?" Or as Socratic scholars in recent decades continue to ask, "Can we legitimately speak of 'Socratic citizenship'?"[63]

Most often scholars tackle this question by in effect trying to determine whether the Socratic *elenkhos* constitutes a valid citizen script in the Athenian democracy. And whether Socrates' commitment to the *psykhê*'s healthy functionings, with its injunctions to commit no injustice toward others and to avoid contradicting one's own reasoning, can flourish as a species of the dominant paradigm of citizenship during his lifetime. These were two versions of the Protagorean–Periclean

---

have decided; Palamedes and Ajax, like Socrates, die due to unjust verdicts (41a2–3, b1–2).

[62] Mead in fact acknowledges Socrates as the earliest embodiment of the "I" (1934: 217–218). Taylor reinforces this historical link between Socrates and what Mead calls the "I" when he attributes to the Socratic self the centering, unification, and internalization typical of our modern senses of the self (1989: 115–20).

[63] Among studies on this question I include Villa 2001, Wallach 2001, Colaiaco 2001, Weiss 1998, Euben 1997, Mara 1997, Vlastos 1994 and 1991, and Kraut 1984.

citizen, one under the ideology of popular sovereignty (450s–420s) and the other (after ca. 420) under the ideology of the sovereignty of law.[64] But there is a more fundamental issue. Can the democracy accommodate a citizen body peopled with Socratic "strangers"? By this I mean a community of individuals who must retreat into the shelter of *physis* to exercise a moral autonomy oriented toward eudaimonistic goals – goals defined by a personal sense of the good that threatens to preclude the need for "recognition" from the dominant social other in Taylor's and Habermas' senses. Or might each individual self negotiate with *nomos* an agreement securing both its recognition and "inimitability"?

We need to answer these questions by reducing our focus to just one choice the citizen as *psykhê* confronts: "Can I negotiate with the dominant social other a peculiar, idiosyncratic form of the social contract?" Our key text is the *Crito*, a dialogue dramatizing one of Socrates' final conversations before his death. In response to Crito's plea that the philosopher permit wealthy friends to spring him from prison into exile, Socrates explains his reasons for staying put and choosing to accept his impending execution. The dialogue's goal is therefore to make visible and comprehensible to others the strange goings on inside Socrates' *psykhê* when he deliberates with himself and makes moral choices. To achieve this Plato has Socrates put on within the dialogue a little drama of his own, a dialogue within a dialogue (50a6–54d1), which performs the thoroughly interior and private process of autonomous moral deliberation in the form of an external, public or semi-public *elenkhos*.

By its very nature this smaller dialogue nested within the larger one is already somewhat anomalous, and it will unfold as an *elenkhos* conducted not by Socrates but by someone else wiser and more

---

[64] E.g., Villa argues that Socrates "transforms" or "transvalues" the Periclean paradigm of citizenship into a "conscientious, moderately alienated citizenship" (2001: 5, 2).

authoritative than he. His interlocutor likewise takes the anomalous form not of a real human being but of another grandiose figure, this time a personification of the many laws of Athens. Since the dialogue is set in 399, we may reasonably suppose that Plato's dramatic decision reflects the growing influence of the ideology of the sovereignty of law. More importantly, in deliberating with these Laws, I suggest that Socrates identifies an alternative interlocutor to his *to daimonion* and an alternative selfobject for his sense of an integrated self.[65]

Because Socrates converses with *Nomos* personified – or in Mead's terms with the dominant social other personified – this embedded dialogue with the Laws returns us to the hypothetical sort of deliberation we have seen before, when individuals struggle to transform a familiar citizen script of deliberation and judgment into a creative, even unique, kind of deliberation and judgment we equate with the exercise of moral autonomy. As with the previously discussed hypothetical deliberations, in his conversation with the Laws Socrates necessarily confuses the distinction between a citizen's outer and inner life, thereby taking a step toward a rule-breaking, paranomological citizenship.[66] But is this truly the case? The Laws insist on exploring with Socrates a critical moment when a citizen deliberates morally, makes a choice, and commits himself to it. Actually they telescope a variety of such moments from a citizen's life into a single script, which they call the

---

[65] Kraut sees the Laws as a mouthpiece for Socrates' arguments, describing them as something like a selfobject: they represent Socrates' legal philosophy "propounded – for dramatic and philosophical purposes – by his imaginary adversaries." He adds, "But in order not to prejudge the issue, I will continue to speak of Socrates and the Laws as two separate characters" (1984: 41). More recently Weiss thinks that Plato adds the Laws as a new speaker (like a rhetorician) to the dialogue because they represent a position radically opposed to Socrates' (1998: 84ff. and 162–69).

[66] Note Kraut's emphasis on the hypothetical, imaginary nature of the Laws (1984: 81–82).

reaching of agreement (*homologein*), and they represent it figurally as the establishing of a contract (*sunthêkai*).[67]

I speculated in Chapter 6 that Antiphon may have pioneered the notion that *nomos* rests purely on a contractual foundation. But for Socrates this type of deliberation is more radical and critical because it forces the individual citizen to choose either obedience to the Laws, and acceptance of the "me" roles they dictate, or to engage in reasonable dissent. For an Athenian this means attempting to persuade one's fellow citizens – or, within the ideology of the sovereignty of law, the Laws themselves (figuratively speaking) – to adjust their never-ending negotiations over *nomos* so that the dominant social other might recognize the peculiar choice (*hêirou*, 52c1) of one person's "I" to play the citizen's role. Through such dissent, an individual attempts, by reaching consensus with others (*homonoia*), to transform his or her personal, private sense of the good into a public sense others may share.

Socrates and the Social Contract

The dialogue does not, however, spell out the nature of this choice by the individual citizen, nor does it attempt to negotiate with the Laws how "sharable" his private sense of the good might be. Kraut claims that Socrates' individually negotiated social contract constitutes an "implied agreement" because Socrates never said "in so many words, 'I agree to do whatever the city commands,' or 'I agree to be a citizen'" (1984: 152). Kraut provides the analogy of opponents at a chess game who agree to play but never verbally promise one another to abide by the rules. Should one opponent leave the room, and the other cheat

---

[67] The dialogue introduces the concept of "agreement" at 49e6 and hammers away at the notion that an individual's citizenship originates and rests on an agreement "to play the role of citizen" (*politeusesthai*, 52c2) and to "frame both contracts and agreements with us [the Laws] to play the role of citizen" (52d1–2 and 8, 53a6 and 54c3).

by illegally moving the pieces on the board, a true violation occurs because the act of sitting down to play implies agreement to follow the rules (152–53). Applying this analogy to the democratic game of *pessoi* called *polis*, does it accurately reflect the sort of agreement each citizen contracts when he enters the citizen ranks? Kraut wants to identify a key "act of assent," a "single, mutually understood, voluntary act [that] bears the entire burden of conveying one's agreement" (162).

And he does notice that in the *Crito* the Laws refer specifically to a voluntary act by which a young man decides to apply for citizenship status: this is the *dokimasia* or official scrutiny which, we saw in Chapter 5, a prospective citizen underwent in his deme (and again when the Council ratified the deme's decision) as he approached the age of eighteen. In order to identify the origin of the contract, the Laws move back to this very first crucial script of a citizen's life: "we proclaim that we have provided the free opportunity to anyone among the Athenians who wishes, after he's passed his *dokimasia* (*dokimasthêi*) and gotten some idea of political activities in the city-state and of us laws, if we don't please him and he wishes to depart, to take all his personal property and go where he wishes" (51d1–5; Kraut 1984: 154–60).

Does the script of *dokimasia* stage the voluntary act of assent Kraut believes a citizen must perform so that his contract with the dominant social other might constitute more than just an "implied agreement"? Kraut answers in the negative because he sees the *dokimasia* as merely the first stage in implicitly agreeing to citizenship, one initiating a series of actions the Laws loosely define over a considerable period of time. These include "[getting] some idea of political activities in the city-state and of us laws" (51d3–4), "seeing the way we render a *dikê* in lawsuits and other ways we manage the city-state" (51e2–3), and residing in the city-state for an unspecified period of time. But Kraut finds the lack of an explicit verbal agreement, a discrete speech act, as decisive for his conclusion that the Athenian citizen has not contracted a binding agreement to obey all its laws. As a result, a citizen could reasonably object to some of the laws and practice legitimate dissent. In particular he claims, "Agreements only exist when offers are made and accepted, but after the citizen has passed his *dokimasia*, it is no longer true to say that the city is still making him an offer" (191). Despite his acute perception that the Laws refer explicitly to the *dokimasia* of a prospective citizen, Kraut overlooks the wider context of the complete script of the ephebe's progress toward citizenship. These probably include a year's instruction in Athens' major military, religious, and political institutions, including their locations, to which the Laws seem to refer when they speak of "[getting] some idea of political activities in the city-state of us laws" and "seeing the way we render a *dikê* in lawsuits."

Most importantly, Kraut overlooks the crucial event, in the form of a speech act, of the ephebic oath. As discussed in the Introduction and in Chapter 5, this oath was probably administered one year after the *dokimasia*, and its wording was echoed in numerous fifth-century texts, including Aeschylus, Sophocles, and Thucydides. It also appears that its wording, recorded in a fourth-century inscription, had changed little from the Archaic period. Kraut's oversight is all the more surprising because in their dialogue with Socrates the Laws evoke promissory portions of the oath concerning the ephebe's relation to his fatherland, his role as a hoplite warrior, and especially his obedience to the laws of Athens. Soon after the Laws introduce the citizen script "reaching an agreement" (*homologêsêi*, 49e6), they summarize key stages in a citizen's progress from birth to full citizenship. They describe the crucial piece of information that needed to be established when a child was presented to the phratry and again at the *dokimasia*: his birth and parentage (50d2–4); they then pass to reminding Socrates of laws concerning a father's obligation to educate his child (50d11–12); and finally they focus on the mature citizen's relation to his fatherland (*patris*) and its laws (51a4).

It is at this point that they introduce the injunction that a citizen must "persuade or do what [the fatherland] commands" when it becomes angry at him (51b4). Among possible commands the fatherland might give a citizen, the Laws single out to be wounded or die in battle (51b6–7) and "not to yield or retreat or abandon [*leipteon*] formation." As we saw in the Introduction, in the ephebic oath the ephebe first promised, "I will not disgrace these sacred weapons, nor will I abandon [*leipsô*] the man at my side wherever I may be stationed" (1–2). Outside of war the Laws insist that a citizen obey "in a law court and everywhere else whatever city-state and fatherland command," and especially that he not attempt violently to harm (*biazesthai*) the fatherland (51b9–c3). In the ephebic oath a young citizen promised, "I will protect our sacred and public institutions, and I will not pass on my fatherland (*patris*) in worse condition but greater and better, by myself or with everyone's help" (3–4). The ephebe then turned to the question of obeying persons and laws, promising, "I will obey those who for now hold authority reasonably [*emphronôs*], and the established laws [*tôn thesmôn tôn hidrumenôn*], and those they will establish reasonably (*emphronôs*) in the future, either by myself or with everyone's help" (5). (We will return in a moment to the implications of this double qualification of "reasonableness.") Finally, if we recall the Laws' opening accusation to Socrates, that he was intending to "destroy" (*apolesai*) them (50b1), we will recognize an echo in the ephebe's promise, "And if anyone should try to do away [*anairei*] with them [the established laws], I will not let them, either by myself or with everyone's help" (6).

Kraut's argument that the individual citizen's contract with the laws forms only an implied agreement relies heavily on the need to construe consent from a citizen's nonverbal actions over an unspecified period of time. He does not believe that, after the *dokimasia*, the city-state presents the citizen with an "offer" he may choose to accept or refuse (1984: 191). As we saw, his argument made much of the fact that Socrates never said "in so many words, 'I agree to do whatever the city commands,' or 'I agree to be a citizen'" (152). I maintain that in their conversation with Socrates the Laws indeed remind him of the ephebic oath as a specific verbal agreement he made after his *dokimasia* – and that Plato's audience would have remembered and recognized this agreement. Most surprisingly, Kraut actually hypothesizes about the possibility that the city-state might require mature citizens at the age of thirty to swear an "oath of allegiance" by which they promise to "obey or persuade" the city-state or lose their citizenship (191–92). He concludes, "if Socrates had taken this oath, then of course he would have broken an agreement had he escaped from jail without persuading the city" (192).

Despite this logical conclusion, however, Kraut then dismisses the validity of such a specific verbal agreement – an agreement whose absence convinced him that citizens only had an implied contract with the city-state – because he does not believe that, once citizenship has been conferred based on the *dokimasia*, a citizen can be deprived of his "rights" on the basis of a specific verbal agreement (192). I suggest that his failure to consider the ephebic oath as a condition of entry into full citizenship renders the example of this hypothetical oath irrelevant. In the *Crito* Socrates concedes that the individual must explicitly, verbally and publicly agree to the necessity of obeying all the city-state's laws without exception. What we still need to understand, however, is this concession's strategic value to Socratic practice.

If we understand Socrates' dialogue with the Laws as in fact another instance of boundary crossing – the external version of an internal deliberation within his *psykhê* – then the Laws can represent a self-object reflecting back to him the dominant social other who proposes the most fundamental "me" roles a citizen's "I" might evaluate and consent to play.[68] In this dialogue their stern, paternal voices in effect

---

[68] Plato stages the dialogue as the external version of internal deliberation. Early on Crito urges Socrates to "deliberate" (*bouleuou*) whether to flee the prison and Athens – actually he urges Socrates to cap off a prior, ongoing deliberation

replace the divine force (*to daimonion*) Socrates usually relies on to conclude his internal deliberations about justice. If this is the case, such a substitution has major implications for determining whether we can "save" Socratic citizenship. Once the ephebe swears his oath, he in effect seals a voluntary contract with the city-state to adopt these fundamental "me" roles – and their adoption becomes off limits to any need his "I" might have to disagree. Now the repeated qualification in the oath to obey those who "reasonably" hold authority and "reasonably" establish laws (*emphronôs*) does seem to invite the citizen's "I" to renegotiate that contract.

Who determines the criteria for such reasonableness? It's been claimed that it is "certainly not the [ephebic] hoplite," but prior to Ephialtes' reforms in 462 it must refer to a corporate group, namely, the Council of the Areopagus (Siewert 1977: 103–4). After Ephialtes' reforms this determination clearly fell to citizens who adhered to the Protagorean–Periclean paradigm under the ideology of popular sovereignty. We know that Socrates has, however, habitually arrogated this sovereignty to his own *psykhê* and specifically to his "I." As he tells Crito, "For this is not now the first time, but has always been the case, that I'm the sort of person [*toutos oios*] who lets himself be persuaded [*peisesthai*] by nothing within me [*ton emon*] other than the argument that seems to me, as I reason it out [*logizomenôi*], to be the best" (46b4–6). Nevertheless, the remainder of the dialogue permits the Laws and their "me" roles to replace the sovereignty of the "I."

The crux of Socratic citizenship lies right here. Antiphon, we saw, believes that in negotiating a personal social contract with the dominant social other and its "me" roles, the individual citizen needs to negotiate

---

(*bebouleusasthai*) with one last decision to flee or stay (*mia . . . boulê*, 46a4–5). Since no earlier interlocutors are mentioned, Crito must assume Socrates has been deliberating with himself.

and test the value of his *physis* by changing its worth into the currency of *nomos*. As a result, as Ostwald paraphrased Antiphon, "to be able to enjoy the advantages provided by the laws we have to sacrifice something of our nature" (1990: 300).[69] What Socrates is willing to sacrifice to the Laws, the terms of the personal contract he is willing to negotiate, amounts to this: he concedes to the Laws the power of life and death over each individual. This move requires his "I" to yield its sovereignty concerning what Antiphon prized as the criterion of the *psykhê's* health: an individual's psycho-physiological well-being. Once this move has been made, the "I" can continue to exercise sovereignty even when deciding on political matters, as when Socrates refused in 406 to vote in favor of an illegal trial for the generals at Arginusae or in 403 to arrange the arrest of Leon of Salamis (*Apology* 32b and d). In this way he acknowledges the reality Antiphon exposed, namely that the state's legal machinery cannot prevent one citizen from inflicting injustice on another, cannot guarantee the victim of injustice an advantage over its perpetrator, cannot prevent one citizen's truthful testimony from harming another, and so on, in a perpetual cycle of citizen wrongdoing (*On Truth* 44[B6–C2]).

Why is Socrates willing to concede this? Because he recognizes the importance, when an individual plays the game of *polis*, of personal risk – a risk that concedes the priority of "me" roles in order to secure something more important: the freedom in a democratic society to

---

[69] The second of the three conversations Xenophon imagined between Socrates and Antiphon concerned Socrates' refusal to charge a fee for his teaching – or more exactly, for his company or willingness to share himself with others (*sunousia*, *Mem.*1.6.11). From *On Harmony* we can recognize here Antiphon's insistence that a citizen should, after reflection and reasoned judgment (*gnômê*), risk testing his value (*axia*) or usefulness to others in public life. Xenophon distorts the seriousness of this principle by depicting it as Antiphon's venality (as had others, including Aristophanes in *Wasps* 1267–71).

create novel scripts of deliberation, both with others and with one-self. Through this risk the self purchases an insurance policy for a component that deserves even higher priority: the "I." This explains why Socrates identifies Achilles as an acceptable selfobject just at that moment of moral duress when the hero faces the risk of death and laughs in its face (28c–d). Socrates stages this risk in his own life as a question by an anonymous citizen, "Aren't you simply ashamed, Socrates, to have committed yourself to the sort of moral life [*epitêdeuma epitêduesas*] where you're risking death?" (28b2–4). Life and death mean nothing, he replies in effect, to the sort of "I" who decides whether the self acts justly or unjustly and for good or evil (28b4–6). I think it's accurate to say that Socrates looks to the ephebic oath as a model for his pecu-liar version of the social contract, for in the oath every young citizen promises to risk his life for the laws in order to play out a necessary set of "me" roles. Socrates too believes the citizen must explicitly, verbally, and publicly agree to the necessity of these "me" roles. However it's his understanding that, even though these roles may imperil the *living* indi-vidual's self-interest – so cherished by Antiphon – they also guarantee the chance that in Athens the *moral* self-interest of the "I" will flour-ish independently of those roles. And if this results, it doesn't matter whether the dominant social other recognizes the self by deciding that the dissent of the "I" is legitimate or not. In other words Socrates advises his followers to play the *polis* version of *pessoi* and to enter the social contract demanded by that game. Hence Socratic citizenship appears viable.

But what results is a paradox: by agreeing to observe the rules, he enables them at the same time to outwit their opponent and break the rules; like Alcibiades he secretly switches games from the democratic *polis* to a version of *pente grammai*, where the piece called the *basileus* hopes to reign supreme. How can this be so? Because he definitively separates the "I" from its compulsory "me" roles by keeping it sheltered in a deliberation peculiar to its own *physis* – and therefore out of play. Since every contest or game dictated by *nomos* must be dominated by a citizen's "me" roles, when the moral agent who actually agrees to play – the "I" – enters the fray, it manages to remain off the board. In this way the philosopher realizes what a statesman like Alcibiades never could: the narcissist's ability to keep others permanently at bay from what he takes to be the core of the self, which need never be exposed to their threats to its well-being. To this need the "I" alone can tend. In a strange consensus with Alcibiades, his erstwhile lover and student, Socrates too declares to the Athenians his partisan support for *physis*: "When it comes to the self, sacrifice nothing!"

CONCLUSION

◎▣◎

CHAPTERS 5 THROUGH 7 EXAMINED A NUMBER OF COMPETING MODELS for citizenship and selfhood appearing in democratic Athens during the seven decades between around 470 and 399. We saw in Chapter 5 that, after defeating the Persians in 480–479, Athenian democrats in the early days of popular sovereignty wrestled with the demands and risks of public deliberation and decision making under the guidance of elite leaders. Aeschylus' Danaid trilogy frames these demands and risks in the form of a contest citizens face between competing senses of community, types of personal identity, and the reason giving on which each depends. On one hand a "real" man and citizen furthers the interests of his political community by distinguishing himself from foreigners and women and by forming alliances with an eye to the city-state's strategic advantage and autonomy. On the other hand, as a human being, the same citizen cannot resist the pull of compassion and fear drawing him to acknowledge a sense of nonpolitical community with foreigners and women, even when alliance with them imperils his political freedom and civic autonomy. In *Suppliants*, I suggested, Aeschylus seems repeatedly to be prompting his spectators to think long and hard about Mead's conundrum, about what it might mean in Athens in the 460s to need to be another if one is to be oneself. In slightly different terms, he encourages them to ponder well the consequences of the boundaries they choose to draw around various senses of community and self.

In Chapter 6 we saw that in the 440s–430s a different model of citizen and self seemed to dominate Athens under the tutelage of Protagoras and Pericles, when faith ran high that the boundaries defining community and the individual need not conflict and might even converge. According to this nomological model, a shared set of collective practices and "habits of the heart" could stimulate citizens to lead lives whose public conduct was free yet regulated by civic norms and whose private inclinations varied freely according to whim without testing the limits of civic tolerance. Nevertheless, the 420s did see other models of citizenship and selfhood emerge. Some, like the anonymous "Old Oligarch's" impassioned yet reasoned diatribe, stridently opposed the Protagorean–Periclean model on political and moral grounds, while Antiphon offered an intellectual and moral alternative to *nomos* in his carefully argued legitimation of *physis* as an ontological and cognitive frame.[1] Again boundaries are at issue: for Antiphon individual well-being depends on first delimiting self-interest within a *nomos*-free zone before reentering the space of civic interactions. And in a sense that Aeschylus' spectators would probably not have understood, Antiphon too asks his listeners to practice a citizenship that harbors within it a self whose interests will be alien to those of his peers.

By today's lights the nomological qualities of the Protagorean–Periclean model incarnate the purity of the communitarian archetype for shared values, political participation, and collective moral solidarity.[2] If Pericles' Funeral Oration articulates ideals of citizenship and

---

[1] This *Constitution* (Politeia) *of the Athenians*, usually dated ca. 430 or to the 420s, was formerly attributed to Xenophon. Ober discusses the treatise in the context of "dissident" Athenian political writing (1998: 14–27), and Yunis in the context of criticizing democratic deliberation (1996: 46–50).

[2] I say this despite Phillips' argument that democratic Athens fails to meet some of the criteria communitarian theorists posit in their nostalgic ideal of community. "There was . . . practically nothing in Athenian society – taken as a whole – that resembled community," he concludes (1993: 143), though for the roughly twenty percent of its inhabitants who were citizens, and compared to other models before the nineteenth century, Athens "very much resembles a full-fledged community" (147).

selfhood that embody communitarianism in our contemporary sense, then it's not too anachronistic for us to see Antiphon's model as an attempt at a "liberal" correction. As Havelock puts it in *The Liberal Temper in Greek Politics*, because of *physis* "within the city-state, an area of private resource and judgment has now been defiantly asserted," enabling Antiphon to "declare war" on the city-state's grip over citizens' "allegiance" and the civic "ideal of the good life" (1957: 270). I've argued that Antiphon opens a breach within Protagorean–Periclean citizenship, first (in *On Truth*) when he encourages each citizen to search for individual senses of the good through an inner deliberation engineered by the will (*gnômê*); then (in *On Harmony*) when he advises the citizen, now transformed and armed for a return to social life with a superior sort of wisdom (*sôphrosynê*), to negotiate the worth of those goods.

If in Chapter 7 I labeled Alcibiades and Socrates "narcissistic" citizens, it was not to designate a perverse type of either citizenship or selfhood. Both individuals instead demonstrate to what extremes an Athenian might take a life-long practice (in MacIntyre's sense) devoted to pursuing self-interested goods that not only are incompatible with the communitarian priority of shared political values but also rely on forms of inner deliberation other Athenians find mysterious, magical, and threatening. Within the Athenian context, both look like poster-boys for the logical limits of liberal self-fashioning. Of course neither Alcibiades nor Socrates embraces an extra-social life; each prefers to form voluntary interpersonal ties – what today we call "networks" and "personal communities" in private life and civil society, and whose relationships some find more significant, more "truly our own," than those based on ascribed membership.[3] But in late fifth-century Athens

---

[3] See Phillips' liberal defense of voluntary associations as alternatives to communitarian memberships (1993: 190–94); on voluntary associations and civil society, see

the alternative communities of an Eros-cult and a Socratic circle piv-
oted around one extraordinary self's ability to enshrine its mysterious
will and intelligence in the grandiose icon of a personal divinity, an
alien god. And because the followers of Alcibiades and Socrates take
this icon for a selfobject, they search for a transformed sense of self
in the guise of a strange other who performs no "me" role society can
endorse or recognize.

Socrates is accurate, however, when in the *Apology* he points to
Achilles as a prototype and selfobject (28b–d). Both he and the hero
find clarity in their second-order reasoning about choosing to pursue
a moral commitment (*epitêdeuma epitêduesas*, 28b) that laughs in the
face of death, for at that point both stand beyond the limit of mortal
life. (Achilles knows from Thetis' prophecy that he will die if he stays
at Troy; Socrates has no intention of bargaining for his life by abjur-
ing the practice of philosophy.) From this extraordinary perspective
so cherished by liberal philosophy, the self is momentarily liberated
from ends embedded in a shared social context: it is now "prior to its
ends" and free to choose them as it will (Sandel 1998: 58–59).

In Chapter 1 we explored the fruitful consequences of Achilles' coura-
geous decision. These include the ability to harness impulsive insights
of the "I" in order to discover a hypothetical sort of more malleable
man, one owing the moral force behind his proclamation of self-worth
to the female peformance of lament and the moral legitimacy of his will
to his preference for one woman rather than another. More importantly
Achilles projects his version of this self into the vision of a new kind of
more malleable community, one ideally peopled by like-minded selves:
a state and its citizens. I contrasted this in Chapter 2 with the privileged

Kymlicka 2002: 305–6. From the perspective of deliberative democracy, Warren
provides a deliberative democrat critique of the importance attributed to voluntary
associations in civil society (2001: 56–59) and of their voluntary nature (96–109).

role of the *basileus* during the Formative period surrounding state formation, when one individual monopolized the performance of justice by assuming the positions in dispute settlement of all litigants and the community. Odysseus in Chapter 3 extends Achilles' demonstration of how powerfully the "I" can operate as a will and transform the self through interior deliberation. Here the new man Odysseus becomes on Calypso's isle emerges from a communitarian's cognitive ability to *rediscover* former ends he once enjoyed but voluntarily abandoned – again in the form of a wife, household, and local community. In other words Odysseus' transformed self decides it's worthless unless it risks embedding itself in social relations as both an object of other men's hybris and as a judge of their hybris.

Each remarkable individual we've examined in this study therefore finds himself under duress, faced with a painful but fruitful dilemma. To decide a question of justice, each confronts both an imperative and a fantastic hypothesis: "In order to decide this question, who *must* I become, and who do I *wish* to become?" The quandary, I suggested in the Introduction, highlights those choices that establish our individual personhood and autonomy. In contemporary terms it brings us to a point where the liberal, communitarian, and deliberative democrat scripts of selfhood and citizenship oppose one another but potentially converge. Speaking of liberals versus communitarians, Kymlicka indicates the nub of the matter: "They disagree over where, within the person, to draw the boundaries of the self" (2002: 227). But as we learned from Aeschylus, the quandary also implicates communities and the ways they choose to draw their boundaries and define their citizens. In Antiphon's language, how are we to draw boundaries for the self which respect *physis* and *nomos*? For while on one hand we might hear a self-interested call from the impulses of the "I" to deliberate over needs that are universal and yet of pressing concern to us as individuals, on the other hand civic membership demands we own up to the obligations of "me" roles compatible with our community's need to draw and maintain its boundaries. How do we coordinate the claims of these potentially conflictual boundaries?

For this reason the questions discussed in Chapter 4 remain pivotal – as well as unresolved. There we encountered Solon, a figure whose reality easily gets confused in a kaleidoscope of self-fashioned historical and performance roles. We isolated him in three poses or personae that in my opinion best illustrate the lawgiver's lesson to future citizen jurors, each pose illustrating an Archaic Greek version of Rawls' unencumbered self: Solon as a boundary stone (*horos*) between competing parties (fr. 37.9–10); Solon holding up a shield to protect warring factions (5.5–6); and Solon as a wolf keeping dogs at bay (36.26–27). Each captures the "I" as a floundering ego having trouble asserting itself as a "subject of possession" in Sandel's sense (1998: 54), yet each captures as well the potency of the law's impersonality. Because each models the scapegoat's self-destruction, Solon drives home to his listeners the personal cost they face when as "cognitive joiners" they play the agent of justice, the juror who applies the law. In effect he tells them that, in deciding questions of justice, you must no longer be yourself so that you may become nobody and everybody.

What then are the arts of cognitive joinery and of being a *horos*-stone other than the know-how to coordinate borders, to indicate those points where borders meet, overlap, or disappear? Here we seem to be close to the fundamental sense of participating in a *dikê*, which in Chapter 1 was linked to *deiknunai* in the sense of "to indicate" a boundary or portion (*moira, aisa*) (Palmer 1950: 160–63). But of course this is not a talent restricted to jurors and law courts: we practice it too as the art of owning up to our roles as citizens and also of dissolving modes of citizenship into modes of selfhood when we so choose. By nature this is a confusing business, for, as has been demonstrated throughout this study, both selves and communities are malleable, given to readily shifting borders. And nowhere is this confusion more apparent than in democracies, where ideals of equality and personal freedom cherish the undoing of differences. It's fitting then to discuss, as an emblem of this confusion, one final democratic text on the law and the individual.

At some point between 338 and 324 a speech was written to prosecute an Athenian politician (rhetor) named Aristogeiton for illegally practicing citizenship while deeply in debt to the state. (Its authorship is disputed and probably not to be attributed to Demosthenes, in whose corpus it appears as Demosthenes 25.) Whoever wrote the speech felt inspired to transform this prosecution into a potpourri of philosophical, rhetorical, and legal commonplaces about law, community, and individual human psychology. In fact, while the speech does contain surprises, the speaker openly tells the jurors that his presentation consists of nothing but a bouquet of ideological clichés: "I'm not saying anything new, extraordinary or original, but what you all know just as well as I do" (25.20). To explain its eclecticism and "intellectually contaminated" arguments, scholars have even surmised that it's a philosophical treatise on law or the work of a sophist masquerading as a court speech (Romilly 2001: 156–58). But the speech's interest for us lies in its return to the Solonian quandary of drawing boundary lines if we wish to perform justice, only it uses more contemporary terms to instruct jurors how to apply the law by frame-switching between *nomos* (the law and custom) and *physis* (the individual *psykhê*).

This frame-switching is so confusing that it permits two different reactions from jurors and two different arguments for the speech's claim to the "sovereignty of law" over everything and everyone in Athens. Its primary argument boldly proclaims an anthropological truth: "The entirety of human life in states large or small is managed by *physis* and *nomos*" (15). The relationship between these two spheres is a hostile one: *physis* represents all that is disorganized and peculiar to each individual, while *nomos* is collective and orderly in the same way for everyone (15).

As expressions of idiosyncracy, evil and crime originate within *physis*, specifically in the self's voluntarist dimension (16); and if the laws did not possess a will to counteract this wickedness (16–17) – that is, if everyone could do as he or she wished – human society would revert to bestial conditions (20–21). The defendant Aristogeiton exemplifies this when he claims that in a democracy people are free to say and do what they wish so long as they don't care about their reputations (25). In fact, the speaker claims, democracy prompts each citizen to imagine that his wish (*boulêsis*) is a law (*nomos*) and an authority (*archê*) (26). When wishes become laws, I would say that individuals confuse the boundaries of self with those of the state; and the frame of *physis* engulfs *nomos*.

This paranoid worldview is a far cry from Pericles' confidence a century before that *nomos* could temper citizens' expressions of individual taste and will, and it would not be a mistake to read the speech as a long-delayed rebuttal to the legitimacy Antiphon conferred on the frame of *physis* alongside *nomos*.[4] For the speaker is sure that the wickedness and refusal of criminals to feel shame permits the disorder of their inner lives to infect and fragment the community's collective self: "everything [in the state] would come undone, break up, and run together" (25) if the criminal's hybris, rule-breaking (*paranomia*) and bad-mouthing (*blasphêmia*) spill out into public space (26). To reinforce his claims about the power of law and its rule over citizens, the speaker concocts a genealogy of law which first locates its origin in transcendent sources such as gods, exceptional lawgivers, and the power of reason: "Every law is a divine discovery and gift, a teaching of intelligent humans, a corrective for voluntary and involuntary crimes" (16). But when the speaker completes his genealogy by claiming that every law is also

---

[4] For comparisons between Demosthenes 25 and Antiphon, see Romilly 2001: 166 and 168.

"a social contract [*sunthêkê koinê*] by which everyone in the state should live" (16–17), we touch the seam of a very different ideology, one deriving the law's authority from the jurors themselves. In effect the speaker acknowledges that this potent rule of law, charged with the task of rooting out the evil that *physis* breeds within citizens like Aristogeiton, is nothing. In a fashion typical of fourth-century forensic orators, he represents the law as useless without the ability of jurors to understand and apply it.[5] And where does a juror achieve this cognitive ability? The answer to this question is surprising, but the speaker provides it in his opening remarks when he tells the jurors that this case rests not on the prosecution's arguments . . . but on the *physis* of each individual juror: "I assume that this case has already been decided long ago by the *physis* inside each one of you" (*hypo tês hekastou phuseôs oikothen*, 2).

What does he mean? His use of *physis* refers to each juror's own character, just as he soon says he'll spin arguments for them based on his own nature and discursive habits (*hôs pephuka kai proêirêmai*, 14). His goal of course is for the jurors to use their character and his to recognize the degenerate *physis* of Aristogeiton (45) in all its bestial manifestations – as a political figure (rhetor) the man is a scorpion and snake in the agora (52), nicknamed "Dog" but more a predator of citizens than their guardian (40). So the law's power, its capacity to prevent criminal behavior and correct wickedness (17), seems to depend largely on how individuals think and feel within the frame of *physis*, for it is the jurors who must protect and strengthen the laws (25) and not permit the inherent *weakness* of a criminal like Aristogeiton from feeding off their energetic support (7–8). It's indeed confusing to speak about how public are

---

[5] Both D. Cohen (1995b) and Allen (2000: 179–90) place this speech within the context of fourth-century philosophical theory about the law (Plato's *Republic*, *Statesman* and *Laws*; Aristotle's *Politics*). Both emphasize the divide between the philosophers' justifications for the sovereignty of law and the appeals in fourth-century forensic oratory to the sovereignty of public judgment; they attribute the sovereignty of law to the philosophers and not to democratic practice.

the consequences of private thoughts, feelings, and inner deliberations; but our speaker seems intent on dramatizing the malleability of borders that expand and contract when *physis* and *nomos* interact. This is especially so with Aristogeiton's character, for as a rhetor his intellect and soul are liable to have a significant impact on state welfare. In one phrase the speaker evaluates both Aristogeiton's *physis* and his performance of citizenship, his personal *politeia*, by asking, "Don't you see there's no rationality [*logismos*] or any shame/respect [*aidôs*] in his *physis* and *politeia?*" (32). What commands (*hêgeitai*) his conduct is nothing but "mindlessness" (*aponoia*): "His entire performance of citizenship [*politeia*] is nothing but *aponoia!*" (32).

Clearly we see here a convergence of borders: Aristogeiton's inner self and his behavior in performing the "me" role of a citizen achieve congruence. But what surprises me most in this speech is that our speaker claims the same is true of the jurors. For he says that, in using their *physis* to perform the law and evaluate Aristogeiton accurately, they are simultaneously submitting to a test of their citizenship. He in fact warns them of this right away, claiming that *they* are on trial as much as Aristogeiton that day, that they are risking *their* citizenship in judging the defendant's joint performance of *physis* and *politeia*. As noted in Chapter 5, he threatens them with regressing beneath the threshold of citizenship if the resources of their *physis* do not enable them to deliberate properly: "It seems to me that it wouldn't be a mistake to say that while Aristogeiton is being tried today, *you're* undergoing scrutiny [*dokimazesthe*] and risking your reputation" (*doxa*, 6). Performing the law evidently amounts to facing either a new *dokimasia* and becoming ephebes again or an imagined *dokimasia* like that of state officials.[6]

---

[6] I opt for the ephebes' *dokimasia* because there was in fact no such scrutiny for jurors. But in addition to calling his audience *dikastai* (jurors), the speaker refers to them as "guardians of the laws" (*phulakes tôn nomôn*, 6–7). While this designation sounds informal, it does recall the traditional privilege of the Council of the Areopagus which gradually devolved to the Council, the Assembly and law courts, possibly as

I have argued in this study that Achilles' and Odysseus' heroic efforts at self-evaluation helped them imagine new types of self and society conducive to citizenship and statehood. These hypothetical speculations of theirs also seem to have fueled a tradition about imagining oneself to be another when deciding a question of justice. Soon after, the impersonality of statute law demands as much from citizens, urged by Solon's cognitive joinery to become nobody and everybody. But the speaker of Demosthenes 25 claims that in trying to do just this, in opening oneself to the otherness of a citizen like Aristogeiton, jurors submit their self-fashioned individuality to scrutiny by the dominant social other. The spheres of *physis* and *nomos* converge on one another: whoever you've chosen to be, he says, your deliberation and judgment today will expose you to one another's scrutiny. The critical moment occurs as each juror looks at Aristogeiton: what does he see? Does he form an empathic relation to a selfobject that is a scorpion, snake and "Dog," or does he prefer to seek out a "someone with whom [*hotôi*] he shares [*koinônêsousin*]" qualities that are antidotes to Aristogeiton's mindlessness: "intelligence [*nous*], a sound mind [*phrenôn agathôn*] and much forethought [*pronoia*]," (33)?

And so when it comes to performing justice, *physis* and *nomos* appear to be not hostile forces but convergent. Despite this anomalous speech's at times confusing and even contradictory play with boundaries and frames, it indicates how performing the law might assume a privileged place in our own conceptions of citizenship and selfhood. For while we may take it as just one rhetorical ploy among many, the possibility that citizen and self are interdependent emerges from the claim that

---

a result of Ephialtes' reforms in 462 (*Ath.Pol.*3.6, 4.4, 8.4: Andoc.1.84). Shortly before 323, however, a board of seven "guardians of the laws" was appointed; see Rhodes 1981: 315–17. Whichever *dokimasia* he refers to, however, the point is the same, for that of state officials constituted an examination of one's character as a citizen as well as credentials for office; see Adeleye 1983: 297–300.

in evaluating another's *timê* (social worth) on the basis of his or her *physis* (personality), we put our own *physis* and *timê* to the test. Despite the Solonian imperative to be impersonal when performing justice and the law, we are judged on the basis of whoever it is with whom we feel empathy or whomever it is we repudiate. Here lies a point, a boundary marker, with which to coordinate the borders of today's competing ideologies of liberalism, communitarianism, and deliberative democracy. This point makes more of a claim on us than a general conclusion that our public and private virtues are "interdependent" (Macedo 1990: 265), or that we're "interdependent" on others by determining which virtues we'll contribute to others and which virtues of theirs we'll adopt for ourselves (Norton 1991: 113), or that we transform ourselves from liberal rights bearers into enlightened republican citizens by acknowledging our dependence on others for some measure of independence (Dagger 1997: 39).

The jurors of Demosthenes 25 face a more concrete imperative and hypothesis, one we might wish to own up to. They must decide the case against Aristogeiton by comparing the person they've chosen to become against two alternatives: one is the person they believe he has chosen to become, the other is a hypothetical someone they imagine to possess the virtues on which their community's well-being depends – a person they might wish to be. In this way judging others at the same time subjects them to a deliberation they must use to evaluate themselves and to be evaluated by others – a deliberation that not only demonstrates the interdependence of citizenship and selfhood but also offers each juror an opportunity for self-transformation.

Some Greeks do therefore enact versions of our three contemporary scripts. In so doing they also model kinds of social contract that aren't foreign to Rawls' unencumbered self in its original position. If the social contract's primary goal (as Rawls revived it) is to put oneself in the position of others and imagine equality with them through a version of the interchangeability of fates, then some of our remarkable Greeks have achieved this too. Most importantly they demonstrate in concete ways how interdependent their citizenship and selfhood can be when performing justice and the law, for through these scripts they help us demystify Mead's conundrum, "We must be others if we are to be ourselves."

REFERENCES

ABBREVIATIONS

AC	Antiquité classique
AJA	American Journal of Archaeology
BICS	Bulletin of the Institute for Classical Studies
BMCR	Bryn Mawr Classical Review
CA	Classical Antiquity
CJ	Classical Journal
CP	Classical Philology
CQ	Classical Quarterly
CR	Classical Review
CW	Classical World
GR	Greece and Rome
GRBS	Greek, Roman and Byzantine Studies
HCSP	Harvard Studies in Classical Philology
JHS	Journal of Hellenic Studies
MH	Museum Helveticum
PCPS	Proceedings of the Cambridge Philological Society
QUCC	Quaderni urbinati di cultura classica
REG	Revue des études grecs
RM	Rheinisches Museum für Philologie
SMEA	Studii micenei ed egeo-anatolici
SO	Symbolae osloenses
TAPA	Transactions of the American Philological Association

Adcock, F. E. 1927. "Literary Tradition and the Early Greek Code-Makers." *Cambridge Historical Journal* 2: 95–109.

Adeleye, Gabriel. 1983. "The Purpose of the *Dokimasia*." *GRBS* 24: 295–306.

Adkins, A. W. H. 1960. *Merit and Responsibility: A Study in Greek Values*. Oxford.

———. 1972. *Moral Values and Political Behaviour in Ancient Greece From Homer to the Fifth-Century BC*. New York.

Alexiou, Margaret. 1974. *The Ritual Lament in Greek Tradition*. Cambridge, MA.

Alford, Fred C. 1991. *The Self in Social Theory: A Psychoanalytic Account of its Construction in Plato, Hobbes, Locke, Rawls and Rousseau*. New Haven.

———. 1993. "Greek Tragedy and Civilization: The Cultivation of Pity." *Political Research Quarterly* 46: 259–80.

Allen, Danielle S. 2000. *The World of Prometheus: The Politics of Punishing in Democratic Athens*. Princeton.

Almeida, Joseph J. 2003. *Justice as an Aspect of the Polis Idea in Solon's Political Poems: A Reading of the Fragments in Light of the Researches of the New Classical Archaeology*. Leiden.

Andersen, Ø. 1976. "Some Thoughts on the Shield of Achilles." *SO* 51: 5–18.

Anderson, Greg. 2003. *The Athenian Experiment: Building an Imagined Political Community in Ancient Attica, 508–490, B.C.* Ann Arbor.

Anhalt, Emily Katz. 1993. *Solon the Singer: Politics and Poetics.* Lanham, MD.

Antonaccio, Carla. 1993. "The Archaeology of Ancestors," in C. Dougherty and L. Kurke (eds.), *Cultural Poetics in Archaic Greece*, Cambridge.

————. 1994. "Contesting the Past: Hero Cult, Tomb Cult, and Epic in Early Greece." *AJA* 98: 389–410.

————. 1995a. *An Archaeology of Ancestors: Tomb Cult and Hero Cult in Early Greece.* Lanham, MD.

————. 1995b. "Homer and Lefkandi," in O. Andersen and M. Dickie. (eds.), *Homer's World: Fact, Fiction and Reality.* Bergen.

Arrowsmith, William. 1973. "Aristophanes' *Birds*: The Fantasy Politics of Eros." *Arion.* n.s. 1: 119–67.

Bakker, Egbert J. 1993. "Discourse and Performance: Involvement, Visualization and 'Presence' in Homeric Poetry." *CA* 12: 1–29.

————. 1997a. *Poetry in Speech: Orality in Homeric Discourse.* Ithaca.

————. 1997b. "The Study of Homeric Discourse," in Ian Morris and Barry Powell, (eds.), *A New Companion to Homer.* Leiden. 1997.

Bakhtin, Mikhail. 1981. *The Dialogic Imagination.* Trans. C. Emerson and M. Holquist. Austin.

————.1986. *Speech Genres and Other Late Essays.* Trans. V. McGee. Austin.

Balot, Ryan K. 2001. *Greed and Injustice in Classical Athens.* Princeton.

Barnouw, Jeffrey. 2004. *Odysseus, Hero of Practical Intelligence: Deliberation and Signs in the* Odyssey. Lanham, MD.

Bassi, Karen. 1998. *Acting Like Men: Gender, Drama, and Nostalgia in Ancient Greece.* Ann Arbor.

Bauman, Richard. 1977. *Verbal Art as Performance.* Prospect Heights, IL.

Beiner, Ronald (ed.). 1995. *Theorizing Citizenship.* Albany.

Bellah, Robert, Richard Madsen, William M. Sullivan, Ann Swidler, and Steven M. Tipton. 1995. *Habits of the Heart: Individualism and Commitment in American Life.* Second edn. Berkeley.

Bérard, Claude, et al. (eds.). 1989. *A City of Images: Iconography and Society in Ancient Greece.* Trans. D. Lyons. Princeton.

Bergren, Ann. 1975. *The Etymology and Usage of Peirar in Early Greek Poetry.* American Classical Studies 2. New York.

Bertrand, Jean-Marie. 1999. *De l'écriture à l'oralité: lectures des* Lois *de Platon.* Paris.

Beye, C. R. 1970. "Sophocles' *Philoctetes* and the Homeric Embassy." *TAPA* 101: 63–75.

Blaise, Fabienne. 1995. "Solon fragment 36 W: pratique et fondation des normes politiques." *REG* 108: 24–37.

Boedeker, Deborah, and Kurt Raaflaub (eds.). 1998. *Democracy, Empire and the Arts in Fifth-Century Athens.* Cambridge, MA.

Boegehold, Alan, and Adele Scafuro (eds.). 1994. *Athenian Identity and Civic Ideology.* Baltimore.

Bohman, James. 1996. *Public Deliberation: Pluralism, Complexity and Democracy.* Cambridge, MA.

Bohman, James, and William Rehg (eds.). 1997. *Deliberative Democracy: Essays on Reason and Politics.* Cambridge, MA.

Bonner, Robert J., and Gertrude Smith. 1930. *The Administration of Justice from Homer to Aristotle.* 2 vols. Chicago.

Bowie, A. M. 1993. *Aristophanes: Myth, Ritual and Comedy.* Cambridge.

––––––. 1997. "Tragic Filters for History: Euripides' *Supplices* and Sophocles' *Philoctetes*," in C. Pelling (ed.), *Greek Tragedy and the Historian.* Oxford.

Bowie, E. L. 1986. "Early Greek Elegy, Symposium and Public Festival." *JHS* 106: 13–35.

Brenne, Stefan. 1994. "Ostraka and the Process of Ostrakaphoria," in W. D. E. Coulson (ed.), *The Archaeology of Attica under the Democracy.* Oxford.

Brickhouse, Thomas C., and Nicholas D. Smith. 1989. *Socrates on Trial.* Princeton.

Brown, Gillian, and George Yule. 1983. *Discourse Analysis.* Cambridge.

Burian, Peter. 1974. "Pelasgus and Politics in Aeschylus' Danaid Trilogy." *Wiener Studien* n.s. 8: 5–14.

Burkert, Walter. 1983. *Homo Necans: The Anthropology of Ancient Greek Sacrificial Ritual and Myth.* Trans. P. Bing. Berkeley.

––––––. 1985. *Greek Religion.* Trans. J. Raffan. Cambridge, MA.

Butler, Judith. 1990. *Gender Trouble: Feminism and the Subversion of Identity.* New York.

Cairns, Douglas L. 1993. Aidôs*: The Psychology and Ethics of Honour and Shame in Ancient Greek Literature.* Oxford.

––––––. 1996. "*Hybris*, Dishonour, and Thinking Big." *JHS* 116: 1–32.

Calame, Claude. 1986. *Le Récit en Grèce ancienne: énonciations et représentations des poètes.* Paris.

––––––. 1990. *Thésée et l'imaginaire athénien: légende et culte en Grèce antique.* Lausanne.

Calder, W. M. 1971. "Sophoclean *Apologia: Philoctetes.*" *GRBS* 12: 153–74.

Caldwell, Richard S. 1989. *The Origin of the Gods.* Oxford.

Calligas, Peter. 1988. "Hero-Cult in Early Iron Age Greece," in R. Hägg, N. Marinatos, and G. C. Nordquist (eds.), *Early Greek Cult Practice.* Stockholm.

Camassa, Giorgio. 1992. "Aux origines de la codification écrite des lois en Grèce," in *Les savoirs de l'écriture en Grèce ancienne*, ed. M. Detienne. Rev. edn. Lille.

Cantarella, Eva. 1979. *Norma e sanzione in Omero: contribuito alla protostoria del diritto greco.* Milan.

––––––. 2001. "Préface," in Louis Gernet, *Recherches sur le développement de la pensée juridique et morale en Grèce: étude sémantique.* Paris.

––––––. 2003. *Ithaque: De la Vengeance d'Ulysse à la naissance du droit.* Trans. P-E. Dauzat. Paris.

Carawan, Edwin. 1998. *Rhetoric and The Law of Draco.* Oxford.

Carey, C. 1996. "*Nomos* in Attic Rhetoric and Oratory." *JHS* 116: 33–46.

Carey, C., and R. A. Reid (eds.). 1985. *Demosthenes: Private Speeches.* Cambridge.

Carr, David. 1986. *Time, Narrative and History.* Bloomington.

Cartledge, Paul, Paul Millett, and Stephen Todd (eds.). 1990. *Nomos: Essays in Athenian Law, Politics and Society.* Cambridge.

Cartledge, Paul, Paul Millett, and Sitta von Reden. 1998. *Kosmos: Essays on Order, Conflict, and Community in Classical Athens.* Cambridge.

Cassin, Barbara. 1995. *L'Effet sophistique.* Paris.

Casson, Lionel. 1971. *Ships and Seamanship in the Ancient World.* Princeton.

———. 1994. *Ships and Seafaring in Ancient Times.* London.

Castriota, David. 1992. *Myth, Ethos and Actuality: Official Art in Fifth-Century BC Athens.* Madison.

———. 1998. "Democratic Art in Late Sixth- and Fifth-Century Athens," in I. Morris and K. Raaflaub (eds.), *Democracy 2500? Questions and Challenges.* Dubuque.

Cavanaugh, W., and C. Mee. 1995. "Mourning Before and After the Dark Age," in C. Morris, Klados: *Essays in Honour of J. N. Coldstream. BICS* Supplement 63: 45–61.

Cavanaugh, W. G., M. Curtis, J. N. Coldstream, and A.W. Johnston (eds.). 1998. *Post-Minoan Crete: Proceedings of the First Colloquium.* BSA Studies 2. London.

Chamoux, François. 1953. *Cyrène sous la monarchie des Battiades.* Paris.

Chantraine, Pierre. 1953. "Reflexions sur les noms des dieux hélleniques." *AC* 32: 65–78.

Christ, Matthew. 1998. *The Litigious Athenian.* Baltimore.

Clark, R. J. 1978. *Catabasis: Virgil and the Wisdom Tradition.* Amsterdam.

Claus, David. 1975. "Aidôs in the Language of Achilles." *TAPA* 105: 13–28.

Clay, Jenny Strauss. 1983. *The Wrath of Athena: Gods and Men in the Odyssey.* Princeton.

Cobb-Stevens, Vera. 1985. "Opposites, Reversals and Ambiguities: The Unsettled World of Theognis," in T. Figueira and G. Nagy (eds.), *Theognis of Megara: Poetry and the Polis.* Baltimore.

Cogan, Marc. 1981. *The Human Thing: The Speeches and Principles of Thucydides' History.* Chicago.

Cohen, David. 1995a. *Law, Violence and Community in Classical Athens.* Cambridge.

———. 1995b. "The Rule of Law and Democratic Ideology in Classical Athens," in W. Eder (ed.), *Die Athenische Demokratie im 4 Jahrhundert v. Chr.* Stuttgart.

———. 2002 (ed). *Demokratie: Recht und soziale Kontrolle im klassischen Athen.* Munich.

———. 2005. "Crime, Punishment, and the Rule of Law in Classical Athens," in Michael Gagarin and David Cohen (eds.), *The Cambridge Companion to Ancient Greek Law.* Cambridge.

Cohen, Edward E. 2000. *The Athenian Nation.* Princeton.

Cohen, Joshua. 1998. "Democracy and Liberty," in Jon Elster (ed.) *Deliberative Democracy.* Cambridge.

Cohen, Joshua, and Andrew Arato. 1992 (eds.), *Civil Society and Political Theory.* Cambridge, MA.

Colaiaco, James. 2001. *Socrates against Athens: Philosophy on Trial.* New York.

Cole, Susan Guettel. 1996. "Oath Ritual and Male Community at Athens," in J. Ober and C. Hedrick (eds.), *Dêmokratia: A Conversation on Democracies, Ancient and Modern*. Princeton.

Conacher, D. J. 1996. *Aeschylus: The Earlier Plays and Related Studies*. Toronto.

Connor, W. R. 1992. *The New Politicians of Fifth-Century Athens*. Indianapolis [rpt. 1971].

————. 1996. "Civil Society, Dionysiac Festival, and the Athenian Democracy," in J. Ober and C. Hedrick (eds.), *Dêmokratia: A Conversation on Democracies, Ancient and Modern*. Princeton.

Cook, Erwin F. 1995. *The* Odyssey *in Athens: Myths of Cultural Origins*. Ithaca.

Corsaro, Marinella. 1988. *Themis: la norma e l'oracolo nella Grecia antica*. Lecce.

Coulson, W. D. E. (ed.). 1994. *The Archaeology of Attica under the Democracy*. Oxford.

Craik, Elizabeth M. 1987. "'One for the Pot': Aristophanes' *Birds* and the Anthesteria." *Eranos* 85: 25–34.

Crane, Gregory. 1988. *Calypso: Backgrounds and Conventions of the* Odyssey. *Beiträge zur Klassischen Philologie* 91. Frankfurt.

————. 1998. *Thucydides and the Ancient Simplicity*. Berkeley.

Croiset, Maurice. 1973. *Aristophanes and the Political Parties at Athens*. Trans. J. Loeb. New York [o.p. 1909].

Crotty, Kevin. 1994. *The Poetics of Supplication: Homer's* Iliad *and* Odyssey. Ithaca.

Dagger, Richard. 1997. *Civic Virtues: Rights, Citizenship, and Republican Liberalism.* Oxford.

Dahl, Robert A. 1989. *Democracy and Its Critics*. New Haven.

Decleva Caizzi, F. 1986. "Hysteron Proteron: la nature et les lois selon Antiphon et Platon." *Revue de métaphysique et de morale* 91: 291–310.

———— (ed.). 1989. *Corpus dei papiri filosifici greci e latini*. Parte I, vol. 1. Florence.

Derderian, Katharine. 2001. *Leaving Words to Remember: Greek Mourning and the Advent of Literacy*. Brill.

Detienne, Marcel. 1992. "L'écriture et ses nouveaux objets intellectuels en Grèce," in M. Detienne (ed.), *Les savoirs de l'écriture en Grèce ancienne*. Rev. edn. Lille.

Dewald, Carolyn. 2003. "Form and Content: The Question of Tyranny in Herodotus," in Kathryn A. Morgan (ed.), *Popular Tyranny: Sovereignty and Its Discontents in Ancient Greece*. Austin.

Diggle, J. (ed.). 1998. *Tragicorum graecorum: fragmenta selecta*. Oxford.

Dillery, John. 1995. *Xenophon and the History of His Times*. London.

Dobrov, Gregory. 1998a. *The City as Comedy: Society and Representation in Athenian Drama*. Charlotte.

————. 1998b. "Language, Fiction and Utopia," in G. Dobrov (ed.), *The City as Comedy: Society and Representation in Athenian Drama*. Charlotte.

Dodds, E. R. 1951. *The Greeks and the Irrational*. Berkeley.

Donlan, Walter. 1980. *The Aristocratic Ideal in Ancient Greece: Attitudes of Superiority from Homer to the End of the Fifth Century B.C.* Lawrence.

————. 1982a. "The Politics of Generosity in Homer." *Helios* 9: 1–15.

————. 1982b. "Reciprocities in Homer." *CW* 75: 137–75.

———. 1985a. "*Pistos Philos Hetairos*," in T. Figueira and G. Nagy (eds.), *Theognis of Megara: Poetry and the Polis.* Baltimore.

———. 1985b. "The Social Groups of Dark Age Greece." *CP* 80: 293–308.

———. 1989. "The Pre-State Community in Greece." *SO* 64: 5–29.

———. 1994. "Chief and Followers in Pre-state Greece," in C. A. M. Duncan and D. W. Tandy (eds.), *From Political Economy to Anthropology* 3. Montreal.

———. 1998. "Political Reciprocity in Dark Age Greece: Odysseus and his *hetairoi*," in C. Gill, N. Postlethwaite, and R. Seaford (eds.), *Reciprocity in Ancient Greece.* Oxford.

Donlan, Walter, and Carol G. Thomas. 1993. "The Village Community of Ancient Greece: Neolithic, Bronze and Dark Ages." *SMEA* 31: 61–72.

Dougherty, Carol. 2001. *The Raft of Odysseus: The Ethnographic Imagination of Homer's Odyssey.* Oxford.

Dougherty, Lillian E. 1995. *Siren Songs: Gender, Audiences and Narrators in the Odyssey.* Ann Arbor.

Dover, Kenneth J. 1974. *Greek Popular Morality in the Time of Plato and Aristotle.* Indianapolis [rpt. 1994].

Dryzek, John. 2000. *Deliberative Democracy and Beyond: Liberals, Critics, Contestations.* Oxford.

Dunbar, Nan. 1995. *Aristophanes:* Birds. Oxford.

Dupont, Florence. 1977. *Le plaisir et la loi.* Paris.

Earle, Timothy, 1987. "Chiefdoms in Archaeological and Ethnological Perspective." American Review of Anthropology 16: 279–308.

———.1997. *How Chiefdoms Come to Power: The Political Economy in Prehistory.* Stanford.

Easterling, P. E. 1990. "Constructing Character in Greek Tragedy," in C. Pelling (ed.), *Characterization and Individuality in Greek Literature.* Oxford.

———. 1991. "Men's *Kleos* and Women's *Goos*: Female Voices in the *Iliad*." *Journal of Modern Greek Studies* 9: 145–51.

———. (ed.) 1997. *The Cambridge Companion to Greek Tragedy.* Cambridge.

Eder, Walter (ed.). 1994. *Democracy in Fourth-Century Athens: Decline or Zenith of a Constitution?* Stuttgart.

Edmonds, J. M. 1957. *The Fragments of Attic Comedy* 1. Leiden [1978–94].

Edmunds, Lowell. 1975. "Thucydides' Ethics as Reflected in the Description of Stasis (3.82–3)." *HSCP* 79: 73ff.

Edmunds, Lowell, and Robert Wallace (eds.). 1997. *Poet, Public and Performance in Ancient Greece.* Baltimore.

Edwards, Anthony T. 2004. *Hesiod's Ascra.* Berkeley.

Else, Gerald. 1958. "'Imitation' in the Fifth Century." *CP* 53: 73–90.

Elster, Jon (ed.). 1998. *Deliberative Democracy.* Cambridge.

Euben, Peter. 1990. *The Tragedy of Political Theory: The Road Not Taken.* Princeton.

———. 1997. *Corrupting Youth: Political Education, Democratic Culture, and Political Theory.* Princeton.

Euben, Peter, Robert Wallach, and Josiah Ober (eds.). 1994. *Athenian Political Thought and the Reconstruction of American Democracy.* Ithaca.

Farenga, Vincent. 1998. "Narrative and Community in Dark Age Greece: A Cognitive and Communicative Approach to Early Greek Citizenship." *Arethusa* 32: 179–206.

Farrar, Cynthia. 1988. *The Origins of Democratic Thinking: The Invention of Politics in Classical Athens.* Cambridge.

Faulkner, Thomas M., Nancy Felson, and David Konstan (eds.). 1999. *Contextualizing Classics: Ideology, Performance, Dialogue: Essays in Honor of John J. Peradotto.* Lanham, MD.

Felson-Rubin, Nancy. 1996. "Penelope's Perspective: Character from Plot," in Seth Schein (ed.), *Reading the* Odyssey: *Selected Interpretive Essays.* Princeton.

Fenik, Bernard. 1974. *Studies in the* Odyssey. Hermes Einzelschriften 30. Wiesbaden.

Fernández-Galiano, Manuel. 1992. "Commentary, Books XXI–XXII," in Joseph Russo, Manuel Fernández-Galiano, and Alfred Heubeck, *A Commentary on Homer's* Odyssey. *Vol. 3. Books XVII–XXIV.* Oxford.

Ferguson, Y. H. 1991. "Chiefdoms to City-States: The Greek Experience," in T. K. Earle (ed.), *Chiefdoms: Power, Economy and Ideology.* Cambridge.

Fine, John. 1983. *The Ancient Greeks: A Critical History.* Cambridge, MA.

Finley, John H. 1978. *Homer's* Odyssey. Cambridge, MA.

Finley, M. I. 1975. *The Use and Abuse of History.* New York.

————. 1979 (1954). *The World of Odysseus.* Second rev. edn. New York.

————. 1982. "Authority and Legitimacy in the Classical City-State." *Danske Videnskab. Selbskab. Hist.-Filos. Meddel.* 50.3. Copenhagen.

————. 1983. *Politics in the Ancient World.* Cambridge.

————. 1985a. *Ancient History: Evidence and Models.* New York.

————. 1985b. *Democracy Ancient and Modern.* New Brunswick.

Fisher, N. R. E. 1992. *Hybris: A Study in Values of Honour and Shame in Ancient Greece.* Warminster.

————. 1998. "Gymnasia and the Democratic Values of Leisure," in Paul Cartledge, Paul Millett, and Sitta von Reden (eds.), *Kosmos: Essays in Order, Conflict and Community in Classical Athens.* Cambridge.

Foley, Helene P. 1995. "Penelope as Moral Agent," in B. Cohen (ed.), *The Distaff Side: Representing the Female in Homer's* Odyssey. Oxford.

————. 2001. *Female Acts in Greek Tragedy.* Princeton.

Föllinger, Sabine. 2003. *Genosdependenzen: Studien zur Arbeit am Mythos bei Aischylos. Hypomnemata* 148. Göttingen.

Fontenrose, Joseph. 1981. *Orion: The Myth of the Hunter and Huntress.* University of California Publications in Classical Studies 23. Berkeley.

Ford, Andrew. 1992. *Homer: The Poetry of the Past.* Ithaca.

Forde, Steven. 1989. *The Ambition to Rule: Alcibiades and the Politics of Imperialism in Thucydides.* Ithaca.

Fouchard, Alain. 2003. *Les états grecs*. Paris.

Foxhall, Lin. 1997. "A View from the Top: Evaluating the Solonian Property Classes," in Lynette G. Mitchell and P. J. Rhodes (eds.), *The Development of the Polis in Archaic Greece*. London.

Fränkel, Hermann. 1975. *Early Greek Poetry and Philosophy*. Trans. M. Hadas and J. Willis. New York.

Friedrich, Paul, and James Redfield. 1978. "Speech as a Personality Symbol: The Case of Achilles." *Language* 54: 263–68.

Friedrich, Rainer. 1987. "Thrinakia and Zeus' Ways to Men in the *Odyssey*." *GRBS* 28: 375–400.

Friis Johansen, H., and E. W. Whittle (eds.). 1980. *Aeschylus: The Suppliants*. 3 vols. Copenhagen.

Gagarin, Michael. 1973. "*Dike* in the Works and Days." *CP* 68: 81–94.

———. 1974. "Hesiod's Dispute with Perses." *TAPA* 104: 103–11.

———. 1981a. *Drakon and Early Athenian Homicide Law*. New Haven.

———. 1981b. "The *Thesmothetai* and the Earliest Athenian Tyranny Law." *TAPA* 111: 71–77.

———. 1986. *Early Greek Law*. Berkeley.

———. 1990. "The Nature of Proofs in Antiphon." *CP* 85: 22–32.

———. 1992. "The Poetry of Justice: Hesiod and the Origin of Greek Law." *Ramus* 21: 61–78.

———. 1994. "Probability and Persuasion: Plato and Early Greek Rhetoric," in I. Worthington (ed.), *Persuasion: Greek Rhetoric in Action*. New York.

———. 1997. *Antiphon: The Speeches*. Cambridge.

———. 2002. *Antiphon the Athenian: Oratory, Law and Justice in the Age of the Sophists*. Austin.

———. 2005a. "The Unity of Greek Law," in Michael Gagarin and David Cohen (eds.), *The Cambridge Companion to Ancient Greek Law*. Cambridge.

———. 2005b. "Early Greek Law," in Michael Gagarin and David Cohen (eds.), *The Cambridge Companion to Ancient Greek Law*. Cambridge.

Garland, Robert. 1985. *The Greek Way of Death*. London.

Garnsey, P., and I. Morris. 1989. "Risk and the *Polis*: The Evolution of Institutionalised Responses to Food Supply Problems in the Ancient Greek State," in P. Halstead and J. O'Shea (eds.), *Bad Year Economics*. Cambridge.

Garvie, A. F. 1969. *Aeschylus' Supplices: Play and Trilogy*. Cambridge.

Gaskin, Richard. 1990. "Do Homeric Heroes Make Real Decisions?" *CQ* 40: 1–15.

Gauthier, Philippe. 1976. Symbola*: les étrangers dans le monde grec*. Nancy.

Gehrke, Hans-Joachim. 1995. "Der Nomosbegriff der Polis" in O. Behrends and W. Sellert (eds.), *Nomos und Gesetz: Ursprunge und Wirkungen des griechishen Gesetzesdenkens*. Göttingen.

Gentili, Bruno. 1988. *Poetry and Its Public in Ancient Greece*. Trans. A. T. Cole. Baltimore.

Gernet, Louis. 1955. *Droit et société dans la Grèce ancienne*. Paris.

———. 1981. *The Anthropology of Ancient Greece*. Trans. J. Hamilton and B. Nagy. Baltimore [o.p. 1968].

———. 2001. *Recherches sur le développement de la pensée juridique et morale en Grèce: étude sémantique*. Paris [o.p. 1917].

Gill, Christopher. 1996. *Personality in Greek Epic, Tragedy and Philosophy*. Oxford.

Giordano, Manuela. 1999. *La Supplica: rituale, istituzione sociale e tema epico in Omero*. AION Quaderni 3. Naples.

Gnoli, G., and Jean-Pierre Vernant (eds.). 1982. *La mort, les morts dans les sociétés anciennes*. Cambridge.

Gödde, Susanne. 2000. *Das Drama der Hikesie: Ritual und Rhetorik in Aischylos' Hiketiden*. Munster.

Goff, Barbara (ed.). 1995. *History, Tragedy, Theory: Dialogues on Athenian Drama*. Austin.

Goffman, Erving. 1974. *Frame Analysis: An Essay on the Organization of Experience*. Boston.

Goldhill, Simon. 1990. "The Great Dionysia and Civic Ideology," in J. Winkler and F. Zeitlin (eds.), *Nothing to do with Dionysos: Athenian Drama in its Social Context*. Princeton.

———. 1991. *The Poet's Voice: Essays in Poetics and Greek Literature*. Cambridge.

———. 1999. "Programme Notes," in S. Goldhill and R. Osborne (eds.), *Performance Culture and Athenian Democracy*. Cambridge.

———. 2000. "Civic Ideology and the Problem of Difference: The Politics of Aeschylean Tragedy, Once Again." *JHS* 120: 34–56.

Goldhill, Simon, and Robin Osborne (eds.). 1999. *Performance Culture and Athenian Democracy*. Cambridge.

Gould, John. 1973. "Hiketeia." *JHS* 93: 74–103.

Gribble, David. 1999. *Alcibiades and Athens: A Study in Literary Presentation*. Oxford.

Griffin, Jasper. 1977. "The Epic Cycle and the Originality of Homer." *JHS* 97: 39–53.

———. 1980. *Homer on Life and Death*. Oxford.

———. 1995. *Homer:* Iliad *Book Nine*. Oxford.

———. 1998. "The Social Function of Greek Tragedy." *CQ* 48: 39–61.

———. 1999. "Sophocles and the Democratic City," in. J. Griffin (ed.), *Sophocles Revisited: Essays Presented to Sir Hugh Lloyd-Jones*. Oxford.

Griffith, Mark. 1983. "Personality in Hesiod." *CA* 2: 37–65.

Guthrie, W. K. C. 1971. *The Sophists*. Cambridge.

Habermas, Jürgen. 1979. *Communication and the Evolution of Society*. Trans. T. McCarthy. Boston.

———. 1984. *The Theory of Communicative Action*. Vol. 1. Trans. T. McCarthy. Boston.

———. 1987. *The Theory of Communicative Action*. Vol. 2. Trans. T. McCarthy. Boston.

———. 1990. *Moral Consciousness and Communicative Action*. Trans. C. Lenhardt and S. W. Nicholsen. Cambridge, MA.

———. 1992. *Postmetaphysical Thinking: Philosophical Essays.* Trans. W. M. Hohengarten. Cambridge, MA.

———. 1996a. *Between Facts and Norms: Contributions to a Discourse Theory of Law and Democracy.* Trans. W. Rehg. Cambridge, MA.

———. 1996b. "Three Normative Models of Democracy," in Seyla Benhabib (ed.), *Democracy and Difference: Contesting the Boundaries of the Political.* Princeton.

Haggis, D. C. 1993. "Intensive Survey, Traditional Settlement Patterns and Dark Age Crete: the Case of Early Iron Age Kavousi." *Journal of Mediterranean Archaeology* 6: 131–74.

Hall, Edith. 1995. "Lawcourt Dramas: The Power of Performance in Greek Forensic Oratory." *BICS* 40: 39–58.

Hammer, Dean. 1998. "The Cultural Construction of Chance in the *Iliad.*" *Arethusa* 31: 125–48.

———. 2002. *The* Iliad *as Politics: The Performance of Political Thought.* Norman, OK.

Hansen, M. H. 1987. *The Athenian Assembly in the Age of Demosthenes.* Oxford.

———. 1990. "Solonian Democracy in Fourth-Century Athens," in W. R. Connor, M. Hansen, et. al. (eds.), *Aspects of Athenian Democracy.* Copenhagen.

———. 1991. *The Athenian Democracy in the Age of Demosthenes: Structure, Principle and Ideology.* Oxford.

———. 1996. "The Ancient Athenian and Modern Liberal View of Liberty as a Democratic Ideal," in J. Ober and J. Hedrick (eds.), *Dêmokratia: A Conversation on Democracies Ancient and Modern.* Princeton.

———. 1998. *Polis and City-State: An Ancient Concept and Its Modern Equivalent.* Copenhagen.

Hanson, Victor. 1989. *The Western Way of War: Infantry Battle in Ancient Greece.* Berkeley.

Harris, Edward M. 1994. "Law and Oratory," in I. Worthington (ed.), *Persuasion: Greek Rhetoric in Action.* New York.

———. 2000. "Open Texture in Athenian Law." *Dike* 3: 27–79.

Harris, Edward M., and Lene Rubinstein (eds.). 2004. *The Law and the Courts in Ancient Greece.* London.

Harrison, A. R. W. 1971a. *The Law of Athens Vol. 1: The Family and Property.* Indianapolis.

———. 1971b. *The Law of Athens Vol. 2: Procedure.* Indianapolis.

Harrison, Jane. 1912. *Themis: A Study of the Social Origins of Greek Religion.* Cleveland [rpt. 1962].

Haubold, Johannes. 2000. *Homer's People: Epic Poetry and Social Formation.* Cambridge.

Havelock, Eric A. 1957. *The Liberal Temper in Greek Politics.* New Haven.

———. 1978. *The Greek Concept of Justice.* Cambridge, MA.

Heinimann, F. 1945. *Nomos und Physis: Herkunft und Bedeutung einer Antithese in griechischen Denken des 5. Jahrhunderts.* Basel.

Held, David. 1996. *Models of Democracy.* Second edn. Stanford.

Helm, James J. 2004. "Aeschylus' Genealogy of Morals." *TAPA* 134: 23–54.

Henderson, Jeffrey. 1998a. "Attic Old Comedy, Frank Speech, and Democracy," in D. Boedeker and Kurt A. Raaflaub (eds.), *Democracy, Empire and the Arts in Fifth-Century Athens*. Cambridge, MA.

———. 1998b. "Mass vs. Elite and the Comic Heroism of Peisetairos," in G. Dobrov (ed.), *The City as Comedy: Society and Representation in Athenian Drama*. Charlotte.

———. 2003. "Demos, Demagogue, Tyrant in Attic Old Comedy," in Kathryn A. Morgan (ed.), *Popular Tyranny: Sovereignty and Its Discontents in Ancient Greece*. Austin.

Herington, John. 1985. *Poetry into Drama: Early Tragedy and the Greek Poetic Tradition*. Berkeley.

Herman, Gabriel. 1987. *Ritualised Friendship in the Greek City*. Cambridge.

Hesk, Jon. 2000. *Deception and Democracy in Classical Athens*. Cambridge.

Heubeck, Alfred. 1989. "Commentary Books IX–XII," in Alfred Heubeck and Arie Hoekstra, *A Commentary on Homer's Odyssey, vol. 2: Books 9–16*. Oxford.

———. 1992. "Commentary Books XXIII–XXIV," in Alfred Heubeck and Arie Hoekstra, *A Commentary on Homer's Odyssey, vol. 2: Books 9–16*. Oxford.

Hirzel, R. 1966. *Der Eid: Eine Beiträge zur seiner Geschichte*. Stuttgart [rpt. 1902].

Hölkeskamp, Karl-Joachim. 1992. "Written Law in Archaic Greece." *PCPS* 38: 87–117.

———. 1993. "Arbitrators, Lawgivers and the 'Codification of Law' in Archaic Greece: Problems and Perspectives." *Metis* 8: 48–81.

———. 1999. *Schiedsrichter, Gesetzgeber und Gesetzgebung im archaischen Griechenland*. Stuttgart.

Horkheimer, Max, and Theodore W. Adorno. 1972. *Dialectic of Enlightenment*. Trans. J. Cumming. New York.

Hornblower, Simon. 1983. *The Greek World 479–323 BC*. London.

———. 1991. *A Commentary on Thucydides. Vol. 1*. Oxford.

Horton, R. 1993. *Patterns of Thought in Africa and the West: Essays on Magic, Religion and Science*. Cambridge.

Hubbard, Thomas K. 1991. *The Mask of Comedy: Aristophanes and the Intertextual Parabasis*. Ithaca.

———. 1998. "Utopianism and the Sophistic City," in G. Dobrov (ed.), *The City as Comedy: Society and Representation in Athenian Drama*. Charlotte.

Humphreys, S. C. 1978. *Anthropology and the Greeks*. London.

———. 1983. "The Evolution of Legal Procedure in Ancient Attica," in E. Gabba (ed.), *Tria corda: Studi in onore di Arnaldo Momigliano*. Como.

———. 1988. "The Discourse of Law in Archaic and Classical Greece." *Law and History Review* 6: 465–93.

———. 1990. Review of I. Morris 1987, *Burial in Ancient Society: The Rise of the Greek City-State. Helios* 17: 263–68.

Hunter, Virginia. 1994. *Policing Athens: Social Control in the Attic Lawsuits, 420–320 BC*. Princeton.

Hunter, Virginia, and Jonathan Edmonson (eds.). 2000. *Law and Social Status in Classical Athens*. Oxford.

Hurwit, Jeffrey M. 1999. *The Acropolis*. Cambridge.

Ireland, S. 1974. "The Problem of Motivation in the Supplices of Aeschylus." *RM* 117: 14–29.

Irwin, Terence. 1977. *Plato's Moral Theory: The Early and Middle Dialogues*. Oxford.

———. 1995. *Plato's Ethics*. Oxford.

Iser, Wolfgang. 1978. *The Act of Reading: A Theory of Aesthetic Response*. Baltimore.

Jaeger, Werner. 1966. "Solon's Eunomia," in *Five Essays*, trans. A. M. Fiske. Montreal [o.p. 1926].

Jameson, M. H. 1956. "Politics and the *Philoctetes*." *CP* 51: 217–24.

Jeanmaire, Henri. 1939. *Couroi et Courètes: essai sur l'éducation spartiate et sur les rites de l'adolescence dans l'antiquité héllenique*. Lille.

Joas, Hans. 1985. *G. H. Mead: A Contemporary Re-examination of his Thought*. Trans. R. Meyer. Cambridge, MA.

Johnson, Allen W., and Timothy Earle. 2000. *The Evolution of Human Societies from Foraging Group to Agrarian State*. Second edn. Stanford.

Johnstone, Steven. 1999. *Disputes and Democracy: The Consequences of Litigation in Ancient Athens*. Austin.

Jones, Nicholas F. 1999. *The Associations of Classical Athens: The Response to Democracy*. Oxford.

Just, Roger. 1989. *Women in Athenian Law and Life*. London.

Kahn, Charles H. 1981. "The Origins of Social Contract Theory in the Fifth Century BC," in G. B. Kerferd (ed.), *The Sophists and Their Legacy*. Hermes Einzelschriften 44. Wiesbaden.

Kant, Immanuel. 1788. *Critique of Practical Reason*. Trans. L. W. Beck. Indianapolis.

Kassel, R., and C. Austin. 1983–. *Poetae comici graeci: fragmenta*. 7 vols. Berlin.

Katz, Barry. 1976. The *Birds* of Aristophanes and Politics." *Athenaeum* 54: 353–81.

Kaufmann-Bühler, Dieter. 1955. *Begriff und Funktion der Dike in den Tragödien des Aischylos*. Bonn.

Kekes, John. 1997. *Against Liberalism*. Ithaca.

Kerferd, G. B. 1981. *The Sophistic Movement*. Cambridge.

Kim, Jinyo. 2000. *The Pity of Achilles: Oral Style and the Unity of the* Iliad. Lanham, MD.

Kinzl, Konrad H., and Kurt A. Raaflaub (eds.). 1995. *Demokratia: Der Weg zur Demokratie bei den Griechen*. Wege der Forschung 657. Darmstadt.

Kirk, G. S. 1985. *The* Iliad*: A Commentary, vol. 1: Books 1–4*. Cambridge.

Kleingunther, Adolf. 1933. Protos Heuretes: *Untersuchungen zu Geschichte einer Fragstellung*. New York [rpt. 1976].

Kohlberg, Lawrence. 1981. *Essays on Moral Development. Vol. 1*. San Francisco.

Kohut, Heinz. 1977. *The Restoration of the Self*. New York.

———. 1984. *How Does Analysis Cure?* Ed. A. Goldberger with P. Stepansky. Chicago.

———. 1985. *Self Psychology and the Humanities*. Ed. C. B. Strozier. New York.

Koller, H. 1954. *Die Mimesis in der Antike*. Bern.

Konstan, David. 1998. "The Greek Polis and Its Negations: Versions of Utopia in Aristophanes' *Birds*," in G. Dobrov (ed.), *The City as Comedy: Society and Representation in Athenian Drama*. Charlotte.

———. 2000. "Pity and the Law in Greek Theory and Practice," *Dike* 3: 25–45.

———. 2001. *Pity Transformed*. London.

Kraut, Richard. 1984. *Socrates and the State*. Princeton.

Kullman, Wolfgang. 1985. "Gods and Men in the *Iliad* and *Odyssey*." *HSCP* 89: 1–23.

Kurke, Leslie. 1999. *Coins, Bodies, Games and Gold: The Politics of Meaning in Archaic Greece*. Princeton.

Kymlicka, Will. 2002. *Contemporary Political Philosophy: An Introduction*. Second edn. Oxford.

Kymlicka, Will, and Wayne Norman. 1995. "Return of the Citizen: A Survey of Recent Work on Citizenship Theory," in Ronald Beiner (ed.), *Theorizing Citizenship*. Albany.

Lambert, S. D. 1993. *The Phratries of Attica*. Ann Arbor.

Lambrinoudakis, V. K. 1988. "The Veneration of Ancestors in Geometric Naxos," in R. Hägg, N. Marinatos, and G. C. Nordquist (eds.), *Early Greek Cult Practice*. Stockholm.

Lape, Susan. 2003. "Radicalizing Democracy: The Politics of Sexual Reproduction in Classical Athens." *Parallax* 9: 52–62.

———. 2004. *Reproducing Athens: Menander's Comedy, Democratic Culture, and the Hellenistic City*. Princeton.

Latacz, Joachim. 1993. *Einführung in die griechische Tragödie*. Göttingen.

Levine, David B. 1985. "Symposium and the Polis," in T. Figueira and G. Nagy (eds.), *Theognis of Megara: Poetry and the Polis*. Baltimore.

Lévy, Edmond. 1995. "*Arétè, timè, aidôs* et *némésis*: le modèle homérique." *Ktema* 20: 177–211.

Lewis, John. 2001. " 'Dike,' 'Moira,' 'Bios' and the Limits of Understanding in Solon, 13 (West)." *Dike* 4: 113–35.

L'Homme-Wéry, Louise-Marie. 1996. "La Notion d'harmonie dans la pensée politique de Solon." *Kernos* 9: 145–54.

Liddell, H. G., R. Scott, and Henry Stuart Jones. 1940. *A Greek-English Lexicon*. Ninth edn. Oxford.

Lloyd-Jones, Hugh. 1971. *The Justice of Zeus*. Berkeley.

Loraux, Nicole. 1986. *The Invention of Athens: The Invention of the Funeral Oration in the Classical City*. Trans. A. Sheridan. Cambridge, MA.

———. 1987. *Tragic Ways of Killing a Woman*. Trans. A. Forster. Cambridge, MA.

———. 1992. "Solon et la voix de l'écrit," in M. Detienne (ed.), *Les savoirs de l'écriture en Grèce ancienne*. Rev. edn. Lille.

———. 1998. *Mothers in Mourning*. Trans. C. Pache. Ithaca.

———. 2002a. *The Divided City: On Memory and Forgetting in Ancient Athens*. Trans. C. Pache with J. Fort. New York.

———. 2002b. *The Mourning Voice: An Essay on Greek Tragedy*. Trans. E. T. Rawlings. Ithaca.

Louden, Bruce. 1999. *The Odyssey: Structure, Narrative, and Meaning*. Baltimore.

Ludwig, Paul. 2002. *Eros and Polis: Desire and Community in Greek Political Theory*. Cambridge.

Luginbill, Robert D. 1997. "Rethinking Antiphon's *Peri Aletheias*." *Apeiron* 30: 163–87.

———. 1999. *Thucydides on War and National Character*. Boulder.

Ma, John. 1994. "Black Hunter Variations." *PCPS* 40: 49–80.

McAfee, Noëlle. 2000. *Habermas, Kristeva, and Citizenship*. Ithaca.

McClure, Laura. 1999. *Spoken Like a Woman: Speech and Gender in Athenian Drama*. Princeton.

McDonald, William A., William D. E. Coulson, and John Rosser (eds.). 1983. *Excavations at Nichoria in Southwest Greece. Vol. 3. Dark Age and Byzantine Occupation*. Minneapolis.

MacDowell, Douglas M. 1976. "Hybris in Athens." *GR* 23: 14–31.

———. 1978. *The Law in Classical Athens*. Ithaca.

———. 1995. *Aristophanes and Athens: An Introduction to the Plays*. Oxford.

Macedo, Stephen. 1990. *Liberal Virtues: Citizenship, Virtues and Community in Liberal Constitutionalism*. Oxford.

McGlew, James. 1993. *Tyranny and Political Culture in Ancient Greece*. Ithaca.

———. 2002. *Citizens on Stage: Comedy and Political Culture in the Athenian Democracy*. Ann Arbor.

MacIntyre, Alasdair. 1984. *After Virtue: A Study in Moral Theory*. Second edn. South Bend.

Mackie, C. J. (ed.). 2004. *Oral Performance and Its Contexts*. Mnemosyne Supplement 248. Leiden.

Macleod, C. W. (ed.) 1982. *Homer: Iliad Book 24*. Cambridge.

Maffi, Alberto. 1992a. "Ecriture et pratique juridique dans la Grece classique," in M. Detienne (ed.), *Les savoirs de l'écriture dans la Grèce ancienne*. Lille.

———. 1992b. "Leggi scritte et pensiero giuridico," in G. Gambiano, L. Canfora, and D. Lanza (eds.), *Lo spazio letterario della Grecia antica I*. Rome.

Malkin, Irad. 1998. *The Returns of Odysseus: Colonization and Ethnicity*. Berkeley.

Mansfeld, Jaap. 1981. "Protagoras on Epistemological Obstacles and Persons," in G. B. Kerferd (ed.), *The Sophists and Their Legacy. Hermes Einzelschriften* 44. Wiesbaden.

Manuwald, B. 1989. "Zu Solons Gedankenwelt." *RM* 132: 1–25.

Manville, Philip Brook. 1990. *The Origins of Citizenship in Democratic Athens*. Princeton.

———. 1994. "Toward a New Paradigm of Athenian Citizenship," in Alan Boegehold and Adele Scafuro (eds.), *Athenian Identity and Civic Ideology*. Baltimore.

Mara, Gerald M. 1997. *Socrates' Discursive Democracy: Logos and Ergon in Platonic Political Philosophy.* Albany.

Martin, Richard. 1989. *The Language of Heroes: Speech and Performance in the* Iliad. Ithaca.

———. 1994. "The Seven Sages as Performers of Wisdom," in Carol Dougherty and Leslie Kurke (eds.), *Cultural Poetics in Ancient Greece.* Cambridge.

Mead, George Herbert. 1934. *Mind, Self and Society.* Chicago.

———. 1964. *Selected Writings: George Herbert Mead.* Ed. A. J. Reck. Chicago.

Meier, Christian. 1991. *De la tragédie grecque comme art poétique.* Trans. M. Carlier. Paris [o.p. 1988].

Meiggs, Russell, and David Lewis (eds.). 1969. *A Selection of Greek Historical Inscriptions to the End of the Fifth Century BC.* Oxford.

Millett, Paul. 1984. "Hesiod and his World." *PCPS* n.s. 30: 84–115.

Mills, Sophie. 1997. *Theseus, Tragedy and the Athenian Empire.* Oxford.

Minchin, Elizabeth. 1992. "Scripts and Themes: Cognitive Research and the Homeric Epic." *CA* 11: 229–41.

———. 1996. "The Performance of Lists and Catalogues in the Homeric Epics," in Ian Worthington (ed.), *Voice Into Text: Orality and Literacy in Ancient Greece. Mnemosyne* Supplement 157, Leiden.

———. 2001. *Homer and the Resources of Memory: Some Aspects of Cognitive Theory in the* Iliad *and the* Odyssey. Oxford.

Minsky, M. 1975. "A Framework for Representing Knowledge," in P. H. Winston, *The Psychology of Computer Vision.* New York.

Mitchell, Lynette G. "New Wine in Old Wineskins: Solon, *Arete* and the *Agathos,* in Lynette G. Mitchell and P. J. Rhodes (eds.), *The Development of the Polis in Archaic Greece.* London.

Monoson, Sara S. 2000. *Plato's Democratic Entanglements: Athenian Politics and the Practice of Philosophy.* Princeton.

Monsacré, Hélène. 1984. *Les larmes d'Achille: le héros, la femme et la souffrance dans la poésie d'Homère.* Paris.

Morgan, Catherine. 1990. *Athletes and Oracles: The Transformation of Olympia and Delphi in the Eighth Century BC.* Cambridge.

———. 2003. *Early Greek States Beyond the Polis.* London.

Morris, Ian. 1987. *Burial in Ancient Society: The Rise of the Greek City-State.* Cambridge.

———. 1988. "Tomb Cult and the 'Greek Renaissance': The Past in the Present in the Eighth Century BC." *Antiquity* 62: 750–61.

———. 1989a. "Attitudes Toward Death in Archaic Greece." *CA* 8: 296–320.

———. 1989b. "Circulation, Deposition, and the Formation of the Early Greek Iron Age." *Man* n.s. 24: 502–519.

———. 1991. "The Early Polis as City and State," in J. Rich and A. Wallace-Hadrill (eds.), *City and Country in the Ancient World.* London.

————. 1996. "The Strong Principle of Equality and the Archaic Origins of Greek Democracy," in J. Ober and J. Hedrick (eds.), *Demokratia: A Conversation on Democracies, Ancient and Modern*. Princeton.

————. 1998a. "Archaeology and Archaic Greek History," in N. Fisher and H. van Wees (eds.), *Archaic Greece*. London.

————. 1998b. *"Burial and Ancient Society* after Ten Years," in S. Marchegay, M.T. Le Dinahet, and J. F. Salles (eds.), *Nécropoles et pouvoir: idéologies, pratiques, et interpretations*. Paris.

————. 2000. *Archaeology as Cultural History: Words and Things in Iron Age Greece*. Malden, MA, and Oxford.

Morris, Ian, and Kurt Raaflaub (eds.). 1998. *Democracy 2500? Questions and Challenges*. Dubuque.

Morrison, J. S. 1972. "Antiphon." Introduction and Translation in Rosamond Kent Sprague (ed.), *The Older Sophists*. Indianapolis. Rpt. 2001.

Mossé, Claude. 2004. "How a Political Myth Takes Shape: Solon, 'Founding Father' of the Athenian Democracy," in P. J. Rhodes (ed.), *Athenian Democracy*. Oxford [o.p. 1979].

Moulton, Carroll. 1972. "Antiphon the Sophist, *On Truth*." *TAPA* 103: 329–66.

Muellner, Leonard. 1976. *The Meaning of Homeric* eukhomai *Through Its Formulas*. Innsbruck.

Mülke, Christoph. 2002. *Solons politische Elegien und Iamben (Fr. 1–13; 32–37 West): Einleitung, Text, Übersetzung, Kommentar*. Munich and Leipzig.

Munn, Mark. 2000. *The School of History: Athens in the Age of Socrates*. Berkeley.

Musti, Domenico. 1995. *Demokratía: origini di un'idea*. Bari.

Naddaf, Gerard. 2005. *The Greek Concept of Nature*. Albany.

Nagler, Michael. 1990. "Odysseus: the Proem and the Problem." *CA* 9: 335–56.

————. 1996. "Dread Goddesses Revisited," in S. Schein (ed.), *Reading the* Odyssey: *Selected Interpretive Essays*. Princeton.

Nagy, Gregory. 1979. *The Best of the Achaeans: Concepts of the Hero in Archaic Greek Poetry*. Baltimore.

————. 1983. "*Sêma* and *Noêsis*: Some Illustrations." *Arethusa* 16: 35–55.

————. 1985. "Theognis and Megara: A Poet's Vision of His City," in T. Figueira and G. Nagy (eds.), *Theognis of Megara: Poetry and the Polis*. Baltimore.

————. 1990. *Pindar's Homer: The Epic Possession of a Lyric Past*. Ithaca.

————. 1996. *Poetry as Performance: Homer and Beyond*. Cambridge.

Naiden, F. S. 2004. "Supplication and the Law," in Edward M. Harris and Lene Rubinstein (eds.), *The Law and the Courts in Ancient Greece*. London.

Neer, Richard. 2002. *Style and Politics in Athenian Vase-Painting: The Craft of Democracy, ca. 530–460 BCE*. Cambridge.

Nehamas, Alexander, 1999. *Virtues of Authenticity: Essays on Plato and Socrates*. Princeton.

Nilsson, M. P. 1967. *Geschichte der griechischen Religion*. Vol. 1. Munich.

Nimis, Steve. 1986. "The Language of Achilles: Construction vs. Representation." *CW* 79: 217–25.

North, Helen. 1966. *Sophrosyne: Self-knowledge and Self-restraint in Greek Literature.* Ithaca.

Norton, David L. 1991. *Democracy and Moral Development: A Politics of Virtue.* Berkeley.

Nussbaum, Martha. 1976–77. "Consequences and Character in Sophocles' *Philoctetes.*" *Philosophy and Literature* 1: 25–53.

———. 1986. *The Fragility of Goodness: Luck and Ethics in Greek Tragedy and Philosophy.* Cambridge.

———. 2001. *Upheavals of Thought: The Intelligence of Emotions.* Cambridge.

Ober, Josiah. 1989. *Mass and Elite in Democratic Athens.* Princeton.

———. 1994. "Civic Ideology and Counterhegemonic Discourse: Thucydides on the Sicilian Debate," in Alan Boegehold and Adele Scafuro (eds.), *Athenian Identity and Civic Ideology.* Baltimore.

———. 1995. "Greek *Horoi:* Artifactual Texts and the Contingency of Meaning," in D. Small (ed.), *Methods in the Mediterranean: Historical and Archaeological Views on Texts and Archaeology.* Leiden.

———. 1996. *The Athenian Revolution: Essays on Ancient Greek Democracy and Political Theory.* Princeton.

———. 1998. *Political Dissent in Democratic Athens: Intellectual Critics of Popular Rule.* Princeton.

———. 2005. *Athenian Legacies: Essays on the Politics of Going on Together.* Princeton.

Ober, Josiah, and John Hedrick (eds.). 1996. *Dêmokratia: A Conversation on Democracies, Ancient and Modern.* Princeton.

Ober, Josiah, and Barry Strauss. 1990. "Drama, Political Rhetoric and the Discourse of Athenian Democracy," in John J. Winkler and Froma I. Zeitlin (eds.), *Nothing to Do with Dionysus? Athenian Drama in its Social Context.* 1990. Princeton.

Ogden, Daniel. 2001. *Greek and Roman Necromancy.* Princeton.

Osborne, Robin. 1985. "Law in Action in Classical Athens." *JHS* 105: 40–58.

———. 1997. "Law and Laws: How We Join Up the Dots," in Lynette G. Mitchell and P. J. Rhodes (eds.), *The Development of the Polis in Archaic Greece.* London.

Osborne, Robin and Simon Goldhill (eds.). 1994. *Ritual, Finance, Politics: Athenian Democratic Accounts Presented to David Lewis.* Oxford.

Ostwald, Martin. 1969. Nomos *and the Beginnings of the Athenian Democracy.* Oxford.

———. 1982. *Autonomia: Its Genesis and Early History. American Classical Studies* 11.

———. 1986. *From Popular Sovereignty to the Sovereignty of Law: Law, Society and Politics in Fifth-Century Athens.* Berkeley.

———. 1990. "*Nomos* and *Phusis* in Antiphon's *Peri Aletheias,*" in M. Griffith and D. Mastronarde (eds.), *Cabinet of the Muses: Essays on Classical and Comparative Literature in Honor of Thomas G. Rosenmeyer.* Atlanta.

Page, Denys. 1976. *The Homeric Odyssey.* Oxford. [rpt. 1955].

Palmer, L. R. 1950. "The Indo-European Origins of Greek Justice." *Transactions of the Philological Society* 1950: 149–68.

Parke, H. W. 1977. *Festivals of the Athenians.* Ithaca.

Parry, Adam. 1956. "The Language of Achilles." *TAPA* 87: 1–7.

Patterson, Cynthia. 2000. "The Hospitality of Athenian Justice," in Virginia Hunter and Jonathan Edmondson (eds.), *Law and Social Status in Classical Athens*. Oxford.

Pedrick, Victoria. 1982. "Supplication in the *Iliad* and *Odyssey*." *TAPA* 112: 125–40.

Pélékides, Chrysis. 1962. *Histoire de l'éphébie attique des origines à 31 avant J-C.* Paris.

Pelling, Christopher (ed.). 1990. *Characterization and Individuality in Greek Literature*. Oxford.

———. 1997a. "Aeschylus' Persae and History," in C. Pelling (ed.), *Greek Tragedy and the Historian*. Oxford.

———. (ed.). 1997b. *Greek Tragedy and the Historian*. Oxford.

Pellizer, Elio. 1981. "Per una morfologia della poesia giambica arcaica," in U. Schulz-Buschaus et al., *I canoni letterari: storia e dinamica*. Trieste.

———. 1983. "Della zuffa simpotica," in M. Vetta (ed.), *Poesia e simposio nella Grecia antica: guida storica e critica*. Rome.

———. 1990. "Outlines of a Morphology of Sympotic Entertainment," in O. Murray (ed.), *Sympotica: A Symposium on the Symposion*. Oxford.

Pendrick, Gerard J. 1987. "Once Again Antiphon the Sophist and Antiphon of Rhamnus" *Hermes* 115: 47–60.

———. 1993, "The Ancient Tradition on Antiphon Reconsidered." *GRBS* 34: 215–29.

———. 2002. *Antiphon the Sophist: The Fragments*. Cambridge.

Peradotto, John. 1990. *Man in the Middle Voice: Name and Narration in the Odyssey*. Princeton.

Petrey, Sandy. 1990. *Speech Acts and Literary Theory*. New York.

Pettit, Philip. 1997. *Republicanism: A Theory of Freedom in Government*. Oxford.

Phillips, Derek L. 1993. *Looking Backward: A Critical Appraisal of Communitarian Thought*. Princeton.

Pocock, J. G. A. 1995. "The Idea of Citizenship Since Classical Tiimes," in R. Beiner (ed.), *Theorizing Citizenship*. Albany.

Podlecki, Anthony J. 1986. "Polis and Monarch in Early Attic Tragedy," in P. Euben (ed.), *Greek Tragedy and Political Theory*. Berkeley.

———. 1990. "*Kat'arkhês gar philaitios leôs*: The Concept of Leadership in Aeschylus," in A. H. Sommerstein, S. Halliwell, J. Henderson, and B. Zimmermann (eds.), *Tragedy, Comedy and the Polis*. Bari.

Pope, Maurice. 1988. "Thucydides and Democracy." *Historia* 37: 276–96.

Postlethwaite, Norman. 1998. "Akhilleus and Agamemnon: Generalized Reciprocity," in C. Gill, N. Postlethwaite, and R. Seaford (eds.), *Reciprocity in Ancient Greece*. Oxford.

Pouncey, Peter. 1980. *The Necessities of War: A Study of Thucydides' Pessimism*. New York.

Pucci, Pietro. 1987. *Odysseus Polutropos: Intertextual Readings in the Odyssey and the Iliad*. Ithaca.

Qviller, Bjorn. 1981. "The Dynamics of the Homeric Society." *SO* 56: 109–55.

Raaflaub, Kurt. 1983. "Democracy, Oligarchy and the Concept of the Free Citizen in Late Fifth-century Athens." *Political Theory* 2: 517–44.

———. 2000. "Poets, Lawgivers, and the Beginnings of Political Reflection in Archaic Greece," in *The Cambridge History of Greek and Roman Political Thought*. Cambridge.

Rawls, John. 1971. *A Theory of Justice*. Rev. edn. 1999. Oxford [page references are to the revised edn.].

———. 1993. *Political Liberalism*. New York.

Redfield, James. 1975. *Nature and Culture in the Iliad: the Tragedy of Hector*. Chicago.

———. 1983. "The Economic Man," in C. Rubino and C. W. Shelmardine (eds.), *Approaches to Homer*. Austin.

Reeve, C. D. C. 1989. *Socrates in the Apology*. Indianapolis.

Rehg, William. 1994. *Insight and Solidarity: The Discourse Ethics of Jurgen Habermas*. Berkeley.

Reinmuth, O. W. 1971. *The Ephebic Inscriptions of the Fourth Century BC*. Mnemosyne Supplement 14. Leiden.

Rheinhardt, Karl. 1961. *Die Ilias und Ihr Dichter*. Göttingen.

———. 1996. "The Adventures in the *Odyssey*," in Seth Schein (ed.), *Reading the* Odyssey: *Selected Interpretive Essays*. Princeton [o.p. 1942].

Rhodes, P. J. 1981. *A Commentary on the Aristotelian* Athenaion Politeia. Oxford.

———. 1998. "Enmity in Fourth-Century Athens," in Paul Cartledge, Paul Millett, and Sitta von Reden (eds.), *Kosmos: Essays in Order, Conflict and Community in Classical Athens*. Cambridge.

———. 2003a. *Athenian Democracy and Modern Ideology*. London.

———. 2003b. "Nothing to Do with Democracy: Athenian Drama and the *Polis*." *JHS* 123: 104–19.

———. (ed.). 2004. *Athenian Democracy*. Oxford.

Rickert, G. 1989. *Hekon and Akon in Early Greek Thought*. American Classical Studies 20. Atlanta.

Ridley, R. T. 1979. "The Hoplite as Athenian Citizen: Military Institutions in Their Social Context." *AC* 48: 508–48.

Roberts, Jennifer Tolbert. 1994. *Athens on Trial: The Antidemocratic Tradition in Western Thought*. Princeton.

Robertson, Bruce. 2000. "The Scrutiny of New Citizens at Athens," in V. Hunter and J. Edmonson (eds.), *Law and Social Status in Classical Athens*. Oxford.

Robertson, D. S. 1924. "The End of the *Supplices* Trilogy of Aeschylus." *CR* 38: 51–53.

Rohde, Erwin. 1987. *Psyche: The Cult of Souls and Belief in Immortality among the Ancient Greeks*. Trans. W. B. Hillis. Rpt. 1925. Chicago.

Rohweder, Christine. 1998. *Macht und Gedeihen: eine politische Interpretation der* Hiketiden *des Aischylos*. Frankfurt.

Romilly, Jacqueline de. 1988. *Les Grands sophistes dans l'Athènes de Pericles*. Paris.

———. 1995. *Alcibiade*. Paris.

_____. 2001. *La Loi dans la pensée grecque des origines à Aristote.* Paris [o.p. 1971].

Rose, Peter W. 1992. *Sons of the Earth, Children of the Gods: Ideology and Literary Form in Ancient Greece.* Ithaca.

Rösler, Wolfgang. 1993. "Der Schluss des 'Hiketiden' und die Danaiden Trilogie des Aischylos." *RM* 136: 1–22.

Rossi, Luigi. 1983. "Feste religiose e letterature: Stesicoro o dell'epica alternativa." *Orpheus* 4: 5–31.

Rubin, David. 1995. *Memory in Oral Tradition.* Cambridge, MA.

Ruck, Carl A. P. 1986. "Mushrooms and Philosophers," in R. Gordon Wasson, Stella Kamrisch, Jonathan Ott, and Carl A. P. Ruck (eds.), *Persephone's Quest: Entheogens and the Origins of Religion.* New Haven.

Ruschenbusch, E. 1966. *Solonis Nomoi.* Historia Einzelschriften 9.

Russo, Joseph. 1999. "Sicilian Folktales, Cognitive Psychology, and Oral Theory," in T. Faulkner, N. Felson, and D. Konstan (eds.), *Contextualizing Classics: Ideology, Performance, Dialogue: Essays in Honor of John J. Peradotto.* Lanham, MD.

Rusten, J. S. 1985. "Two Lives or Three? Pericles on the Athenian Character (Thucydides 2.40.1–2)." *CQ* 35: 14–19.

Rüter, Klaus. 1969. *Odyseeinterpretationen: Untersuchungen zum ersten Buch und Phaiakis.* Hypomnemata 19. Göttingen.

Rutherford, R. B. 1986. "The Philosophy of the *Odyssey.*" *JHS* 106: 145–62.

_____. 1992. *Homer:* Odyssey *Books XIX and XX.* Cambridge.

Ruzé, Françoise. 1992. "Aux debuts de l'écriture politique: le pourvoir de l'écrit," in M. Detienne (ed.), *Les savoirs de l'écriture dans la Grèce ancienne.* Rev. edn. Lille.

_____. 1997. *Déliberation et pouvoir dans la cité grecque de Nestor à Socrate.* Paris.

Sagan. Eli. 1991. *The Honey and the Hemlock: Democracy and Paranoia in Ancient Athens and Modern America.* New York.

Saïd, Suzanne. 1979. "Les Crimes des prétendants, la maison d'Ulysse et les festins de l'*Odyssée,*" in S. Saïd, F. Desbordes, et al., *Etudes de littérature ancienne.* Paris.

_____. 1990. "Tragic Argos," in A. H. Sommerstein, S. Halliwell, J. Henderson, and B. Zimmermann (eds.), *Tragedy, Comedy and the Polis.* Bari.

_____. 1998. *Homère et l'Odyssée.* Paris.

Samons Lauren J. 2004. *What's Wrong with Democracy? From Athenian Practice to American Worship.* Berkeley.

Sandel, Michael. 1984. "The Procedural Republic and the Unencumbered Self." *Political Theory* 12: 81–96.

_____. 1998. *Liberalism and the Limits of Justice.* Second edn. Cambridge.

Sanford, A. J., and S. C. Gawod. 1981. *Understanding Written Language.* Chichester, NY.

Santas, Geriasmos. 2001. *Goodness and Justice: Plato, Aristotle, and the Moderns.* Malden, MA.

Saxonhouse, Arlene. 1992. *Fear of Diversity: The Birth of Political Science in Ancient Greek Thought.* Chicago.

Scafuro, Adele. 1994. "Introduction: Bifurcations and Intersections," in Alan Boegelhold and Adele Scafuro (eds.), *Athenian Identity and Civic Ideology,* Baltimore.

Schank, R., and R. Abelson. 1977. *Scripts, Plans, Goals and Understanding: An Inquiry into Human Knowledge Structures.* Hillsdale, NJ.

Schaps, David M. 1998. "Review of Tandy 1997." *BMCR* (Nov. 11).

Scheidel, Walter. 2003. "The Greek Demographic Expansion: Models and Comparisons." *JHS* 123: 120–40.

Schein, Seth. 1984. *The Mortal Hero: An Introduction to the* Iliad. Berkeley.

———. 1996. "Introduction," in S. Schein (ed.), *Reading the* Odyssey: *Selected Interpretive Essays.* Princeton.

Schnapp, Alain. 1997. *Le chasseur et la cité: chasse et érotique dans la Grèce ancienne.* Paris.

Schneewind, J. B. 1998. *The Invention of Autonomy: a History of Modern Moral Philosophy.* Cambridge.

Schofield, Malcolm. 1986. "*Eubolia* in the *Iliad.*" *CQ* 36: 6–31.

Schwartz, Joel D. 1993. "Pity and Judgment in Greek Drama. A Response to Prof. Alford." *Political Research Quarterly* 46: 281–87.

Scullion, Scott. 2002. "Tragic Dates." *CQ* 52: 81–101.

Scully, Stephen. 1990. *Homer and the Sacred City.* Ithaca.

Seaford, Richard. 1987. "The Tragic Wedding." *JHS* 107: 106–30.

———. 1994. *Reciprocity and Ritual: Homer and Tragedy in the Developing City-State.* Oxford.

Sealey, Raphael. 1976. *A History of the Greek City-States 700–338 BC.* Berkeley.

———. 1984. "The *Tetralogies* Ascribed to Antiphon." *TAPA* 114: 71–85.

———. 1987. *The Athenian Republic: Democracy or the Rule of Law?* University Park, PA.

———. 1994. *The Justice of the Greeks.* Ann Arbor.

Segal, Charles. 1982. *Dionysiac Poetics and Euripides' Bacchae.* Princeton.

———. 1994. *Singers, Heroes and Gods in the* Odyssey. Ithaca.

———. 1996. "*Kleos* and Its Ironies in the *Odyssey,*" in S. Schein (ed.), *Reading the* Odyssey: *Selected Interpretive Essays.* Princeton.

———. 1998. "Frontières, étrangers, et éphébes dans la tragédie grecque," in F. Hartog, P. Schmitt, and A. Schnapp (eds.), *Pierre Vidal-Naquet: un historien dans la cité.* Paris.

———. 1999. "Euripides' Ion: Generational Passage and Civic Myth," in M. W. Padilla (ed.), *Rites of Passage in Ancient Greece: Literature, Religion, Society.* Lewisburg, PA.

Seligman, Adam B. 1997. *The Problem of Trust.* Princeton.

Shapiro, H. A. 1989. *Art and Cult under the Tyrants.* Mainz.

Sharples, R. 1983. "'But Why Has My Spirit Broken Me Thus?' Homeric Decision-Making." *GR* 30: 1–17.

Shell, Marc. 1978. *The Economy of Literature*. Baltimore.

Shotter, John. 1980. "Action, Joint Action and Intentionality," in M. Bremer (ed.), *The Structure of Action*. New York.

———. 1993. "Psychology and Citizenship: Identity and Belonging," in B. Turner, (ed.), *Citizenship and Social Theory*. London.

Sicherl, Martin. 1986. "Die Tragik der Danaiden." *MH* 43: 81–110.

Sickinger James. 2004. "The Laws of Athens: Publication, Presentation, Consultation," in Edward M. Harris and Lene Rubinstein (eds.), *The Law and the Courts in Ancient Greece*. London.

Siewert, P. 1977. "The Ephebic Oath in Fifth-Century Athens." *JHS* 97: 102–11.

Simon, Bennett. 1978. *Mind and Madness in Ancient Greece: The Classical Roots of Modern Psychiatry*. Ithaca.

Sinclair, Patrick. 1988. *Democracy and Participation in Athens*. Cambridge.

Slater, Philip E. 1968. *The Glory of Hera: Greek Mythology and the Greek Family*. Boston.

Slatkin, Laura. 1991. *The Power of Thetis: Allusion and Interpretation in the* Iliad. Berkeley.

Smith, Gertrude. 1922. "Early Greek Codes." *CP* 17: 187–201.

Smith, S. P. 1921. *Hawaiki: The Original Home of the Maori*. Auckland.

Snell, Bruno. 1960. *The Discovery of the Mind: The Greek Origins of European Thought*. Trans. T. Rosenmeyer. New York [o.p. 1953].

Snodgrass, Anthony. 1980. *Archaic Greece: The Age of Experiment*. Berkeley.

———. 1987. *An Archaeology of Greece: The Present State and Future Scope of a Discipline*. Berkeley.

Sommerstein, A. H. 1987. *Aristophanes: Birds*. Warminster.

———. 1995. "The Beginning and the End of Aeschylus' Danaid Trilogy," in B. Zimmermann (ed.), *Griechische-römische Komödie und Tragödie, Drama* 3. Stuttgart.

———. 1997. "The Theatre Audience, the *Demos* and the *Suppliants* of Aeschylus," in C. Pelling (ed.), *Greek Tragedy and the Historian*. Oxford.

Sommerstein, A. H., S. Halliwell, J. Henderson, and B. Zimmermann (eds.). 1990. *Tragedy, Comedy and the Polis*. Bari.

Sourvinou-Inwood, Christiane. 1981. "To Die and Enter the House of Hades: Homer, Before and After," J. Whaley (ed.), *Mirrors of Mortality: Studies in the Social History of Death*. London.

———. 1983. "A Trauma in Flux: Death in the Eighth Century and After," in R. Hagg (ed.), *The Greek Renaissance of the Eighth Century BC: Tradition and Innovation*. Stockholm.

———. 1986. "Crime and Punishment: Tityos, Tantalos and Sisyphos in *Odyssey* 11." *BICS* 33: 37–58.

———. 1995. *'Reading' Greek Death to the End of the Classical Period*. Oxford.

Stadter, Philip. 1989. *A Commentary on Plutarch's* Pericles. Chapel Hill.

Stanford, W. B. 1963. *The Ulysses Theme*. Ann Arbor.

Stears, Karen. 1998. "Death Becomes Her: Gender and Athenian Death Ritual," in S. Blundell and M. Williamson (eds.), *The Sacred and the Feminine in Ancient Greece*. London.

Steiner, Deborah Tarn. 2001. *Images in Mind: Statues in Archaic and Classical Greek Literature and Thought*. Princeton.

Stewart, Andrew. 1990. *Greek Sculpture: An Exploration. Vol. 1: Text*. New Haven.

Stockton, David. 1990. *The Classical Athenian Democracy*. Oxford.

Stoddard, Kathryn B. 2003. "The Programmatic Message of the 'Kings and Singers' Passage: Hesiod, *Theogony* 80–103." *TAPA* 133: 1–16.

Strauss, Barry S. 1993. *Fathers and Sons in Athens: Ideology and Society in the Era of the Peloponnesian War*. Princeton.

Stroud, Ronald. 1968. *Drakon's Law on Homicide*. Berkeley.

Svenbro, Jesper, and Marcel Detienne. 1979. "Les Loups au festin ou la cité impossible," in Jesper Svenbro and Marcel Detienne (eds.), *La Cuisine du sacrifice en pays grec*. Paris.

Szegedy-Maszak, Andrew. 1978. "Legends of the Greek Lawgivers." *GRBS* 19: 199–209.

Tandy, David W. 1997. *Warriors into Traders: The Power of the Market in Early Greece*. Berkeley.

Taplin, Oliver. 1977. *The Stagecraft of Aeschylus: The Dramatic Use of Exits and Entrances in Greek Tragedy*. Oxford.

———. 1980. "The Shield of Achilles within the *Iliad*." *Greece and Rome* 27: 1–21.

———. 1992. *Homeric Soundings: The Shaping of the* Iliad. Oxford.

Taylor, Charles. 1985a. *Human Agency and Language: Philosophical Papers 1*. Cambridge.

———. 1985b. *Human Agency and Language: Philosophical Papers 2*. Cambridge.

———. 1989. *Sources of the Self: The Making of the Modern Identity*. Cambridge, MA.

———. 1994. "The Politics of Recognition," in Amy Gutmann (ed.), *Multiculturalism: Examining the Politics of Recognition*. Princeton.

———. 1995. *Philosophical Arguments*. Cambridge, MA.

Tedeschi, Gennaro. 1982. "Solone e lo spazio della communicazione elegiaca." *QUCC* n.s. 10: 33–46.

Teffeteller, Annette. 2003. "Homeric Excuses." *CQ* 53: 15–31.

Thalmann, W. G. 1992. *The* Odyssey*: An Epic of Return*. New York.

———. 1998. *The Shepherd and the Bow: Representations of Class in the Odyssey*. Ithaca.

Thomas, Carol G. and Craig Conant. 1999. *Citadel to City-State: The Transformation of Greece, 1200–700 BCE*. Bloomington.

Thomas, Carol G., and Edward Kent Webb. 1994. "From Orality to Rhetoric: An Intellectual Transformation," in I. Worthington (ed.), *Persuasion: Greek Rhetoric in Action*. New York.

Thomas, Rosalind. 1994. "Law and the Lawgiver in Athenian Democracy," in R. Osborne and S. Hornblower (eds.), *Ritual, Finance, Politics: Athenian Democratic Accounts Presented to David Lewis.* Oxford.

———. 1996. "Written in Stone? Liberty, Equality and the Codification of Law," in L. Foxhall and A. D. E. Lewis (eds.), *Greek Law in its Political Setting: Justifications and Justice.* Oxford.

———. 2005. "Writing, Law, and Written Law," in Michael Gagarin and David Cohen (eds.), *The Cambridge Companion to Ancient Greek Law.* Cambridge.

Thornton, Agathe. 1984. *Homer's* Iliad: *Its Composition and the Motif of Supplication.* Göttingen.

Thür, Gerhard. 1996. "Oaths and Dispute Settlement in Ancient Greek Law," in L. Foxhall and A. D. E. Lewis (eds.), *Greek Law in its Political Setting: Justifications and Justice.* Oxford.

Todd, Stephen. 1990. "The Purpose of Evidence in Athenian Courts," in P. Cartledge, P. Millett, and S. Todd (eds.), Nomos: *Essays in Athenian Law, Politics and Society.* Cambridge.

———. 1993. *The Shape of Athenian Law.* Oxford.

Tsagarakis, Odysseus. 2000. *Studies in* Odyssey *11. Hermes Einzelschriften* 82. Stuttgart.

Turner, Chad. 2001. "Perverted Supplication and Other Inversions in Aeschylus' Danaid Trilogy." *CJ* 97: 27–50.

Turner, Victor. 1995. *The Ritual Process: Structure and Anti-Structure.* Rpt. 1969. New York.

Van Compernolle, René. 1981. "La législation aristocratique de Locres Épizéphyrienne, dite Législation de Zaleukos." *AC* 50: 759–69.

van Effenterre, Henri. 1985. *La Cité grecque des origines à la défaite de Marathon.* Paris.

van Effenterre, Henri, and Françoise Ruzé (eds.). 1994. Eds. Nomima: *Receuil d'inscriptions politiques et juridiques de l'archäisme grec.* Rome.

van Groningen, B. A. 1957. "Hésiode et Persès." *Med. Ned. Akad. Wet.* 20: 153–66.

van Wees, Hans 1998. "The Law of Gratitude: Reciprocity in Anthropological Theory," in C. Gill, N. Postlethwaite, and R. Seaford (eds.), *Reciprocity in Ancient Greece.* Oxford.

Vasunia, Phiroze. 2001. *The Gift of the Nile: Hellenizing Egypt from Aeschylus to Alexander.* Berkeley.

Vermeule, Emily. 1979. *Aspects of Death in Early Greek Art and Poetry.* Berkeley.

Vernant, Jean-Pierre. 1988 [1972]. "Intimations of the Will in Greek Tragedy," in J. P. Vernant and P. Vidal-Naquet (eds.), *Myth and Tragedy in Ancient Greece.* Trans. J. Lloyd. New York.

———. 1996. "The Refusal of Odysseus," in S. Schein (ed.), *Reading the* Odyssey: *Selected Interpretive Essays.* Princeton.

Vickers, Michael. 1987. "Alcibiades on Stage: *Philoctetes* and *Cyclops.*" *Historia* 36: 171–97.

————. 1997. *Pericles on Stage: Political Commentary in Aristophanes' Early Plays.* Austin.

Vidal-Naquet, Pierre. 1986a. *The Black Hunter: Forms of Thought and Forms of Society in the Greek World.* Trans. A. Szegedy-Maszak. Baltimore [o.p. 1981].

————. 1986b. "The Black Hunter Revisited." *PCPS* n.s. 32: 126–44.

————. 1988. "Sophocles' *Philoctetes* and the Ephebeia," in J. P. Vernant and P. Vidal-Naquet, *Myth and Tragedy in Ancient Greece.* Trans. J. Lloyd. New York.

————. 1990. *Le Démocratie grecque vue d'ailleurs: essais d'historiographie ancienne et moderne.* Paris.

————. 1995. *Politics Ancient and Modern.* Trans. J. Lloyd. Cambridge [in part Vidal-Naquet 1990].

————. 1997. "The Place and Status of Foreigners in Athenian Tragedy," in C. Pelling (ed.), *Greek Tragedy and the Historian.* Oxford.

————. 2000. *Les Grecs, les historiens, la démocratie: le grand écart.* Paris.

Villa, Dana. 2001. *Socratic Citizenship.* Princeton.

Vlastos, Gregory. 1983. "The Historical Socrates and Athenian Democracy." *Political Theory* 11: 495–516.

————. 1991. *Socrates, Ironist and Moral Philosopher.* Ithaca.

————. 1994. *Socratic Studies.* Ed. M. Burnyeat. Cambridge.

————. 1995. *Studies in Greek Philosophy Vol. 1: The Presocratics..* Ed. Daniel W. Graham. Princeton.

Vos, Harm. 1979. "Themis," in *Homerisches Recht* (Rudolf Koestler) *and Themis* (H. Vos). New York [rpt. 1956].

Walker, Henry J. 1995. *Theseus and Athens.* Oxford.

Wallace, Robert W. 1994. "Private Lives and Public Enemies: Freedom of Thought in Classical Athens," in Alan Boegehold and Adele Scafuro (eds.), *Athenian Identity and Civic Ideology.* Baltimore.

————. 1996. "Law, Freedom and the Concept of Citizens' Rights in Democratic Athens," in Josiah Ober and John Hedrick (eds.), *Dêmokratia: A Conversation on Democracies, Ancient and Modern.* Princeton.

————. 1997. "Solonian Democracy," in Ian Morris and Kurl Raaflaub (eds.), *Democracy 2500? Questions and Challenges.* Dubuque.

Wallach, John R. 2001. *The Platonic Art: A Study of Critical Reason and Democracy.* University Park, PA.

Walzer, Michael. 1990. "The Communitarian Critique of Liberalism." *Political Theory* 18: 6–24.

Warren, Mark E. 1992. "Democratic Theory and Self-Transformation." *American Political Science Review* 86: 8–23.

————. 1995. "The Self in Discursive Democracy," in Stephen K. White (ed.), *The Cambridge Companion to Habermas.* Cambridge.

————. 2001. *Democracy and Association.* Princeton.

Weiss, Roslyn. 1998. *Socrates Dissatisfied: An Analysis of Plato's Crito.* Oxford.

West, M. L. 1974. *Studies in Greek Elegy and Iambus*. Berlin.

_____. (ed.) 1978. *Hesiod: Works and Days*. Oxford.

_____. 1985. *The Hesiodic Catalogue of Women: Its Nature, Structure and Origins*. Oxford.

_____. 1993. *Greek Lyric Poetry*. Oxford.

West, Stephanie. 1989. "Laertes Revisited." *PCPS* 35: 113–43.

Westbrook, Raymond. 1988. *Studies in Biblical and Cuneiform Law*. Paris.

_____. 1992. "The Trial Scene in the *Iliad*." *HSCP* 94: 53–76.

Westlake, H. D. 1968. *Individuals in Thucydides*. Cambridge.

Whitehead, David. 1977. *The Ideology of the Athenian Metic*. Cambridge Philological Society Supplement 4. Cambridge.

_____. 1986. *The Demes of Attica 508/7–ca. 250 BC: A Political and Social Study*. Princeton.

Whitley, James. 1991a. "Social Diversity in Dark Age Greece." *BSA* 86: 341–65.

_____. 1991b. *Style and Society in Dark Age Greece: The Changing Face of a Pre-literate Society 1100–700 BC*. Cambridge.

_____. 1995. "Tomb Cult and Hero Cult: The Uses of the Past in Archaic Greece," in N. Spencer (ed.), *Time, Tradition and Society in Greek Archaeology*. London.

_____. 1997. "Cretan Laws and Cretan Literacy." *AJA* 101: 635–61.

_____. 2001. *The Archaeology of Ancient Greece*. Cambridge.

Whitman, Cedric. 1958. *Homer and the Heroic Tradition*. Cambridge, MA.

_____. 1964. *Aristophanes and the Comic Hero*. Warminster.

Williams, Bernard. 1993. *Shame and Necessity*. Berkeley.

Williams, Mary Frances. 1998. *Ethics in Thucydides: The Ancient Simplicity*. Lanham MD.

Wilson, Donna F. 2002. *Ransom, Revenge, and Heroic Identity in the* Iliad. Cambridge.

Winkler, John J. 1990. "The Ephebes' Song: Tragôidia and the Polis," in John J. Winkler and Froma I. Zeitlin (eds.), *Nothing to Do with Dionysus? Athenian Drama in its Social Context*. Princeton.

Winkler, John J., and Froma I. Zeitlin (eds.) 1990. *Nothing to Do with Dionysus? Athenian Drama in its Social Context*. Princeton.

Winnington-Ingram, R. P. 1983. *Studies in Aeschylus*. Cambridge.

Wohl, Victoria. 1999. "The Eros of Alcibiades." *CA* 18: 349–85.

_____. 2002. *Love Among the Ruins: The Erotics of Democracy in Classical Athens*. Princeton.

Wolff, H. J. 1946. "The Origin of Judicial Litigation Among the Greeks." *Traditio* 4: 31–88.

Wolin, Sheldon. S. 1994. "Norm and Form: The Constitutionalizing of Democracy," in P. Euben, R. Wallach, and I. Ober (eds.), *Athenian Political Thought and the Reconstruction of American Democracy*. Ithaca.

Wood, Ellen Meiksins, and Neal Wood. 1978. *Class Ideology and Ancient Political Theory: Socrates, Plato and Aristotle in Social Context*. Oxford.

Yamagata, Naoko. 1994. *Homeric Morality.* Brill.

Yunis, Harvey. 1996. *Taming Democracy: Models of Political Rhetoric in Classical Athens.* Ithaca.

———. 2005. "The Rhetoric of Law in Fourth-Century Athens," in Michael Gagarin and David Cohen (eds.), *The Cambridge Companion to Ancient Greek Law.* Cambridge.

Zanker, Graham. 1994. *The Heart of Achilles: Characterization and Personal Ethics in the* Iliad. Ann Arbor.

———. 1998. "Beyond Reciprocity: The Achilles and Priam Scene in *Il.* 24," in Christopher Gill, Norman Postlethwaite and Richard Seaford (eds.), *Reciprocity in Ancient Greece.* Oxford.

Zeitlin, Froma I. 1990. "Theater of Self and Society in Athenian Drama," in John J. Winkler and Froma I. Zeitlin (eds.), *Nothing to Do with Dionysus? Athenian Drama in its Social Context.* Princeton.

———. 1996. *Playing the Other: Gender and Society in Classical Greek Literature.* Chicago.

INDEX